ADHD - NEW DIRECTIONS IN DIAGNOSIS AND TREATMENT

Edited by **Jill M. Norvilitis**

ADHD - New Directions in Diagnosis and Treatment

http://dx.doi.org/10.5772/59348
Edited by Jill M. Norvilitis

Contributors

Herbert Obu, Josephat Chinawa, Julián González, Guzmán Alba, Soledad Mañas, Almudena González, Ernesto Pereda, Jae Hoon Cheong, June Bryan dela Pena, Catia Scassellati, Cristian Bonvicini, Aili Hashim, Yongning Song, Murat Yüce, Filiz Ucar, Gokce Nur Say, Carlos De Cabo De La Vega, María Carmen Carrascosa-Romero, Sarina Grosswald, Pavel Theiner, Tomáš Kašpárek, Tomáš Skřont, Martin Bareš, Libor Ustohal, Alison Poulton, Akira Yasumura, Masumi Inagaki, Esra Guney, Fatih Hilmi Cetin, Elvan Iseri, Gulser Senses Dinc, Ozden Sukran Uneri, Zeynep Goker, Jill M. Norvilitis, Yi-Yuan Tang, Rongxiang Tang

Published by InTech

Janeza Trdine 9, 51000 Rijeka, Croatia

Copyright © 2015 InTech

Notice

Publishing Process Manager Iva Lipovic

Technical Editor InTech DTP team

Cover InTech Design team

First published September, 2015

Printed in Croatia

Additional hard copies can be obtained from orders@intechopen.com

ADHD - New Directions in Diagnosis and Treatment, Edited by Jill M. Norvilitis

p. cm.

ISBN 978-953-51-2166-4

For EU product safety concerns:
IN TECH d.o.o., Prolaz Marije Krucifikse Kozulić 3, 51000 Rijeka, Croatia,
info@intechopen.com or visit our website at intechopen.com.

Meet the editor

Jill M. Norvilitis, Ph.D., is Professor and Chair of Psychology at SUNY Buffalo State in Buffalo, NY. She earned her undergraduate degree in Psychology from Hope College in Holland, Michigan, and her M.A. and Ph.D. in Clinical Psychology from Wayne State University in Detroit, Michigan. She has been recognized with the Buffalo State President's Award for Excellence in Teaching and the SUNY Chancellor's Award for Excellence in Teaching. Dr. Norvilitis is a Clinical Psychologist who specializes in behavior disorders of childhood. Her research focuses on predictors of social and academic adjustment among students with Attention Deficit Hyperactivity Disorder (ADHD) and perceptions of ADHD cross-culturally. She is the author of over 40 journal articles, book chapters, and edited volumes, and she has given over 100 conferences and invited presentations.

Contents

Preface

Attention Deficit Hyperactivity Disorder (ADHD) is one of the most widely diagnosed behavior disorders in childhood, with a recent study identifying a worldwide pooled prevalence of 7.2 % (Thomas, Sanders, Doust, Beller, & Glasziou, 2015). Although the disorder is quite common, much remains unknown and researchers strive to examine the disorder, its causes and correlates, and its treatment. Our understanding of the biopsychosocial origins of ADHD is not definitive, and much remains to be learned in a variety of domains. While some scientists work to unlock these answers, others work to improve the lives of those with ADHD through understanding their daily functioning and through improving treatment options. Equally critical, this applied work addresses many quality-of-life concerns.

The goal of this volume is to explore the state of the art in research in ADHD around the world. The 16 chapters in this volume represent the work of 42 researchers in countries spanning the globe from Malaysia to Spain to Turkey to the United States. This broad survey covers issues ranging from comorbidity to advances in the search for biomarkers; to executive, cognitive, and social functioning; to the use of new and alternative therapies.

The first section of the book provides an overview of the disorder from a variety of perspectives. The first chapter, "Epidemiology of Attention Deficit Hyperactivity Disorder," provides an introduction to the diagnosis, covering prevalence, treatment, gender differences, and comorbidity. Chapter 2, "The Role of Environmental Factors in Etiology of ADHD," examines a variety of nongenetic risk factors, such as prenatal exposure to substances and psychosocial factors, suggesting avenues for further research and, potentially, avenues for prevention. One challenge in the field is that, to date, there are no definitive diagnostic techniques. Two chapters address advances in this area. Chapter 3, "Assessment of ADHD through Electroencephalographic Measures of Functional Connectivity," explores the use of recording and imaging techniques in diagnosis. Chapter 4, "Role of Dopaminergic and Noradrenergic Systems as Potential Biomarkers in ADHD Diagnosis and Treatment," examines a variety of biochemical markers to identify the most promising for future exploration. Another challenge for the field is understanding how ADHD relates to other conditions in terms of both diagnosis and treatment. The final two chapters of the first section examine the role of comorbidity. Chapter 5, "Comorbid Conditions in Child and Adolescent Patients Diagnosed with Attention Deficit Hyperactivity Disorder," provides an overview of some of the most common conditions found with ADHD, highlighting treatment recommendations. Chapter 6, "The Comorbidity of ADHD and Autism Spectrum Disorders (ASDs) in Community Pre-schoolers," explores one particular comorbid condition in depth. With the recent changes in DSM 5, children may now be diagnosed with ADHD and ASDs simultaneously. This chapter discusses the current research in symptomatology, assessment, and treatment of these two disorders.

The second section of the book considers how ADHD affects different areas of everyday functioning in those with the disorder. Chapter 7, "Executive Function in Children with Attention Deficit Hyperactivity Disorder," argues that executive function deficits are a core symptom of ADHD and goes on to address the assessment and treatment implications of this, particularly through the use of imaging techniques. In Chapter 8, "Cognitive Functions in Attention Deficit Hyperactivity Disorder, Predominantly Inattentive Type (ADHD-I)," Yongning Song studies patterns of executive function deficits in a group of children with ADHD-I. Results indicate that executive function deficits are found in ADHD-I, similar to ADHD-Hyperactive/Impulsive and ADHD-Combined. Chapter 9, "The Quality of Life in Attention Deficit Hyperactivity Disorder," examines the impact of ADHD on well-being and quality of life. The authors cover strengths and weaknesses of the various measures of quality of life as well as the impact of treatment on quality of life. Chapter 10, "Predictors of College Success: Symptoms of ADHD, Psychological Well-being, Appreciation of the Liberal Arts, and Understanding of College Policies," addresses another area of life, college success, impacted by ADHD. Results indicate that inattentive symptoms were more predictive of adjustment to college than other mental health factors, such as depression and anxiety. Chapter 11, "Family Difficulties in Children with ADHD, the Role of Integrated Psychopharmacology-Psychotherapy Treatment," uses a case study to highlight the importance of the role of the family in the onset, maintenance, and treatment of ADHD.

The final section of the book explores advances in the prevention and treatment of ADHD. Although some well-established treatments exist, such as behavior modification and psychostimulant medication, these treatments are not always available or effective for everyone. Thus, work continues to identify new and alternative treatments for the disorder and its prevention. Chapter 12, "Evolution of a Disorder and Insights into Prevention," examines some of the limitations of medication as a treatment for ADHD and considers potential alternatives for both prevention and treatment, such as improving sleep, the use of meditation, and omega-3 supplementation. Chapter 13, "Mindfulness Meditation—A New Preventive Intervention for ADHD," reviews the literature on the efficacy of mindfulness as a technique to improve attention and self-regulation. The authors conclude that this is a promising intervention in need of further research. In Chapter 14, "Therapy for ADHD Directed towards Addressing the Dual Imbalances in Mental Effort and Reward as Illustrated in the Mental Effort-Reward Imbalance Model (MERIM)," Alison Poulton offers a new model for understanding ADHD that incorporates mood and the experience of reward. This new model leads to strategies to improve self-regulation and overall functioning. Chapter 15, "Repetitive Transcranial Magnetic Stimulation in ADHD," examines the potential role for this novel treatment. Although results from the handful of existing studies are equivocal, through the use of a case study the authors argue that further rigorous research may be fruitful. Chapter 16, "Updates on the Use of Natural Treatments for Attention Deficit Hyperactivity Disorder," reviews the literature on a variety of alternatives. The authors note that some of these are better supported than others and offer suggestions for future study.

Overall, the chapters included here cover much of this diverse field. Both the professional and the casual reader alike will find something of interest, whether learning about ADHD for the first time or looking for inspiration for new research questions or potential interventions. I hope that the chapters spark new thoughts and, perhaps, debates.

This book is the result of the work of many individuals. I am particularly grateful to Ms. Iva Lipović for her assistance in coordinating this book. I also thank all of the authors who contributed to this volume: I have learned from you and been inspired by your work.

References

Thomas, R., Sanders, S., Doust, J., Beller, E., & Glasziou, P. (2015). Prevalence of Attention-Deficit/Hyperactivity Disorder: A systematic review and meta-analysis. Pediatrics, 135, 994-1001. doi: 10.1542/peds.2014-3482

Jill M. Norvilitis
Department of Psychology
SUNY Buffalo State
Buffalo, NY
USA

Section 1

Epidemiology, Etiology and Diagnosis of ADHD

Chapter 1

Epidemiology of Attention Deficit/Hyperactivity Disorder

Josephat M. Chinawa and Herbert A. Obu

Additional information is available at the end of the chapter

http://dx.doi.org/10.5772/61016

Abstract

Attention deficit/hyperactivity disorder (ADHD) is a neuropsychiatric disorder characterized with attention deficits, hyperactivity, or impulsiveness. The prevalence of ADHD varies from country to country and from various cultural and geographical zones. The pattern and distribution of ADHD also vary with gender and age. It has also been noted that some factors are associated with ADHD. For instance, some central nervous system anomalies had been associated with ADHD. Genetic and environmental risk factors have also been implicated. Some conduct and learning disorders have also been associated with ADHD. Of recent, some cardiac anomalies and behavioral disorders such as enuresis and encopresis have all been associated with children with ADHD.

Conclusion: Attention deficit/hyperactivity disorder (ADHD), a neuropsychiatric disorder, varies in prevalence from one country to another with several associations.

Keywords: Attention deficit/hyperactivity disorder (ADHD), prevalence, associated factors

1. Introduction

Attention deficit/hyperactivity disorder (ADHD) is a neurological condition which more often than not is genetically influenced [1]. It is characterized by impulsivity and restlessness or hyperactivity [1]. It is the most frequently encountered childhood-onset neurodevelopmental disorder in the primary care setting. Symptoms usually emerge before 7 years of age [2].

There are three types of ADHD, depending on which symptoms are prominent in an individual. In the predominantly inattentive type, an affected child finds it difficult to organize or finish a task, to pay attention to details, or to follow instructions. Such a child is easily distracted or forgets details of daily routines [3,4]. The second type is the predominantly hyperactive–impulsive type; a child with this type tends to fidget and talk a lot. Children find it hard to sit still for long. The child also feels restless and has trouble with impulsivity [4]. The combined type is the third variety and is associated with symptomatology of the other two types in varying degrees [3,4].

ADHD affects children and adolescents in various ways and extents; however, the effects of the condition usually impact greatly on patients and their families and relations. When not treated, ADHD is frequently associated with underachievement in school, increased rates of criminality and accidents, and development of comorbid psychiatric symptoms, including anxiety, depression, and substance use and misuse [5].

It is important to note that not all children with ADHD will have all the symptoms, and the severity of ADHD and the level of impairment will vary between individuals. In addition, ADHD symptoms and severity can change with age [6]. Some symptoms, such as hyperactivity–impulsivity, may decrease with age. In the corollary, other symptoms, like inattention, are more likely to continue till adulthood [6]. It is pertinent to know that children with ADHD may present with other psychiatric disorders, such as learning difficulties or anxiety [6]. The long-term sequel in children with ADHD is variable. For most subjects with ADHD, the disorder will persist through childhood into adolescence and adulthood. Although children with ADHD may present with no issues later in life, they are at increased risk of a range of adverse outcomes [6]. These include poor academic performance, poor social interaction, and low self-esteem.

Prevalence varies from country to country. In Nigeria, for instance, the latest prevalence is 3.2% [6], while in other African countries, such as South Africa, Democratic Republic of Congo, and Ethiopia, the reported prevalence varies from 5.4% to 8.7% [7]. The reported prevalence from other continents follows a similar trend. For instance, the prevalence of ADHD in Saudi Arabian primary schools is reported to be as low as 2.7%, while that in Iran is reported to be as high as 13% [8]. In South America, the prevalence of ADHD in children is about 6%, while in Germany, ADHD has been reported with a prevalence of 4.8% [9–12].

Although variation in prevalence has been shown to be associated with geographic origin, this trend has been refuted in recent times. For example, it was postulated that ADHD is an American dictum, yet recent findings showed that the variation in prevalence with geographic origin did not fit a pattern consistent with the notion that ADHD is a byproduct of American culture [12]. For instance, the North American prevalence rate of 6.2% only slightly exceeded the European rate (4.6%) [12]. The highest rates emerged from Africa (8.5%) and South America (11.8%). In a collaborative study using a dimensional ADHD scale and in which 21 countries were involved, Japanese and Finnish children scored lowest, Jamaican and Thai children scored highest, while American children scored about average [13].

It has been argued that the variability in ADHD/HD prevalence figures obtained from different countries in different continents may be best explained by the use of different case definitions and methodologies. It is further argued that the actual prevalence across geographic sites should not vary when case definitions are identical. For instance, it has been documented that the main difference in ADHD prevalence between North America and Europe was explained by methodology [12]. North American researchers used the *Diagnostic and Statistical Manual of Mental Disorders* (DSM) for their case definition, whereas many European researchers had preferred the *International Classification of Diseases* (ICD). The ICD-10 strictly requires that a child must show symptoms in all three dimensions (inattention, hyperactivity, and impulsivity) and must meet all criteria at home and at school, while the DSM-IV is more "lenient." It is possible to diagnose a child who shows symptoms in only one dimension (inattention) using the DSM-IV criteria, for instance [13].

2. Sex

ADHD usually occurs more in boys than in girls. The male-to-female ratio ranges between 3:1 and 4:1 [14]. Diagnosis of ADHD has improved in recent years, with decreasing male-to-female ratio [14]. This is due to increased recognition of inattentive ADHD [14].

3. Age

There are conflicting data that a child with ADHD will also have the disorder as an adult. For instance, approximately 30–80% of children with ADHD have the disorder as adults. Most experts noted a rate well above 50%. However, many adults with ADHD were never diagnosed as children [15]. That their symptoms were missed in childhood is conjectural.

Hyperactive symptoms tend to decrease with age [16]. This is due to developmental trends toward self-control and changes in neural connections in the brain that occurs during late adolescence.

However, inattentive symptoms do not appear to have a similar developmental advantage and tend to remain the same into adulthood [16].

3.1. Risk factors

These include central nervous system involvement, genetics, and environmental risk factors.

4. Central nervous system involvement

It is a well-known fact that abnormalities in the frontal–striatal circuits and the prefrontal cortex (PFC) affect attention and hyperactivity [17]. Furthermore, neurohormonal aberrations are implicated as triggers of ADHD. For instance, abnormalities in norepinephrine, dopamine, and norepinephrine α-$_{2A}$ inhibits cortical, cerebellar, and striatal processing, which in turn causes inattention and hyperactivity [18,19]. Structural imaging studies have also shown smaller volumes in prefrontal cortex, caudate, splenium of corpus callosum, and cerebellum, as well as smaller total cerebral volume in children with ADHD [20].

5. Genetic influence in ADHD

A higher incidence of ADHD among first-degree family members of ADHD has been reported [21]. ADHD inheritance is estimated at 0.76, which makes it one of the most genetic psychiatric disorders [21].

6. Environmental risk factors

It is worth noting that concordance rate of 33% in dizygotic twins, points to environmental risk factors incurred during the prenatal course [22]. Environmental factors usually implicated in ADHD include maternal smoking during pregnancy, emotional distress or family adversity during pregnancy and early in life, birth weight <1500 g, lead exposure, hypoxemia, encephalitis, trauma, and brain injury from some metabolic disorders [22].

Of all these risk factors, pregnancy-associated risk seems to be the most common. For instance, nicotine (tobacco smoking), alcohol, and caffeine intake during pregnancy pose a greater risk of ADHD-related disorders among children whose mothers smoked during pregnancy. It is noted that in Finnish population, children prenatally exposed to maternal smoking had twice the risk of being diagnosed with ADHD than children of non-smokers [23].

Bekdas, however, used children born after different types of *in vitro* fertilization techniques with egg donation as a way to distinguish between genetic and exposure effects. They found no association between smoking and ADHD phenotype in genetically unrelated mother–child pairs [24].

It has also been documented that patients with ADHD showed higher titer of measles IgG while adolescents with ADHD showed higher levels mumps [24]. When patients with subtypes of ADHD were compared in terms of seropositivity, it was found that patients with ADHD-combined/hyperactive–impulsive subtypes had significantly elevated reactions for Rubella [24].

7. Prevalence of prescribing drugs in the treatment of ADHD

There is varying prevalence of methods of prescription in the management of ADHD. For instance, a trend of increasing prescribing prevalence of ADHD drug treatment has been observed over time in various countries [25]. It is noted that the annual prevalence of any psychotropic medication in youth was significantly greater in the United States (6.7%) than that in the Netherlands (2.9%) and in Germany (2.0%) [26]. These differences in psychotropic medication practice patterns could be due to differences in diagnostic systems, practice guidelines, drug regulations, availability of funds, and more often than not cultural beliefs [26].

More recent studies from the United States include a study by Zuvekas et al. [27], who used the Medical Expenditure Panel Survey database. They reported that the prevalence of use of stimulants in children aged 6–12 years is about 2.7%.

Furthermore, there exist gender differences in methods of prescription of these drugs with a male preponderance. These findings are in keeping with that reported in a study, where differences in prescribing between the genders ranging from a ratio of 2:1 to 9 were documented [28].

Physicians treating ADHD in European countries noted long-acting methylphenidate as a drug of choice in the management of ADHD. This was prescribed to more than half of patients. It was noted that only a third of the patients showed "complete symptom control" on current treatment, and another third were satisfied with their current treatment [29–30].

8. Prevalence of associated disorders

Furthermore, it is important to note that there exists an overwhelming proof to support the fact that children with ADHD are at increased risk for other psychiatric disorders [31]. For instance, children with ADHD have other associated psychiatric disorders in 66% of cases [31]. The most common of these disorders are oppositional defiant disordes and conduct disorders. It is an established fact that children with ADHD had ODD and CD in about 50% and 20% of cases, respectively [32]. There is also evidence that children and adolescents with ADHD are at risk of depressive disorders. Studies have shown increased prevalence rates of 9% to 38% for depressive disorders in children with ADHD [33,34].

In addition, children with ADHD may present with other medical conditions, for instance, Tourette syndrome (TS) often in tandem with ADHD. This is called co-occurring conditions [35].

Findings from the national Centers for Disease Control and Prevention (CDC) study showed that 86% of children with Tourette syndrome also had ADHD [36]. Furthermore, about 5% of children with Tourette syndrome had ADHD without learning disorder (LD), while 5% had LD without ADHD and 4% had both conditions [36]. Approximately 1 in 360 U.S. children aged 6–17 years ever had TS and are more likely than other children to also have another neurobehavioral condition or a learning disability [36].

9. Epidemiology of gender associations of ADHD

There may be gender differences in the types of comorbid disorders seen in children with ADHD. Findings had suggested higher rates of separation anxiety disorder in females and ODD and CD in males [37]. "This study also found differences between ADHD subtypes," with separation anxiety disorder more common in females with the inattention subtype and generalized anxiety disorder more common in females with the combined subtype [37].

10. Epidemiology of other co morbid problems

Children with ADHD may experience other problems. They have reduced intelligence than other children of the same age [38]. Several studies had reported varying findings on incidence of learning disorders among children with ADHD [38].

Children with ADHD are exposed to both accidental and nonaccidental injuries. Szatmari et al. [39] noted that 7.3% of children with ADHD experienced accidental poisoning with 23.2% having bone fractures, compared to 2.6% and 15.1%, respectively, in children without ADHD [39].

There exists high prevalence in criminality among children with ADHD later in life. Male children with ADHD always grow up as adult offenders ending up with high incidence of arrests (44%), convictions (29%), and incarcerations (26%). A U.S. longitudinal study among African American youth revealed that those who reported committing an offence in adolescence were more likely to have had ADHD symptoms in late childhood when compared to those who had never did [40].

11. Prevalence of ADHD and co morbidities among offenders

Studies have shown that about a fifth of prisoners with ADHD present with other psychiatric condition. These include substance use and misuse and personality disorder [41]. Learning disorders and personality were most common among them [41]. Furthermore, the prevalence of ADHD among adolescent offenders varies, although this is higher than the general population [42]. Psychiatric comorbidity among adolescents with ADHD is paramount. This include CD, major depressive disorder, dysthymia, mood disorder, anxiety, posttraumatic stress disorder, adjustment disorder, summarization disorder, and substance abuse disorder [42].

12. Prevalence of ADHD in childhood autism spectrum disorders

Autism spectrum disorders (ASD) and ADHD often coexist. It is noted that about 28–44% of adults diagnosed with ASD also meet criteria for ADHD [43]. Both conditions when they coexist can have a large negative impact on the quality of life of affected individuals and their families. A better understanding of the etiology of this co-occurrence is therefore important [43]. Much is not known on the etiology of the associations between ASD and ADHD in adults. In addition, recent works were unable to eke out any differences in the etiology and associations of ASD and ADHD with respect to gender [43–44].

13. ADHD in children with heart disease

ADHD is found to be more prevalent in children with heart disease than in the general pediatric population. Inattention was identified in 45% of children and hyperactivity in 39% of children with heart disease based on the responses of parents and teachers on the DSM-IV Rating Scale and Behavior Assessment System for Children [45]. It is important to note that more than two thirds of children with hypoplastic left heart syndrome were found to have attention/hyperactivity problems. In the corollary, it was found that 50% of children with total anomalous pulmonary venous return fulfilled the criteria for abnormal hyperactivity and/or attention deficits [45]. This link could be due to chronic or intermittent hypoxia experienced by children with heart disease which culminates into adverse effects on development, academic achievement, and behavior.

14. Enuresis and ADHD

ADHD does not cause enuresis nor is it known to be a symptom of ADHD [46]. However, there seems to be a higher prevalence rate of enuresis in children with ADHD. Children with ADHD had a 2.7 times higher incidence of enuresis and a 4.5 times higher incidence of daytime enuresis [46,47] than children without ADHD.

15. Encopresis and ADHD

Children with ADHD who are about 7.3 ± 1.3 years were twice more likely to meet DSM-IV criteria for enuresis than non-ADHD controls; they were 1.8 times more likely to do so than children without ADHD [48].

16. Conclusion

Attention deficit/hyperactivity disorder (ADHD), a neuropsychiatric disorder, varies in prevalence from one country to another. These variations could be due to geographical and cultural construct. It could also be due to the criteria used in the diagnosis of ADHD.

In addition, ADHD had been known to have a varying epidemiology in gender with a fast reducing gap between male–female ratio probably due to increased recognition of inattentive ADHD. Attention deficit/hyperactivity disorder (ADHD) is indeed a behavioral disorder with several epidemiological associations. Clinicians, especially in developing countries, should therefore manage an individual with ADHD with a view that there could be other associated behavioral disorders, thus the need for multidisciplinary involvement.

Moreover, the fact that abnormalities in the frontal–striatal circuits and the prefrontal cortex (PFC) affect attention and hyperactivity could be a tell tale sign for neuropsychological intervention. In addition, drugs that can completely modify the frontal–striatal circuits and the prefrontal cortex (PFC) in attention and hyperactivity will be worthwhile and a template for future studies.

Acknowledgements

My gratitude extends to my lord Jesus and my dear wife Awoere, who has been very supportive.

Author details

Josephat M. Chinawa* and Herbert A. Obu

*Address all correspondence to: awoerechinawa@yahoo.com

Department of Pediatrics, College of Medicine, University of Nigeria, University of Nigeria Teaching Hospital (UNTH), Ituku-Ozalla, Enugu State, Nigeria

References

[1] American Academy of Pediatrics Clinical. Practice guideline: diagnosis and evaluation of the child with attention-deficit/hyperactivity disorder. Pediatrics 2000; 105: 1158–1170.

[2] National Institute of Neurological Disorders and Stroke (2012). National Institute of Health. Available at http://www.clinicaltrials.gov/ct/search?term=ADHD. Accessed July 25, 2013.

[3] Attention-Deficit/Hyperactivity Disorder (ADHD): Symptoms and Diagnosis. Centers for Disease Control and Prevention 2010. National Center on Birth Defects and Developmental Disabilities. Available at http://en.wikipedia.org/wiki/Attention_deficit_hyperactivity_disorder. Assessed on July 29, 2013

[4] Merrell C, Tymms PB. Inattention, hyperactivity and impulsiveness: their impact on academic achievement and progress. British Journal of Educational Psychology 2001; 71: 43–56.

[5] Bakare MO. Attention deficit hyperactivity symptoms and disorder (ADHD) among African children: a review of epidemiology and co-morbidities. African Journal of Psychiatry 2002; 15: 358–361

[6] Ambuabunos EA, Ofovwe EG, Ibadin MO. Community survey of attention-deficit/hyperactivity disorder among primary school pupils in Benin City, Nigeria. Annals of African Medicine 2011; 1: 91–96

[7] Alqahtani MM. Attention-deficit hyperactive disorder in school-aged children in Saudi Arabia. European Journal of Pediatrics 2010; 169: 1113–1117

[8] Talaei A, Mokhber N, Abdollahian E, Bordbar MR, Salari E. Attention deficit/hyperactivity disorder: a survey on prevalence rate among male subjects in elementary school (7–9 years old) in Iran. Journal of Attention Disorders 2010; 13: 386–390.

[9] Rohde LA, Biederman J, Busnello EA, Zimmermann H, Schmitz M, Martins S, Tramontina S. ADHD in a school sample of Brazilian adolescents: a study of prevalence, comorbid conditions, and impairments. Journal of the American Academy of Child and Adolescent Psychiatry 1999; 38: 716–722.

[10] Childhood ADHD rate increases 22% in the U.S. Can the TM. Available at http://www.tm.org/blog/research/adhd-transcendental-meditation/. Assessed on May 22, 2014.

[11] Gadow KD, Nolan EE, Litcher L, Carlson GA, Panina N, Golovakha E, Sprafkin J, Bromet EJ. Comparison of attention-deficit/hyperactivity disorder symptom subtypes in Ukrainian schoolchildren. Journal of the American Academy of Child and Adolescent Psychiatry 2000; 39: 1520–1527.

[12] Epidemiology of Attention Deficit Hyperactive Disorder. Wikipedia. Available at http://en.wikipedia.org/wiki/Epidemiology_of_attention_deficit_hyperactive_disorder. Assessed May 22, 2014.

[13] Willcutt EG. The prevalence of DSM-IV attention-deficit/hyperactivity disorder: a meta-analytic review. Neurotherapeutics 2012; 9: 490–499.

[14] Gaub M, Carlson C. Gender differences in ADHD: a meta-analysis and critical review. Journal of the American Academy of Child and Adolescent Psychiatry 1997; 36: 1036–1045, 1436–1441.

[15] American Psychiatric Association. Diagnostic and Statistical Manual of Mental Disorders, Fifth Edition: DSM-5. Washington: American Psychiatric Association, 2013.

[16] Margaret A. Onset and Prevalence of ADHD. Available at www.mentalhelp.net/poc/view_doc.php?type=doc&id=13850&cn=3. Accessed March 25, 2015.

[17] Emond V, Joyal C, Poissant H. Structural and functional neuroanatomy of attention-deficit hyperactivity disorder (ADHD). Encephale. 2009; 35: 107–114

[18] Pliszka SR, McCracken JT, Maas JW. Catecholamines in attention-deficit hyperactivity disorder: current perspectives. Journal of the American Academy of Child and Adolescent Psychiatry. 1996; 35: 264–272.

[19] Cooper JR, Bloom FE, Roth RH. The Biochemical Basis of Neuropharmacology, Eighth Edition. New York, NY: Oxford University Press; 2003.

[20] Mary G, Michael S, Meaghan M, Wendy S, Deanna G, Francois L, et al. Developmental trajectories of the corpus callosum in attention-deficit/hyperactivity disorder. Biological Psychiatry 2011; 69: 839–846.

[21] Deeann W, Heather F, Maximilian M. Review: genetics of attention deficit/hyperactivity disorder. Journal of Pediatric Psychology 2008; 33: 1085–1099.

[22] Carsten O, Jørn O, Tine BH, Alina R, Marjo-Riitta J, Irma M, et al. Is maternal smoking during pregnancy a risk factor for hyperkinetic disorder?—findings from a sibling design. International Journal of Epidemiology 2011; 40: 338–345.

[23] Linnet KM, Dalsgaard S, Obel C, Wisborg K, Henriksen TB, Rodriguez A, et al. Maternal lifestyle factors in pregnancy risk of attention deficit hyperactivity disorder and associated behaviors: review of the current evidence. American Journal of Psychiatry 2003; 160: 1028–1040.

[24] Bekdas M, Tufan AE, Hakyemez IN, Tas T, Altunhan H, Demircioglu F, et al. Subclinical immune reactions to viral infections may correlate with child and adolescent diagnosis of attention-deficit/hyperactivity disorder: a preliminary study from Turkey. African Health Sciences 2014; 14: 439–445.

[25] Cox ER, Halloran DR, Homan S, Welliver S, Mager DE. Trends in the prevalence of chronic medication use in children: 2002–2005. Pediatrics 2008; 122: 1053–1061. http://www.biomedcentral.com/sfx_links?ui=1471-2431-12-78&bibl=B22#.75;.75

[26] Schirm E, Tobi H, Zito J, de Jong-van den Berg L. Psychotropic medication in children: a study from the Netherlands. Pediatrics 2001, 108: 25.

[27] Zuvekas S, Vitiello B, Norquist G. Recent trends in stimulant medication use among U.S. children. American Journal of Psychiatry 2006; 163: 579–585.

[28] Hodgkins P, Sasane R, Meijer WM. Pharmacologic treatment of attention deficit/hyperactivity disorder in children: incidence, prevalence, and treatment patterns in the Netherlands. Clinical Therapeutics 2011; 33: 188–203. http://www.biomedcentral.com/sfx_links?ui=1471-2431-12-78&bibl=B24#.75;.75

[29] Rushton J, Whitmire T. Pediatric stimulant and selective serotonin reuptake inhibitor prescription trends: 1992 to 1998. Archives of Pediatrics and Adolescent Medicine 2001; 155: 560–565.

[30] Barkley RA. Attention-Deficit Hyperactivity Disorder a Handbook for Diagnosis and Treatment, 3rd edition. New York Guilford Press, 2006.

[31] Walitza S, Drechsler R, Ball J. The school child with ADHD. Therapeutische Umschau 2012; 69: 467–473.

[32] McBurnett K, Pfiffner LJ. Treatment of aggressive ADHD in children and adolescents: conceptualization and treatment of comorbid behavior disorders. Postgraduate Medicine 2009; 121: 158–165.

[33] Anderson JC, Williams S, McGee R, et al. DSM-III disorders in preadolescent children: prevalence in a large community sample. Archives of General Psychiatry. 1998; 44: 69–76.

[34] Biederman J, Newcorn J, Sprich S. Comorbidity of attention deficit hyperactivity disorder with conduct, depressive, anxiety, and other disorders. American Journal of Psychiatry 1991; 148: 564–577.

[35] Bitsko RH, Holbrook JR, Visser SN, Mink JW, Zinner SH, Ghandour RM, et al. A national profile of Tourette syndrome, 2011–2012. Journal of Developmental and Behavioral Pediatrics 2008; 35: 317–322.

[36] Bitsko RH, Holbrook JR, Visser SN, Mink JW, Zinner, Samuel H, et al. A National Profile of Tourette Syndrome, 2011–2012. Journal of Developmental and Behavioral Pediatrics 2014; 35; 317–322.

[37] Florence L, David AH, Kellie SB, Michael M. Gender differences in ADHD subtype comorbidity. Journal of the American Academy of Child and Adolescent Psychiatry 2005; 44; 368–376.

[38] Altarac M, Saroha E. Lifetime prevalence of learning disability among US children. Pediatrics 2007; 119: S77–S83.

[39] Szatmari P, Offord DR, Boyle MH. Correlates, associated impairments and patterns of service utilization of children with attention deficit disorder: findings from the Ontario Child Health Study. Journal of Child Psychology and Psychiatry 1989; 30: 205–217.

[40] Messer J, Maughan B, Quinton D, Taylor A. Precursors and correlates of criminal behaviour in women. Criminal Behaviour and Mental Health 2004; 14: 82–107.

[41] Gunter TD, Arndt S, Riggins-Caspers K, Wenman G, Cadoret RJ. Adult outcomes of attention deficit hyperactivity disorder and conduct disorder: are the risks independent or additive? Annals of Clinical Psychiatry 2006; 18: 233–237.

[42] Satterfield JH, Schell A. A prospective study of hyperactive boys with conduct problems and normal boys: adolescent and adult criminality. Journal of the American Academy of Child and Adolescent Psychiatry 1997; 36: 1726–1735.

[43] Ronald A, Larsson H, Anckarsäter H, Lichtenstein P. A twin study of autism symptoms in Sweden. Molecular Psychiatry 2011; 16: 1039–1047.

[44] Lichtenstein P, Carlström E, Råstam M, Gillberg C, Anckarsäter H. The genetics of autism spectrum disorders and related neuropsychiatric disorders in childhood. American Journal of Psychiatry 2010; 167: 1357–1363.

[45] Victoria L, Josephine E, Christopher E, Stuart B, Nathan B, Karen U, et al. Cardiovascular monitoring of children and adolescents with heart disease receiving medications for attention deficit/hyperactivity disorder. Circulation 2008; 117: 2407–2423.

[46] ADD/ADHD and Bedwetting—Enuresis Treatments—Bed Wetting. Available at www.nobedwetting.com/.../addadhd--bedwetting.html. Assessed on 11/12/2014.

[47] Mellon MW, Natchev BE, Katusic SK, Colligan RC, Weaver AL, Voigt RG, et al. Incidence of enuresis and encopresis among children with attention-deficit/hyperactivity disorder in a population-based birth cohort. Academic Pediatrics 2013; 13: 322–327.

[48] Johnston BD, Wright JA. Attention dysfunction in children with encopresis. Journal of Developmental and Behavioral Pediatrics 1993; 14: 381–385.

Chapter 2

The Role of Environmental Factors in Etiology of Attention-Deficit Hyperactivity Disorder

Esra Guney, Fatih Hilmi Cetin and Elvan Iseri

Additional information is available at the end of the chapter

http://dx.doi.org/10.5772/61025

Abstract

Environmental factors in etiology of ADHD Attention deficit and hyperactivity disorder (ADHD) is one of the most common developmental disorders of childhood. It was reported that it is a disease that affects 5.29% of children and adolescents in the entire world. Although ADHD is a disorder with high inheritability, genetic factors are not the only explanation to ADHD etiology. ADHD is a disorder etiology which has genetic and environmental components and gene-environment interaction. In spite of the fact that many environmental factors are linked to ADHD, the number of environmental factors that are proven to be in significant cause-effect relation is too small. In other words, in presence of proper genetic basis, disease appears in presence of many environmental factors each of which have a slight effect, its severity or prognosis is variable. Environmental factors that are most commonly linked to ADHD pathophysiology are; complications during pregnancy, natal and postnatal period, several toxins and food substances. It has been considered that exposure to risk factors that may affect development of the brain in any of these periods will have long-term effects on behavior. Along with mother's cigarette or alcohol use during pregnancy, emotional difficulties, medical diseases and complications of pregnancy; natal complications, low birth weight, premature birth, post mature birth, physical traumas that may affect brain development in early childhood, psychosocial difficulties are also found to be related to ADHD. Studies of gene-environment interaction also note the importance of environmental factors. For example, a study showed that in cases which carry 7 repeated alleles of DRD4, exposure to prenatal cigarettes causes more severe symptoms of ADHD. The purpose of this paper is to evaluate the role of environmental factors in etiology of ADHD, review these factors in the light of related literature and, lastly, to mention gene-environment interaction.

Keywords: ADHD, risk factors, enviromental factors, etiology

1. Introduction

Attention deficit hyperactivity disorder (ADHD) is a disorder with strong genetic origins, and a number of factors play a role in its etiology [1]. Although ADHD is characterized by the symptoms of attention deficit, hyperactivity, and impulsivity, it was reported that it might have a phenotypic etiological heterogeneity, and all those variables might affect the outcomes of the disorder [2].

The studies on the etiology of ADHD have focused on genetic, neurochemical, and brain imaging methods, as well as the environmental risk factors. Similar to many psychiatric disorders, it appears that interactions of the small effects of a number of genes with each other and the environment result in the development of the disorder [1-3]. Determining the environmental risk factors that play a role in the etiology of the disorder or affect the outcomes negatively is important to provide more comprehensive interventions starting from early developmental periods, and to take required precautions in those patients [4]. It has been currently shown that various environmental risk factors probably increase the incidence of childhood ADHD. In this paper, we mentioned the environmental risk factors that were most commonly associated with ADHD etiology.

2. Pre- and perinatal complications

Complications related to gestation, labor, and the neonatal period are the most common environmental risk factors that were associated with ADHD pathophysiology. Problems that occur before, during, or after birth were supposed to play a role in the development of ADHD. It has been supposed that the risk factors that affect brain development negatively in critical periods would have long-term effects on cognitive functions and behaviors [5]. ADHD has been associated with maternal smoking and alcohol consumption, emotional stress and medical diseases during pregnancy, and gestational complications as well as complications during labor, low birth weight, prematurity or postmaturity, early childhood physical trauma that could affect brain development negatively, and psychosocial challenges [6-9]. The complications that were associated with ADHD include gestational maternal health problems, toxemia or eclampsia, maternal age, intrauterine infections, fetal postmaturity or prematurity, difficult traumatic labor, fetal stress, low birth weight, prenatal bleeding, and all postnatal complications that can negatively affect brain development [9, 10]. Şenol et al. (2001) analyzed prenatal and perinatal histories of 121 patients with ADHD, 50 patients with oppositional defiant disorder (ODD), and 99 patients with conduct disorder (CD) and reported hypoxia in 5.6%, preterm labor in 9.3%, post-term labor in 4.4%, and unplanned pregnancy in 22.6% of the cases [11]. Prenatal, natal, and postnatal characteristics of the patients and the season of birth were investigated in an unpublished thesis study performed by us, and labor problems (difficult traumatic labor, maternal psychosocial stress and smoking, hypoxia, postnatal jaundice, gestational hypertension) and Cesarean section rate in ADHD group were found significantly higher than the control group [12]. Those findings are in accordance with the previous studies that reported low birth weight, and gestational and neonatal complications were risk factors for ADHD [13, 14].

Pre- and perinatal risk factors may cause hypoxic injury and neuronal developmental defects at the early developmental periods of the brain. Basal ganglions that have usually been linked to with ADHD are one of the most metabolically active structures of the brain, and they are sensitive to hypoxic injury [10]. Any perinatal injury to the frontal lobe has been reported to probably affect cognitive functions such as attention, motivation, and planning, and cause ADHD symptoms [15].

Although some studies reported a strong correlation between low birth weight and ADHD [16, 17], some other studies did not rule out potential familial confounding and gene-environment interactions [18-20], and suggested that children with low birth weight were more often inattentive, had social problems, and low self-esteem. Another study found that children who were born preterm were at risk for reduced cognitive test scores at school age [21]. A previous large twin study reported that birth weight accounted for less than one percent of the variance in ADHD symptoms, and it was not a major risk factor for ADHD [22]. Some previous studies reported that low birth weight affected inattention more than hyperactivity [17, 21]. However, a recent comprehensive twin study reported that a lower birth weight was significantly correlated with increased severity of all ADHD symptoms including inattention, hyperactivity-impulsivity, and total scores, and those findings supported the results of previous positive studies. This large recent study is important for demonstrating the correlation of low birth weight with ADHD, which remained after being controlled for gestational age, and shared environmental and genetic confounds [16]. In a longitudinal follow-up study it was found that low birth weight increased the development of ADHD 2.11-fold compared with the general population [23]. In accordance with these data, it could be concluded that low-birth weight is an important risk factor for the development of ADHD.

In a recent study that investigated the relation between maternal age at childbirth and risk for ADHD in the offspring, it was reported that women giving birth at younger ages (teenage mothers) were more likely to have children with ADHD. The relation of early maternal age with ADHD was explained by genetic confounding, which means genetic factors transmitted from mothers to children contributed to both mother's age of childbirth and ADHD in the offspring [24].

More gestational psychosocial stress was reported in mothers of the children with ADHD [8, 25]. Mother's depression, stress, or nervousness during pregnancy are associated with a broad spectrum of negative outcomes including emotional problems, ADHD symptoms, and defects in the cognitive development of the child. Prenatal anxiety and depression were supposed to contribute 10–15% of the burden attributed to emotional and behavioral negative outcomes. The biological mechanisms underlying the relation of prenatal stress and negative outcomes in the child have been recently started to be enlightened. Exposure to prenatal stress was supposed to cause changes in the behavior of the child by increasing the levels of corticotropin releasing hormone, and by disturbing functions of hypothalamic pituitary adrenal (HPA) axis. Disturbed HPA functions were closely associated with neurobiological development and the risk for psychiatric disorders [25, 26]. Although increased exposure to high levels of cortisol in fetus was shown in animal models, some authors commented that HPA axis operated differently in humans, and responded to stress less as the gestational age increased [27]. On the other hand, some others reported that stress increased fetal transfer of maternal cortisol through placenta, decreased the levels of placental enzyme (11β-HSD2) that converted cortisol to inactive cortisone, and the cognitive development of the fetus was affected negatively as the cortisol levels in the amniotic fluid increased [27]. The sympathetic nervous system that is activated during stress was reported to decrease blood flow to the fetus by increasing the resistance of uterine artery, and a decreased blood flow could affect the brain development of the fetus [28]. Those findings may explain the relation of exposure to prenatal stress with the development of ADHD.

3. Prenatal maternal smoking

Prenatal maternal smoking was reported to be a risk factor for hyperactivity in the offspring. It was reported that 25% of the mothers who gave birth smoked in the United States, and only a small proportion of them quit smoking after they had learned that they were pregnant [29]. The rate of smoking during pregnancy was reported between 3% and 37% in Turkey [30-33]. Millberger et al. (1996) reported that 22% of children with ADHD had a history of prenatal cigarette smoke exposure whereas 8% of children without ADHD had the same exposure history. Smoking disturbs normal placental functions by decreasing uterine blood flow [34]. Decreased oxygen supply and nourishment of fetus results in hypoxia-ischemia and malnutrition [35]. As a result, intrauterine growth retardation occurs [36]. A number of studies reported that prenatal exposure to cigarette smoke affected pre- and postnatal growth negatively, damaged neuronal pathways, caused abnormalities in cellular proliferation and differentiation, inhibited development of cholinergic and catecholaminergic systems, and hence increased the risk for cognitive developmental defects and behavior problems in children and adolescents [37, 38]. Prenatal exposure to nicotine stimulates fetal pre-synaptic high affinity $\alpha_4\beta_2$ neuronal nicotinic receptor complex, and alterations appear in neurite growth and branching through DRD4 receptors as a result of increased release of dopamine (DA) from the dopaminergic neurons. Those developmental changes in neuronal maturation result in permanent alterations in neuronal organization and functions [39]. Milberger et al. (1998) found that maternal smoking increased the risk of ADHD by 2.7-fold [36]. A subsequent study by Hjern et al. (2010) reported that maternal smoking during pregnancy increased ADHD prevalence by 2.86-fold [40]. Interestingly, Han et al. (2014) showed that a non-smoking mother's exposure to environmental tobacco smoke, which reflected paternal smoking during pregnancy, was also associated with increased risk of ADHD [41]. Kotimaa et al. (2003) reported a dose-response relationship between maternal smoking during pregnancy and hyperactivity [42].

Dopaminergic and noradrenergic systems were found to be hypoactive and unresponsive to exogenous stimulation after prenatal nicotine exposure [43]. Prenatal nicotine exposure was also shown to decrease nicotine-triggered norepinephrine release [44]. It has been supposed that this disturbance in the development of catecholaminergic system may be related to increased ADHD prevalence [10].

The interactions of environmental factors with genetic factors are important for the clinical presentation and developmental course of ADHD. DRD4 7 repeat allele is the most commonly associated allele with ADHD, and it is known that it increases the sensitivity of the child to environmental factors [45]. Neuman et al. (2007) reported that prenatal cigarette smoke exposure caused more severe ADHD symptoms in subjects carrying DRD4 7 repeat allele [46]. Subsequently, a similar study performed by Altink et al. (2008) did not find any significant gene-environment interaction [47]. When the relation of DAT1 gene with ADHD was considered, Neuman et al. (2007) reported that the odds ratio for ADHD was 2.9 among twins with DAT1 440 allele and prenatal cigarette smoking exposure. The odds ratio for ADHD was 3.0 among twins with DRD4 7 repeat allele who were exposed to prenatal cigarette smoke [46]. In a subsequent study conducted by Becker et al. (2008), it was shown that neither DAT1 nor prenatal cigarette smoke exposure was related to ADHD symptoms; however, males exposed to prenatal cigarette smoke and homozygous for DAT1 gene 10 repeat allele had higher hyperactivity-impulsivity [48]. On the other hand, further maternal risk factors (young age, low level of education, poor prenatal care, maternal behavioral problems) besides maternal smoking were supposed to be influential for the relation between nicotine and ADHD in addition to a direct cause-and-effect relationship [49].

In summary, it is now known that prenatal nicotine exposure is an important environmental risk factor for the development of ADHD. The next step will be to determine which epigenetic mechanisms are responsible.

4. Prenatal alcohol exposure

Maternal alcohol consumption is one of the risk factors for the development of ADHD. Prenatal alcohol exposure is neurotoxic and gives rise to brain abnormalities [50, 51]. Prenatal alcohol exposure increases the risks for hyperactivity, destructive-offense oriented or impulsive behavior, and psychiatric disorders in children. Disturbed cognitive abilities include overall intellectual performance, learning and memory, language, attention, reaction time, visual-spatial abilities, executive functions, fine and gross motor skills, and adaptive and social behaviors [52]. Streissguth et al. (1990) reported that moderate levels of prenatal alcohol exposure might have long-lasting effects on IQ, and led to learning problems in school aged children [53].

Various studies showed that prenatal alcohol exposure increased the risk for ADHD [41, 54]. Some other studies did not report any association between prenatal alcohol exposure and Continuous Performance Taskperformance in school aged children [55]. Similarly, Rodriguez et al. (2009) did not report any significant association between ADHD and prenatal alcohol exposure [56]. In another study, maternal alcohol consumption was suggested to be associated with a higher rate of conduct problems, but not with ADHD [57]. In a recent review article, it was suggested that heavy prenatal alcohol exposure was associated with symptom characteristics of ADHD including externalizing problems, inattention, impulsivity, as well as the diagnosis of ADHD. However, the association of low to moderate levels of prenatal alcohol exposure with ADHD was less conclusive [58]. The data so far indicate that there is no strong evidence showing that prenatal alcohol exposure plays as much of a role in the development of ADHD as prenatal nicotine exposure. Therefore, longitudinal follow-up studies with large samples are needed to understand the exact effect of prenatal alcohol exposure on ADHD development.

5. Prenatal substance exposure

Various studies showed that gestational exposure to cocaine was associated with behavioral problems and attention disorders in preschool and school aged children [59]. Exposure to cocaine may cause behavioral alterations by changing the monoaminergic system [58]. Disruption of the monoaminergic system's development in the prenatal period may result in changes in various cognitive and behavioral processes such as emotional regulation, arousal, and attention [60]. Cocaine exposure in the first trimester was reported to be significantly associated with increased behavioral problems in 3-year-old children [61]. Another study evaluated 6-year-old, cocaine and non-cocaine exposed children's mental health outcomes, and showed that cocaine exposed children were more likely to self-report ADHD and oppositional defiant disorder symptoms [62]. A large maternal lifestyle study performed by Bada et al. (2011) reported that prenatal cocaine exposure as declared by teacher and parents predicted (or was associated with) externalizing behavior problems in preadolescent children [63].

In a series of studies, Richardson et al. showed that prenatal cocaine exposure was associated with neurobehavioral and neurophysiological alterations at birth [64], temperament at 1 year [65], and temperament, memory, and behavior at 3 years of age [61]. Same authors reported that children exposed to cocaine during pregnancy had more behavior problems at 7 years of age when compared to the children of women who stopped using cocaine at pregnancy's early stages or who never used cocaine prenatally. Therefore, it was emphasized that third trimester use reflecting use throughout pregnancy was associated with significantly more externalizing behavior problems and inattention [66]. On the other hand, follow up analysis performed when the children were 10 years old did not show any significant effect of prenatal cocaine exposure on externalizing problems [67]. As it was commented, the latter result indicated that the results of prenatal cocaine use might differ in relation with methodological factors such as the type of assessment and observer [67], as well as developmental stage [58].

The data on the long-term effects of heroin use are more scarce [58]. Wilson et al. (1979) reported parent-reported uncontrollable tempers and impulsiveness in 3- to 6-year-old children exposed to prenatal heroine, and indicated that those children were more hyperkinetic [68]. Another study reported that children with prenatal methadone exposure were considered to have parent-reported hyperactivity and externalizing behavior problems [69].

Slinning (2004) reported that foster placed children prenatally exposed to poly-substances had significantly elevated levels of impulsivity and attention problems at preschool ages [70]. The presence of environmental changes in studied children such as adoption or accommodation in foster care homes, and comparing those children with healthy controls living together with their biological parents appear as limitations of the studies investigating the effects of prenatal substance exposure on behavior and the attention of children. On the other hand, living with foster-parents may imply the presence of an adequate care, and it may be considered as a protective factor against postnatal risk factors. Contrary to this hypothesis, Ornoy et al. (2010) reported that adoption did not relieve the effects of prenatal exposure to drugs [71]. Another study showed that children born to heroin-dependent parents and raised at home had lower cognitive abilities and higher attention problems at preschool and school ages. However, children who were born to heroin-dependent mothers, adopted, and being raised in an ideal environment had high frequencies of attention and behavioral problems, but normal intellectual functions. Finally, it was found that all school aged children born to heroin-dependent parents including the ones raised at home and adopted had a high rate of ADHD, but an ideal environment after birth had a positive effect on intellectual abilities [72]. Although this result was interpreted as ADHD symptoms might be directly associated with heroin exposure and originated from fetal brain injury related to heroin [71, 72], the high incidences of hyperactivity and inattention in children born to heroin-dependent fathers [72] suggest that different environmental factors contribute to this association.

When it is considered that caretaker characteristics, home environment, and community factors are also risk factors for later behavior problems [63], it is clear that prenatal substance abuse may be a predisposing factor for those risk factors as well as other environmental risk factors such as presence of other maternal psychopathologies, malnutrition during pregnancy, exposure to other abused substances, and unfavorable postnatal living conditions.

6. Toxins and food additives

Various toxins and food additives were investigated in the etiology of ADHD. Exposure to toxins such as lead, mercury, and manganese, or food additives such as dyes and preservatives, as well as sugars was reported to result in the development of ADHD [73-75]. Braun et al. (2006) reported that higher blood lead concentrations in children had a significant correlation with ADHD, and children with a blood lead level >2.0 μg/dL had 4.1-fold increased risk for ADHD [76]. It was emphasized that blood lead levels under 10 μg/dL which is the level set by Centers for Disease Control and Prevention was associated with an increased risk of ADHD in children [76, 77]. Exposure to lead and polychlorinated biphenyls (PCBs) was shown to cause cognitive deficits similar to those seen in children with ADHD, and disturbed attention and executive functions [78]. Studies on children and animal models indicated that lead disrupted both response inhibition and attention processes [79-81], however PCBs tended to disturb response inhibition to a greater degree than attention [78, 82-84]. In a recent study, Neugebauer et al. (2015) investigated the effects of prenatal polychlorinated dibenzo-p-dioxins and furan (PCDD/F), PBC, and lead exposure on attention performance in school-aged children [85]. They found that pre- and perinatal PCDD/F and PBC exposure might affect attention performance in healthy children at low environmental levels while PCDD/F or PBC exposure were negatively associated with ADHD-related behavior, and prenatal lead exposure had an effect on attention deficits [85]. However, cumulative findings on the association between lead exposure and attention deficits are less consistent.

The data on relation of environmental mercury exposure and ADHD are not consistent [86-88]. A recent meta-analysis by Yoshimasu et al. (2014) suggested that environmental perinatal mercury exposure (exposure sources were air pollution, maternal fish consumption during pregnancy estimated by maternal hair samples, or childhood environmental exposure measured by blood sample) was significantly associated with an increased risk of ADHD. On the other hand, the mercury exposure of embryos or young infants related to thimerosal containing vaccines were not associated with an increased risk for ADHD [89]. Studies that investigated the association between postnatal pyrethroid pesticide exposure and ADHD revealed diverse findings. Rodríguez (2012) reported a correlation between urine levels of pyrethroid pesticide's metabolite 3-phenoxy-benzoic acid (3-PBA) and ADHD in girls [90] whereas Quirós- Alcalá et al. (2014) showed that postnatal pyrethroid exposure was not associated with the parental report of ADHD in children [91].

In fact, exposure to those toxins and food additives cannot be determined in many of the children with ADHD, and many children who are exposed to those substances do not develop ADHD. Therefore, scientific evidence related to those substances need to be further clarified [10].

7. Season of birth

It was suggested that season of birth was one of the environmental risk factors. It was reported that season of birth paved the way for seasonal viral infections, and it might play an important role in the etiology and pathophysiology of ADHD [92]. Chotai et al. (2003) reported that season of birth variations were different for schizophrenia and affective disorders in tryptophan hydroxylase, serotonin transporter, and DRD4 gene polymorphisms. Therefore, it was reported that season of birth could be a confounding variable when investigating the role of the candidate genes in susceptibility to psychiatric disorders [93]. Being born in spring or summer was associated with an increased risk for neurodevelopmental disorders [94]. This period was associated with the presence of a short sunlight time for a long period and decreased sex hormones as well as increased pineal gland activity and melatonin release. Melatonin is synthesized from serotonin by N-acetyltransferase enzyme. Melatonin synthesis peaks at night, and it is at minimum during the day. It has been supposed that melatonin inhibits DA synthesis in many regions of the brain including striatum, and DA inhibits melatonin production via DRD4. It was reported that melatonin-DA interaction during pregnancy might result in decreased postsynaptic DRD4 receptor sensitivity [95]. Mick et al. (1996) reported significant relations of winter births and ADHD children with learning disabilities, and no psychiatric comorbidity [92]. Some studies investigated the relation between DRD4 gene and season of birth. Seeger et al. (2004) performed a study on patients with ADHD and comorbid DB, and claimed that seven-repeat allele could be associated with a relative risk only in the ones who were born in summer [96]. On the contrary, another study by Brookes et al. (2008) found a significant relation between winter births and seven-repeat allele in a large sample group [97].

In conclusion, in light of these data, it is not clear that any of the birth seasons are related to an increased risk for ADHD development. The main reason for the inconsistent results in this area might be that the birth season has an indirect effect on ADHD by affecting the exposure to other environmental risk factors such as seasonal viral infections or hormonal changes. When the role of gene-environment interactions and various epigenetic mechanisms on ADHD etiology are taken into account, it is obvious that there is a need to consider all these interactions and the effects of secondary environmental factors on the results.

8. Iron deficiency

The relation between iron deficiency and ADHD symptoms was investigated in some studies [98]. A direct correlation was proposed between iron and dopamine dysfunction, which was suggested to be the case in ADHD. Iron is a cofactor of tyrosine hydroxylase enzyme that plays a role in the rate limiting step of dopamine synthesis [99], and animal studies showed that iron deficiency could affect dopamine receptor density in brain [100]. Konofal et al. (2004) reported low ferritin levels in 84% of the children diagnosed with ADHD, and found a negative correlation between ferritin levels and ADHD symptom severity [101]. Another study found a correlation between low ferritin levels and hyperactivity scores in children with ADHD, however no relation was found with cognitive functions [102]. Karakurt et al. (2011) reported a significant negative correlation between behavior problems and ferritin levels in children with ADHD [98].

Although the results of studies are conflicting, iron supplementation was reported to decrease ADHD symptoms [103]. A large study that investigated the effects of iron deficiency and ferritin levels on treatment of ADHD with stimulants reported that neither iron deficiency nor ferritin levels had significant correlations with short-term response to stimulant therapy, and the authors claimed that the relation between iron metabolism and ADHD was more complex contrary to the popular belief [104].

The results of the researches investigating the relationship of iron deficiency with ADHD etiology show promise and form the basis of further studies to investigate the levels of iron in brain tissue by various neuroimaging methods or classified patients according to the factors that may affect the iron parameters in different ways. However, in this instance, before drawing any conclusions in this area, there is a need for further research.

9. Psychosocial stress factors

Psychosocial challenges such as maltreatment, emotional trauma, and sexual abuse were correlated with ADHD development [105, 106]. Familial factors associated with childhood mental disorders including severe marital discord, low social status, a large family, paternal criminality, maternal mental disorders, lack of family consolidation, and living in nursing homes were described as adversity factors [7]. In a recent retrospective study that aimed to determine the parameters predictive of later diagnosis of ADHD in infants and toddlers, one of the identified factors was psychosocial risk factors, including stress, marital conflicts, separation and divorce, and maternal depression [107]. In a systematic review that investigated environmental risk factors for disruptive behavior disorders (ADHD, ODD, CD), psychosocial risk factors such as parental stress, maternal depression, early deprivation, separation, and adoption were reported to be associated with disruptive behavior disorders [108]. In a prospective cohort study conducted with the general population and consisting of 2,057 children followed up from 5 months to 8 years, as well as other various environmental risk factors, three important psychosocial risk factors were found to be associated with ADHD development: non-intact family, paternal history of antisocial behavior, and maternal depression [23]. Comparison of the families with children with ADHD and the families without children with ADHD revealed more interpersonal conflicts, increased maternal stress and marital discord, separation and divorce, less family dialogues and positive family experiences in ADHD families [109]. In a study investigating how early-life deprivation might cause ADHD, it was reported that early-life deprivation disrupted cortical development and caused reduced cortical thickness and atypical functioning in regions associated with regulation of attention. The increased rates of ADHD among children raised in institutional settings were reported to be possibly associated with this mechanism [110].

Although some authors did not believe in a causative role of parental discipline on the development of ADHD [111], some others believe that discipline problems played an important role in the development of ADHD symptoms, and observing behavior problems and oppositional defiant disorder in children with ADHD [112]. Gathering negative factors rather than the presence of any of those factors was reported to affect development in a negative way. Psychosocial factors were reported to have effects on preparation and fast manifestation in the development of ADHD [113].

10. Conclusion

The most important challenges in studies investigating the environmental factors in ADHD etiology include subjectivity of retrospective assessment, common intermingling of the risk factors, possibility of observer bias, and methodological differences among studies. However, the results of most current studies grew stronger owing to prospective and longitudinal study design, obtaining information from multiple sources such as parents and teachers, use of standardized scales, planning of the study by considering secondary and even tertiary risk factors in addition to the primary risk factor, and analyzing multiple factors in statistical analysis. In this regard, the cumulative evaluation of all studies performed to date indicates the significance of environmental risk factors in the development of ADHD. However, while some of these environmental risk factors are well established, others still require more investigation. Although the association of pre- and perinatal complications that cause hypoxic injury, low birth weight, prenatal nicotine exposure, various perinatal psychosocial risk factors such as maternal depression and parental stress with etiology of ADHD are more clear, the study results associated with prenatal alcohol exposure, toxins, and food additives or iron deficiency are contradictory.

In summary, different from the other etiologic factors, relatively controllable and preventable characteristics of environmental risk factors put forward their importance once again. Determination of the environmental risk factors that play a role in the etiology of ADHD and other neurodevelopmental disorders is important for possible prevention of those diseases, as well as for the execution of comprehensive interventions starting from early developmental stages, and for taking necessary precautions.

Author details

Esra Guney[1], Fatih Hilmi Cetin[2] and Elvan Iseri[1]

1 Department of Child and Adolescent Psychiatry, Gazi University Medical Faculty, Ankara, Turkey

2 Department of Child and Adolescent Psychiatry, Kayseri Training and Research Hospital-Emel Mehmet Tarman Children's Clinic, Ankara, Turkey

References

[1] Faraone SV, Perlis RH, Doyle AE, Smoller JW, Goralnick JJ, Holmgren MA, et al. Molecular genetics of attention-deficit/hyperactivity disorder. Biological Psychiatry 2005; 57: 1313-23.

[2] Rohde LA, Halpern R. Recent advances on attention deficit/hyperactivity disorder. Jornal de Pediatria 2004; 80: 61-70.

[3] Stahl SM. Stahl's essential psychopharmacology: neuroscientific basis and practical applications. Cambridge University Press; 2013.

[4] Kessler RC, Adler LA, Barkley R, Biederman J, Conners CK, Faraone SV, et al. Patterns and predictors of attention-deficit/hyperactivity disorder persistence into adulthood: results from the national comorbidity survey replication. Biological Psychiatry 2005; 57: 1442-51.

[5] Amor LB, Grizenko N, Schwartz G, Lageix P, Baron C, Ter-Stepanian M, et al. Perinatal complications in children with attention-deficit hyperactivity disorder and their unaffected siblings. Journal of Psychiatry and Neuroscience 2005; 30: 120.

[6] Biederman J, Milberger S, Faraone SV, Kiely K, Guite J, Mick E, et al. Impact of adversity on functioning and comorbidity in children with attention-deficit hyperactivity disorder. Journal of the American Academy of Child & Adolescent Psychiatry 1995; 34: 1495-503.

[7] Biederman J, Milberger S, Faraone SV, Kiely K, Guite J, Mick E, et al. Family-environment risk factors for attention-deficit hyperactivity disorder: a test of Rutter's indicators of adversity. Archives of General Psychiatry 1995; 52: 464-70.

[8] McIntosh DE, Mulkins RS, Dean RS. Utilization of maternal perinatal risk indicators in the differential diagnosis of ADHD and UADD children. International Journal of Neuroscience 1995; 81: 35-46.

[9] Sprich-Buckminster S, Biederman J, Milberger S, Faraone SV, Lehman BK. Are perinatal complications relevant to the manifestation of ADD? Issues of comorbidity and familiality. Journal of the American Academy of Child & Adolescent Psychiatry 1993; 32: 1032-7.

[10] Banerjee TD, Middleton F, Faraone SV. Environmental risk factors for attention-deficit hyperactivity disorder. Acta Paediatrica 2007; 96: 1269-74.

[11] Senol S, Sener S, Ergenekon E, Gücüyener K. The impact of pre-and perinatal factors on attention-deficit and disruptive behavior disorders. The Turkish ournal of Pediatrics 2000; 43: 231-6.

[12] Guney E. Dikkat Eksikliği Hiperaktivite Bozukluğunda İzlem: Klinik Özelliklerin Değişimi, Seyir Üzerinde Etkili Faktörler ve Genetik Korelasyon. In: Uzmanlık Tezi Gazi Üniversitesi Ankara; 2009.

[13] Hultman CM, Torrång A, Tuvblad C, Cnattingius S, Larsson J-O, Lichtenstein P. Birth weight and attention-deficit/hyperactivity symptoms in childhood and early adolescence: a prospective Swedish twin study. Journal of the American Academy of Child & Adolescent Psychiatry 2007; 46: 370-7.

[14] Sasaluxnanon C, Kaewpornsawan T. Risk factor of birth weight below 2,500 grams and attention deficit hyperactivity disorder in Thai children. Journal-Medıcal Assocıatıon of Thaıland 2005; 88: 1514.

[15] Levy F, Barr C, Sunohara G. Directions of aetiologic research on attention deficit hyperactivity disorder. Australian and New Zealand Journal of Psychiatry 1998; 32: 97-103.

[16] Pettersson E, Sjölander A, Almqvist C, Anckarsäter H, D'Onofrio BM, Lichtenstein P, et al. Birth weight as an independent predictor of ADHD symptoms: a within-twin pair analysis. Journal of Child Psychology and Psychiatry 2014; 56:453-9.

[17] Indredavik M, Vik T, Heyerdahl S, Kulseng S, Fayers P, Brubakk A. Psychiatric symptoms and disorders in adolescents with low birth weight. Archives of Disease in Childhood-Fetal and Neonatal Edition 2004; 89: F445-50.

[18] Thapar A, Rutter M. Do prenatal risk factors cause psychiatric disorder? Be wary of causal claims. The British Journal of Psychiatry 2009; 195: 100-1.

[19] Elgen I, Sommerfelt K, Markestad T. Population based, controlled study of behavioural problems and psychiatric disorders in low birthweight children at 11 years of age. Archives of Disease in Childhood-Fetal and Neonatal Edition 2002; 87: F128-32.

[20] D'Onofrio BM, Lahey BB, Turkheimer E, Lichtenstein P. Critical need for family-based, quasi-experimental designs in integrating genetic and social science research. American Journal of Public Health 2013; 103: S46-55.

[21] Bhutta AT, Cleves MA, Casey PH, Cradock MM, Anand K. Cognitive and behavioral outcomes of school-aged children who were born preterm: a meta-analysis. JAMA 2002; 288: 728-37.

[22] Ficks CA, Lahey BB, Waldman ID. Does low birth weight share common genetic or environmental risk with childhood disruptive disorders? Journal of Abnormal Psychology 2013; 122: 842.

[23] Galéra C, Côté SM, Bouvard MP, Pingault J-B, Melchior M, Michel G, et al. Early risk factors for hyperactivity-impulsivity and inattention trajectories from age 17 months to 8 years. Archives of General Psychiatry 2011; 68: 1267-75.

[24] Chang Z, Lichtenstein P, D'Onofrio BM, Almqvist C, Kuja-Halkola R, Sjölander A, et al. Maternal age at childbirth and risk for ADHD in offspring: a population-based cohort study. International Journal of Epidemiology 2014: dyu204.

[25] Talge NM, Neal C, Glover V. Antenatal maternal stress and long-term effects on child neurodevelopment: how and why? Journal of Child Psychology and Psychiatry 2007; 48(3-4): 245-61.

[26] Weinstock M. Alterations induced by gestational stress in brain morphology and behaviour of the offspring. Progress in Neurobiology 2001; 65: 427-51.

[27] Glover V. Prenatal stress and its effects on the fetus and the child: possible underlying biological mechanisms. In: Perinatal Programming of Neurodevelopment. Springer; 2015, p. 269-83.

[28] Teixeira J, Fisk NM, Glover V. Association between maternal anxiety in pregnancy and increased uterine artery resistance index: cohort based study. BMJ 1999; 318: 153-7.

[29] Pauly JR, Slotkin TA. Maternal tobacco smoking, nicotine replacement and neurobehavioural development. Acta Paediatrica 2008; 97: 1331-7.

[30] Alp H, Selimoğlu MA, Yaman S, Energin M, Altınkaynak S, Orbak Z. Gebelikte sigara kullanımının fetüsa etkileri. İstanbul Çocuk Kliniği Dergisi 1995; 30: 80-3.

[31] Özsoy S. Gebelikte sigara içme alışkanlığı ve evde sigara içilmesinin doğum şekli ve bebeğin doğum tartısı üzerine etkisi. Hemşirelik Bülteni 1992; 6: 25; 26.

[32] Semiz O, Sözeri C, Cevahir R, Şahin S, Kılıçoğlu SS. Sakarya'da bir sağlık kuruluşuna başvuran gebelerin sigara içme durumlarıyla ilgili bazı özellikler. STED 2006; 15: 149-52.

[33] Marakoğlu K, Sezer RE. Sivas' ta gebelikte sigara kullanımı. Cumhuriyet Üniversitesi Tıp Fakültesi Dergisi 2003; 25: 157-64.

[34] Milberger S, Biederman J, Faraone SV, Chen L, Jones J. Is maternal smoking during pregnancy a risk factor for attention deficit hyperactivity disorder in children? The American Journal of Psychiatry 1996; 153(9):1138-1142.

[35] Suzuki K, Minei L, Johnson E. Effect of nicotine upon uterine blood flow in the pregnant rhesus monkey. American Journal of Obstetrics Gynecology 1980; 136: 1009-13.

[36] Milberger S, Biederman J, Faraone SV, Jones J. Further evidence of an association between maternal smoking during pregnancy and attention deficit hyperactivity disorder: findings from a high-risk sample of siblings. Journal of Clinical Child Psychology 1998; 27: 352-8.

[37] Wasserman RC, Kelleher KJ, Bocian A, Baker A, Childs GE, Indacochea F, et al. Identification of attentional and hyperactivity problems in primary care: a report from pediatric research in office settings and the ambulatory sentinel practice network. Pediatrics 1999; 103: e38-e.

[38] Ernst M, Moolchan ET, Robinson ML. Behavioral and neural consequences of prenatal exposure to nicotine. Journal of the American Academy of Child & Adolescent Psychiatry 2001; 40: 630-41.

[39] Todd RD, Neuman RJ. Gene–environment interactions in the development of combined type ADHD: evidence for a synapse-based model. American Journal of Medical Genetics Part B: Neuropsychiatric Genetics 2007; 144: 971-5.

[40] Hjern A, Weitoft GR, Lindblad F. Social adversity predicts ADHD-medication in school children–a national cohort study. Acta Paediatrica 2010; 99: 920-4.

[41] Han J-Y, Kwon H-J, Ha M, Paik K-C, Lim M-H, Lee SG, et al. The effects of prenatal exposure to alcohol and environmental tobacco smoke on risk for ADHD: a large population-based study. Psychiatry Research 2014; 225(1):164-168.

[42] Kotimaa AJ, Moilanen I, Taanila A, Ebeling H, Smalley SL, Mcgough JJ, et al. Maternal smoking and hyperactivity in 8-year-old children. Journal of the American Academy of Child & Adolescent Psychiatry 2003; 42: 826-33.

[43] Slotkin TA. Fetal nicotine or cocaine exposure: which one is worse? Journal of Pharmacology and Experimental Therapeutics 1998; 285: 931-45.

[44] Seidler F, Levin E, Lappi S, Slotkin T. Fetal nicotine exposure ablates the ability of postnatal nicotine challenge to release norepinephrine from rat brain regions. Developmental Brain Research 1992; 69: 288-91.

[45] Sheese BE, Voelker PM, Rothbart MK, Posner MI. Parenting quality interacts with genetic variation in dopamine receptor D4 to influence temperament in early childhood. Development and Psychopathology 2007; 19: 1039-46.

[46] Neuman RJ, Lobos E, Reich W, Henderson CA, Sun L-W, Todd RD. Prenatal smoking exposure and dopaminergic genotypes interact to cause a severe ADHD subtype. Biological Psychiatry 2007; 61: 1320-8.

[47] Altink ME, Arias-Vásquez A, Franke B, Slaats–Willemse DI, Buschgens CJ, Rommelse NN, et al. The dopamine receptor D4 7-repeat allele and prenatal smoking in ADHD-affected children and their unaffected siblings: no gene–environment interaction. Journal of Child Psychology and Psychiatry 2008; 49: 1053-60.

[48] Becker K, El-Faddagh M, Schmidt MH, Esser G, Laucht M. Interaction of dopamine transporter genotype with prenatal smoke exposure on ADHD symptoms. The Journal of Pediatrics 2008; 152: 263-9. e1.

[49] Button TMM, Maughan B, McGuffin P. The relationship of maternal smoking to psychological problems in the offspring. Early Human Development 2007; 83: 727-32.

[50] Olney J, Ishimaru M, Bittigau P, Ikonomidou C. Ethanol-induced apoptotic neurodegeneration in the developing brain. Apoptosis 2000; 5: 515-21.

[51] Sowell ER, Mattson S, Thompson P, Jernigan T, Riley E, Toga A. Mapping callosal morphology and cognitive correlates Effects of heavy prenatal alcohol exposure. Neurology 2001; 57: 235-44.

[52] Huizink AC, Mulder EJ. Maternal smoking, drinking or cannabis use during pregnancy and neurobehavioral and cognitive functioning in human offspring. Neuroscience & Biobehavioral Reviews 2006; 30: 24-41.

[53] Streissguth AP, Barr HM, Sampson PD. Moderate prenatal alcohol exposure: effects on child IQ and learning problems at age 7 1/2 years. Alcoholism: Clinical and Experimental Research 1990; 14: 662-9.

[54] Knopik VS, Heath AC, Jacob T, Slutske WS, Bucholz KK, Madden PA, et al. Maternal alcohol use disorder and offspring ADHD: disentangling genetic and environmental effects using a children-of-twins design. Psychological Medicine 2006; 36: 1461-71.

[55] Leech S, Richardson GA, Goldschmidt L, Day N. Prenatal substance exposure: effects on attention and impulsivity of 6-year-olds. Neurotoxicology and Teratology 1999; 21: 109-18.

[56] Rodriguez A, Olsen J, Kotimaa A, Kaakinen M, Moilanen I, Henriksen TB, et al. Is prenatal alcohol exposure related to inattention and hyperactivity symptoms in children? Disentangling the effects of social adversity. Journal of Child Psychology and Psychiatry 2009; 50: 1073-83.

[57] D'Onofrio BM, Van Hulle CA, Waldman ID, Rodgers JL, Rathouz PJ, Lahey BB. Causal inferences regarding prenatal alcohol exposure and childhood externalizing problems. Archives of General Psychiatry 2007; 64: 1296-304.

[58] Yolton K, Cornelius M, Ornoy A, McGough J, Makris S, Schantz S. Exposure to neurotoxicants and the development of attention deficit hyperactivity disorder and its related behaviors in childhood. Neurotoxicology and Teratology 2014; 44: 30-45.

[59] Whitaker R. Anatomy of an epidemic: magic bullets, psychiatric drugs, and the astonishing rise of mental illness in America. Broadway LLC; 2011.

[60] Meyer JS, Shearman LP, Collins LM. Monoamine transporters and the neurobehavioral teratology of cocaine. Pharmacology Biochemistry and Behavior 1996; 55(4): 585-93.

[61] Richardson GA, Goldschmidt L, Willford J. Continued effects of prenatal cocaine use: preschool development. Neurotoxicology and Teratology 2009; 31: 325-33.

[62] Linares TJ, Singer LT, Kirchner HL, Short EJ, Min MO, Hussey P, et al. Mental health outcomes of cocaine-exposed children at 6 years of age. Journal of Pediatric Psychology 2006; 31: 85-97.

[63] Bada HS, Bann CM, Bauer CR, Shankaran S, Lester B, LaGasse L, et al. Preadolescent behavior problems after prenatal cocaine exposure: relationship between teacher and caretaker ratings (Maternal Lifestyle Study). Neurotoxicology and Teratology 2011; 33: 78-87.

[64] Richardson GA, Hamel SC, Goldschmidt L, Day NL. The effects of prenatal cocaine use on neonatal neurobehavioral status. Neurotoxicology and Teratology 1996; 18: 519-28.

[65] Richardson GA, Goldschmidt L, Willford J. The effects of prenatal cocaine use on infant development. Neurotoxicology and Teratology 2008; 30: 96-106.

[66] Richardson GA, Goldschmidt L, Leech S, Willford J. Prenatal cocaine exposure: effects on mother-and teacher-rated behavior problems and growth in school-age children. Neurotoxicology and Teratology 2011; 33: 69-77.

[67] Richardson GA, Larkby C, Goldschmidt L, Day NL. Adolescent initiation of drug use: effects of prenatal cocaine exposure. Journal of the American Academy of Child & Adolescent Psychiatry 2013; 52: 37-46.

[68] Wilson GS, McCreary R, Kean J, Baxter JC. The development of preschool children of heroin-addicted mothers: a controlled study. Pediatrics 1979; 63: 135-41.

[69] De Cubas MM, Field T. Children of methadone-dependent women: developmental outcomes. American Journal of Orthopsychiatry 1993; 63(2):266-76.

[70] Slinning K. Foster placed children prenatally exposed to poly-substances. European Child & Adolescent Psychiatry 2004; 13: 19-27.

[71] Ornoy A, Ergaz Z. Alcohol abuse in pregnant women: effects on the fetus and newborn, mode of action and maternal treatment. International Journal of Environmental Research and Public Health 2010; 7: 364-79.

[72] Ornoy A. The impact of intrauterine exposure versus postnatal environment in neurodevelopmental toxicity: long-term neurobehavioral studies in children at risk for developmental disorders. Toxicology Letters 2003; 140: 171-81.

[73] Kanarek RB. Does sucrose or aspartame cause hyperactivity in children? Nutrition Reviews 1994; 52: 173-5.

[74] Needleman HL. Lead and impaired abilities. Developmental Medicine & Child Neurology 1982; 24: 196-7.

[75] Collipp P, Chen S, Maitinsky S. Manganese in infant formulas and learning disability. Annals of Nutrition and Metabolism 1983; 27: 488-94.

[76] Braun JM, Kahn RS, Froehlich T, Auinger P, Lanphear BP. Exposures to environmental toxicants and attention deficit hyperactivity disorder in US children. Environmental Health Perspectives 2006: 1904-9.

[77] Control CfD, Prevention. Blood lead levels--United States, 1999-2002. MMWR Morbidity and Mortality Weekly Report 2005; 54: 513.

[78] Eubig PA, Aguiar A, Schantz SL. Lead and PCBs as risk factors for attention deficit/hyperactivity disorder. Environmental health perspectives 2010; 118: 1654-67.

[79] Chiodo LM, Jacobson SW, Jacobson JL. Neurodevelopmental effects of postnatal lead exposure at very low levels. Neurotoxicology and Teratology 2004; 26: 359-71.

[80] Morgan RE, Garavan H, Smith EG, Driscoll LL, Levitsky DA, Strupp BJ. Early lead exposure produces lasting changes in sustained attention, response initiation, and reactivity to errors. Neurotoxicology and Teratology 2001; 23: 519-31.

[81] Stewart PW, Lonky E, Reihman J, Pagano J, Gump BB, Darvill T. The relationship between prenatal PCB exposure and intelligence (IQ) in 9-year-old children. Environmental Health Perspectives 2008; 116(10):1416-22.

[82] Jacobson JL, Jacobson SW. Prenatal exposure to polychlorinated biphenyls and attention at school age. The Journal of Pediatrics 2003; 143: 780-8.

[83] Stewart P, Fitzgerald S, Reihman J, Gump B, Lonky E, Darvill T, et al. Prenatal PCB exposure, the corpus callosum, and response inhibition. Environmental Health Perspectives 2003; 111: 1670.

[84] Stewart P, Reihman J, Gump B, Lonky E, Darvill T, Pagano J. Response inhibition at 8 and 9 1/2 years of age in children prenatally exposed to PCBs. Neurotoxicology and Teratology 2005; 27: 771-80.

[85] Neugebauer J, Wittsiepe J, Kasper-Sonnenberg M, Schöneck N, Schölmerich A, Wilhelm M. The influence of low level pre-and perinatal exposure to PCDD/Fs, PCBs, and lead on attention performance and attention-related behavior among German school-aged children: results from the Duisburg Birth Cohort Study. International Journal of Hygiene and Environmental Health 2015; 218: 153-62.

[86] Boucher O, Jacobson SW, Plusquellec P, Dewailly É, Ayotte P, Forget-Dubois N, et al. Prenatal methylmercury, postnatal lead exposure, and evidence of attention deficit/hyperactivity disorder among Inuit children in Arctic Québec. Environmental Health Perspectives 2012; 120: 1456-61.

[87] Sagiv SK, Thurston SW, Bellinger DC, Amarasiriwardena C, Korrick SA. Prenatal exposure to mercury and fish consumption during pregnancy and attention-deficit/hyperactivity disorder–related behavior in children. Archives of Pediatrics & Adolescent Medicine 2012; 166: 1123-31.

[88] Ha M, Kwon H-J, Lim M-H, Jee Y-K, Hong Y-C, Leem J-H, et al. Low blood levels of lead and mercury and symptoms of attention deficit hyperactivity in children: a report of the children's health and environment research (CHEER). Neurotoxicology 2009; 30: 31-6.

[89] Yoshimasu K, Kiyohara C, Takemura S, Nakai K. A meta-analysis of the evidence on the impact of prenatal and early infancy exposures to mercury on autism and attention deficit/hyperactivity disorder in the childhood. Neurotoxicology 2014; 44: 121-31.

[90] Rodríguez T. Environmental pesticide exposure and neurobehavioral effects among children of Nicaraguan agricultural workers. Uppsala, Acta Universitatis Upsaliensis, 2012.

[91] Quirós-Alcalá L, Mehta S, Eskenazi B. Pyrethroid pesticide exposure and parental report of learning disability and attention deficit/hyperactivity disorder in US Children: NHANES 1999–2002. Environmental Health Perspectives 2014; 122: 1336.

[92] Mick E, Biederman J, Faraone SV. Is season of birth a risk factor for attention-deficit hyperactivity disorder? Journal of the American Academy of Child & Adolescent Psychiatry 1996; 35: 1470-6.

[93] Chotai J, Serretti A, Lattuada E, Lorenzi C, Lilli R. Gene–environment interaction in psychiatric disorders as indicated by season of birth variations in tryptophan hydroxylase (TPH), serotonin transporter (5-HTTLPR) and dopamine receptor (DRD4) gene polymorphisms. Psychiatry Research 2003; 119: 99-111.

[94] Liederman J, Flannery KA. Fall conception increases the risk of neurodevelopmental disorder in offspring. Journal of Clinical and Experimental Neuropsychology 1994; 16: 754-68.

[95] Tosini G, Dirden JC. Dopamine inhibits melatonin release in the mammalian retina: in vitro evidence. Neuroscience Letters 2000; 286: 119-22.

[96] Seeger G, Schloss P, Schmidt MH, Rüter-Jungfleisch A, Henn FA. Gene–environment interaction in hyperkinetic conduct disorder (HD+ CD) as indicated by season of birth variations in dopamine receptor (DRD4) gene polymorphism. Neuroscience Letters 2004; 366: 282-6.

[97] Brookes KJ, Neale B, Xu X, Thapar A, Gill M, Langley K, et al. Differential dopamine receptor D4 allele association with ADHD dependent of proband season of birth. American Journal of Medical Genetics Part B: Neuropsychiatric Genetics 2008; 147: 94-9.

[98] Karakurt MN, Karabekiroğlu MK, Akbaş S, Bilgici B, Kılıç M, Şenses A, et al. Association between symptom profiles and iron and ferritine serum levels in children with attention deficit hyperactivity disorder research article. 2011; 48:125-128.

[99] Wigglesworth J, Baum H. Iron dependent enzymes in the brain. In: Brain iron: neurochemical and behavioural aspects. New York: Taylor and Francis, 1988; p. 25-66.

[100] Erikson KM, Jones BC, Hess EJ, Zhang Q, Beard JL. Iron deficiency decreases dopamine D1 and D2 receptors in rat brain. Pharmacology Biochemistry and Behavior 2001; 69(3): 409-18.

[101] Konofal E, Lecendreux M, Arnulf I, Mouren M-C. Iron deficiency in children with attention-deficit/hyperactivity disorder. Archives of Pediatrics & Adolescent Medicine 2004; 158: 1113-5.

[102] Oner O, Alkar OY, Oner P. Relation of ferritin levels with symptom ratings and cognitive performance in children with attention deficit–hyperactivity disorder. Pediatrics International 2008; 50: 40-4.

[103] Konofal E, Lecendreux M, Deron J, Marchand M, Cortese S, Zaïm M, et al. Effects of iron supplementation on attention deficit hyperactivity disorder in children. Pediatric Neurology 2008; 38: 20-6.

[104] Oner P, Oner O, Cop E, Munir KM. Effect of ferritin on short-term treatment response in attention deficit hyperactivity disorder. Bulletin of Clinical Psychopharmacology 2012; 22: 325-31.

[105] Famularo R, Kinscherff R, Fenton T. Psychiatric diagnoses of maltreated children: preliminary findings. Journal of the American Academy of Child & Adolescent Psychiatry 1992; 31: 863-7.

[106] McLEER SV, Callaghan M, Henry D, Wallen J. Psychiatric disorders in sexually abused children. Journal of the American Academy of Child & Adolescent Psychiatry 1994; 33: 313-9.

[107] Gurevitz M, Geva R, Varon M, Leitner Y. Early markers in infants and toddlers for development of ADHD. Journal of Attention Disorders 2014; 18: 14-22.

[108] Latimer K, Wilson P, Kemp J, Thompson L, Sim F, Gillberg C, et al. Disruptive behaviour disorders: a systematic review of environmental antenatal and early years risk factors. Child: Care, Health and Development 2012; 38: 611-28.

[109] Kendall J, Leo MC, Perrin N, Hatton D. Modeling ADHD child and family relationships. Western Journal of Nursing Research 2005; 27: 500-18.

[110] McLaughlin KA, Sheridan MA, Winter W, Fox NA, Zeanah CH, Nelson CA. Widespread reductions in cortical thickness following severe early-life deprivation: a neurodevelopmental pathway to attention-deficit/hyperactivity disorder. Biological Psychiatry 2014; 76: 629-38.

[111] Whalen CK, Henker B. The child with attention-deficit/hyperactivity disorder in family contexts. In: Handbook of disruptive behavior disorders. Springer; 1999, p. 139-55.

[112] Danforth JS. The outcome of parent training using the behavior management flow chart with mothers and their children with oppositional defiant disorder and attention-deficit hyperactivity disorder. Behavior Modification 1998; 22(4): 443-73.

[113] Weiss G, Hechtman LT. Hyperactive children grown up: ADHD in children, adolescents, and adults. Guilford Press, New York;1993.

Chapter 3

Assessment of ADHD Through Electroencephalographic Measures of Functional Connectivity

Julián J. González, Guzmán Alba, Soledad Mañas,
Almudena González and Ernesto Pereda

Additional information is available at the end of the chapter

http://dx.doi.org/10.5772/60559

Abstract

The main objective of the chapter is to review the types of electroencephalographic measures of functional connectivity that have been used so far in the study/diagnosis of ADHD. The review will include the methods and results so far reported in the literature as well as those conducted by our research group.

Keywords: ADHD, EEG Connectivity, Synchronization measures

1. Introduction

Quantitative EEG analysis techniques have been used since the beginning of 1990s to investigate the neural correlates of attention deficit hyperactive disorder (ADHD). Early works in this field analysed changes in univariate EEG linear measures, the main focus of these studies being the absolute or relative spectral power in different EEG frequency bands (see, e.g., [1-3]). Over the years, other univariate measures coming from the analysis of nonlinear systems have been incorporated into the study of ADHD. These measures are dedicated, among other factors, to assessing the complexity of EEG channels [4, 5]. Together with univariate measures, quantitative measures assess the linear or nonlinear interdependence between two EEG channels (bivariate measures) or a set of pairs of channels (multivariate measures) have been developed and used for the investigation of ADHD [4, 6-9]. These measures represent an estimate of the functional connectivity (FC, to be defined below) between the signals recorded from different electrodes of the subject under study and appear to offer a better perspective with regard to the clinical diagnosis of ADHD than univariate measures [4, 10]. This chapter is dedicated to describing and explaining the most commonly used multivariate EEG measures to date in the context of ADHD, as well as the most relevant results that have been derived from their implementation.

2. Functional connectivity from EEG

Functional connectivity (FC) refers to the existence of a statistical dependence between some of the features of two signals, be it their amplitudes, their phases or their reconstructed state spaces [11]. Among the linear methods most commonly used to assess the existence of such dependence, we can mention the cross correlation function and magnitude squared coherency (see description below), which analyses the relationship between signals in the time and frequency domains, respectively. At the end of the previous century and the beginning of the present one, different nonlinear methods stemming from the field of complex dynamical systems theory began to be used to characterize the existence of functional connectivity in EEG (see [12, 13] for reviews). Despite the usefulness of these methods and the potential interest of assessing the degree of interdependence between two EEG channels as a proxy of the relationship between two brain areas, its application in EEG studies is not straightforward [13]. On the one hand, the effect of volume conduction in extracranial EEG recordings, whereby the activity of one neural source is picked up by different electrodes, creates a spurious (i.e., not due to *true* interaction between two sources) FC between the electrodes [14]. Different strategies have been proposed to deal with this problem [14-18] but none of them are perfect.

On the other hand, the very nature of EEG, which includes a reference signal in the recordings, may also affect the FC estimators if the reference is active; this is a problem that has been well-documented in coherency studies [19, 20]. Current source density estimators may alleviate but not completely cure this flaw [21, 22]. Thus, in the case of EEG, interpretation of the results from FC analysis should be done very carefully and one should talk about a pattern of FC with a given reference and connectivity measure, rather than directly extrapolating the results to the existence of synchronization between the areas immediately below the electrodes. Such FC patterns are often further analysed by using the matrix of interdependence indices ξ_{ij} (where i, j = 1,..., n, are the number of recorded signals) as the adjacency matrix of a complex brain network, which can be characterized in terms of its different topological properties, which are known to be altered in different pathologies (see [13, 23] for recent reviews). Therefore, FC is still a useful tool for analysing EEG records, which provides insight into EEG changes associated with different pathologies such as ADHD.

3. Functional Connectivity in ADHD: A view from fMRI

FC between different brain regions can be studied with good spatial resolution using image analysis techniques such as positron emission tomography (PET), positron emission tomography simple (PETS) and functional magnetic resonance imaging (fMRI). Although this chapter covers EEG FC, for the sake of completeness, we will show some results of FC in ADHD obtained with analyses performed using fMRI, which has been the most widely used technique to study FC in different pathologies

This image technique provides excellent spatial resolution, as it perfectly identifies (up to 1-3 mm resolution) the most active brain areas, depending on oxygen levels in the blood. However, since some time is required to obtain the images (about 5-8 seconds), the activation sequence of cortical areas involved in the task can only be displayed at a low sampling rate. Therefore, fMRI provides a low temporal resolution for dynamic analysis of brain activity.

FC analysis of fMRI data assesses the existence of statistical dependence between voxel time series. fMRI studies on ADHD have been addressed using two different paradigms: resting state and task-based studies. In resting-state studies, the correlation of the activity of different brain regions is assessed at rest with the subjects having their eyes either open or (most often) closed. In the second case, researchers investigate the correlation of the activity of the brain regions that supposedly co-activate during the performance of a given task. In both cases, the fMRI is generally carried out by comparing an ADHD group with a healthy control group.

One difficulty when establishing a profile of FC of ADHD in fMRI studies arises from the different methodology used for analysing the correlation of activity among brain regions; this has led to heterogeneous results in terms of the networks that are altered in ADHD. The primary brain areas that have been reported to exhibit altered FC in ADHD are the dorsal anterior cingulate cortex (dACC) [24-26], the frontostriatal circuit [27, 28], the default mode network (DMN) [25, 29-32] and the reward circuit [30, 33]. The increasing connectivity between the dACC and the thalamus, cerebellum, insula and pons bilateral in ADHD has been associated with abnormal autonomic activity [26], whereas reduced connectivity between the dACC and posterior components of the DMN is associated with symptoms of inattention and poor performance of working memory in ADHD [25]. This heterogeneity in results is due to methodological differences between studies and appears to be task-dependent, because when comparing resting-state with task-based fRMI studies, the dACC connectivity is enhanced in the first condition and reduced in the second [24]. Regarding the frontostriatal network, ADHD subjects presented reduced connectivity compared to controls, which has been linked to deficits in cognitive functions characteristic of this disorder, primarily the inhibitory control deficit [27, 28]. In the case of the DMN, the ADHD presented lower connectivity, which has been ascribed to the deficits in executive functions that are frequently observed in these subjects [25, 29, 30, 32, 34]. Finally, concerning the reward network, some studies [30, 33] suggest that it is highly connected in the case of ADHD, which is related to the symptoms of impulsivity and delay reward difficulty.

The results in this section demonstrate the existence of distinctive traits in the FC fMRI patterns of ADHD. Although these results cannot be directly extrapolated to EEG, which directly measures neural activity with high temporal but poor spatial resolution, it is clear that comparing brain activity in ADHD with that of healthy controls in terms of changes in FC and beyond the simple activation of individual areas/channels provides useful information about the neural correlates of this pathology.

4. Measures of interdependence between EEG signals for estimating functional connectivity in ADHD

4.1. Linear measures

The magnitude squared coherence is a measure of the linear correlation, both in amplitude and phase, between two signals at a given frequency. It is obtained from the (complex) coherency function between two signals x and y as follows:

$$C_{xy}(f) = \frac{S_{xy}(f)}{S_{xx}(f)S_{yy}(f)} \tag{1}$$

where $S_{xy}(f)$ is the cross-spectrum between these signals, $S_{xx}(f)$ and $S_{yy}(f)$ are the respective auto-spectra and f is the discrete frequency.

The coherence is simply the squared modulus of $C_{xy}(f)$. For each f, coherence values range between 0 (no correlation) and 1 (full linear correlation). The mean value of the coherence for all the frequencies included in that band is normally taken for the coherence in a certain frequency band.

The argument of coherency provides an estimate of the phase delay between the signals:

$$\phi_{xy}(f) = \text{arctag}\frac{\text{Im}\left\{C_{xy}(f)\right\}}{\text{Re}\left\{C_{xy}(f)\right\}} \tag{2}$$

where *Im()* and *Re*() are the imaginary and the real part of $C_{xy}(f)$. Note that the imaginary part of coherency has been suggested as a robust index of interdependence between EEG data that is insensitive to volume conduction [14]; to the best of our knowledge, this idea has not yet been applied to ADHD research.

4.2. Non-linear measures

4.2.1. The concept of generalized synchronization

The first nonlinear indices of FC applied to EEG data were based on the concept of mutual or conditioned neighbours in the state spaces of two time series, which is a practical consequence of the existence of generalized synchronization (GS) between two dynamic systems [35]. Briefly, given a reference state space vector$\boldsymbol{x}_n$ in system *X*, their *k* mutual neighbours are those vectors in *X* that share the time indices of the nearest neighbours of y_n in system *Y*. Since GS manifests itself as the existence of a functional relationship between the state variables of *X* and *Y*, vectors close in *X* tend to also be close in *Y*. Thus, mutual neighbours are more similar to the reference vector than randomly selected vectors, which can be numerically quantified in a number of ways [36-38].

To date, two of these indices have been mainly applied to the EEG analysis of ADHD [4, 6]. The first [6] is a modified fuzzy version of the well-known synchronization likelihood (*SL*) method developed by [38]. The second [4] uses an advanced estimation of distances in the reconstructed state spaces, which is based on rank rather than on true Euclidean distance, as described in [37]. We will briefly describe each of these indices below, after describing how to reconstruct the state spaces from time series.

4.2.2. Reconstructing the state space from data

The first step needed to estimate FC from GS-based methods entails the reconstruction of the state spaces of the systems from the signals that they generate (in this case, the EEGs). Such a reconstruction is based on Takens' theorem [39], which ensures that under general conditions (see also [40]), the delayed vectors defined as:

$$X_i = \left(x(i), x(i-\tau), x(i-2\tau),..., x\left(i-(m-1)\tau\right)\right) \tag{3}$$

are equivalent to the original state vectors. In (3), m is the embedding dimension, which should be at least equal to the dimension of the system, and τ is the delay time, which has to ensure that two consecutive components of the vector are (almost) independent. Normally, m is obtained using a heuristic approach called *"false nearest neighbours"*, whereas τ is estimated using the autocorrelation or the auto mutual information function of the data (see [41] for a review of practical considerations of state space reconstructions).

4.2.3. Fuzzy synchronization likelihood

Many of the originally derived indices of GS in the state spaces are asymmetric [42] and thus potentially able to provide information on the directionality of the interaction (i.e., which system acts as driver). However, the initial enthusiasm about the abilities of these indices cooled after some studies [43, 44] showed that differences in their values in X and Y may be simply due to differences in the complexity of the individual systems. In light of these results, [38] defined the synchronization likelihood (*SL*) index as a measure of GS in the reconstructed state spaces, which sacrifices the (possibly misleading) information about directionality in the interaction in return for obtaining an unbiased, symmetric quantitative estimation of the interdependence between two signals. Although intrinsically multivariate in nature (it measures the degree of similitude among M>2 signals), *SL* is almost invariably used to estimate the FC between two time series and is arguably one of the most widely used indices of FC in EEG studies (see [10, 38, 45] for technical details on the estimation of *SL* in both broad and narrow band signals, respectively).

In the framework of EEG studies of ADHD, [6, 46, 47] have proposed a modified version of the *SL* algorithm, termed fuzzy synchronization likelihood (*FSL*). Briefly, given a reconstructed reference vector in signal x_k such as (3), a window $W_{w_2}^{w_1}(k, i)$ around this vector contains all the $2(w_2 - w_1)$ state vectors $\boldsymbol{X}_{i,m}$ whose indices satisfy the condition $w_1 < |i-m| < w_2$, where w_1 is the

Theiler correction [48] and w_2 determines the temporal resolution of the window. The *fuzzy* in the *FSL* comes from the fact that, in this window, a Gaussian membership (a Gaussian kernel) with a centre at $X_{k,i}$ and a standard deviation of $\varepsilon_{k,i}$ is used [6]:

$$\mu_{k,i}\left(X_{k,m}\right) = \exp\left(-\left(\left|X_{k,m} - X_{k,i}\right|2 / \varepsilon_{k,i}\right)\right) \tag{4}$$

where $\mu_{k,i}(X_{k.m})$ is the membership of $X_{k.m}$ in the window and $|X_{k.m} - X_{k,n}|$ is the Euclidean distance. Then, the probability that $X_{k,m}$ is closer to $X_{k,i}$ than $\varepsilon_{k,i}$ is computed:

$$P_{k,i}^{\varepsilon_{k,i}} = \frac{1}{2(w_2 - w_1)} \sum_m \mu_{k,i}(X_{k,m}) \tag{5}$$

Finally, the *FSL* between X_A and X_B for time index i is computed as follows:

$$FSL_{A-B,i} = \frac{1}{2P_{ref}(w_2 - w_1)} \sum_m \frac{\mu_{A,i}(X_{A,m})}{\mu_{B,i}(X_{B,m})} \tag{6}$$

where $P_{ref} \ll 1$ is a reference probability. Sliding the window along the time series, the *FSL* is computed in each shifted window and is finally averaged for all shifted windows, which leads to the *FSL* between X_A and X_B.

4.2.4. FC estimation based on rank of distances

In the above section, we described a modified version of the *SL* index, the *FSL*, which in the same way as the original *SL*, sacrifices directional information in return for being unbiased. Instead of *SL* or *FSL*, it is possible to compute a robust estimator of directionality based on the GS concept using rank distances [37], the so-called *L* index. In order to compute $L(X_A | X_B)$, delayed state vectors $X_{A,i}$ and $X_{B,i}$ are reconstructed from X_A and X_B as in (3). Then, let $a_{i,j}$ (respectively, $b_{i,j}$) be the time indices of the k nearest neighbours of $X_{A,i}$ (resp. $X_{B,i}$); for each $X_{A,i}$, let $g_{i,j}$ be the rank that the distance between $X_{A,i}$ and $X_{A,j}$ takes in the sorted ascending list of distances of each vector to $X_{A,i}$; the $X_{B,,i}$ -conditioned mean rank is then $G_i^k(X_A | X_B) = \frac{1}{k}\sum_{j=1}^{k} g_{i,b_{i,j}}$ and the measurement L is defined as:

$$L(X_A | X_B) = \frac{1}{N}\sum_{i=1}^{N} \frac{G_i(X_A) - G_i^k(X_A | X_B)}{G_i(X_A) - G_i^k(X_A)} \tag{7}$$

Dummy Text where $N = n - (m-1)\tau$, $G_i(X_A) = \frac{N}{2}$ and $G_i^k(X_A) = \frac{k+1}{2}$. $L(X_B | X_A)$ can be calculated analogously. Finally, the index L of interdependence between the two signals is obtained by averaging both estimations. L ranges between 0 (independence) and 1 (identical signals interdependence).

5. Estimating the reliability of the interdependence measures

As mentioned above, estimating FC from extracranial EEG data is a complicated issue, due to, e.g., volume conduction and reference effects. There is, however, another more general problem associated with the estimation of interdependence measures from finite, noisy experimental data. Due to these two features (shortage and noise), any interdependence index (whether coherence, FSL, *L* or any other one) may be greater than 0 even for two completely independent signals. In order to tackle this issue, it is possible to use the bivariate surrogate data test [12, 49, 50]. This method tests the reliability of an interdependence measure (IM) between two EEGs X_A and X_B, by repeating the calculation of IM after replacing one of the signals (e.g., X_A) with *s* modified (surrogate) versions of it (X^s_A), which share most of its features (amplitude distribution, spectrum and even its nonlinear properties, if any) with X_A but are independent from X_B by construction (see [49] for details on how to construct different types of surrogate data). The IM (e.g., the *L* index) from the original signals is then compared with the distribution of surrogate L indices obtained from the *s* surrogates, which can be done either parametrically or non-parametrically. Parametrically, the following Z-score index (σ) is calculated:

$$\sigma = \frac{| IM_{orig} - IM_{surr} |}{SD_{surr}} \tag{8}$$

where IM_{orig} is the value of IM for the original data and IM_{surr} and SD_{surr} are the mean and the standard deviation of the distribution of the values for the *s* surrogates, respectively. If this distribution is Gaussian, σ follows a student's t-test distribution with *p* degrees of freedom. We need $s = (1/\alpha)-1$ surrogate data for a statistical level of significance of $100^*(1-\alpha)\%$ and it is sufficient to take s=19 for testing the difference at the 95% level of statistical significance ($p<0.05$). We must have $\sigma > 2.1$ to reject the null hypothesis of independence in the original EEG signals for this statistical level. Lack of significance ($\sigma \leq 2.1$) is taken into account by setting the corresponding index to zero. If, however, the distribution is non-Gaussian, then the p-value for the rejection of the null hypothesis of independence is estimated as the ratio

$$p = \frac{1 + Ns}{1 + s} \tag{9}$$

where N_s is the number of surrogate data for which the value of the IM is greater than that of the original data, $IM_{orig.}$ Note that, in either case (parametric or nonparametric method), we are only testing the hypothesis that the original data present some type of interdependence, yet the effect of both volume conduction and the active reference cannot be examined with this approach.

6. Results

The results of the main works in the literature of EEG connectivity as applied to ADHD research are summarized in Table 1 below.

First Auth.	Subjects	Method	Conditions	Main results and trends
Montague (1975)	10 Hyperkinetic 10 CONT	Coherence profile	Resting	Interhemispheric Coh ↓↓. Intrahemispheric Coh ↑↑.
Chabot (1996 a, b)	407 ADHD 310 CONT	Coherence in δ, θ, α and β bands	Resting EC	Coh in ADHD ↑↑ or ↓↓ depend on brain regions paired.
Lubar (1999)	23 ADHD	Coherence in δ, θ, α and β bands.	Resting EO	MPH ↓↓ Coh alterations.
Barry (2002)	40 ADHDcom 40 ADHDinat 40 CONT	Coherences in δ, θ, α and β bands.	Resting EC	Coh in ADHD ↑↑ or ↓↓ depend on inter-channels distances.
Barry (2005)	40 ADHDcom 40 ADHDinat 40 CONT	Coherences in δ, θ, α and β bands.	Resting EC	ADHD boys display coherence anomalies age-dependent & differing between subtypes.
Clarke (2005)	20 ADHDcom 20 CONT	Coherences in δ, θ, α and β bands.	Resting EC	MPH does not affect Coh.
Barry (2006)	40 ADHDcom 40 ADHDin 40 CONT	Coherences in δ, θ, α and β bands.	Resting EC	ADHD Coh is age and gender-dependent. ADHD girls no differences between subtypes.
Barry (2007)	40 ADHD+ODD 40 ADHD-ODD 40 CONT	Coherences in δ, θ, α and β bands.	Resting EC	Coh intrahemisph in ADHD + ODD ↓↓ versus ADHD-ODD
Clarke (2007)	30 ADHD 30 ADHD + ↑↑ β	Coherences in δ, θ, α and β bands.	Resting EC	There are differences between ADHD and ADHD + ↑↑ β.
Murias (2007)	42 ADHD 21 CONT	Coherence in frequencies of 2-12 Hz.	ERP word processing task	Deficient connectivity in ADHD and a stimulus-induced state frontal overconnectivity.
Dupuy (2008)	20 ADHD 20 CONT	Coherences in δ, θ, α and β bands.	Resting EC	Medication ↑↑ Coh.
Barry (2009)	20 ADHD+RD 20 ADHD-RD 20 CONT	Coherences in δ, θ, α and β bands.	Resting EC	ADHD+RD ↓↓ Coh δ and α.
Dupuy (2010)	18 ADHDg 17 ADHDp	Coherences in δ, θ, α and β bands.	Resting EC	ADHDg ↑↑ Coh β.

http://dx.doi.org/10.5772/60559

First Auth.	Subjects	Method	Conditions	Main results and trends
	18 CONT			
Ahmadlou (2010)	47 ADHD 7 CONT	SL Radial Basis Function (RBF)	Resting EC	ADHD ↓↓ SL.
Ahmadlou (2011)	12 ADHD 12 CONT	FSL Graph Theory	Resting EC	Deficient connection of posterior and anterior areas in ADHD.
Ahmadlou (2011b)	47 ADHD 7 CONT	FSL and conventional SL in δ, θ, gamma, α and β bands.	Resting EC	ADHD had anomalies in δ and θ SLs. FSL better than conventional SL.
Barry (2011)	40 ADHD 40 CONT	Coherences in δ, θ, α and β bands.	Resting EC	Coh in ADHD ↑↑ or ↓↓ depend on inter-channels distances.
Ahmadlou (2012a)	15 ADHDg 15 ADHDp	FSL Graph Theory	Resting EC	ADHDg ↓↓ FSL in β band after treatment.
Ahmadlou (2012b)	12 ADHD 12 CONT	FSL Small-world network	Resting EC	ADHD FSL ↑↑ C and ↓↓ L in δ band.
González (2013)	22 ADHD 21 CONT	Coherence Index L	Resting EC and EO	ADHD ↑↑ Coh and index L in certain brain regions.
Liu (2014)	13 ADHD 13 CONT	SL in δ, θ, α and β bands	Resting	ADHD ↑↑ SL in α and β bands

Vertical arrows ↑↑ / ↓↓ indicate increasing or decreasing trends; Coh for coherence; ODD for comorbid Oppositional Defiant Disorder, RD for Reading Disabilities; SL for synchronization likelihood; FSL for fuzzy synchronization likelihood; EC closed eyes, EO open eyes; index L for the nonlinear index of GS; Greek letters δ, θ, α and β for EEG delta, theta, alpha and beta frequency bands, respectively. ERP – event related potential.

Table 1. Review of the literature on EEG functional connectivity in ADHD.

6.1. Results from coherence

The first study where the profile of EEG coherence is analysed in the context of ADHD was conducted 40 years ago [51]. By using a group of behavioural and physiological measures, the author found that EEG coherence was the measure that best differentiated between a group of hyperkinetic children and a control group. Specifically, he reported that the hyperkinetic group had greater intrahemispheric coherence than controls in the low frequency band (up to 8 Hz). Later, [1, 52] analysed patients already diagnosed with ADHD and reported altered values of coherence in almost every frequency band (delta, theta, alpha and beta) in subjects with ADHD compared to subjects with normal development. Coherence in ADHD can be enhanced or reduced depending on the brain regions that are paired for calculating this index.

Over the past 15 years, the study of EEG FC in ADHD using coherence has been carried out primarily by researchers of the Brain & Behaviour Research Institute and Department of Psychology at the University of Wollongong in Australia, who have studied coherence, both intra- and interhemispheric, by planned contrast and by considering short, medium and long distances between electrodes. They have reported that ADHD subjects, compared to healthy controls, present higher intrahemispheric coherences in short/medium distances in delta, theta and beta frequency bands [7-9, 53-55], reduced laterality in the theta band [8, 53, 55, 56] and increased frontal interhemispheric values in the delta and theta bands [8, 9, 53-55]. Coherence results found from our group [4] indicate, in agreement with previous results, that for certain pairs of channels at short (e.g., C3-C4, O1-O2) and medium (e.g., C3-T4, T3-C4, O1-C4) interhemispheric distances, FC was clearly greater for the ADHD group than for controls, whereas for large interhemispheric distances (e.g., Fp1-O2), the reverse was true during both EC and EO.

When the focus was not on pairwise FC but on seed-based connectivity (that of one channel with a certain set of channels or cortical areas (intra or inter-hemispheric)) the results differed, because of the inherent averaging involved. Thus, for example, the intrahemispheric FC of the C3 channel was estimated by averaging coherence from the electrode pairs C3-T3, C3-F3 and C3-P3; interhemispheric coherence of C3, in turn, required averaging the values of C3-C4, C3-F4 and C3-P4. Figure 1 (A) and (B) show the seed-based interhemispheric coherence for the C4 electrode (average of C4-C3, C4-T3, C4-Fp1 and C4-O1) for the delta, theta, alpha and beta bands during EC and EO, respectively, for the same groups of subjects analysed in our former study [4]. This interhemispheric coherence for ADHD was greater than the control during EC in the higher frequency bands; this was also true for the low frequency bands during EO. Therefore, an increase in interhemispheric EEG coherence for ADHD subjects – in this example for the C4 electrode – is associated with higher frequency bands, regardless of the resting condition (EC, EO) and with low frequency bands only for the EO condition. Figure 2 shows a topographic map of the seed-based interhemispheric connectivity of each channel or cortical area for a standard configuration of 16 EEG channels. Once more, the connectivity of ADHD were greater than for controls for certain areas, resting conditions and connectivity indices.

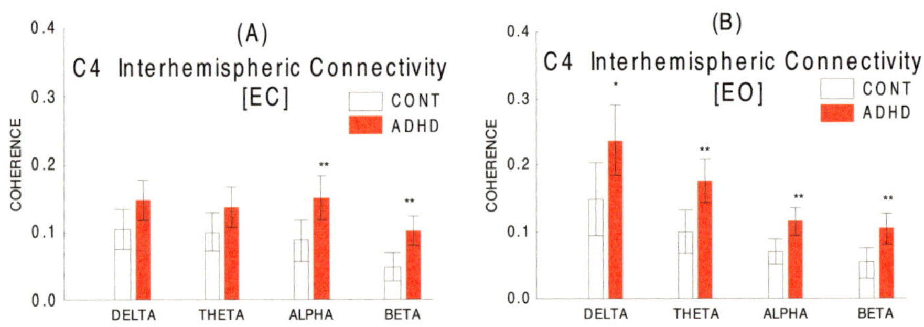

* p<0.05 and ** p<0.01.

Figure 1. (A) Seed-based interhemispheric coherence (C4 area) during EC estimated by averaging the coherence between channel pairs C4-Fp1, C4-C3, C4-T3 and C4-O1. (B) The same results as in (A) but during EO. Results are for coherence in DELTA, THETA, ALPHA and BETA frequency bands. Asterisks indicate the statistical significance of a paired t-test between ADHD and controls (CONT).

http://dx.doi.org/10.5772/60559

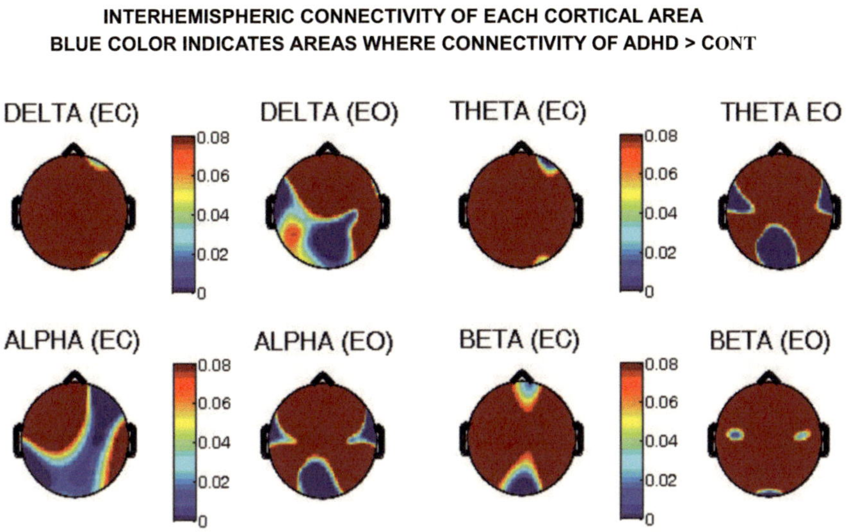

Figure 2. Topographic maps of the seed-based interhemispheric coherence of each cortical area (16 EEG channel configuration) in the DELTA, THETA, ALPHA and BETA EEG frequency bands during EC and EO. Color bar indicates *p* values obtained by comparing ADHD and CONT using a t-test, applied to each cortical area separately, and corrected for multiple comparisons. Blue color indicates areas where connectivity of ADHD was greater than CONT.

The analysis of EEG coherence in subjects with ADHD has also been used to study the effects on the cortical connectivity of factors such as gender, age and comorbid disorders, as well as to understand the influence of certain pharmacological treatments used in ADHD therapy. Thus, a study on the effect of age on EEG coherence [57] analysed three groups of boys, one with ADHD of a combined type, another with ADHD of an inattentive type and a third consisting of control subjects; within each group, the authors studied four subgroups by age (range 8-12 years). They found that there were age-dependent differences in EEG coherence among the three groups. The same authors carried out a similar study involving girls to analyse gender differences [58] and found differences in EEG coherence between ADHD groups and the control group, but not between the ADHD subtypes. Furthermore, this study revealed that such differences were also age-dependent in girls, but not in the same way as they were in boys, in both healthy and ADHD children. The authors concluded from these results that changes in EEG coherence associated with ADHD are different for both genders.

Regarding comorbid disorders, boys with ADHD and oppositional defiant disorder (ODD) presented lower intrahemispheric coherences in shorter distances than ADHD without reading disabilities in delta, theta and beta bands [9]. Furthermore, children with ADHD and reading disabilities had lower intrahemispheric coherences in shorter distances than ADHD without ODD in delta bands [7].

Regarding pharmacological treatments of ADHD, the most commonly used drug to treat the disorder is methylphenidate (MPH), a CNS stimulant that reduces ADHD symptoms. Although its action mechanism is not entirely clear, MPH is known to increase the levels of norepinephrine and dopamine in the frontal cortex and subcortical regions associated with motivation and reward [59]. The results of the effect of MPH on the profile of coherence in ADHD are contradictory. In fact, [60] have found that it reduces the alterations found in EEG coherence profiles in children with ADHD; in contrast, other authors have found neither that MPH ingestion produces changes in the EEG coherence of ADHD, nor that the coherence profile comes closer to that of the controls after treatment [53]. In another study, [56] reported a change in the profile of EEG coherence after MPH ingestion in girls with ADHD and specifically an increase in the delta band between intrahemispheric cortical areas at short distances, resulting in a reduction of the differences between the ADHD and control groups. In [55], the authors reported that ADHD boys showing good response to MPH differed from those unresponsive to the drug, in that MPH produced greater intrahemispheric coherence (shorter and medium distances) in the delta band of the ADHD good response group.

Finally, research on EEG evoked related potentials (ERP) studied the differences in the coherence between ADHD subjects and healthy controls (coherence between different cortical areas for certain frequency bands) during a word-processing task [60]. The ADHD group presented greater differences during the stimulus interval, a deficient connectivity during both intervals and an increase in frontal connectivity within and between hemispheres during a stimulus interval. The intake of medication in this study improved the connectivity pattern of the ADHD group.

6.2. Results from the nonlinear analysis and complex network methods

With regard to the nonlinear indices of FC, these are being increasingly used in the study of EEG of subjects with ADHD. Thus, *SL* was the first nonlinear index used to study the EEG connectivity of ADHD patients [10]. These authors found that, by using filtered EEG (by wavelet decomposition techniques), the SL of the ADHD group was lower than that of the control group for posterior cortical areas at certain EEG bands. In another work by the same authors [6], they applied the FSL index described above and found that ADHD subjects had a lower FC than controls on the centreline of the brain, which could affect the communication between anterior and posterior lobes. In a parallel study [46], these authors compared the SL with the FSL and found that FSL discriminated ADHD from controls better than the non-fuzzy version. Later, the same research group [47, 62] conducted two further studies; in the first [47], they calculated the matrix of FSL values for all possible pairs of channels and then used it to estimate the characteristics of the FC network using graph theoretic-measures. They found that network segregation, as assessed by the clustering index C, was higher in ADHD in the delta band, while network integration, as assessed by the average shortest path length (L) was lower in the same band, thereby suggesting that the small-world character [63] of the FC brain network of ADHD subjects is enhanced in this band, compared to control subjects. Interestingly, increased small-worldness in low frequency bands is a trademark of different neurological pathologies [23]. In the second work [62], the researchers assessed the differences in FSL before and after neurofeedback treatment in a group of ADHD subjects with positive response to treatment and in another group of subjects without response; they found that the former group presented a greater reduction in beta band synchronization compared to that of the group without changes.

Results from our group [4] using the L index described in section 4.2.3 indicated that, as already indicated by coherence, the nonlinear FC of the ADHD subjects was greater than that of controls for short (C3-C4, O1-O2) and medium range (C3-T4, T3-C4, O1-C4) connections during EC. When considering intra- or interhemispheric seed-based FC between one channel and the remaining ones of the same or opposite hemisphere, respectively, we found in the 8 EEG channels configuration that the interhemispheric FC of C3, C4 and O1 was greater in ADHD than in control subjects during EC (see Figure 3 for C4). Figure 4 shows a topographic map of the interhemispheric FC of each channel or cortical area for a standard configuration of 16 EEG channels. As for the corresponding coherence figure (Figure 2), values were obtained by averaging the L indices of the eight pairs that each channel has with the eight channels of the opposite hemisphere. Once more, connectivity in ADHD was only greater than controls for certain areas and resting conditions (EC, EO).

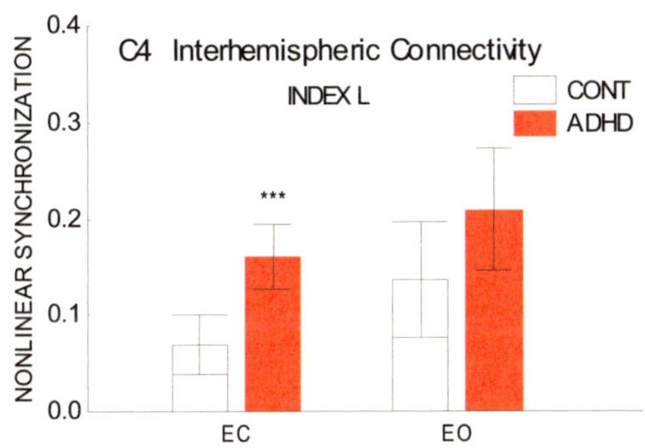

Figure 3. Interhemispheric connectivity of C4 area during EC and EO estimated by averaging the nonlinear synchronization index L between the channel pairs C4-Fp1, C4-C3, C4-T3, C4-O1. Asterisks are for the statistical significance from t-test between ADHD and control (CONT) groups (*** p<0.001).

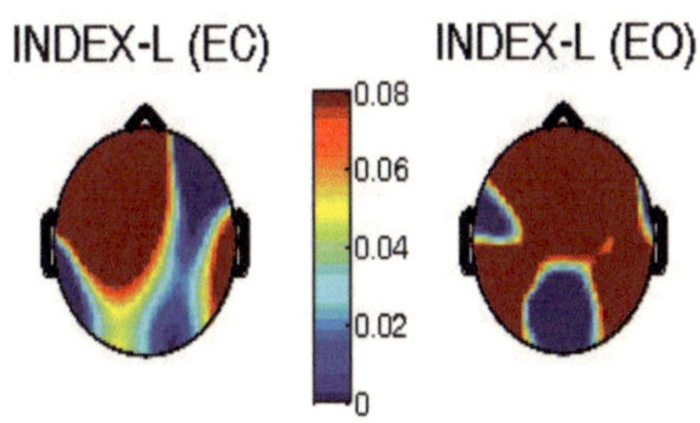

Figure 4. Topographic maps of the interhemispheric connectivity of each cortical area (16 EEG channels configuration). Here connectivities were estimated from the nonlinear synchronization index L. Color bar indicates p values obtained by comparing ADHD and CONT through a t-test applied to each cortical area separately. Blues colors indicate cortical areas where connectivity of ADHD was greater than CONT.

A recent work [64] studied the strength of the connections and the variability of SL, as well as the organization of functional brain networks as described by this index. The researchers found that the strength of connections was greater in the ADHD group in the fronto-occipital networks and that this group also presented a higher SL variability. Other research [65] studied SL in delta, theta, alpha and beta bands and found that this index was greater in the ADHD group for alpha and beta bands.

The results of cortical FC estimated from different nonlinear indices are dependent on the index considered to estimate connectivity and the method used to compute the connectivity of each cortical area with other zones, i.e., whether individual channel pairs or averaging intra- and/or interhemispheric channels pairs are considered. Although the results initially appeared to be heterogeneous, they show some consensus in indicating that the EEG of ADHD subjects are hypersynchronized when compared to that of healthy controls. This is also confirmed by applying graph theory methods to the connectivity matrix of FC patterns.

6.3. Results from diagnostic procedures based on connectivity measures

The section above reviewed the current state of the literature on nonlinear FC indices as applied to the EEG of ADHD subjects. In all cases, the analysis strategy was similar: a set of statistical comparisons was used to study the existence of differences between one (or more) group of ADHD subjects and age- or gender-matched healthy controls. An alternative approach, which has become very popular in recent years, consists of regarding the matrices of FC indices as connectivity patterns that can be used as training vectors for a machine learning classification algorithm [4, 10, 46]. This approach not only allows for determination, of which FC features are the most discriminative for deciding whether a subject's EEG presents any ADHD traits, but also renders unnecessary any discussion on the true relationship between FC of two EEG channels and the existence of synchronization between the underlying cortical networks.

In this framework, the studies cited above [4, 10, 46] have shown that the nonlinear measures of EEG FC present a high degree of accuracy and sensitivity. Thus, [10, 46] combined the radial basis function neural network as classification algorithm and the leave one out cross validation method (see, e.g., [66] for details on the methodologies) to learn from SL and FSL patterns of EEG FC. The researchers found that SL reached an accuracy of 95.6% for diagnosis of ADHD with a variance of 0.7%, whereas the FSL index reached an accuracy of 87.50%.

As for the diagnostic usefulness of the L index, in a recent work, [4] combined the well-known receiver operating characteristic curves and the binomial logistic regression classification technique to verify the diagnostic utility of the EEG FC measures. These results showed that ADHD children are best discriminated from age-matched healthy controls by using inter-hemispheric interdependence measures computed from a few single EEG channel pairs, rather than by using the corresponding inter-hemispheric averages. In fact, the coherence in the beta band between inter-occipital regions and between left/occipital-right/central regions provided an overall accuracy classification rate of 74.4%, but even greater accuracy (86.7%) was obtained by using the *L* index between left/occipital-right/central regions and left/central-right/temporal regions during resting state with EC.

7. Conclusions and future perspectives

The results presented here clearly suggest that the EEG FC of ADHD subjects presents a complex pattern of significant alterations when compared to that of healthy controls across different frequency bands. For instance, depending on the distance between the paired brain regions, the EEG FC in the ADHD group can be greater or smaller than that of the healthy control group. Additionally, the coherence in resting state is influenced by/for age, sex, comorbid disorders and medication. In ERP analysis, the scarcity of results to date indicates that ADHD differences in coherence are more discriminative in the stimulus interval than in the alert interval.

As for the nonlinear FC measures, the results are also heterogeneous; however, when the different nonlinear methodologies are compared, it can be concluded that: the *FSL* is a better discriminator than *SL* and that the use of graph theoretic measures increases the sensibility of these measures for distinguishing between the EEG of ADHD and that of healthy controls. Furthermore, the index *L* seems to present a good perspective that can be applied to distinguishing between ADHD and controls.

Bearing in mind all these results and the usefulness of EEG patterns of FC for classification, it is somewhat surprising that other popular nonlinear FC methods such as those based on the concept of phase synchronization [67] have been applied less often in this field. Moreover, new and improved methods for the study of GS from time series [36, 68], which allow for the estimation of causal interdependence from multivariate data, has recently been successfully applied to EEG data [69]. In addition, recent results (e.g., [70]) have demonstrated that FC indices can be successfully combined with graph theoretic methods and advanced machine learning algorithms such as support vector machines, which can handle high dimensional feature vectors, in order to diagnose neurological pathologies using multivariate neurophysiological data. In fact, another interesting (yet relatively unexplored possibility) entails the combination of data from different modalities such as EEG, MRI and neurophysiological testing [64] to describe the effects of the pathology on different data. This would be very helpful both at applied and basic levels. Taken together, all these old and new results pave the way for further studies regarding the patterns of EEG FC, which can provide further insight into the EEG correlates of ADHD.

Acknowledgements

The authors acknowledge the financial support of the European Regional Development Fund (ERDF) through a grant from the Instituto de Salud Carlos III, (FIS) (Spanish Ministry of Health and Consumption, Grant No. PS09/00856) and the Spanish Ministry of Economy and Competitiveness through grant TEC2012-38453-CO4-03.

Author details

Julián J. González[1*], Guzmán Alba[1], Soledad Mañas[2], Almudena González[1] and Ernesto Pereda[3]

*Address all correspondence to: jugonzal@ull.edu.es

1 Physiology Unit, Health Sciences Faculty. La Laguna University, Spain

2 Clinical Neurophysiology Unit, University Hospital La Candelaria, Tenerife, Spain

3 Department of Industrial Engineering, School of Engineering and Technology, University of La Laguna, Tenerife, Spain

References

[1] Chabot, R.J. and G. Serfontein, *Quantitative electroencephalographic profiles of children with attention deficit disorder.* Biol Psychiatry, 1996. 40(10): p. 951-63.

[2] Clarke, A.R., et al., *EEG analysis in Attention-Deficit/Hyperactivity Disorder: a comparative study of two subtypes.* Psychiatry Res, 1998. 81(1): p. 19-29.

[3] Mann, C.A., et al., *Quantitative analysis of EEG in boys with attention-deficit-hyperactivity disorder: controlled study with clinical implications.* Pediatr Neurol, 1992. 8(1): p. 30-6.

[4] González, J.J., et al., *Performance analysis of univariate and multivariate EEG measurements in the diagnosis of ADHD.* Clinical neurophysiology: official journal of the International Federation of Clinical Neurophysiology, 2013. 124: p. 1139-50.

[5] Sohn, H., et al., *Linear and non-linear EEG analysis of adolescents with attention-deficit/hyperactivity disorder during a cognitive task.* Clin Neurophysiol, 2010. 121(11): p. 1863-70.

[6] Ahmadlou, M. and H. Adeli, *Fuzzy synchronization likelihood with application to attention-deficit/hyperactivity disorder.* Clin EEG Neurosci, 2011. 42(1): p. 6-13.

[7] Barry, R.J., et al., *EEG coherence and symptom profiles of children with Attention-Deficit/Hyperactivity Disorder.* Clin Neurophysiol, 2011. 122(7): p. 1327-32.

[8] Barry, R.J., et al., *EEG coherence in attention-deficit/hyperactivity disorder: a comparative study of two DSM-IV types.* Clin Neurophysiol, 2002. 113(4): p. 579-85.

[9] Barry, R.J., et al., *EEG coherence in children with attention-deficit/hyperactivity disorder and comorbid oppositional defiant disorder.* Clin Neurophysiol, 2007. 118(2): p. 356-62.

[10] Ahmadlou, M. and H. Adeli, *Wavelet-synchronization methodology: a new approach for EEG-based diagnosis of ADHD.* Clin EEG Neurosci, 2010. 41(1): p. 1-10.

[11] Friston, K.J., *Functional and effective connectivity: a review.* Brain Connect, 2011. 1(1): p. 13-36.

[12] Pereda, E., R.Q. Quiroga and J. Bhattacharya, *Nonlinear multivariate analysis of neurophysiological signals.* Prog Neurobiol, 2005. 77(1-2): p. 1-37.

[13] van Diessen, E., et al., *Opportunities and methodological challenges in EEG and MEG resting state functional brain network research.* Clin Neurophysiol, 2014. In press.

[14] Nolte, G., et al., *Identifying true brain interaction from EEG data using the imaginary part of coherency.* Clin Neurophysiol, 2004. 115(10): p. 2292-307.

[15] Stam, C.J., G. Nolte and A. Daffertshofer, *Phase lag index: assessment of functional connectivity from multi-channel EEG and MEG with diminished bias from common sources.* Hum Brain Mapp, 2007. 28(11): p. 1178-93.

[16] Ewald, A., et al., *Estimating true brain connectivity from EEG/MEG data invariant to linear and static transformations in sensor space.* Neuroimage, 2012. 60(1): p. 476-88.

[17] Ewald, A., F.S. Avarvand and G. Nolte, *Identifying causal networks of neuronal sources from EEG/MEG data with the phase slope index: a simulation study.* Biomed Tech (Berl), 2013. 58(2): p. 165-78.

[18] Chella, F., et al., *Third order spectral analysis robust to mixing artifacts for mapping cross-frequency interactions in EEG/MEG.* Neuroimage, 2014. 91: p. 146-61.

[19] Marzetti, L., et al., *The use of standardized infinity reference in EEG coherency studies.* Neuroimage, 2007. 36(1): p. 48-63.

[20] Haufe, S., et al., *A critical assessment of connectivity measures for EEG data: a simulation study.* Neuroimage, 2013. 64: p. 120-33.

[21] Cohen, M.X., *Effects of time lag and frequency matching on phase-based connectivity.* J Neurosci Methods, 2015. 250:p. 137-46.

[22] Cohen, M.X., *Comparison of different spatial transformations applied to EEG data: A case study of error processing.* Int J Psychophysiol, 2015. In press.

[23] Stam, C.J., *Modern network science of neurological disorders.* Nat Rev Neurosci, 2014. 15(10): p. 683-95.

[24] Zang, Y.F., et al., *Altered baseline brain activity in children with ADHD revealed by resting-state functional MRI.* Brain Dev, 2007. 29(2): p. 83-91.

[25] Castellanos, F.X., et al., *Cingulate-precuneus interactions: a new locus of dysfunction in adult attention-deficit/hyperactivity disorder.* Biol Psychiatry, 2008. 63(3): p. 332-7.

[26] Tian, L., et al., *Enhanced resting-state brain activities in ADHD patients: a fMRI study.* Brain Dev, 2008. 30(5): p. 342-8.

[27] Rubia, K., et al., *Methylphenidate normalises activation and functional connectivity deficits in attention and motivation networks in medication-naive children with ADHD during a rewarded continuous performance task.* Neuropharmacology, 2009. 57(7-8): p. 640-52.

[28] Cao, X., et al., *Abnormal resting-state functional connectivity patterns of the putamen in medication-naive children with attention deficit hyperactivity disorder.* Brain Res, 2009. 1303: p. 195-206.

[29] Qiu, M.G., et al., *Changes of brain structure and function in ADHD children.* Brain Topogr, 2011. 24(3-4): p. 243-52.

[30] Tomasi, D. and N.D. Volkow, *Abnormal functional connectivity in children with attention-deficit/hyperactivity disorder.* Biol Psychiatry, 2012. 71(5): p. 443-50.

[31] Fair, D.A., et al., *Atypical default network connectivity in youth with attention-deficit/hyperactivity disorder.* Biol Psychiatry, 2010. 68(12): p. 1084-91.

[32] Uddin, L.Q., et al., *Network homogeneity reveals decreased integrity of default-mode network in ADHD.* J Neurosci Methods, 2008. 169(1): p. 249-54.

[33] Costa, A., et al., *Methylphenidate effects on neural activity during response inhibition in healthy humans.* Cereb Cortex, 2013. 23(5): p. 1179-89.

[34] Sonuga-Barke, E.J. and F.X. Castellanos, *Spontaneous attentional fluctuations in impaired states and pathological conditions: a neurobiological hypothesis.* Neurosci Biobehav Rev, 2007. 31(7): p. 977-86.

[35] Rulkov, N.F., et al., *Generalized synchronization of chaos in directionally coupled chaotic systems.* Physical Review E, 1995. 51(2): p. 980-994.

[36] Sugihara, G., et al., *Detecting causality in complex ecosystems.* Science (New York, N.Y.), 2012. 338(6106): p. 496-500.

[37] Chicharro, D. and R.G. Andrzejak, *Reliable detection of directional couplings using rank statistics.* Physical Review E, 2009. 80(2): p. 26217.

[38] Stam, C.J. and B.W. Van Dijk, *Synchronization likelihood: An unbiased measure of generalized synchronization in multivariate data sets.* Physica D, 2002. 163: p. 236-251.

[39] Takens, F. *Detecting strange attractors in turbulence.* 1980. Springer.

[40] Sauer, T., J.A. Yorke and M. Casdagli, *Embedology.* Journal of Statistical Physics, 1991. 65: p. 579-616.

[41] Pecora, L.M., et al., *A unified approach to attractor reconstruction.* Chaos, 2007. 17(1): p. 013110.

[42] Quiroga, R.Q., J. Arnhold and P. Grassberger, *Learning driver-response relationships from synchronization patterns.* Physical Review. E, 2000. 61(5 Pt A): p. 5142-5148.

[43] Pereda, E., et al., *Assessment of changing interdependencies between human electroencephalograms using nonlinear methods.* Physica D, 2001. 148(1-2): p. 147-158.

[44] Quiroga, R.Q., et al., *Performance of different synchronization measures in real data: A case study on electroencephalographic signals.* Physical Review E, 2002. 65(4 Pt 1): p. 41903-41903.

[45] Montez, T., et al., *Synchronization likelihood with explicit time-frequency priors.* NeuroImage, 2006. 33(4): p. 1117-25.

[46] Ahmadlou, M. and H. Adeli, *Functional community analysis of brain: a new approach for EEG-based investigation of the brain pathology.* Neuroimage, 2011. 58(2): p. 401-8.

[47] Ahmadlou, M., H. Adeli and A. Adeli, *Graph theoretical analysis of organization of functional brain networks in ADHD.* Clin EEG Neurosci, 2012. 43(1): p. 5-13.

[48] Theiler, J., *Spurious dimension from correlation algorithms applied to limited time-series data.* Phys Rev A, 1986. 34(3): p. 2427-2432.

[49] Andrzejak, R.G., et al., *Bivariate surrogate techniques: Necessity, strengths, and caveats.* Physical Review E, 2003. 68(6): p. 66202.

[50] Prichard, D. and J. Theiler, *Generating surrogate data for time series with several simultaneously measured variables.* Phys Rev Lett, 1994. 73(7): p. 951-954.

[51] Montague, J.D., *The hyperkinetic child: a behavioural, electrodermal and EEG investigation.* Dev Med Child Neurol, 1975. 17(3): p. 299-305.

[52] Chabot, R.J., et al., *Sensitivity and specificity of QEEG in children with attention deficit or specific developmental learning disorders.* Clin Electroencephalogr, 1996. 27(1): p. 26-34.

[53] Clarke, A.R., et al., *Effects of methylphenidate on EEG coherence in attention-deficit/hyperactivity disorder.* Int J Psychophysiol, 2005. 58(1): p. 4-11.

[54] Clarke, A.R., et al., *Coherence in children with Attention-Deficit/Hyperactivity Disorder and excess beta activity in their EEG.* Clin Neurophysiol, 2007. 118(7): p. 1472-9.

[55] Dupuy, F.E., et al., *EEG coherence in children with attention-deficit/hyperactivity disorder: differences between good and poor responders to methylphenidate.* Psychiatry Res, 2010. 180(2-3): p. 114-9.

[56] Dupuy, F.E., et al., *EEG coherence in girls with attention-deficit/hyperactivity disorder: stimulant effects in good responders.* Int J Psychophysiol, 2008. 70(3): p. 151-7.

[57] Barry, R.J., et al., *Age and gender effects in EEG coherence: II. Boys with attention deficit/hyperactivity disorder.* Clin Neurophysiol, 2005. 116(4): p. 977-84.

[58] Barry, R.J., et al., *Age and gender effects in EEG coherence: III. Girls with attention-deficit/hyperactivity disorder.* Clin Neurophysiol, 2006. 117(2): p. 243-51.

[59] Volkow, N.D., et al., *Evidence that methylphenidate enhances the saliency of a mathematical task by increasing dopamine in the human brain.* Am J Psychiatry, 2004. 161(7): p. 1173-80.

[60] Lubar, J.F., et al., *Methylphenidate effects on global and complex measures of EEG.* Pediatr Neurol, 1999. 21(3): p. 633-7.

[61] Murias, M., J.M. Swanson and R. Srinivasan, *Functional connectivity of frontal cortex in healthy and ADHD children reflected in EEG coherence.* Cereb Cortex, 2007. 17(8): p. 1788-99.

[62] Ahmadlou, M., R. Rostami and V. Sadeghi, *Which attention-deficit/hyperactivity disorder children will be improved through neurofeedback therapy? A graph theoretical approach to neocortex neuronal network of ADHD.* Neurosci Lett, 2012. 516(1): p. 156-60.

[63] Strogatz, S.H., *Exploring complex networks.* Nature, 2001. 410(6825): p. 268-76.

[64] Barttfeld, P., et al., *Functional Connectivity and Temporal Variability of Brain Connections in Adults with Attention Deficit/Hyperactivity Disorder and Bipolar Disorder.* Neuropsychobiology, 2014. 69: 65-75.

[65] Liu, T., et al., *Electroencephalogram synchronization analysis for attention deficit hyperactivity disorder children.* Biomed Mater Eng, 2014. 24(1): p. 1035-9.

[66] Marsland, S., *Machine Learning: An Algorithmic Perspective, Second Edition.* 2nd ed. Chapman & Hall/CRC Machine Learning & Pattern Recognition. 2014: Chapman & Hall/CRC.

[67] Vinck, M., et al., *An improved index of phase-synchronization for electrophysiological data in the presence of volume-conduction, noise and sample-size bias.* Neuroimage, 2011. 55(4): p. 1548-65.

[68] Kugiumtzis, D., *Direct-coupling information measure from nonuniform embedding.* Physical Review E, 2013. 87(6): p. 062918.

[69] Wan, X., B. Crüts and H.J. Jensen, *The Causal Inference of Cortical Neural Networks during Music Improvisations.* PloS one, 2014. 9(12): p. e112776-e112776.

[70] Zanin, M., et al., Optimizing functional network representation of multivariate time series. Sci Rep, 2012. 2: p. 630.

Chapter 4

Role of Dopaminergic and Noradrenergic Systems as Potential Biomarkers in ADHD Diagnosis and Treatment

Catia Scassellati and Cristian Bonvicini

Additional information is available at the end of the chapter

http://dx.doi.org/10.5772/60860

Abstract

This chapter aims to identify, among the dopaminergic and noradrenergic molecules strongly associated to aetiopathogenesis of the disorder, potential genetic and biochemical markers linked to ADHD diagnosis and to assess whether treatments can change peripheral levels of a biomarker, to be then useful, if tested, as a response predictor.

The results, based on literature research, evidenced a role of some molecules such as SLC6A3, DRD4, MHPG, MAOA, NE, SLC6A2, DBH, COMT that could represent, in this order, a hypothetical signature of genetic and biochemical markers useful for ADHD diagnosis. From this hypothetical signature, the NE metabolite MHPG resulted, after a meta-analytic approach, the main molecule whose urinary levels were influenced by the d-AMP treatment. Urinary MHPG levels were decreased after stimulants administration only in the responder patients, indicating that MHPG could be a useful predictor of the response to these drugs. This, along with the well-reported correlation between decrease in MHPG and behavioral improvements after d-AMP treatment, focuses attention on MHPG as a potential mediator of stimulant drug response, in addition to a potential useful biological marker for diagnostic assessment.

Future studies on specificity, sensitivity and replication of these findings are needed.

Keywords: dopaminergic systems, noradrenergic systems, biomarkers, ADHD, diagnosis, treatment

1. Introduction

The attention-deficit-hyperactivity disorder (ADHD) is one of the most frequently diagnosed psychiatric disorders in children with an estimated worldwide-pooled prevalence of about

5.3–8.7% [1–3], persisting through adolescence and adulthood with a prevalence of up to 5% [4, 5]. The core symptoms include increased inattention and/or hyperactivity and impulsivity as well as lack of emotional self-control and motivation.

ADHD is a complex and heterogeneous disorder and its aetiology is not yet completely understood [6]. Despite evidence that environmental factors (i.e. maternal smoking, low birthweight, prematurity) play a significant role in its aetiology, classical genetics studies support a strong genetic contribution for ADHD. The risk of ADHD among parents of children with ADHD is increased by twofold to eightfold compared with the population rate [7]. A meta-analysis of 20 pooled twin studies estimated an average hereditability of 76%, suggesting that ADHD is one of the disorders with the strongest genetic component in psychiatry [7]. Despite these high heritability estimates, identification of genes that confer susceptibility to ADHD has been a slow and difficult process and current findings from both candidate gene studies and genome-wide association studies (GWAS) suggest that ADHD is a polygenic disorder with minor contribution from each individual susceptibility gene [for reviews, see 8, 9]. In particular, it seems likely that the high heritability of ADHD is determined by common variants as well as by rare deletions or duplications known as copy number variants (CNVs) [10]. A useful database on the genomic studies in ADHD is to date available (http://adhd.psych.ac.cn/index.do).

Multiple neural pathways have been implicated in the development of ADHD and the most studied is the dopaminergic neurotransmission based on the observed dopamine (DA) deficiency in children with ADHD and on the therapeutic benefits provided by methylphenidate (MPH), a DA agonist. A meta-analysis of commonly studied candidate genes has revealed associations between ADHD and variants of the dopamine transporter (DAT1) gene (*SLC6A3*) and the dopamine D4 and D5 receptor genes (DRD4, DRD5) [11]. Moreover, significant peripheral alterations in norepinephrine (NE) levels and its main metabolites have been observed in ADHD patients [12]. This along with pharmacological evidence support that the noradrenergic system also plays a significant role in the aetiopathogenetic mechanisms of this illness.

1.1. Diagnosis

The clinical characterizations, underlying concepts, and nomenclature of the dysfunctions have changed over the time and hyperactive, inattentive, and impulsive children have been described by several authors during the past 200 years. First clinical description of attentional disorders was reported by the German physician, Melchior Adam Weikard, in 1775, and the successive mentioning of ADHD was described in 1902 by the British pediatrician, Sir George Still. In 1952, the APA issued the first DSM but only the second edition included "hyperkinetic impulse disorder". This name was further changed in attention deficit disorder (ADD) with/without hyperactivity in 1980 (DSM-III). The APA released a revised version of the DSM-III in 1987 where they changed the name definitively to attention-deficit-hyperactivity disorder (ADHD). The three subtypes (combined type ADHD, predominantly inattentive type ADHD, predominantly hyperactive-impulsive type ADHD) were established in 2000 (DSM-IV) (for review, see [13]). Recently, NIMH approved the Research Domain Criteria (RDoC) project where a set of assumptions permit to find a new classification system, by integrating genetics, imaging and cognitive information [14]. The RDoC suggests that a biomarker approach to diagnosis may be a more valid way to classify complex mental disorders such as ADHD. Biomarkers offer the opportunity to standardize and improve diagnostic assessment while providing insights into aetiological mechanisms. To date, although biomarkers are successfully used in predicting diseases such as cancer, there is no laboratory test that is used clinically for the diagnosis of ADHD.

1.2. Treatment

Pharmacotherapy has an essential role in the treatment of ADHD [15].

Stimulants, such as MPH and dextro-amphetamine (d-AMP), are the most widely used medications approved by the Unites States Food and Drug Administration (US-FDA) for the treatment of ADHD in children [16], and more than 70% of children with ADHD respond to these drugs [17]. These medications improve both the cognitive (inattention and impulsivity) and the non-cognitive (hyperactivity) domains of the disorder [18]. They have virtually identical clinical effects, although AMP formulations are modestly more efficacious than MPH [19]. Usually, a child who responds to one stimulant drug also responds to the other, presumably because of the similar effect of the drugs on brain monoamine metabolism, and it is generally assumed that the mechanism of at least some effects of these drugs involves DA. In fact, preclinical studies have shown that both stimulants block the re-uptake of DA and NE into the pre-synaptic neuron, and increase the release of these monoamines into the extraneuronal space.

Other drugs used are the monoamine oxidase inhibitors (MAOIs) that block the breakdown of serotonin (5-HT), NE, DA and increase the availability of these monoamines.

Proven alternate choices to stimulant medications include atomoxetine, guanfacine and bupropion. Atomoxetine is a non-stimulant approved by the FDA for the treatment of ADHD. It is in the class of medications known as selective NE re-uptake inhibitors. There is good level of evidence provided by meta-analysis of efficacy for this drug [20–22]. Long-acting guanfacine is in the group of medications known as alpha agonists. These medications were developed for the treatment of high blood pressure but have also been used to treat children with ADHD who have tics, sleep problems and/or aggression. It has recently been approved by the FDA for the treatment of children with ADHD. Finally, bupropion is a unique type of antidepressant that has been less frequently studied as a treatment for ADHD. Like stimulants and atomoxetine, it inhibits the re-uptake of both DA and NE but does not carry the potential risk of abuse and dependence seen with stimulants.

Other alternative treatments, in addition to the behavioural therapy, regard the use of pycnogenol, a herbal dietary supplement derived from French maritime pine bark extract [23] or pemoline, a central nervous system (CNS) stimulant, structurally different from AMP and MPH, that acts via enhancing central dopaminergic transmission [24].

Although there are several treatments for ADHD, the mechanisms of action of these agents are still unknown and to date no biological predictors of treatment response are available that can be used in treatment planning.

1.3. Definition of a biomarker

The identification of genetic and biochemical markers might facilitate the differential diagnosis of ADHD as well as allow better monitoring of treatment response or prediction of disorder progression, and help to determine treatment strategy and the development of individualized therapies.

According to US-FDA, a biomarker is defined as a characteristic that can be objectively measured and evaluated as an indicator of a normal biological process, a pathogenic process or a response to a therapeutic intervention [25, 26].

In other words, the identification of genetic and peripheral biomarkers, which provide molecular signatures of disease, could potentially improve diagnostic classification. Also, the identification and validation of biomarkers for a disorder have the potential application as indicators of disease status, course of the illness and potentially as targets to monitor and predict response to therapeutics.

A desirable diagnostic biomarker should meet several characteristics. In particular, (a) high specificity and sensitivity (80 % for both); (b) reliability, reproducibility, inexpensiveness and easy use; (c) independent confirmations by qualified researchers published in peer-reviewed journals; (d) biomarker interpretation should allow comparison with other neurological observations; (e) information provided by a biomarker should be timely and cost-effective with significant clinical usefulness; (f) technology for a test should be available and tolerated by the general target population; (g) methodology should be cheap, simple and easily integrated into a clinical care practice [27].

To date, it is well accepted that a single biomarker is very unlikely to provide enough information to identify cellular and metabolic pathways involved in a particular individual. Thus the identification of a signature set of biomarkers for a disorder each based on their underlying biological pathways will be the most effective for diagnosis and treatment selection [28].

Biological samples useful for a diagnostic test should be ideally non-invasive, which is especially important in psychiatric disorders, since patients often have conditions that should typically not be exacerbated by additional stress. Some studies utilize fluids such as brain tissue or cerebrospinal fluid (CSF), which represent an invasive procedure, whereas urine and saliva are the best non-invasive procedures.

On this basis, the main aims of this chapter are: (a) to identify, among the dopaminergic and noradrenergic molecules strongly associated to aetiopathogenesis of the disorder, potential genetic and biochemical markers linked to ADHD diagnosis; (b) to assess whether treatments can change peripheral levels of a biomarker, to be then useful, if tested, as a response predictor.

2. Role of dopaminergic and noradrenergic systems as potential genetic and biochemical markers in ADHD diagnosis

In this paragraph, we report evidence on the involvement of the most relevant components of dopaminergic and noradrenergic pathways with ADHD aetiopathogenesis as well as with neuropsychological, neuroimaging, treatment response, biochemical and gene expression features. This is to identify, among these molecules, the best potential markers linked to ADHD diagnosis and thus to characterize a putative signature set of genetic and biochemical markers for ADHD. Here, we report positive associations of polymorphisms (single-nucleotide polymorphisms – SNPs and variable number of tandem repeats – VNTR) in different genes (genomics) or alterations in peripheral levels of different proteins (metabolomics) with ADHD.

2.1. Method

The literature research was conducted by using two online electronic databases (PubMed http://www.ncbi.nlm.nih.gov/pubmed/, database ADHD http://adhd.psych.ac.cn/index.do) from inception until December 2014, for all available studies on genomics, metabolomics neuropsychological, neuroimaging, dopamine, norepinephrine, metabolites, metabolism enzymes, levels, biochemical, expression, response and "ADHD" or "Attention Deficit Hyperactivity Disorder". Once articles had been collected, bibliographies were manually searched for additional eligible studies. The literature search was performed by two individuals independently.

2.2. Results

2.2.1. Dopamine neurotransmitter system

The DA hypothesis for ADHD's neurological mechanism is the most probable and studied theory. It is based on a malfunctioning or decreased functioning of the DA system in particular regions of the brain, supported by data derived from pharmacological and neuroimaging studies, from animal models as well as for its involvement in the regulation of functions such as attention or psychomotor activity, which are impaired in ADHD [29].

2.2.1.1. Dopamine Transporter Gene (DAT1, SLC6A3)

The main function played by DAT1 is to regulate DA availability. In particular, it removes DA from the synaptic cleft into the pre-synaptic neuron or releases DA into the extracellular space. Its involvement in the aetiopathogenetic mechanisms of ADHD is supported by the evidence that dopaminergic neurotransmission is controlled by the DAT1 protein, DAT1 is the main target for MPH and AMP, knockout mice for DAT1 present hyperactivity and deficits in inhibitory behaviour, DAT1 has been mapped near to 5p13, a susceptibility locus for ADHD.

The most studied DAT1 variant is a VNTR of 40 base pairs located at the 3′-untranslated region (3′-UTR) of the gene. The ten repeat (10R) and nine repeat (9R) alleles are the most common. A recent meta-analysis that pooled 34 studies on this polymorphism demonstrated an association between the 10R allele and ADHD susceptibility [11]. A single successive study replicated this association, with the 10R allele conferring greater risk for ADHD symptoms [30]. This allele has a functional effect because it correlates with increased DA concentrations in CSF [31] and with higher DAT density in ADHD children in basal ganglia, a brain area participating in inhibitory behaviours [32].

As reported in [33, 34], 10R allele was linked to specific neuropsychological and neuroimaging functions and treatment response. In particular, this allele was associated to (a) sustained attention, (b) executive functions, (c) response inhibition, (d) spatial attentional bias, (e) abnormal reward-related ventral striatum activity, (f) diverse patterns of EEG responses, (g) lower IQ, (h) reduced caudate volume, (i) abnormalities in vigilance and EEG activity in response to MPH, (l) higher regional cerebral blood flow and poorer treatment response (Table 1).

2.2.1.2. Dopamine D4 Receptor (DRD4) gene

The DRD4 is a G-protein-coupled receptor belonging to the DA D2-like receptor family, which acts to inhibit adenyl cyclase. It is involved in ADHD aetiopathogenetic mechanisms because of its high expression in brain regions implicated in attention and inhibition such as anterior cingulate cortex. Moreover, DRD4 was the first to be associated with personality trait common in ADHD (novelty-seeking).

A highly polymorphic functional VNTR in the third exon has been frequently studied in association studies. It comprises 11 copies of a 48-bp repeat sequence, where 4, 7 and 2R repeat alleles are the most prevalent. Two meta-analyses confirmed that the 7R allele was associated with ADHD susceptibility [11, 35]. Recently, rare variants and non-synonymous mutations in the VNTR region of 7R allele have been identified in ADHD subjects [36], suggesting an allelic heterogeneity in the VNTR as an important factor in the pathophysiology of ADHD.

As summarized in [33], this allele was associated to (a) cognitive markers such as speed of processing, set shifting, and cognitive impulsiveness, (b) thinner pre-frontal and parietal cortex, (c) enhanced response to MPH. Moreover, mRNA expression levels of DRD4 were lower in ADHD [37] (Table 1).

2.2.1.3. Dopamine D5 Receptor (DRD5) Gene

The DRD5 is a G-protein-coupled receptor that belongs to the D1 class of DA receptors and serves to stimulate adenyl cyclase activity. Some studies support its involvement in ADHD aetiopathogenesis: (a) the expression of this gene is higher in hippocampus, a brain area involved in ADHD pathogenesis; (b) DRD5 is implicated in synaptic strength in hippocampal memory formation. The association between ADHD and a highly polymorphic dinucleotide repeat of DRD5 ((CA)n), at the 5′ flanking region, has been the most studied. This variant comprises 12 alleles and the 148-bp and 136-bp alleles are the most common. The 148-bp allele is a risk factor for ADHD according to two meta-analyses [11, 35]. Moreover, it was found associated to some neuropsychological features such as commission errors, omission errors and reaction time variability [33] (Table 1).

Systems		Potential biomarkers	Gene function	Location polymorphism risk allele functionality	Neuro-Psychological features	Variations in brain anatomy (structural MRI)	Variations in brain function (functional MRI)	Gene expression	Drugs response	Peripheral levels	Correlations behavioural modifications and peripheral levels	Drugs effect on peripheral levels: MPH	d-AMP	MAOIs
Genomics	Dopaminergic system	Dopamine transporter DAT1 (*SLC6A3*)	Encodes a transmembrane transport protein mediating the active reuptake of DA from the synapse and serves as a critical regulator of dopaminergic neurotransmission in the brain.	3'-UTR VNTR 10R higher expression levels	Yes	Yes	Yes		Yes					
		Dopamine D4 receptor (DRD4)	A member of the dopamine D2-like receptor family inhibiting adenylcyclase. Expressed in frontal lobe regions (orbitofrontal cortex and anterior cingulated regions).	Exon III VNTR 7R less responsive	Yes	Yes		Yes	Yes					
		Dopamine D5 receptor (DRD5)	A member of the dopamine D1-like receptors family. Expressed in amygdala, frontal cortex, hippocampus, striatum, basal forebrain, hypothalamus, cerebellum and thalamus.	5' Flank dinucleotide repeat 148 bp	Yes									
Metabolomics		Dopamine (DA)	In ADHD, the turnover is reduced with excessive re-uptake and intra-synaptic monoamine concentrations are decreased.							No		No	No	No
		Dihydroxy phenylacetic acid (DOPAC)	Main DA metabolite.							No		No	No	No (BC)
		Homovanillic acid (HVA)	Main DA metabolite.							No		No	No	Yes
Genomics	Noradrenergic system	Norepinephrine transporter protein 1 NET1 (*SLC6A2*)	Codes for a protein responsible for the re-uptake of NE from the synaptic cleft back into the pre-synaptic neuron. Expressed in the frontal lobes. It is actively involved in both noradrenergic and dopaminergic re-uptake and regulation in this region.	Exon 9 rs5569 no risk allele Other polymorphisms	Yes				Yes Yes					
Metabolomics		Norepinephrine (NE)	It is released by noradrenergic neurons located in the specific central nervous system neurons.							Yes	Yes after PYC	No	No	No
		3-Methoxy-4-hydroxyphenyl Glycol (MHPG)	Main metabolite of NE.							Yes	Yes after d-AMP	No	Yes (yes RES)	Yes
		Normetanephrine (NM)	Main metabolite of NE.							No (BC)		No	No	Yes
		Vanillylmandelic acid (VMA)	Other metabolite of NE.							Yes/No		No	No(BC)	Yes
		Neuropeptide Y (NPY)	Co-localizes with catecholamine systems.				Yes			Yes				
	Trace Amines	Phenylethylamine (PEA)	A DA receptor agonist, synthesized by the decarboxylation of phenylalanine.							Yes	Yes -no after d-AMP	No	Yes	No
Genomics/ Metabolomics	Enzymes metabolism	Monoamine oxidase A (MAOA)	Encodes a protein involved in the metabolism of DA, 5-HT, NE.	Promoter VNTR no risk allele Other polymorphisms	Yes				Yes	Yes	Yes			
		Dopamine beta hydroxylase (DBH)	Catalyzes the conversion of DA into NE. Expressed in the PFC.	Intron V rs2519152 (TaqI) no risk allele 5' Flank rs1611115 (-1021 C/T) No risk allele	Yes					Yes/No	Yes			
		Catechol-O-methyltransferase (COMT)	Enzyme catalyzing the inactivation of DA within the PFC. Expressed in frontal lobe regions of brain.	Exon IV rs4680 158Val/Met) no risk allele	Yes				Yes					

Note: VNTR: variable number of tandem repeats; UTR: untranslated region; DA: dopamine; MRI: magnetic resonance imaging; MPH: methylphenidate; d-AMP: d-Amphetamine; MAOIs: Monoamine oxidase Inhibitors; Pycnogenol (PYC); Res: responders; BC: after Bonferroni correction

Table 1. Data from genomic and metabolomic studies in dopaminergic, noradrenergic and biogenic trace amines systems and metabolism enzymes classified according to neuropsychological, neuroimaging, treatment response, biochemical and gene expression findings. Results from meta-analyses on the effects of treatments and peripheral levels of the biomarkers.

2.2.1.4. DA, Dihydroxyphenylacetic Acid (DOPAC) and Homovanillic Acid (HVA)

DA and its main metabolites DOPAC and HVA showed no difference in urine excretion in ADHD patients compared with controls [12] (Table 1).

2.2.2. Noradrenergic neurotransmitter system

In 1971, Wender et al. [38] was the first to propose that symptoms usually present in ADHD, such as hyperactivity, inattention and impulsivity, could be the result of abnormalities in the dopaminergic and in noradrenergic neurotransmission system. The authors suggested that noradrenergic system was disturbed in ADHD and that the stimulant medication used to treat these symptoms acted on this neurotransmitter to compensate for the deficit. Indeed after treatment with low dose of MPH, NE efflux increased within the pre-frontal cortex (PFC). Moreover, the presumed method of action of atomoxetine is to increase extracellular levels of NE in PFC.

2.2.2.1. Norepinephrine Transporter Gene (NET1, SLC6A2)

The *SLC6A2* gene codes for the norepinephrine transporter, which is responsible for the re-uptake of NE from the synaptic cleft back into the pre-synaptic neuron and is targeted by atomoxetine. NET1 is most highly expressed in the frontal lobes where it plays a role in noradrenergic and dopaminergic re-uptake. Although the meta-analysis of the most studied polymorphism of rs5569 or G1287A (exon 9) showed negative results [11], an association was observed in a genome-wide association study [39]. Moreover, allele G was linked to decreasing in mean omission error scores after MPH administration [33] (Table 1).

Although few studies are available, other and different polymorphisms in this gene were associated independently to some neuropsychological tasks and MPH or atomoxetine response [33] (Table 1).

2.2.2.2. Norepinephrine (NE)

A recent meta-analysis [12] on peripheral urinary levels indicated higher concentrations in ADHD compared with controls. (Table 1).

2.2.2.3. 3-Methoxy-4-Hydroxyphenylglycol (MHPG)

MHPG is the main metabolite of NE. According to a meta-analysis on its urinary levels [12], the data showed a significant decrease in ADHD patients as compared to controls (Table 1).

2.2.2.4. Normetanephrine (NM) and Vanillylmandelic Acid (VMA)

Other metabolites studied are NM and VMA. According to a recent meta-analysis [12], the urinary levels of NM showed no alterations in patients as compared to controls after Bonferroni correction. Concerning VMA metabolite, contrasting results were reported on its urinary levels [12] (Table 1).

2.2.2.5. Neuropeptide Y (NPY)

NPY frequently co-localizes with catecholamine systems. It participates in the regulation of feeding, circadian rhythms, reproduction, and thermoregulation. Some studies reported in [12] confirmed increased plasma NPY concentrations in ADHD children compared with controls and an association was observed between gene dose-dependent increases in NPY and emotion processing (Table 1).

2.2.3. Biogenic trace amines

2.2.3.1. Phenylethylamine (PEA)

PEA is considered a trace amine because its urinary excretion rate and brain concentration are very low compared to the other catecholamines. In dopaminergic neurons of the nigrostriatal system, PEA is synthesized by the decarboxylation of phenylalanine and has the function to stimulate the release of DA. According to some studies summarized in [12], urinary levels of PEA are significantly lower in patients with ADHD compared with controls. Interestingly, decreased levels of PEA have also been associated with symptoms of inattentiveness (Table 1).

2.2.4. Metabolism enzymes

Molecular studies have provided compelling evidence for the association of ADHD with genes that encode enzymes involved in the metabolism of catecholamine and serotonin [8, 9].

2.2.4.1. Monoamine Oxidase A (MAOA)

The MAOA gene encodes a protein involved in the metabolism of DA, 5-HT and NE. Different evidence link this gene to aetiopathogenetic mechanisms of ADHD including a MAOA knockout mouse, showing an aggressive behaviour and higher monoaminergic neurotransmitter levels. Recent studies have focused mainly on a functional 30-bp VNTR 1.2 kb upstream of the gene, but according to the meta-analysis [11], no association was found. This VNTR was, however, linked to commission errors attenuated after MPH administration [33]. Other polymorphisms, independently or in combination of haplotypes, were found associated to specific neuropsychological tasks (i.e. motor control or visuo-spatial working memory, reward deficiency or insufficient response inhibition) [33]. Concerning blood levels, the meta-analysis [12] indicated reduced levels in ADHD compared with controls. MAO levels were associated with increased inattention and impulsivity [12] (Table 1).

2.2.4.2. Dopamine Beta Hydroxylase (DBH)

The DBH gene encodes an enzyme that catalyzes the conversion of DA into NE which is particularly expressed in the pre-frontal cortex. The polymorphism intron 5 TaqI (rs2519152) was the most studied, whereas A–1021C/T variant (rs1611115), although a functional polymorphism, was less investigated. A meta-analysisof these variants reported no association with ADHD [11].

However, A2/T allele was found associated with several neuropsychological tasks (poorer performances on a temporal order judgment task, more commission and omission errors and greater reaction time variability, more errors on measures of problem-solving and cognitive impulsiveness). An association between neuropsychological measures of executive function in children with ADHD and the –1021C/T variant has also been reported [33]. Concerning the studies on its peripheral levels, patients with ADHD showed lower activities of DBH in serum and urine, whereas no alterations were observed in plasma levels. It was suggested that decreased DBH levels correlate with ADHD symptoms [12] (Table 1).

2.2.4.3. Catechol-O-Methyltransferase (COMT)

The COMT is an enzyme responsible for the degradation of DA and NE. It is highly expressed in frontal lobe where it regulates synaptic DA levels. Most of the association studies between COMT and ADHD susceptibility were focused on the well-known functional polymorphism in exon 4 valine158 methionine (Val158Met). This SNP influences its enzyme activity because homozygotes for the valine allele show greater activity than homozygotes for the methionine allele. A recent meta-analysis [40] indicates no association between ADHD and the Val158Met. However this polymorphism was found associated to (a) some neuropsychological tasks, (b) antisocial and aggressive behaviours of ADHD, (c) response to MPH treatment [33] (Table 1).

3. Effects of ADHD treatments on peripheral levels of a biomarker in dopaminergic and noradrenergic systems

Although several treatments for ADHD are available, there are no biological predictors of treatment response that can be used in treatment planning. To address this gap in the literature, we, for the first time, meta-analyzed studies assessing the effects of treatment on biomarkers in dopaminergic, noradrenergic, biogenic trace amines systems and their principal metabolites. The effects of treatments on biomarkers may give insights into their mechanisms of action and could be useful for developing hypotheses about biomarkers that might predict treatment efficacy.

3.1. METHODS

3.1.1. Literature Search

To identify eligible studies for the meta-analysis, we searched two online electronic databases (PubMed and Human Genome Epidemiology Network, HuGeNet), from inception until December 2014, for all available studies on biomarkers and ADHD treatments in childhood. The diagnostic search terms used to query the databases were "ADHD" and "Attention Deficit Hyperactivity Disorder". These two terms were used to conduct searches with all relevant names of the biomarkers of interest along with different combinations of the following keywords: dopamine, norepinephrine, metabolites, levels, peripheral, blood, urine, treatment, clinical trial, methylphenidate, amphetamine, pemoline, pycnogenol, aspartame. Once articles had been collected, bibliographies were manually searched for additional eligible studies. The literature search was performed by two individuals independently.

3.1.2. Inclusion and Exclusion Criteria

We included studies that (a) investigated one or more of the peripheral biomarkers described; and (b) provided the features needed for performing meta-analyses. We excluded studies that: (a) compared cases with ADHD with controls; (b) were case reports, (c) were commentaries or reviews, (d) were not in English, (e) used adults or animal models, (f) selected samples based on a disorder other than ADHD.

3.1.3. Data Extraction for Meta-analyses

For all studies suitable for meta-analyses, we extracted the following data from the original publications: first author and year of publication, the number of participants, percent males, mean age in years, study designs, biomarkers analyzed, drugs, dosage, treatment time duration, results obtained (Table 2).

3.1.4. Statistical Analyses

Review Manager was used to analyze the data (RevMan Version 5.1.6; Copenhagen, The Nordic Cochrane Centre, The Cochrane Collaboration, 2008). As reported in [12], we used the fixed-effects model to generate a pooled effect size and 95% confidence interval (CI) from individual study effect sizes (the standardized mean difference [SMD]) using the inverse variance method. The significance of the pooled effect sizes was determined by the z-test. Between study, heterogeneity was assessed using a $\chi 2$ test of goodness of fit test and the I^2 statistic. We used a p value of 0.05 to assert statistical significance. In instances where the results showed a significant effect in the presence of significant between-study heterogeneity, a random effects model was used, with effect sizes pooled using the DerSimonian and Laird method.

Publication bias was estimated by the method of Egger et al. [41] which uses a linear regression approach to measure funnel plot asymmetry on the natural logarithm scale of the OR. The significance of the intercept (a) was determined by the t test [41]. The rank correlation method and regression method tests were conducted by MIX version 1.7. (http://www.mix-for-meta-analysis.info).

Because we conducted 8 meta-analyses to assess the significance of biomarkers, our Bonferroni corrected significance level was 0.006.

3.1.5. Behavioural methods

The main scales to address behavioural modifications/response to drugs were Conners Teacher/Parent Rating Scales [42–54, 23]. Moreover, other tests/scales were used: Physical and Neurological Examination for Soft Signs [47, 53, 46, 55], Multigrade Inventory for Teachers, Matching Familiar Figures Test, Children's Checking Task, Wisconsin Card Sorting Test, Airplane Test [42], Children's Global Assessment and Impression Scales, Child (Attention Problems) Teacher Rating scale, Wechsler Intelligence Scale for Children [47, 54, 23].

First author, Published year	Patients sample size	%Males	Age *	Study design	Biomarkers	Treatments	Dosage	Treatment time duration	Results
Wender et al. [38]	9	89	9 y	P vs. T	HVA, NE, NM, VMA, MHPG	d-AMP	10–20 mg/day	1 week	d-AMP increased NM
Shekim et al. [55]	6	100	9 y	P vs. T	MHPG, NM, HVA	d-AMP	0.5 mg/kg/day	2 weeks	d-AMP depressed MHPG, NM
Rapoport et al. [46]	13	100	9 y	P vs. T	MHPG, HVA, NE, DA	d-AMP	0.5 mg/kg/day	nr	d-AMP decreased MHPG, HVA
Shekim et al. [56]	10	100	9 y	B vs. T	MHPG	d-AMP	0.5 mg/kg/day	2 weeks	d-AMP decreased MHPG
Shekim et al. [51]	21	100	9 y	B vs. T	MHPG, NM	d-AMP	0.5 mg/kg/day	2 weeks	d-AMP decreased MHPG (R)
Shekim et al. [53]	15	100	9 y	B vs. T	MHPG	d-AMP	0.5 mg/kg/day	2 weeks	d-AMP decreased MHPG (R)
Brown et al. [50]	8	100	7 y	P vs. T	MHPG, HVA	d-AMP	0.74±0.98 mg/kg/day	1 week	d-AMP decreased MHPG
Shekim et al. [54]	21	100	9 y	R vs. NR	MHPG, HVA	d-AMP	0.5 mg/kg/day	2 weeks	d-AMP decreased MHPG (R)
Shekim et al. [49]	9	100	13 y	B vs. T	MHPG, HVA	d-AMP	0.5 mg/kg/day	2 weeks	d-AMP decreased MHPG, increased HVA
Shen and Wang [52]	38	95	9 y	B vs. T	MHPG	MPH	0.3 mg/kg/day	3 weeks	MPH decreased MHPG
Zametkin et al. [58]	12	100	9 y	P vs. T	PEA	d-AMP	0.75 mg/kg/day	2 weeks	d-AMP increased PEA
Zametkin et al. [44]	10	100	9 y	B vs. T	NE, VMA, NM, MHPG, DA, DOPAC, HVA, PEA	MPH, d-AMP	0.85±0.12 mg/kg/day 0.69 mg/kg	2 weeks	d-AMP decreased DA, DOPAC,HVA, NE, MHPG,VMA
Zametkin et al. [45]	5	100	9 y	B vs. T	MHPG, NE, NM, VMA, DA, HVA, DOPAC, PEA	d-AMP, MAOIs	13.21±2.5 mg 12.13±4.5 mg clorgyline, 10.40±1.1 mg tranylcypromine sulfate	4 weeks	d-AMP decreased MHPG, NE, NM, VMA MAOIs decreased MHPG, VMA, HVA, DOPAC; increased NM
Zametkin et al. [43]	11	100	8 y	B vs. T	NE, NM, MHPG, VMA, DA, HVA, PEA	Pemoline	2.9±0.31 mg/kg/day	4 weeks	No alterations
Zametkin et al. [48]	11	100	9 y	B vs. T	NE, NM, MHPG, VMA, HVA, DOPAC	MPH	0.74±0.21 mg/kg	2 weeks	MPH decreased NM
Elia et al. [47]	24	100	8 y	P vs. T	NE, MHPG, VMA, HVA, NM, DOPAC	d-AMP, MPH	up to 1.5 mg/kg/day up to 3 mg/kg/day	3 weeks	d-AMP decreased MHPG, VMA
Shaywitz et al. [42]	15	73	9 y	P vs. T	NE, DA, HVA	Aspartame	34 mg/kg	2 weeks	No alterations
Kusaga et al. [57]	22	nr:nr	9 y	R vs. NR	MHPG, PEA, HVA	MPH	0.3 to 0.5 mg/kg/day	Nr	No alterations (R, NR)
Dvokovka et al. [23]	40	82	10 y	P vs. T	NE, DA	Pycnogenol	1 mg/kg/day	4 weeks	Pyc decreased NE

Note: * age is represented in mean/years; y = years; nr = not reported; DA = dopamine; HVA = homovanillic acid; DOPAC = 3,4-dihydroxyphenylacetic acid; NE = norepinephrine; MHPG = 3-methoxy-4-hydroxyphenylethylene glycol; NM = normetanephrine; VMA = vanillylmandelic acid; MPH = methylphenidate; d-AMP = dextro-amphetamine; MAOIs = monoamine oxidase inhibitors; P = placebo; T = treatment; B = baseline; R = responders; NR = no responders

Table 2. Summary of studies on the ADHD treatments and peripheral levels of biomarkers in dopaminergic, noradrenergic and biogenic trace amines systems included in the meta-analyses.

http://dx.doi.org/10.5772/60860

3.2. Results

After screening of papers according to the inclusion/exclusion criteria, 35 ADHD treatments studies that focused on alterations in the principal metabolites and metabolism enzymes of dopaminergic and noradrenergic neurotransmission pathways were reported.

The main studies suitable for performing meta-analyses on ADHD treatments and peripheral biomarkers in dopaminergic, noradrenergic and biogenic trace amines systems are described in Table 2.

All the analyses presented below use the SMD as the effect size.

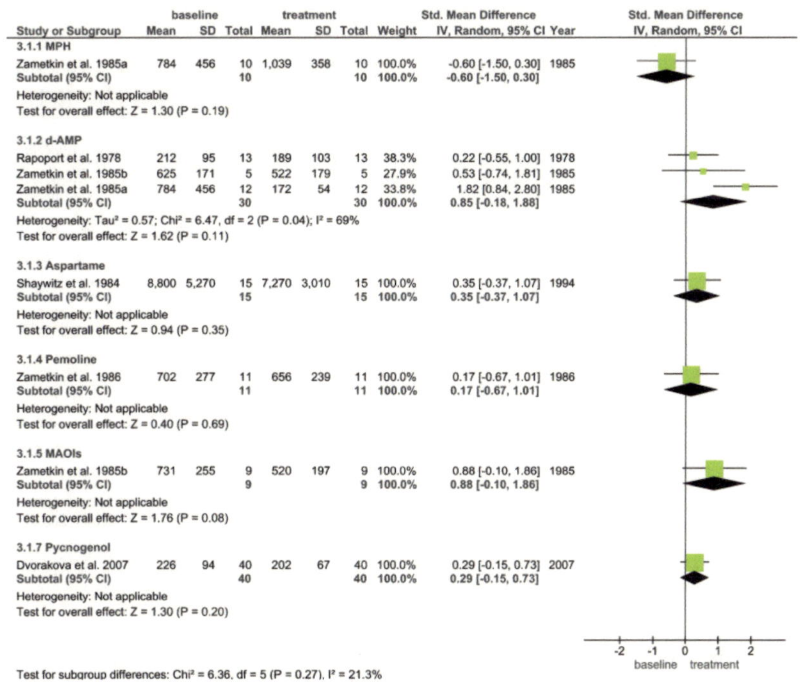

Captions: Chi² = χ^2 test of goodness of fit; Tau² = estimate of the between-study variance in a random-effects meta-analysis; methylphenidate (MPH); dextroamphetamine (d-AMP); monoamine oxidase inhibitors (MAOIs).

Figure 1. Random forest plot for standard mean differences (SMD) from meta-analysis of urinary dopamine (DA) levels.

3.2.1. Dopamine neurotransmitter system

3.2.1.1. DA and DOPAC

Urinary levels of DA [23, 42-46] and its metabolite DOPAC [47, 48, 44, 45] were investigated in several studies included in the meta-analyses. The results indicated no alteration in DA levels after d-AMP treatment ($Z = 1.62$ $p = 0.11$), with a slight heterogeneity in effect sizes among the studies ($p = 0.04$, I^2=69%). Other treatments (MPH, aspartame, pemoline, MAOIs, pycnogenol) did not influence its levels (Figure 1). No clinically significant effect on the behaviour and cognitive status of children with ADHD was observed after aspartame, pemoline, pcynogenol and MAOIs [42, 45, 43, 23], as well as in relation to d-AMP treatments.

Similarly, urinary DOPAC levels were similar between treated and not-treated patients with ADHD both after MPH ($Z = 0.08$, $p = 0.93$) and after d-AMP ($Z = 1.10$, $p = 0.27$) treatment. Significant heterogeneity in effect sizes across studies was observed for d-AMP ($p = 0.0001$, $I^2 = 89\%$). The difference observed after MAOIs treatment ($Z = 2.38$, $p = 0.02$) was lost after Bonferroni correction (Figure 2) and no clinical effect in children with ADHD was observed [45]. Similarity, there were no correlations between DOPAC levels and behavioural improvements after MPH and d-AMP treatments.

Study or Subgroup	baseline Mean	baseline SD	baseline Total	treatment Mean	treatment SD	treatment Total	Weight	Std. Mean Difference IV, Random, 95% CI	Year
4.1.1 MPH									
Zametkin et al. 1985a	1.7	0.7	10	2	1	10	22.0%	-0.33 [-1.22, 0.55]	1985
Zametkin et al. 1988	2.7	1	11	2.8	0.9	11	24.5%	-0.10 [-0.94, 0.74]	1988
Elia et al. 1990	4.7	1.7	24	4.4	2.2	24	53.5%	0.15 [-0.42, 0.72]	1990
Subtotal (95% CI)			45			45	100.0%	-0.02 [-0.43, 0.40]	
Heterogeneity: Tau² = 0.00; Chi² = 0.86, df = 2 (P = 0.65); I² = 0%									
Test for overall effect: Z = 0.08 (P = 0.93)									
4.1.2 d-AMP									
Zametkin et al. 1985b	2,891	1,280	5	2,808	966	5	31.7%	0.07 [-1.17, 1.31]	1985
Zametkin et al. 1985a	1.7	0.7	12	0.2	0.05	12	32.0%	2.92 [1.71, 4.13]	1985
Elia et al. 1990	4.7	1.7	24	4.6	2.3	24	36.4%	0.05 [-0.52, 0.61]	1990
Subtotal (95% CI)			41			41	100.0%	0.97 [-0.76, 2.70]	
Heterogeneity: Tau² = 2.05; Chi² = 18.35, df = 2 (P = 0.0001); I² = 89%									
Test for overall effect: Z = 1.10 (P = 0.27)									
4.1.3 MAOIs									
Zametkin et al. 1985b	3,289	1,312	9	1,699	1,090	9	100.0%	1.26 [0.22, 2.29]	1985
Subtotal (95% CI)			9			9	100.0%	1.26 [0.22, 2.29]	
Heterogeneity: Not applicable									
Test for overall effect: Z = 2.38 (P = 0.02)									

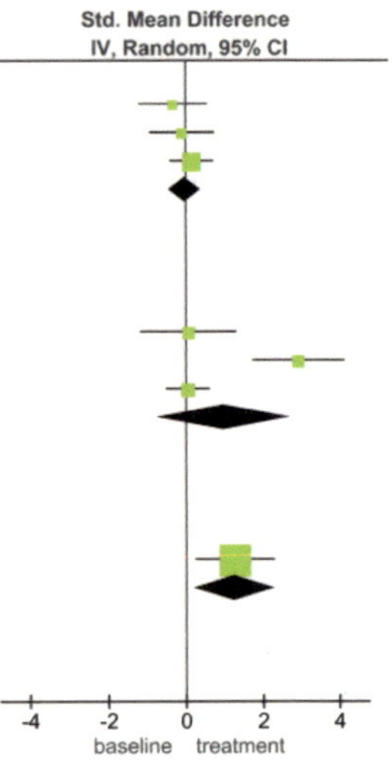

Test for subgroup differences: Chi² = 5.83, df = 2 (P = 0.05), I² = 65.7%

Captions: $Chi^2 = \chi^2$ test of goodness of fit; Tau^2 = estimate of the between-study variance in a random-effects meta-analysis; methylphenidate (MPH); dextroamphetamine (d-AMP); monoamine oxidase inhibitors (MAOIs).

Figure 2. Random forest plot for standard mean differences (SMD) from meta-analysis of urinary metabolite dihydroxyphenylacetic acid (DOPAC) levels.

3.2.1.2. Homovanilic Acid (HVA)

Eleven studies assessed the DA metabolite HVA in urine [42, 47, 48, 43-45, 49, 50, 46, 55, 38]. No alterations in HVA levels were observed after MPH ($Z = 0.09$, $p = 0.93$) and after d-AMP ($Z = 1.76$, $p = 0.08$) treatment. Significant heterogeneity in effect sizes across studies was observed after d-AMP treatment ($p = 0.0001$, $I^2 = 76\%$). Only one study [45] reported reduced HVA levels after MAOIs treatment ($Z = 3.46$, $p = 0005$), but no correlation with behavioural features was observed (Figure 3). No clinical effect on the behaviour and cognitive status of children with ADHD was observed after aspartame, pemoline and MAOIs [42, 45, 43], as well as after MPH and d-AMP treatments.

http://dx.doi.org/10.5772/60860

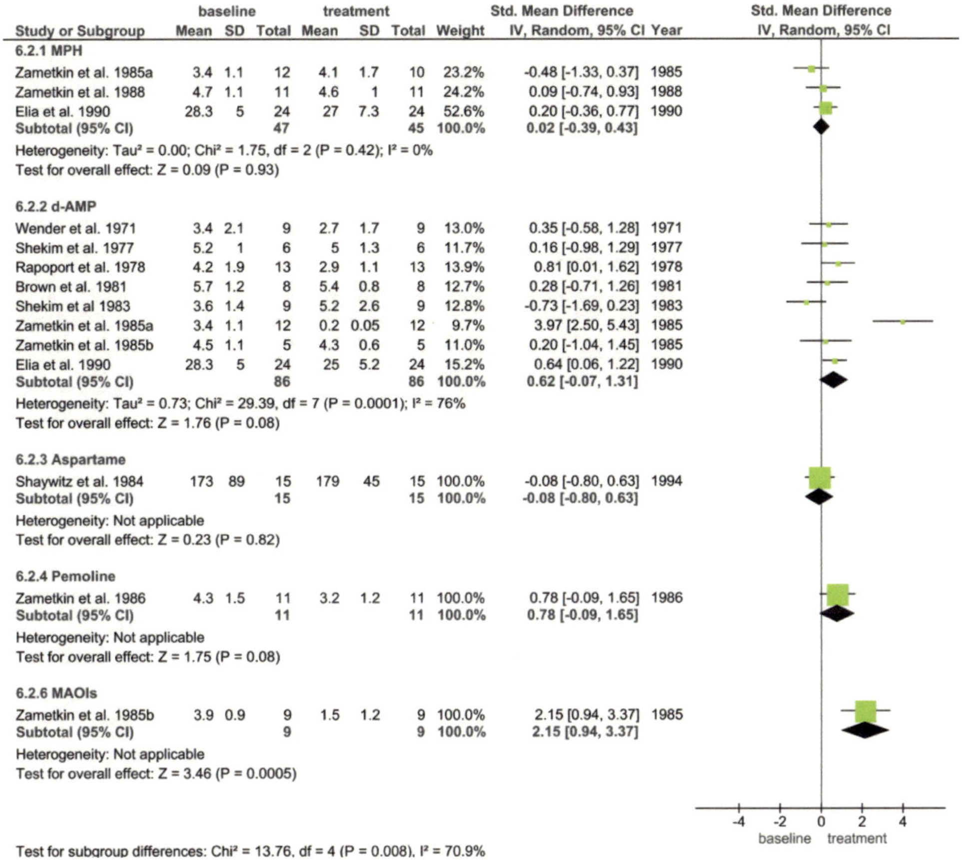

Captions: Chi² = χ^2 test of goodness of fit; Tau² = estimate of the between-study variance in a random-effects meta-analysis; methylphenidate (MPH); dextroamphetamine (d-AMP); monoamine oxidase inhibitors (MAOIs).

Figure 3. Random forest plot for standard mean differences (SMD) from meta-analysis of urinary homovanilic acid (HVA) levels.

3.2.2. Noradrenergic neurotransmitter system

3.2.2.1. NE

Our meta-analyses for NE included nine studies [23, 42, 47, 48, 43–46, 38] and showed no difference in urinary levels in treated patients with ADHD compared with those not treated (MPH: Z = 0.81, $p = 0.42$; d-AMP Z = 1.55, $p = 0.12$), with heterogeneity in effect sizes across studies for d-AMP ($p = 0.0002$, $I^2 = 82\%$) (Figure 4). Significant reduction of urinary NE was observed after pycnogenol treatment (Z = 3.08, $p = 0.002$) (Figure 4), with consequently less hyperactivity [23] (Table 1). No clinical effect on the behaviour and cognitive status of children with ADHD was observed after aspartame, pemoline and MAOIs [42, 45, 43] and similarly with MPH and d-AMP treatments.

Study or Subgroup	baseline Mean	baseline SD	baseline Total	treatment Mean	treatment SD	treatment Total	Weight	Std. Mean Difference IV, Random, 95% CI	Year
9.2.1 MHP									
Zametkin et al. 1985a	120	38.3	10	177	62.5	10	26.3%	-1.05 [-2.00, -0.10]	1985
Zametkin et al. 1988	76.5	17.4	11	75.5	15.9	11	30.4%	0.06 [-0.78, 0.89]	1988
Elia et al. 1990	0.4	0.2	24	0.4	0.3	24	43.3%	0.00 [-0.57, 0.57]	1990
Subtotal (95% CI)			**45**			**45**	**100.0%**	**-0.26 [-0.88, 0.36]**	
Heterogeneity: Tau² = 0.15; Chi² = 3.95, df = 2 (P = 0.14); I² = 49%									
Test for overall effect: Z = 0.81 (P = 0.42)									
9.2.2 d-AMP									
Wender et al. 1971	38.3	5.2	9	41.5	13.6	9	20.5%	-0.30 [-1.23, 0.63]	1971
Rapoport et al. 1978	31.2	12.8	13	25.3	11.5	13	21.7%	0.47 [-0.31, 1.25]	1978
Zametkin et al. 1985a	120	38.3	12	32.4	10.2	12	17.9%	3.02 [1.79, 4.25]	1985
Zametkin et al. 1985b	96.4	25.4	5	66.8	24.8	5	16.6%	1.07 [-0.31, 2.44]	1985
Elia et al. 1990	0.4	0.2	24	0.4	0.2	24	23.3%	0.00 [-0.57, 0.57]	1990
Subtotal (95% CI)			**63**			**63**	**100.0%**	**0.76 [-0.20, 1.72]**	
Heterogeneity: Tau² = 0.94; Chi² = 22.39, df = 4 (P = 0.0002); I² = 82%									
Test for overall effect: Z = 1.55 (P = 0.12)									
9.2.3 Aspartame									
Shaywitz et al. 1984	897	977	15	614	324	15	100.0%	0.38 [-0.34, 1.10]	1994
Subtotal (95% CI)			**15**			**15**	**100.0%**	**0.38 [-0.34, 1.10]**	
Heterogeneity: Not applicable									
Test for overall effect: Z = 1.03 (P = 0.31)									
9.2.4 Pemoline									
Zametkin et al. 1986	112	55	11	101	40	11	100.0%	0.22 [-0.62, 1.06]	1986
Subtotal (95% CI)			**11**			**11**	**100.0%**	**0.22 [-0.62, 1.06]**	
Heterogeneity: Not applicable									
Test for overall effect: Z = 0.51 (P = 0.61)									
9.2.5 Pycnogenol									
Dvorakova et al. 2007	24.1	1.1	40	19.9	8.2	40	100.0%	0.71 [0.26, 1.16]	2007
Subtotal (95% CI)			**40**			**40**	**100.0%**	**0.71 [0.26, 1.16]**	
Heterogeneity: Not applicable									
Test for overall effect: Z = 3.08 (P = 0.002)									
9.2.6 MAOIs									
Zametkin et al. 1985b	99	22.6	9	85.1	84.7	9	100.0%	0.21 [-0.71, 1.14]	1985
Subtotal (95% CI)			**9**			**9**	**100.0%**	**0.21 [-0.71, 1.14]**	
Heterogeneity: Not applicable									
Test for overall effect: Z = 0.45 (P = 0.65)									
Test for subgroup differences: Chi² = 6.95, df = 5 (P = 0.22), I² = 28.1%									

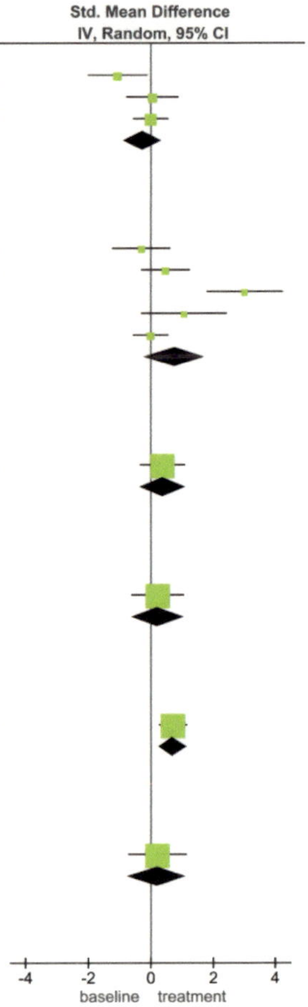

Captions: Chi² = χ^2 test of goodness of fit; Tau² = estimate of the between-study variance in a random-effects meta-analysis; methylphenidate (MPH); dextroamphetamine (d-AMP); monoamine oxidase inhibitors (MAOIs).

Figure 4. Random forest plot for standard mean differences (SMD) from meta-analysis of urinary norepinephrine (NE) levels.

3.2.2.2. Methoxy-4-hydroxyphenylglycol (MHPG)

Another widely studied metabolite of NE is MHPG. Fourteen studies provided data for our meta-analysis [47, 48, 43-45, 52, 49, 50, 56, 51, 53, 46, 55, 38]. We found significantly lower urinary MHPG levels in treated compared with not-treated patients after d-AMP treatment ($d = 0.89$, $Z = 6.23$, $p < 0.00001$), significant after Bonferroni correction. No heterogeneity of effect sizes across studies was observed. Concerning the results about MPH, a trend of significance was reported ($Z = 1.85$, $p = 0.06$), but it was lost after Bonferroni correction. Only one study reported a significant decrease after MAOIs treatment ($Z = 4.21$, $p < 0.0001$) [45] (Figure 5).

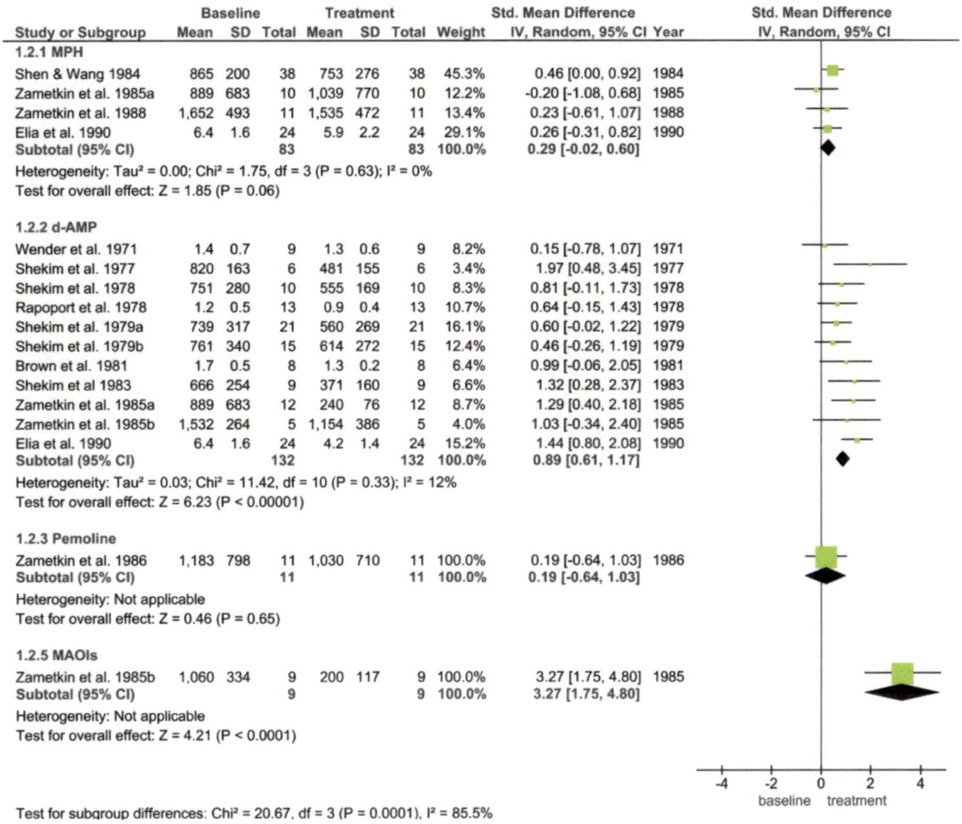

Captions: $Chi^2 = \chi^2$ test of goodness of fit; Tau^2 = estimate of the between-study variance in a random-effects meta-analysis; methylphenidate (MPH); dextroamphetamine (d-AMP); monoamine oxidase inhibitors (MAOIs).

Figure 5. Random forest plot for standard mean differences (SMD) from meta-analysis of urinary 3-methoxy-4-hydroxyphenylethylene glycol (MHPG) levels.

Moreover, with the aim to assess whether MHPG can be a potential predictor of the treatment response, we have meta-analyzed studies that reported MHPG urinary levels among responders and no responders pre- and post-treatment [57, 54, 53, 51]. The results indicated that MHPG urinary levels are reduced by stimulants in the responders ($Z = 2.66$, $p = 0.008$) but not in the no-responders ($Z = 0.16$, $p = 0.87$) (Figure 6).

Significant correlations were observed between lower levels of MHPG and behavioural improvements after d-AMP administration [45, 49, 54, 50, 51, 53] (Table 1), whereas no significant correlation was observed after MPH [48], or MAOIs [45] or pemoline [43] treatments.

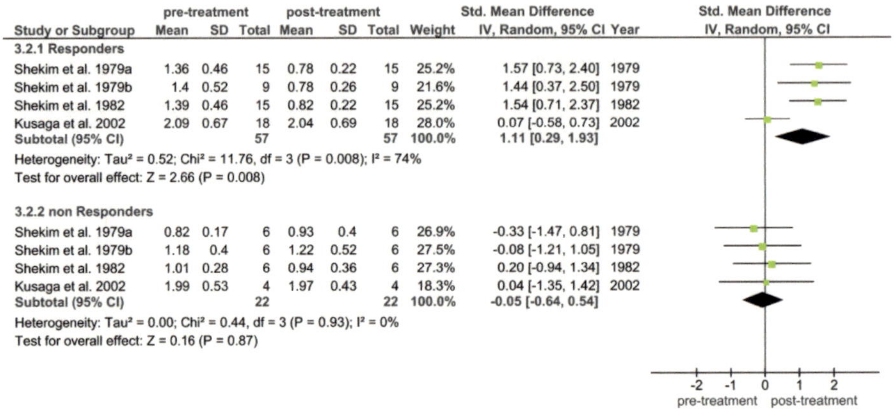

Captions: Chi² = χ² test of goodness of fit; Tau² = estimate of the between-study variance in a random-effects meta-analysis.

Figure 6. Random forest plot for standard mean differences (SMD) from meta-analysis of urinary 3-methoxy-4-hydroxyphenylethylene glycol (MHPG) levels in responders and no responders and pre-post d-AMP treatment.

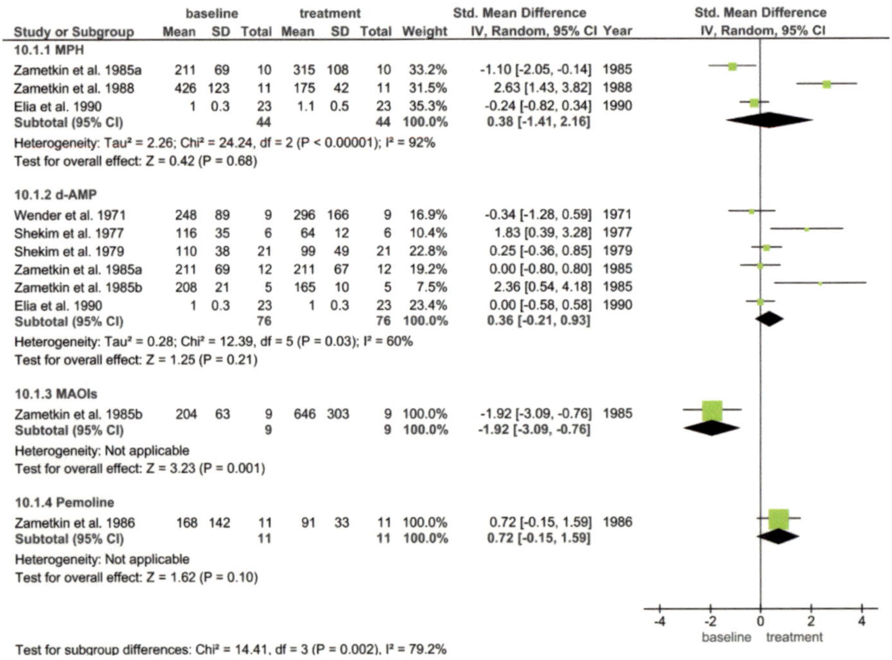

Captions: Chi² = χ² test of goodness of fit; Tau² = estimate of the between-study variance in a random-effects meta-analysis; methylphenidate (MPH); dextroamphetamine (d-AMP); monoamine oxidase inhibitors (MAOIs).

Figure 7. Random forest plot for standard mean differences (SMD) from meta-analysis of urinary normetanephrine (NM) levels.

Following the Egger et al. [41] method, we have tested the presence of publication bias (is a bias with regard to what is likely to be published, among what is available to be published) for all biomarkers analyzed. Only in the case of MHPG, we observed a slight significant presence of publication bias (p = 0.05, data not shown). However when the study from Zametkin et al. [45] was excluded, this difference disappears (p = 0.21, data not shown).

3.2.2.3. Normetanephrine (NM)

The main metabolite of NE is NM. The meta-analysis of NM included eight studies [47, 48, 43–45, 51, 55, 38]. No differences in urinary NM levels were observed between treated and not-treated patients after MPH (Z = 0.42, p = 0.68) and after d-AMP (Z = 1.25, p = 0.21) treatments, with heterogeneity of effect sizes across studies for MPH (p < 0.00001, I^2 = 92%). One study reported no alteration after pemoline treatment, with no correlation with behavioural improvements [43] and one study indicated increased levels of NM after MAOIs treatment with no evidence of correlation with behavioural features (Z = 3.23, p = 0.001) [45] (Figure 7).

3.2.2.4. Vanillylmandelic Acid (VMA)

Other metabolites studied are VMA. Six studies were available for meta-analyses [47, 48, 43–45, 38] and the results indicated significant difference after d-AMP treatment (Z = 2.12, p = 0.03) but lost after Bonferroni correction. Significant difference was observed for the presence of heterogeneity in effect size across the studies (p < 0.0001, I^2 = 86%). Reduced levels of VMA after MAOIs treatment were observed in only one study [45] (Z = 4.45, p < 0.00001), in absence of significant correlation with behavioural improvements. Moreover, no alteration was observed after pemoline treatment along with no clinically significant effect on the behaviour of children with ADHD [43] (Figure 8).

3.2.3. Biogenic trace amines

3.2.3.1. PEA

Although there are not enough studies for performing meta-analysis, administration of d-AMP resulted in an increased urinary excretion of PEA [44, 58, 57]. However, no correlation was observed between PEA levels and the ADHD severity [57, 58] (Table 1). No alterations were observed after MPH, MAOIs, and pemoline treatments [43–45].

4. Discussion and future research

This chapter has two main aims: (a) to define a hypothetical signature of a set of genetic and biochemical markers useful for the ADHD diagnosis; (b) to determine whether the treatment changes the levels of a biomarker to be useful, if tested, as a predictor of treatment response. In Table 1, we summarized the results obtained from this work, providing an overview of the significant findings that emerged by the different analyses.

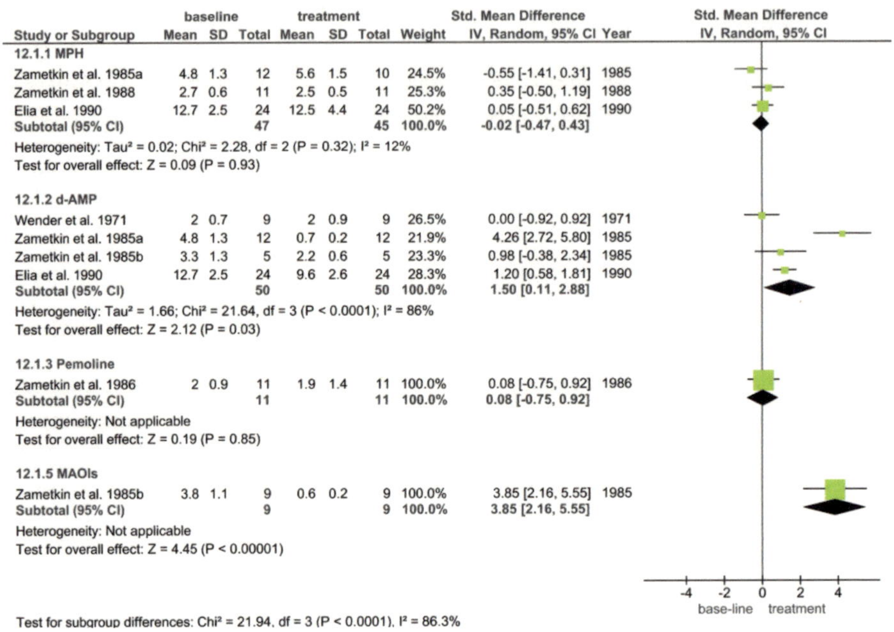

Captions: Chi² = χ^2 test of goodness of fit; Tau² = estimate of the between-study variance in a random-effects meta-analysis; methylphenidate (MPH); dextroamphetamine (d-AMP); monoamine oxidase inhibitors (MAOIs).

Figure 8. Random forest plot for standard mean differences (SMD) from meta-analysis of urinary vanillylmandelic acid (VMA) levels.

Starting from the literature, we support evidence that *SLC6A3* and DRD4 represent the best potential genetic markers for ADHD diagnosis. As reported in [33], allele 10R in *SLC6A3* gene, susceptibility risk allele and associated to higher DA concentrations and higher DAT1 density in basal ganglia, is linked to different and specific neuropsychological tasks, generates more activation in specific brain areas, reduced brain structure and is associated to drugs response. Interestingly a reverse association has been seen for ADHD adults where it is the 9R instead of 10R, the risk allele [59]. This suggests that this allele can be a good candidate also for discriminating ADHD in children vs. ADHD in adults.

Similarly 7R in DRD4 gene, susceptibility risk allele and linked to less responsivity to DA, is involved in some cognitive features, brain structure and functioning, drugs response and expression levels of DRD4.

In the second line, we co-localize the metabolite MHPG, the enzyme MAOA, NE and *SLC6A2* as good candidates as markers for ADHD. They were found associated to peripheral levels altered in ADHD, to some neuropsychological tasks, treatment response and symptomatology.

In the third line, interesting results come from DBH and COMT enzymes. Although the meta-analyses of Taq1 and –1021 T/C in DBH gene and 158Val/Met in COMT gene have not identified susceptibility alleles, variants of these genes are associated with neuropsychological performance, peripheral levels, treatment response and symptomatology.

http://dx.doi.org/10.5772/60860

Although the studies are often opposite or contradictory due to the heterogeneity of the disorder, *SLC6A3*, DRD4, MHPG, MAOA, NE, *SLC6A2*, DBH, COMT could represent, in this order, a hypothetical signature of a set of genetic and biochemical markers useful for ADHD diagnosis. In the absence of medications, peripheral levels of MAOA, DBH and also PEA were observed correlated with ADHD behaviour. Of this hypothetical signature, SLC6A3 10R, DRD4 7R, COMT val158met, MAOA were also associated to major depressive disorder (MDD), schizophrenia, schizophrenia/anxiety disorders/bipolar disorder and obsessive-compulsive disorder, respectively [60]. Moreover, peripheral levels of MHPG have been found associated to manic syndrome in bipolar disorder [61], to microstructural changes within the cerebellum in first-episode schizophrenia [62] and to melancholic MDD, even though without correlation with duration/severity of depressive symptoms [63]. However, these findings, if they are lacking specificity, on the other hand, suggest the common biological mechanisms linked to dopaminergic and noradrenergic systems shareable with different psychiatric disorders, as recently supported [60].

In relation to the meta-analyses on the peripheral alterations of a biomarker after treatment, the results located, for the first time, the NE metabolite MHPG as the main molecule whose urinary levels are influenced by the d-AMP treatment. This association was significant also after Bonferroni correction. The other molecules such as DA, DOPAC, HVA, NE, NM, VMA are not modified by the stimulants treatment and they are not correlated with behavioural modifications after different drugs. Although there are not enough studies, suggestive results have been obtained for PEA molecule, even though no evidence of correlation between peripheral levels and behavioural features was observed after d-AMP treatment (see Table 1). Moreover, we found a slight evidence of publication bias for MHPG and a significant heterogeneity of effect sizes across studies for all biomarkers that significantly differentiated treated ADHD patients from untreated.

Considering the present data along with the recent meta-analysis [12], MHPG could be a potential biomarker for ADHD diagnosis and a potential predictor of treatment response. Indeed, when we compared urinary levels of MHPG among patients with ADHD and control subjects, the meta-analysis [12] indicated a significant decrease in patients. Similarly, the administration of d-AMP significantly reduced the urinary levels of MHPG (present data). This, along with the well-reported correlation between decrease in MHPG and behavioural improvements after d-AMP treatment [45, 49, 54, 50, 51, 53] (see Table 1), focuses attention on MHPG as a potential mediator of stimulant drug response, in addition to a useful biological marker for diagnostic assessment. More interestingly, urinary MHPG levels are decreased after stimulants administration only in the responders patients, indicating that MHPG could be a useful predictor of the stimulants response.

The metabolite MHPG is a major product of NE breakdown. A significant fraction of urinary MHPG (as much as 30–50%) comes from the metabolism of NE in the CNS in man. This is supported by some evidence that destruction of NE terminals in the CNS of animals resulted in decreased urinary levels of MHPG. Moreover, MHPG excretion in urine has been shown to vary in response to changes in sympathetic activity or stressful situations. According to some authors [51], reduced MHPG may be considered linked to decreased activity of MAO enzyme.

Indeed, the results of the meta-analysis [12] demonstrated lower MAO and MHPG and higher NE concentrations in patients with ADHD, supporting the current hypothesis that reduced MAO activity impairs the degradation of NE and leads to lower levels of MHPG in patients with ADHD.

Our results on the treatment contribute also to clarify the mechanism of action of d-AMP on the MHPG levels. In agreement with some authors [51], we hypothesized that d-AMP, by inhibiting the re-uptake of NE by the pre-synaptic nerve terminal and the intraneuronal MAO, tends to decrease MHPG. A similar mechanism could be hypothesized also for MPH because, although the results are negative ($p = 0.06$ see Figure 5), three studies [52, 48, 44] confirmed lower levels of MHPG in treated patients with ADHD. This supports also the evidence that d-AMP and MPH are remarkably similar in their clinical effects.

Few studies have been conducted on other medications such as pycnogenol, pemoline and MAOIs, which make it difficult to interpret the lack of statistical significance for these medications. To date, the current evidence is insufficient to support the use of pycnogenol for the treatment of any chronic disorder including ADHD and well-designed, adequately powered trials are needed to establish the value of this treatment [64]. Concerning pemoline, because 15 cases of acute fulminant hepatic failure with this treatment have been reported, its use has been relegated to only rare circumstances [65, 66]. Moreover, MAOIs are a group of antidepressants that can treat ADHD with some benefit, but are rarely used because they have significant and sometimes dangerous side effects and can dangerously interact with foods and other medications. Finally, one study [42] reported the biochemical monoamine determinations in relation to aspartame treatment. They demonstrated that aspartame at greater than 10 times usual consumption has no effect on the cognitive and behavioural status of children with ADHD. In addition, aspartame does not appear to affect the urinary excretion rates of monoamines and metabolites [42].

These data in general suffer of one important limitation that is specificity/sensitivity. All papers reported in the review and in the different meta-analyses are lacking this information. It is also important to highlight that most of these studies were conducted around '80s, '90s. Moreover, the data related to meta-analyses analyzing the effects of the treatment on a biomarker have some further limitations. In particular, (a) we found significant heterogeneity in effect size across the studies for all biomarkers analyzed. This could be due to several issues: (1) no homogeneity in the study designs because some studies used a placebo or baseline approach; (2) different concentrations of drugs used in the several studies; (3) different treatment time duration (from 1 week to 15 weeks); (4) methods to value the treatment response; (5) methodological procedures: repeated measurements on each child were not performed in all studies; over time, several methods for measuring catecholamines were used [67] (studies include a wide temporal range: urine levels of DA: from 1978 to 2007; HVA: from 1971 to 1994; NE: from 1971 to 2007; VMA: from 1971 to 1988); (6) many of the studies were generated by the same group (Shekim and Zametkin); (7) low significant effect sizes [68]. (b) The presence of publication bias for MHPG. This was due by the paper from Zametkin et al. [45]. However, when this paper was eliminated, the Egger test was not significant ($p = 0.21$ data not shown) and the meta-analysis for this metabolite was still significant ($d = 0.62$, $Z = 6.27$, $p < 0.00001$ with less heterogeneity $p = 0.09$, $I^2 = 34\%$, data not shown).

Future research should be focused on the replication of these findings, to assess their specificity for ADHD, and to quantify the degree to which they are sufficiently precise to be useful in clinical settings. Thus more work is needed to determine whether the statistical significance of our findings translate into diagnostic utility. Moreover, future studies will have to take into account the deep integration of "omics" sciences such as the "pharmacogenomics", "phenomics", "epigenomic", "proteomics", "transcriptomic", "metabolomics". To date, the use of high–throughput computational methods such as learning machinery permits to integrate the complex network of genes (DNA, RNA), proteins and biochemical interactions along with clinical and endophenotype profiling including therapeutic response to identify a set of biomarkers useful for the diagnostic assessment and for the personalization of therapies.

5. Conclusion

Currently, no biomarkers for ADHD have achieved the status of clinical utility as a diagnostic tool. This chapter supports evidence for a role of some dopaminergic and noradrenergic molecules, their metabolites and metabolism enzymes such as *SLC6A3*, DRD4, MHPG, MAOA, NE, *SLC6A2*, DBH, COMT that could represent, in this order, a hypothetical signature of a set of genetic and biochemical markers useful for ADHD diagnosis. Moreover, this chapter demonstrates, for the first time, with a meta-analytic method, that d-AMP influences urinary MHPG levels and that, if it is tested, MHPG could be a useful predictor of response to stimulants. Although further studies are needed mainly in relation to specificity and sensitivity, we speculate that MHPG could be the best potential candidate as biomarker for ADHD.

Author details

Catia Scassellati * and Cristian Bonvicini

*Address all correspondence to: cscassellati@fatebenefratelli.eu

Genetics Unit, IRCCS – Centre Saint John of God, Fatebenefratelli, Brescia, Italy

References

[1] Polanczyk G, de Lima MS, Horta BL, Biederman J, Rohde LA. The worldwide prevalence of ADHD: a systematic review and metaregression analysis. Am J Psychiatr 2007;164(6):942–8.

[2] Willcutt EG. The prevalence of DSM-IV attention-deficit/hyperactivity disorder: a meta-analytic review. Neurotherapeutics 2012;9(3):490–9.

[3] Polanczyk GV, Willcutt EG, Salum GA, Kieling C, Rohde LA. ADHD prevalence estimates across three decades: an updated systematic review and meta-regression analysis. Int J Epidemiol 2014;43(2):434–42.

[4] Simon V, Czobor P, Balint S, Meszaros A, Bitter I. Prevalence and correlates of adult attention-deficit hyperactivity disorder: metaanalysis. Brit J Psychiatr 2009;194(3): 204–11.

[5] Ramos-Quiroga JA, Nasillo V, Fernández-Aranda F, Casas M. Addressing the lack of studies in attention-deficit/hyperactivity disorder in adults. Exp Rev Neurotherapeutics 2014;14(5):553–67.

[6] Thapar A, Cooper M, Eyre O, Langley K. What have we learnt about the causes of ADHD? J Child Psychol Psychiatr 2013;54(1):3–16.

[7] Faraone SV, Perlis RH, Doyle AE, Smoller JW, Goralnick JJ, Holmgren MA, Sklar P. Molecular genetics of attention-deficit/hyperactivity disorder. Biol Psychiatr 2005;57(11):1313–23.

[8] Li Z, Chang SH, Zhang LY, Gao L, Wang J. Molecular genetic studies of ADHD and its candidate genes: a review. Psychiatr Res 2014;219(1):10–24.

[9] Akutagava-Martins GC, Salatino-Oliveira A, Kieling CC, Rohde LA, Hutz MH. Genetics of attention-deficit/hyperactivity disorder: current findings and future directions. Exp Rev Neurotherapeutics 2013;13(4):435–45.

[10] Yang L, Neale BM, Liu L, Lee SH, Wray NR, Ji N, et al. Psychiatric GWAS Consortium: ADHD Subgroup. Polygenic transmission and complex neuro developmental network for attention deficit hyperactivity disorder: genome-wide association study of both common and rare variants. Am J Med Genet B, Neuropsychiatr Genet 2013;162B(5):419–30.

[11] Gizer IR, Ficks C, Waldman ID. Candidate gene studies of ADHD: a metaanalytic review. Human Genetics 2009;126(1):51–90.

[12] Scassellati C, Bonvicini C, Faraone SV, Gennarelli M. Biomarkers and attention-deficit/hyperactivity disorder: a systematic review and meta-analyses. J Am Acad Child Adolesc Psychiatr 2012;51(10):1003–19.

[13] Lange KW, Reichl S, Lange KM, Tucha L, Tucha O. The history of attention deficit hyperactivity disorder. Attention Deficit Hyperactivity Disorders 2010;2(4):241–55.

[14] Insel T. Director's Blog: transforming diagnosis. 2013 http://www.nimh.nih.gov/about/director/2013/transforming-diagnosis.shtml

[15] Kornfield R, Watson S, Higashi AS, Conti RM, Dusetzina SB, Garfield CF, Dorsey ER, Huskamp HA, Alexander GC. Effects of FDA advisories on the pharmacologic treat-

ment of ADHD, 2004–2008. Psychiatric Services (Washington, D.C.) 2013;64(4):339–46.

[16] Findling RL. Evolution of the treatment of attention-deficit/hyperactivity disorder in children: a review. Clin Therapeut 2008;30(5):942–57.

[17] Spencer T, Biederman J, Wilens T, Harding M, O'Donnell D, Griffin S. Pharmacotherapy of attention-deficit hyperactivity disorder across the life cycle. J Am Acad Child Adoles Psychiatr 1996;35(4):409–32.

[18] Swanson J, Baler RD, Volkow ND. Understanding the effects of stimulant medications on cognition in individuals with attention-deficit hyperactivity disorder: a decade of progress. Neuropsychopharmacology 2011;36(1):207–26.

[19] Faraone SV, Buitelaar J. Comparing the efficacy of stimulants for ADHD in children and adolescents using meta-analysis. Eur Child Adoles Psychiatr 2010;19(4):353–64.

[20] Faraone SV. Using meta-analysis to compare the efficacy of medications for attention-deficit/hyperactivity disorder in youths. P & T: J Formul Manage 2009;34(12): 678–94.

[21] Cheng JY, Chen RY, Ko JS, Ng EM. Efficacy and safety of atomoxetine for attention-deficit/hyperactivity disorder in children and adolescents-meta-analysis and meta-regression analysis. Psychopharmacology (Berl) 2007;194(2):197–209.

[22] Hazell PL, Kohn MR, Dickson R, Walton RJ, Granger RE, Wyk GW. Core ADHD symptom improvement with atomoxetine versus methylphenidate: a direct comparison meta-analysis. J Attent Disorders 2011;15(8):674–83.

[23] Dvoráková M, Jezová D, Blazícek P, Trebatická J, Skodácek I, Suba J, Duracková Z. Urinary catecholamines in children with attention deficit hyperactivity disorder (ADHD): modulation by a polyphenolic extract from pine bark (pycnogenol). Nutrit Neurosci 2007;10(3-4):151–7.

[24] De Sousa A, Kalra G. Drug therapy of attention deficit hyperactivity disorder: current trends. Mens sana Monographs 2012;10(1):45–69.

[25] Biomarkers Definitions Working Group. Biomarkers and surrogate endpoints: preferred definitions and conceptual framework. Clin Pharmacol Therapeut 2001;69(3): 89–95.

[26] Schmidt HD, Shelton RC, Duman RS. Functional biomarkers of depression: diagnosis, treatment, and pathophysiology. Neuropsychopharmacol 2011;36(12):2375–94.

[27] Sokolowska I, Ngounou Wetie AG, Wormwood K, Thome J, Darie CC, Woods AG. The potential of biomarkers in psychiatry: focus on proteomics. J Neural Transmiss (Vienna, Austria: 1996) 2013;20.

[28] Singh I, Rose N. Biomarkers in psychiatry. Nature 2009;460(7252):202–7.

[29] Genro JP, Kieling C, Rohde LA, Hutz MH. Attention-deficit/hyperactivity disorder and the dopaminergic hypotheses. Exp Rev Neurotherapeut 2010;10(4):587–601.

[30] Bidwell LC, Willcutt EG, McQueen MB, DeFries JC, Olson RK, Smith SD, Pennington BF. A family based association study of DRD4, DAT1, and 5HTT and continuous traits of attention-deficit hyperactivity disorder. Behavior Genet 2011;41(1):165–74.

[31] Horn A, Scheller C, du Plessis S, Arendt G, Nolting T, Joska J, Sopper S, Maschke M, Obermann M, Husstedt IW, Hain J, Maponga T, Riederer P, Koutsilieri E. Increases in CSF dopamine in HIV patients are due to the dopamine transporter 10/10-repeat allele which is more frequent in HIV-infected individuals. J Neural Transmiss (Vienna, Austria: 1996) 2013;120(10):1411–9.

[32] Cheon KA, Ryu YH, Kim JW, Cho DY. The homozygosity for 10-repeat allele at dopamine transporter gene and dopamine transporter density in Korean children with attention deficit hyperactivity disorder: relating to treatment response to methylphenidate. Eur Neuropsychopharmacol: J Eur College Neuropsychopharmacol 2005;15(1):95–101.

[33] Faraone SV, Bonvicini C, Scassellati C. Biomarkers in the diagnosis of ADHD--promising directions. Current Psychiatr Rep 2014;16(11):497; DOI 10.1007/s11920-014-0497-1.

[34] Koutsilieri E, Riederer P, du Plessis S, Scheller C. A short review on the relation between the dopamine transporter 10/10-repeat allele and ADHD: implications for HIV infection. Attent Deficit Hyperactivity Disorders 2014;6(3):203–9.

[35] Wu J, Xiao HF, Sun HJ, Zou L, Zhu LQ. Role of dopamine receptors in ADHD: a systematic meta-analysis. Molecular Neurobiol 2012;45(3):605–20.

[36] Tovo-Rodrigues L, Rohde LA, Menezes AM, Polanczyk GV, Kieling C, Genro JP, Anselmi L, Hutz MH. DRD4 rare variants in attention-deficit/hyperactivity disorder (ADHD): further evidence from a birth cohort study. PLoS One 2013;8(12):e85164.

[37] Taurines R, Segura M, Schecklmann M, Albantakis L, Grünblatt E, Walitza S, Jans T, Lyttwin B, Haberhausen M, Theisen FM, Martin B, Briegel W, Thome J, Schwenck C, Romanos M, Gerlach M. Altered mRNA expression of monoaminergic candidate genes in the blood of children with attention deficit hyperactivity disorder and autism spectrum disorder. World J Biol Psychiatr: Off J World Fed Soc Biol Psychiatr 2011;12(Suppl 1):104–48.

[38] Wender PH, Epstein RS, Kopin IJ, Gordon EK. Urinary monoamine metabolites in children with minimal brain dysfunction. Am J Psychiatr 1971;127(10):1411–5.

[39] Lasky-Su J, Anney RJ, Neale BM, Franke B, Zhou K, Maller JB, Vasquez AA, Chen W, Asherson P, Buitelaar J, Banaschewski T, Ebstein R, Gill M, Miranda A, Mulas F, Oades RD, Roeyers H, Rothenberger A, Sergeant J, Sonuga-Barke E, Steinhausen HC, Taylor E, Daly M, Laird N, Lange C, Faraone SV. Genome-wide association scan of quantitative traits for attention deficit hyperactivity disorder identifies novel associa-

tions and confirms candidate gene associations. Am J Med Genet B, Neuropsychiatr Genet 2008;147B(8):1345–54.

[40] Sun HJ, Yuan FF, Shen XM, Xiong GL, Wu J. Role of COMT in ADHD: a systematic meta-analysis. Molecular Neurobiol 2014;49(1):251–61.

[41] Egger M, Smith GD, Phillips AN. Meta-analysis: principles and procedures. Brit Med J 1997;315(7121):1533–7.

[42] Shaywitz BA, Sullivan CM, Anderson GM, Gillespie SM, Sullivan B, Shaywitz SE. Aspartame, behavior, and cognitive function in children with attention deficit disorder. Pediatrics 1994;93(1):70–5.

[43] Zametkin AJ, Linnoila M, Karoum F, Sallee R. Pemoline and urinary excretion of catecholamines and indoleamines in children with attention deficit disorder. Am J Psychiatr 1986;143(3):359–62.

[44] Zametkin AJ, Karoum F, Linnoila M, Rapoport JL, Brown GL, Chuang LW, Wyatt RJ. Stimulants, urinary catecholamines, and indoleamines in hyperactivity. A comparison of methylphenidate and dextroamphetamine. Arch Gen Psychiatr 1985;42(3):251–55a.

[45] Zametkin A, Rapoport JL, Murphy DL, Linnoila M, Karoum F, Potter WZ, Ismond D. Treatment of hyperactive children with monoamine oxidase inhibitors. II. Plasma and urinary monoamine findings after treatment. Arch Gen Psychiatr 1985;42(10): 969–73 b.

[46] Rapoport JL, Mikkelsen EJ, Ebert MH, Brown GL, Weise VK, Kopin IJ. Urinary catecholamines and amphetamine excretion in hyperactive and normal boys. J Nervous Mental Disease 1978;166(10):731–7.

[47] Elia J, Borcherding BG, Potter WZ, Mefford IN, Rapoport JL, Keysor CS. Stimulant drug treatment of hyperactivity: biochemical correlates. Clin Pharmacol Therapeut 1990;48(1):57–66.

[48] Zametkin AJ, Hamburger SD. The effect of methylphenidate on urinary catecholamine excretion in hyperactivity: a partial replication. Biol Psychiatr 1988;23(4):350–6.

[49] Shekim WO, Javaid J, Davis JM, Bylund DB. Urinary MHPG and HVA excretion in boys with attention deficit disorder and hyperactivity treated with d-amphetamine. Biol Psychiatr 1983;18(6):707–14.

[50] Brown GL, Ebert MH, Hunt RD, Rapoport JL. Urinary 3-methyoxy-4-hydroxyphenylglycol and homovanillic acid response to d-amphetamine in hyperactive children. Biol Psychiatr 1981;16(8):779–87.

[51] Shekim WO, Dekirmenjian H, Chapel JL, Javaid J, Davis JM. Norepinephrine metabolism and clinical response to dextroamphetamine in hyperactive boys. J Pediatr 1979;95(3):389–94a.

[52] Shen YC, Wang YF. Urinary 3-methoxy-4-hydroxyphenylglycol sulfate excretion in seventy-three schoolchildren with minimal brain dysfunction syndrome. Biol Psychiatr 1984;19(6):861–70.

[53] Shekim WO, Dekirmenjian H, Chapel JL. Urinary MHPG excretion in minimal brain dysfunction and its modification by d-amphetamine. Am J Psychiatr 1979;136(5):667–71b.

[54] Shekim WO, Javaid J, Dekirmenjian H, Chapel JL, Davis JM. Effects of d-amphetamine on urinary metabolites of dopamine and norepinephrine in hyperactive boys. Am J Psychiatr 1982;139(4):485–8.

[55] Shekim WO, Dekirmenjian H, Chapel JL. Urinary catecholamine metabolites in hyperkinetic boys treated with d-amphetamine. Am J Psychiatr 1977;134(11):1276–9.

[56] Shekim WO, Dekirmenjian H, Chapel JL. Urinary MHPG excretion in the hyperactive child syndrome and the effects of dextroamphetamine [proceedings]. Psychopharmacol Bull 1978;14(2):42–4.

[57] Kusaga A, Yamashita Y, Koeda T, Hiratani M, Kaneko M, Yamada S, Matsuishi T. Increased urine phenylethylamine after methylphenidate treatment in children with ADHD. Ann Neurol 2002;52(3):372–4.

[58] Zametkin AJ, Brown GL, Karoum F, Rapoport JL, Langer DH, Chuang LW, Wyatt RJ. Urinary phenylethylamine response to d-amphetamine in 12 boys with attention deficit disorder. Am J Psychiatr 1984;141(9):1055–8.

[59] Franke B, Hoogman M, Arias Vasquez A, Heister JG, Savelkoul PJ, Naber M, Scheffer H, Kiemeney LA, Kan CC, Kooij JJ, Buitelaar JK. Association of the dopamine transporter (SLC6A3/DAT1) gene 9-6 haplotype with adult ADHD. Am J Med GenetB, Neuropsychiatr Genet 2008;147B(8):1576–9.

[60] Gatt JM, Burton KL, Williams LM, Schofield PR. Specific and common genes implicated across major mental disorders: a review of meta-analysis studies. J Psychiatr Res 2015;60:1–13.

[61] Kurita M, Nishino S, Numata Y, Okubo Y, Sato T. The noradrenaline metabolite MHPG is a candidate biomarker from the manic to the remission state in bipolar disorder I: a clinical naturalistic study. PLoS One 2014;27(6):e100634.

[62] Nishimura J, Kakeda S, Abe O, Yoshimura R, Watanabe K, Goto N, Hori H, Sato T, Takao H, Kabasawa H, Nakamura J, Korogi Y. Plasma levels of 3-methoxy-4-hydroxyphenylglycol are associated with microstructural changes within the cerebellum in the early stage of first-episode schizophrenia: a longitudinal VBM study. Neuropsychiatr Disease Treat 2014;10:2315–23.

[63] Cubała WJ, Landowski J, Wielgomas B, Czarnowski W. Low baseline salivary 3-methoxy-4-hydroxyphenylglycol (MHPG) in drug-naïve patients with short-illness-duration first episode major depressive disorder. J Affective Disorders 2014;161:4–7.

[64] Schoonees A, Visser J, Musekiwa A, Volmink J. Pycnogenol(®) for the treatment of chronic disorders. Cochrane Database Syst Rev 2012;15;2:CD008294; doi: 10.1002/14651858.

[65] Markowitz JS, Patrick KS. Pharmacokinetic and pharmacodynamic drug interactions in the treatment of attention-deficit hyperactivity disorder. Clin Pharmacokinet 2001;40(10):753–72.

[66] Safer DJ, Zito JM, Gardner JE. Pemoline hepatotoxicity and postmarketing surveillance. J Am Acad Child Adoles Psychiatr 2001;40(6):622–9.

[67] Marc DT, Ailts JW, Campeau DC, Bull MJ, Olson KL. Neurotransmitters excreted in the urine as biomarkers of nervous system activity: validity and clinical applicability. Neurosci Biobehavioral Rev 2011;35(3):635–44.

[68] Zakzanis KK. Brain is related to behavior (p<.05). J Clin Experiment Neuropsychol 1998;20(3):419–27.

Chapter 5

Comorbid Conditions in Child and Adolescent Patients Diagnosed with Attention Deficit/Hyperactivity Disorder

Murat Yüce, Filiz Uçar and Gökçe Nur Say

Additional information is available at the end of the chapter

http://dx.doi.org/10.5772/61112

Abstract

Attention deficit/hyperactivity disorder (ADHD) is one of the most common childhood psychiatric disorders. The worldwide prevalence of ADHD in children has been reported at 4-7%. Numerous population- and clinical-based studies have reported that more than half of cases of ADHD have at least one psychiatric comorbidity. The presence of psychiatric comorbidities complicates the diagnosis, treatment, and prognosis of ADHD; thus, diagnosis of comorbidities is of great importance. Possible comorbidities should therefore be investigated in cases diagnosed with ADHD before treatment planning.

Keywords: Attention deficit/hyperactivity disorder, psychiatric comorbidity

1. Introduction

Attention deficit/hyperactivity disorder (ADHD) is one of the most common childhood psychiatric disorders. This disorder is multifactorial in origin and clinically heterogeneous, leads to socioeconomic burdens, and has undesirable academic and occupational outcomes [1]. The worldwide prevalence of ADHD in children is reported to be 4-7% [2]. Results of long-term studies have revealed that a substantial proportion of individuals suffering from ADHD during childhood continue to exhibit symptoms of ADHD during adolescence and adulthood [2, 3]. Numerous population-based and clinical studies have reported that more than half of the patients suffering from ADHD have at least one psychiatric comorbidity and that this rate increases with age [4-6].

These comorbidities may be different manifestations of the same disorder or may have different diagnoses while sharing a common disposition. Similarly, ADHD may be an early manifestation of another disorder and may place the individual at risk of developing the same [7].

These comorbid psychiatric conditions are more common in boys than in girls [1, 8-11]. One study conducted in Switzerland reported at least one comorbidity in 87% of the ADHD cases and more than one comorbidity in 67% [4]. Biederman et al. [7] have reported two or more comorbidities in 20% of ADHD patients admitted to clinics. A study from Iran found at least one psychiatric comorbidity in 73% of the childhood and adolescent cases of ADHD [12]. A clinical study from Turkey also documented the presence of at least one comorbid psychiatric disorder in 96% of the children diagnosed with ADHD, assessed according to KSADS-PL [13].

The presence of psychiatric comorbidities complicates the diagnosis, treatment, and prognosis of ADHD, and thus, the diagnosis of comorbidities is of great importance [14]. Possible comorbidities should therefore be investigated in patients diagnosed with ADHD before planning treatment regimens, and the possibility of comorbidities arising during follow-up should be taken into account [13].

2. Disruptive behavior disorder

Disruptive behavior disorders (DBD) are the most common comorbidities accompanying ADHD. Individuals with oppositional defiant disorder (ODD) and conduct disorder (CD) share many characteristics. For example, their conduct is socially unacceptable, they cause disruption or distress to others more than to themselves (i.e., they "externalize" their problems), they are more likely to be male, and they find it difficult to learn from experience. ODD and CD are commonly investigated together in most studies to highlight their similarities and differences. Biederman et al. [15] studied the prevalence of comorbidities in children and adolescents with ADHD aged 6-17 years and reported high rates for ODD (46% in children and 33% in adolescents) and CD (25% in children and 42% in adolescents).

One study that investigated the effect of gender on the clinical features of ADHD reported that girls with ADHD are at reduced risk for developing comorbid major depression, conduct disorder, and oppositional defiant disorder compared to boys with ADHD [16]. In clinical practice, disruptive behavior disorders have a poorer prognosis when they are comorbid with ADHD rather than alone and other accompanying comorbid psychiatric disorders. One population-based prospective study in a broad sample reported an increased risk of unipolar depression and bipolar disorder in ADHD, and that the risk was greatest in the group with ADHD and comorbid CD or ODD [17]. ODD is the most common comorbid psychiatric disorder and is associated with an increase in intrafamilial and social problems, irrespective of whether or not CD accompanies ODD [18]. Disruptive behavior disorders that are comorbid with ADHD are an important factor in determining the clinical picture. Adolescents diagnosed with DBD and ADHD are at a higher risk of undergoing psychiatric hospitalization at some time in their life [19].

The overlap of ADHD and conduct problems is explained by common genetic and non-shared environmental factors that influence both disorders. Nevertheless, the two disorders appear to be partly distinct, in that additional environmental factors influence the severity of the behavioral problems. It appears that ADHD+CD is a genetically more severe variant of ADHD [20].

One study compared patients with ODD/CD, comorbid ADHD, and those with only ODD/CD. Both the patient subgroups had deficits in visuospatial working memory compared to the control subjects, indicating that children with ODD/CD have deficits in visuospatial working memory that are independent of the comorbid ADHD, and that a deficient working memory may be an underlying factor in the development of ODD/CD [21].

Two subtypes of ODD are associated with ADHD, one that is prodromal to CD and another that is subsyndromal to ADHD and unlikely to progress into CD in the later years. These ODD subtypes have different correlates, courses, and outcomes. In a large, well-characterized, cross-sectional sample of children with ADHD assessed at baseline and 4 years later at midadolescence, Biederman et al. found that the majority of the children with ODD did not have comorbid CD. In contrast, CD was almost always comorbid with ODD. When ODD co-occurred with CD, it preceded the onset of CD by several years. These findings indicate that the two subtypes of ODD within ADHD can be distinguished as either being prodromal to CD or not. The study also found that CD and ODD had similar correlates, and that these were less severe in children suffering from ODD than CD, thus supporting the initial hypothesis that ODD is a subsyndromal form of CD. This notion assumes that both disorders are part of the same disease process in which CD is the more severe form while ODD is the less severe form of the same disorder. Their findings, that CD is almost always comorbid with and precede ODD, are also consistent with the second hypothesis that a subtype of ODD is prodromal to CD. This subtype differs from the other type of ODD in that there is significantly higher risk of familial antisocial disorders, comorbidity with mood and anxiety disorders, earlier age at onset of ODD, higher number of comorbid psychiatric disorders, and greater number of ODD symptoms [22].

One study involving the long-term monitoring of CD and ODD patients identified an increased risk of long-term depression in patients with ODD and comorbid ADHD. The same study also reported that patients with accompanying CD are at risk of developing psychoactive substance use disorders and bipolar disorder in the long term [23]. Increased conflict, impaired communication, and incompatibilities between parents and the child also lead to an increased risk of ODD and CD in adolescents with ADHD [24]. While ODD is a precursor of CD, certain additional risk factors are required for ODD to progress to CD. The clinical features of young people with CD include a predominance in males, low socioeconomic status, and familial aggression [25]. Wilson and Morcotte divided ADHD patients aged between 14 and 18 years into two groups as with or without CD and compared these two groups in terms of success at school, self-perception, behavior problems, alcohol and substance abuse, and adaptive behaviors. They reported that patients with CD exhibit significantly lower rates of success in school, greater externalizing behaviors and emotional difficulties, and lower adaptive behaviors compared to patients without CD [26].

The response to treatment in patients with ODD and CD comorbid with ADHD may vary, and there is a greater need for integrative therapeutic approaches in these cases. A higher dose of ADHD drugs may be required, apart from combined drug use, particularly atypical antipsychotics. Atypical antipsychotics are very frequently used in patients exhibiting ADHD and disruptive behavior, and studies have mainly focused on risperidone. One meta-analysis published recently reported that among the atypical antipsychotics, risperidone has a positive effect on aggression and behavioral disorders in the 5- to 18-year age-group; however, similar data on other atypical antipsychotics are not available [27]. Another recent study also compared risperidone and placebo in 168 patients aged 6-12 years diagnosed with ADHD+ODD/CD who were prescribed methylphenidate and a parental education program. A reduction in aggression and attacks on peers was observed when risperidone was added, but it was not particularly effective in relieving the symptoms of the behavior disorder [28]. One open study from Turkey suggested that aripiprazole reduce anger and guilt in cases of ADHD+CD [29]. Nondrug therapies are of great importance in the treatment of ODD and CD, and multidimensional therapies are indicated since the basis of these conditions lie in familial dysfunction, societal problems, and disorganized families. Studies have shown that parental education programs, when combined with a behavioral approach, have a positive effect on children with ODD with respect to nonrule governed actions, anger, and negativism. In addition, enrollment in sports programs also has a positive effect on this group of patients [30], and patient participation in other therapeutic approaches increases following an effective drug therapy.

3. Learning disorders

Learning disorder (LD) is a common comorbid condition in ADHD. One review of the studies on ADHD/LD comorbidity conducted between 2001 and 2011 reported wide differences in comorbidity rates, and rates of LD comorbidity in patients ranged between 8% and 76%. Greater difficulties in writing, but not in reading or mathematics in particular, were reported by the studies on patients with high comorbidity rates [31-33]. Morgan et al. [34] reported that the type of mathematical learning disorder that is more common in cases with ADHD is predominantly the inattentive type. The median prevalence rate of LD was 45% in another study, indicating that, on an average, one out of every two children with ADHD also have LD [35].

Several studies have investigated the etiology of ADHD+LD comorbidity, and structural and functional neuroimaging studies, and behavioral, genetic, and molecular research has revealed the existence of a complex relationship between these two disorders [36].

ADHD and LD share some common symptoms. For example, an attention deficit may have an adverse effect on a child's concentration and learning process. The inability to concentrate on details and making of careless errors also have a negative effect on knowledge acquisition and accurate information gathering. Confusion between alphabets (such as between b and d seen in children with a reading disorder) may also be seen in inattentive children. They may also have difficulties in solving mathematical problems due to their inability to concentrate on details and errors may occur while writing. Thus, children with a learning disorder are reluctant to study because they cannot acquire effective reading, writing or mathematical skills, and similarly, children with ADHD avoid tasks that require uninterrupted attention. As children with a learning disorder have problems transferring information from their short-term memory to their long-term memory and in processing that information, they may forget the information after some time, thus feeling as if they had never acquired it to begin with. Forgetfulness can also be seen in children with ADHD.

Academic difficulties associated with an attention deficit may increase over the course of time in children with ADHD, and this can be confused with LD [37]. Symptoms of an attention deficit in children with ADHD have an adverse impact on the learning processes and lead to the clinical manifestation of learning disorders. If these two disorders are comorbid, then the symptoms may follow a more severe course. Therefore, the presence of LD should be investigated when ADHD is diagnosed, and a differential diagnosis should be performed.

Children with ADHD and LD together are also more resistant to treatment. Comorbid LD must be considered in patients with ADHD who do not show improvement despite treatment. A 6-week randomized, double-blinded, place-controlled study that compared the effectiveness of methylphenidate in ADHD with or without comorbid LD reported that behavior and performance improved with oral methylphenidate in both the groups [38]. The effectiveness of methylphenidate in alleviating the core symptoms of ADHD is clear, but there is insufficient evidence supporting its efficacy in LD alone.

Another study assessed the response to atomoxetine therapy in ADHD and ADHD accompanied by dyslexia and reported a significant improvement in ADHD symptoms and reading scores in both the groups. A correlation analysis performed in the same study showed that improvement in reading was not by itself sufficient to account for the decrease in symptoms of ADHD. Further research is needed to ascertain the potential effects of atomoxetine on reading in children with ADHD+dyslexia or dyslexia alone [39].

Pharmacotherapy alone is insufficient to treat children with ADHD+LD. Psychological therapies can be added to pharmacological treatment, but more research is required to clarify their role in the treatment of ADHD and comorbid learning disability [40]. Special education techniques also need to be used in such cases.

4. Intellectual disability

ADHD is a widespread clinical condition in individuals with intellectual disability (ID). One study that investigated psychiatric comorbidities in groups with or without ID reported that the greatest difference between the two groups was in the rate of meeting the diagnostic criteria for ADHD (ratio = 3.21:1). The same study also reported a correlation between high stability of externalizing behavior problems at age 3 to a diagnosis of ADHD at age 5 in both the groups [41]. Another longitudinal study investigated ADHD in children with or without accompanying ID and monitored these children from the age of 5 till the age of 8 years. ADHD was three or more times prevalent in the ID group compared to typical development across ages 5, 6, 7, and 8 years, and ADHD tended to be diagnosed earlier and was more stable in the ID group [42].

Children with ID exhibit a greater risk for developing ADHD, and the disorder may follow a longer and more persistent course, apart from increasing the risk of developing further psychiatric problems. These findings highlight the need for making available the interventions necessary for early treatment of ADHD in children with ID.

One study on the effectiveness of stimulant drug therapy in children diagnosed with ADHD and ID reported that the symptoms of ADHD could be successfully treated in children with ADHD and ID [43]. A randomized, controlled, double-blind study of children with severe ADHD and ID suggested that methylphenidate is effective in reducing the symptoms of ADHD in these children [44]. Stimulants have a similar effect on improving impulsivity, hyperactivity, and attention deficit in children with IQ ranging between 45 and 75 compared to normal children; however, they may exhibit fewer improvements in learning and memory. Stimulants appear to have a positive effect in preschool children, albeit with more side effects [45]. Reduced appetite, nausea, and irritability are the most common adverse events reported in children with developmental disabilities (DD); clinicians should be aware that, as with stimulants, irritability appears to occur much more commonly in children with DD than in normally developing children. Initial splitting of the dose, starting below the recommended dose, and slowly titrating the dose may prevent or ameliorate these side effects [46].

Only one open-label study has investigated the effectiveness of atomoxetine (ATX) in children with ADHD and ID not accompanied by the autism spectrum disorder (ASD). Atomoxetine appears to be useful in improving ADHD symptoms in individuals with ID. Larger, randomized, controlled, double-blind studies are required to confirm the efficacy of ATX in children with ID without ASD [47].

Clinicians must carefully consider the following when treating cases of ID with ADHD. As patients in this group may have a lower tolerance to side effects, greater care must be taken during dose titration, and drugs must be started at low doses and gradually increased. Antipsychotic agents such as risperidone can lead to an improvement in irritability. Many children with ID may have a micronutrient imbalance that could benefit from an RDA/RDI multivitamin/mineral supplement, especially if appetite has been suppressed by the stimulant [48].

5. Depression and anxiety disorder

Prospective studies show that children and adolescents diagnosed with ADHD are also more frequently diagnosed with major depressive disorder (MDD) compared to control subjects

[49]. Additionally, ADHD is more common in children with major depressive disorder [50]. Studies that have investigated internalizing problems, such as depression and anxiety in the subtypes of ADHD, have shown that internalizing problems are more common in the attention deficit ADHD subtype [51]. CD and ODD seem to appear in early childhood in ADHD, while the symptoms of depression and anxiety appear later [52].

Several studies have been performed to explain the etiology of comorbid ADHD and depression. These studies have shown a genetic overlap between ADHD and depression, and both disorders involve dopamine reward circuit problems and difficulty in emotional regulation. A dysfunctional relationship with parents has also been shown to play a role in the etiology of comorbidities in children with ADHD [51].

Symptoms of depression, such as sleep disorders, difficulty concentrating, and irritability, and symptoms of anxiety disorders, such as sustained anxiety and failure to concentrate, may be confused with ADHD and lead to a misdiagnosis. Depression or anxiety accompanying ADHD make diagnosis difficult and result in greater severity of symptoms [53]. Depression is 2.5 times more frequently diagnosed during adolescence and early adulthood in girls previously diagnosed with ADHD, and the onset of depression is earlier and is more protracted. Depression leads to greater depression-related loss in functionality, increases disposition to suicide, and requires more hospitalization [54]. The adverse effect of comorbid ADHD on the prognosis of depression and the higher incidence of attempted suicide in hyperactive young people make the identification of comorbid depression and ADHD particularly important. It is also important not to overlook the depressive disorder comorbidity in children diagnosed with ADHD as the depressive disorder can increase the severity of attention problems in ADHD [55]. One study showed that the probability of developing comorbid bipolar affective disorder or major depression is higher in patients with ADHD than in patients suffering from major depression alone [56]. One study, intended to determine which children with ADHD subsequently develop depression, showed that ADHD patients with comorbid anxiety and/or disruptive behavior disorders have a higher probability of developing depression [57]. Measures can be taken to avoid the development of depression in ADHD patients who are diagnosed with comorbid anxiety and/or disruptive behavior disorders. While the existence of anxiety in ADHD has an improving effect on DBD, performance anxiety and feelings of inadequacy are thought to be more prominent [58]. Although anxiety reduces the inhibition response in anxiety ADHD and impulsivity, it can worsen work memory test performance [59]. A detailed investigation of the psychiatric symptoms in the family will assist physicians with the diagnosis and treatment of these patients.

Recent familial, genetic, and long-term follow-up studies have demonstrated that ADHD and major depressive disorder share a common familial risk [60]. Comorbidity of ADHD and emotional disorders (such as anxiety) determines the severity of the clinical symptoms and leads to severe social maladaptations.

Since environmental factors make a significant contribution to the development of depression in individuals with ADHD, overcoming these environmental factors and relational problems is an important part of treatment. If the depressive symptoms are mild, treatment starts with assuaging ADHD, and this itself frequently leads to a resolution of the depressive symptoms.

If no improvement in the depressive symptoms is observed, SSRIs may be added. Appropriate dosage and gradual titration are important when using SSRIs.

Depression-related nondrug therapies, particularly cognitive behavioral therapy, may be started along with ADHD drugs in this group. One study on adolescents diagnosed with depression compared the relative effectiveness of three therapeutic approaches, namely, fluoxetine, CBT, and combined treatment, with a placebo. Only combined treatment emerged superior to the placebo in patients with depression alone, but fluoxetine, CBT, and combined treatment were all better than the placebo in adolescents with ADHD and comorbid MDD [61].

The form of treatment that should be undertaken when these disorders are comorbid with ADHD is controversial, and the disorder dominating the general picture should be treated primarily. If there is no doubt regarding the diagnosis of both disorders and the clinical picture is sufficiently severe to require treatment, then such treatments may be started together. Despite a scarcity of well-designed treatment studies in youth with ADHD and comorbid depression, there is increasing preliminary evidence on the role of stimulants, selective serotonergic reuptake inhibitors, bupropion, and atomoxetine in targeting either or both disorders. There is also some indirect evidence on the benefits of combining pharmacological treatments with psychosocial interventions that specifically target relevant environmental factors and functional impairments [62].

In cases of comorbid ADHD and anxiety disorder, therapeutic priority is determined on the basis of the severity of both disorders and the extent of their negative impact on life. If the anxiety is not very severe, then priority must be attached to treating ADHD. In addition, if the patient is amenable to psychotherapy, then this can also be recommended for improving the anxiety disorder in parallel with ADHD treatment. If the anxiety disorder symptoms are very severe, however, SSRIs must be added to the treatment regimen. CBT has been shown to be effective in both adolescents and adults. In addition, psychosocial therapies should be advised in patients with anxiety disorder [30].

6. Bipolar affective disorder (BAD)

Comorbidity or merging of ADHD and BAD is not yet fully understood. There are a number of questions concerning the relationship between these two disorders, such as is there symptomatic similarity between ADHD and BAD, is one a precursor of the other, are ADHD and BAD familial subtypes, are there any similarities in terms of comorbidity and course?

The three symptoms sufficient for diagnosing a manic attack in children, namely, distractibility, excessive talking, and hyperactivity, are also compatible with a diagnosis of ADHD, and given these overlapping symptoms, it is possible that BAD may be misdiagnosed as ADHD or vice versa. The rate of ADHD comorbidity in children diagnosed with BAD ranges from 11% to 98% [63], while BAD comorbidity is lower in individuals with ADHD. This variation may be because ADHD is more commonly diagnosed in children rather than BAD. The prevalence of ADHD in children is higher than BAD, and the predictors of bipolarity may not be completely determined in the presence of comorbid ADHD.

Biederman et al. [63] conducted a 4-year follow-up study and found that the rate of comorbid bipolar disorder increased by an additional 12% at the end of the 4 years; 11% of the children with ADHD had comorbid bipolar disorder at baseline, and these prevalence rates were significantly higher compared to control groups without ADHD. Furthermore, significantly higher rates of additional psychopathology, psychiatric hospitalization, and severely impaired psychosocial functioning were observed in children with ADHD and comorbid BAD, compared to children with ADHD alone both at baseline and at follow-up assessment. The authors also suggested that comorbid ADHD and bipolar disorder do not result from overlapping symptoms.

Co-occurrence of these two disorders is associated with poorer global functioning, greater symptom severity, and additional comorbidity compared to either disorder alone [64].

Available data strongly suggest that the prepubertal onset of BAD is a nonepisodic, chronic, rapid-cycling, mixed manic state that may be comorbid with ADHD and CD [65]. Several studies have reported that pediatric BAD is characterized by irritable and dysphoric moods, mixed episodes, explosive behavior accompanied by anger attacks, and rapid and ultrarapid cycling with a chronic course [66].

There is a significant loss of functionality in both the disorders. An investigation of the etiology of these two disorders, their effective diagnosis, and treatment are important to keep this loss in functionality to a minimum. One familial study that investigated comorbid ADHD and BAD reported higher rates of ADHD diagnoses in families of subjects with BAD and higher rates of BAD diagnosis in families of subjects diagnosed with ADHD [67]. In addition to genetic factors, potential environmental risk factors for comorbidity have also been investigated [68].

As the presence of comorbidities has an adverse effect on the course of both disorders, early identification and prompt treatment are critical. Different classes of psychopharmacological medications are employed in the treatment of ADHD and BAD, such as stimulants or atomoxetine for ADHD and mood stabilizers or antipsychotics for mania. Problems in differentiating between the two disorders and deciding on the best form of clinical management have important clinical implications for patients. Research also suggests that incorrect treatment may result in nonresponsiveness or worsening of symptoms in the case of ADHD and BAD [69].

7. Disruptive mood dysregulation disorder

Researchers regard emotional instability as a core deficit in children diagnosed with ADHD [70]. Therefore, affective instability in children diagnosed with ADHD does not directly indicate the presence of a comorbid mood disorder [71]. The National Institute of Mental Health (NIMH) created a construct for Severe Mood Dysregulation (SMD) to describe such children who do not meet the criteria for a formal mood disorder. Disruptive mood dysregulation disorder (DMDD) took its place in DSM V as a modification of SMD.

ADHD, ODD, and CD are the most common accompanying Axis I diagnoses in children with DMDD [72]. Children with ADHD and SMD experience greater morbidity than children with externalizing behavior disorders alone and are in need of specialized treatment to optimize their functioning [73]. Various behavior modifying therapies and stimulation therapy combinations have been developed for children with comorbid ADHD and SMD, and they have been shown to be effective and acceptable. Research has repeatedly shown that subjects with a diagnosis of SMD exhibited significantly higher levels of functional impairment after a 3-week therapeutic process compared to those with no such diagnosis [74]. It is also important for the parents of children with both these disorders to be referred to parenting programs and family therapy. One study on children with both ADHD and SMD used stimulation therapy at optimal doses prior to their randomization into two groups. One group received treatment involving psychosocial measures for 11 weeks, while the other group took part in group therapy. A significant decrease in suicidal ideation was observed in children receiving group therapy, and their parents also exhibited a more positive parenting behavior [71].

To date, there are too few studies to establish a specific treatment guideline for SMDD. ADHD, the prominent problem in comorbid ADHD and SMDD, can be improved with stimulation therapy. Low-dose antipsychotics can be tried when the basic problems are arousal symptoms and behavioral difficulties.

8. Alcohol and substance use disorder

Significantly high rates of development of substance use disorder (SUD), involving use of nicotine, alcohol, marijuana, cocaine, or other drugs, during adolescence have been reported in individuals diagnosed with childhood ADHD [75]. One 10-year study of patients with ADHD showed that the probability of these patients developing substance dependence was twice as high as that of the control group [76]. A study of comorbid psychiatric disorders in subjects with substance abuse disorder reported that half of the adolescents aged under 15 years met the diagnostic criteria for ADHD [77]. Further, early onset and a more severe substance use disorder have been correlated with ADHD. One recent meta-analysis found that childhood ADHD is associated with nicotine use in adolescence and alcohol and drug use disorder in adulthood [78].

As anxiety, depression, and aggression are frequently seen in children and adolescents with ADHD, these patients use substances such as nicotine to self-treat symptoms of anxiety and depression, and nicotine suppresses symptoms of ADHD. Thus, individuals with ADHD use addictive substances to treat psychiatric comorbidities.

One twin study reported that a substance use disorder did not develop in subjects with ADHD without CD [79]. In children diagnosed with ADHD, the group with comorbid CD and/or BAD was at highest risk of developing a substance use disorder [80]. This marked association between ADHD and substance use disorder shows the importance of diagnosing and treating childhood ADHD to avoid the later development of a severe substance use disorder.

In light of the high comorbidity between ADHD and substance use disorder, it is possible that there are common underlying neurological factors, and ADHD and substance problems also have several common causes.

Variations in dopamine genes that affect attention, arousal, and reinforcement sensitivity are possible common risk factors for the development of ADHD and substance use disorder [81], and altered dopamine (DA) neurotransmission is central to current models of how ADHD and substance abuse disorder develop [82].

As substance abuse itself leads to changes in the brain, it is impossible to determine if individuals with a substance use disorder also exhibit characteristics similar to ADHD or not. However, the changes occurring in the brain due to a substance use disorder are thought to make these individuals more inclined to engage in impulsive behavior, similar to individuals with ADHD but before the onset of the disorder and before the substance abuse. A recent review of neuroimaging studies in humans with ADHD and SUD found repeated evidence of a blunted striatal DA release and a disruption in neural circuitry between the anterior cingulate cortex, the striatum, and the prefrontal cortex. ADHD and SUD-related craving share some neurobiological similarities, which may be because patients with an addiction show increased craving if they also suffer from ADHD [83].

Recent studies have shown that effectively treating ADHD symptoms may be protective in patients with a substance use disorder. The claim that treating ADHD symptoms with stimulants increases the risk for future substance abuse has not been verified, and in fact, the opposite effect is typically seen in medication-treated individuals. Children treated with stimulants appear to have a significantly lower risk of developing a substance use disorder than those who were not pharmacologically treated.

This finding suggests that ADHD does in fact contribute to the development and maintenance of substance use problems, as the successful treatment of ADHD symptoms results in a reduction of the substance use problem [84].

9. Developmental coordination disorder

Several studies show a high correlation between ADHD and developmental coordination disorder (DCD). ADHD-DCD comorbidity can be as high as 50% in children [85]. In a study of 477 cases of ADHD, Blondis et al. [86] have reported the presence of a comorbid developmental coordination disorder in at least 33% of the subjects.

Maladroitness in children with ADHD frequently decreases with age, and the children may successfully engage in sporting activities. However, this does not occur in the presence of a comorbid developmental coordination disorder, and it generally persists along with the inattention [86]. Clinical research has shown that maladroitness, clumsiness, and ponderousness seriously affect a child in numerous areas, and that these children find it difficult to perform certain activities at the same speed as their peers in school.

The possible treatment consists of psychological and educational support. Tervo et al. [87] compared the response to methylphenidate in subjects with developmental coordination disorder and ADHD and ADHD alone. They reported that the response to the drug was similar in both the groups and that the stimulant was also effective in treating ADHD.

There are two hypotheses concerning the decrease in symptoms following treatment with methylphenidate. The first is that methylphenidate increases attention, and that increased attention leads to an improvement in motor deficits, while the second is that drug therapy has distinct effects on attention and motor skills.

The proportion of children with ADHD who could improve their motor skills to the normal range upon medication varies from 28% to 67% among reported studies. While the symptoms of patients with a mild motor deficit before treatment improve to normal levels with therapy, in patients with a more severe motor deficit before treatment, the symptoms only decrease in severity and they may still continue to meet the diagnostic criteria for DCD.

It is important to assess motor skills among children with ADHD because of the risk of their reduced participation in daily activities that require motor coordination and attention [88].

10. Enuresis and encopresis

ADHD and incontinence are common diseases in childhood, are commonly seen together, and also affect one another. Nocturnal enuresis (NE) is seen in 10% of children aged 7 years, daytime urinary incontinence (DUI) in 2-3% and fecal incontinence (FI), or encopresis in 1-3%. Baeyens et al. [89] have investigated the prevalence of ADHD in 120 children with primary enuresis using parent and teacher questionnaires and diagnostic interviews. Their results indicate that 15% of the children met the criteria for ADHD, and a further 22.5% of them met the criteria for the ADHD inattentive type. A 2-year follow-up study of the same cohort indicated that 73% of those initially diagnosed with ADHD had the diagnosis reconfirmed at follow-up [90]. The authors also noted that the probability of a child with ADHD still having episodes of nocturnal enuresis at 2-year follow-up were 3.2 times higher than that for a child who did not have comorbid ADHD.

There are several hypotheses to explain the comorbidity of ADHD and NE. There is evidence that genetic factors occupy an important place in the etiology of ADHD and NE, as the heritability of NE and ADHD as individual disorders is high. However, the only formal molecular genetics study on both the disorders indicates that NE and ADHD are genetically independent, separate entities that do not share a common genetic basis.

Neuroimaging studies have established a great overlap in brain structures involved in ADHD and NE (and to a lesser extent in DUI and FI); however, a possible interaction between functional brain activity in combined incontinence and ADHD has not yet been studied. It is therefore unclear why and how ADHD and incontinence together affect central nervous system (CNS) functioning. From the few studies on ADHD and NE, it can be speculated that complex neural networks, including cortical, subcortical, and brainstem regions, will most likely be responsible for the clinically evident interaction effects [91].

Incontinence must be investigated in children with ADHD, and ADHD must be investigated in children with incontinence. The management of enuresis includes supportive approaches such as educating parents about enuresis, reducing fluids, keeping a dry bed chart, and awakening the child to void during the night, conditioning with a urine alarm, or medications such as imipramine or desmopressin acetate [92]. Treatment must be adapted to include both supportive approaches and pharmacotherapy in patients with ADHD and incontinence.

One double-blind, placebo-controlled study investigating the effectiveness of atomoxetine in children with NE reported a significant decrease in symptoms. Atomoxetine, a highly specific inhibitor of the presynaptic norepinephrine transporter, increases the effects of norepinephrine in many brain areas. Atomoxetine-mediated decrease in symptoms of NE supports the hypothesis that these drugs, with their noradrenergic effect, may be beneficial in the treatment of this disease [93]. NE and ADHD may improve with both methylphenidate and atomoxetine. Many hypotheses have been proposed—involving central neurochemical dysfunctions (dopaminergic and noradrenergic), anticholinergic, and reduced sleep arousal effects of these drugs—to account for the effects of these medications in the treatment of enuresis and ADHD [94, 95].

Studies aimed at understanding the relationship between ADHD and elimination disorders may identify common, underlying neurological alterations that may lead to a more effective treatment for both the disorders [96].

11. Tic disorders

Tic disorders are quite rare in the general population but are common in the population with ADHD. Tic comorbidity in patients with ADHD ranges between 8% and 10% [97, 98], and ADHD is the most common accompanying disorder in tic patients [99].

Tic disorders have little effect on the psychosocial functioning of subjects with ADHD [100]. There is no definitive evidence regarding the course of ADHD being affected by the tic disorder. However, accompanying obsessive-compulsive symptoms have been reported in a significant proportion of individuals with ADHD and comorbid tic disorders. Tics, OCD, and ADHD are related in a number of complex ways and have common demographic and psychopathological risk factors [101].

Greater psychopathology and social and academic impairment have been reported when ADHD is comorbid with Tourette's disease [102]. Earlier age at onset, greater difficulty of anger control, sleep problems, ODD, mood disorders, deficient social skills, inappropriate sexual behavior, and self-harming behaviors are seen when Tourette's syndrome is comorbid with ADHD [103].

The pathophysiology of ADHD and the tic disorder is unclear, although their comorbidity suggests that they have similar mechanisms or at least that they are compatible to varying degrees [104]. These two disorders share a number of genetic, neuronal, and cognitive risk factors, and several dopamine and serotonin genes have been studied as potential risk factors. Genes and environmental risk factors are also thought to cause both disorders. Abnormalities in the same anatomical cycle, such as cortical thinning, frontal system abnormalities, and basal ganglia abnormalities, have been shown in children with Tourette's and ADHD [105].

A comprehensive treatment program for Tourette's syndrome and comorbid ADHD should include measures other than medication such as cognitive-behavioral, psychoeducational, and psychosocial interventions.

Three classes of drugs are currently used in the treatment of Tourette's syndrome and comorbid ADHD: α-agonists (clonidine and guanfacine), stimulants (amphetamine enantiomers, methylphenidate enantiomers or slow release preparations), and selective norepinephrine reuptake inhibitors (atomoxetine). It has been recently suggested that in a few selected cases partial dopamine agonists (aripiprazole) could be useful, and there is evidence supporting the use of noradrenergic agents (clonidine). Reuptake inhibitors (atomoxetine) and stimulants (methylphenidate) could also be used for the treatment of Tourette's syndrome and comorbid ADHD [106]. Although the evidence is insufficient, there are studies that suggest using aripiprazole in children with mild ADHD [107].

12. Conclusion

ADHD is associated with several comorbid psychiatric diseases and conditions, and these comorbid conditions may cause a worsening of the symptoms of ADHD. Greater loss of functionality is observed in patients with a comorbid condition. It is important to diagnose and treat these comorbid conditions to effectively treat ADHD.

Author details

Murat Yüce*, Filiz Uçar and Gökçe Nur Say

*Address all correspondence to: muryuce@yahoo.com

Department of Child and Adolescent Psychiatry, Faculty of Medicine, Ondokuz Mayis University, Samsun, Turkey

References

[1] Biederman J. Attention-deficit/hyperactivity disorder: a selective overview. Biological Psychiatry. 2005;57(11):1215-20.

[2] Spencer TJ, Biederman J, Mick E. Attention-deficit/hyperactivity disorder: diagnosis, lifespan, comorbidities, and neurobiology. Journal of Pediatric Psychology. 2007;32(6):631-42.

[3] Biederman J, Petty CR, O'Connor KB, Hyder LL, Faraone SV. Predictors of persistence in girls with attention deficit hyperactivity disorder: results from an 11-year controlled follow-up study. Acta Psychiatrica Scandinavica. 2012;125(2):147-56.

[4] Jensen PS, Martin D, Cantwell DP. Comorbidity in ADHD: implications for research, practice, and DSM-V Journal of the American Academy of Child and Adolescent Psychiatry. 1997;36(8):1065-79.

[5] Gau SS-F, Ni H-C, Shang C-Y, Soong W-T, Wu Y-Y, Lin L-Y, et al. Psychiatric comorbidity among children and adolescents with and without persistent attention-deficit hyperactivity disorder. Australian and New Zealand Journal of Psychiatry. 2010;44(2):135-43.

[6] Huh Y, Choi I, Song M, Kim S, Hong SD, Joung Y. A comparison of comorbidity and psychological outcomes in children and adolescents with attention-deficit/hyperactivity disorder. Psychiatry Investigation. 2011;8(2):95-101.

[7] Biederman J, Newcorn J, Sprich S. Comorbidity of attention deficit hyperactivity disorder with conduct, depressive, anxiety, and other disorders. American Journal of Psychiatry. 1991.

[8] Pliszka SR. Psychiatric comorbidities in children with attention deficit hyperactivity disorder. Pediatric Drugs. 2003;5(11):741-50.

[9] Kessler RC, Adler LA, Barkley R, Biederman J, Conners CK, Faraone SV, et al. Patterns and predictors of ADHD persistence into adulthood: results from the National Comorbidity Survey Replication. Biological Psychiatry. 2005;57(11):1442.

[10] Semerci Z. Attention deficit hyperactivity disorder comorbidity in children and adolescents with Gilles de La Tourette syndrome. Çocuk ve Gençlik Ruh Sağlığı Dergisi/ Turkish Journal of Child and Adolescent Mental Health. 2001;8(1):19-26.

[11] Wiśniewska B, Baranowska W, Wendorff J. The assessment of comorbid disorders in ADHD children and adolescents. Advances in Medical Sciences. 2006;52:215-7.

[12] Ghanizadeh A. Psychiatric comorbidity differences in clinic-referred children and adolescents with ADHD according to the subtypes and gender. Journal of Child Neurology. 2009;24(6):679-84.

[13] Yuce M, Zoroglu SS, Ceylan MF, Kandemir H, Karabekiroglu K. Psychiatric comorbidity distribution and diversities in children and adolescents with attention deficit/ hyperactivity disorder: a study from Turkey. Neuropsychiatric Disease and Treatment. 2013;9:1791-9.

[14] Waxmonsky J. Assessment and treatment of attention deficit hyperactivity disorder in children with comorbid psychiatric illness. Current Opinion in Pediatrics. 2003;15(5):476-82.

[15] Biederman J, Faraone SV, Taylor A, Sienna M, Williamson S, Fine C. Diagnostic continuity between child and adolescent ADHD: findings from a longitudinal clinical sample. Journal of the American Academy of Child and Adolescent Psychiatry. 1998;37(3):305-13.

[16] Biederman J, Mick E, Faraone SV, Braaten E, Doyle A, Spencer T, et al. Influence of gender on attention deficit hyperactivity disorder in children referred to a psychiatric clinic. American Journal of Psychiatry. 2002;159(1):36-42.

[17] Chen M-H, Su T-P, Chen Y-S, Hsu J-W, Huang K-L, Chang W-H, et al. Higher risk of developing mood disorders among adolescents with comorbidity of attention deficit hyperactivity disorder and disruptive behavior disorder: a nationwide prospective study. Journal of Psychiatric Research. 2013;47(8):1019-23.

[18] Greene RW, Biederman J, Zerwas S, Monuteaux MC, Goring JC, Faraone SV. Psychiatric comorbidity, family dysfunction, and social impairment in referred youth with oppositional defiant disorder. American Journal of Psychiatry. 2002;159(7):1214-24.

[19] Nordström T, Hurtig T, Moilanen I, Taanila A, Ebeling H. Disruptive behaviour disorder with and without attention deficit hyperactivity disorder is a risk of psychiatric hospitalization. Acta Paediatrica. 2013;102(11):1100-3.

[20] Thapar A, Harrington R, McGUFFIN P. Examining the comorbidity of ADHD-related behaviours and conduct problems using a twin study design. British Journal of Psychiatry. 2001;179(3):224-9.

[21] Saarinen S, Fontell T, Vuontela V, Carlson S, Aronen ET. Visuospatial working memory in 7-to 12-year-old children with disruptive behavior disorders. Child Psychiatry and Human Development. 2014:1-10.

[22] Biederman J, Faraone SV, Milberger S, Jetton JG, Chen L, Mick E, et al. Is childhood oppositional defiant disorder a precursor to adolescent conduct disorder? Findings from a four-year follow-up study of children with ADHD. Journal of the American Academy of Child and Adolescent Psychiatry. 1996;35(9):1193-204.

[23] Biederman J, Petty C, Dolan C, Hughes S, Mick E, Monuteaux M, et al. The long-term longitudinal course of oppositional defiant disorder and conduct disorder in ADHD boys: findings from a controlled 10-year prospective longitudinal follow-up study. Psychological Medicine. 2008;38(07):1027-36.

[24] Barkley RA, Fischer M, Edelbrock C, Smallish L. The adolescent outcome of hyperactive children diagnosed by research criteria—III. Mother-child interactions, family conflicts and maternal psychopathology. Journal of Child Psychology and Psychiatry. 1991;32(2):233-55.

[25] Steiner H. Practice parameters for the assessment and treatment of children and adolescents with conduct disorder. American Academy of Child and Adolescent Psychiatry. Journal of the American Academy of Child and Adolescent Psychiatry. 1997;36(10 Suppl):122S-39S.

[26] Wilson JM, Marcotte AC. Psychosocial adjustment and educational outcome in adolescents with a childhood diagnosis of attention deficit disorder. Journal of the American Academy of Child and Adolescent Psychiatry. 1996;35(5):579-87.

[27] Loy JH, Merry SN, Hetrick SE, Stasiak K. Atypical antipsychotics for disruptive behaviour disorders in children and youths. Cochrane Library. 2012.

[28] Gadow KD, Arnold LE, Molina BS, Findling RL, Bukstein OG, Brown NV, et al. Risperidone added to parent training and stimulant medication: effects on attention-deficit/hyperactivity disorder, oppositional defiant disorder, conduct disorder, and peer aggression. Journal of the American Academy of Child and Adolescent Psychiatry. 2014;53(9):948-59. e1.

[29] Ercan ES, Uysal T, Ercan E, Ardıc U. Aripiprazole in children and adolescents with conduct disorder: a single-center, open-label study. Pharmacopsychiatry. 2012;45(1): 13-9.

[30] NM M. Yaşam Boyu Dikkat Eksikliği Hiperaktivite Bozukluğu ve Eşlik Eden Durumlar. Nobel Tıp Kitabevi. 2015.

[31] Mayes SD, Calhoun SL. Similarities and differences in Wechsler Intelligence Scale for Children—Third Edition (WISC-III) profiles: support for subtest analysis in clinical referrals. Clinical Neuropsychologist. 2004;18(4):559-72.

[32] Mayes SD, Calhoun SL. Frequency of reading, math, and writing disabilities in children with clinical disorders. Learning and Individual Differences. 2006;16(2):145-57.

[33] Mayes SD, Calhoun SL. Wechsler Intelligence Scale for Children—Third and Fourth Edition: predictors of academic achievement in children with attention-deficit/hyperactivity disorder. School Psychology Quarterly. 2007;22(2):234.

[34] Morgan AE, Hynd GW, Riccio CA, Hall J. Validity of DSM-IV ADHD predominantly inattentive and combined types: relationship to previous DSM diagnoses/subtype differences. Journal of the American Academy of Child and Adolescent Psychiatry. 1996;35(3):325-33.

[35] DuPaul GJ, Gormley MJ, Laracy SD. Comorbidity of LD and ADHD: implications of DSM-5 for assessment and treatment. Journal of learning disabilities. 2012:0022219412464351.

[36] Sexton CC, Gelhorn H, Bell J, Classi P. The co-occurrence of reading disorder and ADHD: epidemiology, treatment, psychosocial impact, and economic burden. Journal of Learning Disabilities. 2011:0022219411407772.

[37] ABALI O. Attention deficit hyperactivity disorder and learning disorder. Turkiye Klinikleri Journal of Pediatrical Sciences. 2010;6(2):22.

[38] Williamson D, Murray DW, Damaraju C, Ascher S, Starr HL. Methylphenidate in children with ADHD with or without learning disability. Journal of Attention Disorders. 2014;18(2):95-104.

[39] Shaywitz BA, Williams DW, Fox BK, Wietecha LA. Reading outcomes of children and adolescents with attention-deficit/hyperactivity disorder and dyslexia following atomoxetine treatment. Journal of Child and Adolescent Psychopharmacology. 2014;24(8):419-25.

[40] Bolea-Alamañac B, Nutt DJ, Adamou M, Asherson P, Bazire S, Coghill D, et al. Evidence-based guidelines for the pharmacological management of attention deficit hyperactivity disorder: update on recommendations from the British Association for Psychopharmacology. Journal of Psychopharmacology. 2014;28(3):179-203.

[41] Baker BL, Neece CL, Fenning RM, Crnic KA, Blacher J. Mental disorders in five-year-old children with or without developmental delay: focus on ADHD. Journal of Clinical Child and Adolescent Psychology. 2010;39(4):492-505.

[42] Neece C, Baker B, Blacher J, Crnic K. Attention-deficit/hyperactivity disorder among children with and without intellectual disability: an examination across time. Journal of Intellectual Disability Research. 2011;55(7):623-35.

[43] Pearson DA, Santos CW, Roache JD, Casat CD, Loveland KA, Lachar D, et al. Treatment effects of methylphenidate on behavioral adjustment in children with mental retardation and ADHD. Journal of the American Academy of Child and Adolescent Psychiatry. 2003;42(2):209-16.

[44] Simonoff E, Taylor E, Baird G, Bernard S, Chadwick O, Liang H, et al. Randomized controlled double-blind trial of optimal dose methylphenidate in children and adolescents with severe attention deficit hyperactivity disorder and intellectual disability. Journal of Child Psychology and Psychiatry. 2013;54(5):527-35.

[45] Weber P, Lütschg J. Methylphenidate treatment. Pediatric Neurology. 2002;26(4): 261-6.

[46] Aman MG, Smith T, Arnold LE, Corbett-Dick P, Tumuluru R, Hollway JA, et al. A review of atomoxetine effects in young people with developmental disabilities. Research in Developmental Disabilities. 2014;35(6):1412-24.

[47] Fernández-Jaén A, Fernández-Mayoralas DM, Calleja Pérez B, Muñoz Jareño N, del Rosario Campos Díaz M. Atomoxetine for attention deficit hyperactivity disorder in mental retardation. Pediatric Neurology. 2010;43(5):341-7.

[48] Eugene Arnold L. Commentary: filling out the evidence base for treatment of attention-deficit hyperactivity disorder symptoms in children with intellectual and devel-

opmental disability: conclusions for clinicians—a response to Simonoff et al. (2013). Journal of Child Psychology and Psychiatry. 2013;54(6):701-3.

[49] Biederman J, Faraone S, Milberger S, Guite J, Mick E, Chen L, et al. A prospective 4-year follow-up study of attention-deficit hyperactivity and related disorders. Archives of General Psychiatry. 1996;53(5):437-46.

[50] Biederman J, Faraone S, Mick E, Lelon E. Psychiatric comorbidity among referred juveniles with major depression: fact or artifact? Journal of the American Academy of Child and Adolescent Psychiatry. 1995;34(5):579-90.

[51] Meinzer MC, Pettit JW, Viswesvaran C. The co-occurrence of attention-deficit/hyperactivity disorder and unipolar depression in children and adolescents: a meta-analytic review. Clinical Psychology Review. 2014.

[52] Connor DF, Edwards G, Fletcher KE, Baird J, Barkley RA, Steingard RJ. Correlates of comorbid psychopathology in children with ADHD. Journal of the American Academy of Child and Adolescent Psychiatry. 2003;42(2):193-200.

[53] Cohen R, Lohr I, Paul R, Boland R. Impairments of attention and effort among patients with major affective disorders. Journal of Neuropsychiatry and Clinical Neurosciences. 2001;13(3):385-95.

[54] Biederman J, Ball SW, Monuteaux MC, Mick E, Spencer TJ, McCreary M, et al. New insights into the comorbidity between ADHD and major depression in adolescent and young adult females. Journal of the American Academy of Child and Adolescent Psychiatry. 2008;47(4):426-34.

[55] Di Trani M, Di Roma F, Elda A, Daniela L, Pasquale P, Silvia M, et al. Comorbid depressive disorders in ADHD: the role of ADHD severity, subtypes and familial psychiatric disorders. Psychiatry Investigation. 2014;11(2):137-42.

[56] Chen MH, Chen YS, Hsu JW, Huang KL, Li CT, Lin WC, et al. Comorbidity of ADHD and subsequent bipolar disorder among adolescents and young adults with major depression: a nationwide longitudinal study. Bipolar Disorders. 2014.

[57] Roy A, Oldehinkel AJ, Verhulst FC, Ormel J, Hartman CA. Anxiety and disruptive behavior mediate pathways from attention-deficit/hyperactivity disorder to depression. Journal of Clinical Psychiatry. 2014;75(2):e108-13.

[58] Jensen PS, Hinshaw SP, Kraemer HC, Lenora N, Newcorn JH, Abikoff HB, et al. ADHD comorbidity findings from the MTA study: comparing comorbid subgroups. Journal of the American Academy of Child and Adolescent Psychiatry. 2001;40(2): 147-58.

[59] Schatz DB, Rostain AL. ADHD with comorbid anxiety a review of the current literature. Journal of Attention Disorders. 2006;10(2):141-9.

[60] Faraone SV, Biederman J. Do attention deficit hyperactivity disorder and major depression share familial risk factors? Journal of Nervous and Mental Disease. 1997;185(9):533-41.

[61] Kratochvil CJ, May DE, Silva SG, Madaan V, Puumala SE, Curry JF, et al. Treatment response in depressed adolescents with and without co-morbid attention-deficit/ hyperactivity disorder in the Treatment for Adolescents with Depression Study. Journal of Child and Adolescent Psychopharmacology. 2009;19(5):519-27.

[62] Daviss WB. A review of co-morbid depression in pediatric ADHD: etiologies, phenomenology, and treatment. Journal of Child and Adolescent Psychopharmacology. 2008;18(6):565-71.

[63] Biederman J, Faraone S, Mick E, Wozniak J, Chen L, Ouellette C, et al. Attention-deficit hyperactivity disorder and juvenile mania: an overlooked comorbidity? Journal of the American Academy of Child and Adolescent Psychiatry. 1996;35(8):997-1008.

[64] Arnold LE, Demeter C, Mount K, Frazier TW, Youngstrom EA, Fristad M, et al. Pediatric bipolar spectrum disorder and ADHD: comparison and comorbidity in the LAMS clinical sample. Bipolar Disorders. 2011;13(5-6):509-21.

[65] Geller B, Luby J. Child and adolescent bipolar disorder: a review of the past 10 years. Journal of the American Academy of Child and Adolescent Psychiatry. 1997;36(9): 1168-76.

[66] LUŞ MG. Bipolar Bozukluk ve Dikkat Eksikliği Hiperaktivite Bozukluğu. Türkiye Klinikleri Pediatrik Bilimler Dergisi. 2010;6(2):31-7.

[67] Faraone SV, Biederman J, Mennin D, Wozniak J, Spencer T. Attention-deficit hyperactivity disorder with bipolar disorder: a familial subtype? Journal of the American Academy of Child and Adolescent Psychiatry. 1997;36(10):1378-90.

[68] Surman CB, Biederman J, Spencer T, Yorks D, Miller CA, Petty CR, et al. Deficient emotional self-regulation and adult attention deficit hyperactivity disorder: a family risk analysis. American Journal of Psychiatry. 2011;168(6):617-23.

[69] Skirrow C, Hosang GM, Farmer AE, Asherson P. An update on the debated association between ADHD and bipolar disorder across the lifespan. Journal of Affective Disorders. 2012;141(2):143-59.

[70] Martel MM. Research review: a new perspective on attention-deficit/hyperactivity disorder: emotion dysregulation and trait models. Journal of Child Psychology and Psychiatry. 2009;50(9):1042-51.

[71] Waxmonsky JG, Wymbs FA, Pariseau ME, Belin PJ, Waschbusch DA, Babocsai L, et al. A novel group therapy for children with ADHD and severe mood dysregulation. Journal of Attention Disorders. 2012:1087054711433423.

[72] Brotman MA, Schmajuk M, Rich BA, Dickstein DP, Guyer AE, Costello EJ, et al. Prevalence, clinical correlates, and longitudinal course of severe mood dysregulation in children. Biological Psychiatry. 2006;60(9):991-7.

[73] Anastopoulos AD, Smith TF, Garrett ME, Morrissey-Kane E, Schatz NK, Sommer JL, et al. Self-regulation of emotion, functional impairment, and comorbidity among children with AD/HD. Journal of Attention Disorders. 2011;15(7):583-92.

[74] Waxmonsky J, Pelham WE, Gnagy E, Cummings MR, O'Connor B, Majumdar A, et al. The efficacy and tolerability of methylphenidate and behavior modification in children with attention-deficit/hyperactivity disorder and severe mood dysregulation. Journal of Child and Adolescent Psychopharmacology. 2008;18(6):573-88.

[75] Lee SS, Humphreys KL, Flory K, Liu R, Glass K. Prospective association of childhood attention-deficit/hyperactivity disorder (ADHD) and substance use and abuse/dependence: a meta-analytic review. Clinical Psychology Review. 2011;31(3):328-41.

[76] Biederman J, Monuteaux MC, Mick E, Spencer T, Wilens TE, Silva JM, et al. Young adult outcome of attention deficit hyperactivity disorder: a controlled 10-year follow-up study. Psychological Medicine. 2006;36(02):167-79.

[77] Chan Y-F, Dennis ML, Funk RR. Prevalence and comorbidity of major internalizing and externalizing problems among adolescents and adults presenting to substance abuse treatment. Journal of Substance Abuse Treatment. 2008;34(1):14-24.

[78] Charach A, Yeung E, Climans T, Lillie E. Childhood attention-deficit/hyperactivity disorder and future substance use disorders: comparative meta-analyses. Journal of the American Academy of Child and Adolescent Psychiatry. 2011;50(1):9-21.

[79] Disney ER, Elkins IJ, McGue M, Iacono WG. Effects of ADHD, conduct disorder, and gender on substance use and abuse in adolescence. American Journal of Psychiatry. 1999;156(10):1515-21.

[80] Wilens TE, Morrison NR. The intersection of attention-deficit/hyperactivity disorder and substance abuse. Current Opinion in Psychiatry. 2011;24(4):280.

[81] Milberger S, Faraone SV, Biederman J, Chu MP, Wilens T. Familial risk analysis of the association between attention-deficit/hyperactivity disorder and psychoactive substance use disorders. Archives of Pediatrics and Adolescent Medicine. 1998;152(10):945-51.

[82] Volkow N, Fowler J, Wang G, Baler R, Telang F. Imaging dopamine's role in drug abuse and addiction. Neuropharmacology. 2009;56:3-8.

[83] Frodl T. Comorbidity of ADHD and substance use disorder (SUD): a neuroimaging perspective. Journal of Attention Disorders. 2010;14(2):109-20.

[84] Looby A. Childhood attention deficit hyperactivity disorder and the development of substance use disorders: valid concern or exaggeration? Addictive Behaviors. 2008;33(3):451-63.

[85] Kadesjo B, Gillberg C. Developmental coordination disorder in Swedish 7-year-old children. Journal of the American Academy of Child and Adolescent Psychiatry. 1999;38(7):820-8.

[86] Blondis TA. Motor disorders and attention-deficit/hyperactivity disorder. Pediatric Clinics of North America. 1999;46(5):899-913.

[87] Tervo RC, Azuma S, Fogas B, Fiechtner H. Children with ADHD and motor dysfunction compared with children with ADHD only. Developmental Medicine and Child Neurology. 2002;44(6):383-90.

[88] Kaiser M-L, Schoemaker M, Albaret J-M, Geuze R. What is the evidence of impaired motor skills and motor control among children with attention deficit hyperactivity disorder (ADHD)? Systematic review of the literature. Research in Developmental Disabilities. 2015;36:338-57.

[89] Baeyens D, Roeyers H, Hoebeke P, Verte S, Van Hoecke E, Walle JV. Attention deficit/hyperactivity disorder in children with nocturnal enuresis. Journal of Urology. 2004;171(6):2576-9.

[90] Baeyens D, Roeyers H, Demeyere I, Verte S, Hoebeke P, Walle JV. Attention-deficit/hyperactivity disorder (ADHD) as a risk factor for persistent nocturnal enuresis in children: a two-year follow-up study. Acta Paediatrica. 2005;94(11):1619-25.

[91] von Gontard A, Equit M. Comorbidity of ADHD and incontinence in children. European Child and Adolescent Psychiatry. 2014:1-14.

[92] Action AO. Practice parameters for the assessment and treatment of children and adolescents with enuresis. Journal of the American Academy of Child and Adolescent Psychiatry. 2004;43:1540-50.

[93] Sumner CR, Schuh KJ, Sutton VK, Lipetz R, Kelsey DK. Placebo-controlled study of the effects of atomoxetine on bladder control in children with nocturnal enuresis. Journal of Child and Adolescent Psychopharmacology. 2006;16(6):699-711.

[94] Williamson LB, Gower M, Ulzen T. Clinical case rounds in child and adolescent psychiatry: enuresis and ADHD in older children and an adolescent treated with stimulant medication: a case series. Journal of the Canadian Academy of Child and Adolescent Psychiatry. 2011;20(1):53.

[95] Crimmins C, Rathbun S, Husmann D. Management of urinary incontinence and nocturnal enuresis in attention-deficit hyperactivity disorder. Journal of Urology. 2003;170(4):1347-50.

[96] Mellon MW, Natchev BE, Katusic SK, Colligan RC, Weaver AL, Voigt RG, et al. Incidence of enuresis and encopresis among children with attention-deficit/hyperactivity disorder in a population-based birth cohort. Academic Pediatrics. 2013;13(4):322-7.

[97] Steinhausen H-C, Nøvik TS, Baldursson G, Curatolo P, Lorenzo MJ, Pereira RR, et al. Co-existing psychiatric problems in ADHD in the ADORE cohort. European Child and Adolescent Psychiatry. 2006;15(1):i25-i9.

[98] Swanson J, Lerner M, March J, Gresham FM. Assessment and intervention for attention-deficit/hyperactivity disorder in the schools: lessons from the MTA study. Pediatric Clinics of North America. 1999;46(5):993-1009.

[99] Freeman RD, Fast DK, Burd L, Kerbeshian J, Robertson MM, Sandor P. An international perspective on Tourette syndrome: selected findings from 3500 individuals in 22 countries. Developmental Medicine and Child Neurology. 2000;42(7):436-47.

[100] Spencer T, Biederman J, Coffey B, Geller D, Wilens T, Faraone S. The 4-year course of tic disorders in boys with attention-deficit/hyperactivity disorder. Archives of General Psychiatry. 1999;56(9):842-7.

[101] Peterson BS, Pine DS, Cohen P, Brook JS. Prospective, longitudinal study of tic, obsessive-compulsive, and attention-deficit/hyperactivity disorders in an epidemiological sample. Journal of the American Academy of Child and Adolescent Psychiatry. 2001;40(6):685-95.

[102] Gorman DA, Thompson N, Plessen KJ, Robertson MM, Leckman JF, Peterson BS. Psychosocial outcome and psychiatric comorbidity in older adolescents with Tourette syndrome: controlled study. British Journal of Psychiatry. 2010;197(1):36-44.

[103] Freeman RD. Tic disorders and ADHD: answers from a world-wide clinical dataset on Tourette syndrome. European Child and Adolescent Psychiatry. 2007;16(9):15-23.

[104] Steeves TD, Fox SH. Neurobiological basis of serotonin-dopamine antagonists in the treatment of Gilles de la Tourette syndrome. Progress in brain research. 2008;172:495-513.

[105] Murphy T, Muter V. Risk factors for comorbidity in ADHD and GTS: looking beyond a single-deficit model. Applied Neuropsychology: Child. 2012;1(2):129-36.

[106] Rizzo R, Gulisano M, Calì PV, Curatolo P. Tourette Syndrome and comorbid ADHD: current pharmacological treatment options. European Journal of Paediatric Neurology. 2013;17(5):421-8.

[107] Masi G, Gagliano A, Siracusano R, Berloffa S, Calarese T, Ilardo G, et al. Aripiprazole in children with Tourette's disorder and co-morbid attention-deficit/hyperactivity disorder: a 12-week, open-label, preliminary study. Journal of Child and Adolescent Psychopharmacology. 2012;22(2):120-5.

Chapter 6

The Comorbidity of ADHD and Autism Spectrum Disorders (ASDs) in Community Preschoolers

Maria Carmen Carrascosa-Romero and Carlos De Cabo- De La Vega

Additional information is available at the end of the chapter

http://dx.doi.org/10.5772/61400

Abstract

Symptoms of inattention and hyperactivity, features of attention-deficit/hyperactivity disorder (ADHD), have been frequently documented in children with autism spectrum disorders (ASDs) and often co-occur. Evidence indicates that 20-50% of children with ADHD meet criteria for ASD, and 30-80% of ASD children meet criteria for ADHD.

According to the DSM-IV, the essential features of Autistic Disorder (AD) are "the presence of markedly abnormal or impaired development in social interaction and communication and a markedly restricted repertoire of activity and interests". Differential diagnosis of "Pervasive Developmental Disorder" (PDD: Autistic Disorder, Rett's Disorder, Childhood Disintegrative Disorder, Asperger's Disorder) and "Pervasive Developmental Disorder-Not Otherwise Specified"(PDD-NOS) is often difficult in the preschool child. This is particularly true when assessing verbal and nonverbal communication since both expressive and cognitive language are not yet established and there are many differences in their acquisition period among these children (before the age of three). As a result, many of these children are diagnosed with PDD-NOS not meeting the criteria for a specific type of PDD; this category includes "atypical autism" presentations that do not meet the criteria for AD. As a result, the concept of PDD-NOS has become a mixed bag. Often, diagnosis cannot be established before age three, delaying therapeutic interventions. Moreover, differential diagnosis between ADHD and PDD-NOS can be especially difficult, mainly in infant and young children. However, and following the recommendations of the DSM- IV, the ASDs diagnosis has been included among the exclusion criteria for the ADHD. Such exclusion has generated considerable controversy regarding the necessity and benefits of maintaining these separations.

At present, a new edition of the DSM has been published: DSM-5® (Fifth Edition, 2013). Among the advantages that this new manual provides are: i) further categorization of the persons affected and ii) the possibility of diagnosis before the age of three. The DSM-5 takes into account that limitations in language are not specific to autism. The new diagnostic category "Social Communication Disorder" appears separate from ASD, which does not seek to create a new subcategory.

In light of the new DSM-V criteria which allow a dual diagnosis of ASD and ADHD behaviors, in this chapter we will review the clinical overlap of these two conditions, particularly regarding their comorbidities in community pre-schoolers (generally categorized as PDD-NOS). We will also look into possible future research directions necessary to enhance our understanding of the etiology/genetics factors as well as the appropriate sequence of therapeutic interventions and pharmacological treatment (psychostimulant and nonstimulant medications) for the co-occurrence of these disorders.

Keywords: Autism, Attention-deficit/ hyperactivity disorder, co-ocurrece, comorbidities, pre-schoolers, dual diagnosis, therapy, research

1. Introduction

Symptoms of inattention and hyperactivity are features of attention-deficit/hyperactivity disorder (ADHD) that have been frequently documented in children with autism spectrum disorders (ASDs). Evidence indicates that 20–50% of children with ADHD fulfilled the criteria for ASD, particularly at preschool age, and 30–80% of ASD patients fulfilled the criteria for ADHD [1]. A shared genetic susceptibility has been suggested for both neurodevelopmental disorders [2].

According to the DSM-IV-TR [3], the essential features of autistic disorder (AD) are "the presence of markedly abnormal or impaired development in social interaction and communication and a markedly restricted repertoire of activity and interests". Differential diagnosis of pervasive developmental disorder (PDD: autistic disorder, Asperger disorder, childhood disintegrative disorder, Rett disorder) and pervasive developmental disorder-not otherwise specified (PDD-NOS) can often be difficult in preschool children. This is particularly true when assessing verbal and nonverbal communication, since both expressive and cognitive language are not yet established and there are many differences in their acquisition period among these children (before the age of three). As a result, many of these children are diagnosed with PDD-NOS not meeting the criteria for a specific type of PDD. This category includes atypical autism presentations not fulfilling the criteria for AD. As a result, the concept of PDD-NOS has become a mixed bag; overuse of PDD-NOS has led to confusion in the diagnosis and contributed to the autism "epidemic". Often, diagnosis cannot be established before age three, delaying therapeutic interventions. Moreover, differential diagnosis between ADHD and PDD-NOS can be especially difficult, mainly in infants and young children. However, following the recommendations of the DSM-IV, the ASD diagnosis has been included among the exclusion criteria for ADHD. Such exclusion has generated considerable controversy regarding the necessity and benefits of maintaining these separations. (For the conceptual history of modern-day ADHD and ASD, see Table 1).

At present, a new edition of the DSM (Diagnostic and Statistical Manual of Mental Disorders from the American Psychiatric Association) has been published: the DSM-5® (APA. Fifth Edition, 2013) [4]. The DSM-5 is principally intended as a handbook for clinical staff, making

http://dx.doi.org/10.5772/61400

reviews accesible for daily practice. Disorders have been classified with associated criteria to improve the accurate diagnosis of these syndromes. It should be noted that among the major changes in childhood disorders contained in the new edition are the following [5, 6] (see Table 2).

DSM	ASD	ADHD
DSM-I (1952) & DSM-II (1968)	No terminology for Pervasive Developmental Disorder or Autism. Closest denomination: Schizophrenic Reaction (Childhood category)	No term for attention deficit Minimal brain dysfunction Hyperactive Child Syndrome Hyperkinetic reaction of children
DSM-III (1980)	Pervasive Developmental Disorders (PDD): Atypical Autism, Infantile Autism, Childhood Onset PDD	ADD: Attention Deficit Disorder
DSM-III-R (1987)	Pervasive Developmental Disorders (PDD): Autistic Disorder, PDD-NOS	ADHD: Attention Deficit Hyperactivity Disorder
DSM-IV (1994)	Pervasive Developmental Disorders (PDD): Asperger disorder, Rett syndrome, Childhood Disintegrative Disorder, Autistic Disorder, PDD-NOS	ADHD: Attention Deficit Hyperactivity Disorder Identifies three ADHD subtypes: Predominantly Hyperactive-Impulsive type, Predominantly Inattentive type, Combined type
DSM-IV-TR (2000)	Diagnoses are the same, text amendment for PDD-NOS	Same diagnoses
DSM 5 (May 2013)	ASD is a new single condition with different levels of symptom severity. New diagnostic category: Social Communication Disorder	Presentation specifiers that map directly to the prior subtypes. Different levels of symptom severity

Table 1. Nosology Evolution and DSM History

DSM-5 vs. DSM IV	ADHD	ASD
CHANGES	ADHD does not fade at a specific age. The definition ADHD has been updated in DSM-5 to characterize more precisely the experience of affected adults.	One of the main changes in DSM-5 concerns ASD. The present revision of diagnosis constitutes a new, more accurate, and scientifically and medically useful way to diagnose subjects with autistic disorders.
CORE DOMAINS	The criteria have not changed from DSM-IV. Symptoms remain classified into two categories: inattention and hyperactivity/ impulsivity (including behaviors such as excessive talking,	According to DSM-IV, subjects were diagnosed with four separate conditions: Childhood disintegrative disorder Asperger disorder Autistic disorder

DSM-5 vs. DSM IV	ADHD	ASD
	impaired organization skills, failing to pay close attention to details, wriggling, or inability to sit still and remain seated) In DSM-5 subtypes have been substituted with presentation specifiers that relate directly to the prior subtypes.	Pervasive developmental disorder not otherwise specified Using DSM 5 the different groups disappear. ASD is a new DSM-5 term reflecting the scientific consensus that the previously four separate conditions are actually one disorder, with several degrees of symptom severity within two core areas: 1) Deficits in social interaction and social communication 2) Restricted repetitive behaviors, activities and interests (RRBs) (*)
SYMPTOMS	DSM-5 uses the same 18 symptoms employed in DSM-IV and persist the classification into two symptom domains (hyperactivity/impulsivity and inattention). Children have to present with at least six symptoms from either (or both) the hyperactivity or impulsivity group of criteria and inattention criteria, whereas adolescents and adults (over 17 years of age) must have five.	ASD patients often present communication impairments that include incorrect interpretation of nonverbal interactions, inappropriate responses in conversation, or inability to build age-appropriate friendships. Besides, people with ASD tend to be highly dependent on routines, hypersensitive to environmental change, or focus intensely on inappropriate items. ASD symptoms seem to fall on a continuum ranging from mild to much more severe.
AGE OF ONSET	According to DSM-5, a number of the subject's ADHD symptoms have to appear before 12 years of age, whereas when using DSM-IV the age of onset was 7 years old.	According to the new DSM-5 criteria, ASD diagnosis requires the early presence of symptoms during childhood, even if such symptoms cannot be detected until a more advanced age. The present modification in the criteria promotes earlier diagnosis of ASD but also permits including subjects whose symptoms are not completely identified until social tasks surpass their capabilities. It is a relevant improvement from the DSM-IV criteria, which was focused on diagnosing school-age children with autism-related disorders. However, it still falls short to identify ASD in younger children.
EXCLUSION CRITERIA	ADHD symptoms can not appear only during the course of schizophrenia or another psychotic disorder and should	DSM-5 does not include exclusion criteria for subjects with ASD, because symptoms of ASD and ADHD tend to co-occur.

http://dx.doi.org/10.5772/61400

DSM-5 vs. DSM IV	ADHD	ASD
	not be better explained by another psychiatric condition.	(*) Since both domains are required for ASD diagnosis, "social communication disorder" is diagnosed when no RRBs appear.

Table 2. Highlights of Changes of ADHA/ASD from DSM-IV-TR to DSM-5

- The chapter that includes "Diagnoses usually first made in infancy, childhood, or adolescence" in DSM-IV has been deleted and substituted in Section II (Diagnostic criteria and codes) of DSM-5 by the referred "neurodevelopmental disorders".
- Both ADHD and ASD are now classified together as neurodevelopmental disorders, which also includes some former DSM-IV "disorders first diagnosed in infancy, childhood, or adolescence" appearing across DSM-5.
- DSM-5 replaces the term "mental retardation" with *intellectual disability,* and the term *intellectual developmental disorder* appears between brackets to refer to the classification system of the World Health Organization.
- The DSM-5 communication disorders include a new condition: social (pragmatic) communication disorder.
- ASD is a new term in DSM-5 reflecting the scientific consensus that Asperger disorder, AD/autism, PDD-NOS, and childhood disintegrative disorder (formerly considered separate disorders) are actually all the same entity.
- Criteria for diagnosis of ADHD in the new edition are similar to those in DSM-IV. However, several subtle, but very important changes have been made in the DSM-5. Among the most notable are that diagnostic criteria now allow a comorbid diagnosis of ADHD with ASD. DSM-IV required "clear evidence of clinically significant impairment in social, academic, or occupational functioning"; this has been changed in DSM-5 to: "There is clear evidence that the symptoms interfere with, or reduce, the quality of social, academic, or occupational functioning." In addition, ADHD is now included in the neurodevelopmental disorders chapter of the text, rather than being grouped with the disruptive behavior disorders as it was previously.

Among the advantages that this new manual provides are: 1) further categorization of the persons affected and 2) the possibility of diagnosis before the age of three. DSM-5 takes into account that limitations in language are not specific to autism. The new diagnostic category, "social communication disorder", appears separate from ASD, which does not seek to create a new subcategory.

Keeping in mind the new criteria from DSM-5 that allow a dual diagnosis of ASD and ADHD behaviors, in this chapter we will review the clinical overlap of these two conditions, particularly regarding their comorbidities in early preschoolers (before the age of three, generally categorized as PDD-NOS). We will also look into possible new research perspectives to gain futher insights into the etiology/genetic factors, as well as the appropriate sequence of therapeutic interventions and pharmacological treatment (psychostimulant and non-stimulant medications) for the co-occurrence of these disorders.

2. Differential diagnosis of neurodevelopmental disorders

Neurodevelopmental disorders (NDDs) are impairments in the growth, development, and function of the brain that affect emotion, learning ability, and memory, and that unfold as the individual grows. This disorder is highlighted by characteristic deficiencies: cognitive impairment, delays in maturationally-influenced psychological features, overlap among NDDs, and genetic predisposition,

In DSM-IV, the chapter that includes "Diagnoses usually first made in infancy, childhood, or adolescence" has been deleted and substituted in DSM-5 by the referred "Neurodevelopmental Disorders" [4, pp. 229-272], which includes six categories:

- Specific Learning Disorder
- Communication Disorders
- Intellectual Disability (Intellectual Developmental Disorder)
- Autism Spectrum Disorder
- Motor Disorders
- Attention-Deficit/Hyperactivity Disorder

The recognition of the prevalence of comorbidities in NDD, particularly during the preschool years, is important in order to obtain a more complete and comprehensive vision of the range of abilities and deficits of a child without being limited by the possibilities of exclusion obsolete diagnostic criteria of DSM-IV. Especially since these conditions often overlap, an accurate differential diagnosis is needed to provide appropriate services. Where once our diagnostic manual (DSM-IV-TR) prevented comorbid diagnoses of disorders such as autism and ADHD, this exclusion is no longer present in DSM-5. This is the recognition that although symptoms can overlap, a child with autism and ADHD is clearly different from a child with autism alone and therefore, may require different intervention services [1, 5, 6].

In these early ages, neurodevelopment must be taken into account in all situations that may involve both learning difficulties and communication. In this way, NDDs in early childhood, as we highlight in their differential diagnosis, mainly include: intellectual disability, communication disorders, ASD, and ADHD.

2.1. Intellectual disabilities

The DSM-5 subclass includes:

- Intellectual Disability (Intellectual Developmental Disorder)

- Unspecified Intellectual Disability (Intellectual Developmental Disorder)
- Global Developmental Delay

"The choice of which category to use is determined in large part by the strength or clarity of the evidence that criteria are met" [4, pp 229].

- **Intellectual Disability (ID, Intellectual Developmental Disorder) 319**

DSM-5 introduces changes in name and criteria for intellectual disability, including a shift away from primary reliance on IQ scores:

Name. "Mental retardation" is replaced by *intellectual disability.* ID includes both intellectual and adaptive functioning deficits. The onset of this disorder takes place during development. Three domains are employed to assess severity: practical, conceptual, and social life skills.

Elimination of IQ-based Subtypes. In DSM-IV, intellectual function is standardly evaluated using culturally appropriate, comprehensive, psychometrically valid, and sound tests of intelligence that are individually administered (Mild = IQ 55–70; Moderate = IQ 40–55; Severe = IQ 25–40; Profound = IQ < 25). DSM-5 does not list mild, moderate, severe, and profound subtypes; but mild, moderate, and severe severity levels. Severity codes indicate the vision of the diagnosing clinician regarding the severity of adaptive functioning. IQ test scores are conceptual functioning approximations that may not be instrumental to evaluate the performnace of practical tasks reasoning in real-life situations. However, according to the new DSM-5, a subject with severe social impairment (enough to be placed under the moderate category, for example) can be placed in the mild category due to the fact that they present an IQ reaching 80–85. DSM-5 puts less stress on the level of impairment (i.e., IQ scores) and more on the size and type of the intervention that has to be applied.

- **Mild intellectual disability**: This group includes roughly 85% of the individuals with ID, and it is more or less equivalent to the educational category previously refered to as "educable", namely individuals within this group have the capacity to achieve some academic success.
- Children with this ID usually develop communication and social skills during the preschool period (0–5 years of age) and frequently cannot be distinguished from children without ID deficits until they are older. Therefore, initially learning problems can be attributed to deficits in attention, especially if also present with hyperactivity.
- When they reach their late teens, they usually meet elementary academic levels (up to grade six, approximately) or beyond if they count with enough support. Often, they manage to live independent lives in the context of their communities receiving minimal additional support, such as assistance with life decisions. For other skills such as nutrition, transportation, shopping, and finances, additional reminders, instructions, and time may be necessary
- **Moderate, Severe and Profound intellectual disability: Usually, there will be no confusion in the differential diagnosis with** ADHD, but comorbidity with ASD may exist.

Therefore, diagnosis of ASD now requires reference to intellectual ability: "ASD with or without accompanying intellectual impairment".

- **Global Developmental Delay 315.8 (F 88)**

"This diagnosis is reserved for individuals < 5 years old, when clinical severity cannot be reliably assessed during early childhood" [4, p 230]. Criteria:

- failure to meet developmental milestones
- unable to be assessed using standardized tests
- re-assessment is required

- **Unspecified Intellectual Disability (Intellectual Developmental Disorder) 319 (F79)**

"This diagnosis is reserved for individuals > 5 years old, when assessment of the degree of ID by means of locally available procedures is rendered difficult or impossible because of associated sensory or physical impairments" [4, pp 231].

2.2. Communication disorders

Communication disorders in DSM-5 include novel and updated syndromes:

- Language disorder, which is a combination of DSM-IV mixed receptive-expressive, and expressive language disorders.
- Speech sound disorder replaces what was known as phonological disorder.
- Childhood-onset fluency disorder replaces the term stuttering.
- Social (pragmatic) communication disorder (SCD) is a newly coined pathology consisting of constant difficulties in the social uses of nonverbal and verbal communication (ASD must be ruled out).

We only make reference in this chapter to the new category, SCD.

- **Social (pragmatic) Communication Disorder (SCD) 315.39 (F80.89).**

SCD is a pragmatic disability, whose diagnosis is based on deterioration in the social usage of verbal and nonverbal communication in the child´s natural environment, which influences the development of discourse comprehension and social relationships and cannot be explained by poor skills in the areas of grammar, word structure, or overall cognitive capacity. Symptoms include problems with inappropriate responses in conversation, as well as difficulty in the acquisition and use of spoken and written language. Since the symptoms described in SCD were not defined in previous editions of DSM, many individuals with these symptoms may have been classified under the not otherwise specified category of pervasive development disorder [for review see 7].

Social communication can be defined as "the synergistic emergence of social interaction, social cognition, pragmatics (verbal and nonverbal), and receptive and expressive language processing" [8]. Pragmatics [in 9] is defined as "the range of communicative functions (reason for talking), the frequency of communication, discourse skills (turn taking, topic maintenance and change), and flexibility to modify speech for different listeners and social situations". Rapin and Allen [10] coined the term "semantic-pragmatic deficit syndrome" to describe children who are notably loquacious, exhibit problems finding words, and have difficulty conversing, including maintaining the thread of discourse. Correspondingly, Bishop and Rosenbloom [11] began using the term semantic-pragmatic disorder to characterize children with difficulties to understand and follow conversation rules and could use unusual language or choice of words in their speech. However, it has been proposed that semantic deficits may not always co-occur with pragmatic deficits. Thus, the term "pragmatic language impairment" was coined to define subjects with deficits in pragmatics (though not necessarily semantics) [12].

Social communication disorders may correspond to a different diagnosis or may take place associated to other conditions. Pragmatic language impairment has been described in a variety of neurological diseases such as epilepsy [13], children with behavioral problems [14,15], and also in psychiatric and NDDs, including, among others, language learning disabilities, intellectual disabilities, ASD [16], and ADHD [17]. Children with pragmatic language impairment may be placed within a continuum between individuals with specific language impairment and those with the social communication deficits of ASD [16]. With respect to ADHD, it has been suggested that the primary symptoms of the disorder (e.g., hyperactivity, impulsiveness, inattention) may also impair their social communication skills, which, in turn, may cause further limitations in academic achievement, communication, and social participation [18, 19]. The standardized measures available for Test of Pragmatic Language are usually performed in children over 3 years old. A preschool version (birth to 4 years old) [20] provides exclusively descriptive information that can be employed to recognize weaknesses and strengths and to establish treatment aims.

In SCD, the reduced social communication capabilities are the cause of functional limitations in academic achievement, effective communication, occupational performance, or social participation, alone or in any combination of the aforementioned characteristics.

Symptoms have to appear in the early ages even if they are not identifed until they are older when communication, language, or speech demands are beyond their capabilities. It should not be assigned to the ASD section because it corresponds to a type of patient showing related, but distinguishable symptoms (see [3]).

Advantages:

- Including SCD in DSM-5 may drive further research into social (pragmatic) communication disorders using the operationalized diagnostic criteria, and thus aid in reaching a better understanding and documentation of the fundamental features and validity of SCD.

- Will help individuals with these symptoms access suitable treatment adapted to their impairment.

- Field trials from DSM-5 provided evidence of SCD, indicating that the lower ASD diagnoses in DSM-IV could be explained by a shift to the SCD diagnostic category [21].

- It is likely that individuals with social communication and/or pragmatic language disability were diagnosed as DSM-IV PDD-NOS.

Drawbacks:

- The scarcity of longitudinal research reduces our chances to extrapolate from previous literature to SCD.
- The standardized measures available for Test of Pragmatic Language are usually performed in children over 3 years, and a preschool version for children from birth to 4 years old.
- The steps to follow would be to confirm the efficacy of the criteria for SCD, as well as assessing the impact of cultural and socio-demographic factors on its appearance.

2.3. Autism spectrum disorder (ASD) 299.00 (f84.0)

Autism, a debilitating neurological handicap in children, is a highly heterogeneous set of disorders with wide variations in symptom severity, intellectual level, and functional disability. It is a multifactorial disorder implicating a wide range of environmental risk factors and genetic predispositions. No definitive biological markers are available for autism, therefore, in most cases, diagnosis is based on a variety of behavioral signs. Since autistic patients may present with very diverse symptoms and features, autism is thought of as a spectrum disorder [22].

The ASD diagnosis is of great concern to the practicing pediatrician because its frequency has been increasing for decades, with a surprising 556% rise in pediatric prevalence reported between 1991 and 1997 (higher than that of Down syndrome, cancer, or spina bifida). Researchers cannot agree on whether the trend is a result of increased awareness, improved detection, and changing diagnostic criteria with expanding definition, or of new environmental influences [23, 24].

In multiple communities in the United States [CDC surveillance data 2010, see 25], the overall prevalence of ASD was 14.7 per 1,000 (one in 68) 8-year-old children. Overall, prevalence estimations for ASD ranged across locations from 5.7 to 21.9 per 1,000 8-year-old children. Consistent with previous reports, there was significant variety in ASD prevalence according to gender, geographic region, racial/ethnic group, and intellectual ability. It is unclear in this study to what degree the variation in prevalence might be due to diagnostic methods, lack of recognition of ASD symptoms in certain ethnic/racial groups, socioeconomic disparities in access to therapeutic and community services, and regional differences in clinical or school-based practices.

The relevance of accurate diagnosis of autism has become greater than ever, particularly in view of the increasing prevalence [26], elevated costs for both family and society [27], and accepted importance of early identification and intervention in individuals with autism. The classification systems used strongly affect prevalence studies, and it is important to consider the changes that have occurred at this level when analyzing the possible causes of the increase in pervasive developmental disorders [28].

- **Classically in DSM-IV**, Pervasive developmental disorders (PDD) encompass a heterogeneous group of children typified by severe and pervasive impairment in a number of developmental areas: 1) communication skills, 2) reciprocal social interaction skills, and 3) the presence of stereotyped activities, behavior, and interests. The qualitative discapacities described for these conditions vary considerably according to mental age or developmental level of each child. The specific pathologies included five subtypes in this section: autistic disorder (AD), Asperger disorder, childhood disintegrative disorder (CDD), Rett disorder (RD), and pervasive developmental disorder-not otherwise specified (PDD-NOS). These conditions normally become apparent in the early postnatal years and are frequently associated with certain level of mental retardation (now called *intellectual disability*).

DSM-IV is not the "Gold Standard". Among the concerns that have arisen on the application of DSM-IV that stand out [29–31] are:

- Validity of the PDD category. Symptoms are not pervasive. They are specific (selective or greater) impairment in social interaction plus restricted, repetitive behaviors/fixated interests.
- Validity of certain diagnoses (e.g., childhood disintegrative disorder category)
- Consistency in diagnosing (e.g., high-functioning autistic disorder vs. Asperger).
- Current diagnostic guidelines may not fulfill all needs from community evaluators [32].
- The usage of some diagnoses may not be completely appropriate (e.g., PDD-NOS as mild NDD, Asperger as "odd" behaviors)

Recommendations from the Autism and Developmental Disabilities Monitoring (ADDM) Network include improving strategies that meet the needs for 1) amply accepted standardized, methods for documenting both ASD diagnosis functional limitations and the severity of ASD; 2) improved documentation and recognition of ASD symptoms, concretely among both boys and girls, children from all racial/ethnic backgrounds, and children with no intellectual disability; 3) reducing the age of first evaluation for and diagnosis of ASD, including the age at which children are enrolled in community-based support systems [25].

- **The new DSM-5: Changes in the diagnosis of autism** (see [4])

These changes arise to unify and standardize the criteria to better define ASD, to increase validity and appropriateness of the use of diagnoses, and to obtain an earlier diagnosis [33–35].

1. **There is a single category of ASD** instead of five subtypes (Figure 1). The term PDD has been deleted. Scientific evidence and clinical practice indicate that the single spectrum is a better reflection of the symptom picture, time course, and response to therapy. While it is reliable and valid to distinguish ASD from typical development, differentiating between conditions within the spectrum is not. Thus, Asperger and PDD-NOS are used interchangeably, as it also happens with high-functioning autism (HFA) and Asperger [29].

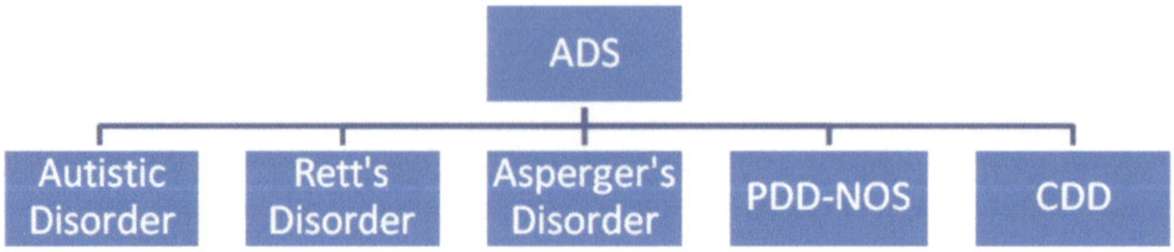

Figure 1. From PDD to ASD.

- Deletion of Asperger disorder: Still, to date, there is little clinical or research evidence that Asperger disorder is qualitatively distinct from other autism diagnoses at the symptom level, or that the new criteria will under-identify high-functioning ASD [36]. This situation has led to difficulties in deciding whether to use the terms "HFA" or "Asperger" for diagnosis. Diagnostic biases are apparent, with rich, white males receiving Asperger dx, while poorer, non-Caucasian populations receive PDD-NOS diagnosis (See site differences in CDC surveillance data [25]).

- Elimination of childhood disintegrative disorder (CDD): New data show that developmental regression in ASD is a continuous variable, encompassing a wide range in the timing and types of skills lost, as well as in the developmental milestones that were accomplished before regression. Since CDD is a rare diagnosis, systematic evaluation is difficult; however, review of accumulated literature indicates that CDD differs notably from other ASDs, including in the abruptness and severity of the deterioration, as well as co-occurrence with physical symptoms such as loss of bladder and bowel control. Thus, CDD diagnosis requires searching **for the neurological impairments** associated with it.

- PDD-NOS: This subset should be employed when there is severe and widespread impairment of reciprocal social interaction in the presence of disability in either verbal or nonverbal communication skills, or associated with stereotyped behavior, activities, and interests without meeting the criteria for a specific PDD. The distinctions among the disorders have been inconsistent and often based on variables other than the criteria for the diagnosis. For example, this category includes "atypical autism" (presentations that do not meet the criteria for autistic disorder because of late age of onset, atypical symptomatology, or subthreshold symptomatology). These changes were necessary taking into account: 1) Overuse of PDD-NOS leads to diagnostic confusion (and may have contributed to the autism "epidemic"); 2) Overlap of PDD-NOS and Asperger disorder.

- At present, ASD is defined by "specific sets of behaviors, not etiologies", therefore, inclusion of Rett disorder is atypical. Patients with Rett disorder can be diagnosed as having ASD but the specifier "ASD associated with a known medical or genetic condition or environmental factor" should be used to indicate that ASD are related to Rett.

2. The three domains are combined into two.

Nowadays, ASD is considered an NDD diagnosed according to a shared group of behaviors and is best defined as a new single condition/diagnostic category showing diversity in the severity of its symptoms that can be assigned to two core domains (Figure 2):

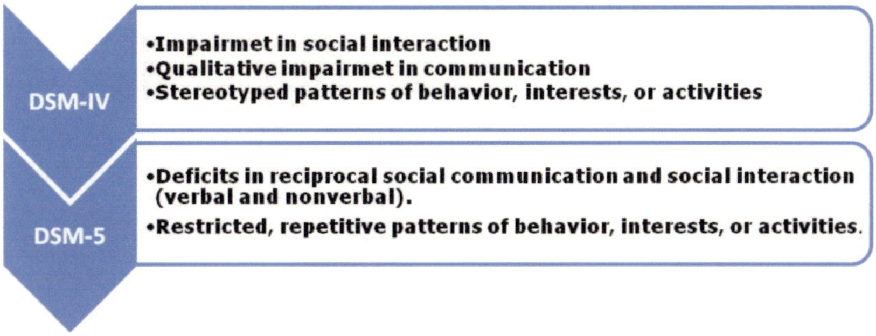

Figure 2. ASD: The three domains are combined into two.

a. Social interaction and social communication deficits. The rationale is that deficits in communication and social behaviors are inseparable. The social communication domain results from combining the principal symptoms from the DSM-IV social and communication domains. By doing this, language skills not employed in the context of social communication reduce the relevance.

b. The second major criterion remains restricted repetitive behaviors, interests, and activities (RRBs).

ASD by definition encompasses pragmatic communication problems, but also includes RRBs. Because both components are required for diagnosis of ASD, taking all this into consideration, SCD is diagnosed if no RRBs are present.

3. **Diagnostic Criteria:** 12 symptom-items in the DSM-IV are reduced to 7. Symptoms are not deleted, but those criteria that describe similar characteristics are merge. There must be five out of seven criteria to make the diagnosis of ASD.

4. **Sensory processing:** RRBs are expanded to include "abnormalities in sensory processing".

5. **The broadened age of onset criteria:** Symptoms must be present in the early developmental period. To meet the requirements for criterion C in DSM-IV, symptoms must start prior to 3 years of age. DSM-5 only stipulates that symptoms start in early childhood, cautioning that they "may not be fully manifest until social demands exceed capacity", that is to say during middle-school years, late adolescence, or young adulthood. The results of Guthrie et al. [37] may be helpful to illustrate the manifestations of autistic symptoms during development. They assessed a sample of 237 children with ASD, between 12 and 30 months of age using ADOS-T, and found that autism symptoms can be divided and best deconstructed into the two-factor DSM-5 model, which supports the DSM-5′s reorganization of symptoms. The fact that these results in young children coincide with earlier studies in older children and adults indicates that the structure of autistic symptomatology may be similar across the developmental stages.

6. **Specify current severity:** Level 3: Requiring very substantial support; Level 2: Requiring substantial support; and Level 1: Requiring support.

7. **The addition of "specifiers"** to describe features such as "with or without intellectual impairment", "with or without language impairment", "associated with known medical or genetic condition" (deletion of Rett syndrome as a specific ASD), and "with catatonia".

Advantages:

- They are specific to the social-communication domain plus restricted, "repetitive behaviors/ fixated interests". The criteria "Qualitative impairment in communication" disappears.
- ASD is a single spectrum disorder; however, it presents important individual variations. DSM-5 incorporates: cognitive abilities (IQ), clinical course and pattern of onset, severity of ASD symptoms, etiologic factors, and associated conditions. Clinicians will be likely to include these observations as "diagnostic specifiers".
- DSM-5 criteria present higher specificity when compared to DSM-IV-TR criteria (0.97 vs. 0.86). This superior specificity may decrease false positive diagnoses, which is especially important in clinical settings where base rate tends to be low [38].

Drawbacks:

- Sensitivity is lower (0.81 vs. 0.95) in DSM-5. Therefore, sensitivity has been "sacrificed" to increase specificity. Loosening the DSM-5 criteria by reducing one symptom criterion improved sensitivity (0.93 vs. 0.81), causing a minor specificity decrease (0.95 vs. 0.97). It would be advisable that Phase II of DSM-5 testing would incorporate loosened criteria, which will prevent up to 12% of ASD-affected people, mainly females, from being potentially overlooked. Less stringent DSM-5 criteria may improve ASD diagnosis, reducing societal costs via adequate early identification and improving treatment resources [38]. Other studies demonstrate that a diagnostic algorithm following the DSM-5 criteria and adapted to age and ability level variations is able to achieve good levels of both specificity and sensitivity [39].
- Merging Asperger disorder and PDD-NOS into a single broad ASD ignores singularity and identity of the Asperger disorder. There is at least one study indicating that the DSM-5 draft criteria were less sensitive identifying patients that were already diagnosed with AS with an ASD [40]. Thus, this proposed change has generated considerable apprehension from both patients and their families, who are concerned that individuals diagnosed with Asperger disorder will be orphaned or receive inappropriate service provision [41]. Due to the fact, that AS patients possess at least average intelligence, they may find themselves a therapeutic "no man's land" and not considered for disability services [42]. By contrast, other studies evaluate an important aspect of this controversy, namely symptom continuity between individuals with Asperger disorder and other ASD cases, by explicitly testing conflicting views of the nature of autism symptom structure. They have suggested that most children diagnosed with ASD using the DSM-IV would also be diagnosed as such employing the DSM-5 criteria [38, 43].
- Research studies from before and after DSM-5 will not be comparable. Important discontinuities in diagnostic practice create significant problems both for the clinical and research fields. It is not yet clear what the impact that these changes in the DSM-5 may have [31].

http://dx.doi.org/10.5772/61400

2.4. Attention-deficit/hyperactivity disorder (ADHD)

ADHD is considered the most frequent neurobehavioral childhood disorder. According to DSM-IV TR criteria, between 8% to 12% of school-age children could be diagnosed with ADHD [44]. However, there is a wide spread notion that ADHD is overdiagnosed. Although, the review of prevalence studies and research on the diagnostic process does not support the concept that ADHD is systematically overdiagnosed [45]. Some authors have proposed that ADHD should not be a disease as such, but rather a group of symptoms converging in a behavioral pathway for a series of psychological, emotional, and/or learning problems [46].

ADHD now falls under the Neurodevelopmental Disorders chapter, instead of being included within the disruptive behavior disorders, i.e., Oppositional Defiant Disorder and Conduct Disorder. This change accords better with the current concept of ADHD. ADHD is identified by a behavioral pattern, present in a variety of settings (e.g., school and home) that may affect performance issues in educational, work, or social settings. The threshold for meeting the diagnostic criteria for ADHD has been lowered slightly [47, 48].

Changes to ADHD in DSM-5:

1. **Core symptoms:** The general structure of the two dimensions of ADHD, inattention and hyperactivity/impulsivity, remains unchanged and DSM-5 retains the exact DSM-IV wording of all 18 symptoms. However, DSM-5 adds developmentally appropriate new exemplars to the criterion items to facilitate the application of these symptoms across the life span, more appropriate for children, adolescents, and adults.

2. **Age of onset criteria** of the disorder: The onset criterion has been changed from "symptoms that caused impairment were present before age 7 years" to "several inattentive or hyperactive-impulsive symptoms were present prior to age 12". Furthermore, DSM-5 only requires that symptoms are present by age 12, not that they necessarily create impairment by this age, as in DSM-IV. The combination of older age of onset and removing the impairment requirement is clearly more lenient.

3. **Number of symptoms required and duration of symptoms:** A symptom threshold change has been made for adults by reducing the number of criteria that patients aged 17 years or older must fulfill for diagnosis, with a cutoff of five symptoms instead of the six required for younger persons, both for inattention and for hyperactivity/impulsivity. As in DSM-IV, it is required that symptoms last for 6 months or more, and keeping at a level that would not overlap with the standard development

4. **Multiple settings requirement:** The cross-situational requirement has been reinforced with "several" symptoms for every setting.

5. **Need for clinically significant impairment.** In DSM-IV, symptoms had to affect least two settings ("the behaviors must create significant difficulty in at least two areas of life, such as home, social settings, school, or work"). Therefore, symptoms were required to cause impairment in several contexts (e.g., both home and school), as well as affecting the functional ability of the child in more than one context. DSM-5 has revised this to "several inattentive or hyperactive-impulsive symptoms are present in two or more settings".

Therefore, symptoms only have to appear in more than one setting and it is not required that they affect the subject's functioning in several contexts. This is less demanding too, and increases the chance to receive a full ADHD diagnosis, thus raising the percentage of the population who meets the diagnostic criteria.

6. **Presentations:** In DSM-5, subtypes have been substituted by presentation specifiers that correspond to the former subtypes in order to employ terms that accord with the change and fluidity that the disorder may display in a given patient across time. DSM-5 defines three presentations of ADHD according to the presence or absence of specific symptoms: hyperactive-Impulsive presentation, inattentive presentation, and combined presentation.

7. **New requirement to specify severity:** DSM-5 requires the severity of the disorder to be graded in the affected person, since ADHD symptoms impact each individual in varying degrees. Clinicians can specify the severity of ADHD presentation as mild, moderate, or severe, according to DSM-5 criteria:

- Mild: A minimal number of symptoms are present that result in only minor impairment at school, work, home, and/or in social contexts.
- Moderate: The impairment or symptoms are between mild and severe.
- Severe: A large number of symptoms show a higher level than required to have diagnostic value, or various symptoms are markedly grave, or they severely undermine the person at school, work, home, and/or in social settings.

It must also be recognized that the degree of severity and how ADHD manifests itself can vary during the patient's lifespan, which implies the chance of a partial remission of ADHD.

8. **Comorbidity:** DSM-5 introduces an important and, generally, positive change related to comorbidity: the elimination of ASD as an exclusion criterion for the diagnosis of ADHD. In its revised ADHD diagnostic criteria, DSM-5 recognizes the frequency of this co-occurrence (particularly at a young, pre-school age), and allows, for the first time, a co-morbid diagnosis of ADHD with ASD.

9. **New categories for persons not meeting full criteria.** The DSM-IV included a category called ADHD Not Otherwise Specified (NOS) for subjects showing notable symptoms but falling short of the required criteria. This has been revised to Other Specified ADHD and Unspecified ADHD in the DSM-5. The Other Specified category is employed when full the criteria are not reached, the clinician is able to determine the reason why full criteria were not met and the symptoms that do appear impair functioning in a clinically significant way.

Advantage:

- Comorbid diagnosis with ASD. This new disposition will pave the way for a more scientific approach to the overlap of these disorders, as well as enable a more appropriate clinical treatment of these children.

Drawbacks:

- The modifications introduced will probably raise the prevalence of ADHD, particularly in adolescents and adults, and perhaps also in children [49]. However, those changes are supported by clinical and epidemiological data and are unlikely to result in over-diagnosis [48].

3. Developmental period in preschool children

In the field of psychiatric disorders there has been a traditional delay in the systematic research dealing with infants and preschoolers (0 to 5-year-old children) in comparison with that studying school-age children, adolescents, and adults. To facilitate research on the preschool and infant ages, the development of clear and specific diagnostic criteria that can be confidently utilized within standardized measurements across a variety of samples is essential. In 2000–2002, an independent research committee elaborated the first Research Diagnostic Criteria-Preschool Age (RDC-PA), with the aim of promoting systematic study of psychiatric disorders in younger children [50].

The DSM model, with some revision to address the child′s developmental level, appears to provide a valid means of differentiating typical behavior problems in preschool children from atypical disruptive conduct that is impairing. Systematic research is required to standardize the revision of current assessment tools so that they can be adapted for use with preschool children and to develop methods that are more clinically sensitive for determining a child′s development level and for employing observational data in assessment [51].

Therefore, in young children, it is very important to recognize changes that may occur in the early stages of learning, especially in language acquisition and behavioral symptoms, which could already be identified as prodromal symptoms, followed by a correct differential diagnosis of these entities.

3.1. Development of language according to the stages of acquisition

The development of both language and communication is an intricate process affected by multiple genetic and environmental factors. Diagnostic criteria for NDDs (e.g., communication disorders, language Impairment, dyslexia, ASD, and ADHA) often include impairments in communication and language skills. These complex disorders are polygenic with a relevant genetic contribution to both types of skills. Language acquisition is the process by which human beings acquire the capacity to perceive, comprehend, produce, and use words and sentences to communicate. Humans' the early years, beginning at birth, are critical to future development of the skills required. Language acquisition needs to be stimulated in every way to generate a solid base to build upon as the child develops. There have been numerous investigations in this area, and several models for learning language have been developed based on neural networks, computational models, and other connectionist approaches [for review see 52–55]

Subject literature provides guidelines for when age-specific language features are acquired on average, but different authors cite different milestone dates, depending on where they conducted their research. Therefore, it is important to note that dates, in terms of specific linguistic milestones, are not concrete and can vary slightly from child to child. In accordance with published data, we can identify six basic stages of language acquisition occurring between ages 0 to 5 years, which coincide with the preschool stage. These ages are divided into two cycles: first cycle, between 0 and 3 years (in toddlers); and a second cycle, ranging from 3 to 5 or 6 years old, prior to the start of mandatory education.

The first cycle

- **Prelingual stage (0-6 mo):** Occurs before the use, acquisition, or development of language. Infants practice the pragmatic component of language use (e.g., by making eye contact with adult caretakers and exchanging sounds in something resembling a conversation). The "normal" child concentrates on the center of the face, or the region of the eyes. In NDD, there is a continuous and general deficiency in reciprocal social interaction. A notable disability in a myriad of nonverbal forms of social interaction and communication may occur (e.g., facial expressions, eye-to-eye contact, gestures, and body postures).
- **Babbling and canonical babbling stage(6–12 mo):** Babbling (also known as twaddling) is a stage of language acquisition during development when the child seems to be exploring their capability to produce articulate sounds, but still not being able to utter recognizable words. Syllable patterns start to emerge. Infants begin to distinguish between the different sounds, from vowels (V) to consonant and vowel (CV) syllables. This phase is considered to be the beginning of the canonical stage. During the canonical stage, babbling consists of repeated sounds containing alternations of consonants and vowels, progressing through such syllable types as VCV, VC, and redup of syllables (CVCV) and variegated syllables; children start to acquire the phonemes of the language.
- **One-wordutterances/holophrastic stage** (12–18 months): By about one year of age, infants start saying their first words. These one-word utterances are defined in the literature as "holophrastic" since they have been interpreted as to serve the same purpose of longer word expressions in adults.
- **Two-word utterances (approx.** 18–24 months**):** The two-word stage is defined as a child using (quite obviously, as stated in the title) two words to form a sentence.
- **Telegraphic stage (2–3 years):** When children have acquired and start to use multiple-word utterances. At this stage, some of the children's utterances are grammatically correct.

The second cycle

- By about 5–6 years of age, children have acquired almost normal speech, with good command of syntax and semantics. In later stages, development of vocabulary and pragmatics takes place. Pragmatic development highlights children's motivation to acquire language in the first place, as it serves different purposes and functions. Pragmatics are not acquired immediately, nor does it take a short period of time for a child to acquire them. This process is on-going until the age of approximately 10 years. In AD patients that have

http://dx.doi.org/10.5772/61400

acquired speech, it can be found either repetitive, stereotyped/idiosyncratic language, or pronounced disability sustaining or initiating a conversation with other individuals.

As already mentioned, developmental milestones and particularly social communication abilities, language acquisition, and proper speech occur at different age ranges amongst children, therefore diagnosis of pathology at early ages can be hindered. In AD, there may be either total absence or a delay in the development of speech.

The classical criteria for AD require abnormal functioning in communication skills, which has been one of the reasons that AD was not usually diagnosed until the second cycle of preschool age. Therefore, although many children did not meet all the criteria, they were included in AD generally categorized as PDD-NOS; overuse of PDD-NOS has lead to misdiagnosis and may have helped in the autism "outbreak". In the new classification of ASD, communication (verbal and nonverbal skills) is excluded; by removing this requirement, possibility of diagnosis before the age of 3 is increased.

In recent years, work on identifying prodromal symptoms of ASD has offered a powerful avenue for studying the emergence of "*ASD in statu nascendi*". At 6 months, ASD prodromal symptoms include a reduced capability to spontaneously pay attention to people and their activities [56–59]. At 12 months, a large proportion of infants posteriorly diagnosed with ASD show clinically relevant delays as well as dysfunction in various fields, including: vocalizations, social smiling, and eye contact [60–63], initiation of requesting and joint attention [62], object exploration [64], response to name [65], and responses to others' distress [66–68]. However, many of these symptoms described for ASD can also occur in children with ADHD or intellectual deficit, so caution is needed before a definitive diagnosis [69].

Sociocultural and individual factors influence body language, facial expressions and eye contact, and social communication behaviors in preschoolers and there is an ample spectrum of norms that are considered acceptable within and across cultures, families, and individuals [70]. Young children with SCD can sometimes present with symptoms similar to ADHD or ASD, so it is necessary to establish screening tests for comorbid conditions. Children diagnosed with pragmatic language impairment may be placed within a continuum between individuals with social communication deficits associated with ASD and those presenting with the specific language impairment [16].

The criteria for PDD-NOS diagnosis according to DSM-IV required the presence of impaired reciprocal social interaction and either deficient communication skills or stereotyped behavior, activities, and interests. Subclinical symptoms were also allowed in the PDD-NOS category. It is therefore possible that, when applying the DSM-IV criteria, children with social communication and/or pragmatic language impairment were diagnosed as PDD-NOS.

The DSM-5 Communication Disorders include a new condition, SCD; so far fewer studies have been conducted to determine the extent of the problem. Additional research is necessary to discern the consequences that pragmatic language impairments and SCD have on neuropsychiatric disorders, problematic behaviors, and the acquisition of academic skills. To reliably diagnose SCD, children must have already acquired suitable language and speech capabilities (i.e., present by 4–5 years of age in standard language development) in order to identify particular verbal pragmatic deficiencies. Therefore, samples from preschool- and school-age children should be employed in future research to establish a baseline for symptom manifestations. Developing and/or validating assessment tools to track and measure SCD traits will be invaluable to follow the course of the disease [7].

3.2. Control processes in behavioral domains

Although autism tends to appear during the first 1–2 years of life, ADHD is nearly impossible to diagnose along this period. Hyperactivity and inattentiveness are features shown by almost all toddlers, thus making ADHD very difficult to diagnose reliably until early childhood (although it is often possible during the preschool period) [71]. Children demonstrate dramatic gains in control processes between the ages of 3 and 6. During this developmental period, children begin to actively develop rudimentary regulation skills in affective, cognitive, and behavioral domains via rapidly developing limbic and neocortical circuitry [72] and in the context of parental socialization [73]. The determination of clinical significance of behavioral symptoms in the preschool period is complex due to the ample diversity usually found for these features.

Clinical experience and empirical data indicate that the criteria proposed for ADHD are largely applicable to children 3–5 years of age, whereas there is less evidence regarding their applicability to children under 3 years of age. Preschool children diagnosed with ADHD are similar with school-age ADHD youths in impaired functioning, high rates of comorbid psychopathology, and the quality of the disorder, despite the age difference [74]. Disorders of dysregulation can be first reliably diagnosed during this developmental period [50]. Hyperactivity-impulsivity may be a particularly prominent behavioral manifestation of preschool ADHD at home, whereas inattention may be more salient at the school setting [75]. Cognitive control has been found to be significantly associated with affective control (but not with effortful control) as a prominent form of control during early childhood in children with ADHD [76].

Furthermore, in a prospective population-based study, the Avon Longitudinal Study of Parents and Children (ALSPAC), in which subjects were recruited in the prenatal period (13,988 children alive at 12 months), results for boys indicated that autism overlaping with hyperactivity symptoms may contribute to problems with pragmatic language. This was not the case for girls or for socio-emotional difficulties [77]. In adults, by contrast, the co-occurrence of autistic and ADHD traits is not characterized by hyperactivity or impaired social skills, routine preferences or imagination. Instead, the connection between AD and ADHD is determined by common attention-related deficiencies (attentional switching capacity and lack of attention) [78].

Other studies have also found impaired facial affect recognition and empathy in children with ADHD [79, 80]. Some of the symptoms, such as lack of eye contact, can occur in different diseases and can be used to diagnose various behavioral and reading disorders: visual disturbances, intellectual disability, autism, ADHD, and dyslexia. In early childhood, when "impairment in social interaction or restricted repetitive and stereotyped patterns of behavior" is still not well established, sometimes it is particularly difficult to establish an appropriate differential diagnosis between these categories. There is little research available on pre-school children with ADHD for the purpose of determining early ASD comorbidity, possibly because while ASD is often diagnosed at pre-school age, diagnosis of primary ADHD is frequently postponed to late pre-school or early school age [1]. No population-based study on ASD diagnoses in children with a primary clinical diagnosis of ADHD has been performed to date [81].

4. Overlap of ADHD and ASD

Although their core diagnostic criteria do not explicitly overlap, lately, an increasing number of studies provide evidence for an elevated degree of corbidity between ADHD and ASD, with different levels of symptom severity. In DSM-5, the diagnoses of AD and ADHD will not be mutually exclusive any longer. This provides the basis for more differentiated studies on overlap and distinction between both disorders. [For review see 1, 81–85].

ADHD and ASD are more frequent in boys than in girls, and both emerge, at least to a certain degree, at preschool age. Research on the co-occurrence of ASD and ADHD has focused on older children despite the fact that characteristic ADHD and autistic behaviors appear already in early childhood. Clinicians have been able to recognize behavioral characteristics, such as social deficits, in children with ADHD hyperactivity among children with ASD for a long time. However, it is only in recent years that research investigating their comorbidity has burgeoned [82].

For example, the percentage of subjects with ASD meeting the criteria for ADHD was 30–31% for autism [86, 87] and 45% for PDD-NOS [88]. In a parallel way, high levels of autistic traits have been found in populations of children with ADHD [89] and with hyperkinetic disorder [90]; these autistic symptoms in ADHD are higher than in healthy control children [91]. Studies of clinical samples with ASD have also differentiated between ADHD subtypes and observed a prevalence of approximately 20% inattentive and 10% combined ADHD subtype in children with ASD [92]. The overlap was also significant for suspected cases (22% of children with suspected ADHD met criteria for ASD, 41% who met criteria for ASD had suspected ADHD) [93].

Contrary to the common belief that PDD-NOS is heterogeneous, the vast majority (97%) of patients presenting PDD-NOS had the same distinct pattern of symptoms, which consisted of deficiencies in social communication and reciprocity, unaccompanied by relevant repetitive and stereotyped behaviors (RSB). They had comparably severe, but more circumscribed, social communication deficiencies than AD or ASD patients, with lower number of non-social autistic symptoms, e.g., visual-spatial, feeding, and sensory impairments. These subjects seem to present a different type of autism that is more than just a less severe form of one symptomatology continuum. According to the current guidelines for DSM-5, requiring the existence of RSBs for every PDD diagnosis, PDD-NOS should be excluded from the autistic spectrum [94].

Currently, there is increasing interest in investigating the overlap of ADHD and ASD in terms of common neurobiological substrates, associated clinical comorbidities/neuropsychological deficits, neural correlates, and shared genetic susceptibility. Therefore, we should ask some questions: Are both disorders distinct manifestations of the same underlying risk factor(s)? Is it possible that different subtypes within and across disorders do exist, for example, a subtype of ADHD combined with atypical autism or PDD-NOS, which may also show specific underlying risk factors? Do the disorders share neuronal circuitry?

4.1. Associated clinical comorbidities ADHD/ASD

The diagnosis of both ADHD and ASD is based on behavioral symptoms. Both conditions frequently encompass deficiencies in communication with peers, attention, various degrees of restlessness or hyperactivity, and impulsivity. The significance of the presence of clinical overlap regarding the underlying neurobiology and phenotype is not well known. Both syndromes are known to present genetic susceptibility, showing comorbidity across family members as well as within the same individual, and both conditions bring about significant academic, behavioral, adaptive, and emotional impairment at home, at school, and in other places [95].

ADHD behaviors and autistic-like features have been reported to present a positive significant correlation in a sample of community two-year-old children. The correlation between ADHD behaviors and autistic-like features was found lower in older children when compared with young adults ($r=0.23$–0.26 vs. $r=0.48$–0.57), indicating that the covariance of ADHD/ASD increases with age [96]. This can possibly be attributed to the fact that not all the characteristic behavioral types for ADHD and ASD have appeared yet in children, which makes less reliable the measurement of these behaviors when compared to adults.

Most reports using factor analysis to study ASD have found at least one factor connected with RRBs or "non-social" behavior and an independent factor connected with separate social-communicative features [97]. To the best of our knowledge, there are no publications employing factor analysis investigating autistic features in groups of children diagnosed with ADHD and, therefore, whether the existence of ADHD has any effect on the type of autistic traits remains to be elucidated.

Preliminary results suggest that, particularly in young children between 2 and 5 years, a worsening of ASD syndrome in children with ADHD is related to lower full-scale IQ, enhanced anxiety, oppositional and conduct symptoms, general motor problems, and working memory deficits [79, 98]. The risk for increased severity of psychosocial problems increases, as well as greater delays in adaptive functioning [99, 100]. These connections remained after correcting for ADHD severity, indicating that the severity of comorbid autistic traits is regulated independently from ADHD [101].

Existing data indicate that pragmatic language deficiencies seem to be similar both in children in the ASD spectrum and ADHD [102]. Both conditions also often show executive function (EF) attention deficits as well as response inhibition impairment. HFA and ADHD hardly differ in their EF measures. However, the HFA group showed more impairment in planning and cognitive flexibility when compared to the ADHD group [101]. Another study found that children with ASD and children with ADHD were indistinguishable as far as emotional recognition and theory of mind, which further underlines the neuropsychological similarities between these two syndromes [103].

Although social difficulties are not considered central for ADHD diagnosis, the truth is that children with ADHD present significant social problems: they tend to be more frequently rejected by their peers (approximately 50–60%), and they do not have as many friends [104]. Research in the recent years indicates that many individuals with ADHD may present social deficiencies that are in line with those found in ASD. Cantwell [105] described a form of social impairment in ADHD as a "lack of savoir faire," and calculated that this social ingenuousness may be present in about 20% of children and adolescents with ADHD. In children with ADHD as their primary diagnosis, the degree of autistic condition related to the severity of ADHD subtype, subjects with the combined type of ADHD showed the most autistic symptoms [106].

RRBs seem to appear less often than communication and social deficits in ADHD children [83]. Recently, it has been found that the separation between RRB and social-communicative dimensions is not affected by ADHD in children; these results highlight that they are distinct dimensions, as shown in children with ASD and in the general population [97, 107]. These data indicate that the existence (or non-existence) of ADHD in children does not impinge upon social-communicative deficiencies and RRBs expression. This finding also justifies the DSM-5 ′s change from a triad to a dyad of diagnostic impairments [35, 38]. However, there appears to be some overlay across RRB traits and hyperactive-impulsive symptoms in children with ADHD [107].

Therefore, it is essential to know to the extent of hyperactivity/overactivity in its most severe form in young children fosters development of autistic traits such as pragmatic language impairment and RRB traits. Future studies conducted on these issues in light of the new criteria in DSM-5 will be of maximum interest.

4.2. Common risk factors susceptibility in ADHD/ASDS

The etiopathogenesis of NDDs appears to be the result of the combined actions of both environmental and genetic risk factors on the developmental process. NDDs display highly complex pathophysiological processes as well as considerable (epi-) genetic heterogeneity. However, NDDs present some phenotypic overlapping in their traits, show a substantial comorbidity and share a number of environmental and genetic risk factors. The current heritability estimates of ASD and ADHD also imply the relevance of common environmental and disorder-specific risk factors for one or both disorders [108].

4.2.1. Genetic risk factors

In recent years, numerous scientific and technical advances have been developed on the human genome. This has allowed an exponential progress in understanding the molecular pathways of genetic expression, which has revealed the pathogenesis of many diseases. In NDD such as ASD and ADHD, these genetic and epigenetic risk factors are very wide, which makes it difficult to give simple answers at the present time. Up to now, genome-wide association studies (GWASs, genome-wide single nucleotide polymorphism (SNP) association studies and genome-wide copy number variants (CNV) studies), assessments of chromosomal variations, as well as candidate-gene and linkage analyses have revealed an ample spectrum of genes presenting polymorphisms and susceptibility mutations related to ADHD and ASD.

- **Genetic** ASD

We now know that a number of Mendelian syndromes seem to be connected to autism. The most common of these single-gene defects, including CGG repeats within the FMR1 gene as the cause of Fragile X syndrome, mutations in the MECP2 gene in Rett syndrome, tuberous sclerosis, and PTEN mutation, account for but a small minority of cases (for up to 5% of ASDs) [109]. Further, even pooling these syndromes together with cytogenetic abnormalities and other diagnosable medical conditions still only account for <10% of cases. The latest advances made in genetics and technology, mainly the widespread use of molecular techniques by chromosomal Microarray Studies and Next-generation Sequencing, have increased the diagnostic cost-effectiveness of conventional techniques (karyotype, subtelomeric analyses, etc.) from 3–5% to 30–40% in patients with intellectual disability or ASD. Cytogenetic abnormalities at the 15q11-q13 and the 7q22-q37 locus seems most strongly linked to autism. Children presenting congenital abnormalities, dysmorphic traits, mental retardation, or with a family history of developmental disorders are the main population expected to profit from genetic consultation and extensive medical testing. Increased diagnosis of ASD associated with genetic abnormalities has allowed its new specification in DSM-5: "associated with known medical or genetic condition".

However, for children with "nonsyndromic or idiopathic" ASD, the studies of genetic risk factors have been less conclusive. The rate of recurrence of ADS in siblings of affected children is about 2% [110], which is 16 times higher than in the general population but much more reduced than in single-gene diseases. There is a remarkable concordance in monozygotic twins (60% to 95.2%) as well as in dizygotic twins (0% to 10%), indicating a strong genetic component. Nevertheless, despite the high heritability of ASDs (~90%), the genetic substrate of these syndromes still remains to be fully elucidated [111]. So, only a few loci show recurrent mutations, and these recurrent mutations account for only about 1–2% of patients [112]

Recently, rare, highly penetrant single nucleotide variants (SNV) have been receiving increasing attention as potential sources of "idiopathic autism" [113-117]. Furthermore, most of the uncovered genetic basis for ASDs correspond to rare variants, mainly the X-linked DDX53-PTCHD1 locus, as well as CNVs involving numerous ASD genes such as DLGAP2, SHANK2, and SYNGAP1 [118]. But this only represents a selected sample of examples of the numerous studies in this field, in as much as these CNVs are widely distributed across the genome at more than 100 different loci. The statistical distribution of influences across the genome suggests that hundreds of different human genes can mutate to influence autism risk [117]. Present calculations indicate that CNVs and SNVs occurring in X-linked, recessive or dominant models represent a small proportion of ASD (as many as 15% of cases), and common SNPs constitute almost 50% of the diversity in autism. Several GWASs [119–122] have been performed to decipher the genetic etiology of autism that is attributable to common variants (i.e., SNPs), with only a few variants having shown significant associations and replicated in an independent population or in endophenotypes. Examining the data from individual SNPs as well as their overall effect that may be deduced from the allele score results, it is acceptable to assume that common variants are implicated in the risk for ASD but individually considered, their effects are moderate

Furthermore, current progress in next-generation sequencing and exome sequencing has allowed the finding of an astounding amount of de novo mutations that increase the risk for ASD. Some of them are copy number variations or rare mutations in synaptic proteins including ProSAPs/Shanks proteins (with a crucial role in the assembly of the postsynaptic density during synaptogenesis, in synaptic plasticity, and in the regulation of dendritic spine morphology) [123], and neuroligins/neurexins (synaptic cell adhesion molecules that play a pivotal role in the assembling of both inhibitory GABAergic and excitatory glutamatergic synapses in the brain) [124]. It has been proposed that genes implicated in "monogenic" variants of syndromic and nonsyndromic ASD coincide on molecular pathways and mechanisms related to synaptic dysfunction (developmental synaptopathies). These genes would regulate synaptic protein degradation and synthesis including neurotransmitter receptors and postsynaptic scaffold structure, and would be involved in synaptic development, plasticity, and signaling [125].

It is not yet clear whether the same group of genes that are involved in the usual genetic risk factors are the same genes that can also cause ASD through rare, highly penetrant mutations. Besides, despite all the research devoted so far to identifying the biochemical pathways involved in ASDs to unify diverse genes, conclusive, well-replicated evidence is not yet available. The mechanisms by which these mutations produce ASD syndromes have only been very partially elucidated [for review see 126, 127]. Hence, genetic factors in most cases still remain unknown, but may potentially include complicated processes such as gene-environment interaction or gene-gene interaction, or even less penetrant rare variants. In this way, one might conclude that the interplay between a variety of genes can produce "idiopathic" autism but that exposure to environmental modifiers as well as “epigenetic factors” may add up to a varying expression of autistic features [128].

- **ADHD and its candidate genes.**

ADHD clinical expression presents a high degree of heterogeneity and not only genetic but also environmental factors are implicated in its etiology. A meta-analysis of 20 pooled twin studies estimated an average heritability of 76%, suggesting that ADHD is one of the disorders with the strongest genetic component in psychiatry [129]. In spite of its high heritability estimates, identifying the genes responsible for ADHD susceptibility has become a complicated and slow task. In recent years, numerous molecular genetic studies (more than 300, including: genome-wide CNV studies as well as genome-wide and candidate-gene association studies) have been devoted to find susceptibility loci for ADHD. The first genetic studies in this field focused on genes related to the dopaminergic system. However, only small effects were found and they could explain just a small fraction of ADHD heritability. The latest studies are trying to identify new genes and pathways underlying ADHD [for review see 130, 131].

The release of linkage studies has provided more than 100 different regions for ADHD including 6q12, 4q13.1, 16p13, and 17p11. Until now, candidate-gene association studies (CGASs) have been able to propose close to 180 candidate genes. The foremost types of pathways involved are the neurotransmission systems: dopaminergic neurotransmission system (mainly DRD4 and dopamine transporter gene DAT1 or SLC6A3), serotoninergic candidate genes (HTR2A, DDC, and MAOB), and noradrenergic genes (SLC6A2, ADRA1B). Other neurotransmitter transporters, such as serotonin receptors HTR1B, HTR2A, and HTR2C; adrenergic receptors ADRA2A and ADRA2C; and cholinergic receptor CHRNA4 were also on the list of "hot genes". In addition, common variants in 16 genes implicated in the control of neurotransmitter release were evaluated [132], as well as a member of the cytokine family of NTFs (CNTF), 10 genes encoding for four neurotrophins (NTF3, NTF4/5, BDNF, and NGF), and their receptors (CNTFR, NGFR, NTRK1, NTRK2, and NTRK3) [133]. Other promising genes: identification of the *LPHN3* gene, a member of the latrophilin subfamily of G-protein-coupled receptors involved in GABA-ergic neurotransmission. Furthermore, the influence of gender factors such as neurosteroids has been of interest, as well as the STS gene.

The results from the five GWASs of ADHD published so far show 85 genes presenting single nucleotide polymorphisms connected with ADHD at a p value <0.0001. Data showed that 45 out of the 85 top-ranked ADHD candidate genes encoded proteins pertaining to a neurodevelopmental pathway implicated in directed axonal outgrowth. SNPs with nominal associations have been identified for several candidate genes such as CHRNA4, SYT1, ADRB2, DRD2, HTR2A, SLC9A9, SLC6A2, TPH2, and BDNF. SLC9A9 seemed to be the most promising candidate out of these findings [130]. Of the identified genes, some (i.e., BMP2, NRXN1, SERPINI1, NAP5, NOS1, ZNF423, SERPINI1, ERK1, NEDD4L, and CTNNA2) are placed within copy number variations and are therefore duplicated/deleted in ADHD patients. Several network proteins are also directly modulated by stimulants, the most commonly used psychopharmacological treatment for ADHD [134].

- **Shared genetic susceptibility ADHD/ASD**

Numerous family studies have revealed that relatives of patients with either ASD or ADHD frequently display features of the other syndrome [91, 135, 136]. Twin studies have highlighted that quantitative variation in the characteristic behaviors from these two disorders may share genetic risk factors. According to twin studies, which used questionnaire-based data on ADHD and ASD symptoms, about 50–70% of the co-variance of ASD and ADHD symptoms may be explained by shared additive genetic factors [93, 137–139]. Presence of ADHD in the parents can predict ASD in the offspring, but not conversely. Therefore, risk factors at the root of ASD may overlay to a greater extent with ADHD risk factors than vice versa [140].

Even though genetic data support the notion of a shared genetic background for both types of syndromes, not many GWA, candidate gene or linkage studies, have specifically investigated ASD/ADHD co-occurrence. Nonetheless, they are providing some promising, loci SNPs and pleiotropic genes [for review see 1, 83, 84].

- *Linkage and candidate gene association studies:* As potential-specific candidate genes for ADHD (functional), variants predominantly in dopaminergic and serotonergic genes have been described [138, 141]. Several variants in candidate genes of ADHD have also been examined for their potential association with ASD: variants in DAT1, DRD3, DRD4, catechol-O-methyltransferase (COMT), and monoamine oxidase A (MAOA) [142]. Only DRD3 and MAOA variants were nominally associated with ASD symptoms [84].

- *Genome-wide association studies (GWAS):* Interestingly, It has been recently discovered that both rare variations and common polymorphisms in one single gene or genetic locus bear susceptibility for conditions up to now thought to be etiologically and clinically distinct. Results of CNV studies supported evidence of a shared heritability in ADHD and ASD. In ADHD cohorts, CNV enrichment was observed at loci linked with autism. Common genetic risk regions were reported for 1p36, 1q21.1, 15q11.2–q13.1, 15q13.3, 16p11.2, and 22q11, respectively, and the genes CNTN4, SUMF1 (sulfatase modifying factor 1), NLGN1, AUTS2 (autism susceptibility candidate 2), UBE3A, and DPP6 [for review in detail see 81, 84]. ASD/autistic-like traits (ALTs) have been linked to polymorphisms in a number of genes implicated in synaptic physiology in the autism candidate regions (RELN, CNTNAP2, SHANK3, and CDH9/10); however, these findings have not been confirmed in all studies [143].

Thus, the possibility exists that the pathological pathways underlying ASD/ADHD share some genetical background; for example, the serotonin transporter, 5-HTT, has been associated with both conditions [144,145] and SNP (rs4307059), between the genes Cadherin 9 and 10 (*CDH9* and *CDH10*), has been associated with ASD and social interaction impairment [143].

The results of exome sequencing studies support models of significant polygenicity for autism; current studies may allow the identification of these genes and elucidation of the repercussions of their products on brain physiology and development [for review see 2, 109, 112, 120, 146]. In light of research of the etiology of these traits, we may come to understand the high heritability and co-heritability of both disorders. On the other hand, the results cannot rule out that the same genotype may be expressed as a distinct ASD or ADHD phenotype [142].

4.2.2. Non-genetic biological risk factors

Although genetic contributions to autism and ADHD etiology are well accepted, the rising prevalence and inconsistent findings from genetic studies suggest a role for interactions between susceptibility genes and relevance of environmental factors for both disorders. Compared with the magnitude of genetic studies in ASD and ADHD, non-genetic biological risk factors besides the well-known male preponderance in both disorders have rarely been studied. The relationship between sex/gender differences has also attracted a variety of research [147,148].

Among the pregnancy-related risk factors that have been associated simultaneously with ASD and combined ADHD diagnosis or symptoms, are toxic exposures and teratogens (as in the use of valproic acid), maternal diabetes, pre-pregnancy obesity, pre-eclampsia, and viral or bacterial infections; these, however, account for few cases. Similarly, studies on maternal autoimmune disorders during pregnancy have reported different associated disorders (psoriasis with ASD; thyroid antibodies with ADHD). Prenatal inflammation and prematurity must be mentioned, associated simultaneously with both ADHD and autism. [81]. A growing body of literature suggests that certain modifiable risk factors such as maternal metabolic syndrome and intake of certain vitamins such as vitamin D and folic acid either in utero or early life, may be associated with increased risk of autism [24, 149].

Previous research has not been able to prove that administrations of the measles-mumps-rubella vaccine were connected with the **autism upsurge** [23], but it has been suggested that acetaminophen may mediate oxidative stress and neurotoxicity in autism [150, 151], and exposure during pregnancy enhances the probability of appearance of ADHD-like behaviors [152]. These are data from an ecological analysis, not considered optimal as evidence of causality. Nonetheless, there is accumulating clinical and experimental evidence connecting acetaminophen metabolism to biochemical routes known to be relevant for autism and related developmental disorders. Taking into account both ecological and mechanistic evidence, the role of acetaminophen in autism should be formally studied [153].

4.3. Common neurobiological substrates

The human brain is an organ of high biological complexity consisting of many different regions, neural pathways and billions of functionally distinct cells. Moreover, it presents a very complex, highly regulated development that extends for a prolonged period of time and involves deep morphofunctional changes. These processes depend on appropriate gene expression producing unimpaired mRNAs and proteins. Mutations altering gene products or function may favor or lead to psychiatric or neurological disorders [154].

Current knowledge indicates a crucial role for the impairment of strictly regulated and well-determined neurodevelopmental processes in NDDs, principally synapse formation and remodeling and neuronal proliferation and migration, aside from configuration of the neural network, causing impaired connectivity and neurophysiology. Furthermore, the epigenetic mechanisms combined with genetic change may alter many of those developmental events and pathways, thus affecting the vulnerability to, and recovery capacity from, NDDs. As a consequence, disease entities such as ID, ASD, or ADHD that are currently categorically defined, are beginning to be regarded as part of a continuum of neurodevelopmental disorders caused by a large variety of cellular and molecular dysfunctions. As it is, the different types of NDDs present a wide phenotypic variability that could be the result of the combination or interaction of subjacent loss and/or gain of function characteristics [155].

4.3.1. Selective brain imaging findings

As we have already mentioned, the origin of ADHD and ASD is multifactorial, and both the etiology and pathophysiology are as yet incompletely understood. The study of neuropsychological profiles across patients with ASD and ADHD has revealed similarities that, in turn, provided evidence for shared neurobiological substrates. ADHD and autism have been associated with prominent executive dysfunction that can derive from impairment within fronto-parietal and fronto-striatal pathways. The prefrontal cortical circuit is in charge of "top-down" regulation of motivation, inhibition/cognitive control, emotion, and attention via connections with posterior cortical and subcortical nuclei. Inferior and dorsolateral prefrontal cortex (PFC) modulate cognitive/inhibitory control and attention, while ventromedial and orbital nuclei regulate affect and motivation. PFC pathways are highly sensitive to neurochemical conditions, and even modest variations in their neurotransmitter environment (e.g., pharmaceuticals) may cause big effects on their functioning [82, 83].

Neuroimaging work with children with neurodevelopmental syndromes has revealed brain functional and structural impairments in specific pathways regarding this organization [156]. The majority of MRI works investigate just one of the conditions at a time. Several meta-analyses [157–159] have reported decreased brain volume for ADHD patients in most of the studies examined. The main regions affected by volume reductions in ADHD patients were the caudate nucleus, putamen, globus pallidus, and lentiform gyrus. A decrease in total brain volume and grey matter has also been reported in ADHD subjects when compared with standard development control individuals.

It should be pointed out that the development of brain volume alterations differs between ASD and ADHD. In ASD individuals, the brain seems to undergo an accelerated growth stage during the first four years of life, until achieving a plateau level similar to standard development around puberty. However, this is succeeded by a decrease in brain volume towards adulthood in comparison with standard development controls. It is also noteworthy that younger children with autism (2–3 years old) show an increase in white matter (WM) greater than an increase in grey matter (GM) (18% more WM in the cortex and 38% more WM in the cerebellum). This increment in WM found in young children is inverted in 12–16-year-olds with autism whose WM volume is decreased when compared with healthy children [160]. Histopathological analyses have shown that children with autism present an excessive number of neurons in the prefrontal cortex, indicating impairment in prenatal development that can be accompanied by abnormal laminar development and dysmorphic cell types. Qualitative neuropathological developmental changes in 92% of autistic individuals reveal multiregional impairment of maturation, neuronal migration, and neurogenesis in autism, which could be an additional source of heterogeneity in their clinical phenotype [161]. Recent data support a likely failure in the regulation of layer-specific neuronal differentiation and layer formation during the antenatal brain developmental period [162]. Although many cell types and brain areas can be damaged, the main effect of ASD related mutations seems to be on the medium spiny neurons of the striatum and cortical pyramidal neurons and interneurons, suggesting the involvement of corticostriatal and cortical pathways [127].

It seems likely that ASD represents a disorder with more general abnormalities and atypical connectivity compared to ADHD. Functional and structural brain connectivity studies in individuals with these conditions have provided initial evidence regarding apparent overlays in the neuroanatomy of the syndromes. Nonetheless, data have not been consistent across studies, which could explain both the convergent and divergent clinical and behavioral manifestations.

A structural MRI study [163] in 15 children and adolescents with ASD, 15 age-matched ADHD patients and 15 healthy peers described several brain volume variations across both patient groups relative to the control, such as increased GM volume in the left inferior parietal cortex and a decrease in GM in the left medial temporal lobe. Furthermore, they also found an increment in GM volume in the right supramarginal gyrus that was specific for autism. By contrast, Ray et al. [164] suggested that ASD and ADHD display differential large-scale connectivity patterns in intermediate childhood. The ADHD group showed reduced functional connectivity and generalized fractional anisotropy (GFA) inside the rich-club networks, but elevated correlation coefficient values and number of axonal fibers outside the rich-club. Other studies have also identified implication of sub-cortical arousal systems and fronto-parietal attention networks in ADHD pathology, as well as prefrontal cortex malfunction in children with HFA [165].

In a comorbidity study, increasing ASD scores in ADHD were associated with greater GM volume compared with the typically developing population [166]. Recent work by Geurts et al. [167] has found that volume variations in some specific brain areas are often associated with the severity of ASD and ADHD symptoms. Volumetric changes in the left inferior frontal gyrus GM were associated with symptom severity in both conditions. Variations in the left posterior cingulate GM volume appeared to be ASD specific, whereas the bilateral thalamus, left hippocampus/amygdala complex, right temporal frontal cortex, and right parietal lobe seemed to be specifically correlated with ADHD symptom severity This work suggest that ASD and ADHD constitute a continuum expanding into the broad population. Nonetheless, the conclusions were marred by the fact that the directions of the brain-behavior relationships lacked consistency across regions when compared to previous clinical reports.

4.3.2. Neurotransmitter systems

- **Catecholaminergic pathways:** The catecholaminergic pathways have been a usual focus for ADHD neurobiological research on ADHD since they represented the principal target for drug treatments. The neurotrophic factors (NTFs) participate in synapses formation, neuronal survival, and neurodevelopment, whereas the dopaminergic and serotoninergic systems are implicated in neurotransmission, cortical organization, and brain maturation. The "monoamine deficit-hypothesis" of ADHD postulates an imbalance in the interaction of the neurotransmitters dopamine, noradrenaline, and serotonin. The neurotrophic factors as well as the neurotransmitter systems are thought to be good candidates for ASD and frequent allelic variants in the dopamine decarboxylase (DDC) gene may be connected with susceptibility to autism [142].

Notwithstanding, more basic and distal neuronal mechanisms connected with cell functionality and morphology could also play a role, possibly providing an explanation for the coexistence of both specific and diffuse impairment in brain activation patterns and structure [for review in detail see 168]. For both disorders (ADHD/ASD), the association with the serotonergic system is a focus of current research [169].

- **The imbalance of excitatory/inhibitory neurotransmitters**: Excitotoxicity, oxidative stress, and impaired mitochondrial function are mechanisms that potentially serve as convergence points for these genetic, environmental and immunological risk factors in both disorders. A balance between excitatory glutamate and inhibitory GABA neurotransmitter is essential and critical for proper development and functioning of the brain. GABAergic (gamma aminobutyric acid) and glutamatergic interneurons maintain excitability, integrity, and synaptic plasticity. Glutamate is the principal excitatory neurotransmitter in the central nervous system. Glutamate hypersecretion as well as hyperactivity of its NMDA and AMPA receptors are known to produce excitotoxicity via the activation of enzymes that injure cellular components and alter membrane properties and electrochemical gradients [170]. Many synaptic protein genes are linked to the pathogenesis of ASDs, making them prototypical synaptopathologies. For excitatory glutamatergic and inhibitory GABAergic synapses, neurexins (trigger postsynaptic differentiation), and neuroligins (trigger presynaptic differentiation) play a pivotal role in synaptic function, especially at GABAergic synapses. Several works have implicated relative loss of inhibitory GABA with corresponding glutamate-mediated hyper-excitation in the development of ASD and ADHD, which might resemble a common pathological mechanism for these developmental disorders [171].

- **Neurosteroids:** Increasing evidence shows gender differences in the clinical manifestations and pathology of a number neurodevelopmental syndromes, including ADHD and ASD, likely via the effects of sex hormones during critical stages of brain development. Moreover, neuroactive steroids are known to be involved in modulation of neuronal excitability, synaptogenesis, spinogenesis, as well as neuroprotection through binding GABA A-type receptors [172]. Symptoms of cognitive and attention-related deficits have been observed in boys with X-linked ichthyosis caused by a mutation at the STS gene [173]. The STS gene can be found on the distal part of the short arm of the X chromosome (Xp22.3-pter), and a higher prevalence of ADHD in boys than in girls is characteristic of the disorder. This gene is responsible for conversion of the sulfated form of dehydroepiandrosterone (DHEA), known as DHEA-S, to DHEA. Neurosteroids are important neuroactive substrates with demonstrated involvement in ADHD, with significant inverse correlations between levels of both DHEA and pregnenolone and clinical symptomatology [174]. It is interesting to note that the STS gene escapes X-chromosome inactivation, thus a possible differential influence on ADHD in girls should also be considered in future studies.

5. Impact of comorbid ADHD and ASD: A continuum?

Research on co-occurring ADHD and ASD has been limited by diagnostic restraints, since according to DSM-IV, many works have excluded subjects with more than one developmental or psychiatric disorder [175]. The study conducted by Sinzig et al. [176], reveals a large phenotypic overlay between ADHD and ASD. The two identified subtypes, hyperactive-communication impaired and inattentive-stereotyped, follow the DSM classification and could be the manifestation of two distinct neurochemical circuits—dopaminergic and serotonergic—involved in the disorders. In view of this, the division of ASD into two-dimensional scales of social-communication and RRB dimensions, and of ADHD into inattentive and hyperactive-impulsive symptoms has high significance for the classification of developmental conditions.

The debate continues in the literature regarding the clinical implications of these findings; some authors believe that co-occurring symptoms indicate the existence of two distinct syndromes with a common etiology [177], whereas other researches argue that these conditions are better explained as part of one ample spectrum, extending from moderate (ADHD) to more serious (ASD) disability [82]. There is accumulating evidence indicating that ASD and ADHD are at both ends of a continuum, instead of being different entities [139, 178, 179]. It is especially important to establish the diagnosis of co-occurrence of both entities, since symptoms such as limited attentional bias toward people in early development is expected to have deleterious consequences on the appearance of social interaction patterns and the maturation of brain social networks. Further research into the underlying substrates of decreased social attention and its role in the psychopathology of ASD in the first year becomes necessary [57].

6. Therapeutic interventions for co-occurring ADHD and ASD

Recent findings associate co-occurrence of ASD and ADHD in children with poorer quality of life and decreased adaptive functioning in comparison with data from children suffering from ASD only. Adolescents diagnosed with both ASD and ADHD appear to need psychiatric medication more frequently (58%) than young people with ASD (34%) or ADHD (49%) alone. Moreover, co-occurrence of ASD and ADHD seems to make individuals less sensitive to current therapies for either condition than patients with only one of the syndromes [180, 181]. Only a few specific studies on a targeted treatment for children, adolescents, and adults with comorbid ADHD and ASD have been performed to date. The improvement of current treatments will require a better understanding of the mechanisms underlying co-occurrence of ASD and ADHD (for review see 1, 81, 82, 175, 182].

6.1. Psychoeducational/behaviorallybased interventions

ASD/ADHD should allow for more targeted interventions. Parent-mediated interventions can be markedly effective during early infancy, since parental behavior influences both social-communicative learning and the development of executive functions [183]. The identification of common protective factors could be of pivotal importance, since interventions targeting those factors would apply to a wide spectrum of conditions. Furthermore, determining which early risk factors are responsible for cascade effects and which are a mere reflection of the pathological process could be important for identifying the main intervention targets [85]. In preschool children with ASD, the treatment of choice is behaviorally-based early intervention [184, 185]. Likewise, in older schoolage children with ASD, autism-specific social skills training leads to improved social responsiveness [186–188]. Still, despite this treatment intensity, not all children with ASD improve with therapy [189].

By contrast, in a Cochrane Database review of randomized trials studying social skills training for children with ADHD as a standalone therapy or as a complement to pharmacological treatment, the data suggest that there is not enough evidence either to support or refute social skills training for youths with ADHD [190]. In this sense, another meta-analysis [191] compares effect-sizes of psychosocial treatments and methylphenidate and their combination on ADHD, academic functioning, concurrent conduct and oppositional symptoms, and social behaviors.

http://dx.doi.org/10.5772/61400

Both psychosocial treatments and methylphenidate are effective in decreasing ADHD symptoms. However, psychosocial treatment renders more modest results than the other two treatments, and adds no further benefit to methylphenidate for the improvement of teacher-rated oppositional defiant disorder symptoms and ADHD.

In a recent study to evaluate the influence of psychiatric comorbidity on social skill treatment effects in children with ASDs, it was found that while children with ASD and comorbid symptoms of anxiety improved by social skills training, children with ASD and comorbid ADHD did not [180].

6.2. Pharmacological interventions

The clinical impairments associated with ASD are often difficult to alleviate, and are increasingly managed using pharmacologic interventions. While core symptoms of communication deficits and circumscribed interests are difficult to address with medication, other clinical impairments are often targets of treatment, including comorbid anxiety, difficulty with sustained attention, aggressive behaviors, sleep disturbances, and stereotypic movements [for review see 175, 192, 193].

The only medical treatments passed by the United States of America Food and Drug Administration (US FDA) for ASD are the antipsychotic drugs risperidone (Risperdal) and aripiprazole (Abilify). However, these pharmaceuticals only address one symptom connected with ASD, irritability, but none of the core ASD symptoms, and treatments for ASD remain limited. Despite the lack of extensive evidence and unclear effectiveness, examination of prescribing patterns for youth with ASD reveals that pharmacotherapy is very common, and many other medications may be prescribed off-label. The strongest evidence for a positive effect comes from noradrenergic reuptake inhibitors, alpha-adrenergic agonists, antipsychotics, and psychostimulants [193]. Further work is necessary to determine subgroups of children with ASD in which these treatments would be most effective and confirm their efficacy in double-blind, placebo-controlled large-scale multicenter studies.

6.2.1. Antipsychotic medications

The effectiveness of risperidone and aripripazole for irritability associated with autism is supported by several articles reviewing the literature. All conclude that the data supporting effectiveness is strong, while cautioning that behavioral intervention should be tried first, and that side effects including metabolic abnormalities, weight gain, and potential for extrapyramidal side effects warrant caution in their use [192].

6.2.2. Antiepileptic drugs (AEDs)

The impairments in gains of GABAergic transmission could also justify the very high prevalence of epilepsy in autistic patients (about 25%) [194] with respect to the average prevalence of 1% in the general population [195]. Moreover, up to 20–25% of subjects with PDD without epileptic paroxysmal clinical manifestations may present EEG abnormalities, mainly during night polygraphic recordings. A recent large-scale study revealed that ADHD in children is often accompanied by epilepsy; about half (48.3%) of the children with ADHD had abnormal EEG findings and 22.1% of them had epileptiform discharges [196]. Regression in PPDs associated with seizures and epileptiform electroencephalogram correlates have been reported. [197]. Cases of complete recovery or significant improvement following the use of AEDs such as valproate, ethosuximide, clobazam, oxcarbazepine, sulthiame, levetiracetam, topiramate, or lamotrigine in ASD have been reported. It is speculated that the suppression of subclinical epileptiform activity by the early use of AEDs can reverse the changes in behavior, cognition, and language in these patients and, in a similar way, could improve the semiotic nucleus of ASD. Overall, there are few studies and limited evidence for the use of antiepileptic mood stabilizers in improving symptoms of ADHD in children with PDDs and the positive studies in ASD are all uncontrolled. Despite some positive carbamazepine studies in typically developing children, clinical use of these agents for ADHD symptoms in children with PDDs must be considered a personal experiment and should be guided by clinical data [193]. An electroencephalogram (EEG) is recommended in young children with ASD or ADHD, and can help confirm whether a child is having seizures. But even if they are not having seizures, these children may have abnormal EEGs, and additional antiepileptic drug treatment is advisable.

6.2.3. Psychostimulant medications

- **Methylphenidate**: Psychostimulant medication, most commonly the catecholamine agonist methylphenidate (Ritalin®) and OROS-methylphenidate (Concerta®), is the safest and most effective treatment for people with ADHD. The prevalence of stimulant treatment in youth with ASD is 16% [198]. Methylphenidate's mechanism of action implicates the inhibition of catecholamine reuptakes; it acts by arresting the norepinephrine and dopamine transport, leading to elevated concentrations of norepinephrine and dopamine in the synaptic cleft. Methylphenidate is also a 5HT1A receptor agonist. The fMRI analysis showed that methylphenidate significantly enhanced activation in the bilateral inferior frontal cortex/insula during inhibition and time discrimination but had no effect on working memory networks [199]. These areas of the brain are fundamental to cognitive control and the most replicated neurocognitive dysfunctions in ADHD occur here.

Methylphenidate is clearly effective in treating children with ASD and hyperactive symptoms or comorbid ADHD, but a lower daily dose is generally required [200]. However, not all children with ASD benefit from methylphenidate treatment and those who respond present more side effects than children with ADHD. A recent review of randomized and non-randomized trials concluded that, after careful symptom assessment, treatment of comorbid ADHD symptoms with stimulant medication is indicated for youth with ASD [201].

All in all, the stimulants tend to produce highly variable responses in children with PDDs and ADHD symptoms. Such responses range from substantial improvement with minor side effects to more problematic behavior and physical and/or behavioral side effects. Given what we know, stimulants would still be a reasonable first therapeutic choice for previously-untreated children with PDDs and uncomplicated ADHD, even though they do not work as well, on average, as they do in typically-developing children. Any side effects should be reversible on discontinuing the drug. Clinicians should be candid with parents about the lower likelihood of a positive clinical response and elevated risk of adverse events. Treatment should proceed with low initial doses, small dose increments, and a data-based approach. Both clinicians and parents should be prepared to stop the trial if there is clear evidence of behavioral deterioration and/or unacceptable adverse events [193].

- **Lisdexamfetamine dimesylate (LDX)** is a once-a-day medication passed by the US FDA as a possible treatment for ADHD management in children (6–12 years of age) as well as in adults [202]. It is generally employed in children and adolescents with an inadequate response to methylphenidate (MPH) treatment, but to date, there are no studies of its use in ASD.

6.2.4. Nonstimulant Medications

- **Noradrenergic reuptake inhibitor:Atomoxetine** (Strattera®). There is some evidence for effectiveness of non-stimulant ADHD medications in youth with ASD. They also alleviate ADHD symptoms in both disorders; with one randomized controlled trial [203] each for atomoxetine, which showed superiority over placebo. Generally speaking, methylphenidate and atomoxetine present similar efficacy and the same acceptability in treating children and youths with ADHD. Nonetheless, OROS-methylphenidate seems more effective than atomoxetine and can be considered as first line treatment of ADHD in children and adolescents [204].

- **Alpha2 Adrenergic Agonists:** Clonidine and guanfacine act on α2-adrenergic presynaptic receptors to inhibit noradrenergic release and synaptic transmission. Guanfacine has a longer action than clonidine. Guanfacine is an alpha-2 adrenergic agonist traditionally employed for hypertension treatment that has been recently approved to treat ADHD as an extended release formulation. Ituniv® (Shire; Dublin, Ireland) can be used both alone and together with stimulants for the treatment of children with ADHD [205]. Several studies report positive results for guanfacine treatment in children with co-occurring ADHD and ASD symptoms. Reduction in hyperactivity and inattention among cognitively higher-functioning (i.e., not cognitively- impaired) children with ASD was found in a retrospective analysis of 80 clinical patients [206]. Similarly, in an open trial studying children for whom methylphenidate was previously unsuccessful, guanfacine had positive effects on parent- and teacher-rated hyperactivity [207].

- **Selective serotonin reuptake inhibitors (SSRIs):** Although fluoxetine (Prozac) seemed to be beneficial for some autism symptoms, the increase in hyperactivity may be a limiting factor. A Cochrane Review concluded that there was no systematic evidence to support the use of SSRIs to treat ASD [208].

- **Cholinesterase Inhibitors: Donepezil, Galantamine, andRivastigmine Tartrate.** To date, there is no compelling argument for advocating cholinesterase inhibitors for treating either the secondary symptoms or the core features of autism. Rigorous exploratory studies are needed. Galantamine can be of possible benefit for interfering behaviors in children with PDDs, although there was no indication of benefit for ADHD symptoms [209].

- **NMDA receptor Antagonists:**
- **Amantadine**, which impacts the N-methyl-D-aspartate (NMDA) receptor, may act by limiting excitotoxicity of the glutamatergic neurotransmitter system. This receptor class is thought to be essential for modulating synaptic plasticity and represents a new class of pharmacologic targets with the potential to impact neurophysiologic and cognitive functioning. One RCT of amantadine treatment in youth with ASD found improved control of irritability and hyperactivity [210], and another reported beneficial effects for ADHD [211]. Although amantadine is not commonly used, it may be considered when other treatments do not provide adequate symptom control, particularly for distractibility and hyperactivity [192].
- **Memantine** is an NMDA antagonist that is thought to preserve neuronal function. It selectively blocks the excitotoxic effects associated with abnormal glutamate transmission by modulating calcium channels. Treatment with memantine is clearly experimental at this time.
- **Antioxidants:** Oxidative stress and antioxidants can participate in pathobiochemical mechanisms of autism. Chemicals standardly employed for mitochondrial disorder treatment have been shown to alleviate both core and associated ASD symptoms [for review see 212, 213]. Two DBPC studies employing a multivitamin complex containing antioxidants, co-enzyme Q10, vitamin E, and B vitamins showed several improvements in ASD symptoms when compared to placebo administration [214, 215]. Several other antioxidants, including vitamin C [216], methylcobalamin and folinic acid [217–219], N-acetyl-l-cysteine [220–222], ubiquinol [223], and L-carnosine [224], have also caused significant progress in ASD behaviors and may work to enhance mitochondrial function without causing adverse effects; therefore, they could be recommended in younger children.
- **Bioactive lipid mediator:** Many animal and clinical studies have shown the relevance of long-chain polyunsaturated fatty acids (LCPUFA) in neurodegeneration and neural development [225]. Increasing evidence indicates that altered fatty acid metabolic pathways as a result of insufficient dietary supplementation or genetic defects, may affect proper function of the nervous system and contribute to ASDs [226]. Many reports have connected ROS-mediated damage with cell membrane loss of integrity and the consequent elevation of intracellular Ca^{2+}, which, in turn, stimulate a number of Ca^{2+} dependent enzymes such as phospholipases and PKC, damaging membranes directly and initiating the production of lipid mediators, including arachidonic acid and platelet-activating factor (PAF).
- **Omega-3 fatty acids** may improve ADHD symptoms, but large randomized-controlled studies need to be done [227]. A recent Cochrane Review did not find any evidence of effects of Omega-3 fatty acids in ASD [228].
- **Citicoline (cytidine diphosphate-choline):** Although the exact mechanisms by which citicoline produces its neuroprotective effects are unknown, the suggested mechanisms that may explain the neuroprotective actions of citicoline include stimulation of phosphatidylcholine synthesis, prevention of fatty acid release, restoration of Na^+/K^+-ATPase activity, increase of glutathione synthesis and glutathione reductase activity, antiglutamatergic

effects, and preservation of cardiolipin and sphingomyelin levels. Additionally, studies indicate that citicoline supplements elevate dopamine receptor concentrations, and cholinergic neurotransmission, and may possibly be useful in the treatment of ADHD [229, 230].

The relationships between betaine, choline, and energy metabolism in the human species suggest new roles for those molecules. These novel functions may surpass the role of nutrients in gene methylation (epigenetic control.) Research simulating methyl-deficient diets has shown impairment in liver protein synthesis and energy metabolism, as well as muscle disorders and fatty liver. Altered levels of total homocysteine (tHcy) in plasma are a good example of how metabolism can be affected by methyl group deficiency or nutrient supplementations. Both elevation of tHcy and hypomethylation can be reduced if either betaine or choline is available [231].

Citicoline given to youth with ASD led to increased control of hyperactivity, reduced attention deficit and improved communication skills in some children [173]. The use of citicoline in young children (prior to three years), followed by methylphenidate after three years, may be an alternative treatment for community pre-schoolers with ASD.

- **Other Agents:**

- **Oxytocin** has also received attention as a potential treatment for ASD. A recent editorial cautioned against premature clinical use as a treatment modality until more research is done to elucidate long-term implications and potential side effects or problems [232].

- **Opiate Blockers:** Several studies of **naltrexone** were conducted in children with autism, usually with the hope of reducing its core features. No consistent effects were found for autism symptoms. However, what is intriguing is that in all of these studies, reductions in hyperactivity were observed, an often unanticipated finding [211].

- **Sleep medication:** Consistent positive effects for melatonin and clonidine were found in autism. However, given the limited data available, a recent review suggested that the most prudent initial course is to formally evaluate patients for sleep disorders, without clear support for any one particular sleep medication [233].

7. Conclusion: Implications for future research

In light of the new DSM-5 criteria, which allow a dual diagnosis of ASD and ADHD behaviors, further investigation into clinical overlap of these two conditions will possibly enhance our understanding of the etiology/genetics factors and common metabolic pathways of these disorders, and of the appropriate sequence of therapeutic interventions and pharmacological treatment for their co-occurrence, particularly in early preschoolers. It remains to be seen whether early intervention could change the course of "ASD in statu nascendi", interpreted as a continuum with other NDDs such as ADHD or SCD of less than severe character.

8. Nomenclature/abbreviations

AD: Autistic disorder

ADHD: Attention-deficit/hyperactivity disorder

AS: Asperger syndrome

ASD: Autism spectrum disorder

DSM: Diagnostic and statistical manual

HFA: High-functioning autism

GM: Grey matter

NDD: Neurodevelopmental disorders

PFC: Prefrontal cortical circuit

PDD: Pervasive developmental disorder

PDD-NOS: Pervasive developmental disorder-not otherwise specified

RRBs: Restricted repetitive behaviors, interests, and activities

SCD: Social (pragmatic) communication disorder

SNV: Single nucleotide variants

WM: White matter

Author details

Maria Carmen Carrascosa-Romero[1] and Carlos De Cabo- De La Vega[2*]

*Address all correspondence to: carlosd@sescam.jccm.es

1 Department of Neuropediatrics, Albacete General Hospital, Spain

2 Neuropsychopharmacology Unit, Albacete General Hospital, Spain

References

[1] Leitner Y. The co-occurrence of autism and attention deficit hyperactivity disorder in children—what do we know? Front Hum Neurosci. 2014 Apr 29;8:268.

[2] Lichtenstein P, Carlstrom E, Rastam M, Gillberg C, Anckarsater H. The genetics of autism spectrum disorders and related neuropsychiatric disorders in childhood. Am J Psychiatry. 2010;167:1357–1363.

[3] American Psychiatric Association. Diagnostic and statistical manual of mental disorders. Fourth Edition. Washington, DC: American Psychiatric Association; 2000. Text Revision 5.

[4] American Psychiatric Association. The Diagnostic and Statistical Manual of Mental Disorders, Fifth Edition.: DSM 5. American Psychiatric Association, 2013. BookpointUS. [Accessed February 01, 2011] DSM-5 Development. 299.00 Autistic Disorder. 2011. http://www.dsm5.org/ProposedRevisions/Pages/proposedrevision.aspx?rid=94].

[5] Regier DA, Kuhl EA, Kupfer DJ. The DSM-5: Classification and criteria changes. World Psychiatry. 2013;12:92–98.

[6] Regier D, Narrow W, Kuhl E, Kupfer, D. The conceptual development of DSM-V. Am J Psychiatry. 2009 Jun;166(6):645–50.

[7] Swineford LB, Thurm A, Baird G, Wetherby AM, Swedo S. Social (pragmatic) communication disorder: A research review of this new DSM-5 diagnostic category. J Neurodev Disord. 2014;6(1):41.

[8] Adams C. Social communication intervention for school-age children: Rationale and description. Seminars in Speech and Language. 2005;26(3):181–188.

[9] Bloom, P. 2000. How Children Learn the Meanings of Words. Cambridge, MA: MIT Press.

[10] Rapin I, Allen D. Developmental language disorders: Nosologic considerations. Neuropsychol Lang Read Spelling. 1983;155–184.

[11] Bishop D, Rosenbloom L. Classification of childhood language disorders. Lang Dev Disord. 1987;22:61–81.

[12] Bishop DV. Development of the Children's Communication Checklist (CCC): A method for assessing qualitative aspects of communicative impairment in children. J Child Psychol Psychiatry. 1998;39:879–891.

[13] Broeders M, Geurts H, Jennekens-Schinkel A. Pragmatic communication deficits in children with epilepsy. Int J Lang Commun Disord. 2010;45:608–616.

[14] Mackie L, Law J. Pragmatic language and the child with emotional/behavioural difficulties (EBD): A pilot study exploring the interaction between behaviour and communication disability. Int J Lang Commun Disord. 2010;45:397–410.

[15] Ketelaars MP, Cuperus J, Jansonius K, Verhoeven L. Pragmatic language impairment and associated behavioural problems. Int J Lang Commun Disord. 2010;45:204–214.

[16] Bishop DV, Norbury CF. Exploring the borderlands of autistic disorder and specific language impairment: A study using standardised diagnostic instruments. J Child Psychol Psychiatry. 2002;43:917–929.

[17] Geurts HM, Verte S, Oosterlaan J, Roeyers H, Hartman CA, Mulder EJ, et al. Can the Children's Communication Checklist differentiate between children with autism, children with ADHD, and normal controls? J Child Psychol Psychiatry. 2004;45:1437–1453.

[18] Bruce B, Thernlund G, Nettelbladt U. ADHD and language impairment: A study of the parent questionnaire FTF (five to fifteen). Eur Child Adolesc Psychiatry. 2006;15:52–60.

[19] Bellani M, Moretti A, Perlini C, Brambilla P. Language disturbances in ADHD. Epidemiol Psychiatr Sci. 2011;20:311–315.

[20] Dewart H, Summers S. The Pragmatics Profile of Everyday Communication Skills in Children. NFER-Nelson: Slough; 1995.

[21] Regier DA, Narrow WE, Clarke DE, Kraemer HC, Kuramoto SJ, Kuhl EA, et al. DSM-5 field trials in the United States and Canada, Part II: Test-retest reliability of selected categorical diagnoses. Am J Psychiatry. 2013;170:59–70.

[22] Durkin MS, Maenner MJ, Newschaffer CJ, Lee LC, Cunniff CM, Daniels JL, et al. Advanced parental age and risk of autism spectrum disorder. Am J Epidemiol. 2008 Dec 1;168(11):1268–76.

[23] Muhle R, Trentacoste SV, Rapin I. The genetics of autism. Pediatrics. 2004 May; 113(5):e472–86.

[24] Neggers YH. Increasing prevalence, changes in diagnostic criteria, and nutritional risk factors for autism spectrum disorders. ISRN Nutr. 2014 Feb 13;2014: Article ID 514026, 14 pages.

[25] Developmental Disabilities Monitoring Network Surveillance Year 2010 Principal Investigators; Centers for Disease Control and Prevention (CDC). Prevalence of autism spectrum disorder among children aged 8 years—autism and developmental disabilities monitoring network, 11 sites, United States, 2010. MMWR Surveill Summ. 2014 Mar 28;63(2):1–21.

[26] Fombonne E. Epidemiology of pervasive developmental disorders. Pediatr. Res. Jun. 2009;65(6):591–598.

[27] Ganz ML. The lifetime distribution of incremental societal costs of autism. Arch. Pediatr. Adolesc. Med. 2007;161:343–349.

[28] Baird G, Simonoff E, Pickles A, Chandler S, Loucas T, Meldrum D, et al. Prevalence of disorders of the autism spectrum in a population cohort of children in South

Thames: The Special Needs and Autism Project (SNAP). Lancet. 2006 Jul 15;368(9531):210–5.

[29] Kaufmann WE. DSM-5: The New Diagnostic Criteria For Autism Spectrum Disorders.http://www.autismconsortium.org/symposiumfiles/WalterKaufmannAC2012Symposium.pdf.

[30] Huerta M, Bishop SL, Duncan A, Hus V, Lord C. Application of DSM-5 Criteria for Autism Spectrum Disorder to Three Samples of Children With DSM-IV Diagnoses of Pervasive Developmental Disorders. Am J Psychiatry. 2012;169:1056–1064.

[31] Volkmar FR, Reichow B. Autism in DSM-5: Progress and challenges. Mol Autism. 2013 May 15;4(1):13.

[32] Rosenberg RE, Daniels AM, Law JK, Law PA, Kaufmann WE. Trends in autism spectrum disorder diagnoses: 1994-2007. J Autism Dev Disord. 2009 Aug;39(8):1099–111.

[33] Coury DL. DSM-5 and autism spectrum disorders: Implications for families and clinicians. J Dev Behav Pediatr. 2013 Sep;34(7):494–6.

[34] Mahjouri S, Lord CE. What the DSM-5 portends for research, diagnosis, and treatment of autism spectrum disorders. Curr Psychiatry Rep. 2012 Dec;14(6):739-47.

[35] Mandy WP, Charman T, Skuse DH. Testing the construct validity of proposed criteria for DSM-5 autism spectrum disorder. J Am Acad Child Adolesc Psychiatry. 2012 Jan;51(1):41–50.

[36] Miller JN, Ozonoff S. The external validity of Asperger disorder: Lack of evidence from the domain of neuropsychology. J. Abnorm. Psychol. 2000;109:227–238.

[37] Guthrie W, Swineford LB, Wetherby AM, Lord C. Comparison of DSM-IV and DSM-5 factor structure models for toddlers with autism spectrum disorder. J Am Acad Child Adolesc Psychiatry. 2013 Aug;52(8):797–805.e2.

[38] Frazier TW, Youngstrom EA, Speer L, Embacher R, Law P, Constantino J, et al. Validation of proposed DSM 5 criteria for autism spectrum disorder. J Am Acad Child Adolesc Psychiatry. 2012 Jan;51(1):28–40.e3.

[39] Kent RG, Carrington SJ, Le Couteur A, Gould J, Wing L, Maljaars J, Noens I, van Berckelaer-Onnes I, Leekam SR. Diagnosing autism spectrum disorder: Who will get a DSM-5 diagnosis? J Child Psychol Psychiatry. 2013 Nov;54(11):1242–50.

[40] Mattila ML, Kielinen M, Linna SL, Jussila K, Ebeling H, Bloigu R, et al. Autism spectrum disorders according to DSM-IV-TR and comparison with DSM-5 draft criteria: An epidemiological study. J Am Acad Child Adolesc Psychiatry. 2011;50(583–592):e511.

[41] Tanner L. Proposed autism diagnosis changes anger "Aspies". ABC news/health. 2010.

[42] Woods AG, Mahdavi E, Ryan JP. Treating clients with Asperger's syndrome and autism. Child Adolesc Psychiatry Ment Health. 2013 Sep 11;7(1):32.

[43] Huerta M, Bishop SL, Duncan A, Hus V, Lord C: Application of DSM-5 criteria for autism spectrum disorder to three samples of children with DSM-IV diagnoses of pervasive developmental disorders. Am J Psychiatry. 2012;169:1056–1064.

[44] Biederman J, Faraone SV. Attention-deficit hyperactivity disorder. Lancet. 2005;366:237–248.

[45] Sciutto MJ, Eisenberg M. Evaluating the evidence for and against the overdiagnosis of ADHD. J Atten Disord. 2007 Sep;11(2):106–13.

[46] Furman L. What is attention-deficit hyperactivity disorder (ADHD)? J Child Neurol. 2005 Dec;20(12):994–1002.

[47] Bell AS. A critical review of ADHD diagnostic criteria: What to address in the DSM-V. J Atten Disord. 2011 Jan;15(1):3–10.

[48] Coghill D, Seth S. Do the diagnostic criteria for ADHD need to change? Comments on the preliminary proposals of the DSM-5 ADHD and Disruptive Behavior Disorders Committee. Eur Child Adolesc Psychiatry. 2011 Feb;20(2):75–81.

[49] Dalsgaard S. Attention-deficit/hyperactivity disorder (ADHD). Eur Child Adolesc Psychiatry. 2013 Feb;22 Suppl 1:S43–8.

[50] Task Force on Research Diagnostic Criteria: Infancy Preschool. Research diagnostic criteria for infants and preschool children: The process and empirical support. J Am Acad Child Adolesc Psychiatry. 2003 Dec;42(12):1504–12.

[51] Keenan K, Wakschlag LS. Can a valid diagnosis of disruptive behavior disorder be made in preschool children? Am J Psychiatry. 2002 Mar;159(3):351–8.

[52] Astington J W, Baird JA. Why language matters for the theory of mind. New York New York, NY, US: Oxford University Press, Lind, & Bowler. 2009;298–318.

[53] MacWhinney B. Language emergence. In Burmeister P, Piske T, and Rohde A (Eds.). An integrated view of language development. Papers in honor of Henning Wode. WVT *Wissenschaftlicher* Verlag Trier. 2002;17–42.

[54] Daltrozzo J, Conway CM. Neurocognitive mechanisms of statistical-sequential learning: What do event-related potentials tell us? Front Hum Neurosci. 2014 Jun 18;8:437.

[55] Saxton W. 2010. Child Language Acquisition and Development. London: SAGE Publications.

[56] Young GS, Merin N, Rogers SJ, Ozonoff S. Gaze behavior and affect at 6 months: Predicting clinical outcomes and language development in typically developing infants and infants at risk for autism. Developmental Science. 2009;12(5):798–814.

[57] Chawarska K, Macari S, Shic F. Decreased spontaneous attention to social scenes in 6-month-old infants later diagnosed with autism spectrum disorders. Biol Psychiatry. 2013 Aug 1;74(3):195–203.

[58] Wan MW, Green J, Elsabbagh M, Johnson M, Charman T, Plummer F. Parent–infant interaction in infant siblings at risk of autism. Research in Developmental Disabilities. 2012;33(3):924–932.

[59] Gupta AR, State MW. Recent Advances in the Genetics of Autism. Biological Psychiatry. 2007;61(4):429–437.

[60] Zwaigenbaum L, Bryson S, Rogers T, Roberts W, Brian J, Szatmari P. Behavioral manifestations of autism in the first year of life. Int J Dev Neurosci. 2005 Apr-May; 23(2-3):143–52.

[61] Ozonoff S, Iosif AM, Baguio F, Cook IC, Hill MM, Hutman T, et al. A prospective study of the emergence of early behavioral signs of autism. J Am Acad Child Adolesc Psychiatry. 2010 Mar;49(3):256–66.e1-2.

[62] Rozga A, Hutman T, Young GS, Rogers S, Ozonoff S, Dapretto M, et al. Behavioral profiles of affected and unaffected siblings of children with autism: Contribution of measures of mother-infant interaction and nonverbal communication. J Autism Dev Disord. 2011 Mar;41(3):287–301.

[63] Paul R, Fuerst Y, Ramsay G, Chawarska K, Klin A. Out of the mouths of babes: Vocal production in infant siblings of children with ASD. J Child Psychol Psychiatry. 2011 May;52(5):588–98.

[64] Ozonoff S, Macari S, Young GS, Goldring S, Thompson M, Rogers SJ. Atypical object exploration at 12 months of age is associated with autism in a prospective sample. Autism. 2008;12(5):457–472.

[65] Nadig AS, Ozonoff S, Young GS, Rozga A, Sigman M, Rogers SJ. A prospective study of response to name in infants at risk for autism. Arch Pediatr Adolesc Med. 2007 Apr;161(4):378–83.

[66] Hutman T, Rozga A, DeLaurentis AD, Barnwell JM, Sugar CA, Sigman M. Response to distress in infants at risk for autism: A prospective longitudinal study. J Child Psychol Psychiatry. 2010 Sep;51(9):1010–20.

[67] Hutman T, Rozga A, DeLaurentis A, Sigman M, Dapretto M. Infants' pre-empathic behaviors are associated with language skills. Infant Behav Dev. 2012 Jun;35(3):561–9.

[68] Luyster R, Gotham K, Guthrie W, Coffing M, Petrak R, Pierce K, et al. The Autism Diagnostic Observation Schedule—Toddler Module: A new module of a standardized diagnostic measure for autism spectrum disorders. J Autism Dev Disord. 2009;39(9):1305–1320.

[69] Lord C, Rutter M, Le Couteur A. Autism Diagnostic Interview-Revised: A revised version of a diagnostic interview for caregivers of individuals with possible pervasive developmental disorders. J Autism Dev Disord. 1994 Oct;24(5):659–85.

[70] Curenton SM, Justice LM. African American and Caucasian preschoolers' use of decontextualized language: Literate language features in oral narratives. Lang Speech Hear Serv Sch. 2004 Jul;35(3):240–53.

[71] Nelson CA. Commentary: Developmental origins of autism and ADHD—a commentary on Johnson, et al. J Child Psychol Psychiatry. 2015 Mar;56(3):248–50.

[72] Casey BJ, Tottenham N, Liston C, Durston S. Imagining the developing brain: What have we learned about cognitive development? Trends Cogn Sci. 2005 Mar;9(3):104–10.

[73] Eisenberg N, Spinrad TL, Eggum ND. Emotion-related self-regulation and its relation to children's maladjustment. Annu Rev Clin Psychol. 2010;6:495–525

[74] Wilens TE, Biederman J, Brown S, Tanguay S, Monuteaux MC, Blake C, et al. Psychiatric comorbidity and functioning in clinically referred preschool children and school-age youths with ADHD. J Am Acad Child Adolesc Psychiatry. 2002 Mar;41 (3):262–8.

[75] Lahey BB, Pelham WE, Loney J, Lee SS, Willcutt E. Instability of the DSM-IV subtypes of ADHD from preschool through elementary school. Arch Gen Psychiatry. 2005 Aug;62 (8):896–902.

[76] Martel MM, Roberts B, Gremillion ML. Emerging control and disruptive behavior disorders during early childhood. Dev Neuropsychol. 2013;38(3):153–66.

[77] Oliver BR, Barker ED, Mandy WP, Skuse DH, Maughan B. Social cognition and conduct problems: A developmental approach. J Am Acad Child Adolesc Psychiatry. 2011 Apr;50(4):385–94.

[78] Polderman TJ, Hoekstra RA, Vinkhuyzen AA, Sullivan PF, van der Sluis S, Posthuma D. Attentional switching forms a genetic link between attention problems and autistic traits in adults. Psychol Med. 2013 Sep;43(9):1985–96.

[79] Sinzig J, Morsch D, Lehmkuhl G. Do hyperactivity, impulsivity inattention have an impact on the ability of facial affect recognition in children with autism and ADHD? Eur. Child Adolesc. Psychiatry. 2008;17:63–72.

[80] Uekermann J, Kraemer M, Abdel-Hamid M. Schimmelmann B G, Hebebrand J, Daum I, et al. Social cognition in attention-deficit hyperactivity disorder (ADHD). Neurosci. Biobehav. Rev. 2010;34:734–743.

[81] Taurines R, Schwenck C, Westerwald E, Sachse M, Siniatchkin M, Freitag C. ADHD and autism: Differential diagnosis or overlapping traits? A selective review. Atten Defic Hyperact Disord. 2012 Sep;4(3):115–39.

[82] Gargaro BA, Rinehart NJ, Bradshaw JL, Tonge BJ, Sheppard DM. Autism and ADHD: How far have we come in the comorbidity debate? Neurosci Biobehav Rev 2011;35:1081–1098.

[83] Rommelse NN, Geurts HM, Franke B, Buitelaar JK, Hartman CA. A review on cognitive and brain endophenotypes that may be common in autism spectrum disorder and attentiondeficit/hyperactivity disorder and facilitate the search for pleiotropic genes. Neurosci Biobehav Rev. 2011;35:1363–1396.

[84] Rommelse NN, Franke B, Geurts HM, Hartman CA, Buitelaar JK. Shared heritability of attention-deficit/hyperactivity disorder and autism spectrum disorder. Eur Child Adolesc Psychiatry. 2010;19:281–295.

[85] Johnson MH, Gliga T, Jones E, Charman T. Annual Research Review: Infant development, autism, and ADHD—early pathways to emerging disorders. J Child Psychol Psychiatry. 2015 Mar;56(3):228–47.

[86] Simonoff E, Pickles A, Charman T, Chandler S, Loucas T, Baird G. Psychiatric disorders in children with autism spectrum disorders: Prevalence, comorbidity, and associated factors in a population-derived sample. J Am Acad Child Adolesc Psychiatry. 2008;47:921–929.

[87] Leyfer OT, Folstein SE, Bacalman S, Davis NO, Dinh E, Morgan J, et al. Comorbid psychiatric disorders in children with autism: Interview development and rates of disorders. J Autism Dev Disord. 2006;36:849–861.

[88] de Bruin EI, Ferdinand RF, Meester S, de Nijs PF, Verheij F. High rates of psychiatric co-morbidity in PDD-NOS. J Autism Dev Disord. 2007;37:877–886.

[89] Clark T, Feehan C, Tinline C, Vostanis P. Autistic symptoms in children with attention deficithyperactivity disorder. Eur Child Adolesc Psychiatry. 1999;8:50–55.

[90] Santosh PJ, Mijovic A. Social impairment in hyperkinetic disorder–relationship to psychopathology and environmental stressors. Eur Child Adolesc Psychiatry. 2004;13:141–150.

[91] Mulligan A, Anney RJ, O'Regan M, Chen W, Butler L, et al. Autism symptoms inattention-deficit/hyperactivity disorder: A familial trait which correlates with conduct, oppositional defiant, language, and motor disorders. J Autism Dev Disord. 2009;39:197–209.

[92] Gjevik E, Eldevik S, Fjaeran-Granum T, Sponheim E (2011) Kiddie-SADS reveals high rates of DSM-IV disorders in children and adolescents with autism spectrum disorders. J Autism Dev Disord. 41:761–769.

[93] Ronald A, Simonoff E, Kuntsi J, Asherson P, Plomin R. Evidence for overlapping genetic influences on autistic and ADHD behaviours in a community twin sample. J Child Psychol Psychiatry. 2008 May;49(5):535–42.

[94] Mandy W, Charman T, Gilmour J, Skuse D. Toward specifying pervasive developmental disorder-not otherwise specified. Autism Res. 2011 Apr;4(2):121–31.

[95] Rao PA, Landa RJ. Association between severity of behavioral phenotype and comorbid attention deficithyperactivity disorder symptoms in children with autism spectrum disorders. Autism. 2013;18:272–280.

[96] Ronald A, Edelson LR, Asherson P, Saudino KJ. Exploring the relationship between autistic-like traits and ADHD behaviors in early childhood: Findings from a community twin study of 2-yearolds. J Abnorm Child Psychol. 2010;38:185–196.

[97] Mandy WPL, Skuse DH. Research Review: What is the association between the social-communication element of autism and repetitive interests, behaviours and activities? J Child Psychol Psychiatry. 2008;49(8):795–808.

[98] Sikora DM, Vora P, Coury DL, Rosenberg D. Attention deficit/hyperactivity disorder symptoms, adaptive functioning, and quality of life in children with autism spectrum disorder. Pediatrics. 2012;130(Suppl. 2):S91–S97.

[99] Gadow KD, DeVincent CJ, Pomeroy J, Azizian A. Psychiatric symptoms in preschool children with PDD and clinic and comparison samples. J. Autism Dev. Disord. 2004;34: 379–393.

[100] Yerys BE, Wallace GL, Sokoloff JL, Shook DA, James JD, Kenworthy L. Attention deficit/hyperactivity disorder symptoms moderate cognition and behavior in children with autism spectrum disorders. Autism Res. 2009;2:322–333.

[101] Cooper M, Martin J, Langley K, Hamshere M, Thapar A. Autistic traits in children with ADHD index clinical and cognitive problems. Eur Child Adolesc Psychiatry. 2014 Jan;23(1):23–34.

[102] Bishop DV, Baird G. Parent and teacher report of pragmatic aspects of communication: Use of the children's communication checklist in a clinical setting. Dev. Med. Child Neurol. 2001;43:809–818.

[103] Buitelaar JK, van der Wees M, Swaab-Barneveld H, van der Gaag RJ. Verbal memory and performance IQ predict theory of mind and emotion recognition ability in children with autistic spectrum disorders and in psychiatric control children. J. Child Psychol. Psychiatry. 1999;40:869–881.

[104] Barkley RA, DuPaul GJ, McMurray MB. Comprehensive evaluation of attention deficit disorder with and without hyperactivity as defined by research criteria. J. Consult. Clin. Psychol.1990;58:775–789.

[105] Cantwell DP. Attention deficit disorder: A review of the past 10 years. J. Am. Acad. Child Adolesc. Psychiatry. 1996;35:978–987.

[106] Reiersen AM, Constantino JN, Volk HE, Todd RD. Autistic traits in a population-based ADHD twin sample. J. Child Psychol. Psychiatry. 2007;48:464–472.

[107] Martin J, Hamshere ML, O'Donovan MC, Rutter M, Thapar A. Factor structure of autistic traits in children with ADHD. J Autism Dev Disord. 2014 Jan;44(1):204–15.

[108] Kiser DP, Rivero O, Lesch KP. Annual Research Review: The (epi)genetics of neurodevelopmental disorders in the era of whole-genome sequencing—unveiling the dark matter. J Child Psychol Psychiatry. 2015 Feb 11. doi: 10.1111/jcpp.12392. [Epub ahead of print].

[109] Carter MT, Scherer SW. Autism spectrum disorder in the genetics clinic: A review. Clin Genet. 2013;83:399–407.

[110] Ozonoff S, Young GS, Carter A, Messinger D, Yirmiya N, Zwaigenbaum L, et al. Recurrence risk for autism spectrum disorders: A baby siblings research consortium study. Pediatrics. 2011;128:e488–e495.

[111] Bailey A, Le Couteur A, Gottesman I, Bolton P, Simonoff E, Yuzda E, et al. Autism as a strongly genetic disorder: Evidence from a British twin study. Psychol Med. 1995;25(1):63–77.

[112] Abrahams BS, Geschwind DH. Advances in autism genetics: On the threshold of a new neurobiology. Nat. Rev. Genet. 2008;9:341–355.

[113] Iossifov I, Ronemus M, Levy D, Wang Z, Hakker I, Rosenbaum J, De novo gene disruptions in children on the autistic spectrum. Neuron. 2012;74:285–99.

[114] Lim ET, Raychaudhuri S, Sanders SJ, Stevens C, Sabo A, MacArthur DG, Rare complete knockouts in humans: Population distribution and significant role in autism spectrum disorders. Neuron. 2013;77:235–42.

[115] Neale BM, Kou Y, Liu L, Ma'ayan A, Samocha KE, Sabo A. Patterns and rates of exonic de novo mutations in autism spectrum disorders. Nature. 2012;485:242–5.

[116] O'Roak BJ, Deriziotis P, Lee C, Vives L, Schwartz JJ, Girirajan S, Exome sequencing in sporadic autism spectrum disorders identifies severe de novo mutations. Nat Genet. 2011;43:585–9.

[117] Sanders SJ, Murtha MT, Gupta AR, Murdoch JD, Raubeson MJ, Willsey AJ. De novo mutations revealed by whole-exome sequencing are strongly associated with autism. Nature. 2012;485:237–41.

[118] Pinto D, Pagnamenta AT, Kle Li, Anney R, Merico D. Regan R, et al. Functional Impact of Global Rare Copy Number Variation in Autism Spectrum Disorder. Nature. 2010 Jul 15;466(7304):368–72.

[119] Carayol J, Schellenberg GD, Dombroski B, Amiet C, Génin B, Fontaine K, et al. A scoring strategy combining statistics and functional genomics supports a possible role for common polygenic variation in autism. Front Genet. 2014 Feb 18;5:33

[120] Pinto D, Delaby E, Merico D, Barbosa M, Merikangas A, Klei L, et al. Convergence of genes and cellular pathways dysregulated in autism spectrum disorders. Am J Hum Genet. 2014 May 1;94(5):677–94.

[121] Anney R, Klei L, Pinto D, Regan R, Conroy J, Magalhaes TR, et al. A genome-wide scan for common alleles affecting risk for autism. Hum Mol Genet. 2010 Oct 15;19(20):4072–82.

[122] Anney R, Klei L, Pinto D, Almeida J, Bacchelli E, Baird G, et al. Individual common variants exert weak effects on the risk for autism spectrum disorderspi. Hum Mol Genet. 2012 Nov 1;21(21):4781–92.

[123] Boeckers TM, Bockmann J, Kreutz MR, Gundelfinger ED. ProSAP/Shank proteins—a family of higher order organizing molecules of the postsynaptic density with an emerging role in human neurological disease. J Neurochem. 2002 Jun;81(5):903–10.

[124] Südhof TC. Neuroligins and neurexins link synaptic function to cognitive disease. Nature. 2008;455:903–911.

[125] Ebrahimi-Fakhari D, Sahin M. Autism and the synapse: Emerging mechanisms and mechanism-based therapies. Curr Opin Neurol. 2015 Feb 19. [Epub ahead of print].

[126] Won H, Mah W, Kim E. Autism spectrum disorder causes, mechanisms, and treatments: Focus on neuronal synapses. Front Mol Neurosci. 2013 Aug 5;6:19.

[127] Chang J, Gilman SR, Chiang AH, Sanders SJ, Vitkup D. Genotype to phenotype relationships in autism spectrum disorders. Nat Neurosci. 2015 Feb;18(2):191–8.

[128] Stein JL, Parikshak NN, Geschwind DH. Rare inherited variation in autism: Beginning to see the forest and a few trees. Neuron. 2013;77:209–11.

[129] Faraone SV, Perlis RH, Doyle AE, Smoller JW, Goralnick JJ, Holmgren MA, et al. Molecular genetics of attention-deficit/hyperactivity disorder. Biol Psychiatry. 2005 Jun 1;57(11):1313–23.

[130] Akutagava-Martins GC, Salatino-Oliveira A, Kieling CC, Rohde LA, Hutz MH. Genetics of attention-deficit/hyperactivity disorder: Current findings and future directions. Expert Rev Neurother. 2013 Apr;13(4):435–45.

[131] Li Z, Chang SH, Zhang LY, Gao L, Wang J. Molecular genetic studies of ADHD and its candidate genes: A review. Psychiatry Res. 2014 Sep 30;219(1):10–24.

[132] Sánchez-Mora C, Cormand B, Ramos-Quiroga JA, Hervás A, Bosch R, Palomar G. Evaluation of common variants in 16 genes involved in the regulation of neurotransmitter release in ADHD. Eur Neuropsychopharmacol. 2013 Jun;23(6):426–35.

[133] Ribasés M, Hervás A, Ramos-Quiroga JA, Bosch R, Bielsa A, Gastaminza X, et al. Association study of 10 genes encoding neurotrophic factors and their receptors in adult and child attention-deficit/hyperactivity disorder. Biol Psychiatry. 2008 May 15;63(10):935–45.

[134] Poelmans G, Pauls DL, Buitelaar JK, Franke B. Integrated genome-wide association study findings: Identification of a neurodevelopmental network for attention deficit hyperactivity disorder. Am J Psychiatry. 2011 Apr;168(4):365–77.

[135] Nijmeijer JS, Hoekstra PJ, Minderaa RB, Buitelaar JK, Altink ME, Buschgens CJ, et al. PDD symptoms in ADHD, an independent familial trait? J Abnorm Child Psychol. 2009;37:443–453.

[136] Smalley SL, Kustanovich V, Minassian SL, Stone JL, Ogdie MN, McGough JJ, et al. Genetic linkage of attention-deficit/hyperactivity disorder on chromosome 16p13, in a region implicated in autism. Am J Hum Genet. 2002 Oct;71(4):959–63.

[137] Reiersen AM, Constantino JN, Grimmer M, Martin NG, Todd RD. Evidence for shared genetic influences on self-reported ADHD and autistic symptoms in young adult Australian twins. Twin Res Hum Genet. 2008;11:579–585.

[138] Franke B, Neale B, Faraone S. Genome-wide association studies in ADHD. Hum Genet 2009;126:13–50.

[139] Constantino JN. Todd RD. Autistic traits in the general population: A twin study. Archives of General Psychiatry. 2003;60:524–530.

[140] van Steijn DJ, Richards JS, Oerlemans AM, de Ruiter SW, van Aken MA, Franke B, et al. The co-occurrence of autism spectrum disorder and attention-deficit/hyperactivity disorder symptoms in parents of children with ASD or ASD with ADHD. J Child Psychol Psychiatry. 2012 Sep;53(9):954–63.

[141] Gizer IR, Ficks C, Waldman ID. Candidate gene studies of ADHD: A meta-analytic review. Hum Genet. 2009;126:51–90.

[142] Toma C, Hervás A, Balmaña N, Salgado M, Maristany M, Vilella E, et al. Neurotransmitter systems and neurotrophic factors in autism: Association study of 37 genes suggests involvement of DDC. World J Biol Psychiatry. 2013 Sep;14(7):516–27.

[143] Jonsson L, Zettergren A, Pettersson E, Hovey D, Anckarsäter H, Westberg L, et al. Association study between autistic-like traits and polymorphisms in the autism candidate regions RELN, CNTNAP2, SHANK3, and CDH9/10. Mol Autism. 2014 Dec 16;5(1):55.

[144] Manor I, Eisenberg J, Tyano S, Sever Y, Cohen H, Ebstein RP, et al. Family-based association study of the serotonin transporter promoter region polymorphism (5-HTTLPR) in attention deficit hyperactivity disorder. Am. J. Med. Genet. 2001;105:91–95.

[145] Cook EH, Leventhal BL. The serotonin system in autism. Curr. Opin. Pediatr. 1996;8:348–354.

[146] Freitag CM. The genetics of autistic disorders and its clinical relevance: A review of the literature. Mol Psychiatry. 2007 Jan;12(1):2–22.

[147] Frazier TW, Georgiades S, Bishop SL, Hardan AY. Behavioral and cognitive characteristics of females and males with autism in the Simons Simplex Collection. J Am Acad Child Adolesc Psychiatry. 2014 Mar;53(3):329–40.

[148] Lai M, Lombardo MV, Auyeung B, Chakrabarti B, Baron-Cohen S. Sex/Gender Differences and Autism: Setting the Scene for Future Research. J Am Acad Child Adolesc Psychiatry. 2015 Jan;54(1):11–24.

[149] Newschaffer CJ, Croen LA, Daniels J, Giarelli E, Grether JK, Levy SE, et al. The epidemiology of ASD. Annu Rev Public Health. 2007;28:235–58.

[150] Ghanizadeh A. Acetaminophen may mediate oxidative stress and neurotoxicity in autism. Med Hypotheses. 2012 Feb;78(2):351.

[151] Good P. Did acetaminophen provoke the autism epidemic? Altern Med Rev. 2009 Dec;14(4):364–72.

[152] Thompson JM, Waldie KE, Wall CR, Murphy R, Mitchell EA. ABC study group. Associations between acetaminophen use during pregnancy and ADHD symptoms measured at ages 7 and 11 years. PLoS One. 2014 Sep 24;9(9):e108210.

[153] Bauer AZ, Kriebel D. Prenatal and perinatal analgesic exposure and autism: An ecological link. Environ Health. 2013 May 9;12:41.

[154] Tebbenkamp AT, Willsey AJ, State MW, Sestan N. The developmental transcriptome of the human brain: Implications for neurodevelopmental disorders. Curr Opin Neurol. 2014 Apr;27(2):149–56.

[155] Kiser DP, Rivero O, Lesch KP. Annual Research Review: The (epi)genetics of neurodevelopmental disorders in the era of whole-genome sequencing—unveiling the dark matter. J Child Psychol Psychiatry. 2015 Feb 11. doi: 10.1111/jcpp.12392. [Epub ahead of print].

[156] Arnsten AF, Rubia K. Neurobiological circuits regulating attention, cognitive control, motivation, and emotion: Disruptions in neurodevelopmental psychiatric disorders. Am Acad Child Adolesc Psychiatry. 2012 Apr;51(4):356–67.

[157] Valera EM, Faraone SV, Murray KE, Seidman LJ. Meta-analysis of structural imaging findings in attention-deficit/hyperactivity disorder. Biol Psychiatry. 2007;61:1361–1369.

[158] Frodl T, Skokauskas N. Meta-analysis of structural MRI studies in children and adults with attention deficit hyperactivity disorder indicates treatment effects. Acta Psychiatr Scand. 2012;125:114–126.

[159] Nakao T, Radua J, Rubia K, Mataix-Cols D. Gray matter volume abnormalities in ADHD: Voxel-based meta-analysis exploring the effects of age and stimulant medication. Am J Psychiatry. 2011;168:1154–1163.

[160] Courchesne E, Karns CM, Davis HR, Ziccardi R, Carper RA, Tigue ZD, et al. Unusual brain growth patterns in early life in patients with autistic disorder: An MRI study. Neurology 2001 Jul 24;57(2):245–54.

[161] Wegiel J, Kuchna I, Nowicki K, Imaki H, Wegiel J, Marchi E, et al. The neuropathology of autism: defects of neurogenesis and neuronal migration, and dysplastic changes. Acta Neuropathol. 2010 Jun;119(6):755–70.

[162] Stoner R, Chow ML, Boyle MP, Sunkin SM, Mouton PR, Roy S, et al. Patches of disorganization in the neocortex of children with autism. N Engl J Med. 2014 Mar 27;370(13):1209–19.

[163] Brieber S, Neufang S, Bruning N, Kamp-Becker I, Remschmidt H, Herpertz-Dahlmann B, et al. Structural brain abnormalities in adolescents with autism spectrum disorder and patients with attention deficit/hyperactivity disorder. J Child Psychol Psychiatry. 2007;48:1251–1258.

[164] Ray S, Miller M, Karalunas S, Robertson C, Grayson DS, Cary RP, et al. Structural and functional connectivity of the human brain in autism spectrum disorders and attention-deficit/hyperactivity disorder: A rich club-organization study. Hum Brain Mapp. 2014 Dec;35(12):6032–48.

[165] Johnson KA, Robertson IH, Kelly SP, Silk TJ, Barry E, Dáibhis A, et al. Dissociation in performance of children with ADHD and high-functioning autism on a task of sustained attention. Neuropsychologia. 2007 Jun 11;45(10):2234–45.

[166] O'Dwyer L, Tanner C, van Dongen EV, Greven CU, Bralten J, Zwiers MP, et al. Brain volumetric correlates of autism spectrum disorder symptoms in attention deficit/hyperactivity disorder. PLoS One. 2014 Jun 30;9(6):e101130.

[167] Geurts HM, Ridderinkhof KR, Scholte HS. The relationship between grey-matter and ASD and ADHD traits in typical adults. J Autism Dev Disord. 2013;43:1630–1641.

[168] Purper-Ouakil D, Ramoz N, Lepagnol-Bestel AM, Gorwood P, Simonneau M. Neurobiology of attention deficit/hyperactivity disorder. Pediatr Res. 2011 May;69(5 Pt 2): 69R–76R.

[169] Sinzig J, Lehmkuhl G. What do we know about the serotonergic genetic heterogeneity in attention-deficit/hyperactivity and autistic disorders? Psychopathology. 2007;40(5):329–37.

[170] Essa MM, Braidy N, Vijayan KR, Subash S, Guillemin GJ. Excitotoxicity in the pathogenesis of autism. Neurotox Res. 2013 May;23(4):393–400.

[171] Purkayastha P, Malapati A, Yogeeswari P, Sriram D. A Review on GABA/Glutamate Pathway for Therapeutic Intervention of ASD and ADHD. Curr Med Chem. 2015 Feb 9. [Epub ahead of print].

[172] Fanelli F, Marino R, Keller F. Focusing on the interactions between the GABAergic system and neurosteroids in neurodevelopmental disorders. Curr Pharm Des. 2013;19(36):6491–8.

[173] Carrascosa-Romero MC, Suela J, Alfaro-Ponce B, Cepillo-Boluda AJ. X-chromosome-linked ichthyosis associated to epilepsy, hyperactivity, autism and mental retardation, due to the Xp22.31 microdeletion. Rev Neurol. 2012 Feb 16;54(4):241–8.

[174] Strous RD, Spivak B, Yoran-Hegesh R, Maayan R, Averbuch E, Kotler M, et al. Analysis of neurosteroid levels in attention deficit hyperactivity disorder. Int J Neuropsychopharmacol. 2001 Sep;4(3):259–64.

[175] Davis NO, Kollins SH. Treatment for co-occurring attention deficit/hyperactivity disorder and autism spectrum disorder. Neurotherapeutics. 2013;9:518–530.

[176] Sinzig J, Walter D, Doepfner M. Attention deficit/hyperactivity disorder in children and adolescents with autism spectrum disorder: symptom or syndrome? J Atten Disord. 2009 Sep;13(2):117–26.

[177] Grzadzinski R, Di Martino A, Brady E, Mairena MA, O'Neale M, Petkova E, et al. Examining autistic traits in children with ADHD: Does the autism spectrum extend to ADHD? J Autism Dev Disord. 2011 Sep;41(9):1178–91.

[178] Larsson H, Anckarsater H, Ra˚stam M, Chang Z, Lichtenstein P. Childhood attention-deficit hyperactivity disorder as an extreme of a continuous trait: A quantitative genetic study of 8,500 twin pairs. Journal of Child Psychology and Psychiatry. 2011;53(1):73–80.

[179] Levy F, Hay DA, McStephen M, Wood C, Waldman I. Attention-deficit hyperactivity disorder: A category or a continuum? Genetic analysis of a large-scale twin study. J Am Acad Child Adolesc Psychiatry. 1997 Jun;36(6):737–44.

[180] Antshel KM, Polacek C, McMahon M, Dygert K, Spenceley L, Dygert L, et al. Comorbid ADHD and anxiety affect social skills group intervention treatment efficacy in children with autism spectrum disorders. J Dev Behav Pediatr. 2011;32:439–446.

[181] Research Units on Pediatric Psychopharmacology (RUPP) Autism Network. Randomized, controlled, crossover trial of methylphenidate in pervasive developmental disorders with hyperactivity. Arch Gen Psychiatry. 2005;62:1266–1274.

[182] Murray MJ. Attention-deficit/Hyperactivity Disorder in the context of Autism spectrum disorders. Curr Psychiatry Rep. 2010 Oct;12(5):382–8.

[183] McConachie H, Diggle T. Parent implemented early intervention for young children with autism spectrum disorder: A systematic review. J Eval Clin Pract. 2007 Feb; 13(1):120–9.

[184] Freitag CM. Empirically based early intervention programs for children with autistic disorders—a selective literature review. Z Kinder Jugendpsychiatr Psychother. 2010;38:247–256.

[185] Ospina MB, Krebs SJ, Clark B, Karkhaneh M, Hartling L, Tjosvold L, et al. Behavioural and developmental interventions for autism spectrum disorder: A clinical systematic review. PLoS One. 2008;3:e3755.

[186] White SW, Keonig K, Scahill L. Social skills development in children with autism spectrum disorders: a review of the intervention research. J Autism Dev Disord. 2007;37:1858–1868.

[187] Kasari C, Rotheram-Fuller E, Locke J, Gulsrud A. Making the connection: Randomized controlled trial of social skills at school for children with autism spectrum disorders. J Child Psychol Psychiatry. 2012;53:431–439.

[188] Llaneza DC, DeLuke SV, Batista M, Crawley JN, Christodulu KV, Frye CA. Communication, interventions, and scientific advances in autism: A commentary. Physiol Behav. 2010 Jun 1;100(3):268–76.

[189] Howlin P. The effectiveness of interventions for children with autism. J Neural Transm. 2005;Supp 101–119.

[190] Storebø OJ, Skoog M, Damm D, Thomsen PH, Simonsen E, Gluud C. Social skills training for Attention Deficit Hyperactivity Disorder (ADHD) in children aged 5 to 18 years. Cochrane Database Syst Rev. 2011 Dec 7;(12):CD008223.

[191] Van der Oord S, Prins PJ, Oosterlaan J, Emmelkamp PM. Efficacy of methylphenidate, psychosocial treatments and their combination in school-aged children with ADHD: A meta-analysis. Clin Psychol Rev. 2008 Jun;28(5):783–800.

[192] Kodish I, Rockhill CM, Webb SJ. ASD: Psychopharmacologic Treatments and Neurophysiologic Underpinnings. Curr Top Behav Neurosci. 2014;21:257–75.

[193] Aman MG, Farmer CA, Hollway J, Arnold LE. Treatment of inattention, overactivity, and impulsiveness in autism spectrum disorders. Child Adolesc Psychiatr Clin N Am. 2008 Oct;17(4):713–38.

[194] Viscidi EW, Triche EW, Pescosolido MF, McLean RL, Joseph RM, Spence SJ, et al. Clinical characteristics of children with autism spectrum disorder and co-occurring epilepsy. PLoS One. 2013 Jul 4;8(7):e67797.

[195] Giovedí S, Corradi A, Fassio A, Benfenati F.Involvement of synaptic genes in the pathogenesis of autism spectrum disorders: The case of synapsins. Front Pediatr. 2014 Sep 4;2:94.

[196] Kanazawa O. Reappraisal of abnormal EEG findings in children with ADHD: on the relationship between ADHD and epileptiform discharges. Epilepsy Behav. 2014 Dec; 41:251-6.

[197] Tuchman RF, Rapin I. Regression in pervasive developmental disorders: Seizures and epileptiform electroencephalogram correlates. Pediatrics. 1997;99:560–6.

[198] Dalsgaard S, Nielsen HS, Simonsen M. Five-fold increase in national prevalence rates of attention-deficit/hyperactivity disorder medications for children and adolescents with autism spectrum disorder, attention-deficit/hyperactivity disorder, and other psychiatric disorders: A Danish register-based study. J Child Adolesc Psychopharmacol. 2013 Sep;23(7):432–9.

[199] Rubia K, Alegria AA, Cubillo AI, Smith AB, Brammer MJ, Radua J. Effects of stimulants on brain function in attention-deficit/hyperactivity disorder: A systematic review and meta-analysis. Biol Psychiatry. 2014 Oct 15;76(8):616–28.

[200] Aman MG, Arnold LE, Ramadan Y, Witwer A, Lindsay R, McDougle CJ, et al. Randomized, controlled, crossover trial of methylphenidate in pervasive developmental disorders with hyperactivity. Arch Gen Psychiatry. 2005;62:1266–1274.

[201] Mahajan R, Bernal MP, Panzer R, Whitaker A, Roberts W, Handen B, et al. Clinical practice pathways for evaluation and medication choice for attention-deficit/hyperactivity disorder symptoms in autism spectrum Disorders. Pediatrics. 2012;130(Supplement 2):S125–S138.

[202] Najib J. The efficacy and safety profile of lisdexamfetamine dimesylate, a prodrug of d-amphetamine, for the treatment ofattention-deficit/hyperactivity disorder in children and adults. Clin Ther. 2009 Jan;31(1):142–76.

[203] Arnold LE, Aman MG, Cook AM, Witwer AN, Hall KL, Thompson S, Ramadan Y. Atomoxetine for hyperactivity in autism spectrum disorders: Placebo-controlled crossover pilot trial. J Am Acad Child Adolesc Psychiatry. 2006;45:1196–1205.

[204] Hanwella R, Senanayake M, de Silva V. Comparative efficacy and acceptability of methylphenidate and atomoxetine in treatment of attention deficit hyperactivity disorder in children and adolescents: a meta-analysis. BMC Psychiatry. 2011;11:176.

[205] Connor DF, Rubin J. Guanfacine extended release in the treatment of attention deficit hyperactivity disorder in children and adolescents. Drugs Today (Barc). 2010;46:299–314.

[206] Posey DJ, Puntney JI, Sasher TM, Kem DL, McDougle CJ. Guanfacine treatment of hyperactivity and inattention in pervasive developmental disorders: A retrospective analysis of 80 cases. J Child Adolesc Psychopharmacol. 2004;14:233–241.

[207] Scahill L, Aman MG, McDougle CJ, McCracken JT, Tierney E, Dziura J, et al. A prospective open trial of guanfacine in children with pervasive developmental disorders. J Child Adolesc Psychopharmacol. 2006;16:589–598.

[208] Williams K, Wheeler DM, Silove N, Hazell P. Selective serotonin reuptake inhibitors (SSRIs) for autism spectrum disorders (ASD). Cochrane Database of Syst Rev. 2013;(8).

[209] Nicolson R, Craven-Thuss B, Smith J. A prospective, open-label trial of galantamine in autistic disorder. J Child Adolesc Psychopharmacol. 2006;16:621–9.

[210] King BH, Wright D, Handen BL, Sikich L, Zimmerman AW, McMahon W, et al. Double-blind, placebo-controlled study of amantadine hydrochloride in the treatment of children with autistic disorder. J Am Acad Child Adolesc Psychiatry. 2001;40(6):658–665.

[211] Aman MG, Langworthy KS. Pharmacotherapy for hyperactivity in children with autism and other pervasive developmental disorders. J Autism Dev Disord. 2000;30(5): 451–459.

[212] Frye RE, Rossignol DA. Treatments for biomedical abnormalities associated with autism spectrum disorder. Front Pediatr. 2014 Jun 27;2:66.

[213] Rossignol DA. Novel and emerging treatments for autism spectrum disorders: A systematic review. Ann Clin Psychiatry. 2009;21:213–36.

[214] Adams JB, Holloway C. Pilot study of a moderate dose multivitamin/mineral supplement for children with autistic spectrum disorder. J Altern Complement Med. 2004;10:1033–9.

[215] Adams JB, Audhya T, McDonough-Means S, Rubin RA, Quig D, Geis E, et al. Effect of a vitamin/mineral supplement on children and adults with autism. BMC Pediatr. 2011;11:111. doi:10.1186/1471-2431-11-111.

[216] Dolske MC, Spollen J, McKay S, Lancashire E, Tolbert L. A preliminary trial of ascorbic acid as supplemental therapy for autism. Prog Neuropsychopharmacol Biol Psychiatry. 1993;17:765–74.

[217] Nakano K, Noda N, Tachikawa E, Urano MAN, Takazawa M, Nakayama T, et al. A preliminary study of methylcobalamin therapy in autism. J Tokyo Womens Med Univ. 2005;75:64–9.

[218] James SJ, Melnyk S, Fuchs G, Reid T, Jernigan S, Pavliv O, et al. Efficacy of methylcobalamin and folinic acid treatment on glutathione redox status in children with autism. Am J Clin Nutr. 2009;89:425–30.

[219] Frye RE, Melnyk S, Fuchs G, Reid T, Jernigan S, Pavliv O, et al. Effectiveness of methylcobalamin and folinic acid treatment on adaptive behavior in children with autistic disorder is related to glutathione redox status. Autism Res Treat. 2013;609705.

[220] Ghanizadeh A, Derakhshan N. N-acetylcysteine for treatment of autism, a case report. J Res Med Sci. 2012;17:985–7.

[221] Hardan AY, Fung LK, Libove RA, Obukhanych TV, Nair S, Herzenberg LA, et al. A randomized controlled pilot trial of oral N-acetylcysteine in children with autism. Biol Psychiatry. 2012;71:956–6.

[222] Ghanizadeh A, Moghimi-Sarani E. A randomized double blind placebo controlled clinical trial of N-acetylcysteine added to risperidone for treating autistic disorders. BMC Psychiatry. 2013;13:196.

[223] Gvozdjakova A, Kucharska J, Ostatnikova D, Babinska K, Nakladal D, Crane FL. Ubiquinol improves symptoms in children with autism. Oxid Med Cell Longev. 2014;798957.

[224] Chez MG, Buchanan CP, Aimonovitch MC, Becker M, Schaefer K, Black C, et al. Double-blind, placebo-controlled study of L-carnosine supplementation in children with autistic spectrum disorders. J Child Neurol. 2002;17:833–7.

[225] Janssen CI, Kiliaan AJ.Long-chain polyunsaturated fatty acids (LCPUFA) from genesis to senescence: The influence of LCPUFA on neural development, aging, and neurodegeneration. Prog Lipid Res. 2014 Jan;53:1–17.

[226] Tamiji J, Crawford DA. The neurobiology of lipid metabolism in autism spectrum disorders. Neurosignals. 2010;18(2):98–112.

[227] Richardson AJ. Review: Omega-3 fatty acids produce a small improvement in ADHD symptoms in children compared with placebo. Evid Based Ment Health. 2012 May; 15(2):46. doi: 10.1136/ebmental-2011.

[228] James S, Montgomery P, Williams K (2011) Omega-3 fatty acids supplementation for autism spectrum disorders (ASD). Cochrane Database Syst Rev CD007992.

[229] Parikh V, St Peters M, Blakely RD, Sarter M. The presynaptic choline transporter imposes limits on sustained cortical acetylcholine release and attention. J Neurosci. 2013 Feb 6;33(6):2326–37.

[230] English BA, Hahn MK, Gizer IR, Mazei-Robison M, Steele A, Kurnik DM, et al. Choline transporter gene variation is associated with attention-deficit hyperactivity disorder. J Neurodev Disord. 2009;1:252–263.

[231] Obeid R. The metabolic burden of methyl donor deficiency with focus on the betaine homocysteine methyltransferase pathway. Nutrients. 2013 Sep 9;5(9):3481–95.

[232] Harris JC, Carter CS. Therapeutic interventions with oxytocin: Current status and concerns. J Am Acad Child Adolesc Psychiatry. 2013;52(10):998–1000

[233] Malow B, Adkins KW, McGrew SG, Wang L, Goldman SE, Fawkes D, et al. Melatonin for sleep in children with autism: a controlled trial examining dose, tolerability, and outcomes. J Autism Dev Disord. 2012;42(8):1729–1737.

Section 2

Biopsychosocial Functioning in ADHD

Chapter 7

Executive Function in Children with Attention Deficit/ Hyperactivity Disorder

Akira Yasumura and Masumi Inagaki

Additional information is available at the end of the chapter

http://dx.doi.org/10.5772/60669

Abstract

In recent years, deficit in executive function has been noted as a core symptom of attention deficit hyperactivity disorder (ADHD). Previously, with the aim of quantitatively assessing the characteristics of children with ADHD from the viewpoint of inhibition among executive functions, we have considered behavioral and frontal brain functions with regard to inhibition vis a vis color word interference. In this study we also undertook additional collections of data at a number of facilities and investigated usefulness as a differential diagnosis aid. A total of 38 ADHD children and 46 typical developing children, matched in terms of age, gender, dominant arm and non-verbal intelligence, were the subject of analysis in this study. Utilising a Reverse Stroop Task (RST), we measured prefrontal area activity during task performance with near-infrared spectroscopy (OEG-16). Results were: 1) Behavioral results: in the RST, the ADHD children recorded a higher rate of interference than the TD children. 2) Brain activity: as regards brain activity during the RST, right lateral prefrontal activity was significantly lower in the ADHD children than in the TD children. These results suggest that RST results and changes in brain activity during task performance allow quantitative assessment of the clinical symptom of ADHD.

Keywords: attention-deficit hyperactivity disorder, executive function, frontal lobe function, near-infrared spectroscopy (NIRS), children

1. Introduction

Attention deficit hyperactivity disorder (ADHD) is a neurodevelopmental disorder, which specifically affects behaviour. Until the publication of the *Diagnostic and Statistical Manual of Mental Disorders, Fourth Edition, Text Revision (DSM-IV-TR)*, ADHD was classified as a disruptive behaviour disorder, alongside oppositional defiant disorder and conduct disorder. In the most recent version, the fifth edition of the *DSM* (*DSM-5*), ADHD has been re-classified as a neurodevelopmental disorder, alongside autism spectrum disorders (ASD) [1]. As this change shows, in the past, the focus of ADHD was on antisocial and non-adaptive problem behaviours. Currently, however, ADHD is classified as one distinct type of developmental disorder, based on the assumption of a dysfunction in the brain. Thus, the focus is now on a more central cause. In addition, while the *DSM-5* does not present any major changes, compared to the *DSM-IV-TR*, in terms of diagnostic criteria for ADHD, the age of manifestation was revised from 7 years old to 12 years old. Thus, the *DSM-5* emphasizes ADHD as a developmental disease, which can afflict both adolescents and adults.

2. Deficits in executive functions as the core symptom of ADHD

Attention deficit and hyperactivity/impulsivity are cited as the primary clinical symptoms of ADHD [1]. Several studies have suggested that the core symptom is a deficit in executive functions [2]. Executive functions, which are related to high-level cognitive and behavioural control, are cognitive functions that are necessary in order to effectively accomplish human goal-oriented activities. The neural basis of these functions is generally considered to be located in the prefrontal cortex [3, 4]. For example, achieving the goal of "get to school by 9:00 AM" entails going directly to school, while suppressing the impulses to look in a display window of a toy store along the route to school and play with friends.

Based on recent developments in cognitive psychology, various theoretical models of executive functions have been proposed. There are two main models: a simple model, which asserts that executive functions are simple functions, and a complex model, in which executive functions are divided into multiple elements [5, 6]. With regard to the latter model, based on the results of a series of cognitive tasks, Miyake et al. reported that the three crucial components of executive functions are "inhibition", "attention shifting", and "updating (working memory)" [6]. Of these three, it is suggested that the clinical symptoms of ADHD strongly relate to "inhibition" in particular [4, 7, 8]. This function is necessary for intentionally inhibiting inappropriate and predominant behaviours in a given situation. Typical tasks for assessing this function include the Stroop test and the reverse Stroop test [8, 9]. The former test assesses the inhibition of Stroop interference. Stroop interference refers to the interference that occurs when receiving incongruent information regarding a colour and its name. In a Stroop test, when the word "yellow" is written in red, the correct answer is the colour in which the word is written (in this case, red). Providing this answer results in interference from the meaning of the word, known as semantic interference. In the latter reverse Stroop test, the correct answer is the word itself (yellow). Providing this answer results in interference from the colour (colour word interference). Both tests use oral responses and matching responses. Oral responses indicate the fluency and accuracy of reading aloud, while matching responses assess the accuracy and speed of selection by means such as pointing. With oral responses, the reverse Stroop effect (colour word interference) seldom occurs, compared to the Stroop effect (semantic interference). Therefore, reports of the reverse Stroop effect are extremely rare and the development process of its neural basis has yet to be reported. However, in contrast to oral responses, matching responses, in which the subject must select the colour of the word written from among a patch of multiple colours (for example, if the word "red" is written in green, the correct answer would be to point to red), are known to produce reverse Stroop interference [10-12]. Some researchers have indicated that, when a reverse Stroop test is performed on children with ADHD or ADHD tendencies, an ADHD-associated specificity, which is not seen in a Stroop test, is observed [13, 14].

Another typical assessment of inhibition is the Go/No-go task. This cognitive task assesses inhibition by asking subjects to either perform an appropriate action (Go response) or to appropriately withhold a response (No-go response), in accordance with a situation. One previous study compared children with ADHD to typical developing (TD) children, while another compared children with ADHD before and after medication [15, 16]. In the former test, the children with ADHD demonstrated poorer outcomes in No-go responses than the TD children. In the latter test, increased activity was observed in the right prefrontal cortex, following medication.

Another study has reported on the link between symptoms of ADHD and deficit in working memory, which is an element in executive function. Westerberg et al. have stated that the difference in outcomes of non-verbal working memory tasks between TD children and children with ADHD tend to increase with age [17].

These studies suggest that clinical symptoms of ADHD are strongly associated with the executive functions of inhibition and working memory.

3. Brain function measurements for children with ADHD

As can be seen from the English listing of "neurodevelopmental disorder" in the *DSM-5*, the main cause of developmental disorders, including ADHD, is generally considered to be brain function specificity [1]. Thus, in order to aid differential diagnosis of ADHD and assess ADHD before and after intervention, methods for quantitatively measuring brain function are called for. However, many children with ADHD present with hyperactivity and other behavioural problems, which easily result in artefacts that are caused by the child's movement during measurement. Therefore, as it is usually difficult to measure while the child is awake, assessment tools, such as functional magnetic resonance imaging, can only be used when the child is asleep. Of the currently existing testing modalities, near infrared spectroscopy (NIRS) can measure cerebral blood flow even when the head is moving. It is, therefore, capable of reflecting the function of the prefrontal cortex, which is the seat of executive function. Thus, NIRS is well suited for measuring the brain function in children with ADHD.

As previously stated, a number of previous studies have examined inhibition in ADHD. However, there is a dearth of studies on brain function, particularly involving children, which address the differences in results between tasks or support disorders. Therefore, we used the Stroop test (ST) and the reverse Stroop test (RST) in order to assess executive functions, particularly functions that are related to the inhibition of interference (Figure 1).

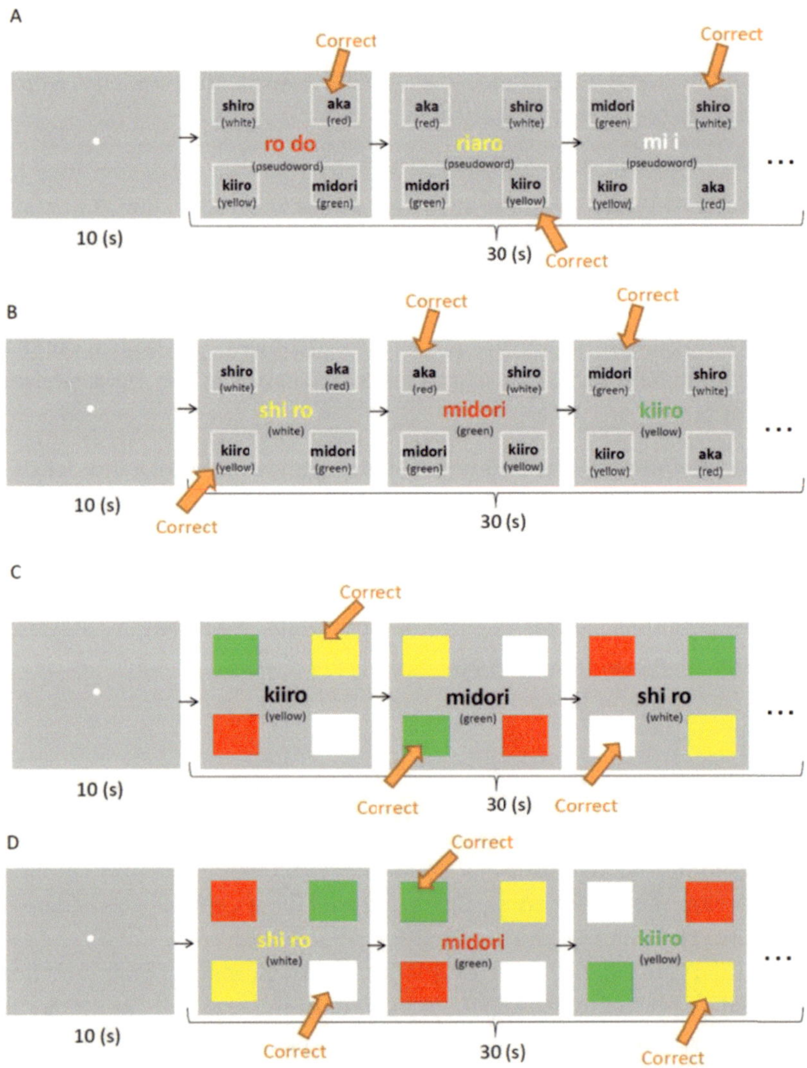

Figure 1. Schematic illustration of the protocol for the neutral condition of the Stroop task (A), incongruent condition of the Stroop task (B), neutral condition of the reverse Stroop task (C) and incongruent condition of the reverse Stroop task (D).

We began our research with the objective of determining the specificity of brain function in children with ADHD [7]. In particular, we also examined children with autism spectrum disorders (ASD), which are considered difficult to differentially diagnose from ADHD, and attempted to abstract differences in the developmental disorders. The subjects were 10 children with ADHD (age: 11.2±2.2), along with 15 TD children (age: 9.6±1.5) and 11 children with ASD (age: 10.5±2.3), who were matched with the children with ADHD in terms of age, sex, intelligence, and verbal capacity (p>0.1). The ST and RST were conducted with touch panels and matching responses. During both tasks, an NIRS device (OEG-16; Spectratech, inc. Japan) was mounted over the prefrontal cortex in order to measure the changes in cerebral blood flow (Figure 2).

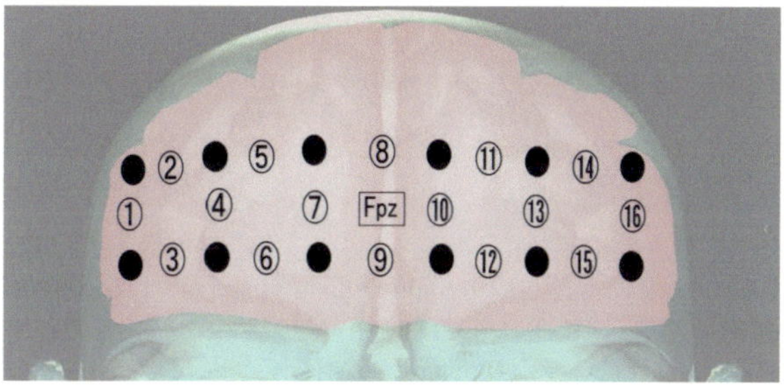

Figure 2. Experimental settings. The NIRS probe was attached to the prefrontal area. The centre of the probe matrix was place on Fpz (International 10-10 system).

We found no differences among the three groups in the ST (p>0.1). However, in the RST, in comparison with the TD children, the children with ADHD demonstrated behavioural abnormalities, i.e., a higher rate of interference (p<0.01) and a greater number of incorrect responses (p<0.05). Furthermore, with regard to changes in brain activity during the RST, the children with ADHD demonstrated lower activation of the prefrontal cortex than the TD children (p<0.05). In addition, the ADHD group demonstrated a tendency towards a negative correlation between brain activity and severity of attention deficit, which were evaluated by the Japanese versions of the Swanson, Nolan and Pelham, version-IV Scale (SNAP- IV) [18] (r=-0.60, p=0.07). These results demonstrated that inhibition of colour word interference is diminished in ADHD children. In addition, the weakness of interference inhibition was suggested to be associated with the severity of attention deficit and affected by the low activity level of the prefrontal cortex.

We also accumulated additional data from multiple institutions in order to investigate the usefulness of NIRS as a differential diagnosis aid. The subjects of this examination were 38 children with ADHD (age: 10.4±2.3, 12 children taking medication) and 46 TD children (age: 10.2±1.7), matched in terms of age, sex, dominant arm and non-verbal intelligence (p>0.1). In order to assess Stroop inhibition, frontal lobe activity was measured with an NIRS device (OEG-16) during the performance of RST. Among behaviour outcomes, we re-confirmed that children with ADHD demonstrated a higher rate of interference on the RST than the TD children (p<0.01). Within the ADHD group, the rate of interference demonstrated positive correlations with the severity of attention deficit (r=0.48, $p<0.01$) and severity of hyperactivity/ impulsivity (r=0.40, $p<0.05$) (Figure 3).

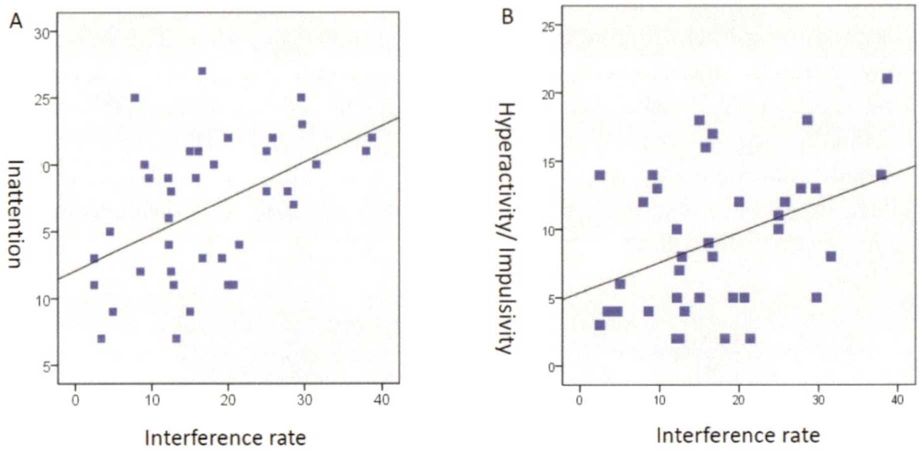

Figure 3. Correlation between the interference rate of the reverse Stroop task and the inattention score from Swanson, Nolan and Pelham scale (SNAP) in children with attention deficit hyperactivity disorder (ADHD) (A). The correlation between the interference rate of the reverse Stroop task and the hyperactivity/ impulsivity score from SNAP in the ADHD group (B).

Among the results related to brain activity, the children with ADHD demonstrated significantly lower activity in the right lateral prefrontal cortex during the RST than the TD children ($p<0.05$) (Figure 4).

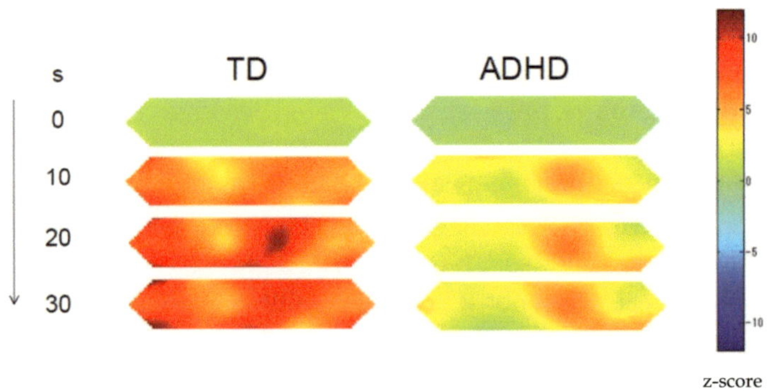

Figure 4. Changes in oxygenated haemoglobin (oxy-Hb) during the reverse Stroop task, using the mean z-scores from all of the subjects, as measured by near-infrared spectroscopy. Pseudocolor images plot regional changes in oxy-Hb across the prefrontal cortex for typically developing children (TD, left) and children with attention deficit hyperactivity disorder (ADHD, right). The bar graphs below each of the pseudocolor image series plot the mean signals over the right and left hemispheres.

Furthermore, when we performed a discriminant analysis, based on the diagnostic results with regard to the rate of interference and prefrontal cortex activity, we obtained an overall discrimination rate of 79.8%. A correlation was observed between the rate of interference and severity of ADHD in the RST. Children with ADHD demonstrated lower right lateral prefrontal cortex activity during the RST than the TD children. These findings suggested that changes in RST outcomes and changes in brain activity during the RST could be used to linearly assess the clinical symptoms of ADHD. In order to construct a linear model with a higher discrimination rate, future studies may need to include greater numbers of participants and additional selection of indicators, as well as children with developmental disorders other than ADHD.

4. Autism spectrum disorders and deficit in executive function

A deficit in executive functions has also been indicated in developmental disorders other than ADHD, such as in ASD. For example, because the stereotypical symptoms of ASD can be understood as sustained, inflexible symptoms, they are suspected to be associated with a deficit in executive functions. Among executive function tasks, particularly tasks that assess attention shifting, which require a flexible conversion of attention, children with ASD are known to demonstrate poorer behavioural outcomes. Therefore, we performed behavioural analysis and examined cerebral blood flow, with the objective of determining the pathology regarding the neural basis of attention shifting in children with ASD [19]. The subjects were 14 children with high-functioning ASD (age: 9.6±1.4), diagnosed in accordance with the diagnostic criteria in the *DSM-IV-TR*, and 20 TD children (age: 9.2±1.6), who matched with the ASD children in terms of age, sex and intelligence. The task we used was a modified version of the Dimensional -Change Card Sort (DCCS) task [20], in which the rules are frequently altered (Figure 5).

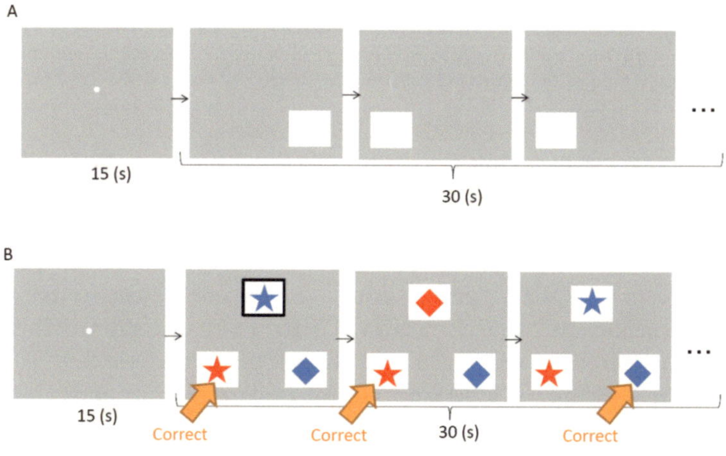

Figure 5. Illustration of the protocol of the baseline (a) and dimensional change card sort (DCCS) (b) tasks. In the baseline task, the participants had to indicate the side of the screen on which the white square appeared. In the DCCS task, if the upper card was hemmed in black, the participants had to select the lower card with the same shape as the one that was printed on the upper card. If the upper card was not hemmed in black, they had to select the lower card of the same colour as that of the upper card.

We also measured the changes in blood flow in the prefrontal cortex during task performance, using NIRS (OEG-16). In addition, in order to assess the guardians' needs in supporting their children with ASD, we asked them to complete a shortened version of the Paediatric Anxiety Rating Scale (PARS) [21]. The results from the PARS showed that children with ASD have greater support needs than TD children. In the DCCS task, the children with ASD had fewer correct responses than the TD children. Furthermore, as for cerebral blood flow, the children with ASD demonstrated less activity than the TD children in the vicinity of the right dorsolateral prefrontal cortex, the frontal pole and the left inferior prefrontal cortex (Figure 6).

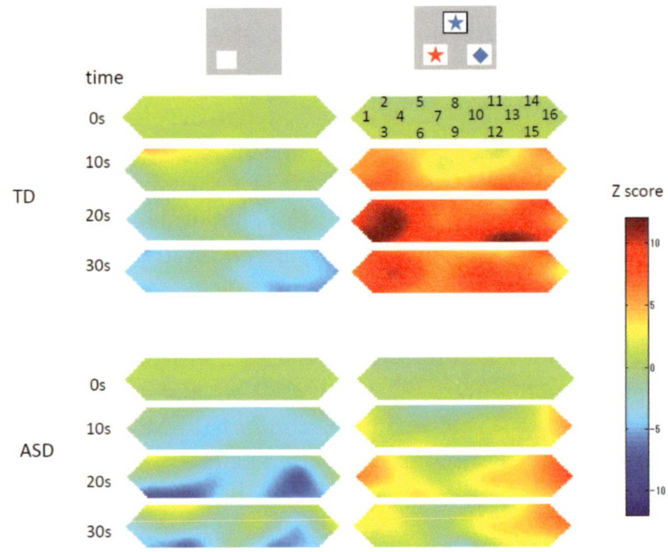

Figure 6. Time course of near-infrared spectroscopy topography using the mean z-scores from all of the subjects. The numbers on the first image on the second row indicate the locations of the channels. The left side of the figure indicates the brain activities during the baseline task - typically developing children (TDC, upper) and autism spectrum disorder (ASD, lower). The right side of the figure indicates the brain activities during the dimensional change card sort task - TDC (upper) and ASD (lower).

The above results suggest that children with ASD have a diminished ability to shift their attention, which is consistent with previous studies [22]. This can be inferred as a reflection of the specific stereotypes in ASD. In addition, the brain function results during the task performance suggested that reduced prefrontal cortex activity is related to the pathology of ASD. This, in turn, suggests that NIRS findings could serve as an objective indicator for clinical diagnoses of ASD in children. Future studies will need to investigate whether the DCCS task can be applied in differential diagnosis of other developmental disorders, as well as whether it can be applied as an indicator for assessing the effects of medication and behavioural therapy.

5. Conclusion

In this report, we discussed the relationships of ADHD and ASD, which are neurodevelopmental disorders, with executive functions. The seat of executive functions is generally considered to be located in the prefrontal cortex. We discussed NIRS as a useful method for measuring this activity. It is possible that the core symptoms of ADHD may be quantified by NIRS. Progress in functional neuroimaging research on ADHD and ASD is expected to enable highly precise measurements of the severity of developmental disorders. In addition to differentiating severity, future research will need to determine the optimal intervention (drug therapy, behavioural therapy, etc.) on a case-by-case basis when selecting treatment.

Acknowledgements

This work was supported in part by the TMC Young Investigator Fellowship and an Intramural Research Grant (25-6; Clinical Research for Diagnostic and Therapeutic Innovations in Developmental Disorders) for Neurological and Psychiatric Disorders of National Center of Neurology and Psychiatry (NCNP); Grant-in-Aid for Young Scientists (A) from JSPS KAKENHI (15H05405 to Akira Yasumura) and Grant-in-Aid for Challenging Exploratory Research from JSPS KAKENHI (15K13167 to Akira Yasumura). We would like to thank the following people for their cooperation in collecting data: Dr. Tasuku Miyajima, Department of Pediatrics, Tokyo Medical University; Dr. Masao Aihara, Department of Pediatrics, University of Yamanashi; Dr. Yushiro Yamashita, Department of Pediatrics, Kurume University; Dr. Tatsuya Koeda, Graduate School of Regional Sciences, Tottori University; and Dr. Toshihide Koike, Department of Special Needs Education, Tokyo Gakugei University.

The authors have no conflicts of interest to declare.

Author details

Akira Yasumura* and Masumi Inagaki

*Address all correspondence to: yasumura@ncnp.go.jp

Department of Developmental Disorders, National Institute of Mental Health, National Center of Neurology and Psychiatry, Kodaira, Tokyo, Japan

References

[1] American Psychiatric Association. Diagnostic and Statistical Manual of Mental Disorders Fifth Edition (DSM-5). American Psychiatric Publishing; 2013.

[2] Barkley RA, et al. Frontal Lobe Functions in Attention Deficit Disorder with and Without Hyperactivity: A Review and Research Report. J Abnorm Child Psychol. 1992; 20(2) 163-188.

[3] Pennington BF, et al. Executive Functions and Developmental Psychopathology. J Child Psychol Psychiatry. 1996; 37(1) 51-87.

[4] Schroeter ML, et al. Prefrontal Activation Due to Stroop Interference Increases During Development - An Event-related fNIRS Study. Neuroimage. 2004; 23(4) 1317-1325.

[5] Baddeley A. The Episodic Buffer: A New Component of Working Memory? Trends Cogn Sci. 2000; 4(11) 417-423.

[6] Miyake A, et al. The Unity and Diversity of Executive Functions and their Contributions to Complex "Frontal Lobe" Tasks: A Latent Variable Analysis. Cogn Psychol. 2000; 41(1) 49-100.

[7] Yasumura A, et al. Neurobehavioral and Hemodynamic Evaluation of Stroop and Reverse Stroop Interference in Children with Attention-Deficit/Hyperactivity Disorder. Brain Dev. 2014; 36(2) 97-106.

[8] Negoro H, et al. Prefrontal Dysfunction in Attention-Deficit/Hyperactivity Disorder as Measured by Near-infrared Spectroscopy. Child Psychiatry Hum Dev. 2010; 41(2) 193-203.

[9] Stroop JR. Studies of Interference in Serial Verbal Reactions. J Exp Psychol. 1935; 18(6) 643-662.

[10] Jensen AR, et al. The Stroop Color-word Test: A Review. Acta Psychol (Amst). 1966; 25(1) 36-93.

[11] MacLeod CM. Half a Century of Research on the Stroop Effect: An Integrative Review. Psychol Bull. 1991; 109(2) 163-203.

[12] Durgin FH. The Reverse Stroop Effect. Psychon Bull Rev. 2000; 7(1) 121-125.

[13] Song Y, et al. An Asymmetric Stroop/Reverse-Stroop Interference Phenomenon in ADHD. J Atten Disord. 2011; 15(6) 499-505.

[14] Ikeda Y, et al. Stroop/Reverse-Stroop Interference in Typical Development and its Relation to Symptoms of ADHD. Res Dev Disabil. 2013; 34(8) 2391-2398.

[15] Inoue Y, et al. Reduced Prefrontal Hemodynamic Response in Children with ADHD During the Go/Nogo Task: A NIRS Study. Neuroreport. 2012; 23(2) 55-60.

[16] Monden Y, et al. Clinically-oriented Monitoring of Acute Effects of Methylphenidate on Cerebral Hemodynamics in ADHD Children Using fNIRS. Clin Neurophysiol. 2012; 123(6) 1147-1157.

[17] Westerberg H, et al. Visuo-spatial Working Memory Span: A Sensitive Measure of Cognitive Deficits in Children with ADHD. Child Neuropsychol. 2004; 10(3) 155-161.

[18] Inoue Y, et al. Psychometric Properties of Japanese Version of the Swanson, Nolan, And Pelham, Version-IV Scale-Teacher Form: A Study of School Children in Community Samples. Brain Dev. 2014; 36(8):700-706.

[19] Yasumura A, et al. Neurobehavioral and Hemodynamic Evaluation of Cognitive Shifting in Children with Autism Spectrum Disorder. JBBS. 2012; 2(4):463-470.

[20] Moriguchi Y, et al. Neural Origin of Cognitive Shifting in Young Children. Proc Natl Acad Sci U S A. 2009; 106(14) 6017-6021.

[21] Adachi J, et al. Reliability and Validity of Short Version of Pervasive Developmental Disorders (PDD)-Autism Society Japan Rating Scale (PARS): A Behavior Checklist for People with PDD. Seishinigaku 2008; 50(5) 431-438 [in Japanese].

[22] Lopez BR, et al. Examining the Relationship Between Executive Functions and Restricted, Repetitive Symptoms of Autistic Disorder. J Autism Dev Disord. 2005; 35(4) 445-460.

Chapter 8

Cognitive Function in Attention Deficit Hyperactivity Disorder

Yongning Song

Additional information is available at the end of the chapter

http://dx.doi.org/10.5772/60785

Abstract

This study examined the hypothesis that individuals with attention deficit hyperactivity disorder, predominantly inattentive type (ADHD-I), show both executive function (EF) deficits and non-EF deficits. A group with ADHD-I (n = 16) and a paired control group (n = 21) completed a battery of tasks covering the major domains of EF (planning, working memory, flexibility and inhibition) and non-EF (alertness, divided attention, flexibility, sustained attention, visual field and visual scanning). EF impairments in planning, spatial working memory, flexibility, and inhibition as well as non-EF impairments in divided attention, flexibility, sustained attention and visual scanning were observed in the ADHD-I group. Our results do not support Barkley's (1997) view of ADHD which postulated that only ADHD-C and ADHD-H, but not ADHD-I, are associated with EF deficits. It suggests that ADHD-I and ADHD-C children had similar profiles of cognitive impairment, and the deficits in cognition are not good markers for the classification of ADHD subtypes in *the Diagnostic and Statistical Manual of Mental Disorders, Fifth Edition (DSM-V).*

Keywords: ADHD-I, Executive function, Non-executive function, Cognitive profile

1. Introduction

Executive function (EF) is an umbrella term that refers to processes that control other cognitive processes [1]. Researchers have identified four distinct domains of EF: planning, working memory, flexibility, and response inhibition [2-6]. The role of EF is debated, but most researchers agree that EF is involved in deliberately managing an appropriate problem solving set to attain a future goal [7-8].

A deficit in EF is postulated to account for core symptoms in psychiatric patients with no focal frontal lesions, such as those diagnosed with attention deficit hyperactivity disorder (ADHD). The evidence supporting a deficiency in EF domains in ADHD comes from a number of sources [8, 9-14].

Clarification of the neuropsychological similarities and differences in ADHD subtypes can contribute to understanding their etiological relationship. *The Diagnostic and Statistical Manual of Mental Disorders* (*DSM-V)* [15] classifies the symptoms of ADHD into three distinct subtypes: predominantly inattentive type (ADHD-I); predominantly hyperactive-impulsive type (HD or ADHD-H), and combined type (ADHD-C). In addition, Barkley (1997) postulated a model of ADHD in which only ADHD-C and ADHD-H, but not ADHD-I, are associated with EF deficits [16]. This is because, ADHD-C and ADHD-H exhibits the symptoms of hyperactivity/ impulsivity which are believed to be caused by the deficit in response inhibition, a key process in EF.

Now, nearly all of the neuropsychological literature on ADHD pertains to the group designated as ADHD combined type (ADHD-C), while the primarily inattentive subtype of ADHD (ADHD-I) remains relatively under-investigated with regard to potentially relevant cognitive functions [17-19]. Nigg (2005) suggested that further studies of children with ADHD-C versus control children on many executive measures might no longer be needed [18]. Instead, studies to examine issues such as neuropsychological process theories of ADHD-I have been proposed.

Previous research has found many non-EF cognitive deficits in ADHD-I, such as the inconsistent alertness and orientation [20], Sluggish cognitive tempo [21], and the poor attention shifting [22]. And many non-EF symptoms rather than EF symptoms were described in DSM-V, such as often fails to give close attention to details or often loses things necessary for tasks or activities. For a long time, we failed to give much attention to the EF domain in ADHD-I, thus it is still unknown whether the EF domain are impaired in ADHD-I. Combining the hypothesis that EF weaknesses are neither necessary nor sufficient to cause all cases of ADHD [8], we predict that individuals with ADHD-I encounter not just difficulties with EF, but also show deficits in other cognitive domains (hereafter termed non-EF).

Thus, the first goal of the present study was to examine the EF weaknesses hypothesis in ADHD-I by comparing children with ADHD-I versus typically developing children in the four distinct EF domains of planning, working memory, flexibility, and inhibition. The second goal was to examine the non-EF deficit hypothesis in children with ADHD-I by comparing them with a control group on six non-EF domains: alertness, divided attention, flexibility, sustained attention, visual field and visual scanning.

2. Methods

2.1. Participants

Children diagnosed with ADHD were recruited from several child psychiatry outpatient services across the Zabei district of Shanghai. Each sample was referred from the Shanghai Pediatric Hospital where the participants were diagnosed with ADHD, primarily inattentive type.

Before testing, we obtain written consent from participants and their parents. Each family completed an unstructured screening interview based on the Child and Adolescent Psychiatric Assessment [23]. We recorded information regarding the children's medical history, developmental history and general symptoms. We excluded children with any significant comorbid psychiatric or neurological conditions, such as epilepsy, severe attention deficit hyperactivity disorder or schizophrenia. We also confirmed that the children had not been on medication for at least 3 months.

All children met DSM-V diagnostic criteria for ADHD. Any child with ADHD-H or ADHD-C was excluded. Furthermore, a 27 items version of Conners' Teacher Rating Scale (CTRS-S) [24] was completed for each child to confirm the pervasiveness of symptoms. Scoring was performed according to the test manual [25] and established cutoff points for possible and likely ADHD, primarily inattentive type were imposed. Furthermore, all children were administered the Raven's Progressive Matrices IQ test. Children exhibiting intellectual disability (IQ scores below 75) were excluded from further experiment. Finally, a total of 16 children with ADHD-I participated in the experiment.

Twenty-one children without ADHD were paired with the ADHD group by gender and age. We administered an unstructured screening interview based on the Child and Adolescent Psychiatric Assessment [23] for the controls and did not find any psychiatric or neurological symptoms. All children did not meet DSM-V diagnostic criteria for ADHD. Furthermore, a teacher completed the CTRS-S [24] for the control group, with t scores below 50 used to confirm the children's non-ADHD status. In addition, the non-ADHD group was administered the IQ test (CRT) to confirm that they did not have intellectual disability. Information on participants is shown in Table 1.

	ADHD-I	Control	P value
N	16	21	
Sex ratio (F/M)	12/4	14/7	Ns
Age	12 (1.43)	12 (1.41)	Ns
Range of age	9-14	9-14	
IQ(CRT-C)	89 (11.3)	92 (12)	p=.51
Range of IQ	75-122	80-123	

Table 1. Group means (*SDs*) for age and IQ

2.2. EF tests

We chose EF tests according to distinct domains of EF: planning, working memory, flexibility, and response inhibition [2-6]. Four EF tests were conducted in this study: the Spatial Working Memory Test (SWM), Stockings of Cambridge Test (SOC), Wisconsin Card Sorting Test (WCST), and Stroop/reverse-Stroop Test. With regard to response inhibition, Barkley (1997) proposed a model suggesting that a deficit in behavioral inhibition, considered a key process in EF, accounts for central impairment of ADHD [16]. In the model, Barkley distinguished three interrelated processes believed to constitute behavioral inhibition: (1) inhibition of a prepotent response; (2) cessation of an ongoing response; and (3) interference control. Researchers have long used Stroop/reverse-Stroop interference as the main paradigm to study interference control. Thus, in this study, we used the Stroop/reverse-Stroop Test [26, 27] to evaluate the level of response inhibition.

Spatial Working Memory Test (altered). This test was designed based on the SWM in the Cambridge Automated Neuropsychological Test Battery (CANTAB) [28, 29]. In this test, participants are asked to search through a number of boxes presented on the screen to find a token. The key instruction states that once a token has been found in a box, that box cannot be used again to hide a token during that particular trial. On each trial, the total number of blue tokens to be found corresponds to the number of boxes on the screen. Once a blue token is found in a particular box, that box cannot be used again to hide a token. Returning to an empty box where a target has already been found is referred to as a "between-search error."

In the original SWM, there were four types of trials with either three, four, six, or eight boxes in each. Several previous studies showed that children with ADHD made significantly more errors compared with controls only on the eight-box problems [30, 31]. Given that between-search errors may appear as a function of the number of boxes in pediatric clinical populations [32], it is possible that children with ADHD also make significantly more errors compared with controls on seven-box problems. Thus, we made a few changes to the original task, in which the independent variable of box consisted of five uninterrupted levels with three, four, five, six, or seven boxes. There were four test trials each with three, four, five, six, and seven boxes. The order of the trials was randomized, with the constraint that the same number of boxes did not occur consecutively. The dependent measure for the SWM test was the number of between-search errors on three-, four-, five-, six-, and seven-box problems.

Stocking of Cambridge Test (altered). This test was designed based on the SOC in the CANTAB [28, 29]. This test is closely related to the Tower of London task developed by Shallice and McCarthy [33]. In this test, two sets of three colored balls (one green, one blue, and one red) were presented on the screen. Participants were asked to rearrange the balls in the bottom display such that their positions matched the "goal" arrangement in the top half of the screen. The starting position of the balls was varied across trials to ensure that in any particular trial a minimum move of two, three, four, or five moves was required. Participants were instructed to examine the original position of the balls and attempt to solve it in the minimum possible number of moves. The time to complete the pattern is taken as a measure of the participant's planning ability.

In the original SOC task, there were four test trials each with two, three, four, and five moves. However, some studies failed to find that children with ADHD made significantly more extra moves than typically developing children on this task (For example, see [30,31,34]). It is possible that the short range of the minimum moves to goal state can account for the above conclusion. Thus, we made a few changes to the original task, such that the minimum moves to goal state ranged from three to seven moves. There were four test trials each with of three, four, five, six, and seven moves, and the order of the trials was randomized. The dependent measure for the SWM test was response times on three-, four-, five-, six-, and seven-move problems.

Wisconsin Card Sorting Test. Flexibility was assessed with the Computerized WCST [35-37], a widely used test to measure cognitive flexibility or set shifting. In this test, participants were asked to match a series of stimulus cards to a set of four target cards that differed by form, color, and number. The display did not disappear until a choice was made. Feedback information followed the choice, and consisted of a "×" sign if the response was correct, or a "∘" sign if the response was incorrect. Response cards could be matched by number (1, 2, 3, 4), shape (triangle, star, cross, circle), or color (red, green, blue, yellow). After participants determined one of the correct dimensions, referred to as "categories" (C), 10 correct responses were required before the category was shifted to the next one. The task was terminated after a maximum of 128 trials was reached. The order of the sorting principles was randomized, with the constraint that the same sorting principles did not occur consecutively.

Continued matching to a category that is no longer correct is considered a perseverative error (PE). Other errors that occur when a participant is required to switch to another sorting principle are referred to as non-perseverative errors (NPE). The variables of interest were the number of categories achieved, percentage of perseverative errors and percentage of non-perseverative errors.

The Stroop/reverse-Stroop Test. The Stroop/reverse-Stroop Test [26, 27, 38] was used to evaluate the level of both Stroop interference and reverse-Stroop interference. The test comprised four subtests in which all color–word combinations and color patches were printed on four separate sheets of paper.

Test 1 was control condition for the Stroop test, in which the color patch was shown on the left side of the test sheet, requiring participants to make a choice from the five matching color–words(written in black ink) corresponding to the color of the color patch. Test 2 was the Stroop test, in which incongruent color–words were shown on the left side of the test sheet, requiring participants to make a choice from the five matching color–words (printed with black ink) according to the ink color of the color–word in the center. If the semantic content of the incongruent color–word does not affect the processing of ink color, the response to Test 1 and Test 2 should not differ. Test 3 was control condition for the Reverse-Stroop test, in which all the color–word combinations were written in black ink, requiring participants to make a choice from the five matching color patches corresponding to the color–words. Test 4 was the RI test, in which all the color–word combinations were written in incongruent ink (e.g., the word blue printed in green ink) on the left side of the test sheet, requiring participants to make a choice from the five matching color patches corresponding to the semantic meaning of the word.

Similarly, if the ink color does not affect semantic processing, the responses to Test 3 and Test 4 should not differ. Thus, we can evaluate the Stroop interference ratio and the reverse-Stroop interference ratio by comparing the responses in the four tests.

Each test consisted of 10 practice trials and 100 test trials. On the basis of the number of correct responses in each subtest (C1, C2, C3, C4), two interference ratios were calculated using the following formulas: Stroop interference ratio, (SI) = (C3–C4)/C3, and reverse-Stroop interference ratio, (RI) = (C1–C2)/C1.

2.3. Non-EF tests

To fully assess non-EF in this study, performance was assessed by a set of computer-assisted psychological tests, the Test for Attentional Performance (TAP), version 2.2, published by Zimmermann and Fimm [39]. The six subtests of alertness, divided attention, flexibility, sustained attention, visual field, and visual scanning were administered. The dependent measure for the TAP was the reaction times.

Alertness Test (TAP, subtest 1). A simple reaction time task measures response readiness to a simple visual target on the computer screen. Simple reaction time has been shown to be a valid measure of general slowness. In this test, a cross (2 cm) appeared in the middle of the screen, and the participant had to press a button as rapidly as possible. The interval between the warning and the imperative stimulus varied randomly between 300 and 700 ms. The reaction times were automatically recorded by the program (a total of 40 trials were presented in this subtest).

Divided Attention Test (TAP, subtest 5). In this subtest, participants had to deal with one visual simultaneous task. The visual task consisted of a matrix of 4 × 4 dots (size: 10 × 10 cm). Seven small Xs were superimposed randomly over the 4 × 4 dots. When four Xs formed a square, the participants had to react as quickly as possible by pressing a button. The task contained 20 visual targets out of 20 visual non-targets.

Flexibility Test (TAP, subtest 6). In this subtest, one letter and one digit were presented simultaneously, one on the left and one on the right. The digit always represented the target stimulus (50 trials). Participants needed to respond to each trial by pressing the corresponding left or right response button as quickly and as accurately as possible to judge which side of the target was displayed. The placement of the target was randomized so that participants could not anticipate where it would be displayed.

Sustained Attention Test (TAP, subtest 9). In this subtest, a sequence of stimuli was presented on the monitor. The stimuli varied in a range of feature dimensions: color, shape, size and filling. A target stimulus occurred whenever it corresponded in one predetermined stimulus dimension with the preceding stimulus (e.g., the same shape but with different color, size and filling), participants needed to respond to each trial by pressing the space key as quickly as possible (test time lasted 10 minutes).

Visual Field Test (TAP, subtest 11). To record vision in circumscribed areas of the visual field, a stimulus was presented at different points of the screen and at varying intervals. Participants were required to fixate on the middle of the screen throughout the entire test run. Whenever the peripheral stimulus appeared the patient was to press the reaction key as quickly as possible. The reaction times to targets were recorded automatically. A total of 40 stimuli were presented in this subtask.

Visual scanning Test (TAP, subtest 12). In this subtest, a matrix-like arrangement of 5 × 5 stimuli was used. Participants were required to detect whether this arrangement included a critical stimulus. One reaction key was used for the answer "present" and another for the answer "not present." The task contained 20 visual targets out of 20 visual non-targets.

2.4. Procedure

Testing took place on four different occasions and was administered in a fixed order for both groups. During the first session, the Stroop/reverse-Stroop Test was administered. In the second testing session, the TAP battery was administered individually. In the third testing session, the WCST and SOC were administered individually. Finally, the SWM was administered individually.

3. Results

In this section, we briefly provide the statistical analyses, focusing on the performance on the EF tests (working memory, planning, flexibility and inhibition) and non-EF tests (alertness, divided attention, flexibility, sustained attention, visual field and visual scanning) between children with ADHD-I and typically developing children.

3.1. EF tests

Working memory. We performed a two-way ANOVA on the number of between search errors with the group type (ADHD-I or difficulty (three- to seven-box problems) as a within subjects factor. Results showed that the two main effects of group type, F (1, 35) = 10.37, p <.01, and task difficulty, F (4, 140) =27.54, p <.01, were significant. The interaction effect between group type and task difficulty was significant, F (4, 140) = 9.01, p <.01. Furthermore, the simple main effect of group type was only significant in six-box problems, F (1, 35) = 4.77, p =.04 and seven-box problems, F (1, 35) = 12.18, p <.01. It was not significant in three-box problems, F (1, 35) =.70, p =.41, four-box problems, F (1, 35) =3.42, p =.07, or five-box problems, F (1, 35) =.01, p =.77. In contrast to three- and four-box problems, in six- and seven-box problems there is a higher memory load of the task. Our findings indicate that the higher memory load task affected the ADHD-I group more than the controls.

Planning. We performed a two-way ANOVA on the reaction times with the group type (ADHD-I or control) as a between subjects factor and the task difficulty (three- to seven-move problems) as a within subjects factor. Results showed that the two main effects of group type, F (1, 35) = 10.17, p <.01, and task difficulty, F (4, 140) =21.32, p <.01, were significant. The interaction effect between group type and task difficulty was significant, F (4, 140) = 2.77, p <.

05. Furthermore, the simple main effect of group type was only significant in five-move problems, F (1, 35) = 5.02, p <.05, six-move problems, F (1, 35) = 6.63, p <.05, and seven-move problems, F (1, 35) =3.80, p <.05. It was not significant in three-move problems, F (1, 35) =3.29, p =.08, and four-move problems, F (1, 35) =.48, p =.23. This showed that with difficulty level of planning task increases, ADHD-I exhibited poor performance on the planning task.

Flexibility. We performed an independent-samples t test on the categories achieved by the two groups. Results showed that the effect of group type, t (35) = 3.06, p <.01, was significant. In addition, we performed a two-way ANOVA on the number of errors with the group type as a between-participants factor and the error type (PE and NPE) as a within participants factor. Results showed that the two main effects of group type, F (1, 35) = 4.20, p <.05, and error type, F (4, 140) =233.91, p <.01, were significant. The interaction effect between group type and test condition was significant, F (4, 140) = 7.05, p <.01. Furthermore, the simple main effect of group type was only significant in PE, F (1, 35) = 6.01, p <.05. It was not significant in NPE, F (1, 35) = 1.42, p =.24. This finding suggests that cognitive flexibility was impaired in ADHD-I.

Inhibition. We performed a two-way ANOVA on the interference ratios with the group type (ADHD-I or control) as a between subjects factor and the interference type (SI and RI) as a within subjects factor. Results showed that the two main effects of group type, F (1, 35) = 3.63, p =.06, and interference type, F (1, 35) =.76, p =.39, were not significant. The interaction effect between group type and interference type was significant, F (1, 35) = 3.52, p <.05. Furthermore, the simple main effect of group type was only significant in reverse-Stroop interference, F (1, 35) = 7.52, p <.01, whereas Stroop interference was not significant, F (1, 35) =.37, p =.55. This finding suggests that ADHD-I showed a selective impairment in interference control.

EF domain	Tasks	ADHD-I	Control	Contrast
Working Memory	SWM			
	BSE on 3-box problems	.13(.34)	.01(.22)	Ns
	BSE on 4-box problems	1.31(1.85)	.43(1.03)	Ns
	BSE on 5-box problems	.88(1.41)	.71(1.82)	Ns
	BSE on 6-box problems	4.38(4.56)	1.81(2.52)	ADHD-I>NC
	BSE on 7-box problems	9.83(7.95)	2.79(4.15)	ADHD-I>NC
Planning	SOC			
	TT on 3-move problems	17.27(6.71)	14.20(3.41)	Ns
	TT on 4-move problems	27.76(15.18)	33.14(11.80)	Ns
	TT on 5-move problems	62.81(38.92)	37.05(31.08)	ADHD-I>NC
	TT on 6-move problems	70.68(30.00)	49.24(20.64)	ADHD-I>NC
	TT on 7-move problems	73.20(39.23)	48.32(37.85)	ADHD-I>NC
Flexibility	WCST			
	C	6.50(2.00)	8.29(1.55)	ADHD-I<NC
	PE	13.94(9.47)	6.76(8.31)	ADHD-I>NC
	NPE	25.44(5.97)	23.10(5.88)	Ns
Inhibition	Stroop/reverse-Stroop Test			

EF domain	Tasks	ADHD-I	Control	Contrast
	SI	.23(.21)	.19(.13)	Ns
	RI	.30(.15)	.17(.11)	ADHD-I>NC

Note: ADHD-I=ADHD Pre-dominantly Inattentive type; SWM: Spatial Working Memory; SOC=Stocking of Cambridge; WCST =Wisconsin Card Sorting Test; BSE=the number of Between Search Errors; TT: Response Times; C= the number of Categories Achieved; PE=the number of Perseverative Errors; NPE= the number of Non-Perseverative Errors; SI=Stroop Interference ratio; RI=reverse-Stroop Interference ratio.

Table 2. Means and standard deviations (*SDs*) for EF test results

3.2. Non-EF tests

We performed multivariate analysis (Pillai's trace) with group type (ADHD group or non-ADHD group) as a fixed factor and reaction times on the six subtests as a dependent factor. Results showed that the effect of group type, F (6, 28) = 4.42, p <.01, was significant. The tests of between-subjects effect indicated that the group type effect was significant for divided attention, F (1, 35) =8.18, p <.01, flexibility, F (1, 35) =8.15, p <.01, sustained attention, F (1, 35) =4.57, p <.05, and visual scanning, F (1, 35) =13.41, p <.01. It was not significant for alertness, F (1, 35) =.07, p =.98, or visual field, F (1, 35) =.06, p =.79.

	Tasks	ADHD-I	Control	Contrast
Alertness	TAP, subtest 1	350.67(54.44)	345.17(64.88)	Ns
Divided attention	TAP, subtest 4	1434.17 (432.73)	1097.09 (265.93)	ADHD-I>NC
Flexibility	TAP, subtest 6	560.75(92.43)	480.00(74.42)	ADHD-I>NC
Sustained attention	TAP, subtest 9	560.56(59.50)	515.96(61.07)	ADHD-I>NC
Visual field	TAP, subtest 11	503.97(107.96)	496.36(90.83)	Ns
Visual scanning	TAP, subtest 12	5454.91(1270.07)	4114.94 (898.77)	ADHD-I>NC

Note: TAP = Test for Attentional Performance.

Table 3. Means and standard deviations (*SDs*) for non-EF test results

4. Discussion

4.1. EF domains

Working memory. Results of the two-way ANOVA indicated a significant group-by-task difficulty interaction: the ADHD-I differed significantly from controls only on six- and seven-box problems. This result is consistent with several previous studies in which children with ADHD-C exhibited deficits in multiple components of working memory [30, 40, 41]. These results suggest that working memory is impaired in both ADHD-C and ADHD-I.

Planning. Analysis of thinking times on three-, four-, five-, six- and seven-move problems indicated that children with ADHD-I took more time to complete the five-, six- and seven-move problems than controls. The current findings are in contrast to previous studies (For example, see [30, 42]) that failed to find a significant divergence between ADHD-C and controls on three difficulty levels of SOC: two or three moves necessary to solve the problem (lowest difficulty level), four moves (medium difficulty level), and five moves (highest difficulty level). We argued that the short level range (the maximum move to goal state is five) may account for the no-difference findings in these studies. Numerous studies (For example, see [8, 31]) have reported poor performance on planning tasks in individuals with ADHD-C. Evidence from our research and previous studies support the hypothesis that planning is impaired in both ADHD-C and ADHD-I. And we made a modification to the original SOC task by changing the minimum moves to goal state ranged from three to seven moves and the results show that the modified SOC task is a more useful tool to evaluate the individual's planning ability.

Flexibility. Results showed that the categories achieved by the ADHD group were fewer than the categories achieved by controls, and the simple main effect of group type was only significant for perseverative errors and not significant for non-perseverative errors. This indicates that the ADHD-I group exhibited a deficit in flexibility relative to typically developing children. Although a few studies have shown no statistically significant differences from controls on the WCST in individuals with ADHD [42-43], more than half of the investigations have shown statistically significant differences from controls [14,45-48]. Moreover, Houghton et al. (1999) found no differences between inattentive and combined subtypes on WCST [49, 50]. These results support the hypothesis that flexibility is impaired in both ADHD-C and ADHD-I.

Inhibition. We found an asymmetric phenomenon between Stroop interference and reverse-Stroop interference for ADHD-I participants. This finding replicated our recent results reporting an ADHD-I impairment in reverse-Stroop interference but not in Stroop interference [37]. A number of studies have used the Stroop test to examine interference control in ADHD, but results have been inconsistent. Recently, Mourik, Oosterlaan, & Sergeant (2005) completed a meta-analytic review that systematically examined 17 studies of Stroop interference control in ADHD [51]. They concluded that the Stroop color-word task does not provide strong evidence for a deficit in interference control in ADHD. Lansbergen, Kenemans, and Van Engeland (2007) conducted another meta-analytic review of 19 studies that administered the Stroop tests to groups with ADHD [52]. In contrast, consistency analysis of ratio scores across those 19 studies revealed that interference control was consistently compromised in individuals with ADHD. We have few studies available on reverse-Stroop interference in ADHD-C. This is possibly because the reverse-Stroop has seldom been discussed in ADHD because it cannot be observed in oral responses [53]. It is difficult to conclude that individuals with ADHD-I or ADHD-C exhibit the same deficit in reverse-Stroop interference until more studies on this question are conducted.

4.2. Non-EF domains

Deficits in divided attention, flexibility, sustained attention, and visual scanning relative to controls indicate that individuals with ADHD-I also exhibited impairment on the non-EF domains. We know that the cognitive and behavioral characters (the attention trait, hyperactivity and impulsivity) are the main criterion for the subtypes of ADHD in DSM-V. However, the DSM-V does not provide specific examples of the cognitive difference between ADHD-C and ADHD-I.

With regard to non-EF domains, previous studies have suggested that ADHD-I shows a deficit in speed of information processing, generally, and in focused or selective attention, specifically [54, 55], while deficits in ADHD-C are characterized as sustained persistence [16]. However, one recent study has shown that ADHD-I and ADHD-C children had similar profiles of vigilance impairment indexing a lack of sustained attention [56]. Furthermore, in the present research, we found that ADHD-I is also associated with a sustained attention deficit. Moreover, Geurts, Vert′ec, Oosterlaana, Roeyersc, and Sergeanta (2005) found no differences between inattentive and combined ADHD subtypes on non-EF tasks, such as response execution, short-term memory, visual-motor integration and categorization [57]. Based on combined results of the current research and previous studies, we wonder whether the deficits in non-EF cognitive abilities can be used as good markers for the validation of ADHD subtypes in DSM-V.

5. General discussion

The present study was designed to investigate the hypothesis that those with ADHD-I exhibit both EF deficits and non-EF deficits by comparing typically developing controls with boys carefully diagnosed with ADHD-I on an extensive battery of tasks that cover the major EF and non-EF domains.

With regard to the EF domains, results are consistent with findings in previous studies of EF and ADHD. That is, ADHD is associated with weaknesses in several key EF domains, but the strongest and most consistent effects are obtained on measures of response inhibition, vigilance, spatial working memory and some measures of planning [8, 41, 56-58]. The deficits on EF domains revealed in ADHD-I also suggest that the pathology of ADHD-I is related to deficits in managing an appropriate problem or attaining a future goal. Furthermore, results did not yield evidence for the model of ADHD in which only ADHD-C and ADHD-H, but not ADHD-I, are associated with EF deficits.

With regard to non-EF domains, findings revealed that the children with ADHD-I also demonstrated deficits in these domains, such as, divided attention, flexibility, sustained attention and visual scanning. This suggests that children with ADHD-I not only show deficits in EF, but also experience deficits in other non-EF domains.

Discriminating among disorders is particularly important. However, there are no objective diagnostic tests for ADHD-I [59]. Considering the fact that neither EF nor non-EF domains distinguish ADHD-I from ADHD-C, examination of other factors, such social, emotional and behavioral characteristics [60, 61] may be needed to support the validity of ADHD subtypes in the DSM-V.

6. Limitations

A limitation of our study findings is the small sample size and potential response bias from those who agreed to participate. To gather more reliable data and validate the results of the present study, future research should focus on selecting larger samples to engage in the same tasks. Furthermore, to examine whether EF and non-EF tests can distinguish ADHD-I from ADHD-C, it would be useful to make a direct comparison between ADHD-C and ADHD-I in the battery of EF and non-EF tests used in the study. Future studies should be conducted using the same tasks with an ADHD-C group.

Acknowledgements

The authors wish to thank all the participants in this experiment. Special thanks go to Yu Jia for her invaluable help. This work was also supported by National Natural Foundation of China (31300839), Grant-in-Aid for JSPS Postdoctoral Fellowship For Foreign Researchers (P13311), Shanghai Pujiang Program (12PJC034), and MOE (Ministry of Education in China) Project of Humanities and Social Sciences (13YJC190020).

Author details

Yongning Song*

Address all correspondence to: ynsong@psy.ecnu.edu.cn

School of Psychology and Cognitive Science, East China Normal University, China

References

[1] Chan RCK, Shum D, Toulopoulou T, Chen EYH. Assessment of executive functions: Review of instruments and identification of critical issues. Archives of Clinical Neuropsychology. 2008; 3 (2): 201-216. DOI: 10.1016/j.acn.2007.08.010

[2] Hughes C. Executive function in preschoolers: Links with theory of mind and verbal ability. British Journal of Developmental Psychology. 1998;16: 233-253. http://dx.doi.org/10.1111/j.2044-835X.1998.tb00921.x

[3] Miyake A, Friedman, N, Emerson, M, Witzki, A, Howerter, A, Wager, T. The unity and diversity of executive functions and their contributions to complex " frontal lobe" tasks: a latent variable analysis. Cognitive Psychology. 2000; 41: 49-100. DOI: 10.1006/cogp.1999.0734

[4] Ozonoff S. Components of executive function in autism and other disorders. In J. Russell (Ed.), Autism as an executive disorder. New York, USA: Oxford University Press; 1997.179–211p.

[5] Robbins TW. Dissociating executive functions of the prefrontal cortex. Philosophical Transactions of the Royal Society London. 1996; 351: 1463-1471. DOI: 10.1098/rstb. 1996.0131

[6] Welsh MC, Pennington BF,Groisser DB. A normative developmental study of executive function: a window on prefrontal function in children. Developmental Neuropsychology. 1991;7: 131-149. DOI: 10.1080/87565649109540483

[7] Welsh MC,Pennington BF. Assessing frontal lobe functioning in children: Views from developmental psychology. Developmental Neuropsychology. 1988; 4: 199-230. DOI: 10.1080/87565648809540405

[8] Willcutt EG, Doyle AE, Nigg JT, Faraone SV,Pennington BF. Validity of the executive function theory of attention-deficit/hyperactivity disorder: A meta-analytic review. Biological Psychiatry. 2005;57: 1336-1346. DOI: 10.1016/j.biopsych.2005.02.006

[9] Boucagnani LL,Jones RW. Behaviors analogous to frontal dysfunction in children with attention deficit hyperactivity disorder. Archives of Clinical Neuropsychology. 1989;4: 161-73. DOI: 10.1093/arclin/4.2.161

[10] Castellanos FX,Tannock R. Neuroscience of attention-deficit/hyperactivity disorder: The search for endophenotypes. Nature Reviews Neuroscience. 2002; 3: 617-628. DOI: 10.1038/nrn896

[11] Levin PM. Restlessness in children. Archives of Neurology and Psychiatry. 1938; 39: 764-770. doi:10.1001/archneurpsyc.1938.02270040120006.

[12] Pennington B,Ozonoff S. Executive functions and developmental psychopathology. Journal of Child Psychology and Psychiatry. 1996; 37: 51– 87. DOI: 10.1111/j. 1469-7610.1996.tb01380.x

[13] Pineda DA, Restrepo MA,Sarmiento RJ. Statistical analyses of structural magnetic resonance imaging of the head of the caudate nucleus in Colombian children with attention-deficit hyperactivity disorder. Journal of Child Neurology. 2002; 17: 97-105. DOI: 10.1177/088307380201700202

[14] Shue KL,Douglas VI. Attention deficit hyperactivity disorder and the frontal lobe syndrome. Special Issue: The role of frontal lobe maturation in cognitive and social development. Brain and Cognition. 1992; 20: 104-124. DOI: 10.1016/0278-2626(92)90064-S

[15] American Psychiatric Association (APA). Diagnostic and statistical manual of mental disorders. 5th ed. Washington, DC: American Psychiatric Association. 2013.

[16] Barkley RA. Behavioral inhibition, sustained attention, and executive function: constructing a unified theory of ADHD. Psychological Bulletin. 1997; 121: 65-94.http://dx.doi.org/10.1037/0033-2909.121.1.65

[17] Milich R, Balentine A,Lynam D. ADHD combined type and ADHD predominantly inattentive type are distinct and unrelated disorders. Clinical Psychology: Science and Practice. 2001; 8: 463-488. DOI: 10.1093/clipsy.8.4.463

[18] Nigg JT. Neuropsychologic theory and findings in attentiondeficit/ hyperactivity disorder: the state of the field and salient challenges for the coming decade. Biological Psychiatry. 2005; 57: 1424-35. DOI: 10.1016/j.biopsych.2004.11.011

[19] Nigg JT, Blaskey LG, Huang-Pollock CL,Rappley MD. Neuropsychological executive functions and DSM-IV ADHD subtypes. Journal of the American Academy of Child and Adolescent Psychiatry. 2002; 41: 59-66. DOI: 10.1097/00004583-200201000-00012

[20] McBurnett K, Pfiffner LJ,Frick PJ. Symptom properties as a function of ADHD type: An argument for continued study of sluggish cognitive tempo. Journal of abnormal child psychology. 2001; 29(3): 207-213. DOI: 10.1023/A:1010377530749

[21] Carlson CL,Mann M. Sluggish cognitive tempo predicts a different pattern of impairment in the attention deficit hyperactivity disorder, predominantly inattentive type. Journal of Clinical Child and Adolescent Psychology. 2002; 31(1): 123-129. DOI: 10.1207/S15374424JCCP3101_14

[22] Song Y,Hakoda Y. The interference of local over global information processing in children with attention deficit hyperactivity disorder of the inattentive type. Brain and Development. 2012; 34(4): 308-317. DOI: 10.1016/j.braindev.2011.07.010

[23] Angold A, Prendergast A, Cox R, Harrington E, Simonoff E,Rutter M. The child and adolescent psychiatric assessment (CAPA). Psychological Medicine. 1995; 25: 739-753. DOI: http://dx.doi.org/10.1017/S003329170003498X

[24] Conners CK. Rating scales in attention deficit hyperactivity disorder use in assessment, and treatment and monitoring. Journal of Clinical Psychiatry. 1998; 59: 24-30.

[25] Conners CK. The Conners rating scales: Instruments for the assessments of childhood psychopathology. Durham, NC: Duke University. 1995.

[26] Hakoda YJ,Sasaki M. Group version of the Stroop and reverse-Stroop test: The effects of reaction mode, order and practice. Japanese Journal of Educational Psychology. 1990; 38: 389-394.

[27] Hakoda YJ,Sasaki MTwo interferences based on new Stroop test and reaction model (Report No. 3). Fukuoka: Japan, Kyushu University, Department of Information Systems. 1991

[28] Luciana M,Nelson CA. Neurodevelopmental assessment of cognitive function using the Cambridge Neurospychological Testing Automated Battery (CANTAB): Validation and future goals. In M. ErnstJ. Rumseyy (Eds.), The foundation and future of

functional neuroimaging in child psychiatry. Cambridge University Press. 2000. http://dx.doi.org/10.1111/1469-7610.00152

[29] Sahakian B,Owen A. Computerised assessment in neuropsychiatry using CANTAB. Journal of the Royal Society of Medicine. 1992; 85: 399-402.

[30] Goldberg MC, Mostofsky SH, Cutting LE, Mahone EM, Astor BC,Denckla MB. Subtle executive impairment in children with autism and children with ADHD. Journal of Autism Developmental Disordors. 2005; 35: 279-293. DOI: 10.1007/s10803-005-3291-4

[31] Kempton S, Vance A, Maruff P, Luk E, Costin J,Pantelis C. Executive function and attention deficit hyperactivity disorder: stimulant medication and better executive function performance in children. Psychological Medicine. 1999; 29: 527-538. DOI: 10.1017/S0033291799008338

[32] Joyce E, Blumenthal S,Wessely S. Memory, attention, and executive function in chronic fatigue syndrome. Journal of Neurology, Neurosurgery and Psychiatry. 1996; 60: 495-503.

[33] Shallice T. Specific impairments of planning. Philosophical Transactions of the Royal Society of London, 1982; 298, 199-209. DOI: 10.1098/rstb.1982.0082

[34] Luciana M. Practitioner Review: Computerized assessment of neuropsychological function in children: Clinical and research applications of the Cambridge Neuropsychological Testing Automated Battery (CANTAB). Journal of Child Psychology and Psychiatry. 2003; 44: 649-663. DOI: 10.1111/1469-7610.00152

[35] Grant DA, Berg EA. A behavioral analysis of degree of reinforcement and ease of shifting to new responses in a Weigl-type card sorting problem. Journal of Experimental Psychology. 1948; 34: 404-411. http://dx.doi.org/10.1037/h0059831

[36] Heaton RK. Wisconsin Card Sorting Test manual. Odessa, FL: Psychological Assessment Resources. 1981

[37] Heaton R.K, Chelune G.J, Talley JL, Kay G.G,Curtiss G. Wisconsin Card Sorting Test manual. Odessa, FL: Psychological Assessment Resources, Inc. 1993.

[38] Song Y,Hakoda Y. An Asymmetric Stroop/Reverse-Stroop Interference Phenomenon in ADHD. Journal of Attention Disorders. 2011; 15(6): 499-505. DOI: 10.1177/1087054710367607

[39] Zimmermann P,Fimm B. A test battery for attentional performance. In: Leclercq M. Applied neuropsychology of attention. London: Psychology Press. 2002.

[40] Corbett BA, Constantine L.J, Hendren R, Rocke D,Ozonoff S. Examining executive functioning in children with autism spectrum disorder, attention deficit hyperactivity disorder and typical development. Psychiatry Research. 2009; 166: 210-222. DOI: 10.1016/j.psychres.2008.02.005

[41] Martinussen R, Hayden J, Hogg-Johnson S,Tannock R. A meta-analysis of working memory impairments in children with attention-deficit/hyperactivity disorder. Jour-

nal of the American Academy of Child and Adolescent Psychiatry. 2005; 44: 377-384. DOI: 10.1097/01.chi.0000153228.72591.73

[42] Geurts HM, Verte S, Oosterlaan J, Roeyers H,Sergeant JA. How specific are executive functioning deficits in attention deficit hyperactivity disorder and autism? Journal of Child Psychology and Psychiatry. 2004; 45: 836-854. DOI: 10.1111/j. 1469-7610.2004.00276.x

[43] Pennington BF, Groisser D,Welsh MC. Contrasting cognitive deficits in attention deficit hyperactivity disorder versus reading disability. Developmental Psychology. 1993; 29: 511-523.

[44] Weyandt LL,Willis WG. Executive functions in school-aged children: Potential efficacy of tasks in discriminating clinical groups. Developmental Neuropsychology. 1994; 10: 27-38. DOI: 10.1080/87565649409540564

[45] Amaral AH,Guerreiro MM. Attention deficit hyperactivity disorder: proposal of neuropsychological assessment. Arq Neuropsiquiatr. 2001; 59 (4): 884-888. DOI: 10.1590/ S0004-282X2001000600009

[46] Reeve WV,Schandler SL. Frontal lobe functioning in adolescents with attention deficit hyperactivity disorder. Adolescence. 2001; 36: 749-765.

[47] Semrud CM, Steingard RJ,Filipek P. Using MRI to Examine Brain-Behavior Relationships in Males With Attention Deficit Disorder with Hyperactivity children. Journal of the American Academy of Child and Adolescent Psychiatry. 2000; 39(4): 477-484. DOI: 10.1097/00004583-200004000-00017

[48] Tripp G, Ryan J,Peace K. Neuropsychological functioning in children with DSM-IV combined type Attention Deficit Hyperactivity Disorder. Australian and New Zealand Journal of psychiatry. 2002; 36: 71-779. DOI: 10.1046/j.1440-1614.2002.01093.x

[49] Houghton S, Douglas G,West J. Differential patterns of executive function in children with attention-deficit hyperactivity disorder according to gender and subtype. Journal of Child Neurology. 1999; 14: 801-805. DOI: 10.1177/088307389901401206

[50] Schmitz M, Cadore, L, Paczko M, Kipper L, Chaves M,Rohde LA. Neuropsychological performance in DSM-IV ADHD subtypes: An exploratory study with untreated adolescents. Canadian Journal of Psychiatry. 2002; 47: 863-869.

[51] Mourik R, Oosterlaan J,Sergeant JA. The Stroop revisited: A meta-analysis of interference control in AD/HD. Journal of Child Psychology and Psychiatry. 2005; 46: 150-165. DOI: 10.1111/j.1469-7610.2004.00345.x

[52] Lansbergen MM, Kenemans JL,Van Engeland H. Stroop interference and attention-deficit/hyperactivity disorder: A review and meta-analysis. Neuropsychology. 2007; 21(2): 251-262. http://dx.doi.org/10.1037/0894-4105.21.2.251

[53] Stroop JR. Studies of interference in serial verbal reactions. Journal of Experimental Psychology. 1935;18: 643-662. http://dx.doi.org/10.1037/0096-3445.121.1.15

[54] Goodyear E,Hynd, G. Attention deficit disorder with (ADD/H) and without (ADD/WO) hyperactivity: Behavioral and neuropsychological differentiation. Journal of Clinical Child Psychology. 1992; 21: 273-304. DOI: 10.1207/s15374424jccp2103_9

[55] Lahey BB,Carlson CL. Validity of the diagnostic category of attention deficit disorder without hyperactivity: A review of the literature. In S.E. ShaywitzB. Shaywitz (Eds), Attention deficit disorder comes of age: Toward the twenty-first century. Austin, TX: Pro-Ed. 1992. 119-144p.

[56] Chhabildas N, Pennington BF,Willcutt EG. A comparison of the Neuropsychological Profiles of the DSM-IV Subtypes of ADHD. Journal of Abnormal Child Psychology. 2001;29: 529-540. DOI: 10.1023/A:1012281226028

[57] Geurts, HM, Vert'ec S, Oosterlaana J, Roeyersc H,Sergeanta HA. ADHD subtypes: do they differ in their executive functioning profile? Archives of Clinical Neuropsychology. 2005; 20: 457-477.DOI: 10.1016/j.acn.2004.11.001

[58] Riccio CA, Homack S, Jarratt KP,Wolfe ME. Differences in academic and executive function domains among children with ADHD Predominantly Inattentive and Combined Types. Archives of Clinical Neuropsychology. 2006; 21: 657-667. DOI: 10.1016/j.acn.2006.05.010

[59] Aaron P, Joshi RM,Phipps J. A cognitive tool to diagnose predominantly inattentive ADHD behaviour. Journal of Attention Disorders. 2004; 7: 125-135. DOI: 10.1177/108705470400700301.

[60] Gadow KD, Sprafkin J,Nolan EE. DSM–IV symptoms in community and clinic preschool children. Journal of the American Academy of ChildAdolescent Psychiatry. 2001; 40: 1383-1392. DOI: 10.1097/00004583-200112000-00008

[61] Graetz BW, Sawyer MG, Hazell PL, Arney F, Baghurst P. Validity of DSM-IV ADHD subtypes in a nationally representative sample of Australian children and adolescents. Journal of the American Academy of Child and Adolescent Psychiatry. 2001; 40: 1410-1417. DOI: 10.1097/00004583-200112000-00011

Chapter 9

The Quality of Life (QoL) in Attention Deficit Hyperactivity Disorder (ADHD)

Ozden Sukran Uneri, Gulser Senses-Dinc and Zeynep Goker

Additional information is available at the end of the chapter

http://dx.doi.org/10.5772/60955

Abstract

Attention-deficit/hyperactivity disorder (ADHD) is a neurodevelopmental disorder characterized by inattention, impulsivity, and hyperactivity of core symptoms, affecting 3-10% of school age children, as well as 4% of adults.

Quality of Life (QoL) is an individual perception in regard to his/her position in life, in the context of culture and value systems in which they live, and in relation to their goals, expectations, standards and concerns. Then it has a multidimensional concept, the core of which consists of the physical, psychological, cognitive, and social aspects of functioning.

Several studies on QoL in ADHD have been published pointing out that QoL domains in ADHD have been found to be negatively affected compared to the healthy persons. This situation suggests that ADHD not only affects academic achievements of a person but it also has a deteriorating effect on all aspects of life, including social and occupational. Mostly used pharmacological agents are atomoxetine, methylphenidate and other stimulants related to QoL and ADHD context. These agents of ADHD treatments have been correlated with an improvement in QoL scores. Non-pharmacological interventions and their effects on QoL in patients with ADHD or the effectiveness of combined treatment modalities should be carried out in the near future.

Keywords: Attention deficit hyperactivity disorder, quality of life, children, treatment

1. Introduction

Quality of life (QoL) and its evaluation have become an increasingly important measure of outcome in all age groups of mental health clinical work and research [1]. WHOQoL group describes QoL as "the individuals' perception of their position in life, in the context of culture and value systems in which they live, and in relation to their goals, expectations, standards and concerns" [2]. QoL is a multidimensional concept, the core of which consists of the physical, psychological, cognitive, and social aspects of functioning [1].

Attention-deficit/hyperactivity disorder (ADHD) is a psychiatric disorder characterized by inattention, impulsivity, and hyperactivity that affects 3–10% of school age children [3]. Although most commonly thought of as a childhood disorder, ADHD affects children, adolescents, and adults. It persists in adolescence in approximately 80% of patients, and approximately 4% of adults are affected with ADHD [4]. ADHD is associated with a significant impairment of cognitive, emotional, and psychosocial functioning [5]. Also, children with ADHD can develop problematic relationships with families, and this pattern may continue into late adolescence and adulthood [6].

Several studies on QoL in ADHD have been published. Available studies confirm that ADHD impairs QoL in the sufferers [7]. QoL has the potential to be an important outcome measure. Understanding the impact of ADHD on QoL can be informative on a number of levels. In this chapter, we provide a review of QoL in adults, adolescents, and children with ADHD. We will be addressing the definition of QoL, providing an overview of what ADHD involves, and discussing four main issues:

1. The impact of ADHD on QoL
2. The relationship between ADHD symptoms and QoL
3. The effects of ADHD treatments on QoL domains
4. Appendix: The QoL measurement tools (generic and health-related scales)

2. The Quality of Life (QoL)

Quality of life (QoL) is a term explaining a satisfaction of life and fulfillment of one's expectations within the social and cultural milieu in which one lives and works. This QoL definition includes physical and mental health, independency levels, social relations, environmental issues, activities, individual beliefs, point of views of life itself and health, expectancy, and habits. All QoL definitions consist of physical, psychological, and social domains [1]. Health-related quality of life (HRQoL), on the other hand, is a multi-dimensional definition that consists of the parts of the QoL domains of the affected person by a disease. HRQoL attempts to measure to what extent the patient's activities are affected on a daily basis due to the disease [2]. In medical literature, it is observed that the terms QoL and HRQoL are used interchangeably. In this section, QoL and HRQoL terms will be used as synonyms in issues related to the quality of life.

The term QoL seems to have existed in sociological and medical terms since antiquity. Aristo and subsequent philosophers noted that the main purpose of life was reaching the optimized state allowed by life itself [3]. Hippocrates, building the foundations of medicine, taught his pupils that they must take responsibility for increasing the state of well-being to the highest point during treatment procedures [4]. Excluding these general teachings, the term QoL was first reported in medical literature in 1960 with Long's article titled "On the quantity and quality of life." Six years later, it was again used in the editorial section of *Annals of Internal Medicine*, "Medicine and the Quality of Life" [5]. In subsequent years, QoL has been at the center of many debates, discussing how to define it, how to measure it, and which scales have the highest levels of validity [6].

Because QoL assessments are a crucial health parameter, it has been necessary to develop QoL measurements for children. Child QoL studies began in the 1980s. Herndon et al. (1986) evaluated the quality of life of 12 children with severe burns that affected physical functioning. This study conducted an evaluation based on the degree of the burn and how it affected psychosocial adjustment [8]. Two studies, conducted by Ditesheim and Templeton (1987) and another one reported by Henning et al (1988), are the very first studies in evaluating children's QoL [9, 10]. These first QoL studies of children were important in leading to the development of QoL scales in child age groups.

QoL scales are evaluated generally under two main headings; a general (generic) evaluation of well-being and the QoL developed after a specific disorder. They have superior and limiting aspects from one another. Generic QoL scales are created by comparing two people: one with any disorder to one who is healthy. Therefore, generic QoL scales have advantages in terms of applicability to public health studies, and comparison studies enabling the evaluation of subjects with disease and subjects without. However, the low sensitivity of generic QoL scales and their long-term evaluation phases can be seen as negative aspects. On the other hand, disease-specific QoL scales are valid only during the evaluation of the disease they have been developed for. This increases the internal consistency of the scale, as well as the sensitivity and specificity. However, a negative aspect of disease-specific QoL scales is, because they are only valid for a single disease, there is the question of which scale should be used for patients with multiple diseases [7]. Both generic and health-related QoL scales are available for evaluating QoL in adults and children with ADHD. All measurement tools mentioned throughout the text can be seen in the appendix.

3. Attention deficit hyperactivity disorder

Attention deficit hyperactivity disorder (ADHD) is a neurodevelopmental disorder consisting of inattention, hyperactivity, and impulsivity, unsuitable for the child's age and developmental level. By far the most common disorder in childhood, it causes impairment in social, cognitive, academic, and emotional domains.

Epidemiological studies have pointed out that ADHD prevalence in children throughout the world is at a 3–10% rate. A large number of studies have shown that the symptoms of ADHD and functional impairment continue during the adulthood period. With age, however, its prevalence decreases. The adult ADHD prevalence rate is 4% [11]. Community-based studies have shown that the frequency of ADHD in boys is 2 to 3 times higher than in girls, and this rate increases up to 9 times in clinical sample studies. The inattention subtype of ADH is seen more frequently in girls, whereas the combined subtype of ADHD is seen more dominantly in boys. Because girls have more prominent inattention symptoms and they have less conduct disorder, they are admitted to the hospital at a lower rate [12].

ADHD, though its etiology is still not clearly understood, is a disorder in which genetic and environmental factors play crucial roles. Family, twin, and orphan studies support the importance of genetic factors in the etiology of ADHD. The heritability rate of ADHD has been found at a 76% rate in genetic studies. Genetic predisposition to ADHD is identified by the combination of the effects of many genes. Environmental factors that lead to ADHD, on the other hand, are more influential in those who have a genetic predisposition to disease [13]. Neuroimaging studies have revealed that there is a relationship between a delay in cortical maturation and ADHD. Previously, a dysfunction located in the prefrontal-striatal pathways was thought to play a crucial role. However, later studies have shown that the etiopathogenesis of ADHD is a widespread dysfunction in a number of locations such as the frontoparietal-cortical pathways, corpus callosum, anterior cingulate cortex, and cerebellum. These areas are responsible for functions such as cognitive processing, attention, motor control, executive functions, response inhibition, reward, and motivation. Neuropsychological problems and behavioral symptoms of ADHD are considered to be a result of structural and functional abnormalities in fronto-striatal-cerebellar circuits [14]. Findings obtained from neuropsychological evaluations and neuroimaging studies are very important but not sufficient to be used in the diagnosis of ADHD. Thus, ADHD is still a clinical diagnosis based on detailed history, clinical observations, and a physical and neurological examination. Clinicians should refer to the information from parents and teachers regarding the symptoms of children. It is important to determine the severity of the symptoms before and after treatment with valid and reliable rating scales [13].

Children, adolescents, and adults diagnosed with ADHD have a high rate of comorbid psychiatric disorders. Studies have rated this comorbidity from 46% to 76%. Oppositional defiant disorder (40–60%), conduct disorder (10–20%), anxiety disorder (30–40%), and mood disorders (20–30%) are the most frequently seen comorbid disorders [15]. Alcohol and substance abuse are two problems patients face in their adolescence or adulthood. The presence of comorbid psychiatric disorders during the progress of ADHD negatively affects both the treatment process and the prognosis.

Even though ADHD is mostly diagnosed during childhood, follow-up studies have pointed out that 60–80% of patients continue to have symptoms of ADHD during adulthood [14]. It is known that during the transition to adolescence and adulthood, the symptoms of ADHD vary. Hyperactivity decreases during and after adolescence, and restlessness, feelings of discomfort or risky behaviors become dominant instead. However, in adulthood, symptoms such as difficulty in maintaining attention, forgetfulness, an inability to organize, an inability to complete plans, frequent change of jobs, marital problems, and changes in mood are seen [16].

The treatment of ADHD is a multifaceted approach that includes psychosocial interventions as well as pharmacotherapy. For adults, cognitive-behavioral therapy (CBT) is seen as an effective intervention method to treat ADHD [17, 18] or as an added approach to the ADHD medication as a supplement, to being effective in ADHD treatment [19, 20]. Similarly, behavioral management is also the most commonly used psychosocial approach in children with ADHD and has different forms for parents (such as behavioral parent training [BPT]), for teachers (such as training of classroom behavior management), and for children (such as summer treatment program [STP] and operant conditioning trails) [21, 22, 23]. STP is a multi-modal intervention, developed by Pelham et al. (1996), consisting of parent training, classroom implementation, practicing and tutoring of academic and sport skills, and social skill training [22]. Using these psychosocial approaches with pharmacotherapy could result in giving lower doses of medication to children with ADHD [23]. In adolescents with ADHD, behavior therapy (BT) was found to be effective compared to the medication, though BT had brought about greater improvement on overall functioning measures than that of medication [24]. CBT is another psychosocial intervention used in adolescents, which mostly relied on behavioral principles and was shown as effective [25, 26].

Pharmacotherapy is needed for many ADHD patients to control the symptoms and to decrease functional deteriorations. The first step in medication for the treatment of ADHD is stimulants. Stimulants are known to be generally safe and effective, and their clinical response rate is considered to be about 70%. Among non-stimulant medications, those frequently used are atomoxetine, alpha-2 agonists (clonidine and guanfacine), tricyclic antidepressants, and bupropion. Beginning the treatment in the very early stages of the disease and using effective dosage positively affects its prognosis and it leads to fewer problems in adulthood [27].

4. The impact of ADHD on QOL

Difficulties stemming mainly from the core symptoms of ADHD (inattention, hyperactivity, and impulsivity), affect many aspects of the lives of children and their families. It has also been long known that there is a relationship between a wide range of developmental, cognitive, social, and academic insufficiencies and ADHD [28]. Children and adolescents with ADHD experience more difficulties in social relations than that of their non-ADHD peers, especially in terms of establishing a relationship [29]. Also, ADHD in adults has been found to have specific and disabling effects on substance abuse, driving, divorce, lost years of schooling, unemployment, underemployment, poor self-esteem, and as a risk for other disorders [30]. Thus, a QoL assessment is especially important in disorders of a chronic nature that cause difficulties in almost every aspect of life such as ADHD. Studies examining the relationship between ADHD and QoL have gained momentum because QoL has become more prominent among health-related indicators.

Evaluating QoL in adults or children with ADHD has ultimately been possible by using generic QoL scales. A study conducted by Mick et al. (2008) showed that the psychometric properties of "Quality of life enjoyment and satisfaction questionnaire (Q-LES-QSF) [31]," one of the generic QoL scales, had internal consistency at a 0.88 rate in adults with ADHD, showing that it would be appropriate for evaluating QoL in ADHD [32]. Studies carried out in adults with ADHD have shown evidence of lower levels of QoL when compared to non-ADHD controls. In a study where the QoL of older patients with ADHD were evaluated with 148 adults aged over 50 years, the quality of life levels, determined by using EurQoL [33], the generic QoL scale, and life satisfaction levels were found to be significantly lower than that of population normative results due to an important decrease in QoL aspects such as mobility, self-care, general activity, pain/discomfort, and anxiety/depression [34]. Similar to this report, a study conducted by Kooij et al (2005) with 1813 adults who had ADHD-DSM-IV symptoms that were obtained from self-report evaluations demonstrated psychosocial impairments [35]. This study revealed that inattentiveness and hyperactivity scores were significantly associated with the measures of impairment, evaluated by using the General Health Questionnaire (GHQ-28) [36], one of the generic QoL scales. Even after controls for the GHQ-28, it was concluded that ADHD is not merely a child psychiatric disorder that persists into young adulthood, but is an important and unique manifestation of psychopathology during the entire lifespan [35]. These findings support the idea that ADHD has significant effects on the QoL measured by generic QoL scales and other questionnaires evaluating daily functions and other aspects of life throughout the world.

As far as children with ADHD and their QoL measurements using generic QoL scales are concerned, a large number of studies pointed out similar findings with that of the adults' reports. A study reviewing other studies related to children with ADHD and their QoL, Danckaerts et al. (2010) revealed that there were a total of 36 QoL and ADHD studies, and 29 of them evaluated the QoL of children with ADHD, using generic QoL scales [37]. Some of these studies have pointed out that there is an important decrease in all measurable areas [38, 39, 41], as well as only the "psychosocial areas" [42, 43] of QoL domains in patients with ADHD compared to healthy subjects. Taking a closer look at these findings, a study, conducted by Varni et al. (1999), showed high reliability in assessing the QoL of children aged 5–16, including 72 with ADHD, 66 cancer patients, 57 cerebral palsy patients, and 3,256 healthy subjects, through the use of the Pediatric Quality of Life Inventory (PedsQL), a generic QoL scale [38]. Similarly, Escobar et al. (2005) conducted a study consisting of 237 children between the ages of 6 and 12, where 124 of them had ADHD, 93 of them had asthma, and 120 were healthy subjects [39]. In this study, QoL assessment was examined with the Child Health Questionnaire (CHQ) [40] scale. The results indicated that children with ADHD showed impaired psychosocial functioning (compared to the asthma group) and an impaired psychosocial and physical functioning (compared to the healthy group). Differences between the ratings for children with ADHD and asthmatic children were smaller than that of the ADHD group and the healthy children.

Another study reported an important difference in connection with QoL between children aged 8–12 with ADHD and healthy controls [41]. In this study, all subscale scores of PedsQoL-parent forms and "psychosocial health" and "total scale" scores of PedsQoL-children forms were found to be significantly lower in ADHD group than that of the healthy controls. Kandemir et al. (2014) examined 76 ADHD children and 59 healthy subjects aged 7–16 years, using PedsQL. As a result, the PedsQL-child scale psychosocial health subscale and total scale scores of the ADHD patients were significantly lower than the control group [42]. Similarly, another study, using CHQ, revealed that ADHD has a deteriorating effect on multiple aspects of QoL [43].

There may also be a distinct difference between parents' reports and their children's with respect to QoL measurements. In a review, 36 QoL studies conducted between the years 1998 and 2008 were evaluated, concluding that parents evaluated their children's QoL parameters lower than their children rated themselves [37]. During the evaluation of QoL parameters and ADHD's effect on it, the question arose of whether or not ADHD subtypes make a difference. According to the assessment of ADHD subtypes and their effect on QoL parameters, Landgraf et al. (2002) found that children with ADHD combined type had a poorer QoL than children with ADHD inattentive type, both in the area of emotional-social well-being and in how they functioned at home [44]. As shown, a great number of factors could affect studies' findings of ADHD and QoL and could lead to different results. Among these factors are the following: sampling's age group, using different types of QoL scales, choosing proxy or self-report scales (whether filled out by parents or children), and different cultural contexts.

There are also a great number of studies evaluating QoL domains through ADHD-specific QoL measures in both adults and children. Brod et al. (2006), for instance, revealed that adults with ADHD had lower QoL scores, when compared to controls and subthreshold groups, using Adult-ADHD Quality of Life scale (AAQoL), a disease-specific QoL [45]. Another report showed that Taiwanese adult subjects with ADHD had a poorer quality of life than that of controls [46]. It also has been pointed out that ADHD subjects took longer to fall asleep, had lower sleep efficiency, and had shorter periods of uninterrupted sleep, which were consistent with subjective complaints. Alongside this, actigraphic measures of ADHD subjects showed continuously elevated day-time activity levels that resulted in a 24-hour pattern that was more stable and less variable than in controls [47].

Gjervan et al. (2012) assessed the relationship between ADHD symptoms and specific QoL areas in 149 adults with ADHD. In this study, there was a negative correlation between all of the components of QoL, and the inattention and hyperactivity scores, though this correlation was most prominent between inattention scores and vitality scales and between hyperactivity symptoms and mental health scale scores. This study concluded that inattention was only significant as a predictor of emotional outcome scores and hyperactivity was significant as a predictor of both mental health outcome scores and social functioning scores. A relationship between age/sex and aforementioned mental components was not found [48]. In contrast to this report, a study revealed the predictors of QoL, reporting a difference in the QoL scores of different sexes and pointing out that the QoL predictors were income levels for men and inattention symptoms for women [49]. Because findings have revealed that the QoL and its effects on sexes differ, there is a need for further evaluation of other environmental issues and their roles in future studies.

Studies carried out with children and adolescents using ADHD-specific QoL scales have highlighted similar conclusions as adult studies. A study conducted by college students showed that the ADHD group reported a lower quality of life compared to the non-ADHD groups [50]. Another study, a pooled analysis of a total of 136 girls and 658 boys (from one Canadian sample and four European samples) with ADHD showed impaired QoL levels [51]. In conclusion, ADHD is associated with a variety of functional impairments in every aspect of daily life, from academic achievements to social and occupational areas in both children and adults, as well as a significantly lower quality of life than of those without ADHD.

5. The relationship between ADHD symptoms and QoL

5.1. Symptom severity

A large number of studies in both adults and children with ADHD have shown that there is a negative correlation between ADHD severity and QoL parameters. A study revealed a relationship between a deteriorated QoL and ADHD symptom severity and unemployment in patients aged over 50. Both the severity of ADHD symptoms and inattention symptoms have been found to be correlated with the general activity levels of QoL scale scores and current health status sub-scores [34]. Similarly, a negative correlation was reported between the number of ADHD symptoms (ASRS) and the AAQoL total score [52]. Another study pointed out that the ADHD-RS-IV scores of 725 adults with ADHD were correlated with an improvement in both ADHD symptoms and its health-related QoL domains. In this study, inattention symptoms were found to be more predictive of QoL scores than that of hyperactivity/impulsivity symptoms [53]. In a study of 369 university students with ADHD symptoms, determined by using the "Diagnostic and Statistical Manual of Mental Disorders (DSM-IV)" criteria, it was reported that their satisfaction with life scale (SWLS)'s scores were negatively correlated with all the other measures. Among males, poor social functions were the best predictor of dissatisfaction with life, whereas among females, it was poor emotional control. This implied that both ADHD symptoms and associated problems are significantly related to a lower satisfaction with life, arguing that ADHD symptoms and associated problems were found to be negatively related to subjective well-being [54]. Similarly, Brod et al. (2006) reported a negative correlation between adult self-report scale (ASRS) scores and QoL, where more severe symptoms of ADHD were associated with lower levels of QoL [45]. Another study evaluated the quality of life of 127 Israeli young adults who were living in community residences, diagnosed with borderline intelligence quotient, and attention-deficit/hyperactivity disorder. They studied the subjects with regard to their personal data, disability data, and social ecology data. Overall, they discovered that the QoL was associated with their inclusive education, the total attention-deficit disorder symptomatology score, the monthly income, the amount of participation in leisure activities, and having a personal friend. Two significant predictors of QoL were found to be attention-deficit disorder symptomatology score and monthly income. Additional analyses indicated that among younger residents, the two significant predictors were inclusive education and a high monthly income, whereas the predictors for older residents were a low level of medical disability and a low attention-deficit disorder symptomatology score [55].

Similar to studies of adults, studies of children with ADHD pointed out a negative correlation between symptoms of ADHD and QoL domains. In their two studies, Wehmeier et al. (2010, 2012) showed a correlation between the ADHD rating scale and CHIP-CE [56] scores, another generic QoL scale, where both were similar in both genders, with low scores at baseline measurement and increased to a moderate level at endpoint assessment [29, 51]. Another study called ADORE, the ADHD Observational Research in Europe, made an important contribution to the evaluation of QoL using parent report forms (PRF) of the Child Health and Illness Profile-Child Edition (CHIP-CE) scales. With the participation of 1,500 parents from 10 European countries, children with ADHD between the ages of 6 and 18 were evaluated. In their conclusions, higher ADHD scores were found to be a predictor of lower QoL scores [57]. Studies using the CHQ-PF-50 scale for evaluating QoL found a statistically significant relationship (from small to moderate range) between QoL and ADHD, where both inattention and hyperactivity symptoms were found to be strongly related to psychosocial health subscale scores [43, 58]. All in all, assessing the above-mentioned results, a negative relationship between ADHD symptom severity and QoL, independent from age, is noticeable.

5.2. Functional impairment

The evaluations of QoL and functional impairment have many similar and different aspects from each other. In adults, ADHD determined by using self-report evaluations was found to be correlated with not graduating or being unemployed and these subjects were much more likely to experience relationship problems than those without ADHD diagnosis [59]. Brod et al. (2012) examined the burden of illness and QoL in 24 patients over the age of 65 and compared the findings of population data of younger adults with ADHD. Older ADHD adults showed a significantly greater impairment in productivity and a better life outlook than younger ADHD adults. In addition, 63% of participants had experienced problems such as financial difficulties, academic failures, poor working performance, and social isolation accumulated over a lifetime of living with ADHD [60]. A community-based study evaluating middle-aged adults with ADHD revealed a correlation between ADHD symptoms and both depression-anxiety scores and functional deterioration (as determined in "health," "subjective well-being," "building of social relationship skills," and "maintaining a healthy relationship" measures). After controlling depression-anxiety symptoms, the relation found between ADHD and functional deterioration was to remain [61]. Similarly, ADHD in young adults (ages 18 to 30) was found to be associated with significant impairments in multiple functional domains [62]. In another study, conducted with 3,400 university undergraduates, those with self-reported ADHD had significantly lower grade point averages, poorer emotional stability, and greater academic and social concerns than students who had never been diagnosed with ADHD [63]. Another study revealed that social functions were the best predictor of dissatisfaction with life, whereas among females it was poor emotional control, and both ADHD symptoms and associated problems are significantly related to a poorer satisfaction with life [53].

Detecting problems at the functional level is mainly carried out by clinicians, while the evaluation of QoL is done by the patient or their parents or caregivers. Rimmer et al. (2007) reported a mild correlation between functional impairment evaluated by a clinician and a QoL assessment carried out by children with ADHD or their parents [64]. In conclusion, studies reported that ADHD causes deterioration in the functioning of patients. However, in each study, the affected life domains were found to be different. This situation could very well stem from the chosen samplings' age groups.

5.3. Comorbidity

A large number of studies pointed out that mental diseases accompanied by ADHD are common, and this affects individuals' QoL levels [37, 65-67, 69, 70]. A high level of psychiatric disorder comorbidity was reported by Lensing et al. at a 70.9% rate in adults with ADHD. QoL scores were found to be negatively affected in those who had comorbid psychiatric disorder. Also, these patients' QoL scores have been found to be lower in terms of their current health status, general activity levels, and mobility [34]. A study examining the effects of depression symptoms on QoL scores in adults with ADHD revealed that a total of 131 Korean soldiers were included, and ADHD symptoms were found to be affected by the symptoms of depression. However, depression symptoms had an indirect effect on QoL scores as a mediator [65]. Similarly, a study evaluating ADHD symptoms and anxiety-depression scores in 1382 of young persons between ages 19 and 30 found that there was a correlation between ADHD symptoms and anxiety or depression scores. The presence of depression or anxiety symptoms was found to have a negative effect on QoL scores [66]. In another study conducted with 319 prisoners where the psychopathology and QoL were evaluated, 68 of them were diagnosed with ADHD [67]. This showed that patients diagnosed with ADHD had more psychiatric comorbid disorders. This study also revealed that although prisoners with ADHD had similar risk factors than non-ADHD prisoners, their mental health, mental summary, emotional role limitations, and social functioning scores, as assessed by SF36-QoL [68], the generic QoL scale, were significantly lower than those of non-ADHD. Liew and Cavanna (2013) showed that those with ADHD with Tourette syndrome (TS) had a lower HR-QoL level than that of patients without it. They set out to compare tic severity and health-related quality of life (HR-QoL) ratings between adult patients with TS versus patients with TS plus ADHD. Comparing 40 patients with only TS to 32 patients with TS plus ADHD using standardized self-report measures of adult ADHD (Adult ADHD Severity Scale), tic severity (MOVES), and disease-specific HR-QoL (Gilles de la Tourette Syndrome Quality of Life Scale, GTS-QoL), they found a highly significant difference in tic severity as measured by the MOVES scale, with the TS plus ADHD group reporting higher scores. Likewise, there were significant differences in GTS-QoL scores, with the TS plus ADHD group demonstrating worse HR-QoL perception. Adult patients with TS and comorbid ADHD tended to have higher tic severity and poorer HR-QOL compared to patients with only TS. As a result, clinicians treating adults with TS should screen their patients for residual ADHD symptoms in order to ensure that appropriate management is provided to prevent potential behavioral difficulties and other functional impairments [69]. A study was reported in relation with psychiatric comorbidity, age, and sex in subjects up to age 18 with treatment-naive ADHD. Results of this study were evaluated after being categorized as dimensional and categorical. A lower self-reported QoL was associated with females, older subjects, more symptoms of anxiety, and trauma-related disorders (in dimensional approach terms), and with comorbid diagnoses of trauma-related disorders and oppositional defiant disorder (ODD)/conduct disorder (CD)(in categorical approach terms). A lower parent-reported QoL was related to older subjects and increasing number of symptoms of mood and anxiety disorders on one hand, and any diagnosis of mood and anxiety disorders and ODD/CD on the other. Consequently, researchers have emphasized that during the evaluation of QoL in ADHD, age and sex variables, as well as both parents' and children's scales should be evaluated altogether [70]. It can be concluded that comorbid psychiatric disorders accompanying ADHD have a negative effect on QoL perceptions.

6. The effects of ADHD treatments on QOL

The concept of QoL has helped us understand the effects of medical conditions on individuals, as well as increasing our awareness of how treatments of diseases affect patients' life domains. ADHD treatment options including psychosocial approaches and pharmacotherapies have been shown to be effective in ameliorating both ADHD symptom scores and QoL measurements in both children and adults.

6.1. Psychosocial approaches and QoL in ADHD

There are a few studies regarding psychosocial programs and their effectiveness in treating ADHD and improving QoL compared to the medication studies. Cognitive-behavioral therapy (CBT) group intervention approach, one of the psychosocial methods, was shown as effective in low self-esteem and self-efficacy domains in adults with ADHD [17]. In another randomized controlled study, including a CBT booster-trial group, a CBT group and a control group, CBT booster sessions were shown to be as effective on Chinese adults with ADHD [18], using WHOQoL, another generic QoL scale [71]. Another study showed that CBT combined with pharmacotherapy of ADHD resulted in improvements of overall functioning assessed by clinical global impression scale (CGI) as well as ADHD symptoms [19]. Similarly, CBT combined with usual ADHD medication improved both the self-rated ADHD symptoms and social and occupational functioning in comparison to ADHD medication alone [20]. The other psychosocial approaches added to the ADHD medication in adults were also reported to be effective, though medication was found to be superior to placebo and psychosocial programs [72]. On the other hand, a review examining the effects of psycho-education interventions on outcomes of children and adolescents with ADHD highlighted that programs focusing on the communication between children and their parents and/or teachers and coping skills of parents had some positive effect on the clinical outcomes [73]. BPT has been shown to be effective in parent-child conflicts to improve child oppositional behavior rather than ADHD symptoms themselves [21]. Teacher training for contingency management procedures such as strategy training and curriculum modifications as well as punishment techniques were also found promising in altering the level of ADHD symptoms [22]. CBT was also shown as more effective in adolescents with pure ADHD or in those with anxiety/depression symptoms comorbidity than that of adolescents with ADHD and in those with comorbid oppositional defiant disorders [26]. Psychosocial interventions added to ADHD medication was reported to be effective in ameliorating the core ADHD symptoms and functional impairments accompanying it [74].

6.2. Atomoxetine (ATX) and QoL in ADHD

Medication use for ADHD treatment and its effects on QoL domains is a well-studied issue. In the literature, studies evaluating QoL and ATX have been noticeably more common than that of other agents. With randomized, double-blind, placebo-controlled studies, ATX had a positive effect on the QoL of both adults and children with ADHD as well as with open-labelled designed reports [29, 51, 53, 57, 62, 74-78].

For adults with ADHD, ATX is the only United States Food and Drug Administration (FDA)-approved, non-stimulant drug. In studies conducted with adults with ADHD, the improvement of ADHD symptoms and QoL domains have been shown in many adult ADHD trials in ATX treatment groups compared to the placebo group [62, 74-78]. These improvements were not only statistically significant, but also showed a clinically meaningful improvement in symptoms [79]. A double-blind, placebo-controlled study, during 12 weeks of ATX treatment consisting of young adults with ADHD, revealed more improvement in ADHD symptoms, executive functions, and QoL scores than that of the placebo group [62]. Similarly, in the first large sampling of placebo-controlled prospective studies, ATX group's QoL total scores and all subscores (except for life outlook subscale) were found significantly improved compared to the placebo group [75]. In the first placebo-controlled design of an Asian sampling study, ATX was found as safe and tolerable in adults with ADHD for 10 weeks. Compared to the placebo, ATX was more effective on ADHD core symptoms and showed more improvement in QoL scores than that of the placebo group [76]. The study examined the effectiveness of ATX in adults with ADHD, at 10 weeks of the treatment and at six months and total QoL scores and ADHD symptom rating scores evaluated by the clinicians and clinical global impression scale scores were found significantly improved over that of the placebo group [78]. The evaluation of adults with both ADHD and comorbid social anxiety disorder after 14 weeks medication with ATX revealed that QoL total scores, state anxiety scores, social anxiety scores, and clinical global impression scores were significantly improved in ATX group over that of the placebo group [80].

For children and adolescents, ATX has also been the most studied pharmacotherapeutic agent in ADHD and QoL. In a randomized, placebo-controlled designed study of Swedish children with ADHD, ATX treatment was found as effective on Child Health and Illness Profile (CHIP) QoL domains [74]. Similar to this study, Escobar et al. (2009) reported that ATX was superior to that of a placebo on CHIP-CE scores [81]. Another randomized, double blind, placebo controlled study, conducted among 180 children and adolescents with ADHD and comorbid ODD/CD for nine weeks, showed that ATX had a positive effect on QoL domains [82]. In another study of comorbid oppositional defiant disorder and ADHD, Dell'Agnello et al. (2009) showed that ATX was more effective on CHIP-CE QoL domains than that of a placebo [83].

Also, with open-label designed studies, ATX has been shown to cause an increase in the QoL of children with ADHD [84, 85]. Montoya et al. (2014) examined the prognostic factors of improvements of ATX treatment in children and adolescents with ADHD, concluding that a baseline level of impairment in health-related QoL could be an early prognostic factor of clinical outcomes of ADHD treatment [86]. Also, another analysis of pooled data (from 5 clinical ATX trials (four from Europe and one from Canada) of similar durations (8- to 12-week follow-ups) and with similar inclusion and exclusion criteria) evaluated whether gender makes a difference in QoL domains with ATX treatments. It showed that there were correlations between HR-QoL and ADHD core symptoms. Boys and girls were similarly impaired at baseline with minor differences in some of the subdomains. The treatment effect of ATX was significant in both groups for the risk-avoidance domain and its subdomains [51].

6.3. Stimulants and QoL in ADHD

There are relatively few studies related to QoL and stimulants such as methylphenidate (MPH), amphetamines and lisdexamfetamine dimesylate (LDX), although they are the most used agents in ADHD treatment. Adult studies with stimulants and QoL in ADHD unanimously pointed out the efficacy of these medications on ADHD symptoms and QoL measurements. Mattos et al. (2013) showed OROS-MPH, a long-acting methylphenidate, was found effective, in a 12-week, multicenter, open-label trial involving 60 patients. All subscales of QoL improved from baseline to week 12, as well as the total score of QoL. In addition, significant improvement was pointed out by the Clinical Global Impression-Improvement (CGI-I) scale, depression scale, state-trait anxiety scale, ADHD symptom rating scale [87]. The placebo-controlled study examined the sleep quality and its relation with MPH treatment in adult patients with ADHD. Then, pre-treatment and after-treatment of sleep parameters, activity, and circadian rhythm were evaluated [47]. Data obtained from ADHD subjects at the beginning were compared with healthy persons. Actigraphic sleep estimates revealed that ADHD subjects took longer to fall asleep, had lower sleep efficiency, and had shorter uninterrupted night sleep. In addition, ADHD subjects showed continuously elevated daytime activity levels, resulting in a 24-hour pattern that was more stable and less variable than in controls. With MPH treatment, a decrease was found in waking throughout the night sleeps, concluding that there was an improvement in sleep quality despite the reduction in total sleep time. Kooij et al. (2001) evaluated the effect of MPH and dextroamphetamine treatments on sleep parameters in 8 adults with ADHD in a case-control study [88]. Actimeters were used to assess nocturnal motor activity for six consecutive nights both at baseline and after three weeks of treatment. ADHD patients slept worse and showed significantly higher nocturnal motor activity at baseline compared with controls. When within-group changes were compared between ADHD subjects and controls, treatment with stimulants tended to be associated with a reduction of Activity Level and Movement Index scores and improved sleep quality in ADHD patients.

An open-labelled designed study examining effectiveness of long-acting amphetamines in adults with ADHD for eight months found strong responses to the amphetamine treatment. This study revealed that changes in the symptoms and treatment satisfaction mediate independently the mental outcome of QoL but not the physical outcome. Inattention symptoms were found as strong mediators for QoL outcomes compared to the disruptive behaviors [53]. A positive correlation between improvement of executive functions and health-related quality of life scores in adults with ADHD treated with triple-bead mixed amphetamine salts (MAS) was pointed out according to the evaluation of two large-sampled, randomized, placebo-controlled and double-blind study results [89]. Similarly, another study in adults with double-blind, placebo-controlled design for seven weeks showed a significant improvement in all subscales of health-specific QoL scores compared to the placebo results [90].

LDX was also shown to be effective in both ADHD core symptoms and in QoL measurements in adults with ADHD who had significant impairments [91]. Adler et al. (2013) examined the effects of LDX on QoL in adults with ADHD and clinically significant executive function deficits (EFD). In this 10-week randomized placebo-controlled trial study, LDX was just as effective on QoL and EFD measurements [92].

Stimulants and their efficacies on QoL parameters in children and adolescents with ADHD were also reported in the literature. Forty-five of treatment-naïve children with ADHD, aged 8–14, were assessed, based on self, parent, and teacher reports at the baseline and at the end of the first and third months of MPH treatment, regarding changes in inattention, hyperactivity, impulsivity, depression, anxiety, and obsessive compulsive symptoms. Symptoms of inattention, hyperactivity, and impulsivity were significantly reduced following a three-month MPH treatment. There were significant decreases in depression, trait anxiety, and checking compulsion symptom scores. Moreover, parents reported significant improvements in psychosocial and total scores of quality of life [93].

Gerwe et al. (2009) showed that in their 8-week, prospective, open-label, non-interventional trial, the impact of therapy with OROS-MPH on functioning in four different areas of life (school, recreation, family life, and peer interaction), severity of disease, and quality of life (QoL) as well as tolerability, were investigated under daily routine care. In this study, 306 patients, aged 10.2±2.3 years, were either transitioned to OROS-MPH from short-acting, immediate-release MPH preparations, or treatment was initiated with OROS MPH in MPH-naive patients. In both groups, therapy with OROS-MPH was associated with significant improvements in daily functioning, severity of disease, and QoL [94]. Another double-blind, open-label study designed with placebo controls examined MPH effects on QoL, conducted with children aged 7–10 who have ADHD and developmental coordination disorder comorbidity, over the course of four weeks. QoL was evaluated by using both children self-reports and parents' proxy-reports. Pre-treatment scores of autonomic, social, motor, cognitive domains of QoL and general well-being scores decreased, and after MPH treatment, scores of health-related QoL domains improved compared to the controls [95].

Lisdexamfetamine dimesylate (LDX) was also shown as effective in QoL measurements. Banaschewski et al. (2014) evaluated the effectiveness of LDX on QoL in a total of 262 children, aged 6–17, with ADHD [96]. CHIP-CE Parent Report Form, as QoL evaluation, was found during the pre-treatment period as lower in 4 of 5 sub-scales as one standard deviation of

http://dx.doi.org/10.5772/60955

normative means. After a treatment of 30–70 mg/day LDX for 26 weeks, all QoL subscale scores were found to be improved compared to the baseline evaluation. After 26 weeks, 76 of 153 patients who used LDX continued to take the same dosage of LDX whereas 77 of them used a placebo instead of LDX. During this new six-week period, QoL scores of all patients who used placebos deteriorated, while there was no difference in QoL scores of patients who continued with the LDX agent. During a six-week period, there was a statistically significant difference in terms of "Avoidance Achievement," and "Satisfaction domains" of QoL scores between two groups (placebo and LDX).

Other pharmacological treatments undergoing clinical trials as are follows [30]:

- Long-acting clonidine hydrochloride (Clonicel) (is in Phase III).
- Pozanicline (ABT-089), a neuronal nicotinic receptor partial agonist, might prove to be promising, as research has shown that this drug significantly improves QoL (measured with AAQoL), improves the core symptoms of ADHD, and also reduces the overall work impairment in the adult ADHD population.
- Sofinicline (ABT-894), another nonstimulant agent, is in clinical trials for ADHD and no QoL data are yet available.

7. Conclusion and summary

QoL is one the most important variables for evaluating health issues. The QoL of subjects who have ADHD has been revealed as decreased in almost all areas of life compared to the healthy persons. This situation suggests that ADHD not only affects academic achievements of a person but it also has a deteriorating effect on all aspects of life, including social and occupational. These findings have the potential to be cornerstones of applying treatment choices and regulating follow-up of ADHD. To be well-understood, the strengths and weaknesses of QoL and ADHD studies are important for designing further studies.

Most studies evaluating the relation between ADHD and QoL seem to have used generic QoL scales. These scales are appropriate and useful to determine QoL in different disease groups or patients who have concurrent diseases. At the same time, it is undeniable that generic QoL scales might not be correlated with the symptoms of ADHD, indicating that there is a need for specific evaluation of core symptoms of ADHD and their probable effects on QoL domains. In this perspective for evaluating adults and adolescents with ADHD and their QoL, self-report ADHD-QoL scales such as "The ADHD Impact Module for Adults (AIM-A)," "The Adult ADHD Quality of Life Scale (AAQoL)," and "The Adult ADHD Quality of Life-29 (AA-QoL-29)" or "The Weiss Functional Impairment Rating Scale WFIRS," and "The ADHD Impact Module-Child; AIM-C" are profitable. For QoL of children with ADHD, it is recommended that both self-report and the parent proxy forms of ADHD-QoL scales be used including "The EuroQoL Five-Dimension Questionnaire-Parent-Proxy Version; Parent-proxy EQ-5D." Because the number of ADHD-specific QoL scales is very limited, an increase in the number of ADHD-specific QoL scales that have high reliability and validity scores will be useful for further application and evaluation of QoL in ADHD.

According to the literature, ADHD symptoms continue through the life span in many of the patients. This situation recalls that following the treatment and symptoms of ADHD in patients with ADHD, the child, adolescent, and adult forms of scales need to be used. In addition, ADHD has one of the most frequently observed comorbidity rates among the psychiatric disorders. In assessing QoL in ADHD, the frequency of comorbidity stands out as an aspect to be taken into consideration.

ADHD treatment consists of both pharmacological and non-pharmacological interventions. There is a specific notification that psychosocial interventions for treating of ADHD in both adults and children are seen at a lesser extent compared to the medication use. It is crucial to examine the further psychosocial approaches and their effects on both ADHD symptoms and QoL in adults and children. The use of many pharmacological agents in ADHD treatments has been correlated with an improvement in QoL scores. However, the presence of a small number of randomized placebo-controlled studies with agents, except atomoxetine, draws attention. In addition, there is a need for further study, including comparisons with different pharmacotherapic agents. In addition, non-pharmacological interventions and their effects on QoL in patients with ADHD or the effectiveness of combined treatment modalities should be carried out in the near future.

Appendix

QoL scales

QoL scales are evaluated generally under two main headings; a general (generic) evaluation of well-being, and the QoL developed after a specific disorder. Generic and health-specific QoL scales both have superior and limiting aspects from one another. Generic QoL scales are created by comparing two people: one with any disorder and one who is healthy. Therefore, generic QoL scales have advantages in terms of applicability to public health studies, and comparison studies enabling the evaluation of subjects with disease and subjects without. However, the low sensitivity of generic QoL scales and their long-term evaluation phases can be seen as negative aspects. Disease-specific QoL scales are valid only during the evaluation of the disease they have been developed for. This increases the internal consistency of the scale, as well as the sensitivity and specificity. However, a negative aspect of disease-specific QoL scales is that they are valid only for a single disease and there is the question of which scale should be used for patients with multiple diseases [7].

Studies of QoL scales first began in adult groups. For evaluating physical functions of adults in QoL measurements, activities such as working conditions, self-care, tasks within the family, the ability to walk up the stairs, and the ability to sweep the house are questioned. From these studies, there are several QoL scales for evaluating the adults' QoL domains. On the other hand, it has since become clear that the evaluation of children's QoL has many different aspects than adult QoL assessments. Activities, for instance, are differently evaluated from children with parameters like being able to eat, going to the toilet on their own, being able to perform minor chores, and gaming activities. Although activities in school or relationships with friends are not crucially important in adults when assessing social functioning, in children activities in school, peer relations, game playing, and adjustments to school are very important. Areas of emotional and cognitive functioning, body image, autonomy, family relations, and expectations of the future should be assessed for each age group (adults, adolescents, and children) differently. For these reasons, during QoL evaluations, using adults' QoL scales to evaluate adolescents or using scales developed for evaluating adolescents or children is not deemed appropriate without making age-appropriate changes [58].

The question of whether or not the assessment of QoL of children should be made by children themselves or their parents has been discussed for many years. Some researchers argue that a subjective assessment is more valuable because it reflects the conditions of children from their own perspective, while others suggest that an objective assessment made by parents with proxy scales has more validity [7, 97]. In general, it is proposed that scales used for evaluating QoL should be filled by the individual himself. However, the necessity of using proxy-report scales instead of self-report scales in persons who are too old, too young, or too sick to fill out the forms themselves has brought about the discussion of who will fill out the QoL scales. In last decade, the idea that children, after 3 years of age, need to self-assess their quality of life as much as possible has become more dominant. If children or adolescents are too young or too sick to answer the questions, or if they do not wish to, then, to evaluate their QoL, the use of the parents' version of QoL scales is recommended. In this case, the negative aspects of using parents' scales should be considered, which are as follows:

- Parents will not be able to know precisely what their child is experiencing from the symptoms, the child's relationship with his peers, or about his concerns for the future.
- Being affected by other children while filling out the scales, or the possibility of being affected by their own expectations and hopes, stress, or mental states at that moment.

Where possible, the use of scales that can be compared between parents and children seems to be the most appropriate solution. However, because these scales are limited in number and the results of the parents and children are not always compatible with each other, there are difficulties in using combined parent proxy and self-reporting. When analyzing parents' and children's scales simultaneously, children, unlike their parents, did not seem to be affected by the cause of the disease or its treatment; they look at their disease more optimistically. Having friends and their ability to run and play are the more important issues for them than the necessity of basic skills and aptitudes. Besides this, it should be noted that the level of the cognitive development of the child affects the ability to fill out the scale [7].

Generic QoL scales

Some generic QoL scales used in adults and children and adolescents are as follows:

For adults

1. The Quality of Life Enjoyment and Satisfaction Questionnaire Short Form (QLESQ-SF): It has five domains of questioning, including physical health, mood, family relationships, ability to function in daily life, and taking any treatment or medication, via a Likert-type order from very poor to very good [31].

2. The EuroQoL-Five Dimension Scale (EurQoL-5D): This is a standardized instrument designed by EurQoL Group evaluating health outcomes and is comprised of five dimensions: mobility, self-care, usual activities, pain/discomfort, and anxiety/depression, each with three response levels: no problems, some problems, and extreme problems. It is also allowed to rate each dimension on a vertical visual analogue scale (VAS) from 0 (worst imaginable health state) to 100 (best imaginable health state) [33].

3. The General Health Questionnaire-28 (GHQ-28): This scale is a summary of GHQ and consists of four subscales: somatic symptoms, anxiety and insomnia, social dysfunction, and severe depression [36].

4. The Short Form-36 General Health Survey Questionnaire (SF-36): This is a short questionnaire with 36 items that measure eight of multi-item variables: physical functioning, social functioning, role limitations due to physical problems, role limitations due to emotional problems, mental health, energy and vitality, pain, and general perception of health. It uses a scale of 0 to 100, with higher scores representing a better quality of life [68].

5. The World Health Organisation Quality of Life Scale (WHOQoL): The WHOQOL has been developed collaboratively in several culturally diverse centers over four years and contains a multi-dimensional profile of scores across 6 domains and 24 subdomains of the quality of life. It assesses individuals' perceptions of their positions in life in the context of the culture and value systems in which they live and in relation to their goals, expectations, standards, and concerns [71].

For children and adolescents:

1. The Pediatric Quality of Life Inventory™4.0 (PedsQL™4.0): This scale was developed by Varni et al. (1999) and is used in children aged 2–18 years. There are both child forms for ages 5 and up, and parallel parent scales for all age groups. In addition, all forms of the scale for age groups 2–4, 5–7, 8–12, and 13–18 have been arranged to contain minor differences according to the age group's characteristics. It has four main domains, including physical, emotional, social, and school-related functioning. A large number of studies in different languages have been carried out to determine the reliability and validity of PedsQL™4.0. It is a Likert-type scale and it can easily be completed within 5–10 minutes [38].

2. The Child Health Questionnaire (CHQ): It was validated by Landgraf, Abetz, and Ware (1996) and was examined for its reliability and validity with a group of children, ages 5–18. It is available in many different languages (Arabic, Bulgarian, Chinese, Danish, English, German, Spanish, etc.). CHQ has 12 subscales and 2 summary scores. It has a child's form (CHQCF-87 items) and two types of parents' forms (CHQ-PF-28, and 50 items). However, these are not parallel versions. CHQCF-87 was developed to be com-

pleted by children aged 10 or older. CHQ is frequently used to assess the QoL of children with different diseases [40].

3. The Child Health and Illness Profile (CHIP): It was developed by Starfield et al. (1995), assessing five domains that include achievement, comfort, resilience, risk avoidance, and satisfaction with health and self. CHIP has three versions: an adolescent form (CHIP-AE; ages 11–17), an illustrated form for children (CHIP-CE; ages 6–11), and a parallel version to measure the parental perspective on children's health and well-being (CHIP-PRF) [56].

4. The Dutch-Child-AZL-TNO-Quality of Life Questionnaire (DUX-25): This scale was validated by Kolsteren et al. (2001) as a generic instrument with identical proxy and self-report forms. It has 25 items and is used for children aged 5 to 16 years [98].

5. TNO-AZL-Child Quality of Life (TACQOL) Questionnaire: It was developed by Vogels et al. (1998) and measures problems in seven domains: (1) bodily functioning (fatigue and pains), (2) motor functioning, (3) autonomic functioning, (4) cognitive functioning (school), (5) social functioning (peers, family), (6) positive moods, and (7) negative moods. All seven domains include eight items [99].

6. The Kinder Lebensqualitatsfragebogen (KINDL, German Quality of Life Questionnaire): It is a validated tool comprised of 24 items, created by Ravens-Sieberer and Bullinger (1998). It has six subscores: physical well-being, emotional well-being, self-esteem, family, friends, and school. Three versions (KID-KINDL; KIDDO-KINDL; KINDL for parents) were used according to the age group. KID-KINDL was used for children aged 6–11 years, KIDDO-KINDL for adolescents aged 12–17 years, and KINDL for parents of patients aged 6–17 years [100].

ADHD-Specific QoL Scales

Because the assessment of QoL with generic measures has the potential disadvantage of emphasizing areas of disability that are inappropriate to the disorder in question, there have been several attempts to construct new evaluation scales, for both adults and children. The generic QoL scales such as SF-36, for instance, may not be correlated with the symptoms of a specific disorder like ADHD, indicating the need for specific QoL instruments [101]. Health-related QoL scales are not purely related with the disease itself, but are also associated with other factors such as family, friends, and socioeconomic and cultural issues. This situation emerges as a complicating factor in evaluating the relationship between the disease and the QoL. Some disease-specific QoL scales used in adults, children, and adolescents with ADHD are as follows:

For adults:

1. The Adult ADHD Quality of Life Scale (AAQoL): This scale, validated by Brod et al. (2006), is a Likert-type scale consisting of 29 items distributed in the following four domains: life productivity (11 items), psychological health (6 items), life outlook (7 items), and relationships (5 items)[45].

2. The Adult ADHD Quality of Life-29 (AAQoL-29): It is a participant-reported outcome measure used to examine disease-specific functional impairments and quality of life in

adults with ADHD. The AAQoL includes "life productivity," "psychological health," "quality of relationships," and "life outlook" subscales. Higher scores on the AAQoL-29 indicate better functioning [75].

3. The ADHD Impact Module for Adults (AIM-A): AIM-A is a validated measurement of the quality of life in adults with ADHD. The AIM-A measures the following multi-item concepts: living with ADHD (10 items), general well-being (11 items), performance and daily functioning (10 items), relationships/communication (8 items), bothersomeness/ concern (9 items), and daily interference (9 items). Like SF-36, it uses a 0-to-100 scale, with higher scores representing a better quality of life [102].

For children and adolescents:

1. The ADHD Impact Module-Child (AIM-C): This is a disease-specific HRQoL survey instrument, consisting of two core multi-item scales to assess HRQL impact on the child and family. The child scale includes 8 items that measure the well-being of the child, and the home scale includes 10 items that assess the impact on the family/parent at baseline and study endpoint. In addition, the AIM-C includes 10 clinical treatment questions, a 6-item school cooperation scale, 9 parent attribute/knowledge items, 4 economic impact items, and 4 demographic questions answered by the subject's parents [44].

2. The Weiss Functional Impairment Rating Scale (WFIRS): This scale evaluates ADHD-related functional impairment. It shares many similarities with measures of QoL. The self-report form of the scale (WFIRS-S) is appropriate for adolescents and adult reporting of functional impairment associated with ADHD. It contains 68 items spanning six functional domains: home, self-concept, learning and work, activities of daily living, social activities, and risky activities. The parent form of the scale (WFIRS-P) consists of 50 items to be filled out by parents. Each item is measured on a four-point Likert scale. It measures functioning across six domains: family, learning and school, life skills, child's self-concept, social activities, and risky activities [103].

3. The ADHD Quality of Life Scale (ADHD/QoLS): It was developed by Dolgun et al. (2005). The ADHD/QoLS is designed for children aged 8–12. It has 30 items and they are on a 5-point Likert scale with five responses ranging from completely false to completely true. The scale is comprised of three subscales: cognitive, social, and psychological [104].

4. The EuroQoL Five-Dimension Questionnaire-Parent-Proxy Version (Parent-proxy EQ-5D): This proxy version of EQ-5D was tested by Matza et al. (2005) in a sample of children with ADHD in the United States and the United Kingdom, measuring of ADHD symptoms based on the DSM-IV criteria. The EQ-5D scales were also significantly correlated with the ADHD-RS scales. The proxy version of the EQ-5D completed by parents was able to detect impairment in children diagnosed with ADHD in the United States and the United Kingdom. Significant correlations were found with an ADHD symptom measure and previously validated multi-dimensional QoL instruments. These results suggest that parent-proxy EQ-5D ratings are feasible and valid to be used as a part of an overall health outcome assessment in clinical studies of childhood ADHD [105].

Study	N & Mean age	Design & Duration	Drug & Dose	Questionnaire	Main outcomes
Wehmeier et al (2012) [36]	794 (136, girls, mean age 9.6; 658 males, mean age 9.7)	5 ATX follow-up trials (4 of Europe, one from Canada 8-to12-week meta-analysis	ATX, up to 1.8 mg/kg/day,	CHIP-CE-PRF, HRQoL, ADHD symptoms	ATX was effective in improving some aspect of HR-QoL in both genders, correlation between core symptoms of ADHD and HR-QoL were low to moderta in both gender.
Wehmeier et al (2011) [80]	180, children and adolescents (6-17 years)	Randomized, double blind, placebo controlled, 9-weeks	ATX, up to 1.2 target dose mg/kg/day,	KINDL-R	Positive effects of ATX on QoL (emotional well-being, self-esteem, friends and family, in children and adolescents with ADHD and comorbid ODD/CD).
Wehmeier et al (2010) [23]	794 (611:children, 183:adolescent)	5 ATX follow-up trials (4 of Europe, one from Canada 8-to12-week meta-analysis	ATX, up to 1.8 mg/kg/day,	ADHD-RS, CHIP-CE	Atomoxetine was effective in improving some aspects of HR-QoL in both age groups. Correlations between core symptoms of ADHD and HR-QoL were low to moderate.
Becker et al (2011) [22]	721, children and adolescents (6-17 years)	Open-label OBSEER study	Once-daily modified-released (MR) MPH	SDQ, KIND(parent, child or adolescent versions)	ADHD had low QoL, independent of core symptom severit. QoL lower in additional conduct disorder, medication was effective.
Gerwe et al (2009) [88]	306, mean age 10.2±2.3	Open-label, non-interventional study, 8 weeks	OROS-MPH, IR-MPH	Non-validated, simplified Likert type scales	The importance of a therapy that covers not only school-time, but also takes other areas of life into account. Initiating treatment with long-acting preparations, such as OROS(®) MPH in MPH-naïve patients might be a feasible option.
Prasad et al (2007) [76]	201	Open-label, 10 weeks	ATX, 0.5-1.8 mg/kg/day	CHIP-CE Parent Report Form ADHD-RS, CGI-S, CGI-I	CHIP-CE score was significantly higher for patients treated with ATX. ADHD-RS, CGI-S, and CGI-I scores were significantly different in favour of ATX.
Dell'Agnello et al (2009) [77]	139	RDBPC, 8 weeks	Atomoxetine, 1.2 mg/kg/day	CHIP-CE Parent Report Form, CGI-ADHD-S,	CHIP-CE scores for risk avoidance domain,

Study	N & Mean age	Design & Duration	Drug & Dose	Questionnaire	Main outcomes
				CPRS-R:S, CTRS-R:S	emotional comfort and individual risk avoidance subdomains were improved by ATX. An improvement in all the subscales of Conners was observed with ATX.
Escobar et al (2009) [78]	149	RDBPC, 12 weeks	Atomoxetine, 1.2 mg/kg/day	CHIP-CE Parent Report Form	ATX improved HRQoL by parents and in the risk avoidance domain by patients. A modest correlation of clinical severity with HRQoL was found in this clinical population.
Svanborg et al (2009) [79]	99	RDBPC, 10 weeks	Atomoxetine, 1.2 mg/kg/day	CHIP-CE Parent Report Form	ATX combined with psychoeducation had a positive effect on coping abilities of the patients and their families.
Perwien et al (2006) [75]	912, 6-17 years	Open-label, 10 week acute, 24 months	ATX	CHQ parent report form	Improvements in HRQL were found both acute and long-term treatment for psychosocial health.
Gurkan et al (2010) [87]	45, 8-14 years	Open-label, 3 months	MPH	PedsQL (parent, children forms)	Depression, trait anxiety and compulsion symptoms decreased and QoL improved along with ADHD symptoms
Flapper et al (2008) [89]	23, 7-10 years	Open-label, 4 week	MPH	DUX-25, TACQoL parent children forms	HRQOL scores improved in 18 children receiving MPH. The ADHD/DCD group also demonstrated a significant improvement in ADHD symptoms and motor functioning.

ADHD-RS-IV: ADHD Rating Scale-IV; YQoL-R: Youth QoL-Research Version; HR-QoL: Health-related quality of life; BRIEF-A: Behaviour Rating Inventory of EF-Adult; GEC: Global Executive Composite; CHIP-CE- PRF: Child Health and Ilness Profile-Child Edition-Parent Rating Form, Weiss functional impairment rating scale-parent report; ADHDRS-IV-Parent: Inv total score; TQoLA: Taiwanese Quality of life questionnaire for adolescents, SDQ: strengths and difficulties questionnaire, CHQ= The Child Health Questionnaire; RDBPC =Randomized,double-blind,placebo controlled; CHIP-CE = Child Health and Illness Profile-Child Edition ; TQOLQA=Taiwanese Quality of Life Questionnaire for Adolescents; PedsQL= Pediatric Quality of Life Inventory; DUX-25= Dutch-Child-AZL-TNO-Quality of Life Questionnaire; TAC-QOL=TNO-AZL-Child Quality of Life; MPH =Methylphenidate, CPRS-R:S: Conners Parents Subscale, CTRS-R:S: Conners Teacher Subscale,

Table 1. Studies of the impact of treatment on QoL of children with ADHD

http://dx.doi.org/10.5772/60955

Study	N & Mean age	Design & Duration	Drug & Dose	Questionnaire	Main outcomes
Altin et al (2014) [44]	18-30 years	randomized, double-blind, plasebo-controlled, 12 weeks	ATX	CAARS-Inv: SV total score, AAQoL-29, CGI-ADHD-S, CGI-I, CAARS and BRIEF-AV Self-Reports	Atomoxetine reduced ADHD symptoms and improved quality of life and executive functioning deficits in young adults compared with placebo.
Adler et al (2013) [97]	159, adults with clinically significant executive function deficits (EFD)	Randomized placebo controlled, 10 weeks	LDX, 30-70 mg/day,	EFD (BRIEF-A, GEC) ADHD-RS-IV, CGI-S, AAQoL, AIM-A	Aduls with ADHD/EFD exhibited self-reported improvement on QoL, AIM-A and AAQoL correlate with medium/ large ES, these improvements parallel by improvements in EF and ADHD symptoms.
Durell et al (2013) [73]	445, 18-30 years	randomized, double-blind, plasebo-controlled, 12 weeks	ATX	the AAQoL-29	Score decreases from baseline to the 12-week end-point greater in ATX group for the AAQoL-29 total score and all the subscale scores, except "life Outlook subscale" score.
Goto et al (2013) [81]	391, adults from Japan, Korea, and Taiwan	Randomized, double-blind, plasebo-controlled, 10 weeks	ATX	CAARS-Inv: SV total score, QoL	ATX effective in improving QoL and executive function as well as ameliorating core ADHD symptoms in adult Asian patients
Mattos et al (2013) [90]	60, adult, mean age 31.1 years	Multicenter, open-label trial, 12 weeks	OROS-MPH	Adult Self-Rating Scale, AAQoL, STAI, HAM-D, CGI	A significant reduction on CGI-I, HAM-D, STAI, and ASRS scores was observed
Weiss et al (2010) [39]	725, adults,	QUEST study, open-label, 8 months	Long-acting mixed amphetamine salts extended release	ADHD symptoms, medication satisfaction mediate quality of life	Symptom change and satisfaction with medication independently mediate change in mental but not

Study	N & Mean age	Design & Duration	Drug & Dose	Questionnaire	Main outcomes
					physical quality of life outcomes. Attention is a stronger mediator of ADHD-specific quality of life outcomes.
Brown and Landgraf (2010) [91]	Adults	2 of randomized, double-blind, placebo-controlled trials,	(MAS (SPD465)	BADDS, AIM-A	Improvement in executive function correlates with reported improvement in HRQOL as assessed in 2 independent clinical trials
Adler et al (2009a) [83]	442, adults with ADHD and social anxiety disorder	Randomized, double-blind, placebo-controlled, 14 weeks	ATX, 40-100 mg	CAARS:Inv:SV, LSAS, CGI-O-S, STAI, SAS, AAQoL-29	CGI-O-S, STAI, AAQoL score changes greater in favour of ATX, STAI scores was comparable. SAS scores were similar with placebo.
Adler et al (2009b) [86]	501, adults	randomized, double-blind, placebo-controlled, 10 weeks, then 6-month trial	once-daily morning-dosed ATX	AISRS, CAARS:Inv:SV, CGI-ADHD-S, AAQoL	Once-daily morning-dosed atomoxetine is efficacious for treating ADHD in adults when measured 10 weeks and 6 months after initiating treatment.
Spencer et al (2008) [92]	274, adults (18-55 years)	Randomized, double-blind, plasebo-controlled, 7 weeks	MAS (SPD465), 12.5-75 mg/day	AIM-A, ADHD-RS-IV, CGI	Triple-bead MAS was significantly more effective than placebo in adult ADHD.
Boonstra et al (2007) [94]	39 normal controls, 33 adults with ADHD for baseline comparison 31 adults with	1) Baseline group comparison; 2) Double blind, placebo-controlled, cross-over medication	MPH, placebo	Actigraphy, sleep log data,	Sleep problems are inherent in adults with ADHD and that methylphenidate reduced total sleep time but improved sleep quality by consolidating sleep.

http://dx.doi.org/10.5772/60955

Study	N & Mean age	Design & Duration	Drug & Dose	Questionnaire	Main outcomes
	ADHD medication				
Adler et al (2005) [82]	384, adults from 31 sites	ongoing, 3-year, open-label study, up to 97 weeks	ATX	CAARS-Inv:SV	Significant improvement was noted with atomoxetine therapy, with mean CAARS-Inv:SV total ADHD symptom scores
Michelson et al (2003) [84]	280 (study 1), adults 256 (study 2), adults	randomized, double-blind, placebo-controlled, 10-week	ATX	Conners' Adult ADHD Rating Scale.	ATX as efficacious treatment for adult ADHD.
Kooij et al (2001) [93]	8 adults,	Open-label, 7 days	MPH (51 mg: 30-90 mg) for 7 cases, dextroamphetamine (30 mg) for one case	Activity level Movement index scores	Treatment with stimulants associated with a reduction of activity Level and movement index scores and improved sleep quality in ADHD.

CAARS-Inv: SV: Conners' Adult ADHD Rating Scale-Investigator Rated: Screening Version; AAQoL: Adult ADHD Quality of Life Scale; STAI:State and Trait Anxiety Inventory, HAM-D: Hamilton Depression Rating Scale, CGI: Clinical Global Impression, MAS: triple-bead mixed amphetamine salts, AIM-A: Adult ADHD Impact Module, ADHD-RS-IV: ADHD Rating Scale-IV, TASS: Time-Sensitive ADHD Symptom Scale, BADDS: Brown Attention-Deficit Disorder Scale, ASRS: Adult ADHD Self-Report Scale, GAF: Global Assessment of Functioning, CGI-I: Clinical-Global-Impressions-Improvement Scale, CGI-ADHD-S: Clinical Global Impression-ADHD-Severity, BRIEF-AV: Behavior Rating Inventory of Executive Function-Adult Version Self-Report, LSAS: Liebowitz Social Anxiety Scale, CGI-O-S: Clinical Global Impression-Overall-Severity, STAI: State-Trait Anxiety Inventory, SAS: Social Adjustment Scale-Self Report, AAQoL-29: Adult ADHD Quality of Life Scale-29, AISRS: Adult ADHD Investigator Symptom Rating Scale, CGI-ADHD-S: Clinical Global Impressions-ADHD-Severity, BADDS: Brown Attention-Deficit Disorder Scale, BRIEF-A: Behaviour Rating Inventory of Executive Function-Adult Version Self-Report.

Table 2. Studies of the impact of treatment on QoL of adults with ADHD

Author details

Ozden Sukran Uneri, Gulser Senses-Dinc* and Zeynep Goker

*Address all correspondence to: gulserdinc@yahoo.com

Ankara Pediatric Hematology Oncology Training and Research Hospital, Child Psychiatry Department, Diskapi-Ankara, Turkey

References

[1] Saxena S, Orley J, WHOQOL Group. Quality of life assesment: The World Health Organization perspective. Eur Psychiatry,1997;12:263-66.

[2] World Health Organization. WHOQoL measuring quality of life: programme on mental health. Division of Mental Health and Prevention of Substance Use. Geneva, WHO (WHO/MSA/MNH/PSF/97.4). 1997;1-15

[3] Osterfeld E. Aristotle on the good life and quality of life. In: Nordenfelt L (ed.), Concepts and measurement of quality of life in health care. Amsterdam, Kluwer, 1994;19-34.

[4] Levine RJ. Quality of life assessments in clinical trials: an ethical perspective. In: Spilker B (ed.), Quality of life and pharmacoeconomics in clinical trials. 2nd edition. Philedelphia, Lippincott-Raven Publishers, 1996;489-95.

[5] Hawthorne G. Measuring the value of health-related quality of life. In: Quality of life impairment in schizophrenia, mood and anxiety disorders. Netherlands, Springer, 2007;99-132.

[6] Pennacchini M, Bertolaso M, Elvira MM, De Marinis MG. A brief history of the quality of life: its use in medicine and in philosophy. Clin Terminol,2011;162.3:e99-103.

[7] Eiser C, Cotter I, Oades P, Seamark D, Smith R. Health-related quality-of-life measures for children. Int J Cancer Suppl,1999;12:87-90.

[8] Herndon DN, LeMaster J, Beard S, Bernstein N, Lewis SR, Rutan TC, Winkler JB, Cole M, Bjarnason D, Gore D, et al. The quality of life after major thermal injury in children: an analysis of 12 survivors with greater than or equal to 80% total body, 70% third-degree burns. J Trauma, 1986;26(7):609-19

[9] Ditesheim JA, Templeton JM. Short-term versus long-term quality of life in children following repair of high imperforate anus. J Pediatr Surg, 1987;22(7):581-7.

[10] Henning P, Tomlinson L, Rigden SP, Haycock GB, Chantler C. Long term outcome of treatment of end stage renal failure. Arch Dis Child, 1988;63(1):35-40.

[11] Chao CY, Gau SS, Mao WC, Shyu JF, Chen YC, Yeh CB. Relationship of attention-deficit-hyperactivity disorder symptoms, depressive/anxiety symptoms, and life quality in young men. Psychiatry Clin Neurosci, 2008;62(4):421-6.

[12] Skounti M, Philalithis A, Galanakis E. Variations in prevalence of attention deficit hyperactivity disorder worldwide. Eur J Pediatr, 2007;166:117-23.

[13] Feldman HM, Reiff MI. Clinical practice. Attention deficit-hyperactivity disorder in children and adolescents, 2014;370(9):838-46.

[14] Sharma A, Couture J. A review of the pathophysiology, etiology, and treatment of attention-deficit hyperactivity disorder (ADHD). Ann Pharmacother, 2014;48(2):209-25.

[15] Cak HT, Dinc GS, Tuzun Z, Evinc SG, Cop E, Cuhadaroglu Cetin F. Comorbidity and continuity of attention deficit hyperactivity disorder (ADHD) from childhood to adolescence in Turkey. Atten Defic Hyperact Disord, 2013;5(4):353-60.

[16] Rösler M, Casas M, Konofal E, Buitelaar J. Attention deficit hyperactivity disorder in adults. World J Biol Psychiatry, 2010;11(5):684-98.

[17] Bramham J, Young S, Bickerdike A, Spain D, McCartan D, Xenitidis K. Evaluation of group cognitive behavioral therapy for adults with ADHD. J Atten Disord, 2009;12(5):434-41.

[18] Huang F, Qian Q, Wang Y. Cognitive behavioral therapy for adults with attention-deficit hyperactivity disorder: study protocol for a randomized controlled trial. Trials, 2015;16(1):161.

[19] Rostain AL, Ramsay JR. A combined treatment approach for adults with ADHD-results of an open study of 43 patients. J Atten Disord, 2006;10(2):150-9.

[20] Dittner AJ, Rimes KA, Russell AJ, Chalder T. Protocol for a proof of concept randomized controlled trial of cognitive-behavioural therapy for adult ADHD as a supplement to treatment as usual, compared with treatment as usual alone. BMC Psychiatry, 2014;14:248.

[21] Antshel KM, Barkley R. Psychosocial interventions in attention deficit hyperactivity disorder. Child Adolesc Psychiatr Clin N Am, 2008;17(2):421-37.

[22] Pelham WE, Hoza B. Intensive treatment: a summer treatment program for children with ADHD. In: Jensen EHP (ed.), Psychosocial treatments for children and adolescent disorders: empirically based strategies for clinical practice. New York, APA Press, 1996:311-40.

[23] Antshel KM. Psychosocial interventions in attention-deficit/hyperactivity disorder: update. Child Adolesc Psychiatr Clin N Am, 2015;24(1):79-97.

[24] Sibley MH, Kuriyan AB, Evans SW, Waxmonsky JG, Smith BH. Pharmacological and psychosocial treatments for adolescents with ADHD: an updated systematic review of the literature. Clin Psychol Rev, 2014;34(3):218-32.

[25] Antshel KM, Olszewski AK. Cognitive behavioral therapy for adolescents with ADHD. Child Adolesc Psychiatr Clin N Am, 2014;23(4):825-42.

[26] Antshel KM, Faraone SV, Gordon M. Cognitive behavioral treatment outcomes in adolescent ADHD. J Atten Disord, 2014;18(6):483-95.

[27] Wu EQ, Hodgkins P, Ben-Hamadi R, Setyawan J, Xie J, Sikirica V, Du EX, Yan SY, Erder MH. Cost effectiveness of pharmacotherapies for attention-deficit hyperactivity disorder: a systematic literature review. CNS Drugs, 2012;26(7):581-600.

[28] Becker A, Roessner V, Breuer D, Döpfner M, Rothenberger A. Relationship between quality of life and psychopathological profile: data from an observational study in children with ADHD. Eur Child Adolesc Psychiatry, 2011;Suppl 2:S267-75

[29] Wehmeier PM, Schacht A, Barkley RA. Social and emotional impairment in children and adolescents with ADHD and the impact on quality of life. J Adolesc Health, 2010;46(3):209-17.

[30] Agarwal R, Goldenberg M, Perry R, Ishak WW. The quality of life of adults with attention deficit hyperactivity disorder: a systematic review. Innov Clin Neurosci, 2012;9(5-6):10-21.

[31] Endicott J, Nee J, Harrison W, Blumenthal R. Quality of life enjoyment and satisfaction questionnaire: a new measure. Psychopharmacol Bull, 1993;29:321-6.

[32] Mick E, Faraone SV, Spencer T, Zhang HF, Biederman J. Assessing the validity of the ouality of life enjoyment and satisfaction questionnaire short form in adults with ADHD. J Atten Disord, 2008;11(4):504-9.

[33] Group EQ. EQ-5D Health Questionnaire. Rotterdam, EuroQol Group; 2009.

[34] Lensing MB, Zeiner P, Sandvik L, Opjordsmoen S. Quality of life in adults aged 50+ with ADHD. J Atten Disord, 2015;19(5):405-13.

[35] Kooij JJ, Buitelaar JK, van den Oord EJ, Furer JW, Rijnders CA, Hodiamont PP. Internal and external validity of attention-deficit hyperactivity disorder in a population-based sample of adults. Psychol Med, 2005;35(6):817-27.

[36] Goldberg DP, Hillier VF. A scaled version of the General Health Questionnaire. Psychol Med, 1979;9(1):139-45.

[37] Danckaerts M, Sonuga-Barke EJ, Banaschewski T, Buitelaar J, Döpfner M, Hollis C, Santosh P, Rothenberger A, Sergeant J, Steinhausen HC, Taylor E, Zuddas A, Coghill D. The quality of life of children with attention deficit/hyperactivity disorder: a systematic review. Eur Child Adolesc Psychiatry, 2010;19(2):83-105.

[38] Varni JW, Seid M, Rode CA.The PedsQL: measurement model for the pediatric quality of life inventory. Med Care, 1999;37(2):126-39.

[39] Escobar R, Soutullo CA, Hervas A, Gastaminza X, Polavieja P, Gilaberte I. Worse quality of life for children with newly diagnosed attention-deficit/hyperactivity disorder, compared with asthmatic and healthy children. Pediatrics, 2005;116(3):e364-9.

[40] Landgraf JM, Abetz L, Ware JE. Child Health Questionnaire (CHQ): a user's manual, 1996:39.

[41] Uneri OS, Turgut S, Oner P, Bodur S, Rezaki B. Quality of life in 8-12 years old children with attention deficit hyperactivity disorder. Turk J Child Adolesc Ment Health, 2010;17(1):27-32.

[42] Kandemir H, Kilic BG, Ekinci S, Yuce M. An evaluation of the quality of life of children with attention-deficit/hyperactivity disorder (ADHD) and their families. Anadolu Psikiyatri Derg, 2014; 5(3):265-71.

[43] Klassen AF, Miller A, Fine S. Health-related quality of life in children and adolescents who have a diagnosis of attention-deficit/hyperactivity disorder. Pediatrics, 2004;114:e541-7.

[44] Landgraf JM, Rich M, Rappaport L. Measuring quality of life in children with attention-deficit/hyperactivity disorder and their families: development and evaluation of a new tool. Arch Pediatr Adolesc Med, 2002;156(4):384-91.

[45] Brod M, Johnston J, Able S, Swindle R. Validation of the adult attention-deficit/hyperactivity disorder quality-of-life Scale (AAQoL): a disease-specific quality-of-life measure. Qual Life Res, 2006;15(1):117-29.

[46] Chao CY, Gau SS, Mao WC, Shyu JF, Chen YC, Yeh CB. Relationship of attention-deficit-hyperactivity disorder symptoms, depressive/anxiety symptoms, and life quality in young men. Psychiatry Clin Neurosci, 2008;62(4):421-6.

[47] Boonstra AM, Kooij JJ, Oosterlaan J, Sergeant JA, Buitelaar JK, Van Someren EJ. Hyperactive night and day? Actigraphy studies in adult ADHD: a baseline comparison and the effect of methylphenidate. Sleep, 2007;30(4):433-42.

[48] Gjervan B, Torgersen T, Nordahl HM, Rasmussen K. Functional impairment and occupational outcome in adults with ADHD. J Atten Disord, 2012;16(7):544-52.

[49] Rimmerman A, Yurkevich O, Birger M, Araten-Bergman T. Quality of life of men and women with borderline intelligence and attention deficit disorders living in community residences: a comparative study. J Atten Disord, 2005;9(2):435-43.

[50] Grenwald-Mayes G. Relationship between current quality of life and family of origin dynamics for college students with attention-deficit/hyperactivity disorder. J Atten Disord, 2002;5(4):211-22.

[51] Wehmeier PM, Schacht A, Escobar R, Hervas A, Dickson R. Health-related quality of life in ADHD: a pooled analysis of gender differences in five atomoxetine trials. Atten Defic Hyperact Disord, 2012;4(1):25-35.

[52] Mattos P, Segenreich D, Dias GM, Nazar B, Saboya E, Broad M. Construct reliability and validity of the Portuguese version of the adult ADHD quality of life questionnaire (AAQoL). Rev Psiq Clin, 2011;38(3):91-6.

[53] Weiss MD, Gibbins C, Goodman DW, Hodgkins PS, Landgraf JM, Faraone SV. Moderators and mediators of symptoms and quality of life outcomes in an open-label study of adults treated for attention-deficit/hyperactivity disorder. J Clin Psychiatry, 2010;71(4):381-90.

[54] Gudjonsson GH, Sigurdsson JF, Eyjolfsdottir GA, Smari J, Young S. The relationship between satisfaction with life, ADHD symptoms, and associated problems among university students. J Atten Disord, 2009;12(6):507-15.

[55] Rimmerman A, Yurkevich O, Birger M, Azaiza F, Elyashar S. Quality of life of Israeli adults with borderline intelligence quotient and attention-deficit/hyperactivity disorder. Int J Rehabil Res, 2007;30(1):55-60.

[56] Starfield B, Bergner M, Riley A, Ensminger M, Green B, Ryan S, Kim S, Johnston D. Child Health and Illness Profile-Adolescent Edition (CHIP-AE). Medical Care, 1995;33(5):553-66.

[57] Riley AW, Coghill D, Forrest CB, Lorenzo MJ, Ralston SJ, Spiel G; ADORE Study Group. Validity of the health-related quality of life assessment in the ADORE study: Parent Report Form of the CHIP-Child Edition. Eur Child Adolesc Psychiatry, 2006;15 (Suppl 1):I63-71.

[58] Matza LS, Rentz AM, Secnik K, Swensen AR, Revicki DA, Michelson D, Spencer T, Newcorn JH, Kratochvil CJ. The link between health-related quality of life and clinical symptoms among children with attention-deficit hyperactivity disorder. J Dev Behav Pediatr, 2004;25(3):166-74.

[59] Biederman J, Faraone SV, Spencer TJ. Functional impairments in adults with self-reports of diagnosed ADHD: a controlled study of 1001 adults in the community. J Clin Psychiatry, 2006;67(4):524-40.

[60] Brod M, Schmitt E, Goodwin M, Hodgkins P, Niebler G. ADHD burden of illness in older adults: a life course perspective. Qual Life Res, 2012;21(5):795-9.

[61] Das D, Cherbuin N, Butterworth P, Anstey KJ, Easteal S. A population-based study of attention deficit/hyperactivity disorder symptoms and associated impairment in middle-aged adults. PLoS One, 2012;7(2):e31500.

[62] Altin M, Alev L, Durell TM, Adler LA, Williams DV, Deldar A, Mcgough JJ, Glaser PE, Rubin RL, Sarkis ES, Pigott TA, Boardman BK. Atomoxetine for the treatment of ADHD in young adults with an assessment of associated functional outcomes. Turkish Association for Psychopharmacology, 4th International Congress on Psychopharmacalogy, [PP-025], 2014.

[63] Blase SL, Gilbert AN, Anastopoulos AD. Self-reported ADHD and adjustment in college: cross-sectional and longitudinal findings. J Atten Disord, 2009;13(3):297-309.

[64] Rimmer M, Campbell C, Murphy S. ADHD: the impact on parent's and children's quality of life. In: American Academy of Child and Adolescent Psychiatry Annual Meeting, 2007: 23-28; Boston.

[65] Seo JY, Lee CS, Park CS, Kim BJ, Cha BS, Lee SJ, Ahn IY. Mediating effect of depressive symptoms on the relationship between adult attention deficit hyperactivity disorder and quality of life. Psychiatry Investig, 2014;11(2):131-6.

[66] Yang HN, Tai YM, Yang LK, Gau SS. Prediction of childhood ADHD symptoms to quality of life in young adults: adult ADHD and anxiety/depression as mediators. Res Dev Disabil, 2013;34(10):3168-81.

[67] Westmoreland P, Gunter T, Loveless P, Allen J, Sieleni B, Black DW. Attention deficit hyperactivity disorder in men and women newly committed to prison: clinical characteristics, psychiatric comorbidity, and quality of life. Int J Offender Ther Comp Criminol, 2010;54(3):361-77.

[68] Jenkinson C, Coulter A, Wright L. Short form-36 (SF-36) health survey questionnaire: normative data for adults of working age. BMJ, 1993;306:143740

[69] Liew A, Cavanna AE. Attention deficit and hyperactivity symptoms in adult patients with Tourette syndrome. J Neurol Neurosurg Psychiatry, 2013;84:e1. http://jnnp.bmj.com/ downloaded on January 11, 2015 - Published by group.bmj.com

[70] Dallos G, Miklósi M, Keresztény A, Velő S, Szentiványi D, Gádoros J, Balázs J. Self- and parent-rated quality of life of a treatment naïve sample of children With ADHD: the impact of age, gender, type of ADHD, and comorbid psychiatric conditions according to both a categorical and a dimensional approach. J Atten Disord, 2014 Jul 11. pii: 1087054714542003.

[71] WHOQOL Group. The World Health Organization quality of life assessment (WHOQOL): position paper from the World Health Organization. Soc Sci Med, 1995;41(10): 1403-9.

[72] Safren SA, Sprich SE, Cooper-Vince C, Knouse LE, Lerner JA. Life impairments in adults with medication-treated ADHD. J Atten Disord, 2010;13(5):524-31.

[73] Montoya A, Colom F, Ferrin M. Is psychoeducation for parents and teachers of children and adolescents with ADHD efficacious? A systematic literature review. Eur Psychiatry, 2011;26(3):166-75.

[74] Svanborg P, Thernlund G, Gustafsson PA, Hägglöf B, Schacht A, Kadesjö B. Atomoxetine improves patient and family coping in attention deficit/hyperactivity disorder: a randomized, double-blind, placebo-controlled study in Swedish children and adolescents. Eur Child Adolesc Psychiatry, 2009;18(12):725-35.

[75] Durell TM, Adler LA, Williams DW, Deldar A, McGough JJ, Glaser PE, Rubin RL, Pigott TA, Sarkis EH, Fox BK. Atomoxetine treatment of attention-deficit/hyperactivity disorder in young adults withy assessment of functional outcomes. A randomized, double blind, placebo-controlled clinical trial. J Clin Psychopharmacol, 2013;33:45-54.

[76] Goto T, Hirata Y, Takita Y, Trzepacz PT, Allen AJ, Song DH, Gau SS, Ichikawa H, Takahashi M. Efficacy and safety of atomoxetine hydrochloride in Asian adults with ADHD: a multinational 10-week randomized double-blind placebo-controlled Asian study. J Atten Disord, 2013 Nov 7. [Epub ahead of print].

[77] Michelson D, Adler LA, Spencer TJ, Reimherr FW, West SA, Allen AJ, Kelsey D, Wernicke J, Dietrich A, Milton D. Atomoxetine in adults with ADHD: two randomized, placebo-controlled studies. Biol Psychiatry, 2003;53(2):112-20.

[78] Adler LA, Spencer TJ, Brown TE, Holdnack J, Saylor K, Schuh K, Trzepacz PT, Williams DW, Kelsey D. Once-daily atomoxetine for adult attention-deficit/ hyperactivity disorder: a 6-month, double-blind trial. J Clin Psychopharmacol, 2009;29:44-50.

[79] Adler LA, Spencer TJ, Milton DR, Moore RJ, Michelson D. Long-term, open-label study of the safety and efficacy of atomoxetine in adults with attention-deficit/ hyperactivity disorder: an interim analysis. J Clin Psychiatry, 2005;66(3):294-9.

[80] Adler LA, Liebowitz M, Kronenberger W, Qiao M, Rubin R, Hollandbeck M, Deldar A, Schuh K, Durell T. Atomoxetine treatment in adults with attention-deficit/hyperactivity disorder and comorbid social anxiety disorder. Depress Anxiety, 2009;26(3): 212-21.

[81] Escobar R, Montoya A, Polavieja P, Cardo E, Artigas J, Hervas A, Fuentes J. Evaluation of patients' and parents' quality of life in a randomized placebo-controlled atomoxetine study in attention-deficit/hyperactivity disorder. J Child Adolesc Psychopharmacol, 2009;19(3):253-63.

[82] Dittmann RW, Schacht A, Helsberg K, Schneider-Fresenius C, Lehmann M, Lehmkuhl G, Wehmeier PM. Atomoxetine versus placebo in children and adolescents with attention-deficit/hyperactivity disorder and comorbid oppositional defiant disorder: a double-blind, randomized, multicenter trial in Germany. J Child Adolesc Psychopharmacol, 2011;21(2):97-110.

[83] Dell'Agnello G, Maschietto D, Bravaccio C, Calamoneri F, Masi G, Curatolo P, Besana D, Mancini F, Rossi A, Poole L, Escobar R, Zuddas A; LYCY Study Group. Atomoxetine hydrochloride in the treatment of children and adolescents with attention-deficit/hyperactivity disorder and comorbid oppositional defiant disorder: a placebo-controlled Italian study. Eur Neuropsychopharmacol, 2009;19(11):822-34.

[84] Perwien AR, Kratochvil CJ, Faries DE, Vaughan BS, Spencer T, Brown RT. Atomoxetine treatment in children and adolescents with attention-deficit hyperactivity disorder: what are the long-term health-related quality-of-life outcomes?. J Child Adol Psychop, 2006;16(6):713-24.

[85] Prasad S, Harpin V, Poole L, Zeitlin H, Jamdar S, Puvanendran K; SUNBEAM Study Group. A multi-centre, randomised, open-label study of atomoxetine compared with standard current therapy in UK children and adolescents with attention-deficit/ hyperactivity disorder (ADHD). Curr Med Res Opin, 2007;23(2):379-94.

[86] Montoya A, Quail D, Anand E, Cardo E, Alda JA, Escobar R. Prognostic factors of improvement in health-related quality of life in atomoxetine-treated children and adolescents with attention-deficit/hyperactivity disorder, based on a pooled analysis. Atten Defic Hyperact Disord, 2014;6(1):25-34.

[87] Mattos P, Louza MR, Palmini AL, de Oliveira IR, Rocha FL. A multicenter, open-label trial to evaluate the quality of life in adults with ADHD treated with long-acting methylphenidate (OROS MPH): Concerta Quality of Life (CONQoL) study. J Atten Disord, 2013;17(5):444-8.

[88] Kooij JJ, Middelkoop HA, van Gils K, Buitelaar JK. The effect of stimulants on nocturnal motor activity and sleep quality in adults with ADHD: an open-label case-control study. J Clin Psychiatry, 2001;62(12):952-6.

[89] Brown TE, Landgraf JM. Improvements in executive function correlate with enhanced performance and functioning and health-related quality of life: evidence from 2 large, double-blind, randomized, placebo-controlled trials in ADHD. Postgrad Med, 2010; 122(5):42-51.

[90] Spencer TJ, Landgraf JM, Adler LA, Weisler RH, Anderson CS, Youcha SH. Attention-deficit/hyperactivity disorder-specific quality of life with triple-bead mixed amphetamine salts (SPD465) in adults: results of a randomized, double-blind, placebo-controlled study. J Clin Psychiatry, 2008;69(1):1766-75.

[91] Brams M, Giblin J, Gasior M, Gao J, Wigal T. Effects of open-label lisdexamfetamine dimesylate on self-reported quality of life in adults with ADHD. Postgrad Med, 2011;123(3):99-108.

[92] Adler LA, Dirks B, Deas P, Raychaudhuri A, Dauphin M, Saylor K, Weisler R. Self-reported quality of life in adults with attention-deficit/hyperactivity disorder and executive function impairment treated with lisdexamfetamine dimesylate: a randomized, double-blind, multicenter, placebo-controlled, parallel-group study. BMC Psychiatry, 2013;13:253.

[93] Gurkan K, Bilgic A, Turkoglu S, Kiliç BG, Aysev A, Uslu R. Depression, anxiety and obsessive-compulsive symptoms and quality of life in children with attention-deficit hyperactivity disorder (ADHD) during three-month methylphenidate treatment. J Psychopharmacol, 2010;24(12):1810-8.

[94] Gerwe M, Stollhoff K, Mossakowski J, Kuehle HJ, Goertz U, Schaefer C, Bogdanow M, Heger S. Tolerability and effects of OROS® MPH (Concerta ®) on functioning, severity of disease and quality of life in children and adolescents with ADHD: results from a prospective, non-interventional trial. Atten Defic Hyperact Disord, 2009;1(2): 175-86.

[95] Flapper BC, Schoemaker MM. Effects of methylphenidate on quality of life in children with both developmental coordination disorder and ADHD. Dev Med Child Neurol, 2008;50(4):294-9.

[96] Banaschewski T, Johnson M, Lecendreux M, Zuddas A, Adeyi B, Hodgkins P, Squires LA, Coghill DR. health-related quality of life and functional outcomes from a randomized-withdrawal study of long-term lisdexamfetamine dimesylate treatment

in children and adolescents with attention-deficit/hyperactivity disorder. CNS Drugs, 2014;28(12):1191-203.

[97] Rajmil L, Herdman M, Fernandez de Sanmamed MJ, Detmar S, Bruil J, Ravens-Sieberer U, Bullinger M, Simeoni MC, Auquier P; Kidscreen Group. Generic health-related quality of life instruments in children and adolescents: a qualitative analysis of content. J Adolesc Health, 2004;34(1):37-45.

[98] Kolsteren MM, Koopman HM, Schalekamp G. Health-related quality of life in children with celiac disease. J Pediatr, 2001;138:593-5.

[99] Vogels T, Verrips GH, Verloove-Vanhorick SP, Fekkes M, Kamphuis RP, KoopmanHM, Theunissen NC, Wit JM. Measuring health-related quality of life in children: the development of the TACQOL parent form. Qual Life Res, 1998;7(5):457-65.

[100] Ravens-Sieberer U, Bullinger M. Assessing health-related quality of life in chronically ill children with the German KINDL: first psychometric and content analytical results. Qual Life Res, 1998;7(5):399-407.

[101] Adler LA, Sutton VK, Moore RJ, Dietrich AP, Reimherr FW, Sangal B, Allen AJ. Quality of life assessment in adult patients with ADHD treated with atomoxetine. J Clin Psychopharmacol, 2006;26:648-52.

[102] Landgraf JM. Monitoring quality of life in adults with ADHD. Reliability and validity of a new measure. J Atten Disord, 2007;11(3):351-62.

[103] Weiss MD, Wasdell MB, Bomben MM. Weiss Functional Impairment Rating Scale-Parent Report (WFIRS-P). University of British Columbia, Vancouver, BC, 2007.

[104] Dolgun G, Savas S, Yazgan Y. Development of the quality of life scale in children of the age group of 8-12 attention deficit/hyperactivity disorder (AD/HD-QOLS). J Res Develop Nursing, 2005;1(2):39-52.

[105] Matza LS, Secnik K, Mannix S, Sallee FR. Parent-proxy EQ-5D ratings of children with attention-deficit hyperactivity disorder in the US and the UK. Pharmacoeconomics, 2005;23(8):777-90.

Chapter 10

Predictors of College Success: Symptoms of ADHD, Psychological Well-being, Appreciation of the Liberal Arts, and Understanding of College Policies

Jill M. Norvilitis and Howard M. Reid

Additional information is available at the end of the chapter

http://dx.doi.org/10.5772/60560

Abstract

The present study was designed to identify predictors of college student success. More specifically, the study examined seven potential predictors for each of three measures of student success. These predictors were year in college, three academic variables and three measures of psychological well-being. It was found that self-identification of ADHD symptoms was a negative predictor of student success, whereas understanding college policies, study skills and appreciation of the liberal arts were all positive predictors of at least one of the measures of student success.

Keywords: college success, well-being, academics

1. Introduction

1.1. Symptoms of ADHD, psychological well-being, appreciation of the liberal arts and college student success

Measures of student success in college have been extensively studied and often focus on grade point average (GPA) and graduation rates. Graduation rate is not only a measure of student success, but is also increasingly being viewed as an overall measure of the success of the college or university. However, an overall measure of college or university success should be based on a broader definition that includes measures such as students' satisfaction with their choice of higher education institution, as well as with their choice of academic major, though these have been much less commonly studied. Regardless of the definition, some students are at an increased risk of experiencing difficulties with success in college. Among these are students with ADHD, who have been found to have lower levels of academic achievement [1], as well as poorer social and emotional adjustment to college [2]. Understanding predictors of college student success from a variety of perspectives will allow for more targeted interventions to improve retention and adjustment, both in the general college population and particularly among students with elevated symptoms of ADHD.

2. Predictors of success in college

Not surprisingly, due to the importance of higher education for both students and society, many studies have examined the predictors of student success. Early studies noted, for instance, that college success, as measured by college grade point average, was positively correlated with high school success as measured by high school GPA, as well as by achievement test scores (reviewed in [3]) and these variables continue to predict academic success [4, 5]. Additional variables such as the mastery of study skills have also been found to be positively associated with college GPA, both in the past and in more recent research [6, 7].

However, college success involves more than simply the student's GPA. More recently, the focus on this subject has broadened to include other factors that define college success. For example, a major factor is how well a student adapts to college life and its demands. To measure this construct, Baker and Siryk [8, 9] developed the Student Adaptation to College Questionnaire. Among the factors that have been found to be related to adaptation to college are student religiosity [10], marriage status [11] and attitudes toward seeking professional counselling [12]. Recently, Norvilitis and Reid [7] examined multiple predictors for several measures of academic success and found that parental encouragement of intellectual curiosity during childhood, ADHD symptomatology and varying motives for attending college were also predictive of success, as indicated by measures of academic adjustment, social adjustment and satisfaction with life.

Although student adaptation to college has been studied in some detail, fewer studies have utilized an overall measure of student satisfaction as a measure of college success [13, 14]. This would seem to be a reasonable measure and though limited, the data available support the view that a general measure of student satisfaction is associated with college GPA and measures of student adaptation to college [13, 14]. A more specific measure, satisfaction with one's major, also appears to be an important correlate of success in college. As expected, the evidence indicates that choice of major and career directedness are both associated with increased student retention [15]. Conversely, frequent change of major is associated with lower levels of college student well-being [16].

Thus, a number of variables have been reported to be associated with college success. The present study incorporates a comprehensive set of measures for student success and focuses on how these relate to an at-risk population of students, i.e., those exhibiting symptoms of ADHD, depression or anxiety. More specifically, the present study sought to explore the predictors of three facets of college student success: GPA, student adaptation to college and satisfaction with one's major. As noted above, many predictors of student success have been examined in the past, while others still require additional research. For example, Norvilitis and Reid [7] noted that an appreciation of the liberal arts is associated with student success. This suggests that the degree of correspondence between the student's educational values and the liberal arts college's educational mission is important; however, to date, this finding has not been replicated. Another underexplored predictor of college student success is the student's understanding of college policies. In order for students to graduate, they must not only maintain an adequate GPA, but they must also adhere to numerous college policies such as those related to repeating courses, the number of credits required to graduate and meeting prerequisites for courses. It is reasonable to expect that students with a better understanding of these policies will be more successful in college.

3. Attention deficit hyperactivity disorder and success in college

College students with ADHD are at a unique disadvantage when it comes to college adjustment. Symptoms of ADHD are associated with poorer study skills; specifically, those with ADHD prefer studying at a surface level, rather than at a deep level both in terms of motives and strategies [17]. Related to this, higher levels of ADHD symptoms have been reported to be negatively associated with college success as measured by academic adjustment and GPA in the US [18, 19] as well as in China [20].

In addition to their academic struggles, college students with more symptoms of ADHD also have difficulties with peers. Those with ADHD report feeling less competent at providing emotional support to and managing interpersonal conflict with their peers who exhibit fewer symptoms, though they do not report more difficulties with initiating social contact or disclosing personal information [21]. This pattern suggests that, although those students with more ADHD symptoms may be able to initiate friendships, subsequently progressing to the deeper, supportive friendships that are critical to success in college – particularly for those living away from home – may be especially challenging.

Further complicating matters, those with more symptoms of ADHD are at an increased risk for other disorders, most notably, anxiety and depression. Estimates show that up to 36% of children and adolescents with ADHD also meet the criteria for anxiety disorders [22]. Although specific rates of anxiety disorders in college students have not been determined, it is clear that many students with ADHD also struggle with anxiety symptoms and disorders. For example, Nelson, Lindstrom and Foels [23] reported that close to half of college students with ADHD reported clinically meaningful levels of test anxiety. Similarly, those with ADHD also experience higher rates of depression than the general college student population [24-26].

As a result, the present study sought to examine a series of predictors of different aspects of college student success with an emphasis on students in at-risk populations. More specifically, predictors of success included indicators of psychological well-being, including measures of ADHD, depression and anxiety, as well as a series of more general predictors including student understanding of college policies, appreciation of the liberal arts and study skills. The study incorporated three measures of student success: GPA, attachment to their college and satisfaction with their academic major. It was predicted that student satisfaction with their choice of academic major and college would be associated with their psychological characteristics, as well as with the match between their academic goals and the mission of the college. More specifically, it was hypothesized that those students with elevated symptoms of ADHD, anxiety and depression would have lower grade point averages and poorer study skills, as well as less satisfaction with their choice of major and college. Finally, it was predicted that at a liberal arts college, students' satisfaction with their academic major and choice of college would be correlated with the degree to which they personally valued the liberal arts.

4. Method

4.1. Participants

A total of 212 participants enrolled in a large, urban, public, liberal arts college completed the survey. Of these, 72 (34%) were male and 140 (66%) were female. There were 48 (23%) freshmen, 40 (19%) sophomores, 70 (33%) juniors, 42 (20%) seniors and 11 (5%) second year seniors. The participants self-identified as 146 (71%) Caucasian, 44 (21%) African American, 13 (6%) Hispanic, 3 (1%) Asian and 1 (.5%) Native American.

Of the 149 students who reported their grade point average, the mean was 3.17 (*SD* =.50). First year students and transfer students in their first semesters did not have GPAs and were therefore unable to report this number. Most students reported that they had not changed their major. Among the participants, 131 (62%) reported no changes in major, 51 (24%) reported one change, 15 (7%) reported two, 11 (5%) reported three and 4 (2%) reported four. Most students had also not changed colleges. Among the participants, 124 (59%) had not changed schools, 70 (33%) had attended one other college prior to their current one, 15 (7%) had attended two prior schools and 3 (1%) had attended three or more prior colleges.

4.2. Materials and procedure

Participants were recruited from courses from a variety of departments across campus and were given the opportunity to receive extra credit for completing the questionnaire. Questionnaires were to be completed outside of class, following informed consent and were collected at the beginning of the next two meetings of the class in which they were handed out. The questionnaire assessed demographic information such as gender, ethnicity, class level and GPA, as well as the following:

4.2.1. Predictors of college student success

The **Current Symptoms Scale [27]** was used to assess the total symptoms of inattention and hyperactivity using a symptom checklist. The 18 items were completed on a scale rating from

1 (*Never or Rarely*) to 4 (*Very Often*). In the present study, internal consistency was .82 for inattention and .77 for hyperactivity. Higher scores indicated more symptoms of ADHD.

IPIP Depression and Anxiety Scales [28] were used to assess symptoms of depression and anxiety. The 10 items measuring depression and 10 items measuring anxiety were completed on a scale of 1 (*Applies very closely to me*) to 5 (*Doesn't apply to me at all*). In the present study, internal consistency was .90 for depression and.84 for anxiety. Higher scores indicated more symptoms of depression or anxiety.

The **Study Skills Scale [19]** is a 14-item measure for assessing one's study habits on a scale from 1 (*Not at all like me*) to 4 (*Always or very much like me*). In the present study, internal consistency was .72. Higher scores indicated better self-reported study skills.

Understanding of College Policies Scale (UCP; created for this study) was used to examine how well students were aware of the requirements for graduation. The 11 multiple choice items were scored as correct or incorrect. Items inquired about such topics as the minimum GPA required for good academic standing, the number of credits required to graduate and policies regarding repeating courses. The score was the total number of items answered correctly.

The **Appreciation of the Liberal Arts Scale-Revised** (ALAS; [27]) is a 24-item scale for assessing how important one feels the liberal arts are to his or her education on a scale from 1 (*Not at all like me*) to 5 (*Definitely describes me*). For the present study, internal consistency was strong (α =.88). Higher scores indicated a greater appreciation of the liberal arts.

4.2.2. Measures of college student success

The **Student Adaptation to College Questionnaire-Attachment Subscale** (SACQ; [9]) assessed a student's attachment to his or her college on a scale of 1 (*Applies very closely to me*) to 5 (*Doesn't apply to me at all*). The 14-item measure had strong internal consistency (α =.81). Higher scores indicate greater attachment to college.

The **College Major Satisfaction Questionnaire** (created for this study) evaluated the individual satisfaction of a student with his or her major on a scale from 1 (*Very untrue for me*) to 5 (*Very true for me*). Statements regarding this 15-item scale included "I am excited by the classes in my major" and "If I had to start college over, I would choose another major." Internal consistency was strong (α =.85). Higher scores indicated greater satisfaction with one's major.

5. Results

5.1. Relations among predictor variables

The predictor variables of inattention, hyperactivity, depression, anxiety, study skills, UCP and ALAS were related to one another, but generally appeared to represent unique constructs. However, the measures for psychological well-being were correlated with one another (See Table 1). In particular, the strong correlation between inattention and hyperactivity was problematic in that collinearity diagnostics for the subsequent regression analyses indicated a strong degree of overlap between the two variables. Therefore, hyperactivity was eliminated from the regression analyses. Although depression and anxiety were also strongly related, collinearity diagnostics did not indicate a substantial overlap and as a result, both measures were included in subsequent analyses.

	Inattention	Hyperactivity	Depression	Anxiety	Study Skills	UCP	ALAS
Inattention	-	.65***	.39***	.25***	-.40***	-.02	-.19**
Hyperactivity	-	-	.29***	.22**	-.16*	.08	-.06
Depression	-	-	-	.57***	-.19**	.06	-.15*
Anxiety	-	-	-	-	-.19**	.09	-.11
Study Skills	-	-	-	-	-	-.01	.21**
UCP	-	-	-	-	-	-	.13

Note: *** p <.001; **p<.01,*p<.05.

Table 1. Relations among predictor variables.

5.2. Relations among measures of student success

The measures of student success, SACQ, GPA and major satisfaction were marginally related to one another, but appeared to largely be tapping independent constructs. SACQ was related to major satisfaction (r =.33, p <.001) but not to GPA (r =.12, p =.16). Major satisfaction was related to GPA (r =.27, p =.001).

5.3. Student success in different populations

ANCOVAs controlling for year in school were used to examine differences in the three student success measures according to whether or not the students had transferred colleges. There were no differences in GPA [F (1, 144) =.42, p =.52, partial η^2 =.003], SACQ [F (1, 207) =.27, p =. 61, partial η^2 =.001], or major satisfaction [F (1, 188) = 1.96, p =.16, partial η^2 =.01] by transfer status.

ANCOVAs controlling for year in school were also used to examine differences in the three student success measures according to whether or not students had changed majors. There were no differences in GPA [F (1, 144) =.42, p =.52, partial η^2 =.003], SACQ [F (1, 207) =.27, p =. 61, partial η^2 =.001], or major satisfaction [F (1, 188) = 1.96, p =.16, partial η^2 =.01] according to major change status. We considered that perhaps students who had changed majors only once (e.g., from undeclared to a major) might be similar to those who had never changed majors. Regrouping the students into those who had never changed majors or who had changed only once and those who had changed more than once did not substantively alter the results.

5.4. Predicting student success

Three simple regressions were completed to examine the relative contributions of inattention, depression, anxiety, study skills, UCP and ALAS in predicting GPA, SACQ and major satisfaction (see Table 2). In each regression, year in college was entered in the first step to control for any effects due to this factor. Different predictors emerged for the three measures of success. GPA was predicted only by the better understanding of college policies. SACQ was predicted by lower levels of inattention, better study skills and greater appreciation of the liberal arts, with an understanding of college policies approaching significance. Greater major satisfaction was predicted by fewer years in college, better study skills, greater understanding of college policies and greater appreciation of the liberal arts.

Predictor Variable	B	SE B	B	*p*
GPA				
Year	-.05	.04	-.12	.22
Inattention	-.09	.13	-.07	.51
Depression	-.06	.07	-.10	.42
Anxiety	.08	.07	.13	.25
Study Skills	.14	.11	.12	.22
UCP	.08	.03	.22	.02
ALAS	.00	.08	.00	.98
SACQ				
Year	.01	.03	.02	.76
Inattention	-.35	.10	-.26	.001
Depression	-.09	.06	-.12	.14
Anxiety	-.09	.06	-.12	.13
Study Skills	.26	.10	.19	.007
UCP	.05	.03	.13	.07
ALAS	.17	.07	.16	.02
Major Satisfaction				
Year	-.10	.04	-.19	.01
Inattention	-.12	.11	-.09	.30
Depression	.01	.07	.02	.85
Anxiety	-.04	.07	-.05	.57
Study Skills	.31	.11	.22	.005
UCP	.06	.03	.15	.05
ALAS	.32	.08	.31	<.001

Note: GPA: R =.30, R^2 =.09, Adj. R^2 =.03, F (7, 117) = 1.60, p =.14.

SACQ: R =.57, R^2 =.33, Adj. R^2 =.30, F (7, 166) = 11.54, p <.001.

Major satisfaction: R =.51, R^2 =.26, Adj. R^2 =.23, F (7, 151) = 7.64, p <.001.

Table 2. Summary of regression analyses predicting student success.

6. Discussion

The present study was designed to identify variables that predict college student success. In addition to GPA, two less common measures of student success were also included, i.e., student adjustment to college and student satisfaction with their choice of academic major. The predictors included year in college, as well as three measures broadly related to academics: student study skills, their understanding of college policies and their appreciation of the liberal arts. Particular emphasis was also placed on students' psychological well-being as a predictor of their college success. This was accomplished by including measures of ADHD symptoms, depression and anxiety. The goal was, therefore, to identify both the academic and psychological predictors of three definitions of college student success.

GPA has been the most widely studied measure of student success. In the present study, regression analyses indicated only one of the seven predictors, students' understanding of college policies, as a significant predictor of GPA. This was surprising, as previous research has indicated, for example, that the mastery of study skills was positively correlated with GPA, while students' self-reports of ADHD symptoms have been found to be negatively correlated with this measure of college student success.

There were three significant predictors for student adjustment to college. Specifically, ADHD was a negative predictor, whereas both study skills and the ALAS were positive predictors. A fourth predictor, an understanding of college policies, approached significance. These outcomes were as expected. Students reporting symptoms of ADHD have been found to have difficulties with peer relations [21]; as such, it is not surprising that they would experience the transition to college as challenging. The positive relationship between adjustment to college and study skills was also expected, as studying is a fundamental activity students engage in while attending college and thus, facility with this skill will likely promote a sense of belonging. Similarly, correspondence between the goals of the college and a student's values also appear as conducive to a smooth adjustment to college. The data for this study were collected at a liberal arts institution and it is therefore not surprising that students who reported higher scores on the ALAS also reported higher scores on the SACQ.

Four of the seven measures were found to be predictors for student satisfaction with their choice of academic major. Of these, only year in college was found to be a negative predictor. The negative direction of this predictor was surprising, as we had assumed students' satisfaction with their major to increase as they advanced toward graduation. However, it appears to be the case that many students' enthusiasm for their major declined as they enrolled in increasingly challenging courses. Not surprisingly, study skills efficacy is positively associated with satisfaction with major. The positive relationship between satisfaction with academic major and an understanding of college policies may reflect students' understanding of the academic requirements needed to graduate, including not only the specific courses that are necessary, but also their prerequisites, as well as a better understanding of the academic expectations inherent in their courses. Finally, we interpreted the positive relationship between major satisfaction and the ALAS as reflecting the correspondence between the students' and the college's goals.

In conclusion, the present study has identified predictors for three measures of college students' success. Perhaps most surprising was the prominence of understanding college policies. This measure was a significant predictor for two of these three measures of student success, GPA, as well as satisfaction with academic major and approached significance for the third, i.e., student adjustment to college. Two other predictors that were significant for two of the three measures of student success were study skills and the ALAS. It appears, therefore, that students perceive effective study skills to be a defining characteristic of what it means to successful in college, as is the fit between their goals and values as measured by the ALAS and those of the college they are attending.

At first glance, the three measures of psychological well-being – ADHD, depression and anxiety – did not appear to be central in determining student success, as only one of these, ADHD, was found to be significantly related to a measure of student success and then only for student adjustment to college. As this was unexpected, we examined these results in more depth. First, it is worth noting that the Shapiro-Wilks Test of Normality indicated that both ADHD and depression were skewed, with somewhat more cases with fewer symptoms than would be expected in a normal distribution. Anxiety was normally distributed. It is possible that this skew may have masked any relationships between ADHD and depression and success in college. This may have happened because students with these conditions had not been enrolled in the classes surveyed or they were not able to complete the survey. Because students in their first semester at the college were not able to enter a GPA and because students with symptoms of ADHD and depression have been reported to have lower rates of retention, it is possible that we had a lower than expected number of students with these disorders who participated. On the other hand, the lack of relationship between ADHD, depression and anxiety and success in college may be encouraging, as it might suggest that college interventions are being effective in accommodating students with psychological concerns. However, as noted above, the previous literature indicates that these psychological variables have repeatedly been associated with GPA. Thus, while it is heartening to view our findings as being an indication of the success of these interventions, we suggest caution and instead encourage additional studies that include multiple measures of student success, as well as a range of potential academic and psychological predictors.

Author details

Jill M. Norvilitis* and Howard M. Reid

*Address all correspondence to: NORVILJM@BuffaloState.edu

Department of Psychology, SUNY Buffalo State, Buffalo, NY, USA

The authors wish to thank Amanda Grenier for her assistance with this project.

References

[1] Frazier TW, Youngstrom EA, Glutting JJ, Watkins MW. ADHD and achievement: Meta-analysis of the child, adolescent, and adult literatures and a concomitant study with college students. Journal of Learning Disabilities. 2007; 40: 49-65.

[2] Shaw-Zirt B, Popali-Lehane L, Chaplin W, Bergman A. Adjustment, social skills, and self-esteem in college students with symptoms of ADHD. Journal of Attention Disorders. 2005; 8: 109-120.

[3] Emme EE. Predicting college success. Journal of Higher Education. 1942; 13: 263-267. doi:10.2307/1974937

[4] Hall C, Smith K, Chia, R. Cognitive and personality factors in relation to timely completion of a college degree. College Student Journal. 2008; 42: 1087-1098.

[5] Zwick R, Sklar JC. Predicting college grades and degree completion using high school grades and SAT scores: The role of student ethnicity and first language. American Educational Research Journal. 2005; 42: 439-464. doi: 10.3102/00028312042003439

[6] McCausland DF, Stewart NE. Academic aptitude, study skills, and attitudes and college GPA. The Journal of Educational Research. 1974; 67: 354-357.

[7] Norvilitis JM, Reid HM. Predictors of academic and social success and psychological well-being in college students. Education Research International. 2012; 2012. DOI: 10.1155/2012/272030.

[8] Baker RW, Siryk B. Measuring adjustment to college. Journal of Counseling Psychology. 1984; 31: 179-189.

[9] Baker RW, Siryk B. Student Adaptation to College Questionnaire (SACQ): Manual. Western Psychological Services, 1989.

[10] Kneipp LB, Kelly KE, Cyphers B. Feeling at peace with college: Religiosity, spiritual well-being, and college adjustment. Individual Differences Research. 2009; 7: 188-196.

[11] Meehan D, Negy C. Undergraduate students' adaptation to college: Does being married make a difference?. Journal of College Student Development. 2003; 44: 670-690. doi:10.1353/csd.2003.0055

[12] Baysden M. International and United States citizen student adaptation to college, opinions about mental illness, and attitudes toward seeking professional counseling help. Dissertation Abstracts International Section A. 2003; 64.

[13] Borrello A. Subjective well-being and academic success among college students. Dissertation Abstracts International. 2005; 66.

[14] Lounsbury JW, Fisher LA, Levy JJ, Welsh DP. An investigation of character strengths in relation to the academic success of college students. Individual Differences Research. 2009; 7: 52-69.

[15] Willcoxson L, Winder M. The relationship between choice of major and career, experience of university, and attrition. Australian Journal of Education. 2010; 54: 175-189.

[16] Norvilitis JM, Reid HM. Frequent change of academic major: A sign of trouble? Paper presented at the 77th Annual Meeting of the Eastern Psychological Association, March 2006. Baltimore, MD.

[17] Simon-Dack SL, Rodriguez PD, Marcum GD. Study habits, motives, and strategies of college students with symptoms of ADHD. Journal of Attention Disorders. 2014. doi: 10.1177/1087054714543369.

[18] Heiligenstein E, Guenther G, Levy A, Savino F, Fulwiler J. Psychological and academic functioning in college students with attention deficit hyperactivity disorder. Journal of American College Health. 1999; 47: 181-185.

[19] Norwalk K, Norvilitis JM, MacLean MG. ADHD symptomatology and its relationship to factors associated with college adjustment. Journal of Attention Disorders. 2009; 13: 251-258. DOI: 10.1177/1087054708320441

[20] Norvilitis JM, Sun L, Zhang J. ADHD symptomatology and adjustment to college in China and the United States. Journal of Learning Disabilities. 2010; 43: 86-94.

[21] McKee, TE. Peer relationships in undergraduates with ADHD symptomatology: Selection and quality of friendships. Journal of Attention Disorders. 2014. doi: 10:1177/1087054714554934.

[22] Tsang TW, Kohn MR, Efrons D, Clarke SD, Clark CR, Lamb C, Williams LM. Anxiety in young people with ADHD: Clinical and self-report outcomes. Journal of Attention Disorders. 2015; 19: 18-26.

[23] Nelson JM, Lindstrom W, Foels PA. Test anxiety and college students with ADHD. Journal of Psychoeducational Assessment. 2014; 32: 548-557.

[24] Blase SL, Gilbert AN, Anastopoulos AD, Costello EJ, Hoyle RH, Swartzwelder HS, Rabiner DL. Self-reported ADHD and adjustment in college: Cross-sectional and longitudinal findings. Journal of Attention Disorders. 2009; 13: 297-309.

[25] Nelson JM, Gregg N. Depression and anxiety among transitioning adolescents and college students with ADHD, dyslexia, and comorbid ADHD/dyslexia. Journal of Attention Disorders. 2012; 16: 44-254. doi:10.1177/1087054711430331

[26] Rabiner DL, Anastopoulos AD, Costello J, Hoyle RH, Swartzwelder HS. Adjustment to college in students with ADHD. Journal of Attention Disorders. 2008; 11: 689-699.

[27] Barkley RA, Murphy KR. Attention deficit hyperactivity disorder: A clinical workbook (3rd ed.). Guilford; 2006.

[28] International Personality Item Pool: A Scientific Collaboratory for the Development of Advanced Measures of Personality Traits and Other Individual Differences. Available from http://ipip.ori.org/.

[29] Reid HM, Kline B, O'Quin K. The revised appreciation of the liberal arts scale (ALAS-R): Development, reliability and validity. *International Journal of Research Studies in Education. 2014; 3:* 63-78.

Chapter 11

Family Difficulties in Children with ADHD, the Role of Integrated Psychopharmacology Psychotherapy Treatment

H.H. Aili, B. Norharlina, K.S. Manveen and W.I. Wan Salwina

Additional information is available at the end of the chapter

http://dx.doi.org/10.5772/61416

Abstract

Children with ADHD and their families face many challenges. The chapter discusses these difficulties with a case illustration. The write up of the case will demonstrate the difficulties faced by children with ADHD and their families; highlighting how the difficulties in the parents impact the child's ADHD symptoms. The case illustration will demonstrate how "normal" the cases can be, and often are missed or dismissed, yet it causes distress to the children and the adults. The chapter hopes to raise awareness that not only does the child needs assistance so do his/ her family members. Helping the parents will significantly aid in the progress of the child.

Keywords: Psychopathology, family difficulties, parents, children with attention-deficit/hyperactivity disorder (ADHD), management

1. Introduction

Children with ADHD have difficulties in their social and adaptive behavior which are related to the core symptoms of the disorder [1, 2]. The difficulties are felt within and outside the family setting [1, 3-5] with factors in their environment increasing the risk of impairment. Families of children with ADHD have consistently been shown to experience more burdens including stress [1, 6, 7].

Her parents brought Alice, a 12-year-old Asian girl to a child and adolescent psychiatry service. Her parents were upset that Alice would not follow their instructions at home. Alice would daydream and procrastinate with her school assignments despite constant reminders, and her grades were deteriorat-

ing. Alice's parents appeared frustrated, as they felt Alice intentionally defy their requests, even in simple day-to-day tasks, and to make matters worse, Alice was disinterested in her studies.

The parents were especially distressed that Alice had posted seductive photos of herself on Facebook, and their daughter had become increasingly moody and irritable over the past couple of months. They described Alice as being lazy, deceitful and dishonest. Her father at this point revealed that since the discovery, he had successfully removed all Internet access at home.

Alice remained quiet, while her parents went on relentlessly in a tirade of dissatisfaction regarding their daughter's behavior. When the clinician could, she asked the parents for qualities they admired in Alice, they were unable to come up with any.

On seeing Alice alone, she was warm and engaging. Alice expressed frustration at not being understood. Alice expressed she had difficulties in concentrating for long periods. She felt angry with herself for not finishing her tasks, and noticed she was often distracted easily. About her being distracted easily, Alice felt, this has been present since as long as she could remember. She later expressed regret over posting pictures of herself on Facebook. She said she was dared by a friend, and did it without thinking. Alice said she was petrified of her dad when he found the pictures, as no one at home chose to annoy her father. Her father, she added, had a "very bad temper".

The difficulties illustrated above may seem common in many children. However, when these difficulties considerably interfere with a child's normal functioning, clinicians should consider the possibility of the child having attention deficit hyperactivity disorder (ADHD). ADHD is a common neurobiological condition affecting 5-8% of school-age children [8]. For children like Alice, the inability to focus, attend to lessons, listen and obey instructions, and the presence of impulsive behavior often impact their functioning and interaction with others [9, 10].

It is often difficult to sort out what difficulties are caused specifically by the disorder and what factors add to the difficulties, and how. Adults often see the problems in the children as the child misbehaving and being under the influence of friends, as this case illustrates. There are many ways of characterizing the difficulties associated with ADHD [11, 12], with some researchers categorizing it as:

1. Emotional component, e.g., they are easily frustrated, impatient and emotionally reactive. The pathology is described as the presence of uncontrolled irritable temperament and has been suggested to be as a result of inability to inhibit responses, with the impulsivity in ADHD thought to drive the emotional component seen [11].

2. Social component, e.g., arguing, defiant. Other than poor behavioral inhibition [12], the social component is often linked to learned behaviors and is frequently related to the reaction of significant others to the child's behavior.

2. Behavioral disinhibition

Alice's parents reported a broad range of behaviors that can be classified as 'behavioral disinhibition". Alice struggled to contain and restrain her behavior. Alice was unable and at times was unwilling to inhibit her impulses, resulting in the emergence of inappropriate or disruptive behaviors. One of the most complained about behaviors by Alice's parents was that Alice was excessively responding to things when she was stressed. This caused their communication and interaction to deteriorate quickly as many times Alice responded by answering back to her parents instead of taking time to assess the task or requests from them and to come to a reasonable response. Alice's reactions angered her parents as they expected Alice to respond to them more appropriately and most importantly to comply with their requests.

Behavioral disinhibition is central to understanding many behavioral complications seen in ADHD, and it is described as being impulsive/ impulsiveness. Behaviors such as uncontrollable silly and clown-like conduct, giggling too much, and involvement in risk- taking behaviors, e.g., sexual misconduct, substance use or abuse, engagement with online friends or interest in prohibited actions, are behaviors often seen as annoying and causing disturbances or distress to others. These behaviors are beyond the definition of normal behavior and signify the impulsive behavior seen in people with ADHD.

Inhibition is defined as the ability to control one's attention, behavior, thoughts, and/or emotions [12]. In humans, the ability to use one's inhibition is necessary to override many strong internal vulnerability and external lure [13]. Inhibition is part of executive function, which is regulated in the frontal lobe [14].

Appropriate regulation of emotions is reliant on having effective behavioral inhibition [12]; and when this is deficient or defective, this often results in many emotional and behavioral problems [3, 15]. Many researchers have emphasized the presence of poor behavioral inhibition as the central impairment of the disorder [12, 16]. The poor behavior inhibition and poor impulse control is evident in people with ADHD having greater disinhibition and being less effective at regulating their emotions [12, 16]. As the consequence, they have the inability to delay responding long enough to consider the social situation and the consequences of their behavior [12, 16, 17]. Thus they make frequent hasty decisions and actions that occur in the moment without them thinking and considering the possibility of high potential of harm, failure or disappointment to the individual. Learning from their mistakes does not often occur or is difficult. They are repeatedly unable to use appropriate self-regulation strategies and social skills [12, 16]. They are unable to persist long enough to complete tasks and are unable to regulate them from being easily distracted.

Children with ADHD are seen as being disruptive and annoying. Again, this is as a consequence of their inability to regulate their behaviors and emotions. Their behaviors are highly intense, unmodulated and often inappropriate in the given context and insensitive to social expectations [3, 5, 18, 19]. They are often described as interrupting and intruding on others. The disruptive behaviors often emerge as early as in the preschool years and in many children persisting into adolescence [20]. Children with ADHD are described as less attentive to social cues, not listening to adults, and ignoring parental requests.

These difficulties impair their academic and social functioning, use of their recreational time as well as the relationship with their parents [21]. They are often seen as being less compliant even oppositional towards adults [22, 23]. It makes it hard for the parent of a child who is often annoyed and over-reacting to things around him/ her. Just as frustrating and worrying, many parents have been called in to their child's school to listen to numerous negative reports of their child and some may have triggered negative reactions from their teachers.

Further neurobiological information on impulsivity and inhibition has been suggested to be as a result multiple pathway models [16, 24, 25] and discussed in-length elsewhere in the book.

Alice felt over controlled being home, and expressed that she chose to keep to herself. Alice added she would usually confide and feel better when she chatted with friends online. She felt miserable, as she had no longer had any access to them after her father cut-off the Internet access.

Alice felt she was walking on eggshells when she was at home. She added that she felt tense at home, and was not able to be herself. She feared that her father would be angry, and he often was angry when he came home. In many of his angry outbursts, father has asked Alice's mother to leave the house.

Alice had symptoms of ADHD, which was clearly impacting her performance at school and putting a strain on her relationship with her parents. Her impulsivity resulted in her making hasty and unwise decisions, as seen in her risk-taking behavior. The dispute and conflict at home between her parents and her, her parent's negative perception of her, further drove her to seek comfort and acceptance with online friends. Her anger and frustration at her predicament appeared to be taking a toll on her ability to regulate her emotions. She was seen to be moody and irritable at the time of presentation, and it worsened the interaction between her and her parents.

3. Diagnosis

ADHD

Oppositional Defiant Disorder

Difficulties with Primary support group

Reactive attachment disorder

The diagnoses arrived at were purely based on detailed psychiatric assessment which involves thorough history taking and mental state examination of the child and her family. No other assessment devices/ rating scales were employed.

The writers were based in a child and adolescent mental health facility where the service has only child and adolescents psychiatrists. There are many such services operating with the lack of staffs e.g. child psychiatrists or allied health personnel, and funding. This should not prevent clinicians or any mental health professionals assessing any child presenting to mental health facilities with symptoms suggestive of ADHD. It is most logical to gather enough data from the parents regarding symptoms of ADHD, i.e. look for any behavioral, emotional and academic difficulties.

Neuropsychological testing, speech-language assessments, and computerized testing of attention or inhibitory control may not be available in many centers or settings. These assessments are not required as part of a routine assessment for ADHD, but may be indicated by the findings of the initial psychological assessment [26]. Having no such assessment tools should not prevent any child and their families to be assessed.

4. Emotional dysregulation

children with ADHD are viewed as being more unsuccessful with regulation and this can be easily seen as they are easily upset when faced with faced with daunting and frustrating tasks [12, 13, 27]. As demonstrated in Alice, they respond impulsively.

Emotion regulation refers to the ongoing process of responding to one's environment with emotions that are both socially acceptable and context-appropriate for any given situation [13]. It is a process that allows the individual to select, attend and appraise emotionally arousing stimuli [28]. The expression of emotions is pertinent and it has to be appropriate to help promote adaptive and goal-oriented behaviors and to fit in with others [29]. These processes trigger behavioral and physiological responses that can be modulated through understanding of what influences these components of emotions, with dysregulation of one's emotion appearing when these adaptive processes are impaired [28, 30].

From the history Alice seemed easily frustrated, moody and irritable. Alice was not able to regulate her emotions adequately, giving rise to her being irritable at home especially when she felt she was confronted by her parents. These clearly complicated things between Alice and her parents; despite them telling her to consider issues brought up by her parents, Alice was not able to delay responding.

Emotional dysregulation can be seen in three domains from temper control, affective lability and emotional over reactivity [31]. Emotion dysregulation is prevalent in ADHD and is a major contributor to impairment [13, 32, 33]. Reports estimates, prevalence of between 24% and 50% children with ADHD has emotional dysregulation [33-35], and it is more severe in males [13].

Furthermore, children with ADHD has been described as emotionally explosive [1, 13]. The difficulties with self-regulating their emotions is seen in them being easily frustrated, and having low frustration tolerance, with frequent temper outbursts and mood lability [16, 36]. They are seen seen to be easily angry, hot-tempered, sensitive thus easily annoyed and reacts to the slightest comments. They fight with parents, teachers and even their peers [1, 37, 38]. Many children end up facing numerous limitations in their activities with friends at school or within the neighborhood, with some children consequently having no friends. Peers avoid being with the child due to their negative, harsh and at times aggressive behavior.

It has been proposed that genetic factors play a role in the etiology of emotional dysregulation in children with ADHD [33, 39, 40]. Failures of parental emotion regulation, high levels of parental criticism contribute to the development of emotion dysregulation in children with ADHD [41, 42], and these issues were illustrated in Alice and her family.

Emotional dysregulation is thought to have a greater impact than hyperactivity and inattention on an individual's well-being and self-esteem [33]. Individuals with combination of ADHD and emotional dysregulation face more impairment in peer relationships, family life, occupational attainment, and academic performance than those with ADHD alone [1, 33]. Other than it is a major source of impairment, the presence of emotional dysregulation indicates poorer clinical outcome [30].

The presence of oppositional behavior and difficulties with self-regulation are often an indication of more serious difficulties [12, 16].

5. Peer and school challenges in ADHD

Having friends is important; children learn to socialize, communicate, cooperate, and negotiate having friends. They also learn to manage disagreements and challenges. Friends are an important source of influence, both positive and negative, especially outside the home environment [43, 44]. Friends play a key role in the development of personal competence and identity, with having friends predictive of the child's later psychological functioning as they are an important source of support [45]. Peer relationships are important especially for adolescents with presence of peer rejection linked to long-term negative outcomes including academic problems, school dropout, delinquency, even cigarette and substance use [5, 19, 45].

The core symptoms of ADHD, i.e. inattention and hyperactivity/impulsivity impede effective functioning with peers [19, 46, 47]. Between 50% and 80% of children with ADHD are rejected by peers [19, 48]. Inattentiveness limits opportunities to acquire social skills through observational learning and to attend to social cues necessary for successful social interaction, while hyperactive and impulsive behaviors contribute to unrestrained and overbearing social behavior that makes children with ADHD highly aversive to their peers [3, 5, 46, 47].

Peers often report children with ADHD exhibit more negative behaviors, such as "interrupting or intruding on others", are noisy and others often find them as socially immature. This is primarily because these children exhibit deficits in social skills such as reduced capacity for social reciprocity and difficulties in understanding social cues [49]. In addition, children with ADHD have reduced ability to monitor and evaluate their own behaviors [19, 50]. They are unable to wait for their turn or to learn from being told before, resulting in them to be lower on social preference among their peers. They are less well-liked and have fewer dyadic friendships [19, 50]. The deficits in peer rejection often occur early in age and these children are often excluded from popular social groups [47].

The presence of ADHD symptoms in children impact the child's school functioning, performance and achievement [26, 51]. A significant proportion of children with ADHD faced significant difficulties in school with learning [52, 53], low academic achievement [54], and absenteeism [21, 55-57].

To add to their challenges in school, even among their teachers, children with ADHD are perceived as being less socially competent [58] and at times challenging. Teachers play an important role in the lives of children, including in children with ADHD. They have daily contact with the children, and they are often the first to notice the difficulties in the children with ADHD. Teachers often make inferences about the child's present and future academic achievement and general classroom behavior of their students, thus creating expectations for and perception of the child [54, 59, 60]. Like parents, teachers report feeling more stressed when handling and interacting with children with ADHD as the interactions are more negative [61]. Similarly the perceptions and expectations of teachers affect their interactions with the children, which in turn affect the children's behavior and academic success [59, 60].

6. Co-morbidity

Approximately two thirds of children with ADHD have at least one other coexisting condition [62, 63]. Disruptive behavior is one of the most common behavioral difficulties with an estimate of between 30% and 50% of children with ADHD have them [63-65]. Children with ADHD, particularly those exhibiting more impulsivity, are likely to be diagnosed with oppositional defiant disorder. They have more difficulties restricting their behavior in conformance with instructions especially from adults, deferring gratification and resisting temptations [12]. Additionally the presence of conduct disorder or oppositional defiant disorder significantly complicates the acute presentation of ADHD and its management. The disruptive behavior is associated with more aggression and delinquency, and disrupts academic achievement [12, 66-69]. The emergence of disruptive behavior in Alice clearly caused a lot of animosity between her parents and Alice.

7. Depression

Alice did not have sufficient symptoms to warrant a diagnosis of a depressive disorder, however she did reveal some symptoms to suggest she was depressed. Many children with ADHD describe chronic unhappiness even though they do not fulfill the criteria of major depression (MD). Presence of depression is common with between 5% and 40% of children with ADHD meeting the criteria for MD [62, 70, 71]. Major depression in children with ADHD is often recurrent and the prevalence increases significantly around puberty [72]. Presence of depression further complicates the picture as it is linked with increasing disruptive behavior, and further impairments in academic performance, peer relationships, and family relationships [71, 73]. The presence of MD in ADHD children is as well associated with significant long-term psychiatric morbidity [72].

Adolescents with ADHD and co-morbid mood disorders are at increased risk for suicide attempts [72, 74]. The rate of suicide is much higher in patients with both ADHD and MD as compared to patients with MD alone because both disorder may aggravate the symptoms of the other [75]. Even though Alice did not have any suicide attempt, she did express death wishes; hence, it was crucial that the clinician closely monitored her mood symptoms. This was done with regular and close follow-up visitation. With the ongoing difficulties within her family still continuing, Alice was at definite risk of developing depression. Noticeably, her relationship with her parents had deteriorated.

Alice found solace in friends online. Both inattention and hyperactive-impulsivity domains in ADHD are important risk factors for excessive use of Internet. Internet addiction is also found to be associated with symptoms of ADHD [76]. Significant associations have been found between the level of ADHD symptoms and the severity of Internet addiction in children [76, 77]. It is postulated that the rapid response and immediate reward of the Internet makes it attractive for children with ADHD who easily bored and have aversion to delaying rewards. Thus it is not surprising the lack of self-control and inhibition makes them vulnerable to Internet Addiction [76, 77].

Other difficulties, i.e., bipolar and substance use and abuse, are discussed elsewhere.

Subsequent Sessions

Over the subsequent sessions, Alice established a comfortable relationship with the clinician. She would walk in and eagerly share her difficulties. In one of the session, Alice shared she was upset that her teacher complained to her parents that Alice had kissed a boy outside school. At this point, her relationship with her parents was at its worst.

Her clinician was able to explore the family dynamics. The authoritarian parenting characteristics, the family environment, its lack of emotional warmth and support, and the parental psychopathology were clearly impacting Alice. Her behaviors may have served an important purpose within the family. It appeared to be an avenue for focus to be directed to her, instead of the very evident conflict between her parents. The clinician felt Alice was attempting to keep her parents together, as they appeared to be united in their stance and approach handling her. The high levels of conflict at home had conferred Alice at a heightened state of anxiety and hypervigilance, which were clearly taking a toll on her ability to regulate her emotions.

The clinician felt at this point it would be essential to make Alice's parents conscious of the dysfunctionality within the family. This was very difficult as her father was suspicious and untrusting of the clinician. To the clinician, it appeared that the father was fearful of the loss of autonomy over his family. Hence it showed showed in the father's presentation to the clinic. Her father portrayed a very defensive and almost aggressive stance. In view of the clinician's difficulty with the client's father, the clinician decided to engage the mother in order to facilitate some changes.

8. Family background

Alice came from an upper class family. Her father was a businessman, while her mother was a housewife. She had an older sister with whom she did not have a close relationship. She felt looked down upon by her sister, and her parents made constant comparison between her and her sister. Her sister was doing exceptionally well.

8.1. Alice's mother

Alice's mother had a difficult childhood. Her father passed away when she was very young. At the age of 10 years, she was expected by her mother to look after her younger siblings, whilst her mother worked.

Mother was expected to be independent and she was constantly reminded of her role as the eldest, and to not be a burden to her mother. Alice's mother lost a normal childhood, and grew up with a mother who showed no warmth, was critical, and imposed huge demands on her that she carried out dutifully. When the clinician asked her what she saw when she looked at her own daughter, mother added that she saw a lazy child, who was so different from how she was, as a child. Upon reflection, mother then added that she indeed had become exactly like her own mum. At this juncture mother became very distressed and tearful.

When the clinician asked her how she felt when she had discovered those letters, mother added that she was not surprised. Alice had, over past 6 months, placed letters of death wishes on mum's pillow. The clinician asked her how she responded to Alice, on reading the letters. Mother mentioned that she never asked Alice about the letters, as she felt her daughter was seeking attention, and if she asked her, it would encourage her further. Once again, she cried upon realizing the impact of what she had just said. It was a difficult session for mother, but one that allowed her to self-reflect, and impelled her to make changes, for the sake of her daughter. Mother realized she did love her daughter still, but mother had great difficulties to express her love, to show she cared, and it affected her bonding and ability to secure a loving relationship.

9. Parenting and parent-child relationship in children with ADHD

Parenting is challenging enough and the case demonstrates the reality that parenting children with ADHD is a big challenge to many parents. Symptoms of the disorder such as hyperactivity, impulsivity and inattention make parenting a child more difficult [65, 78, 79]. Although the presentation may change throughout the developmental years, the difficulties are often ongoing [9, 63]. It is often more challenging during the adolescent years.

For school-going children like Alice, the inability to focus, attend to lessons, listen and obey instructions, difficulties in play or recreational activities and to interact pleasantly with others clearly impairs their academic and social functioning [7, 9] as well as the relationship with their parents [80]. It is stressful dealing with a child's noncompliance and oppositional behavior. Parents frequently misinterpret their child's behavior and intentions, and are often frustrated as "correcting their child's behaviors" is every so often associated with more oppositional behaviors from the child. This was how Alice's parents felt towards their daughter. Children with ADHD tend to exhibit higher than average rates of noncompliance [81], and in adolescents with ADHD, as discussed, it is not uncommon to see an increased in emotionality, especially in the form of anger [82]. This results in parents expressing their child as being non-compliant and oppositional [22, 23, 81]. Parents are not aware of their child having a disorder, or even aware what behaviors are related to the disorder. All they think about is how frustrating it is for them to handle their child.

Alice's parents felt managing their daughter was indeed challenging, especially in her adolescent years; they felt Alice **was the major source of stress** for the family. The problematic parent child interactions are often ongoing and repetitive, characterized by parents requesting for compliance, followed by the child's refusal to comply. This often results in either escalation of parents control and demanding compliance. This eventually leads to occurrence of occurrence of annoyance and increasing control control over the child while in other instances the parents give up. Despite this, there is still presence of frustration and anger in the environment. Many are unaware that the parent child interactions negatively reinforce each other in ways that increase the probability and severity of the child's problematic behaviour(s) and the deterioration of the parent child relationship.

Presence of negative emotions and cognitions, e.g., in a distress parent consistently influences one's evaluations of others with major consequences on their interactions with their children [83-85]. As the case demonstrates, the parents and the child are both angry and distressed with each other. There is as well presence of distrust milieu, both parties perceiving the other as intentionally frustrating resulting in the behavior of being noncompliant with the other. The presence of many conflicting interactions between parents and children often results in angry or distraught interactions, with each perceiving the other as intentionally frustrating, being uncooperative. This often results in both sides trying to out-do the other. The environment is often of greater negative affect, with less positive involvement and parenting responsiveness. It is no wonder that both parties could not exert some control on their own behaviour and emotions, and to try to find a compromise. Each party feel, they are right.

Unresolved parental reactions to their own or family crisis impacts the parents' parenting styles [84, 85]; with Pianta and Marvin [84] and Sheeran, Marvin [85] stating the resolution of the matter, influences their mental representation of strategies in managing their difficulties. The lesser positive parenting responsiveness invariably leads to the use of more harsh and inconsistent discipline, and more coercive exchanges than in families of nonproblematic children [86].

Like any parents, parents of ADHD children may have their own difficulties. However, parents of ADHD children are at increased risk of having other psychiatric disorders as low self-confidence [22, 87] and depression [88, 89]. Presence of parental stress, marital disharmony, high expressed emotions etc. affects parental functioning, family involvement and the parent child interaction [90, 91]. Without doubts, problematic parent child relationships adds to the parenting distress [37, 92].

Aspects of parenting are significant and are often over-shadowed by the difficulties in children with ADHD. **Parenting style** is a constellation of attitudes, behaviors and interactional styles or patterns of parenting practices [93]. Invariably how parents behave and interact with their children creates an emotional climate for the parent–child relationship [20, 93-95]. Parenting practices and behaviors are directly linked to children's emotional, behavioral regulation, social and interpersonal competence [93]; with substantial associations demonstrated between undesirable parenting behaviors/ styles with problems in their off-springs [96]. Other than maladaptive parenting practices [92, 97], parental perceptions and ideas [37, 97], differences in parenting and disagreements between the couple [81, 86, 90, 98] are factors which contribute to the development and escalation of the child's problematic behaviors [99]. These issues distract the parents towards finding a more workable intervention for their child with difficulties.

http://dx.doi.org/10.5772/61416

The psychodynamic model emphasizes the importance of emotional relationships between parents and their child plays a significant role in the development course of children. The emotional relationships between parents and child are thought to be as a result of parenting behaviors and attitudes influencing the parents and their child's behaviors, and later influencing the child's relationships with other adults and peers [100-102]. In this dynamic family system, the internal representation of each party is just as influential [100, 103].

This notion is supported by Maccoby [104] who stated that the parent child interaction is a reciprocal process with parents influencing their children and the children's behaviors may influence the way they are treated by their parents. While it is evident that parents often exhibit a range of emotions toward their children, in Alice's parents there is a predominant and persistent feeling of hostility and displeasure. Their interaction with their daughter was often distant, hostile, and at times disengaged, which supports the hypothesis that parental beliefs and perceptions influence specific parental behaviors and the emotional climates concerning their child [93, 95, 105].

Perception toward the child's symptoms is important as it significantly influences parents' interaction with their children [106]. In parents of ADHD children Alizadeh, Applequist [87] reported parents showed less warmth and involvement in the parenting of their children and they are more prone to greater use of corporal punishment. Similarly, Gau [107] found mothers of children with ADHD were less affectionate, more overprotective and controlling toward their children than mothers of controls. Margari, Craig [108] found parents with ADHD children tend to be more controlling, disapproving and rejecting of their children. The parents tended to use more verbal direction, repeated commands, added with more verbal reprimands and correction of their children. Margari, Craig [108] reported in these parents, they are also less rewarding and responsive than parents of children without ADHD. This is not surprising surprising as having a child with chronic difficulties and different from others affects the parents' beliefs, perceptions, attributions, etc. about the child and of other things faced by the parents.

Parents are often unaware of their reactions to the children's behaviors and emotions, which are often modeled by the children and affecting most notably their self-image. Alice's mother was getting more and more tired and irritable having to deal with her daughter's chronic difficulties and she was feeling alone and unsupported. Having to handle their daughter alone aggravated the marital disharmony. Many parents may not be aware of the symptoms and the severity of the problems that their child has. In this instance, Alice's parents labeled her as "bad, stubborn", they were unable to acknowledge their daughter was struggling as well. The parents' expectations and their beliefs, perceptions, and attribution about the child affect the parents' behavior toward the child. Thus if the parents feel their child is exhausting for them, it creates more tension in their relationship. Some parents may initially be overwhelmed with guilt feelings and blamed themselves for the children's misbehaviors however when the situation deteriorates, and things worsened, feelings of hopelessness and helplessness creep in. In other parents, they may have difficulty accepting the fact that their child is suffering from a disorder, given the stigma attached to the illness.

Mothers are the principal caregivers in many families across different cultures and countries. In countless instances, mothers are the parent who interacts and has to deal with their children in situations where the child exhibits most of the ADHD symptoms. Mothers are the ones most often helping their child do their school work, even organizing their school bag, their room, getting their children organized and to get through their daily activities. Inevitably, mothers are more likely to be blamed for their child's poor academic and social performances [109]. It is not surprising mothers of children with ADHD often report greater psychological distress and receiving lesser support from their families than do mothers of normal children [107, 110].

Maternal affection buffers children with attention problems from developing social and adjustment problems [50], and this was considerably absent in the family discussed. Alice's mother was not able to offer comfort to her daughter, as the mother was distressed with having to handle her daughter on her own. This is not surprising as seen in the case described. As the situation continued and with no end insight, the severity of the difficulties increased. Predictably, the impairment increases, and it seemed the parents are the ones who often feel the impact more than their children [79]. Alice's parents, especially her mother, had become averse to being with Alice. Mother felt distress knowing her daughter was around. By the time the family was seen, the parents were very critical of their daughter, and it worried the clinician. The adults were not able to see any strength in Alice. Their perception of their daughter and the difficulties made the child parent interaction and parenting challenging.

Additionally, the difficulties are complicated by the presence of comorbidity and psychosocial stressors in the parents themselves. Family dysfunction or disadvantage is associated with early conduct complications [20]. This was clearly happening in Alice's family as her parents were struggling in their own marital relationship and often reacted hastily and angrily to their daughter's struggles.

Alice's father was impatient and often angry, and in his outburst he had told his wife to leave their matrimonial home. Unaware to the couple, it made Alice anxious and worried. Alice's father displayed poor emotional regulation resulting in frequent anger outbursts. Further history revealed that the father was brash in his manner with his family. In the clinical sessions, the clinician found father had difficulties to engage in the session. This raised the possibility of undiagnosed ADHD in the father.

ADHD is one of the most heritable psychiatric disorder [111, 112]. Parents of children with ADHD are more likely to have ADHD themselves [113, 114]. Subsequently, the parenting difficulties observed in families of children with ADHD may be accounted for, at least in part, by parental ADHD [114]. Presence of parental ADHD symptoms significantly impairs parents' parenting of their children, affecting the parental and child interactions and relationship [37, 114, 115]. Adults with ADHD have similar impairment in their executive functioning such as self-regulation of attention, inhibition, and organization. This effects their time management, planning, memory, motivation, persistence, and emotional regulation, i.e., they are likely to have more difficulties managing their child particularly those with oppositional behaviors [79, 115, 116].

http://dx.doi.org/10.5772/61416

In most parents, their ADHD symptoms have not been assessed. Many of the adults are not aware of the symptoms and how the symptoms may affect their functioning as parents. The symptoms of inattentiveness and impulsivity are likely to cause adults with ADHD to engage in harsh or lax parenting behaviors when dealing with their child's problems [113, 117]. It is more difficult for parents to refrain themselves during discipline encounters therefore they are likely to use more negative and coercive methods. As the presence of ADHD results in difficulties with self-regulating, this may effect parents ability to think through about long-term gains [113, 118]. The short attention span and impulsivity may make it difficult for a parent to stay focused or be consistent in monitoring or carrying out rules [81, 118]. Additionally, they have problems with decision-making, e.g., they will have hitches with monitoring their child's behaviors, progress, or whereabouts. The consistency of the external feedback provided by parents of ADHD children is an important element for these children to remain on track with tasks, behaviors, etc. Harvey, Danforth [118] reported mothers with ADHD tended to use more repetitions during mothers with ADHD tended to use more repetitions during attempts to get their child to comply. This often results in arguments because repeated and angry requests from mothers are often ignored.

Affective lability is also seen in adult ADHD [113]. Fathers displaying features of impulsivity were found to have more arguments with their children during the interactions [118]. They were more demanding, are more power-assertive and they are less likely to express warmth toward these children [119]. When fathers do attend to their children's noncompliance, they demand more compliance and obedience at the expense of not or less expressing nurturance [118-120]. Similarly in mothers with ADHD, they are more emotionally reactive, causing likely to use more to use harsh or physical forms of punishments [116]. Like-wise maternal ADHD symptoms have been associated with lower level of positive parenting, lesser involvement and inconsistent discipline [113, 118]. In adolescences, this dyadic interaction with their parents often results in the relationship to be hostile or distant.

Fathers are often less talked about as the source of emotional support and attachment. Fathers are equally an important source of support and resource for their children's well-being, cognitive development, and social competence [119, 121-123]. Studies of fathers with ADHD children found fathers' parenting style play a significant role in their interaction with their children [119] including the engagement and progression of adolescent delinquent behaviors [118, 122, 124]. Fathers of children with ADHD, particularly when handling their sons, are more demanding and controlling [125, 126] and argumentative [118]. Other than being demanding, both Buhrmester, Camparo [126] and Gerdes, Hoza [120] reported fathers of ADHD children were less likely to express warmth
towards their children while Harvey, Danforth [118] found in fathers with ADHD, the inattentiveness and impulsivity results in lax parenting. The presence of a supportive father may certainly help lift the burden of mothers handling the child alone. Likewise, support between parents and parenting similarity has been found to be associated with greater marital adjustment and and lesser marital conflict among parents of ADHD children [81].

10. Impact: Why the need to be aware of parenting difficulties?

It is not easy to parent a child with ADHD. Lower quality of life has been reported in families with ADHD children [79, 115, 127], complicated by the presence of adversities, conflicts [23, 128-131], and psychological difficulties [88, 89]. These factors significantly impact family functioning which may precipitate and/or aggravate the child parent relationship and parenting difficulties [131]. Hence it is important for clinicians and mental health workers to consider these difficultieswhen interacting with a family of a child or adolescent with ADHD.

In psychiatry, family factors are taken into consideration in the formulation of clients' presentation and symptoms, i.e., in precipitating, perpetuating, predisposing or aggravating patient's symptoms, in treatment and in prognosis [132]. Over the past decade, much attention has been given to the understanding of the parent child interaction, with regards to attachment styles and parental behaviors, etc. and their impact on children. A significant number of researches have recognized the family environment plays an important role in the development, outcomes, and manifestation of difficulties in children with ADHD [37, 50, 128]. **Both parental psychopathology and parenting behavior** have been identified as important environmental risk and/or protective factors in children with ADHD [37, 133]. Family dysfunction impacts not only the family functioning and certainly clinical outcomes. Family functioning influences continuity and/or exacerbation of the child's ADHD symptoms [37, 86]. The difficulties related to the parents and family dysfunction are often linked to the frequency and severity of ADHD symptoms [20, 134-136]. Whereas improvement in outcomes linked to ongoing family engagement particularly active parental involvement and participatory collaborations between care-givers and healthcare providers [97, 137].

These phenomena can be explained as the family interaction is continuous and ongoing, and invariably children are affected by the dynamics in the family. Parents are the main source of their children's socialization and emotional regulation [44, 96], and children often model their parents' regulation and expression of emotions [44, 138]. Accordingly, positive parenting constitutes having parenting attitudes and behaviors which are accepting and nurturing **(acceptance),** while negative parenting practices encompasses parenting styles which are rejecting and controlling [95]. In negative parenting practices, there is a constant need need for parents set fixed rules with rigid boundaries, with the necessity for constant supervision [139, 140]. The parents often make endless demands on their children and readily confronts the child who disobeys with more continuous demands made [140]. In this style of parenting there is often presence of hostility when dealing with the child [141]. As studies have indicated, parents with ADHD children often are controlling, disapproving and hostile of their children [20, 37, 108].

It is not unusual for parents to react to their child's noncomplaint and disruptive behavior in a less positive manner, and this is often seen among parents with ADHD children [86, 125]. The use of punishment and harsh discipline are often thought to be associated with good parenting. Parents feel using frequent punishment allows them by doing so, they are able to control their children's behaviors. Likewise, parents often exert control on their children in the pretext of having to protect their children from possible harm or from going astray. Many parents often believe their parenting is adequate, appropriate or the best for their for their children. Many parents parenting styles with them having to be able to control and to discipline their child. The reality is, using more control with presence of punitive interactions, often results in retaliation and noncomplaint behavior from the child, especially among adolescents. Many parents are unaware of the importance and the need for them to be equally nurturing and supportive of their children.

Evidence supports findings of reciprocal pathways between child disruptive behavior and parent–child interaction difficulties. Being in a chaotic, harsh, unsupportive or unresponsive family environment exacerbate inattentive, impulsive, and hyperactive behaviors [37]. Cunningham and Boyle [20] found mothers with pre-school children with ADHD and oppositional behavior cope with their children's behaviours using more controlling and negative strategies. The mothers used more reprimands and corporal punishments. Often this does not settle the child. Querido, Warner [142] and Carpenter and Mendez [143] found harsh parenting is predictive of worsening behavior as the presence of punitive interactions and low level of warmth do not offer any comfort, feeling safe, and support to the child [15]. The presence of harsh, punitive, and controlling parenting behaviors as seen in authoritarian parenting styles hinders the development of a child's social competence. This parenting style is linked to the presence of aggressive and defiant behavior in children [15, 69, 136, 142, 144, 145].

Over the recent years, studies have focussed on the attachment theory specifically on the quality of parenting and understanding how socio-emotional dysfunction impacts children's behavior and development. Attachment is the deep and lasting affective and close relationship between a child and their care-giver(s), which is established in the early years of a child's life [100, 101]. The parent child relationship is crucial as it lays the foundation of attachment and socialization which eventually dominates and affects the child's emotional, interpersonal development, and well-being [146]. Consequently in vulnerable children, the presence of secure attachment provides safety and protection through the existence of a trusting, safe, and secure environment [147, 148]. The presence of a secure, supportive, and trustworthy caregiver allows distressed children to use their care-givers as a secure base to regulate their anxiety and distress; the child finds comfort and support when confronted with stressful stimuli or situations [148].

Growing up with an insensitive and unresponsive, or unavailable caregiver often puts the child at risk for developing an insecure attachment relationship [102]. Alice could not find comfort from her parents as the adults were entrapped in their own burden. Her parents were unable to provide relief and nurturance to their daughter, especially in her times of need. This is not surprising as parents who lack or not able to provide self regulation skills are unable to offer the framework necessary for the development of such skills in their children [20, 137]. Thus, they are less able to support their child, which leaves the child feeling insecure and vulnerable. Insecurely attached individuals are indeed more vulnerable to problems concerning affective and behavioral regulation [149]. Lower levels of conduct problems even in children as young as pre-school-going age has been reported in parents exhibiting parental warmth in combination with other positive parenting behaviors [123, 150]. The presence of a secure attachment and base allows a child with with ADHD the awareness and security they will be supported as they work through their difficulties.

11. What elements constitute negative parenting behaviors and interfere with establishment of a secure family base?

Researchers have shown negative parenting behaviors as:

1. Over-controlling [151, 152]: This describes the parenting styles which resembles the no-nonsense parenting with decrease in responsiveness and increase in demandingness. In this parenting style, parents are involved in all decision-making, and are overprotective. There is presence of frequent instructions to children, e.g., on how to behave, think, or feel, in view to influence the child. This style of parenting has been shown to mediate higher risk for anxiety and depression [141] and delinquency in children [123, 136].

2. Harsher discipline characterized by presence of constant yelling, nagging, threatening or the use of physical aggression (hitting, beating). This harsh parenting relates to the emergence and escalation of aggressive and defiant behavior in children [15, 123, 143].

3. Over-indulgent: This style of parenting reduces the child's opportunities for learning. There is constant parental interference with parents over doing their role. Their parenting style interferes with the child's attempts at gaining age normative autonomy and emotional independence. There is no restrictions, and no boundaries to what the child wants and desire [94, 153].

4. Inconsistent parenting [119], often exhibits inconsistent availability and therefore discipline. It is akin to low parental involvement and often may worsen the child's ADHD symptoms [137].

5. Rejection and hostile parenting characterized by presence of disapproval, and low levels of parental warmth and responsiveness. Parents often exhibit coldness or are unresponsive, dismissive and disapproving of their child. They often respond to their children's expressions of needs or emotions with criticizing or minimizing and even nagging. This often convinces a child that positives, especially from a significant other, are difficult to obtain and are independent of the child's actions. Presence of high levels of parental rejection is often associated with poor child emotion regulation [138] and increasing sensitivity to develop anxiety and depression [153].

6. Negative and unreasonable parenting beliefs [106, 154].

7. Dissimilarity in parenting [81]: dissimilarities between parents would not only impact on the problems in the child, it will as well cause higher marital conflicts and dissatisfaction between the couple.

8. Higher levels of parenting stress are often associated with the presence of marital disharmony, divorce, separation, remarriage, parental depression [37, 136]. Stressed

parents exhibit either hostility, over-protectiveness or are unavailable when dealing with their children.

The negative parenting behavior as stated above, i.e., hostile, unavailable, inconsistent parenting along with parental stress and psychopathology often influences the parent child interactions and family functioning. In children these circumstances predict treatment outcomes [110].

Parents from every background love their children and want to protect them from all sorts of harm and misfortune. Qualities in parents such as the presence of parental affection and sensitivity, the amount and nature of control strategies, and monitoring are key aspects of healthy child development [104, 155]. The existence of warmth, acceptance, and communication becomes increasingly important during adolescence. Parents are an important source of support, especially among adolescents. They can still exert influence over their children's behavior by providing the existence of being responsive and sensitive while creating a caring and safe family environment, and not just the presence of strict control. As a matter of fact, strict control, especially during adolescence, is associated with deviance and misconduct [156-158].

The manner in which parents respond to their children's emotions and behaviors, their perception and managing of their children's behaviors impacts the outcomes of the difficulties, the child's self-image and problem-solving skills. Bowlby [159] hypothesized early experiences with primary caregivers are internalized by the child as generalized mental representations or *internal working models* i.e. the child's image of the self as well as the image of others. These cognitive representations of early relationships serve as templates for functioning in future relationships [100, 103] and shapes how the child responds to external events [102, 160]. These mental representations (organize a person's adults' later attachment-related representations and) play a key role in guiding interpersonal behavior and regulating affect during adolescence and adulthood [161, 162].

In positive parenting, parents create an environment of secure attachment by balancing giving the child their attention while creating the presence of a nurturing environment. In this style of parenting, appropriate attention is given, and there is often positive affect felt through the expression presence of positive emotions. Communication is encouraged; there is presence of proper discipline and structure, with clear rules, instructions. There are, and consistent monitoring of how things are balanced with use of praises [163, 164]. Parents react positively, allowing their children to learn to control their impulses using their cognition [149]. This style of parenting serves as protective factor that results in and facilitates the development of proper self-regulation [149].

In dealing with children with ADHD, parents need loads of patience and consistency as the case demonstrates. It is not easy dealing with a child who is active, has difficulties to stay focus to listen to parents, to follow as parents want them to. It is not surprising that parents with ADHD children tend to be more controlling and disapproving of their children. They frequently give their attention to their child's overactive and impulsive behaviors. They invariably repeat their commands, and become increasingly impatient with little reaction from their child. More verbal commands follows accompanied by them attempting to correct their child's behavior and subsequently trailed by verbal reprimands. This is a common scene with parents of children with ADHD.

Positive family environments are crucial in promoting children's emotional and behavioral wellbeing. Positive and secure bonding the child's trust in themselves and others, while inadequate and defective bonding results in patterns of insecurity and self-doubt. Being in a positive family environment also buffers the difficulties associated with the disorder. The authoritative parenting style has been shown to be associated with better social competence, fewer behavioral problems [142, 143, 165], decreases the development of conduct problems [20, 37, 136], and even has impact on aspects of children's school readiness [165, 166]. Parental warmth, in combination with other positive parenting behaviors, has been associated with lower levels of conduct problems [150] even in kindergarten and first grade children [20].

Johnston [125] found among parents with older ADHD children with higher oppositional behaviors, report of feeling less competent as parents than those of ADHD children without or exhibiting less oppositional behaviors. This has been seen in other studies [87, 110, 116]. This is not surprising as it is indeed difficult handling a child with ADHD, and when stressed, parents are often left feeling frustrated or irritable and accompanied by feelings of being powerless and insufficiency. Being in this state often leads to ineffective parenting and often has negative consequences the child.

Qualities in parents such as the presence of parental affection and sensitivity with the existence of warmth, acceptance, and appropriate involvement are key aspects of healthy child development. Appropraite parenting behaviors result in a positive interaction with the child, such that the child feel safe and reassured. There are more active listening, expressions of encouragement, with opportunities and experiences for the child by allowing them to learn through trial and error, while tolerating their child's negative affect.

12. Role of professionals

The families of children with ADHD experience difficulties in many areas of functioning as illustrated with Alice. The presence of the difficulties in the child as well as comorbidities signifies risk factors for insecure attachment with impact on the parent child relationship. The existence of these factors and its consequences **must be recognized**.

ADHD creates a huge impact not only on the child alone but also upon the whole family. From the very initial consultation, parental factors, such as perception of parents/caregivers, the dynamics within the family, emotional difficulties of parents themselves, and their parenting skills, areas
of concernin the family that needs consideration.

In pharmacological treatment of ADHD, the effectiveness of medication has been well established. However, medication alone cannot and should not serve to be the sole modality of treatment. Of recent, increasing evidence has demonstrated the role of multi-modal treatment for effectively addressing the diverse difficulties of children with ADHD [167].

To be most effective in helping children and their families, it is commended that health care professionals have a good understanding of the individual and their family development. Family difficulties are common as discussed in Alice's family, i.e., parental depression, aggression, marital discord, and hostile parent child interactions. While child characteristics are important, the discussion emphasizes on the need to look at what other factors contribute to attachment difficulties and family destabilization. Thus, the assessment should include family factors that may have an impact on the child and their family functioning, which is often related to the origins of behavior problems in the child [135, 136].

Understanding family dynamics is most essential, in order to examine the interactions among family members, and identify factors that are triggering or maintaining undesirable behaviors. These dynamic interactions between social, biological, and psychological factors of the child often lead to longstanding distress in the child and their family. The family environment if often viewed as the earliest setting for dysfunctional attitudes, behaviors and interactional patterns which often results in self-esteem issues, symptoms of depression and anxiety [94, 153, 168] as well as learning antisocial behaviors [169]. In order to facilitate the child's progress towards recovery, positive changes within the child's family must be addressed.

Positive parenting styles are significantly associated with development of more appropriate behavior in children including their inhibition capacities [164]. Parents often misunderstand the use of punishment in changing a child's behavior. It has well been demonstrated that once punishment ceases, children often return to their previous behavior(s). Using harsh punishment does not help establish new and wanted behaviors; in fact, it is linked to the presence of more undesired behavior, including withdrawal of the child from their parents. Additionally, children often model their parents' behavior(s). In clinical setting it is common parents report their children hitting back their parents when in anger or frustrated.

Much of the evidence indicates family therapy being efficacious for children with ADHD refers to multimodal forms of family therapy. This often includes pharmacological treatment along with family therapy or parent training, and individual therapy for children [170-172]. Though further research is still necessary examining the effectiveness of family therapy as an relevant intervention for children with ADHD [173], other clinicians and researchers emphasize the need to routinely focus on children's attachment and attachment difficulties in clinical settings and to incorporate it in the treatment option [149, 172].

There is now increasing evidence of the implication of parent training programs, with results showing the improvement of the child's behavior [170]. In working with children like Alice, parent work and individual therapy with the parent(s), are essential. A broad-based psychodynamic approach was taken working with Alice's mother. To begin with, a client-centered approach was initiated. It was discovered Alice's mother was vulnerable and needed emotional support. Alice's mother needed to work through her own challenging childhood experiences and a conflictual marriage with an over controlling husband. With psychotherapy,

Alice's mother was able to mourn her losses she had sustained since her childhood. It was through reflection that she was finally able to view herself, her needs and the needs of her child, and how pathological her responses to Alice had been. With the employment of object relations theory in therapy, Alice's mother was able to view that she was parenting Alice similarly, to her own mother, whom she had vowed never to become.

Clinicians work to facilitate changes in the internal working model of many of their clients. After several sessions, Alice's mother no longer perceived Alice negatively. Alice too was able to form a more trusting and comfortable relationship with her mother. Parenting skills were later introduced. Alizadeh, Applequist [87] further emphasize the usefulness to educate parents in their recognition that ADHD is not their fault, nor is it a consequence of something that they have done in the past.

The clinician had hoped to engage Alice's father into therapy however, the huge resistance that Alice's father demonstrated made it difficult. Father was unhappy that his wife was attending therapy, and made it apparent. Alice's father's own difficulty in managing his emotions, his own psychological issues and immense need for control, and most immediate, a very high likelihood of Adult ADHD, would need to be addressed at some point.

Current progress:

Alice still attends treatment, where she now is on daily long-acting stimulant, and doing well in school. Her much improved relationship with mum at times does have difficult phases, where she struggles to communicate and at times hides the truth from her mother. Overall their relationship had improved significantly. The difficulties with dad remain.

Alice was noted to be less impulsive, she was more able to think through things carefully, and was able to make wiser choices on her own. One of them was her choosing to end the strained relationship with her boyfriend, who himself had significant emotional difficulties. The triumph for the year for Alice was she was awarded a prize of being the student with the most improvement shown in the year

The purpose of this chapter was to illustrate the magnitude of complexity in dealing with a child with ADHD. The interplay of roles within their families, and the huge impact that family difficulties have on a child with ADHD warrants the need for mental health professionals to look beyond the core symptoms of the disorder. In recognizing, assessing and treating family difficulties of children with ADHD, clinicians often need to incorporate several modalities of treatment demonstrated. This is to increase the likelihood. This brings us back to the very core hallmarks of child psychiatry, which serves to remind us that one cannot treat children without treating their families. There is no denying that the mental well-being of parents is utmost important; the captain of the ship has to be working well to maintain the mental health and well-being of the members of the ship (called family).

In the best attempt to maintain confidentiality, the real name of the child was not used. Her ethnicity, place of residence, the name of her parents, and socio-demographic details have been intentionally omitted. This was in order to preserve, in the best interest of the child and her family, to disguise her identity. This is also in accordance to adhere to the ethics of publishing.

Author details

H.H. Aili[1*], B. Norharlina[2], K.S. Manveen[1] and W.I. Wan Salwina[3]

*Address all correspondence to: childpsy62@gmail.com

1 Psychiatry Adolescent and Child Unit, Department of Psychological Medicine, Faculty of Medicine, University Malaya, Kuala Lumpur, Malaysia

2 Department of Psychiatry and Mental Health, Hospital Selayang, Malaysia

3 Department of Psychiatry, Faculty of Medicine, University Kebangsaan, Malaysia

References

[1] Wehmeier, P.M., A. Schacht, and R.A. Barkley, *Social and emotional impairment in children and adolescents with ADHD and the impact on quality of life*. Journal of Adolescent Health, 2010. 46(3): p. 209-217.

[2] Barkley, R.A., *Major life activity and health outcomes associated with attention-deficit/hyperactivity disorder*. Journal of Clinical Psychiatry 2002. 63 (Suppl 12): p. 10-5.

[3] Nijmeijer, J.S., et al., *Attention-deficit/hyperactivity disorder and social dysfunctioning*. Clinical Psychology Review, 2008. 28: p. 692-708.

[4] Cho, S.C., et al., *Associations between symptoms of attention deficit hyperactivity disorder, depression, and suicide in Korean female adolescents*. Depression And Anxiety, 2008. 25(11): p. E142-E146.

[5] Mrug, S., et al., *Peer rejection and friendships in children with Attention-Deficit/Hyperactivity Disorder: contributions to long-term outcomes*. Journal of Abnormal Child Psychology 2012. 6(6): p. 1013-1026.

[6] Narkunam, N., et al., *Stress among parents of children with attention deficit hyperactivity disorder, a Malaysian experience*. Asia-Pacific Psychiatry, 2012(Aug): p. 1-10.

[7] Coghill, D., et al., *Impact of attention-deficit/hyperactivity disorder on the patient and family: results from a European survey*. Child and Adolescent Psychiatry and Mental Health, 2008. 2(31): p. BioMed Central: Open Access.

[8] Froehlich, T.E., et al., *Prevalence, recognition, and treatment of attention-deficit/hyperactivity disorder in a national sample of US children*. Archives of Pediatric and Adolescent Medicine, 2007. 161: p. 857-864.

[9] Barkley, R.A., *Taking charge of ADHD.The complete, authoritative guide for parents*. Vol. Revised Edition. 2005, New York/London: The Guilford Press

[10] Faraone, S.V. and J. Biederman, *Neurobiology of Attention-Deficit Hyperactivity Disorder.* Biological Psychiatry, 1998. 44: p. 951-958.

[11] Rubia, K., A. Smith, and E. Taylor, *Performance of children with Attention Deficit Hyperactivity Disorder (ADHD) on a test battery of impulsiveness.* Child Neuropsychology, 2007. 13(3): p. 276-304.

[12] Barkley, R.A., *Behavioral inhibition, sustained attention, and executive functions: Constructing a unifying theory of ADHD.* Psychological Bulletin, 1997. 121(1): p. 65-94.

[13] Walcott, C.M. and S. Landau, *The relation between disinhibition and emotion regulation in boys with attention deficit hyperactivity disorder.* Journal of Clinical Child and Adolescent Psychology, 2004. 33(4): p. 772-782.

[14] Wu, K.K., V. Anderson, and U. Castiello, *Neuropsychological evaluation of deficits in executive functioning for adhd children with or without learning disabilities.* Developmental Neuropsychology, 2002. 22(2): p. 501-531.

[15] Stormshak, E.A., et al., *Parenting practices and child disruptive behavior problems in early elementary school.* Journal of Clinical Child Psychology, 2000. 29(1).

[16] Barkley, R.A., *Deficient emotional self-regulation: a core component of attention-deficit/ hyperactivity disorder.* Journal of ADHD Related Disorder, 2010. 1: p. 1-30.

[17] American Psychiatric Association, *Diagnostic and statistical manual of mental disorders (5th ed.; DSM–5).* 2013, Washington, DC.

[18] Mrug, S., B. Hoza, and A.C. Gerdes, *Children with Attention-Deficit/ Hyperactivity Disorder:Peer relationships and peer-oriented interventions* New Directions for Child and Adolescent Development, 2001. 91: p. 51-77.

[19] Hoza, B., et al., *What aspects of peer relationships are impaired in children with attention-deficit/hyperactivity disorder?* Journal of Consulting and Clinical Psychology 2005. 73(3): p. 411-423.

[20] Cunningham, C.E. and M.H. Boyle, *Preschoolers at risk for attention-deficit hyperactivity disorder and oppositional defiant disorder: family, parenting, and behavioral correlates.* Journal of Abnormal Child Psychology, 2002. 30(6): p. 555-569.

[21] Brook, U. and M. Boaz, *Attention deficit and hyperactivity disorder/learning disabilities (ADHD/LD): Parental characterization and perception* Patient Education and Counseling, 2005. 57(1): p. 96-100.

[22] Wells, K.C., et al., *Parenting and family stress treatment outcomes in attention deficit hyperactivity disorder (ADHD): an empirical analysis in the MTA study.* Journal of Abnormal Child Psychology 2000. 28(6): p. 543-553.

[23] DuPaul, G.J., et al., *Preschool children with attention-deficit/hyperactivity disorder: impairments in behavioral, social, and school functioning.* Journal of American Academy of Child and Adolescent Psychiatry, 2001. 40(5): p. 508-515.

[24] Nigg, J.T., *Is ADHD a disinhibitory disorder?* Psychological Bulletin, 2001. 127(5): p. 571-598.

[25] Nigg, J.T., H.H. Goldsmith, and J. Sachek, *Temperament and attention deficit hyperactivity disorder: the development of a multiple pathway model.* Journal of Clinical Child and Adolescence Psychology, 2004. 33(1): p. 42-53.

[26] Pliszka, S. and AACAP Work Group on Quality Issues, *Practice parameter for the assessment and treatment of children and adolescents with attention-deficit/hyperactivity disorder.* Jounal of American Child and Adolescent Psychiatry 2007. 46: p. 894-921.

[27] Fell, C.T., *Crying out for change: A call for a new child abuse hearsay exception in New York state.* Albany Law Review, 2013. 76(3): p. 1853-1889.

[28] Thompson, R.A., *Emotion and emotion regulation: Two sides of the developing coin.* Emotion Review, 2011. 3(1): p. 53-61.

[29] Thompson, R.A., *Emotion regulation: a theme in search of definition.* Monographs for the Society of Research in Child Development 1994. 59(2-3): p. 25-52.

[30] Shaw, P., et al., *Emotion dysregulation in Attention Deficit Hyperactivity Disorder* American Journal of Psychiatry, 2014. 171: p. 276-293.

[31] Vidal, R., et al., *Emotional lability: The discriminative value in the diagnosis of attention deficit/hyperactivity disorder in adults.* Comprehensive Psychiatry 2014. 55(7): p. 1712-1719.

[32] Maedgen, J.W. and C.L. Carlson, *Social functioning and emotional regulation in the Attention Deficit Hyperactivity Disorder subtypes.* Journal of Clinical Child Psychology 2000. 29(1): p. 30-42.

[33] Biederman, J., et al., *Deficient emotional self-regulation and pediatric attention deficit hyperactivity disorder: a family risk analysis.* Psychological Medicine, 2012. 42: p. 639-646.

[34] Spencer, T.J., et al., *Toward defining deficient emotional self-regulation in children with attention-deficit/hyperactivity disorder using the Child Behavior Checklist: a controlled study.* Postgraduate Medicine, 2011. 123(5): p. 50-59.

[35] Stringaris, A. and R. Goodman, *Mood lability and psychopathology in youth.* Psychological Medicine, 2009. 39: p. 1237-1245

[36] Biederman, J., et al., *Longitudinal course of deficient emotional self-regulation CBCL profile in youth with ADHD: Prospective controlled study.* Neuropsychiatric Disease and Treatment, 2012. 8(Open Access): p. 267-276.

[37] Johnston, C. and E.J. Mash, *Families of children with Attention-Deficit/Hyperactivity Disorder: Review and recommendations for future research.* Clinical Child and Family Psychology Review, 2001. 4(3): p. 183-207.

[38] Cunningham, C.E., *A family-centered approach to planning and measuring the outcome of interventions for children with attention-deficit/hyperactivity disorder.* Ambulatory Pediatrics 2007. 7(1 Supplementary): p. 60-72.

[39] Sobanski, E., et al., *Emotional lability in children and adolescents with Attention Deficit/ Hyperactivity Disorder (ADHD): clinical correlates and familial prevalence.* Journal of Child Psychology and Psychiatry, 2010. 51: p. 915-923

[40] Surman, C.B., et al., *Deficient emotional self-regulation and adult attention deficit hyperactivity disorder: a family risk analysis.* American Journal of Psychiatry, 2011. 168: p.: 617-623

[41] Taylor, E., *Developmental neuropsychopathology of attention deficit and impulsiveness.* Development and Psychopathology, 1999. 11: p. 607-628

[42] Peris, T.S. and B.L. Baker, *Applications of the expressed emotion construct to young children with externalizing behavior: stability and prediction over time.* Journal of Child Psychology and Psychiatry, 2000. 41(4): p. 457-462.

[43] Berndt, T.J., *Friendship quality and social development.* Current Directions in Psychological Science, 2002. 11: p. 7–10.

[44] Harris, J.R., *Where is the child's environment? A group socialization theory of development* Psychological Review, 1995. 102(3): p. 458–489.

[45] Poulin, F. and A. Chan, *Friendship stability and change in childhood and adolescence* Developmental Review 2010. 30: p. 257–272.

[46] Chiang, H.-L. and S.S. Gau, *Impact of executive functions on school and peer functions in youths with ADHD* Research in Developmental Disabilities, 2014. 35: p. 5963-5972.

[47] Hoza, B., *Peer functioning in children with ADHD.* Ambulatory Pediatrics 2007. 7(1 Supplement): p. 101-106.

[48] Barkley, R.A., *Attention-Deficit Hyperactivity Disorder. A Handbook for Diagnosis and Treatment.* 3rd Edition ed. 2006, New York: Guilford Press.

[49] Hoza, B., et al., *Attention-deficit/hyperactivity disordered and control boys' responses to social success and failure.* Child Development, 2000. 71(2): p. 432-446.

[50] Kawabata, Y., W.L. Tseng, and S.S.S. Gau, *Symptoms of attention-deficit/hyperactivity disorder and social and school adjustment: The moderating roles of age and parenting.* Journal of Abnormal Child Psychology, 2012. 40: p. 177–188.

[51] Subcommittee On Attention-Deficit/Hyperactivity Disorder, et al., *ADHD: clinical practice guideline for the diagnosis, evaluation, and treatment of attention-deficit/hyperactivity disorder in children and adolescents.* Pediatrics, 2011. 128(5): p. 1007-1022.

[52] Brook, U. and M. Boaz, *Attention deficit and hyperactivity disorder (ADHD) and learning disabilities (LD): adolescents perspective.* Patient Education and Counseling 2005. 58: p. 187–191.

[53] Pastor, P.N. and C.A. Reuben, *Diagnosed attention deficit hyperactivity disorder and learning disability: United States, 2004-2006.* Vital Health Statistics 2008. 10(237): p. 1-14.

[54] Ohan, J.L., et al., *Teachers' and education students' perceptions of and reactions to children with and without the diagnostic label "ADHD"* Journal of School Psychology, 2011. 49(1): p. 81-105.

[55] Muhammad, N.A., et al., *Attention-deficit hyperactive disorder presenting with school truancy in an adolescent: a case report.* Mental Health in Family Medicine, 2011. 8(4): p. 249–254.

[56] Heiligenstein, E., et al., *Psychological and academic functioning in college students with attention deficit hyperactivity disorder.* Journal of American College Health, 1999. 47(4): p. 181-185.

[57] Classi, P., et al., *Social and emotional difficulties in children with ADHD and the impact on school attendance and healthcare utilization.* Child and Adolescent Psychiatry and Mental Health 2012. 6(33): p. Open Access.

[58] DuPaul, G.J., et al., *Elementary school students with AD/HD: predictors of academic achievement.* Journal of School Psychology 2004. 42: p. 285–301.

[59] Batzle, C.S., et al., *Potential impact of ADHD with stimulant medication label on teacher expectations.* Journal of Attention Disorder 2010. 14(2): p. 157-166.

[60] Eisenberg, D. and H. Schneider, *Perceptions of academic skills of children diagnosed with ADHD.* Journal of Attention Disorders 2007. 10(4): p. 390-397.

[61] Greene, R.W., et al., *Are students with ADHD more stressful to teach? Patterns of teacher stress in an elementary school sample.* Journal of Emotional and Behavioral Disorders, 2002. 10(2): p. 79-89

[62] Milberger, S., et al., *Attention deficit hyperactivity disorder and comorbid disorders: issues of overlapping symptoms.* American Journal of Psychiatry 1995. 152(12): p. 1793-1799.

[63] Spencer, T.J., J. Biederman, and E. Mick, *Attention-Deficit/Hyperactivity Disorder: Diagnosis, Lifespan, Comorbidities, and Neurobiology* Ambulatory Pediatrics, 2007. 7(1): p. 73-81.

[64] Adesman, A., *A diagnosis of ADHD? Don't overlook the probability of comorbidity.* Contemporary Pediatrics 2003. 20(12): p. 91-115.

[65] Biederman, J., et al., *The long-term longitudinal course of oppositional defiant disorder and conduct disorder in ADHD boys: findings from a controlled 10-year prospective longitudinal follow-up study.* Psychological Medicine 2008. 38: p. 1027-1036.

[66] Wilens, T.E., et al., *Psychiatric comorbidity and functioning in clinically referred preschool children and school-age youths with ADHD.* Journal of American Academy of Child and Adolescent Psychiatry, 2002. 41: p. 262-268.

[67] Nevels, R.M., et al., *Psychopharmacology of aggression in children and adolescents with primary neuropsychiatric disorders: a review of current and potentially promising treatment options.* Experimental and Clinical Psychopharmacology, 2010. 18(2): p. 184-201.

[68] Waschbusch, D.A., et al., *Reactive aggression in boys with disruptive behavior disorders: behavior, physiology, and affect.* Journal of Abnormal Child Psychology, 2002. 30(6): p. 641-656.

[69] Bauermeister, J.J., et al., *ADHD correlates, comorbidity, and impairment in community and treated samples of children and adolescents.* Journal of Abnormal Child Psychology 2007. 35(6): p. 883-898.

[70] Angold, A., E.J. Costello, and A. Erkanli, *Comorbidity.* Journal of Child Psychology and Psychiatry, 1999. 40: p. 57-87.

[71] Meinzer, M.C., J.W. Pettit, and C. Viswesvaran, *The co-occurrence of attention-deficit/hyperactivity disorder and unipolar depression in children and adolescents: A meta-analytic review* Clinical Psychology Review, 2014. 34(8): p. 595-607.

[72] Biederman, J., E. Mick, and S.V. Faraone, *Depression in attention deficit hyperactivity disorder (ADHD) children: "True" depression or demoralization?* Journal of Affective Disorders 1998. 47: p. 113–122.

[73] Meinzer, M.C., et al., *Attention-deficit/hyperactivity disorder in adolescence predicts onset of major depressive disorder through early adulthood.* Depression And Anxiety, 2013. 30(6): p. 546-553.

[74] Van Eck, K., et al., *ADHD and suicidal ideation: The roles of emotion regulation and depressive symptoms among college students.* Journal of Attention Disorders, 2014: p. 1-12.

[75] Turgay, A. and R. Ansari, *Major depression with ADHD: In children and adolescents.* Psychiatry (Edgmont), 2006. 3(4): p. 20-32.

[76] Yen, J.Y., et al., *The Comorbid psychiatric symptoms of internet addiction: Attention Deficit and Hyperactivity Disorder (ADHD), depression, social phobia, and hostility* Journal of Adolescent Health, 2007. 41(1): p. 93-98.

[77] Yoo, H.J., et al., *Attention deficit hyperactivity symptoms and internet addiction.* Psychiatry and Clinical Neurosciences, 2004. 58: p. 487-494.

[78] Greene, R.W., et al., *Psychiatric comorbidity, family dysfunction, and social impairment in referred youth with oppositional defiant disorder.* The American Journal of Psychiatry, 2002. 159 I(7): p. 1214-1224.

[79] Danckaerts, M., et al., *The quality of life of children with attention deficit/hyperactivity disorder: a systematic review.* European Child and Adolescent Psychiatry, 2010. 19(2): p. 83-105.

[80] Modesto-Lowe, V., J.S. Danforth, and D. Brooks, *ADHD: Does Parenting Style Matter?* Clinical Pediatrics, 2008. 47(9): p. 865-871.

[81] Harvey, E.A., *Parenting smilarity and children with Attention-Deficit/Hyperactivity Disorder.* Child & Family Behavior Therapy, 2000. 22(3): p. 39-54.

[82] Harty, S.C., et al., *Adolescents with childhood ADHD and comorbid disruptive behavior disorders: aggression, anger, and hostility.* Child Psychiatry Human Development 2009. 40(1): p. 85-97.

[83] Lee, P.C., et al., *Parent-child interaction of mothers with depression and their children with ADHD.* Research in Developmental Disabilities, 2013. 34(1): p. 656-668.

[84] Pianta, R.C. and R.S. Marvin, *Mothers' resolution of their children's diagnosis: organized patterns of caregiving representations.* Infant Mental Health Journal, 1996. 17(3): p. 239-256.

[85] Sheeran, T., R.S. Marvin, and R.C. Pianta, *Mothers' resolution of their child's diagnosis and self-reported measures of parenting stress, marital relations, and social support* Journal of Pediatric Psychology, 1997. 22: p. 197–212.

[86] Johnston, C. and J.L. Ohan, *The importance of parental attributions in families of children with Attention-Deficit/Hyperactivity and disruptive behavior disorders.* Clinical Child and Family Psychology Review, 2005. 8(3): p. 167-182.

[87] Alizadeh, H., K.F. Applequist, and F.L. Coolidge, *Parental self-confidence, parenting styles, and corporal punishment in families of ADHD children in Iran* Child Abuse & Neglect, 2007. 31(5): p. 567-572.

[88] Chronis, A.M., et al., *Psychopathology and substance abuse in parents of young children with attention-deficit/hyperactivity disorder.* Journal of the American Academy of Child and Adolescent Psychiatry, 2003 12(12): p. 1424-1432.

[89] Ghanizadeh, A., M.R. Mohammadi, and R. Moini, *Comorbidity of psychiatric disorders and parental psychiatric disorders in a sample of Iranian children with ADHD.* Journal of Attentional Disorder 2008. 12(2): p. 149-155.

[90] Bowen, M., *Family therapy in clinical practice* 1978, New York Jason Aronson.

[91] Harvey, E., B. Stoessel, and S. Herbert, *Psychopathology and parenting practices of parents of preschool children with behavior problems.* Parenting, 2011. 11(4): p. 239-263.

[92] Whalen, C.K., et al., *Dissecting daily distress in mothers of children with ADHD: an electronic diary study.* Journal of Family Psychology 2011. 25(3): p. 402-411.

[93] Darling, N. and L. Steinberg, *Parenting style as context: An integrative model.* Psychological Bulletin, 1993. 113: p. 487–496.

[94] Wood, J.J., et al., *Parenting and childhood anxiety: Theory, empirical findings, and future directions.* Journal of Child Psychology and Psychiatry, 2003. 44(1): p. 134-151.

[95] Bois, J.E., J. Lalanne, and C. Delforge, *The influence of parenting practices and parental presence on children's and adolescents' pre-competitive anxiety.* Journal of Sports Sciences, 2009. 27(10): p. 995-1005.

[96] Belsky, J., *The determinants of parenting: A process model.* Child Development 1984. 55: p. 83-96.

[97] Paidipati, C.P. and J.A. Deatrick, *The role of family phenomena in children and adolescents with Attention Deficit Hyperactivity Disorder.* Journal Of Child And Adolescent Psychiatric Nursing, 2015. 28(1): p. 3–13.

[98] Hollenstein, T., et al., *Rigidity in parent—child interactions and the development of externalizing and internalizing behavior in early childhood.* Journal of Abnormal Child Psychology, 2004. 32(6): p. 595-607.

[99] Barkley, R.A., et al., *The adolescent outcome of hyperactive children diagnosed by research criteria: I. An 8-year prospective follow-up study.* Journal of American Academy of Child and Adolescent Psychiatry, 1990. 29(4): p. 546-557.

[100] Bowlby, J., *A secure base: clinical applications of attachment theory* 1988, Hove and New York: Brunner-Routledge, Taylor & Francis Group

[101] Bowlby, J., *The Making and Breaking of Affectional Bonds.* 1989, New York: Routledge, Taylor and Francis Group.

[102] Ainsworth, M.D., *Attachments across the life span.* Bulletin of the New York Academy of Medicine, 1985 61(9): p. 792-812.

[103] Bowlby, J., *A secure base: Parent-child attachment and healthy human development.* 1988, New York: Basic Books.

[104] Maccoby, E.E., *The role of parents in the socialization of children: A historical review.* Developmental Psychology, 1992. 28: p. 1006–1017.

[105] Baurain, C. and N. Nader-Grosbois, *Socio-emotional regulation in children with intellectual disability and typically developing children in interactive contexts.* ALTER, European Journal of Disability Research 2012. 6: p. 75-93.

[106] Reder, P. and C. Lucey, *Significan issues in parenting assessment,* in *Assessment of parenting: Psychiatric and psychological contributions* P. Reder and C. Lucey, Editors. 2004, Brunner-Routledge: New York. p. 3-17.

[107] Gau, S.S., *Parental and family factors for attention-deficit hyperactivity disorder in Taiwanese children.* Australian New Zealand Journal of Psychiatry., 2007. 41(8): p. 688-696.

[108] Margari, F., et al., *Parents psychopathology of children with Attention Deficit Hyperactivity Disorder*. Research in Developmental Disabilities, 2011. 32(1): p. 1036–1043.

[109] Chao, R.K., *Beyond parental control and authoritarian parenting style: understanding Chinese parenting through the cultural notion of training*. Child Developement 1994. 65(4): p. 1111-1119.

[110] Gau, S.S. and J.P. Chang, *Maternal parenting styles and mother-child relationship among adolescents with and without persistent attention-deficit/hyperactivity disorder*. Research in Developmental Disabilities, 2013. 34(5): p. 1581-1594.

[111] Faraone, S., et al., *A family study of psychiatric comorbidity in girls and boys with attention-deficit/hyperactivity disorder* Biological Psychiatry, 2001. 50(8): p. 586-592.

[112] Faraone, S.V., et al., *Molecular genetics of attention-deficit/hyperactivity disorder*. Biological Psychiatry, 2005. 57(11): p. 1313-1323.

[113] Chronis-Tuscano, A., et al., *Associations between maternal Attention-Deficit/Hyperactivity Disorder symptoms and parenting*. Journal of Abnormal Child Psychology 2008. 36(8): p. 1237-1250.

[114] Lui, J.H.L., C.M. Lee, and S.C. Lee-Flynn, *Parental ADHD symptoms and self-reports of positive parenting* Journal of Consulting and Clinical Psychology, 2013. 81(6): p. 988-998.

[115] Chen, V.C., et al., *Symptoms of attention deficit hyperactivity disorder and quality of life of mothers of school-aged children: the roles of child, mother, and family variables*. Kaohsiung Journal of Medical Sciences 2014. 30(12): p. 631-638.

[116] Chronis-Tuscano, A., et al., *The relation between Maternal ADHD symptoms & improvement in child behavior following brief behavioral parent training is mediated by change in negative parenting*. Journal of Abnormal Child Psychology 2011. 39(7): p. 1047-1057.

[117] Kendziora, K. and S. O'Leary, *Dysfunctional parenting as a focus for prevention and treatment of child behavior problems*. Advances in Clinical Child Psychology, 1993. 15: p. 175-206.

[118] Harvey, E., et al., *Parenting of children with attention-defecit/hyperactivity disorder (ADHD): the role of parental ADHD symptomatology*. Journal of Attention Disorders 2003. 7: p. 31–42.

[119] Chang, L.-R., et al., *Father's parenting and father–child relationship among children and adolescents with attention-deficit/hyperactivity disorder*. Comprehensive Psychiatry, 2013. 54(2): p. 128-140.

[120] Gerdes, A.C., et al., *Child and parent predictors of perceptions of parent–child relationship quality*. Journal of Attention Disorders, 2007. 11: p. 37-48.

[121] Amato, P.R. and F. Rivera, *Paternal involvement and children's behavior problems*. Journal of Marriage and Family 1999. 61: p. 375-384.

[122] Coley, R.L. and B.L. Medeiros, *Reciprocal longitudinal relations between nonresident father involvement and adolescent delinquency.* Child Development 2007. 78(1): p. 132-147.

[123] Rinaldi, C.M. and N. Howe, *Mothers' and fathers' parenting styles and associations with toddlers' externalizing, internalizing, and adaptive behaviors* Early Childhood Research Quarterly, 2012. 27(2): p. 266-273.

[124] Flouri, E., *Fathers' behaviors and children's psychopathology.* Clinical Psychology Review, 2010. 30(3): p. 363-369.

[125] Johnston, C., *Parent characteristics and parent-child interactions in families of nonproblem children and ADHD children with higher and lower levels of oppositional-defiant behavior.* Journal of Abnormal Child Psychology, 1996. 24(1): p. 85-104.

[126] Buhrmester, D., et al., *Mothers and fathers interacting in dyads and triads with normal and hyperactive sons.* Development & Psychopathology, 1992. 28: p. 500-509.

[127] Grenwald-Mayes, G., *Relationship between current quality of life and family of origin dynamics for college students with Attention-Deficit/Hyperactivity Disorder.* Journal of Attentional Disorder, 2002. 5(4): p. 211-222.

[128] Buschgens, C.J., et al., *Differential family and peer environmental factors are related to severity and comorbidity in children with ADHD.* Journal of Neural Transmission 2008. 115(2): p. 177-186.

[129] Schachar, R.J. and R. Wachsmuth, *Family dysfunction and psychosocial adversity: Comparison of attention deficit disorder, conduct disorder, normal and clinical controls.* Canadian Journal of Behavioural Science/Revue canadienne des sciences du comportement,, 1991. 23(3): p. 332-348.

[130] Foley, M., *A comparison of family adversity and family dysfunction in families of children with attention deficit hyperactivity disorder (ADHD) and families of children without ADHD.* Journal of Specialists in Pediatric Nursing 2011. 16(1): p. 39-49.

[131] Biederman, J., S.V. Faraone, and M.C. Monuteaux, *Impact of exposure to parental attention-deficit hyperactivity disorder on clinical features and dysfunction in the offspring.* Psychological Medicine 2002. 32(5): p. 817-827.

[132] Bloch, S., et al., *The Family in Clinical Psychiatry.* 1994, Oxford, New York: Oxford Medical Publications.

[133] Chronis, A.M., et al., *Maternal depression and early positive parenting predict future conduct problems in young children with attentiondeficit/hyperactivity disorder.* Developmental Psychology 2007. 43(1): p. 70-82.

[134] Agha, S.S., et al., *Are parental ADHD problems associated with a more severe clinical presentation and greater family adversity in children with ADHD?* Europen Child and Adolescent Psychiatry, 2013. 22(6): p. 369-377.

[135] Roelofs, J., et al., *On the links between attachment style, parental rearing behaviors, and internalizing and externalizing problems in non-clinical children.* Journal of Child and Family Studies, 2006. 15(3): p. 331-345.

[136] Schroeder, R.D. and T.J. Mowen, *Parenting Parenting style transitions and delinquency.* Youth and Society, 2014. 46(2): p. 228-254.

[137] Johnston, C., et al., *Parenting in adults with attention-deficit/hyperactivity disorder (ADHD).* Clinical Psychology Review, 2012. 32(4): p. 215-228.

[138] Havighurst, S.S., A. Harley, and M. Prior, *Building preschool children's emotional competence: A parenting program.* Early Education and Developmen, 2004. 15(4): p. 423-448.

[139] Baumrind, D., *Current patterns of parental authority.* Developmental Psychology, 1971. 4: p. 1-103.

[140] Baumrind, D., *The influence of parenting style on adolescent competence and substance use* Journal of Early Adolescence 1991. 11(1): p. 56-95.

[141] Rapee, R.M., *Potential role of childrearing practices in the development of anxiety and depression Rapee RM1.* Clinical Psychology Review, 1997. 17(1): p. 47-67.

[142] Querido, J.G., T.D. Warner, and S.M. Eyberg, *Parenting styles and child behavior in African American families of preschool children.* Journal of Clinical Child and Adolescent Psychology, 2002. 31: p. 272-277.

[143] Carpenter, J.L. and J. Mendez, *Adaptive and challenged parenting among African American mothers: Parenting profiles relate to head start children's aggression and hyperactivity.* Early Education and Development, 2013. 24: p. 233–252.

[144] Rothbaum, F. and J.R. Weisz, *Parental caregiving and child externalizing behavior in nonclinical samples: A meta-analysis* Psychological Bulletin, 1994. 116: p. 55-74.

[145] Webster-Stratton, C. and D.L. Deborah Woolley, *Social competence and conduct problems in young children: issues in assessment.* Journal of Clinical Child Psychology, 1999. 28(1): p. 25-43.

[146] Reder, P. and C. Lucey, *Assessment of Parenting: psychiatric and psychological contributions* 1995, Hove and New York: Brunner-Routledge, Taylor and Francis Group.

[147] Levy, T.M. and M. Orlans, *Attachment, trauma and healing: Understanding and treating attachment disorder in children and families.* 1998, Washington, DC: CWLA Press.

[148] Muris, P., et al., *Self-reported attachment style, attachment quality, and symptoms of anxiety and depression in young adolescents.* Personality and Individual Differences 2001. 30: p. 809-818.

[149] Clarke, L., et al., *Attention deficit hyperactivity disorder is associated with attachment insecurity.* Clinical Child Psychology and Psychiatry, 2002. 7(2): p. 179-198.

[150] Patrick, M.R., et al., *The joint contribution of early parental warmth, communication and tracking, and early child conduct problems on monitoring in late childhood.* Child Development, 2005. 76(5): p. 999-1014.

[151] Beck, A.T., *Cognitive therapy and the emotional disorders.* 1976 International Universities Press

[152] Lewinsohn, P.M., et al., *Theoretical issues in behavior therapy* in *An integrated theory of depression,* S. Reiss and R. Bootzin, Editors. 1985, Academic Press: New York. p. 331-359.

[153] McLeod, B.D., J.J. Wood, and J.R. Weisz, *Examining the association between parenting and childhood anxiety: A meta-analysis.* Clinical Psychology Review, 2007. 27: p. 155-172.

[154] Robin, A. and S.L. Foster, *Theoretical orientation,* in *Negotiating parent-adolescent conflict: A behavioral-family systems approach,* A. Robin and S.L. Foster, Editors. 2003, The Guildford Press New York. p. 7-30.

[155] Maccoby, E.E. and J.A. Martin, *Socialization in the context of the family: Parent-child interaction* Handbook of child psychology: Socialization, personality, and social development (4th edition) ed. P.H.M.E.M. Hetherington. Vol. 4. 1983, New York Wiley.

[156] Loeber, R., *Development and risk factors for juvenile antisocial behaviour and delinquency* Clinical Psychology Review, 1990. 10: p. 1-41.

[157] Loeber, R. and M. Stouthamer-Loeber, *Development of juvenile aggression and violence: Some common misconceptions and controversies.* American Psychologist, 1998. 53: p. 242-259.

[158] Hill, N.E., et al., *Developmental commentary: Ecological perspectives on parental influences during adolescence.* Journal of Clinical Child & Adolescent Psychology, 2007. 36(3): p. 367-377.

[159] Bowlby, J., *Attachment and loss.* Second ed. Attachment, ed. T.I.o.H. Relations. Vol. 1. 1969, New York: Basic Books.

[160] Ainsworth, M.S., et al., *Patterns of attachment: A psychological study of the strange situation.* 1978, New York: Lawrence Erlbaum.

[161] Colonnesi, C., et al., *The relation between insecure attachment and child anxiety: a meta-analytic review.* Journal of Clinical Child and Adolescent Psychology 2011. 40(4): p. 630-45.

[162] Jones, J.D., J. Cassidy, and P.R. Shaver, *Parents' self-reported attachment styles: a review of links with parenting behaviors, emotions, and cognitions.* Personality and Social Psychology Review, 2015. 19(1): p. 44-76.

[163] Forehand, R., et al., *Is parenting the mediator of change in behavioral parent training for externalizing problems of youth?* Clinical Psychology Review, 2014. 34(8): p. 608-619.

[164] Roskam, I., et al., *The development of children's inhibition: Does parenting matter?* Journal of Experimental Child Psychology, 2014. 122: p. 166-182.

[165] Fantuzzo, J., et al., *Multiple dimensions of family involvement and their relations to behavioral and learning competencies for urban, low-income children.* School Psychology Review, 2004. 33: p. 467-480.

[166] Gest, S.D., et al., *Shared book reading and children's language comprehension skills: The moderating role of parental discipline practices.* Early Childhood Research Quarterly 2004. 19: p. 319-336.

[167] MTA Cooperative Group, *National Institute of Mental Health Multimodal Treatment study of ADHD follow-up: Changes in effectiveness and growth after the end of treatment.* Pediatrics 2004. 113(4): p. 762-769.

[168] Lee, A. and B.J. Hankin, *Insecure attachment, dysfunctional attitudes, and low self-esteem predicting prospective symptoms of depression and anxiety during adolescence* Journal of Clinical Child and Adolescent Psychology 2009. 38(2): p. 219-231.

[169] Desbiens, N. and M.-H. Gagné, *Profiles in the development of behavior disorders among youths with family maltreatment histories.* Emotional and Behavioural Difficulties, 2007. 12(3): p. 215-240.

[170] Carr, A., *Evidence-based practice in family therapy and systemic consultation: Child-focused problems* Journal of Family Therapy, 2000. 22: p. 29-60.

[171] McMahon, R.J. and J.S. Kotler, *Treatment of conduct problems in children and adolescents* in *Handbook of interventions that work with children and adolescents prevention and treatment*, P.M. Barrett and T.H. Ollendick, Editors. 2004, John Wiley & Sons Ltd: England. p. 396-424.

[172] Zeanah, C.H., L.J. Berlin, and N.W. Boris, *Practitioner Review: Clinical appli*cations of attachment theory and research for infants and young children. Journal of Child Psychology & Psychiatry, 2011. 52(8): p. 819–833.

[173] Bjornstad, G. and P. Montgomery, Family therapy for attention-deficit disorder or attention-deficit/hyperactivity disorder in children and adolescents. Cochrane Database of Systematic Reviews, 2005. 18(2).

Section 3

Advances in ADHD Prevention and Treatment

Chapter 12

Evolution of a Disorder and Insights into Prevention of ADHD

Sarina J. Grosswald

Additional information is available at the end of the chapter

http://dx.doi.org/10.5772/61069

Abstract

Understanding the history of the development of diagnostic criteria for ADHD, the parallel growth of the ADHD drug market, and factors that improve the symptoms of ADHD provides insight into alternative approaches to treatment and the potential for prevention. This chapter sheds light on the rise of ADHD as a diagnostic disorder, and highlights the growth of the ADHD drug market and associated drug sales. The chapter concludes by exploring the potential strategies for preventing ADHD, reviewing research on sleep, omega-3 supplementation, and meditation.

Keywords: ADHD, Executive Function, Meditation, Prevention, Transcendental Meditati

1. Introduction

ADHD is considered the most common chronic disorder of childhood. In the USA, 11% of children aged 4–17 have been diagnosed with ADHD, a 16% increase since 2007 [1]. Some studies suggest that this is a significant underestimation, because the diagnosis may be missed in as many as 50% to 75% of girls (girls often do not exhibit the more disruptive behaviors associated with the disorder). In comparison, all cancers combined affect less than 4% of the population. From this perspective, ADHD might be considered an epidemic among today's children.

Why is it that today greater than 1 in 10 children have ADHD? Where did it come from? When did it appear? What are the possible causes? To gain perspective on the current prevalence of

ADHD, it is useful to follow the history of the disorder. This can also provide insight into the possibilities for prevention.

2. Origins of drug treatment for ADHD

The first documentation of a disorder relating to impulsiveness in children was in Britain in 1902. Dr. George Still suggested that overactivity and defiant behavior was a "defect of moral control" caused by a genetic tendency toward moral deviation, or the result of an injury at birth. Later, in the 1920s, child survivors of the 1917–1926 pandemic of encephalitis exhibited symptoms of severe behavioral disturbances including hyperactivity. Their behaviors were termed "post-encephalitic behavior disorder".

Drug treatment to control behavior and improve attention emerged when in 1937, Dr. Charles Bradley postulated that amphetamines might help calm children who were in a treatment center for behavioral and neurological problems. Dr. Bradley accidently discovered that children taking the drug also happened to do better in school.

The turning point was in the late 1950s when Dr. Leon Eisenberg conducted the first randomized controlled study of the use of Ritalin for children with hyperactivity. He found the drug to be effective, and therefore concluded the children's behavior was a result of impaired brain functioning, coining the phrase "minimal brain dysfunction" to explain the symptoms. This "dysfunction" was then defined as a mental illness in the Diagnostic and Statistical Manual of Mental Disorders (DSM). The DSM, published by the American Psychiatric Association, covers all mental health disorders of children and adults. The book is considered the "bible" of psychiatric diagnoses. Once a condition is labeled and listed in the DSM, it has credibility and legitimacy as a mental disorder.

In 1961, soon after Dr. Eisenberg's results were published, Ritalin was approved by the FDA for use with children. Ten years later, 150, 000 children were taking the drug. There was, however, no actual scientific evidence underlying the assumption that hyperactivity was the result of brain dysfunction. Consequently, in 1979 the FDA ordered that "minimal brain dysfunction" be eliminated as a diagnostic term.

Around this time, psychiatry was moving from the view that behavior problems are the result of environment (home life and parenting) to the belief that the problems are the result of chemical imbalances. Though, again, there was no scientific foundation for this shift in thinking. The growing availability and use of drug treatment was serving as de facto evidence that the problems must be chemically based since they could be treated, with some effect, by chemicals.

3. Initial concerns about drug treatment

By 1980 the description of hyperactivity in the DSM had morphed into ADHD, with a broadening symptom list. It was beginning to encompass what might previously have been accepted as common differences in how children behave. By this time, 500, 000 children were taking Ritalin. Parents were told the drug was mild, safe, and effective.

The active ingredient in Ritalin and most other ADHD medications is methylphenidate, which is an amphetamine. The US government classifies these drugs as Schedule II drugs. Schedule II drugs, which include opiates, are defined as having high potential for abuse, and may lead to severe psychological or physical dependence. ADHD drugs are in the same drug classification as opium, cocaine, morphine, and oxycodone.

From 1990 to 1997, the use of Ritalin increased 700%. In 1996, the US Drug Enforcement Agency (DEA) convened a national conference of experts in research, medicine, public health, and law enforcement to examine the use of the drug with school-age children for the treatment of ADHD. The DEA enforces laws and regulations pertaining to controlled substances. The agency was alarmed by the tremendous increase in the use of Ritalin (the only ADHD drug on the market at the time), and concerned about the dangers of the drug as a Schedule II substance.

Below is an excerpt from comments made by Gene R. Haislip, Deputy Assistant Administrator of the DEA's Office of Diversion Control, at the conclusion of the conference.

> "...there is also strong evidence that the drugs have been greatly over-prescribed in some parts of the country as a panacea for behavior problems. These drugs have been over-promoted, over-marketed and over-sold, resulting in profits of some $450 million annually. This constitutes a potential health threat to many children and has also created a new source of drug abuse and illicit traffic. The data shows that there has been a 1, 000 percent increase in drug abuse injury reports involving methylphenidate for children in the 10 to 14 age group. This now equals or exceeds reports for the same age group involving cocaine. The reported numbers are still small but experts feel that this is only the "tip of the iceberg. "[2]

Though 20 years later there is continued debate as to whether ADHD medication is overprescribed, the issues raised by the DEA remain, as the number of prescriptions for these drugs rise every year.

4. MTA Study

What has been considered the definitive study about treatment for ADHD was published in late 1999. The US government funded Multimodal Treatment Study of Children with ADHD – "MTA" for short – involved 18 nationally recognized authorities in ADHD at 6 different university medical centers and hospitals to evaluate treatments for ADHD. The study followed 579 elementary school children, aged 7–9, who received either (1) medication alone, (2) psychosocial/behavioral treatment alone, (3) a combination of both, or (4) routine community care.

The study reported that the most effective treatment was a combination of medication and psychosocial/behavioral treatment. Second was medication alone, which was reported as more effective than routine community care. The drug and behavioral interventions in the study were very intensive. They included training sessions with the parents as well as regular meetings with the child, parents, and even teachers. The regimens also included behavioral therapy in the classroom by a special teacher's aide, and special summer camp for the children. When compared with community-based programs where the doctor would see the child once or twice a year, these intensive study interventions showed improvements over the community-based treatment.

However, all children actually tended to improve over the course of the study, differing only in the relative amount of improvement. For some outcomes that are important in the daily functioning (e.g., academic performance, familial relations), only the addition of behavioral therapy with medication produced improvements better than community care. Of note, families and teachers reported somewhat higher levels of satisfaction for the treatments that included the behavioral therapy components.

In 2007, several follow-up studies of the children in the 1999 study painted a very different picture than that of the initial study. After three years of treatment, there were no significant differences in symptoms among the children who received the intensive drug treatments and those who did not. Further, those on the drug regimens had significantly higher rates of delinquency and substance use [3]. The study also showed that the children in the drug groups experienced growth retardation.

5. Concerns about safety and long-term effects

Though the MTA study showed that behavioral intervention along with medication was shown to be most effective, it was drug treatment alone that most often became the treatment of choice. By 2004, the market for ADHD-related drugs in the USA had grown to over $3 billion annually.

By 2005, concerns were emerging about the safety of the drugs. The FDA announced safety concerns about the drugs causing hallucinations, suicidal ideation, psychotic behavior, and aggressive and violent behavior. The agency convened an advisory panel to examine the safety issues. The panel recommended that "black box" warnings be placed on all ADHD drug products. Black box warnings tell the consumer that the drug has a significant risk of serious or even life-threatening side-effects.

However, after hearings were held, including testimony from doctors who were often consultants paid by the drug makers, the FDA rejected the advisory panel's recommendation. This was the first time in the history of the FDA that the agency rejected an advisory panel's recommendations. But, in 2006, with the evidence mounting about the potentially harmful effects of the medication, the FDA convened a second pediatric advisory panel, with the objective to examine the relationship to cardiac risk including sudden death. This time the FDA took the panel's advice to require black box warnings on the drugs.

Also in 2005, while concerns were surfacing about the safety of the ADHD drugs for children, the makers of Adderall announced the results of a study showing significant improvement in

http://dx.doi.org/10.5772/61069

ADHD symptoms in adults taking the drug. Magazine articles began appearing about adult ADHD (even though at the time ADHD was defined as a disorder of childhood, with symptoms appearing before age 7).

The effectiveness of drug medication continues to be questionable. In 2009, another follow-up study of the MTA groups was published. Eight years after the original intervention, there was again no difference in symptoms among those who continued on medication and those who did not. And those who continued on the medication were about an inch shorter and six pounds lighter than their counterparts who were not on the drugs [4].

At this point, Dr. William Pelham, one of the original researchers of the 1999 study as well as on the follow-up studies, was quoted as saying "The stance the group took in the first paper was so strong that the people are embarrassed to say they were wrong and we led the whole field astray" [5].

There is now growing exploration of the long-term effects of ADHD medication. In early 2010, the Government of Western Australia Department of Health reported on a study it conducted [6]. They described the study as "the first of its type in the world" and found that "long-term use of drugs such as Ritalin and dexamphetamine may not improve a child's social and emotional well-being or academic performance." In a statement, the Chair of the Ministerial Implementation Committee for Attention Deficit Hyperactivity Disorder in Western Australia said "We found that stimulant medication did not significantly improve a child's level of depression, self-perception or social functioning and they were more likely to be performing below their age level at school by a factor of 10.5 times."

In spite of the growing number of studies indicating the questionable long-term effectiveness of ADHD drugs, there has been little abatement in the number of children prescribed these drugs. A recent study of medication trends reported a 36% increase in ADHD prescriptions from 2008–2012, with the number of adults on these drugs growing even faster, with a 53% increase over the same time period [7]. Drug sales continue to grow, expecting to reach almost $13 billion in 2015, and more children identified with the disorder. With no clear understanding of the causes, it raises the question as to whether this is the result of increased prevalence, better diagnostics, or better marketing.

ADHD is now one of the most researched psychiatric disorders of childhood. Usually, such extensive research leads to a more specifically and more narrowly defined description of a disorder. However, with ADHD, the description has grown broader and more inclusive rather than narrower and exclusive, encompassing a wide variety of temperaments, learning abilities, and social and behavioral responses.

6. Alternative treatments and prevention

For some children and adults, ADHD medication can be life-changing. However, like all medication, ADHD drugs do not work for everyone. In general, medication tends to be effective for some users, not effective for others, and have adverse effects for the remaining users.

Current medications do not cure ADHD. They can help control the symptoms, and can help a child pay attention. It is not clear, however, whether medication helps children learn better. Further, studies do not show long-term functional benefit from medication.

The American Academy of Pediatrics recommends behavioral approaches as the first line of treatment for young children. For elementary school age children and adolescents, if behavioral therapy alone is not sufficient, then medication is recommended – preferably along with behavioral approaches [8]. Though the guidelines recommend behavioral approaches as first-line therapy, or if necessary, both medication and behavioral approaches, less than half of children treated for ADHD receive behavioral therapy. Studies do not show long-term functional benefit from medication. In contrast, behavioral approaches help children learn self-control, critical for functionality and success.

Though millions of adults and children are affected by ADHD, there is little or no study of means of preventing the disorder. While ADHD medication can be effective for a percentage of those with symptoms, medication as prevention would be a dangerous strategy. Studies have shown that for those who do not exhibit symptoms of ADHD and evidence of biochemical imbalance or developmental impairment, these drugs can be harmful. In surveys of nonmedical use, or abuse, of ADHD drugs, adverse events were frequently reported, including sleep difficulties (72%), irritability (62%), dizziness and light-headedness (35%), headaches (33%), stomach aches (33%), and sadness (25%) [9].

Non-pharmaceutical approaches may hold the greatest promise for both prevention and for self-management and learning. Parents and adult sufferers frequently turn to diet and nutrition to treat symptoms following anecdotal reports of the association between food additives, environmental toxins, or nutritional deficiencies, with the expectation that addressing these issues may reduce symptoms or prevent development of ADHD, though there is scant research on the effectiveness. There are however, some alternatives that show promise as both treatment approaches and as potential means of prevention. These will be discussed in the following sections.

7. Omega-3

One notable dietary supplement that has shown research-based benefits is the use of omega-3 fatty acid supplementation [10, 11]. Omega-3 increases myelination, development of a fatty layer around the cell fibers. Myelination increases the speed of information processing. Studies have shown that those with developmental delay in motor and cognitive milestones have significant reductions in myelination [12], offering an explanation for the mechanisms of how omega-3 can improve symptoms of ADHD. Since omega-3 fosters development of myelination, and myelination increases brain processing, supplementation with omega-3 may offer a viable preventive approach.

http://dx.doi.org/10.5772/61069

8. Sleep

Insufficient rest can have serious detrimental effects on learning, mental health, and brain development, including memory. Memory reprocessing during sleep is an important component of how our memories are formed and ultimately shaped [13]. Studies show that sleep facilitates learning, theoretically because it prevents interference from on-going sensory input and cognitive activities that normally occur during waking. Similarly, research has shown that restful waking (e.g., lying in a dark room) also facilitates learning, and can contribute to the facilitation of learning that occurs during sleep [14].

A study of behavioral sleep intervention modestly improved the severity of ADHD symptoms in a community sample of children with ADHD, most of whom were taking stimulant medications. The intervention also improved the children's sleep, behavior, quality of life, and functioning, with most benefits sustained to six months post-intervention [15].

Study of sleep duration found that children having longer duration of sleep per night were at lower risk of ADHD symptoms than those who slept only 7.7 hours or less [16]. Thus, improving the quality of sleep and duration of sleep can have important implications for reduction of ADHD symptoms including behavior regulation and executive function, and importantly, for reducing the risk of ADHD.

9. Stress

Stress can play a significant role in ADHD symptoms. Stress interferes with executive function and behavior regulation [17, 18], resulting in difficulties with working memory, organization, attention, and impulse control. Stress also limits mental flexibility and reduces coping strategies.

Many of the symptoms associated with ADHD are also symptoms of chronic stress (Table 1). The Diagnostic and Statistical Manual of Mental Disorders (DSM-V) symptoms of ADHD can be viewed as the way in which these symptoms appear in children.

Symptoms of Stress	Symptoms of ADHD
Inability to concentrate	Difficulty sustaining attention
	Not listening when spoken to
Difficulty organizing	Difficulty organizing
Memory problems	Forgetfulness
Poor judgment	Speaks without thinking
Short temper	Impulsivity

Table 1. Symptoms of stress closely match symptoms of ADHD

The part of the brain responsible for developing means of adjusting to stress is the prefrontal areas. Children with ADHD have been shown to have impaired function of this area [19]. This region is responsible for developing coping strategies, influencing the ability to handle stress. Children exposed to trauma or other adverse experiences during childhood are almost three times more likely to have ADHD. Chronic acute stress leads to elevated levels of cortisol. In children with ADHD, high cortisol levels interfere with executive function, self-regulation, and learning [20].

Chronic physical or psychological stress can change the brain. The body's natural response to stress is to activate the sympathetic nervous system, or "fight or flight" response. This results in changes to the levels of dopamine, norepinephrine, serotonin, and cortisol. These changes interfere with memory, and lead to increases in irritability, aggression, impulsivity, suicide, and alcohol and drug abuse. Chronic stress damages or kills brain pathways. As much as 34% reduction in cells in the prefrontal cortex have been reported [21]. Modalities that reduce stress can have a positive effect on ADHD symptoms.

In addition, early intervention with stress-reducing strategies in the presence of trauma, emotional or physiological stress, or even severe illness, has the potential to prevent the development of ADHD symptoms. Recognition of the relationship of stress and the symptoms of ADHD helps to understand the underlying factors influencing these symptoms, and helps improve screening and treatment approaches.

10. Stress reduction and meditation

Given the role stress seems to play in the cognitive function and symptoms of ADHD, it is logical to explore stress reduction techniques as a means of minimizing the effects of stress and potentially preventing ADHD. Commonly suggested stress management options include exercise, deep breathing, yoga, and meditation. Research in techniques is limited, but meditation shows promise as both a behavioral strategy for treatment and as prevention through stress reduction.

Recent neuroscience research has shed light on the differences in different forms of meditation, how they work, the areas of the brain affected, and the overall effects. Different techniques use different procedures for reaching a state of relaxation, and have different effects [22, 23].

Meditation practices have been classified into three types based on their EEG results. The three types are (1) techniques of concentration, also called focused attention, (2) mindfulness-type meditation, also called open monitoring, and (3) transcending, also called automatic self-transcending [24].

Techniques of focused attention are concentration techniques, where attention is kept on the object of meditation, such as an event, image, or sound. Open monitoring or mindfulness-based techniques involve dispassionate non-judgmental monitoring of experience. Automatic self-transcending meditation is defined as effortless transcending of the meditation process itself [24, 25]. Each of these techniques has their own unique EEG signatures.

Preliminary research investigated the effects of mindfulness training on 24 adults and 8 adolescents diagnosed with ADHD, who received an 8-week mindfulness training program.

http://dx.doi.org/10.5772/61069

Seventy-five percent of these individuals finished the eight-week program. After the mindfulness training, both adults and adolescents exhibited statistically significant decreases in inattention and hyperactivity [26].

The Transcendental Meditation (TM) technique falls into the category of automatic self-transcending [27]. Concentration and open monitoring meditations both require some mental effort (i.e., holding attention on its object or maintaining attention on an on-going experience, respectively). The Transcendental Meditation technique automatically leads to a relaxed state where the mind is not actively engaged in controlling or directing the thinking process. The awareness actually goes beyond the active level of thought to experience what is referred to as transcendental or pure consciousness.

Transcendental Meditation is practiced for 10–20 minutes twice a day, with eyes closed. The technique is simple, and easy to do. It does not involve concentration or controlling the mind – both of which are difficult for an individual with ADHD.

Measurement of brain function during the Transcendental Meditation technique shows increases in brain coherence both during the practice of the Transcendental Meditation technique and afterwards in activity [24, 28, 29]. The primary areas of the brain activated are the frontal and prefrontal executive areas responsible for attention, executive function, emotional stability, and anxiety (Figure 1) [28, 30].

Study of college students practicing the Transcendental Meditation technique showed reduced stress and anxiety, and improved cognitive processes compared to controls [31, 32]. Effects include balancing the neurohormones including cortisol and serotonin [33, 34, 35] during meditation and during activity.

The use of the Transcendental Meditation technique for stress reduction in adolescents has resulted in improvement in school behavior, decreases in absenteeism and rule infractions, and reduction in suspensions due to behavior-related problems [36]. Students practicing the Transcendental Meditation technique show increased emotional regulation and improved well-being [37], as well as improved academic performance.

Students with ADHD who were practicing the Transcendental Meditation technique in school showed reduced stress and stress-related symptoms including anxiety, anxiousness, and depression. Improvements in behavior regulation and emotional control were also significant. In addition to reduction in stress-related symptoms, there were improvements in cognitive function, including the ability to initiate tasks, working memory, planning, and organizing.

In an effort to more objectively diagnose ADHD, rather than completely relying on subjective questionnaires, the US Food and Drug Administration (FDA) recently approved a device for measuring brain waves that can be used as a means of diagnosing ADHD. The device measures theta/beta brain frequencies ratio. Theta/beta ratios are higher in children with ADHD.

The Transcendental Meditation technique has been shown to improve theta/beta ratios through the effortless practice of the technique. In a randomized controlled trial of the Transcendental Meditation technique, EEG coherence, theta/beta ratio, and executive function were measured in middle school students with ADHD. After three months, the group

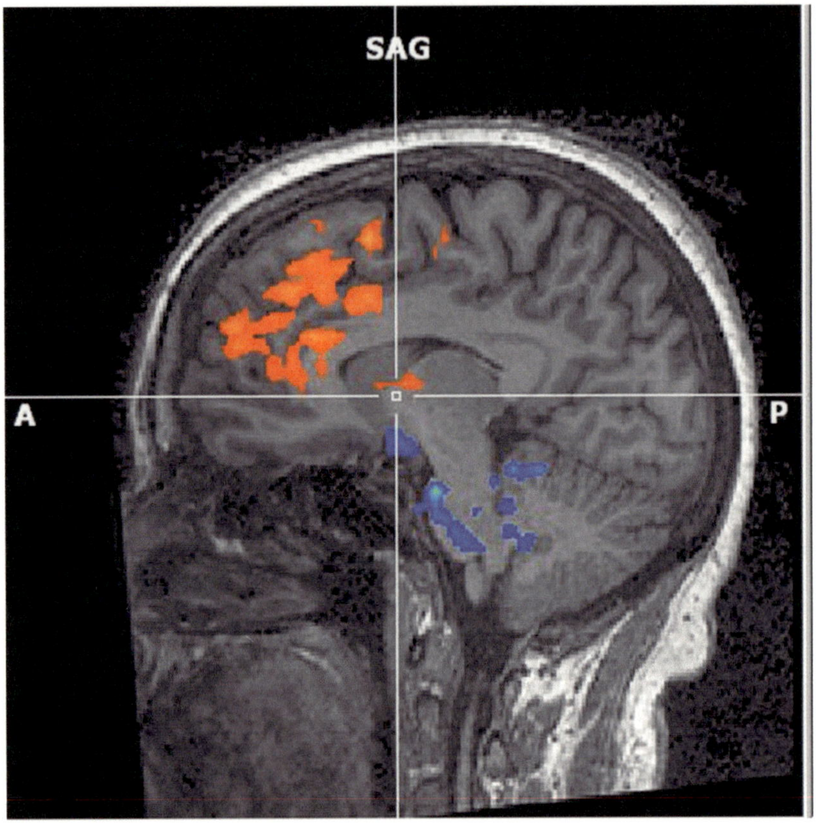

Figure 1. fMRI showing increased activation in the frontal areas of the brain during the practice of the Transcendental Meditation technique (Courtesy of M. Ludwig, 2012)

practicing the Transcendental Meditation technique showed improvements in theta/beta ratios. At the 6-months post-test, theta/beta ratios were in the normal range [38].

11. Conclusion

Understanding the history of the development of diagnostic criteria for ADHD, the parallel growth of the ADHD drug market, and factors that improve the symptoms of ADHD provides insight into alternative approaches to treatment and the potential for prevention.

Recognition of the role fatty acids, sleep, and stress play in cognitive function and behavior regulation in ADHD offers opportunities to intervene to alter the course of the disorder. Interventions that immediately address reducing the effects of the stressors, improve sleep, and enhance myelination have the potential of reducing the damaging effects on the brain, and possibly avoiding manifestation of the symptoms of ADHD.

http://dx.doi.org/10.5772/61069

Initial research supports the value of Transcendental Meditation as a promising behavioral tool not only for reducing symptoms of ADHD in adults and children but also for enhancing brain development, and for potentially preventing the future development of symptoms. Strategies for improved sleep and omega-3 dietary supplementation may also be beneficial strategies for intervention and prevention.

Author details

Sarina J. Grosswald

Address all correspondence to: Sarina@grosswald.com

SJ Grosswald & Associates, Arlington, VA, USA

References

[1] Visser SN, Danielson ML, Bitsko RH, Holbrook JR, Kogan MD, Ghandour RM, et al. Trends in the parent-report of health care provider-diagnosed and medicated attention-deficit/hyperactivity disorder: United States, 2003–2011. J Am Acad Child Adolesc Psychiatr 53(1):34–46.e2.

[2] Haislip GR. Stimulant Use in the Treatment of ADHD. San Antonio, TX; 1996 [cited 2015 Mar 12]. Available from: http://www.chromagen-spain.com/web/component/content/article/54Treatment-ADHD.html

[3] Jensen PS, Arnold LE, Swanson JM, Vitiello B, Abikoff HB, Greenhill LL, et al. 3-Year follow-up of the NIMH MTA study. J Am Acad Child Adolesc Psychiatr 46(8):989–1002.

[4] Molina BSG, Hinshaw SP, Swanson JM, Arnold LE, Vitiello B, Jensen PS, et al. The MTA at 8 years: prospective follow-up of children treated for combined-type ADHD in a multisite study. J Am Acad Child Adolesc Psychiatr 2009;48(5):484–500.

[5] Vedantam S. Debate Over Drugs for ADHD Reigites. Washington Post; 2009 Mar 27; Available from: http://www.washingtonpost.com/wp-dyn/content/article/2009/03/26/AR2009032604018.html

[6] Smith G, Jongeling B, Hartmann P, Russell C, Landau L. Raine ADHD study: long-term outcomes associated with stimulant medication in the treatment of ADHD in children. Western Australia Department of Health.

[7] The Express Scripts Lab. Turning Attention to ADHD: US MedicationTrends for Attention Deficit Hyperactivity Disorder. Express Scripts Lab; 2014 Mar.

[8] Subcommittee on Attention-Deficit/Hyperactivity Disorder, Steering Committee on Quality Improvement and Management. ADHD: clinical practice guideline for the diagnosis, evaluation, and treatment of attention-deficit/hyperactivity disorder in children and adolescents. Pediatrics 2011;128(5):1007–22.

[9] Rabiner D. Misuse & Abuse of ADHD Meds among college students: Updated review of a growing concern [Internet]. Sharp Brains; 2012 [cited 2015 Mar 16]. Available from: http://sharpbrains.com/blog/2013/03/26/misuse-abuse-of-adhd-meds-among-college-students-updated-review-of-a-growing-concern

[10] Richardson AJ. Omega-3 fatty acids in ADHD and related neurodevelopmental disorders. Int Rev Psychiatr 2006;18(2):155–72.

[11] Bloch MH, Qawasmi A. Omega-3 fatty acid supplementation for the treatment of children with attention-deficit/hyperactivity disorder symptomatology: systematic review and meta-analysis. J Am Acad Child Adolesc Psychiatr 2011;50(10):991–1000.

[12] Pujol J, Lopez-Sala A, Sebastian-Galles N, Deus J, Cardoner N, Soriano-Mas C, et al. Delayed myelination in children with developmental delay detected by volumetric MRI. NeuroImage 2004 Jun;22(2).

[13] Stickgold R. Sleep-dependent memory consolidation. Nature 2005;437(7063):1272–8.

[14] Gottselig JM, Hofer-Tinguely G, Borbely AA, Regel SJ, Landolt H-P, Retey JV, et al. Sleep and rest facilitate auditory learning. Neuroscience 2004;127(3):557–61.

[15] Hiscock H, Sciberras E, Mensah F, Gerner B, Efron D, Khano S, et al. Impact of a behavioural sleep intervention on symptoms and sleep in children with attention deficit hyperactivity disorder, and parental mental health: randomised controlled trial. BMJ 2015;350.

[16] Paavonen EJ, Raikkonen K, Lahti J, Komsi N, Heinonen K, Pesonen A-K, et al. Short sleep duration and behavioral symptoms of attention-deficit/hyperactivity disorder in healthy 7-to 8-year-old children. Pediatrics 2009;123(5):e857–64.

[17] McEwen BS. Protective and damaging effects of stress mediators: central role of the brain. Dialogues Clin Neurosci 2006;8(4):367–81.

[18] Arnsten AF. Stress signalling pathways that impair prefrontal cortex structure and function. 2009;10(6):410–22.

[19] Vance A, Silk TJ, Casey M, Rinehart NJ, Bradshaw JL, Bellgrove MA, et al. Right parietal dysfunction in children with attention deficit hyperactivity disorder, combined type: a functional MRI study. Mol Psychiatr 2007;12(9):826–32, 793.

[20] Lupien SJ, McEwen BS, Gunnar MR, Heim C. Effects of stress throughout the lifespan on the brain, behaviour and cognition. Nat Rev Neurosci 2009;10(6):434–45.

[21] Cotter D, Mackay D, Chana G, Beasley C, Landau S, Everall IP. Reduced neuronal size and glial cell density in area 9 of the dorsolateral prefrontal cortex in subjects with major depressive disorder. Cereb Cortex 2002;12(4):386–94.

[22] Orme-Johnson DW, Walton KG. All approaches to preventing or reversing effects of stress are not the same. Am J Health Promot AJHP 1998;12(5):297–9.

[23] Shear J, editor. Experience of Meditation: Experts Introduce the Major Traditions. Paragon House 2006. p. 312.

[24] Travis F, Shear J. Focused attention, open monitoring and automatic self-transcending: categories to organize meditations from Vedic, Buddhist and Chinese traditions. Conscious Cogn 2010;19(4):1110–8.

[25] Travis F, Arenander A, DuBois D. Psychological and physiological characteristics of a proposed object-referral/self-referral continuum of self-awareness. Conscious Cogn 2004;13(2):401–20.

[26] Zylowska L, Ackerman DL, Yang MH, Futrell JL, Horton NL, Hale TS, et al. Mindfulness meditation training in adults and adolescents with ADHD: a feasibility study. J Atten Disord 2008;11(6):737–46.

[27] Travis F, Shear J. Focused attention, open monitoring and automatic self-transcending: categories to organize meditations from Vedic, Buddhist and Chinese traditions. Conscious Cogn 2010;19(4):1110–8.

[28] Dixon C, Dillbeck MC, Travis F, Msemaje H, Clayborne BM, Dillbeck SL, et al. Accelerating cognitive and self-development: longitudinal studies with preschool and elementary school children. J Soc Behav Personal 17:65–91.

[29] So KT, Orme-Johnson DW. Three randomized experiments on the longitudinal effects of the Transcendental Meditation technique on cognition. Intelligence 2001;29:419–40.

[30] Fergusson LC. Field independence, Transcendental meditation, and achievement in college art: a reexamination. Percept Mot Skills 1993;77(3 Pt 2):1104–6.

[31] Travis F, Haaga DAF, Hagelin J, Tanner M, Nidich S, Gaylord-King C, et al. Effects of Transcendental Meditation practice on brain functioning and stress reactivity in college students. Int J Psychophysiol 2009;71(2):170–6.

[32] Travis F, Haaga D, Hagelin J, Tanner M, Arenander A, Nidich S, et al. A self-referential default brain state: patterns of coherence, power, and eLORETA sources during eyes-closed rest and Transcendental Meditation practice. Cogn Process 2010;11(1):21–30.

[33] Jevning R, Wallace RK, Beidebach M. The physiology of meditation: a review. A wakeful hypometabolic integrated response. Neurosci Biobehav Rev 1992;16(3):415–24.

[34] Jevning R, Wilson AF, Davidson JM. Adrenocortical activity during meditation. Horm Behav 1978;10(1):54–60.

[35] MacLean CR, Walton KG, Wenneberg SR, Levitsky DK, Mandarino JP, Waziri R, et al. Effects of the Transcendental Meditation program on adaptive mechanisms: changes in hormone levels and responses to stress after 4 months of practice. Psychoneuroendocrinology. 1997;22(4):277–95.

[36] Barnes VA, Bauza LB, Treiber FA. Impact of stress reduction on negative school behavior in adolescents. Health Qual Life Outcomes 2003;1.

[37] Rosaen C, Benn R. The experience of Transcendental Meditation in middle school students: a qualitative report. Explore N Y N. 2006;2(5):422–5.

[38] Travis F, Grosswald SJ, Stixrud WR. ADHD, brain functioning, and Transcendental Meditation practice. Mind Brain J Psychiatr 2011;2(1):73–81.

Chapter 13

Mindfulness Meditation — A New Preventive Intervention for ADHD

Yi-Yuan Tang and Rongxiang Tang

Additional information is available at the end of the chapter

http://dx.doi.org/10.5772/61213

Abstract

Medication and behavioral treatments have been used for ADHD treatments; however, both have limitations. Mindfulness meditation has been shown to improve attention and self-control, (or self-regulation), which could help the core ADHD symptoms of inattention, impulsivity, and hyperactivity. This chapter aims to review the latest literature on the effectiveness of mindfulness meditation on ADHD, to explore the brain mechanism underlying ADHD intervention, and to propose a mindfulness-based preventive intervention for ADHD symptoms and treatments.

Keywords: Mindfulness meditation, attention, self-control, IBMT, brain mechanism

1. Introduction

People with attention deficit/hyperactivity disorder (ADHD) have problems sustaining attention over prolonged periods of time, have difficulty to hold goals and plans in mind, and have difficulty inhibiting a prepotent response. Consequently, this neurodevelopmental disorder is characterized by symptoms of inattention, impulsivity, and hyperactivity and can influence brain structure and function [1]. Medication (mostly stimulants) and behavioral treatments (e.g., cognitive behavioral therapy) have been used for ADHD treatments; however, both have limitations. For example, medication works only short term and often has side effects, and treatment fidelity is often low [2].

Mindfulness meditation is often described as non-judgmental attention to experiences in the present moment [3, 4]. It has been suggested that mindfulness meditation involves a systematic training of attention and self-control [3]. It is thus reasonable to suggest that the underlying brain mechanisms of mindfulness may involve similar brain regions and networks as these mental processes [3–5]. Mindfulness meditation has been shown to improve attention and self-control [3, 6–10]. Since poor attention functioning is a core symptom of ADHD [11] and executive functioning deficits in ADHD are common [12–14], mindfulness meditation that purportedly strengthen these processes may help the ADHD symptoms and treatments.

In this chapter, we first introduce attention and self-control (or self-regulation) networks and the brain mechanism underlying ADHD intervention. We also summarize the latest literature on the effectiveness of mindfulness meditation on ADHD and then propose a mindfulness-based preventive intervention for ADHD symptoms and treatments.

2. Attention and self-control networks

Attention can be viewed as a system of anatomical areas that consists of three or more specialized networks. These networks carry out the functions of alerting, orienting and executive control, or resolving conflict [15]. Figure 1 illustrates what is known of the anatomy of attention networks that involves in mindfulness practice, especially executive control (attention) network [6,15]. The executive attention network shares with the brain circuits of self-regulation, mainly in the anterior cingulate cortex (ACC) and its adjacent medial prefrontal cortex (mPFC) and striatum/basal ganglia [16–18]. In mindfulness meditation, attentional control is required to stay engaged in the practice, and meditators often report improved attention control as an effect of repeated practice [6, 9]. Research has shown that the executive control (attention) network is heavily involved in mindfulness practice [3–6, 9,10]. In sum, ACC/mPFC and striatum play an important role in attention control and self-control following mindfulness.

3. Brain mechanism involved in ADHD

Functional neuroimaging and structural neuroimaging have identified brain abnormalities involved in ADHD. The hypofunction of the brain regions, including the cingulo-frontal–parietal cognitive attention network, has been consistently observed across studies [19]. Meta-analysis has also shown a ventral–striatal hyporesponsiveness in ADHD [20]. These are major components of neural systems related to ADHD, including attention and self-control networks, motor systems, and reward/feedback-based processing systems. The ADHD neuroimaging research related to these network dysfunction is also associated with the core symptoms of inattention, impulsivity, and hyperactivity. This evidence suggests the biomarkers of diagnosis and treatment in ADHD prevention and intervention. However, these network abnormalities are not the only factors responsible for ADHD; instead, they are only part of the pathophysiology of ADHD [20]. In order to fully characterize the disorder, we should not only consider the dysfunction of prefrontal–striatal circuitry but also consider the large-scale neural

http://dx.doi.org/10.5772/61213

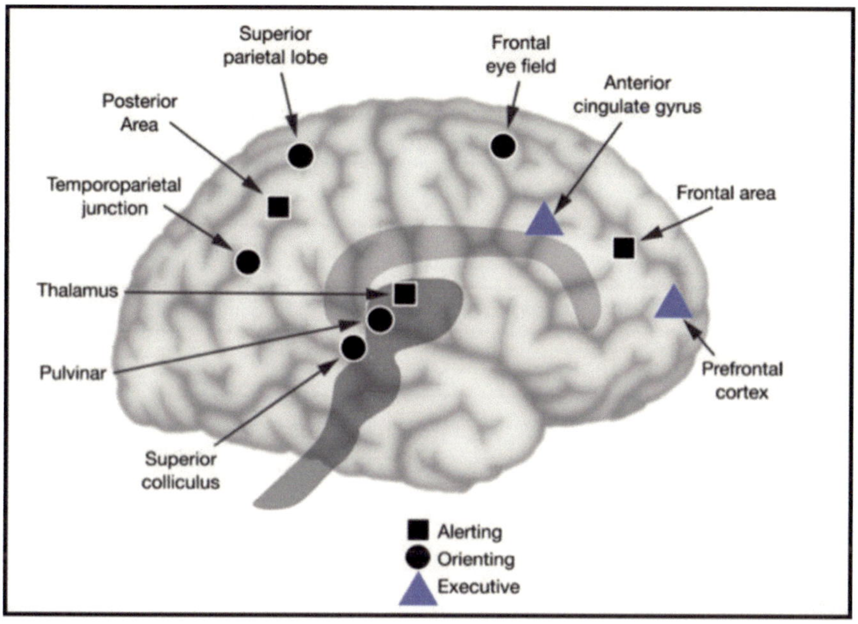

Figure 1. The anatomy of attention and self-control networks. Square, alerting network; circle, orienting network; triangle, executive control network. Executive attention shares with the brain circuits of self-control, mainly in ACC/mPFC. We call this as attention/self-control networks.

systems involved in ADHD based on recent advances in systems neuroscience-based approaches to brain dysfunction [21].

4. Mindfulness-based preventive intervention for ADHD

In addition to the pharmacological and behavioral treatments, mindfulness meditation has also been shown to improve attention and self-control [3, 6–10]. Given that poor attention functioning is a core symptom of ADHD [11] and self-control (executive functioning) deficits in ADHD are common [12–14], mindfulness meditation could strengthen these processes and may help the ADHD symptoms and treatments. We here propose the integrated translational model for mindfulness meditation as prevention strategies on ADHD [3]. As shown in Figure 2, mindfulness meditation includes at least three components that interact closely to constitute a process of enhanced self-regulation: enhanced attention control, improved emotion regulation, and altered self-awareness that targets the core symptoms of ADHD.

Previously in healthy population, we have applied one form of mindfulness meditation, the integrative body–mind training (IBMT) [3, 6], originating from an ancient eastern contemplative tradition, which involves body relaxation, mental imagery, and mindfulness training. Eighty undergraduates were randomly assigned to an experimental group (IBMT) or a control group (relaxation training) for 5 days of short-term training (20 min per day). The IBMT group showed significantly greater improvement of performance in executive attention as measured

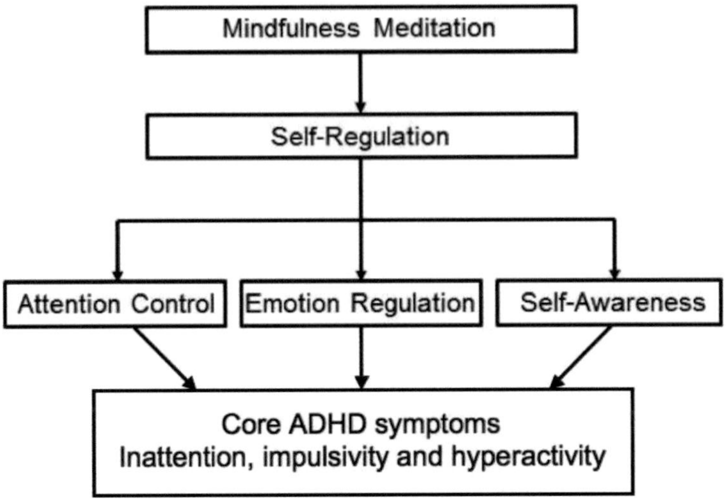

Figure 2. Integrated translational model. Mindfulness meditation includes at least three components that interact closely to constitute a process of enhanced self-regulation: enhanced attention control, improved emotion regulation, and altered self-awareness that targets the core symptoms of ADHD.

by the attention network test (ANT). They also reported lower anxiety, depression, anger, and fatigue and higher vigor. In addition, we found that after a stressful task, IBMT participants showed significantly reduced stress responses, as measured by salivary cortisol, and increased immunoreactivity, as measured by salivary immunoglobulin A [6]. These results indicated that brief mindfulness meditation – IBMT – can improve attention and self-regulation ability. A similar study showed that in comparison with a book listening control group, 4 days of meditation training enhanced the ability to sustain attention [8]. If the participants practiced 1 month of IBMT (10 h in total), we found improved efficiency of executive attention, alertness (sustained attention), and basal cortisol and immune function [3, 22, 23].

We further studied the brain and body mechanisms of IBMT [18]. During and after 5 days of training, the IBMT group showed significantly better physiological responses, including heart rate, respiratory amplitude and rate, and skin conductance response than the relaxation control. In addition, the IBMT group has significant differences in heart rate variability (HRV) and EEG power during and after training, suggesting greater involvement of the autonomic nervous system (ANS). Imaging data demonstrated stronger subgenual/ventral ACC activity in the IBMT group, and ACC theta was correlated with high-frequency HRV, suggesting control by the ACC over parasympathetic activity. These results indicate that after 5 days of training, the IBMT group shows better regulation of the ANS through a ventral midline brain system than does the relaxation group. This altered state probably reflects training in the coordination of body and mind given in the IBMT, but not in the control group [18]. Other studies also showed the ACC involvement [3, 4, 24]. Taken together, these evidences suggest that mindfulness practice is associated with enhanced attention, self-control, and awareness involving neuroplasticity in the ACC/mPFC, striatum, insula, and other brain areas [3, 4]. These biomarkers can be the target of diagnosis and treatment of ADHD.

Children and adolescents with ADHD often receive different formats of mindfulness meditation (e.g., MYmind program), with either the patients receive training only, or the caregivers receive concurrent mindfulness training as well [25, 26]. Overall, results are promising and demonstrate feasibility of mindfulness meditation in ADHD population. However, methodological issues pertaining to small samples, a lack of active comparison groups, and short follow-up periods limit generalizability suggest the need for longitudinal randomized rigorous trials [25, 26].

Studies in adult ADHD samples also provide promising preliminary support for mindfulness meditation (e.g., mindful awareness practices). In addition to mindfulness training, some studies have included mindfulness training as a component also showed the positive results related to ADHD symptoms (e.g., modified dialectical behavior therapy, mindfulness-based cognitive therapy). In sum, existing studies support the acceptability and feasibility in child, adolescent, and adult with ADHD and preliminary effectiveness of mindfulness in the treatment of ADHD [14]. Future studies are required to address methodological limitations of these studies.

5. Other factors in ADHD treatment

As one form of ADHD treatment, mindfulness meditation can be subdivided into methods involving focused attention and those involving open monitoring of present-moment experience [3–5]. These two techniques involve different attention and self-control strategies that may help ameliorate different ADHD symptoms. For example, "attention deficit" means brain hypoactivity that could not support attention functioning (e.g., sustained attention), whereas "attention hyperactivity" indicates overactivity that includes impulsivity. Thus, focused attention and open monitoring mindfulness may sensitize two extremes of attention problems in clinical practice using mindfulness intervention.

Regarding the ADHD different subtypes in responding to mindfulness intervention, clinical observations showed that there are differences in the ease of engaging in mindfulness based on the ADHD subtypes. In general, inattentive subtypes have easier time with quiet sitting practice and combined or hyperactive types struggle more because of restlessness. The latter responds more to body movement-based practice over quiet observation. Once engaged in the mindfulness practices, there also may be differences in outcomes. So far, there has not been enough research (studies with enough power) to tease out the effects of subtypes.

In addition, many other factors such as cultural differences in clinical strategy and social support can further complicate ADHD treatment. For instance, at least 9% school-aged children in the United States have been diagnosed with ADHD and are taking medications because ADHD is thought as a biological disorder with biological causes and the preferred treatment is stimulant medications such as Ritalin [27]. However, only less than 1% kids in France are diagnosed and medicated for ADHD. The drastic difference may due to the fact that in France, ADHD is viewed as a medical condition that has psychosocial and situational causes. Therefore, instead of using medications to treat children, French doctors look for the underlying social issue that is causing the problematic behavior. The common treatment for these underlying social context problems is psychotherapy or family counseling. This is a very different perspective from the American doctors, who tend to attribute all symptoms to a biological dysfunction such as a chemical imbalance in the child's brain [27].

6. Future directions

ADHD has often been thought to reflect dysfunction of prefrontal–striatal circuitry, but the involvement of other circuits has frequently been largely overlooked. Recent systems of neuroscience-based approaches to brain dysfunction have facilitated the development of models of ADHD pathophysiology, which include a number of different large-scale resting-state networks such as prefrontal–striatal, frontoparietal, dorsal attentional, motor, visual, and default networks. A better understanding of large-scale brain systems in ADHD could greatly advance our diagnosis and treatment of ADHD [21].

Recent commercial claims suggest that computer-based cognitive training (e.g., working memory) can remediate ADHD impairments and provide lasting improvement in attention, impulse control, and other cognitive and social functioning. However, the meta-analysis indicates that training attention or executive functions did not significantly improve attention and the targeted executive functions. The future rigorous RCT cognitive training studies may provide the possibility to improve executive function deficits and benefit ADHD [28]. We term this type of training as "network training" that exercises certain brain circuits using repeated cognitive tasks (e.g., working memory). In contrast, mindfulness meditation focuses on changing brain and body state that can affect many networks; we call it as "state training" [9, 10, 22]. Since network training and state training involve different brain networks, the combination of these two methods may be more effective [10]. In sum, a holistic approach to ADHD preventive intervention could be the trend in the field.

It should be noted that although the empirical evidences have shown the promising effects of mindfulness meditation on attention control, emotion regulation, and impulsivity reduction in healthy and ADHD populations, future research should consider the use of longitudinal randomized clinical trial to validate the effectiveness of mindfulness-based intervention for ADHD [29] and how this intervention could better transfer into school and workplace environment. If supported by rigorous studies, the practice of mindfulness meditation could serve as the treatment of clinical disorders and might facilitate the cultivation of a healthy mind and increased well-being.

Acknowledgements

This work was supported by the U.S. Office of Naval Research.

Author details

Yi-Yuan Tang[1,3*] and Rongxiang Tang[2]

*Address all correspondence to: yiyuanbalance@gmail.com

1 Department of Psychological Sciences, Texas Tech University, Lubbock, TX, USA,

2 Department of Psychology, Washington University in St. Louis, St. Louis, MO, USA

3 Department of Psychology, University of Oregon, Eugene, OR, USA

References

[1] Barkley RA. Attention-deficit hyperactivity disorder: a handbook for diagnosis and treatment. New York: Guilford Press; 1998.

[2] Van der Oord S, Bögels SM, Peijnenburg D. The effectiveness of mindfulness training for children with ADHD and mindful parenting for their parents. J Child Fam Stud. 2012; 21:139–147.

[3] Tang YY, Hölzel BK, Posner MI. The neuroscience of mindfulness meditation. Nat Rev Neurosci. 2015; 16:213-25. DOI: 10.1038/nrn3916.

[4] Hölzel, BK, et al. How does mindfulness meditation work? Proposing mechanisms of action from a conceptual and neural perspective. Perspect Psychol Sci. 2011; 6: 537–559.

[5] Lutz A, Slagter HA, Dunne JD, Davidson RJ. Attention regulation and monitoring in meditation. Trends Cogn Sci. 2008; 12: 163–169. DOI: 10.1016/j.tics.2008.01.005.

[6] Tang YY, Ma Y, Wang J, Fan Y, Feng S, Lu Q, Yu Q, Sui D, Rothbart MK, Fan M, Posner MI. Short-term meditation training improves attention and self-regulation. Proc Natl Acad Sci U S A. 2007; 104: 17152–17156.

[7] Chan D, Woollacott M. Effects of level of meditation experience on attentional focus: is the efficiency of executive or orientation networks improved? J. Altern. Complement. Med. 2007; 13: 651–657.

[8] Zeidan F, Johnson SK, Diamond BJ, David Z, Goolkasian P. Mindfulness meditation improves cognition: evidence of brief mental training. Conscious Cogn. 2010; 19: 597–605. DOI: 10.1016/j.concog.2010.03.014

[9] Tang YY, Posner MI. Attention training and attention state training. Trends Cogn Sci. 2009; 13: 222–227.

[10] Tang YY, Posner MI. Training brain networks and states. Trends Cogn Sci. 2014: 18: 345–350.

[11] American Psychiatric Association. Diagnostic and Statistical Manual of Mental Disorders, 5th edition (DSM-5). Washington, DC: American Psychiatric Association; 2013.

[12] Barkley RA. Behavioral inhibition, sustained attention, and executive functions: constructing a unifying theory of ADHD. Psychol Bull. 1997; 121: 65–94. DOI: 10.1037/0033-2909.121.1.65

[13] Boonstra AM, Oosterlaan J, Sergeant JA, Buitelaar JK. Executive functioning in adult ADHD: a meta-analytic review. Psychol Med. 2005; 35:1097–1108. DOI: 10.1017/S003329170500499X

[14] Mitchell JT, Zylowska L, Kollins SH. Mindfulness meditation training for attention-deficit/hyperactivity disorder in adulthood: current empirical support, treatment overview, and future directions. Cogn Behav Pract. 2015; 22:172–191.

[15] Posner MI, Rothbart MK. Educating the human brain. Washington, DC: APA Books; 2007.

[16] Bush G, Luu P, Posner MI. Cognitive and emotional influences in the anterior cingulate cortex. Trends Cogn Sci. 2000; 4: 215–222.

[17] Posner MI, Sheese B, Rothbart M, Tang YY. The anterior cingulate gyrus and the mechanism of self-regulation. Cogn Affect Behav Neurosci. 2007; 7: 391–395.

[18] Tang YY, Ma Y, Fan Y, Feng H, Wang J, Feng S, Lu Q, Hu B, Lin Y, Li J, Zhang Y, Wang Y, Zhou L, Fan M. Central and autonomic nervous system interaction is altered by short-term meditation. Proc Natl Acad Sci U S A. 2009; 106: 8865–8870. DOI: 10.1073/pnas.0904031106.

[19] Bush G. Cingulate, frontal, and parietal cortical dysfunction in attention-deficit/hyperactivity disorder. Biol Psychiatry. 2011; 69:1160–1167. DOI: 10.1016/j.biopsych.2011.01.022.

[20] Plichta MM, Scheres A. Ventral-striatal responsiveness during reward anticipation in ADHD and its relation to trait impulsivity in the healthy population: a meta-analytic review of the fMRI literature. Neurosci Biobehav Rev. 2014; 38:125-34. DOI: 10.1016/j.neubiorev.2013.07.012.

[21] Castellanos FX, Proal E. Large-scale brain systems in ADHD: beyond the prefrontal–striatal model. Trends Cogn Sci. 2012; 16:17–26. DOI: 10.1016/j.tics.2011.11.007.

[22] Tang YY, Rothbart MK, Posner MI. Neural correlates of establishing, maintaining and switching brain states. Trends Cogn Sci. 2012;16: 330–337. DOI: 10.1016/j.tics.2012.05.001.

[23] Tang YY, Posner MI, Rothbart MK. Meditation improves self-regulation over the lifespan. Ann N Y Acad Sci. 2013; 1307: 104–111. http://dx.doi.org/10.1111/nyas.12227.

[24] Tang YY, Lu Q, Geng X, Stein EA, Yang Y, Posner MI. Short-term meditation induces white matter changes in the anterior cingulate. Proc Natl Acad Sci U S A. 2010; 107: 15649–15652. DOI: 10.1073/pnas.1011043107.

[25] Zylowska L. The mindfulness prescription for adult ADHD: an 8-step program for strengthening attention, managing emotions, and achieving your goals. Boston: Shambhala; 2012.

[26] van de Weijer-Bergsma E, Formsma AR, de Bruin EI, Bögels SM. The effectiveness of mindfulness training on behavioral problems and attentional functioning in adolescents with ADHD. J Child Fam Stud. 2012; 21: 775–787. DOI: 10.1007/s10826-011-9531-7

[27] Wedge M. A Disease Called Childhood: Why ADHD Became an American Epidemic. New York: Avery; 2015.

[28] Rapport MD, Orban SA, Kofler MJ, Friedman LM. Do programs designed to train working memory, other executive functions, and attention benefit children with ADHD? A meta-analytic review of cognitive, academic, and behavioral outcomes. Clin Psychol Rev. 2013;33: 1237–1252. DOI: 10.1016/j.cpr.2013.08.005.

[29] Felver JC, Tipsord JM, Morris MJ, Racer KH, Dishion TJ. The effects of mindfulness-based intervention on children's attention regulation. J Atten Disord. 2014; DOI: 10.1177/1087054714548032

Chapter 14

Therapy for ADHD Directed Towards Addressing the Dual Imbalances in Mental Effort and Reward as Illustrated in the Mental Effort-Reward Imbalances Model (MERIM)

Alison Poulton

Additional information is available at the end of the chapter

http://dx.doi.org/10.5772/60814

Abstract

In this chapter we describe a clinical model for ADHD: the Mental Effort Reward Imbalances Model (MERIM). We use this model to explain some of the behaviour commonly observed in children with ADHD and to guide approaches to treatment. The MERIM views the behaviour associated with ADHD as an outcome of two unfavourable imbalances: 1.Imbalance of the level of mental effort required for achievement. 2.Imbalance in the level of reward experienced. These imbalances each contribute to lower levels of achievement and fewer rewarding experiences in ADHD. This results in a poorer mood with less tolerance for frustration, together with seeking rewards that do not involve high levels of effort. The concept of ADHD as dual imbalances in mental effort and reward gives a useful framework for understanding the behaviour and the strategies that individuals use to compensate and improve their mood.

Keywords: attention deficit hyperactivity disorder, oppositional defiant disorder, mental effort reward imbalances model, emotional self regulation, reward deficiency syndrome

1. Introduction

In this chapter we describe a clinical model for ADHD: the Mental Effort-Reward Imbalances Model (MERIM) [1]. We use this model to explain some of the behaviour commonly observed in children with ADHD and to guide approaches to treatment. The MERIM is a clinical model which we have found useful for explaining some of the more difficult behaviour observed in individuals with ADHD. This is particularly valuable for parents and teachers because a better insight into the reason the behaviour works for the child helps promote understanding and empathy.

The MERIM views the behaviour associated with ADHD as an outcome of two unfavourable imbalances:

1. Imbalance of the level of mental effort required for achievement
2. Imbalance in the level of reward experienced

These imbalances each contribute to lower levels of achievement and fewer rewarding experiences in ADHD. This results in a poorer mood with less tolerance for frustration, together with seeking rewards that do not involve high levels of effort. The concept of ADHD as dual imbalances in mental effort and reward gives a useful framework for understanding the behaviour and the strategies that individuals use to compensate and improve their mood.

This chapter is structured with some clinical descriptions and some sections which outline the background and evidence. As much of the descriptive information is based on observation, it cannot be fully referenced. It is therefore up to the readers to draw on their own observations, experience and intuition for validation.

2. Background

2.1. What is ADHD?

ADHD is a common condition with an estimated population prevalence of between 2.6% and 11% in children [2-5], being higher in boys and younger children. It is also common in adults, with estimates varying from 2.8% to 4.7% [6-8]. People with ADHD have impaired functioning due to difficulties with sustaining attention and with controlling impulsive behaviour [9]. They also often have a high level of physical activity.

There is evidence that individuals with ADHD have functional deficits in the prefrontal cortex, which is the part of the brain most involved in executive functioning [10]. Executive functions include working memory, reasoning, planning and resisting distractions [11]. ADHD is also associated with reduced motivation attributable to deficits in the striatum affecting the dopamine reward pathway and it may impact on the functioning of the amygdala, which is associated with the experience of emotions [12, 13]. The stimulant medications used in the treatment of ADHD increase the levels of the neurotransmitters noradrenaline and dopamine, and lead to improvement in the executive functioning deficits and the mood [14, 15].

http://dx.doi.org/10.5772/60814

ADHD is a clinical diagnosis and depends on an individual showing the behavioural features to a greater extent than would be expected for their age or developmental level and having associated problems in functioning. The features of ADHD are not specific, also occurring within the normal population but not with sufficient severity to cause significant impairment. ADHD typically results in difficulty completing tasks, which leads to underachievement and a less rewarding existence. A popular misconception is that individuals with ADHD will tend to be similar in their behaviour. However, within the normal population there is substantial variation in personality types, skills and abilities. When a diagnosis such as ADHD is superimposed, it adds a further source of variability. ADHD can occur in people of all levels of intellectual ability. Intellectual ability is one of the most important personal attributes that modifies the expression of ADHD.

2.1.1. *Inattention*

People with ADHD have more difficulty than others for tasks that involve sustained attention, particularly if the task is mentally demanding. Therefore, they would cope better for tasks that are shorter, easier or have a particular interest that stimulates attention. Individuals with ADHD may be able to concentrate for prolonged periods of time on electronic games. These typically do not involve the effort of independent or creative thought and also provide constant stimulation that catches and keeps the attention.

One characteristic of people with ADHD is that they are easily distracted. This may occur while they are talking and may lead to forgetting what they were going to say or losing the point while telling a story. Alternatively, becoming distracted during a task and then forgetting to go back and get it finished can lead to a person being inefficient and disorganised. People with ADHD often have difficulty ignoring distractions and this may make them particularly intolerant to background noise while trying to concentrate. Losing focus on schoolwork may lead to disruptive behaviour in class as a response to the boredom that comes with having nothing to do. Lack of attention predisposes to missing instructions and making careless mistakes. A child with ADHD may have difficulty with age appropriate play, quickly losing concentration and moving on to the next task or looking around for something more entertaining to relieve boredom.

ADHD is more disabling in children who have learning difficulties. This is because they have to concentrate longer and harder to acquire the same skills. The more difficult the task is for them, the more quickly they will fatigue mentally and give up. Conversely, an able child with ADHD may have no difficulty achieving at school during the early years. However, as the work becomes more demanding in high school, intellectual ability by itself may no longer be sufficient; and if they are unable to concentrate in class and study consistently, their grades may decline. Once a person leaves school, they usually have more opportunity to follow their interests and strengths and ADHD may therefore be less of a problem. However, lack of organisational ability may become more disabling when an individual has to contend with the complexities of functioning in society as an adult.

2.1.2. Hyperactivity

Hyperactivity is common in ADHD and is the most easily recognised feature. The hyperactivity often reflects the changing focus of attention as a child moves rapidly from one distraction to another. The restless energy may make it difficult to remain seated for any length of time, increasing the challenge for table-based activities. A child with ADHD may also be excessively talkative, sometimes apparently talking just for the sake of it and may lack the patience to stop talking and listen. Hyperactivity tends to diminish with age [16] and although some adults with ADHD may be still hyperactive, a hyperactive young child may develop into an underactive, unmotivated adolescent.

2.1.3. Impulsivity

People with ADHD often have quick reactions that occur without having time to stop, think and make a decision. Impulsivity can have an adverse effect on peer relationships as a child may unintentionally hurt or offend or repeatedly get into trouble for the same misdemeanour, such as impulsively calling out in class. Because of the lack of any active decision-making, these unregulated actions may be considered accidental by the child who may be inclined to deny responsibility. The lack of impulse control can lead to anxiety and low self-esteem as the child may suddenly be in trouble without any prior warning or intent.

2.1.4. Oppositional Defiant Disorder (ODD)

ODD is very frequently associated with ADHD. It is a common condition, with a community sample in the United Kingdom showing a prevalence of 2.2% in children aged 8–19 [2]. Among children with ADHD, about 38–52% also meet diagnostic thresholds for ODD [2, 17, 18], and of the remainder many will have symptoms of ODD but not of sufficient severity or consistency to meet the diagnostic criteria. People with ODD typically overreact with anger in response to minor frustrations [9]. The lack of control over impulsive behaviour in ADHD becomes even worse when associated with anger as such children may incorrectly interpret another child's actions as hostile [19]. For example, if accidently pushed, a child may automatically react by hitting. This can make individuals prone to involvement in physical fights and they may show no fear, even fighting with children who are much older and stronger. Other children may find this loss of control amusing and may deliberately provoke or bully such a child for a reaction. ODD is also associated with deliberately annoying people and sometimes with planned acts of spite. ODD is therefore a risk factor for bullying, either as the perpetrator, or the victim, or both. Children with ADHD sometimes consider the features of ODD to be an intrinsic part of their ADHD identity and may view the threat to their peers of their uncontrolled aggression as a source of power or strength rather than a weakness [21]. ODD is also associated with a negative attitude and a tendency to blame others and deny responsibility, argue and oppose authority.

2.1.5. Functional impairment in ADHD

The key to diagnosis of ADHD is not simply a matter of expressing the symptoms but, more importantly, it relates to the consequent impairment in functioning. When assessing the extent of functional impairment, it is useful to consider the level of achievement in the following modalities: academic achievement in relation to ability; peer relationships; ability to function at home and/or at school without generating unreasonable levels of stress or disruption and level of self-esteem.

2.2. Why is ADHD different from normal functioning? – The Mental Effort-Reward Imbalances Model (MERIM)

The most fundamental problem in ADHD is the inability to achieve consistently at a level appropriate to a person's ability. The individual would therefore be intellectually capable of higher achievement and have no physical disability sufficient to explain their level of achievement. For normal people, getting through their daily routine involves a constant stream of tasks that require effort and lead to a series of achievements, most of them small. These achievements are each associated with the satisfaction of task completion – the feeling of a job done well – which all help to sustain a stable and amicable mood. Therefore, for example, you get up in the morning, you put some effort into getting dressed and ready to go. Your assessment is that you look presentable in your clothes. You have achieved and you feel good about yourself and ready to put further effort into the next challenge. Achievement therefore involves some level of effort and is associated with a feeling of satisfaction (reward) which contributes to a good mood and a readiness to attempt the next task. Good mood is important for normal functioning and it has been shown that individuals who have a greater tendency to react with positive emotions have better emotional, psychological and social well-being [22]. They have better physical health and fewer days off work. The cycle of achievement, reward, good mood and further achievement is represented in Figure 1.

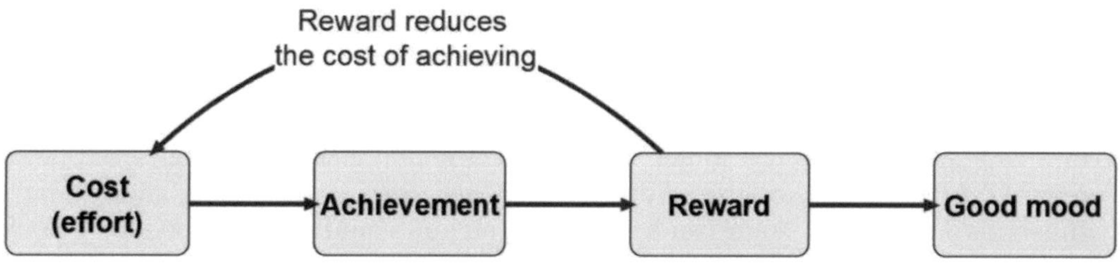

Figure 1. Schematic representation of the achievement and reward sequence

In ADHD the sequential pathway shown in Figure 1 does not work as effectively as it should. According to the MERIM, there are two places where it can malfunction. The first is if the cost or effort required to achieve is disproportionately great, as occurs in association with executive functioning deficits leading to less efficient thought processes in ADHD. The second is if a person experiences an inadequate level of reward. The MERIM views ODD as a deficit in the experience of reward, caused by neurochemical underactivity in the reward pathway. The impact of these two deficits on achievement and reward is illustrated in Figure 2.

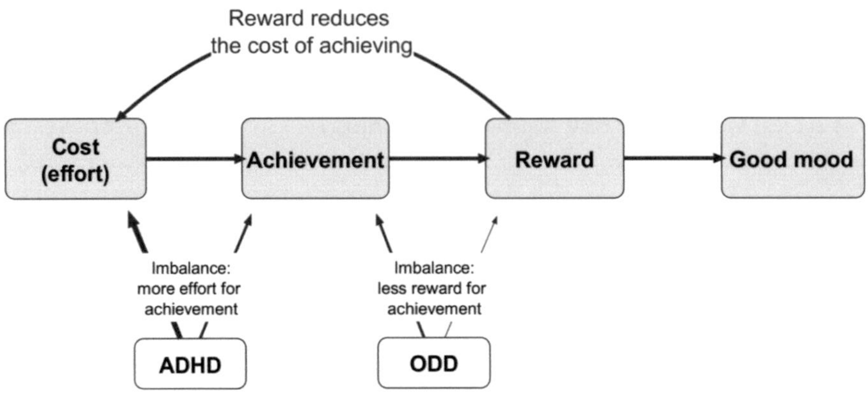

Figure reproduced with permission by Australasian Psychiatry [1]

Figure 2. Mental Effort-Reward Imbalances Model (MERIM)

2.2.1. Inefficient mental processes in ADHD leading to higher cost for achievement

In ADHD, mental processes (executive functions) are less efficient and therefore achievement requires more mental effort. This is like a runner who has to run uphill. It is not that running is a task that is too difficult for him, but he will tire more quickly than others who are running along level ground. He will either keep going but run more slowly, or he will try and run as fast as the others and then have to stop to rest. It is like this for mental tasks for people with ADHD. The mental fatigue is genuine and may affect academic functioning, social interactions and managing the daily routine at home. Children with ADHD often develop various ways of disguising or adapting to it. Some of these could be considered as 'taking mental short-cuts'.

2.2.1.1. Schoolwork

A child with ADHD may rush to get work finished within a time span for which he can concentrate. Alternatively, he may work for a bit and then stop working and appear to daydream, as if his mind is going blank like a computer on standby. Some just limit their rate of mental effort to a manageable level by working slowly. This may be disguised by giving too much attention to neatness and therefore doing very little of the more cognitively demanding aspects of the work. Creating a distraction may also be an effective work avoidance strategy. For example, a little girl developed the pattern of turning around and giving her mother a cuddle whenever she felt under too much pressure to concentrate on her homework. Other more common avoidance strategies include changing the subject or asking an irrelevant question.

2.2.1.2. Social interactions

Conversation demands mental effort, both for listening and for thinking and formulating the sentences required for a response. Children with ADHD often use strategies which conserve their mental effort. If a child is asked about who they have played with at school, this involves the effort of thinking back to an earlier part of the day and it may be easier to respond: 'I don't remember'.

2.2.1.3. Routine tasks

Children with ADHD often have difficulty carrying out instructions, particularly if given several together. A child may try to look as though he is listening, keeping his eyes on the speaker but not fully concentrating and therefore unable to follow an explanation or instruction. Sometimes a child may only listen to part of a sentence and guess the rest. Remembering several instructions often involves the effort of repeating them mentally. Rehearsal strategies and recall may be less efficient in ADHD [23]. If a person is not putting in adequate mental effort or is distracted by other thoughts, instructions may easily be forgotten.

If a person is achieving less on account of the disproportionate or unsustainable effort they have to put into completing a task, they will experience less satisfaction. They may be less ready to put further effort into the next task, with a tendency to give up easily. Inefficient mental processes therefore contribute to the underachievement associated with ADHD and consequent low self-esteem. Some individuals attempt to preserve their self-esteem by reducing their goals in life to a level that is more achievable. This may lead to dropping out of school into unskilled work or state benefits. This may be framed as a deliberate choice rather than failure to achieve.

2.2.2. Inadequate experience of reward from achievement leading to symptoms of ODD

Getting pleasure from the little things in life is important as this helps to maintain a good mood and amicable outlook [24]. However, if the subjective experience of reward is inadequate, a person is likely to feel negative and dissatisfied. The resultant low mood may lead to lack of motivation stemming from the perception that tasks are not worth the effort. Alternatively, a person may compensate by seeking activities that are more highly rewarding or that give reward for less effort. The dissatisfaction associated with inadequate experience of reward predisposes to the characteristic behaviour of ODD.

In this chapter, the term ODD is being used to include all the disruptive, impulse control and conduct disorders (ODD, intermittent explosive disorder, antisocial personality disorder, disruptive mood dysregulation disorder, conduct disorder) [9]. These conditions are associated with temper outbursts (problems in emotional regulation) and with behaviour problems including rule breaking and antisocial acts, with the specific diagnosis designated according to the main symptoms and the relative balance of the mood versus the behavioural dysfunction.

Deficits in reward do not only occur in ADHD/ODD but are also associated with other conditions such as addictions and obesity [25]. These are sometimes termed reward deficiency syndromes and are characterised by the strategies that people use to compensate for their inadequate experience of reward [26]. These may include comfort eating, compulsive gambling, internet or gaming addiction and drug abuse.

2.3. Relating the MERIM to the DSM and other models of ADHD

A formal diagnosis of ADHD is usually made in accordance with specific diagnostic criteria, such as those published by the American Psychiatric Association in their Diagnostic and Statistical Manual of Mental Disorders (DSM), the current edition being DSM-5 [9]. The diagnosis is based on meeting a sufficient number of the DSM-5 criteria for inattention, hyperactivity and impulsivity, with associated impairment in functioning. ADHD is classified as combined type (meets sufficient criteria for inattention and for hyperactivity–impulsivity), predominantly inattentive ADHD (meets criteria for inattention but not for hyperactivity–impulsivity), or hyperactive–impulsive ADHD (does not meet criteria for inattention). The diagnosis of hyperactive–impulsive ADHD tends only to be made in preschool children, who are at a stage of life in which the lack of ability to sustain concentration may be less evident. A diagnosis of hyperactive–impulsive ADHD may therefore be revised to ADHD combined-type as a child matures [27].

Several of the DSM-5 diagnostic criteria for ADHD are outcome-based and relate to lack of achievement in task completion. These do not dictate the causal mechanism and are therefore not specific to underachievement due to executive functioning deficits. Children who under-achieve due to inadequate experience of reward would also qualify. According to the MERIM, the dual deficits in executive functioning and reward experience contribute independently to the lack of achievement associated with ADHD (Figure 2). Because these two mechanisms are both highly prevalent and are additive in their effects on achievement, most people diagnosed with ADHD using the DSM are likely to have some degree of deficit in each. This provides an explanation for the substantial levels of diagnosable ODD among children with DSM-diagnosed ADHD. The MERIM would therefore consider the negative attitude and outlook that is frequently associated with ADHD as evidence of some degree of reward deficiency syndrome contributing to the symptoms of ADHD.

The MERIM is not the only model for ADHD that competes with that described in the DSM. The MERIM is probably the simplest model as it does not attempt to relate the symptoms of ADHD to specific testable modalities of executive functioning. Instead, it starts from the premise that unspecified executive functioning deficits mean that cognition is less efficient in ADHD and therefore requires more mental effort. It also does not really provide any explanation for the hyperactivity or the impulsivity. It has similarities with the model put forward by Douglas, which considers ADHD to be a result of four predispositions: the desire for immediate gratification, reluctance to invest mental effort, impaired impulse control and impairment in modulating arousal or alertness [28]. However, although it does not address arousal and impulse control, in the area of gratification the MERIM goes further than Douglas in that the desire for reward is explained as being an intrinsic deficit that reduces the individual's subjective experience of reward and interacts with the motivation for mental effort.

Barkley postulated the primary problem in ADHD to be inadequate response inhibition [27]. He gave this as the underlying cause for deficits in executive functions that include working memory, inner speech and verbal reasoning, analysis of behaviour and also for deficits in emotional regulation. According to this model, the symptoms of ODD would be explainable as manifestations of the emotional dysregulation associated with ADHD. Therefore, with

Barkley's model there is also no need for any additional diagnosis of ODD. However, although Barkley's model includes ODD in the overall symptomatology of ADHD, unlike the MERIM it does not explain the observation that the main emotional component of ADHD should be negative.

2.4. Striving for happiness: The balance between adequate reward and manageable effort

According to the MERIM, the clinical presentation of a child with ADHD will vary according to the severity of the imbalances in the level of mental effort required for achievement and the level of reward experienced. The particular clinical problems depend partly on the behavioural outcomes resulting from the underlying neurochemical deficits and partly on the strategies an individual develops to compensate and cope with these deficits.

People who have deficits in their experience of reward may feel miserable and moody. However, many develop strategies that make their life more rewarding and result in improving their mood and feeling happier. The particular strategies depend partly on the relative balance of deficits in executive functioning and reward experience and also on a person's intellectual strengths and weaknesses. Symptoms of reward deficit include arguing, deliberately annoying people and being spiteful or vindictive. Although these strategies might not initially appear to be obviously rewarding, there are study data that suggest otherwise. A study of adolescents with aggressive conduct disorder found that they showed an atypical response when observing inflicted pain, with activation in areas of the brain associated with pleasure [29]. Clinical observations also provide intuitive support: why would a child be deliberately spiteful if this were not pleasurable in some way? Humans are a social species and even more fundamental than communicating with language is communication that involves influencing and manipulating others' emotions. This can be done in a positive way, for example, telling a good joke that makes people laugh or giving someone a pleasant surprise that makes them happy. However, positive experiences can be difficult to organise and it is often easier to hurt or upset someone. Parents sometimes say that their child with ADHD will argue that black is white. This implies that arguing may not be a rational debate but rather an end in itself. Perceptive parents may observe that their child would start out in an angry mood but after a prolonged argument that frustrates or even hurts and upsets the parent, the child's mood may have improved. Therefore, the strategy works for the child, but clearly not for the parent. Winning is also a rewarding experience and older teenagers or adults may actively look for opportunities for starting an argument that they think they can win. Alternatively, children may become skilled at annoying or upsetting other family members, or playing one parent off against the other, and then quietly smiling at the resulting chaos. Children with less sophistication may simply resort to unprovoked physical violence when they feel irritable. Eliciting a negative social response by being deliberately difficult may therefore be an effective strategy that compensates for deficits in the subjective experience of reward. In the present context, any such activity that is carried out with the intention of causing pain or distress to another person has been classified as bullying. Therefore, a child may bully a parent or a teacher. The positive impact of bullying on mood is shown in Figure 3.

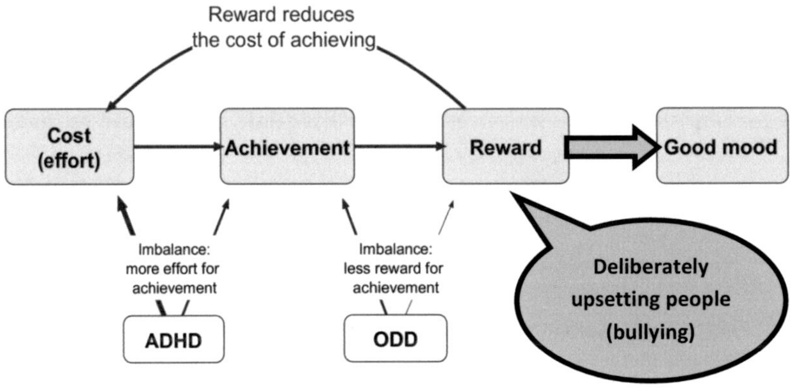

Figure 3. Oppositional behaviour that compensates for lack of reward

Although the behaviour that is typically associated with ODD may be effective for compensating for deficits in reward experience, there are other strategies that can also enhance reward. Figure 4 shows a range of tasks, strategies and achievements that vary in the amount of effort they require and the level of reward experienced. For individuals with the most severe deficits in executive functioning and reward, the level of reward has to be particularly high in relation to the level of effort to make the activity worthwhile.

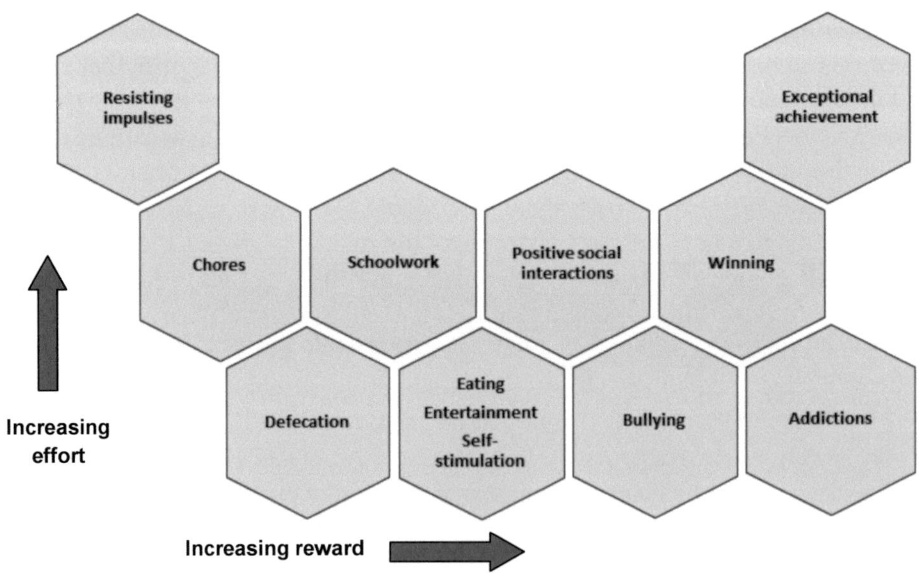

Figure 4. Hypothetical balance of effort and reward for various tasks and pastimes.

http://dx.doi.org/10.5772/60814

Intellectual capacity and tenacity determine an individual's capability for achievement. Individuals with severe ADHD, ODD and intellectual disability may find that going to the toilet for defecation is not sufficiently rewarding to be worth the effort [30]. An individual may indulge in self-stimulation as this provides reward and is not mentally demanding. Eating is also easy and rewarding, which may explain the recognised association of ODD with obesity [31, 32]. Individuals with ODD are particularly susceptible to addictions to substances such as nicotine or illicit drugs [33, 34]. Conversely, resisting impulses requires substantial effort and is not particularly rewarding. An aggressive and irritable child may therefore have no meaningful incentive for putting effort into foregoing the satisfaction of hitting a sibling.

Having a higher level of intellectual ability opens the possibility for higher levels of achievement. Within the broad categories of chores, schoolwork and social interactions, different activities will vary in their level of interest and difficulty for the individual, with some chores and schoolwork being experienced as less arduous and more rewarding than others. The level of effort required for social interaction is often underestimated. Children generally demand a high level of attention from their friends, and even though play and conversation are rewarding, a child with ADHD may find the intensity of the mental effort unsustainable. The child may consequently withdraw to a less demanding pastime, perhaps playing alongside their friend. A child may find relaxation from a low-level, repetitive activity, which can lead to an incorrect diagnostic label of autism spectrum disorder. Alternatively, a child with ADHD may be more comfortable playing with a younger or less intellectually demanding child, or an older child who can make allowances or entertain.

Some individuals with reward deficit may be intensely competitive, striving for the high rewards that accompany high achievement. Those who are intellectually able may appear 'driven' to exceptional achievement, combating their general dissatisfaction by striving for higher levels of reward. Failure may lead to hostility and antagonism towards those who are more successful. In other words, after not managing exceptional achievement, their reward deficit may be addressed by the less exacting activity of bullying. Some children use competition to maintain motivation during play by making every activity into a win–lose situation. Such children may be unable to tolerate losing. However, being competitive may be used adaptively to enhance the reward associated with routine tasks or chores, for example, a child trying to break their record for how quickly they can get dressed.

With the exception of addiction, the higher rewards depend for their value on social recognition or an emotional response from one or more other people. Even exceptional achievement needs a social frame of reference in order to designate its value. The higher rewards associated with more positive achievements tend to require higher levels of effort and aptitude. By contrast, negative behaviour such as bullying has a high balance of reward for the mental effort and is therefore easier for those who are less able. However, the rewards that are associated with low levels of effort and achievement may be associated with low self-esteem. This could negate some of the reward experienced from activities such as bullying. Attributing blame to the victim may reduce this negative effect on the bully's self-esteem[19].

The above figure and paragraphs classify a range pastimes and achievements with a model that assigns to each a comparative level of effort and reward. This model predicts the strategies and behaviours that are likely to characterise deficient internal reward processes. It is important to recognise the function that such behaviours serve for the individual in generating the sense of satisfaction that they crave. An individual's prevailing mood gives a measure of the success of their strategies for achieving adequate reward within a manageable level of effort.

3. Management

Management of ADHD may involve medication, non-pharmacological treatment or a combination of both.

3.1. Non-pharmacological management of ADHD

Non-pharmacological approaches to management usually focus on the areas of functioning which are causing the most problems. This may involve additional learning support or other assistance related to the executive functioning deficits, such as help with organisation. However, the main emphasis is usually on behaviour management strategies. The conventional behavioural strategies used in ADHD are not specific for this condition, but aim to take good parenting and good classroom management to a higher level. Therefore, strategies may be applied to the whole family or to the entire class or even the whole school. An additional but less well utilised modality of non-pharmacological management targets the emotional issues. We suggest a larger role for emotional self-regulation as a means of promoting and maintaining a positive mood and outlook in ADHD.

3.1.1. Addressing the imbalance of the level of mental effort required for achievement

3.1.1.1. Additional learning support

This is designed to address specific problems exacerbated by the executive functioning deficits, for example, additional support with reading, so that this skill becomes easier and accomplished with a more manageable level of effort. Reading is a complex skill that involves several components. Each component requires attention. Therefore, the individual has to recognise the letters, relate them to their sounds and blend the sounds together to decipher the word. The words then have to be remembered so that the sentences can be derived. The sentences have to be understood and their meaning remembered long enough to make sense of the passage. The main reward of the task is in the interest from the information contained in the passage.

When a child is learning to read, the process is slow and laborious and the reward from the information may be lost unless the sentence is very simple. With practice, the child starts to recognise common words without having to sound out each one individually and reading becomes easier and more fluent. This allows more attention to be focussed on the meaning. The information is received at a faster rate and the balance of effort to reward improves. As reading becomes more rewarding, the child may start to read books for pleasure and thereby further practice and develop their skills.

If a child has ADHD, their attention span for concentrating will be less than other children. The learning process may be more laborious and the child may be inclined to give up easily. It may be harder for the child with ADHD to attend to the meaning while simultaneously deciphering the individual words, which reduces the interest of the task for the child. At this stage, additional one-to-one teaching may accelerate the rate at which the child develops reading fluency. As reading is a prerequisite for success in almost every area of schooling, good skills that enable a child to read without putting all their attention and effort into the process will be beneficial in all areas of academic learning.

3.1.1.2. Modifying the tasks and expectations

A child with ADHD is likely to need a higher level of parent or teacher attention and the tasks may need to be modified to make them achievable. Management often involves looking at the particular problems to find modifications that may make the required tasks more manageable within a child's limited attention span. Such strategies may include keeping tasks short and varied and moving on to a new topic before boredom sets in. Instructions need to be easily understood and repeated if necessary, perhaps with a written task list. A child with ADHD may need to be reminded to remain on task. Breaks may be factored in, such as sending the child out on an errand.

3.1.1.3. Teaching organisational strategies

Organisational skills can also be taught. These can include strategies to keep track of homework, including structuring the tasks, using checklists and long-term planning of tasks with their completion dates [20, 35].

3.1.2. Addressing the imbalance in the level of reward experienced: increasing the external rewards with conventional behaviour management

Behaviour management strategies are generally used by the parent or teacher and are designed to make favourable behaviour more rewarding and negative behaviour less rewarding for the child. These strategies usually involve a combination of rewarding desired behaviour and negative consequences for behaviour that is being discouraged. They depend on the individual being able to evaluate in advance the consequences of their behaviour. The particulars of the behavioural strategies have to be carefully thought out.

Conventional behaviour management has the drawbacks that because the rewards and consequences are external and often tied to particular tasks and situations, they may not carry over to other tasks and settings. Conventional behavioural strategies often use emotional rewards, with the parent or teacher praising the child and showing delight if the child has achieved or put considerable effort into the task. The child may respond by trying harder in order to gain the satisfaction of making another person happy. Therefore, it is frequently observed that a child will work better for a teacher who cares and takes more interest in him, but works less well following a change of teacher. The long-term aim of behaviour management is that the behavioural change should become generalised as the child matures [36].

A review evaluating psychological interventions has demonstrated sufficient evidence to consider behaviour management to be an established and effective intervention for ADHD, either when administered by the parent following training or when used in the classroom [36].

In order for behaviour management to be effective, a number of prerequisites must be met.

1. **The child must be capable of carrying out the target behaviour.**

This means that the goals should be realistic. It is important that goals are not too difficult such that the child gives up. Targeting small, manageable tasks is often the more effective approach. In children with a lot of behaviour that is perceived as problematic, goals need to be prioritised. For example, if a child regularly refuses to do any homework, rewarding the child for concentrating for 5 minutes and writing a single sentence and gradually working up to completing their entire half hour of homework may be more successful than choosing homework completion as the initial goal.

2. **The child must understand the rewards and consequences and be able to relate these to their behaviour.**

The child needs to have sufficient capacity to be able to comprehend that there will be consequences. The child also has to make an emotional connection with the consequences. It has been shown that children with ADHD may choose immediate small rewards over larger, delayed rewards [37]. The relevance of this to the clinical setting is that children with ADHD may appear to 'live for the moment'. The child may at be able to recite the consequences for a particular misdemeanour; but at the moment of making a decision, the consequences appear to have little relevance to the child. Afterwards, the child may show no interest in the reason for their punishment, experiencing it only as a frustration. It may not be that the child is intellectually incapable of understanding the connection between an activity and its consequence, but that what is important or relevant to the child is the present.

3. **The rewards and consequences need to be meaningful and appropriate.**

Rewards and consequences should be chosen carefully. A child might be rewarded with time to play on a computer; a meaningful punishment might be taking away the child's favourite toy or game. Rewards and punishments that are small and repeatable are often more effective than larger ones. For example, if a parent is very angry with a child, there may be a temptation to extend the duration of the punishment, perhaps taking away the favourite toy or banning the child from watching television for a week. If the child subsequently misbehaves during that week, the parent has lost one valuable option for punishment. Alternatively, if the punishment is milder, for example, the child is prevented from watching just one show, or loses their game for only five or ten minutes, the same punishment can be repeated as often as necessary. Prolonged punishment with restoration of the item made dependent on good behaviour may be even less effective. To a child with ADHD, a week may be such a long time that they consider the item lost forever; furthermore, it may be unrealistic to expect the child to behave well for a whole week. Withdrawal of attention from a child who has misbehaved can also be effective.

http://dx.doi.org/10.5772/60814

4. **The strategies should be applied consistently.**

Effective behaviour management requires consistent effort from the parent or teacher. If there is any leeway a child may become skilful in picking the time when they can get away with breaking a rule.

5. **The child must choose to co-operate.**

Co-operation is likely to depend on the child's own assessment of the balance of effort to reward. If the effort required is disproportionate due to the executive functioning deficits associated with ADHD, the child may insist on a reward that appears similarly disproportionate. For example, a small reward, such as adding a sticker to a chart for every task completed, may work for a few days until the child realises that the stickers are not worth the effort. At that stage, in order for the behaviour management to continue to be effective, a higher reward may be negotiated. This cycle may continue until the child will not even consider doing any homework unless rewarded with a very substantial sum of money. Alternatively, the child may perceive that he or she will experience greater satisfaction through non-co-operation. Figure 4 categorises bullying – behaviour designed to upset or hurt another person – as being more rewarding than schoolwork. Therefore, if a child can derive an alternative to co-operation that causes pain, this may appear an attractive option. If the child perceives that the parent or teacher is emotionally committed to their co-operation and genuinely wants to see the child carry out the task, this may provide an opportunity for bullying. This might take the form of deliberately destroying their work, for example, by scribbling on the page. Observing the resultant surprise, anger or frustration may be immensely satisfying for the child. Another very common strategy for non-co-operation is arguing. This may be a delaying tactic and a parent may be baffled that their child may spend twenty minutes and considerable effort arguing over ten minutes of homework, which ultimately still has to be done. To the child arguing may serve several purposes. Firstly, time spent arguing may be considered time well-spent because the homework is not actually being done. Secondly, the child may be negotiating a better deal, such as a higher reward or a reward in advance of the task. Winning such a concession would also be rewarding in itself (Figure 4). Thirdly, the child may be bullying the parent, enjoying the effect of the argument on their parent's emotions, for example, observing an increasing level of frustration or anger. It is important for adults to understand the value that a child may place on observing an emotional response. Withdrawing from the child to calm down may minimise the reward the child experiences for their negative behaviour.

3.1.3. Emotional self-regulation

Emotional self-regulation with the aim of improving the mood fits in with the logic of the MERIM because reward deficit resulting in a less positive mood is considered an intrinsic part of the symptomatology of the majority of individuals with ADHD. Although strategies that can lead to a higher level of task completion have merit, an important additional outcome is the effect on mood. Therefore, for example, if a child completes homework under protest and with the sole aim of gaining a tangible external reward, perhaps perceived as a bribe, this might be considered an acceptable outcome as the work is done. However, if the attitude towards the work is poor, it is likely that the child will complete it to the lowest acceptable standard. Therefore, an important additional aim would be to teach the child to value their work and gain internal reward in the satisfaction of a job done well. In other words, the positive aspects of the task that has been undertaken would be used to enhance the mood. Emotional self-regulation could supplement conventional behaviour management based on rewards and punishment, but places less emphasis on targeting particular behaviour, instead focusing on generating a positive mood through achievement. The main aim of this approach is to enhance achievement by promoting the cycle of achievement leading to a feeling of satisfaction, a happier mood and a readiness to take on the next challenge to achieve. Although not directly addressing the reward mechanisms, we have also included in this section anger management strategies.

3.1.3.1. Potentiating the internal reward mechanisms for a positive mood

Individuals may use a number of strategies which regulate their emotions. These strategies are not simply learned in childhood and adolescence but continue to develop, usually in a positive way, over the course of adult life [38]. Self-regulation strategies may be helpful as a long-term intervention for generating and maintaining positive emotions. For example, an intervention study of meditation (Loving Kindness Meditation) found that 35% of participants continued to derive positive emotional benefit from meditation a year after ceasing therapy [39].

Unlike conventional behaviour management, emotional self-regulation aiming to promote positive emotions has a theoretical advantage that its techniques directly address the effects of the underlying reward deficit. Furthermore, it can be applied to all aspects of daily life, and once taught and adopted, it does not rely on any outside sources for reward as individuals evaluate and provide their own reinforcement for their positive behaviour, developing strategies for sustaining their mood and self-esteem. The long-term goal would be for the individual to become independent in using the techniques of emotional self-regulation. This might happen if the individual notices that these strategies are worthwhile because they make him or her feel better. Because the individual has the control, self-regulation in relation to mood promotes individual responsibility and independence.

Positive rumination

Rumination involves repetitive thoughts that can influence an individual's emotional state. Rumination is conventionally considered to be negative in both the content of the ruminant thoughts and the emotional outcome as it focuses on the causes and symptoms of distress without seeking any solution to the perceived problems [40]. Negative rumination not only exacerbates depression and anxiety but is also a risk factor for a range of mental health problems, including aggressive behaviour in boys [41]. However, we suggest that spending time reflecting on a positive achievement could increase the level of enjoyment or satisfaction obtained. We have termed this positive rumination. We suggest that positive rumination may be a strategy used by healthy individuals that helps them to sustain a positive, stable mood and amicable outlook. It is a cognitive process that would involve some mental effort and therefore may come less easily to individuals with ADHD. It also depends on a person being

http://dx.doi.org/10.5772/60814

able to recognise their emotions, which can be a problem in ADHD [42]. Therefore, positive rumination may need to be specifically taught and practised in order for a person with ADHD to be able to use it effectively and understand and recognise its value.

There is evidence that frequent small, positive emotional boosts are associated with enhanced physical and mental well-being [24]. Positive rumination might provide this, but to be a workable strategy it would depend on the individual taking time to consider the good points about a piece of work or an activity and then reflecting on the sense of satisfaction that is generated. For example, after doing a piece of work, even if the work is not perfect, some positive attributes may be identified. These could initially be pointed out by the parent or teacher, but ultimately the individual would be encouraged to identify for themselves the value in their work. Times of reflection may also be built into the daily routine, for example, at bedtime thinking of the positive and enjoyable experiences and achievements of the day. These might include some of the following pleasant activities that are often associated with positive emotions: being helpful, interactions with others, playing, learning, exercise and spiritual activities [24]. In positive rumination, the individual has to be able to pause and reflect and have awareness of their mood, together with mood changes following on from their positive reflection.

Positive re-appraisal

In therapeutic settings, emotional self-regulation has tended to be directed towards dealing with negative emotions, for example, in anxiety, depression and anger [43]. However, a more recent approach to emotional regulation aims to generate and promote positive emotions [39]. Some strategies, such as negative rumination, avoidance and suppression are associated with psychopathology, while re-appraisal, problem solving and acceptance are considered protective. [43]. Positive re-appraisal involves redefining an adverse event in terms of any possible positive aspects [38]. Initially, the parent or teacher would need to assist the child, perhaps with a response such as: 'Although you lost your temper, you only hit him once, you calmed down quickly and you've learned that you should avoid him in future'. With time, the child may learn to practise positive re-appraisal. If the child's mood and self-esteem can so be preserved in times of adversity, he or she may be less tempted to resort to bullying in order to feel better.

3.1.3.2. Anger management

The symptoms of ODD might indicate a valuable role for anger management techniques. Strategies that have been used successfully for anger management include emotion recognition, problem solving, cognitive re-appraisal and relaxation with controlled breathing [44]. Recognition of emotion involves developing an awareness of symptoms associated with physiological arousal, such as feeling hot and having a pounding heart. Cognitive re-appraisal is designed to counteract an aggressive individual's tendency to respond with anger or blame if they have difficulty interpreting another person's actions [19]. The tendency to blame or to attribute hostility to another person in ambiguous situations may be used to justify aggression and can be associated with poor problem solving skills [45]. Therapy may emphasise thinking of non-personal reasons to explain another's behaviour instead of taking offense (for example:

'she must be having a bad day') and also looking for positives in a social situation. Learning to delay responding impulsively while feeling angry or thinking of alternative responses may also be valuable, perhaps by using 'self-instructions', which may be rehearsed and practised [45]. Strategies for managing the arousal include firstly avoiding or moving away from the stimulus and then calming the physiological changes. This may be achieved by controlled breathing, concentrating on taking a deep breath and self-instructions such as 'calm down' or 'relax' during expiration, also imagining reducing the body temperature and heartbeat [45]. Large muscle exercise and relaxation may be beneficial for hyperactive impulsive children [46].

Self-regulation with the aim of promoting good mood would appear to be a logical and promising new approach that is worthy of consideration. If these strategies can be used effectively by people with ADHD, they could lead to improvements in mood, functioning and self-esteem, which would not be linked to specific tasks and situations. The lack of study of emotional regulation in ADHD does not necessarily mean that such strategies are not being used therapeutically and effectively. However, efficacy still needs to be established with further research.

3.2. Pharmacological management of ADHD

The aim of treatment of ADHD is to achieve normal functioning. Non-pharmacological interventions can be successful, but the individual may still have ongoing problems associated with the underlying deficits of ADHD. Therefore, they would still experience mental fatigue with tasks that require sustained concentration. The tendency to act quickly and impulsively without the opportunity for adequate decision-making can greatly reduce the efficacy of behavioural management strategies. This is because behaviour management depends on the child being in a position to make a rational decision based on the pre-determined consequences. Furthermore, the low mood that is associated with reward deficit will tend to reduce the inclination to co-operate. Children who have significant functional impairment due to ADHD are sometimes identifiable as those who do not respond to the management strategies that work well for their siblings or peers. Drug treatment can improve the deficits in executive functioning and reward.

The medical formulations used most frequently in ADHD are based on the stimulants dexamphetamine and methylphenidate. These enhance the levels of neurotransmitters and address the underlying neurochemical deficits. They result in improvements in cognitive functioning which increase as the dose is increased [47]. They also improve the mood and behaviour, which may be an effect of enhancing the activity of the dopamine reward pathway. In clinical settings, the dose is established not by the child's weight but by titration for optimal therapeutic effect [48]. The non-stimulant atomoxetine is also an effective treatment for ADHD [49].

3.2.1. Mechanism of action of the stimulants

Methylphenidate and dexamphetamine increase the synaptic levels of dopamine and noradrenalin in the prefrontal cortex and in sub-cortical structures including the striatum and

http://dx.doi.org/10.5772/60814

nucleus accumbens (a part of the brain involved with appetite control). Dopamine and noradrenalin are neurotransmitters which are released into synaptic clefts and transmit impulses between nerve cells. Higher concentrations may assist with neurotransmission. The stimulants potentiate neurotransmission by three different mechanisms: enhancing neurotransmitter release, blocking reuptake by binding with the transporters and by direct stimulation of the receptors [50]. The actions of the stimulants on the different neurotransmitter systems depend on the amount of neurotransmitter and the affinities of the neurotransmitter receptors and transporters in the different regions of the brain [51]. The striatum is rich in dopamine; and although the dopamine transporter has high affinity for dopamine, it will also bind with noradrenalin. Conversely, noradrenalin is the principal neurotransmitter in the prefrontal cortex where it is taken up by the noradrenalin transporter. Dopamine is also present in the prefrontal cortex but at low levels and is taken up by the noradrenalin transporter, to which it binds with low affinity Dexamphetamine and methylphenidate are both highly effective for reducing the reuptake of dopamine and noradrenalin, but dexamphetamine also enhances the release of stored dopamine and increases serotonin levels [52].

3.2.2. Clinical effects of the stimulants

The beneficial effect of stimulant medications for improving the functioning of children with ADHD was first recognised in the 1930s [53]. The stimulant medications dexamphetamine and methylphenidate have the effect of reducing the level of physical activity and enhancing the ability for sustained attention. They also suppress the appetite [54]. The efficacy of the stimulants for treating the symptoms of ADHD has been well established in placebo controlled trials [48, 55]. In the Multimodal Treatment study of ADHD (MTA Study), it was shown that for the core features of ADHD (inattention, hyperactivity and impulsivity), stimulant medication was more effective than behaviour therapy [18]. Behaviour management was better for comorbid conditions including ODD. Children treated only with stimulant medication required higher doses for optimal improvement than those randomised to a combination of medication and behaviour therapy, suggesting an interaction between behavioural strategies and medication, with differential effects on the different symptom types. The stimulants have been shown to be effective in reducing the symptoms of ADHD in pre-schoolers [56], school-aged children [18], adolescents [55] and adults [57].

Clinical trials treating children with ADHD plus ODD have shown symptomatic improvement on medication for both of these conditions, but children with clinically significant symptoms of ODD required higher doses [55, 58, 59]. This suggests that different types of symptoms respond to different doses of medication. Evidence of two distinct pharmacological effects, each with its own therapeutic window, comes from the work of Sprague and Sleator [60]. They treated children with ADHD on two doses of methylphenidate and found that on the lower dose there was more improvement in learning, suggesting that this dose was targeting executive functioning. The higher dose was associated with greater improvements in social behaviour, but was less good for learning and may therefore have been treating the difficult, negative and hostile behaviour associated with ODD. This suggests that the stimulant effects for improving the deficits in executive functioning and reward are pharmacologically distinct, with different therapeutic windows that do not precisely coincide, reward deficit requiring higher doses for optimal treatment.

The main ongoing concern about the therapeutic use of stimulant medication in ADHD is the risk of abuse and diversion. Although methylphenidate is similar to cocaine in its affinity for the dopamine receptor, the addictive effect is the euphoria and this depends on a rapid rate of binding of the drug with the receptor [61]. Methylphenidate, particularly when taken orally, binds much more slowly than cocaine, which explains its far lower abuse potential. Atomoxetine is also used for treating ADHD. It is not a stimulant; it selectively inhibits noradrenalin reuptake and has minimal dopaminergic effect. It therefore lacks the abuse potential of the stimulants. It is also longer acting than the stimulants, giving a more consistent effect over the course of the day. However, the time taken for the levels to stabilise makes accurate dose titration more difficult.

Aside from their abuse potential, the most significant side effect of stimulant medication is the effect on appetite and weight, with a secondary effect on growth [62, 63]. It is as if the stimulant resets the appetite at a lower level. This results in initial weight loss. If a child remains on stimulant medication, the appetite recovers and weight gain resumes. After a year of treatment, the weight is usually approximately the same as it was at the time that medication was started. Appetite suppression appears to correlate closely with the therapeutic effect and a dose that does not affect weight is likely to be too low to be effective. Because weight gain is important for providing the resources necessary for growth in height, there is slowing of the height velocity, which gradually normalises over two to three years. Adult height appears not to be significantly affected by stimulant treatment, but there is some evidence that puberty may progress more slowly, with a later growth spurt [64, 65]. Stimulant medication also increases the heart rate and blood pressure [66]. Stimulant medications can also cause insomnia, irritability and feelings of sadness [67].

3.2.3. Practical issues of pharmacological treatment

The above section indicates that the actions of the stimulants are complex, that they have different effects in different parts of the brain and that the optimal doses for different aspects of functioning may not coincide. The dose–response curves for cognitive functioning and for mood and behaviour might look like Figure 5. This figure illustrates that the dose can be titrated to maximise either effect, but not both together. Alternatively, the dose giving the best overall effect might fall somewhere between the two peaks. Even if one effect is targeted, the selected dose may still lead to some improvements in the other effect. For example, a child with severe symptoms of ODD may function best on a relatively high dose of medication. Although this dose may be higher than his optimal dose for executive functioning, he may still concentrate substantially better than he would if unmedicated. This is likely to be related to some improvement in his executive functioning on the selected dose and also because his attitude towards cognitive tasks may be better when the deficits in his dopamine neurotransmission are addressed.

http://dx.doi.org/10.5772/60814

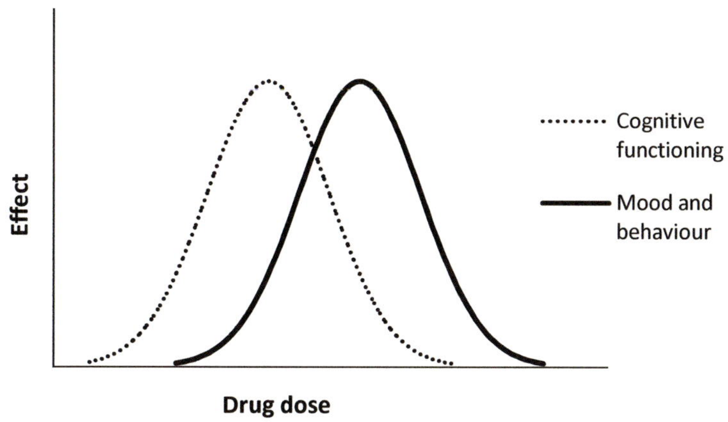

Figure 5. Hypothetical dose–response curves for the improvements in executive functioning and behaviour on stimulant medication

As children mature, they tend to improve in their behaviour [16]. They also outgrow their dose as they gain weight. Therefore, a dose initially selected for optimal improvement in the symptoms of ODD may, with time, gradually progress into a dose that is better for maximising the executive functioning deficits as the drug levels decline with the growth of the child.

The most important aspect of pharmacological management is to find the dose that works best for the individual. Careful dose titration while monitoring the changes in cognitive functioning and behaviour on medication and adjusting the dose to target those symptoms that are most impairing can be very effective. This is usually done by starting at a low dose and gradually increasing the dose while observing the changes in functioning. Behavioural rating scales may assist with comparing effects of different doses of medication. It is important that the rating scale includes items relating to cognitive functioning and to mood and behaviour, for example [68]. Dose titration and its effects are illustrated in Figure 6. Because the reward mechanisms also affect appetite control, the improvement in mood and behaviour correlates with weight loss. However, the dopamine reward pathway is only one of a series of mechanisms that affect energy balance and these other systems become activated as the weight drops, increasing the appetite and limiting further weight loss. [69]

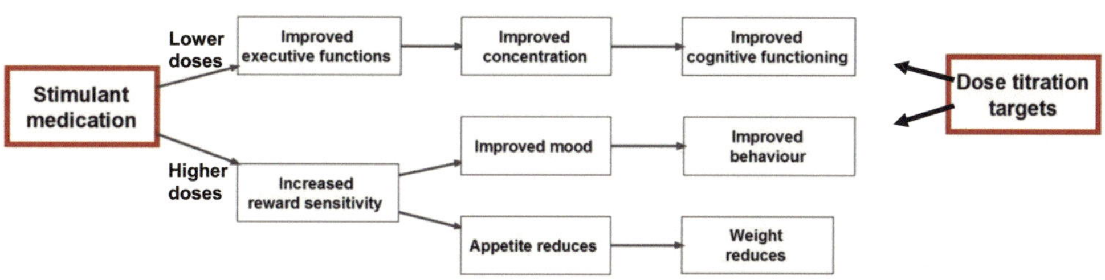

Figure 6. Stimulant medication and the effects of dose titration

The stimulant medications dexamphetamine and methylphenidate are short-acting, with an effect that lasts around 3–4 hours. In children who have significant hyperactivity or oppositional symptoms, the effect is usually obvious within 30 minutes of taking the dose. In children who only have inattention, the effect may be more subtle. As the effect wears off there may be rebound, with irritability and worsening of symptoms. The therapeutic effect may be prolonged by using formulations that release medication slowly over several hours. These may also wear off more slowly, reducing the rebound associated with rapidly falling levels. Because the stimulants can cause difficulty with settling to sleep at night, medication is often targeted to be effective earlier in the day while the child is at school, wearing off into the evening. Although the short duration of action of the stimulants can be inconvenient, it has the advantage that it allows a constant comparison of the child's functioning on and off medication. It is important to monitor the therapeutic effect and make dose adjustments whenever necessary as the dose usually needs to be increased periodically as the child grows.

3.2.4. Changes in treatment requirements with maturity

As children mature, they usually develop more control over their behaviour and this may reduce their reliance on medication. For example, a young hyperactive child may generate so much stress in the family that he or she may need medication every day. As the child matures, the hyperactivity may start to settle and medication may only be needed for school. The school years are often the most difficult stage of life for the individual with ADHD. This is because schoolwork involves prolonged periods of concentration and many of the tasks may not be intrinsically interesting. Once a person is no longer studying, they may be able to cease medication.

Although executive functioning deficits generally persist into adult life, with maturity individuals often become better at developing strategies to help them to function. However, some have ongoing problems with irritability and anger. An understanding of the reward deficit associated with ADHD may encourage such people to practise emotional self-regulation strategies to help promote a better mood and more rewarding existence.

4. Directions for research

The main novel approach to treatment suggested in this chapter is the recommendation for strategies designed to enhance the positive emotional experiences in everyday life for individuals with ADHD. These would clearly need to be evaluated with randomised controlled studies that include a plausible comparison treatment. In young children, behaviour management strategies are generally taught to the parents who then implement them with the child. Therefore, groups of parents could be taught conventional behaviour management using external rewards and punishments or strategies designed to promote positive emotions in the child through their achievement. Outcomes would be assessed using standardised rating scales relating not only to achievement in terms of task completion but also any positive effects on mood. In older children and adults with ADHD, particularly those with anger or oppositional features, there would be value in comparing anger management strategies that are intended to give more control over negative emotions, with strategies designed to enhance the positive experience of reward. Outcomes could be evaluated with standardised rating scales, both self-reported and observer-reported.

5. Conclusions

In this chapter we have described the MERIM, a new way of conceptualising ADHD that emphasises the importance of mood in the overall symptomatology. This naturally leads on to strategies specifically aiming to enhance a person's experience of reward in order to sustain a stable and amicable mood. Although medication can directly address the neurochemical deficits, self-regulation strategies may play a valuable role in enhancing reward, leading to long-term improvements in behavioural functioning.

Author details

Alison Poulton

Address all correspondence to: alison.poulton@sydney.edu.au

The University of Sydney - Sydney Medical School Nepean, Penrith, Australia

References

[1] Poulton A, Nanan R. The attention deficit hyperactivity disorder phenotype as a summation of deficits in executive functioning and reward sensitivity: does this explain its relationship with oppositional defiant disorder? Australas Psychiatry 2014; 22 174-8.

[2] Stringaris A, Goodman R. Mood lability and psychopathology in youth. Psychol Med 2009; 39 1237-45.

[3] Amiri S, Fakhari A, Maheri M, Mohammadpoor Asl A. Attention deficit/hyperactivity disorder in primary school children of Tabriz, North-West Iran. Paediatr Perinat Epidemiol 2010; 24 597-601.

[4] Dopfner M, Breuer D, Wille N, Erhart M, Ravens-Sieberer U. How often do children meet ICD-10/DSM-IV criteria of attention deficit-/hyperactivity disorder and hyperkinetic disorder? Parent-based prevalence rates in a national sample--results of the BELLA study. Eur Child Adolesc Psychiatry 2008; 17 Suppl 1 59-70.

[5] Sawyer MG, Arney FM, Baghurst PA, Clark JJ, Graetz BW, Kosky RJ, Nurcombe B, Patton GC, Prior MR, Raphael B et al. The mental health of young people in Australia: key findings from the child and adolescent component of the national survey of mental health and well-being. Aust NZ J Psychiatry 2001; 35 806-14.

[6] Caci HM, Morin AJ, Tran A. Prevalence and correlates of attention deficit hyperactivity disorder in adults from a French community sample. J Nerv Ment Dis 2014; 202 324-32.

[7] Antshel KM, Faraone SV, Maglione K, Doyle A, Fried R, Seidman L, Biederman J. Is adult attention deficit hyperactivity disorder a valid diagnosis in the presence of high IQ? Psychol Med 2009; 39 1325-35.

[8] de Zwaan M, Gruss B, Muller A, Graap H, Martin A, Glaesmer H, Hilbert A, Philipsen A. The estimated prevalence and correlates of adult ADHD in a German community sample. Eur Arch Psychiatry Clin Neurosci 2012; 262 79-86.

[9] American Psychiatric Association DSMTF. Diagnostic and Statistical Manual of Mental Disorders: DSM-5. Arlington, VA: American Psychiatric Association; 2013.

[10] Rubia K, Smith AB, Halari R, Matsukura F, Mohammad M, Taylor E, Brammer MJ. Disorder-specific dissociation of orbitofrontal dysfunction in boys with pure conduct disorder during reward and ventrolateral prefrontal dysfunction in boys with pure ADHD during sustained attention. Am J Psychiatry 2009; 166 83-94.

[11] Pennington BF, Ozonoff S. Executive functions and developmental psychopathology. J Child Psychol Psychiatry 1996; 37 51-87.

[12] Del Campo N, Chamberlain SR, Sahakian BJ, Robbins TW. The roles of dopamine and noradrenaline in the pathophysiology and treatment of attention-deficit/hyperactivity disorder. Biol Psychiatry 2011; 69 e145-57.

[13] Hulvershorn LA, Mennes M, Castellanos FX, Di Martino A, Milham MP, Hummer TA, Roy AK. Abnormal amygdala functional connectivity associated with emotional lability in children with attention-deficit/hyperactivity disorder. J Am Acad Child Adolesc Psychiatry 2014; 53 351-61.e1.

[14] Gamo NJ, Wang M, Arnsten AF. Methylphenidate and atomoxetine enhance prefrontal function through alpha2-adrenergic and dopamine D1 receptors. J Am Acad Child Adolesc Psychiatry 2010; 49 1011-23.

[15] Sinita E, Coghill D. The use of stimulant medications for non-core aspects of ADHD and in other disorders. Neuropharmacology 2014; 87: 161-72.

[16] Biederman J, Mick E, Faraone S. Age-dependent decline of symptoms of attention deficit hyperactivity disorder: impact of remission definition and symptom type. Am J Psychiatry 2000; 157 816-8.

[17] Greenhill L, Kollins S, Abikoff H, McCracken J, Riddle M, Swanson J, McGough J, Wigal S, Wigal T, Vitiello B et al. Efficacy and safety of immediate-release methyl-

phenidate treatment for preschoolers with ADHD. J Am Acad Child Adolesc Psychiatry 2006; 45 1284-93.

[18] MTA Cooperative Group. A 14-month randomized clinical trial of treatment strategies for attention-deficit/hyperactivity disorder Arch Gen Psychiatry 1999; 56 1073-86.

[19] Fondacaro MR, Heller K. Attributional style in aggressive adolescent boys. J Abnorm Child Psychol 1990; 18 75-89.

[20] Langberg JM, Epstein JN, Graham AJ. Organizational-skills interventions in the treatment of ADHD. Expert Rev Neurother 2008; 8 1549-61.

[21] Singh I. A disorder of anger and aggression: children's perspectives on attention deficit/hyperactivity disorder in the UK. Soc Sci Med 2011; 73 889-96.

[22] Keyes CL. Promoting and protecting mental health as flourishing: a complementary strategy for improving national mental health. Am Psychol 2007; 62 95-108.

[23] O'Neill ME, Douglas VI. Rehearsal strategies and recall performance in boys with and without attention deficit hyperactivity disorder. J Pediatr Psychol 1996; 21 73-88.

[24] Catalino LI, Fredrickson BL. A Tuesday in the life of a flourisher: the role of positive emotional reactivity in optimal mental health. Emotion 2011; 11 938-50.

[25] Volkow ND, Wang GJ, Fowler JS, Telang F. Overlapping neuronal circuits in addiction and obesity: evidence of systems pathology. Philos Trans R Soc Lond B Biol Sci 2008; 363 3191-200.

[26] Downs B, Oscar-Berman M, Waite R, Madigan M, Giordano J, Beley T, Jones S, Simpatico T, Hauser M, Borsten J et al. Have We Hatched the Addiction Egg: Reward Deficiency Syndrome Solution System. Journal of genetic syndrome & gene therapy 2013; 4 14318.

[27] Barkley RA. Behavioral inhibition, sustained attention, and executive functions: constructing a unifying theory of ADHD. Psychol Bull 1997; 121 65-94.

[28] Parry PA, Douglas VI. Effects of reinforcement on concept identification in hyperactive children. J Abnorm Child Psychol 1983; 11 327-40.

[29] Decety J, Michalska KJ, Akitsuki Y, Lahey BB. Atypical empathic responses in adolescents with aggressive conduct disorder: a functional MRI investigation. Biol Psychol 2009; 80 203-11.

[30] Johnston BD, Wright JA. Attentional dysfunction in children with encopresis. J Dev Behav Pediatr 1993; 14(6): 381-5.

[31] Pauli-Pott U, Neidhard J, Heinzel-Gutenbrunner M, Becker K. On the link between attention deficit/hyperactivity disorder and obesity: do comorbid oppositional defiant and conduct disorder matter? Eur Child Adolesc Psychiatry 2014; 23 531-7.

[32] Mustillo S, Worthman C, Erkanli A, Keeler G, Angold A, Costello EJ. Obesity and psychiatric disorder: developmental trajectories. Pediatrics 2003; 111 851-9.

[33] Harty SC, Ivanov I, Newcorn JH, Halperin JM. The impact of conduct disorder and stimulant medication on later substance use in an ethnically diverse sample of individuals with attention-deficit/hyperactivity disorder in childhood. J Child Adolesc Psychopharmacol 2011; 21 331-9.

[34] Modesto-Lowe V, Danforth JS, Neering C, Easton C. Can we prevent smoking in children with ADHD: a review of the literature. Conn Med 2010; 74 229-36.

[35] Abikoff H, Gallagher R, Wells KC, Murray DW, Huang L, Lu F, Petkova E. Remediating organizational functioning in children with ADHD: immediate and long-term effects from a randomized controlled trial. J Consult Clin Psychol 2013; 81 113-28.

[36] Evans SW, Owens JS, Bunford N. Evidence-based psychosocial treatments for children and adolescents with attention-deficit/hyperactivity disorder. J Clin Child Adolesc Psychol 2014; 43 527-51.

[37] Sonuga-Barke EJ, Taylor E, Sembi S, Smith J. Hyperactivity and delay aversion--I. The effect of delay on choice. J Child Psychol Psychiatry 1992; 33 387-98.

[38] Samson AC, Wells WM, Phillips JM, Hardan AY, Gross JJ. Emotion regulation in autism spectrum disorder: evidence from parent interviews and children's daily diaries. J Child Psychol Psychiatry 2014.

[39] Cohn MA, Fredrickson BL. In search of durable positive psychology interventions: Predictors and consequences of long-term positive behavior change. The journal of positive psychology 2010; 5 355-66.

[40] Nolen-Hoeksema S, Wisco BE, Lyubomirsky S. Rethinking Rumination. Perspectives on Psychological Science 2008; 3 400-24.

[41] McLaughlin KA, Aldao A, Wisco BE, Hilt LM. Rumination as a transdiagnostic factor underlying transitions between internalizing symptoms and aggressive behavior in early adolescents. J Abnorm Psychol 2014; 123 13-23.

[42] Conway F. The use of empathy and transference as interventions in psychotherapy with attention deficit hyperactive disorder latency-aged boys. Psychotherapy (Chic) 2014; 51 104-9.

[43] Aldao A, Nolen-Hoeksema S, Schweizer S. Emotion-regulation strategies across psychopathology: A meta-analytic review. Clin Psychol Rev 2010; 30 217-37.

[44] Fuller JR, Digiuseppe R, O'Leary S, Fountain T, Lang C. An open trial of a comprehensive anger treatment program on an outpatient sample. Behav Cogn Psychother 2010; 38 485-90.

[45] Feindler EL. Ideal treatment package for children and adolescents with anger disorders. Issues Compr Pediatr Nurs 1995; 18 233-60.

[46] Klein SA, Deffenbacher JL. Relaxation and exercise for hyperactive impulsive children. Percept Mot Skills 1977; 45 1159-62.

[47] Douglas VI, Barr RG, Amin K, O'Neill ME, Britton BG. Dosage effects and individual responsivity to methylphenidate in attention deficit disorder. J Child Psychol Psychiatry 1988; 29 453-75.

[48] Rapport MD, Denney C. Titrating methylphenidate in children with attention-deficit/hyperactivity disorder: is body mass predictive of clinical response? J Am Acad Child Adolesc Psychiatry 1997; 36 523-30.

[49] Michelson D, Faries D, Wernicke J, Kelsey D, Kendrick K, Sallee FR, Spencer T. Atomoxetine in the treatment of children and adolescents with attention-deficit/hyperactivity disorder: a randomized, placebo-controlled, dose-response study. Pediatrics 2001; 108 E83.

[50] Arnsten AF, Rubia K. Neurobiological circuits regulating attention, cognitive control, motivation, and emotion: disruptions in neurodevelopmental psychiatric disorders. J Am Acad Child Adolesc Psychiatry 2012; 51 356-67.

[51] Madras BK, Miller GM, Fischman AJ. The dopamine transporter and attention-deficit/hyperactivity disorder. Biol Psychiatry 2005; 57 1397-409.

[52] Kuczenski R, Segal DS. Effects of methylphenidate on extracellular dopamine, serotonin, and norepinephrine: comparison with amphetamine. J Neurochem 1997; 68 2032-7.

[53] Bradley C. The behavior of children receiving benzedrine. Am J Psychiatry 1937; 94 577-85.

[54] Greenhill LL, Halperin JM, Abikoff H. Stimulant medications. J Am Acad Child Adolesc Psychiatry 1999; 38 503-12.

[55] Spencer TJ, Abikoff HB, Connor DF, Biederman J, Pliszka SR, Boellner S, Read SC, Pratt R. Efficacy and safety of mixed amphetamine salts extended release (adderall XR) in the management of oppositional defiant disorder with or without comorbid attention-deficit/hyperactivity disorder in school-aged children and adolescents: A 4-week, multicenter, randomized, double-blind, parallel-group, placebo-controlled, forced-dose-escalation study. Clin Ther 2006; 28 402-18.

[56] Greenhill L, Kollins S, Abikoff H, McCracken J, Riddle M, Swanson J, McGough J, Wigal S, Wigal T, Vitiello B. Efficacy and safety of immediate-release methylphenidate treatment for preschoolers with ADHD. J Am Acad Child Adolesc Psychiatry 2006; 45 1284-93.

[57] Jain U, Hechtman L, Weiss M, Ahmed TS, Reiz JL, Donnelly GA, Harsanyi Z, Darke AC. Efficacy of a novel biphasic controlled-release methylphenidate formula in

adults with attention-deficit/hyperactivity disorder: results of a double-blind, placebo-controlled crossover study. J Clin Psychiatry 2007; 68 268-77.

[58] Blader JC, Pliszka SR, Jensen PS, Schooler NR, Kafantaris V. Stimulant-responsive and stimulant-refractory aggressive behavior among children with ADHD. Pediatrics 2010; 126 e796-806.

[59] Newcorn JH, Spencer TJ, Biederman J, Milton DR, Michelson D, Newcorn JH, Spencer TJ, Biederman J, Milton DR, Michelson D. Atomoxetine treatment in children and adolescents with attention-deficit/hyperactivity disorder and comorbid oppositional defiant disorder. J Am Acad Child Adolesc Psychiatry 2005; 44 240-8.

[60] Sprague RL, Sleator EK. Methylphenidate in hyperkinetic children: differences in dose effects on learning and social behavior. Science 1977; 198 1274-6.

[61] Volkow ND, Wang GJ, Fowler JS, Gatley SJ, Logan J, Ding YS, Hitzemann R, Pappas N. Dopamine transporter occupancies in the human brain induced by therapeutic doses of oral methylphenidate. Am J Psychiatry 1998; 155 1325-31.

[62] Poulton A, Briody J, McCorquodale T, Melzer E, Herrmann M, Baur LA, Duque G. Weight loss on stimulant medication: how does it affect body composition and bone metabolism? - A prospective longitudinal study. International journal of pediatric endocrinology 2012; 2012 30.

[63] Poulton A, Cowell CT. Slowing of growth in height and weight on stimulants: a characteristic pattern. J Paediatr Child Health 2003; 39 180-5.

[64] Harstad EB, Weaver AL, Katusic SK, Colligan RC, Kumar S, Chan E, Voigt RG, Barbaresi WJ. ADHD, stimulant treatment, and growth: a longitudinal study. Pediatrics 2014; 134 e935-44.

[65] Poulton AS, Melzer E, Tait PR, Garnett SP, Cowell CT, Baur LA, Clarke S. Growth and pubertal development of adolescent boys on stimulant medication for attention deficit hyperactivity disorder. Med J Aust 2013; 198 29-32.

[66] Stiefel G, Besag FM. Cardiovascular effects of methylphenidate, amphetamines and atomoxetine in the treatment of attention-deficit hyperactivity disorder. Drug Saf 2010; 33 821-42.

[67] Efron D, Jarman F, Barker M. Side effects of methylphenidate and dexamphetamine in children with attention deficit hyperactivity disorder: a double-blind, crossover trial. Pediatrics 1997; 100 662-6.

[68] Pelham W, Milich R, Murphy D, Murphy H. Normative data on the IOWA Conners teacher rating scale. J Clin Child Psychology 1989; 18 259-62.

[69] Cummings DE, Overduin J. Gastrointestinal regulation of food intake. J Clin Invest 2007; 117 13-23.

Chapter 15

Repetitive Transcranial Magnetic Stimulation in ADHD

Pavel Theiner, Libor Ustohal, Tomáš Skřont, Martin Bareš and Tomáš Kašpárek

Additional information is available at the end of the chapter

http://dx.doi.org/10.5772/61158

Abstract

Although there are very effective treatment approaches for ADHD available, the clinical management has its limits and a search for new treatment modalities is useful. rTMS found its use in neurology and is widely applied in psychiatric research and although its effect seems mild, it can be specific to some extend. The text reviews current knowledge on the neurobiology of ADHD symptoms with regard to a possible rTMS treatment. The basics of the rTMS method are described. The use of rTMS is summarized both generally in psychiatric disorders and specifically in ADHD. The safety issues are discussed both in adults and children. The text also brings a case study where rTMS was applied in an adult patient with ADHD.

Keywords: ADHD, rTMS, neurobiology

1. Introduction

1.1. Limits of current treatments for ADHD

Although the current treatment approaches in ADHD are highly supported by research and are very effective, they are not suitable for all patients in need for treatment. Medications used in clinical practice are generally well tolerated; however, they have some safety issues. Cardiovascular effects are the most important of them. Both stimulants and atomoxetine increase heart rate and blood pressure and for some patients it prevents their use. Treatment with stimulants belongs to the most effective within psychiatry. Almost all guidelines recommend stimulants as first-line treatment. However, 20–35% of children and adolescents in clinical trials may have an inadequate response to initial stimulant treatment either due to insufficient efficacy or non-adherence [1]. The response rate in atomoxetine is even lower, with 40% of patients without significant improvement [2]. In adults, the response rates for methylphenidate are around 50% [3]. The long-time studies in adults with ADHD show high rates of non-adherence to medications. Only about half of the patients remain in treatment after two years [4]. As for the psychosocial treatment, the evidence-based efficacy remains unclear, although psychosocial treatments can have some positive impact for children with ADHD beyond the impact of pharmacologic treatment alone. The quality of studies aimed at psychosocial interventions is insufficient, although it improves continuously [5].

Therefore, although specific pharmacotherapies for ADHD exist, they are not always available or suitable for all individuals. Moreover, as for the effect on specific symptom clusters, such as impulsivity, inconsistent data exist with both positive and negative effect of stimulants [6]. Even more, there are other issues, such as parents' non-acceptance of pharmacological treatment, that limit the benefit from pharmacological treatment. The need for novel treatment approaches is clear. Repetitive transcranial magnetic stimulation (rTMS), one of the most recent treatment approaches in psychiatry, allows selective neuromodulation of regions involved in the functional neuroanatomy of individual symptomatic profiles.

1.2. Functional neuroanatomy of ADHD symptoms

Although there exist unifying theories on the nature of symptom clusters in ADHD, the evidence on unequal expression of individual symptoms across clinical samples suggests that at least some symptom clusters are based on distinct neurobiology. This notion is demonstrated by a multivariate analysis of the results of testing of a large sample of ADHD subjects using cognitive battery that focused on cognitive control, reward- and time-processing that showed that these domains form distinct components, and that 80 % of subjects who had a deficit were deficient on only one component [7]. Dysfunctions in these cognitive domains may manifest in distinct symptom profiles in ADHD, i.e. inattention, impulsivity, and hyperactivity. Below, we summarize their functional neuroanatomy to evaluate the potential targets for rTMS treatment.

1.2.1. Impulsivity

Impulsivity is a clinically important feature that accompanies many neuropsychiatric disorders, including ADHD, and constitutes a significant risk for their development, and complicates their course and treatment. In contrast to its frequent manifestation and significant impact, relatively little is known about its neurobiology, and, more importantly, there is no effective specific treatment available at present, except for behavioral modification. This situation may result from inadequate definition of impulsive behaviour with insufficient discrimination between phenomenologically similar, but neurobiologically different, processes.

Indeed, impulsivity is a heterogeneous concept which manifests in many ways, such as personality traits, behavioral features and particular way of behavioural and cognitive task performance. Moreover, in clinical populations, there is rather variable phenomenology of behaviour that is generally labeled as impulsive and a considerable inconsistency of impulsivity concepts in neuropsychiatric disorders exists. It is not clear if there is a single psychological process linked to a distinct neurobiology or if discrete patterns of impulsive behaviour could be found with specific functional neuroanatomy in various clinical contexts.

Impulsive behaviour is the execution of an immediate urge to act, bypassing consideration of possible means and outcomes of available alternatives. In a closer look, there may be several sources of such behaviour. Moreover, behaviours like compulsions or hyperactivity may resemble impulsivity on the phenomenological level while they result from different neuro-biological and psychological processes [8]. Contemporary neuroscience opens new possibilities for objective analysis of neurophysiological sources of behavior. Moreover, it brings new ways of treatment that are guided by detailed knowledge of neurobiology of individual signs and symptoms.

Impulsivity may be expressed in personality traits, cognitive and emotional processes or behaviour control [9]. **Impulsive personality traits** include impulsivity proper, i.e. tendency to act rashly without evaluation of consequences (most frequently measured using the Barrat Impulsivity Scale); furthermore, it is reflected in the concept of *sensation seeking* (search of novel intense experiences without consideration of associated risks), *lack of perseverance, positive and negative urgency* (a tendency to act rashly during intense positive or negative affects) or high *reward sensitivity*.

Cognitive manifestation of impulsivity includes a concept of **behavioural disinhibition**, i.e. inability to suppress irrelevant or unfavourable behaviour ("stop impulsivity" – Go-No go task, Stop signal task), and a concept of **risky decision-making** and **reward processing** with preference of immediate, but in a long run, disadvantageous gains, and inability to postpone reward ("wait impulsivity" – various modifications of Delayed Discounting paradigm, Iowa Gambling task). Compulsion is a repetitive urge to act that leads to a stereotyped behavior; impulsivity, on the other hand, is not stereotypic.

The forms of impulsivity associated with ADHD involve the inadequate control of behaviour, poor sustained inhibition, the inability to delay a response or defer gratification, or the inability to inhibit dominant or prepotent responses. An equal or perhaps greater problem is the delay aversion – children and adults find waiting aversive, and therefore they act impulsively to terminate the delay more quickly. There is a reduction of symptoms of impulsivity with age, but adults still describe some symptoms of it. The clinical manifestations of impulsivity are described as "acts before thinking", "does not learn from mistakes", "says things without thinking" and "does not think about risks or effects of actions" [10, 11]. Impulsivity in individuals with ADHD is associated with greater emotional and behavioral impairments in all stages of life. The consequences of impulsivity often include poor academic and occupational performance, problems in interpersonal relationships. Impulsivity is also associated with an elevated risk for substance abuse, cigarette smoking, driving problems or antisocial behaviors. [12]

1.2.1.1. Functional neuroanatomy of impulsivity

Functional neuroanatomy of symptoms is based on imaging of brain activity during execution of a specific behavioral paradigm. Therefore, there are no studies of impulsivity, hyperactivity, nor any other clinical symptom. Rather, the neuroanatomy is based on associations between a particular pattern of responses during behavioral paradigm that engage specific cognitive processes and clinical manifestation of an illness. Impulsivity is associated with changes in reward processing, behavioral inhibition, and, perhaps, time processing. Failures in any of these processes can manifest as impulsivity. Although it might be difficult sometimes to differentiate what process causes a specific pattern of behavioral responses, for the sake of clarity the functional neuroanatomy of reward, behavioral inhibition, and time processing will be elaborated individually. The evidence suggests that they represent distinct patterns of brain circuit dysfunctions, and, therefore, they may form distinct phenotypes of impulsivity (i.e. "stopping" – "inhibition-dependent" and "waiting" – "reward-dependent" impulsivity).

Test features that require **inhibition** of inappropriate behaviour activate right inferior frontal gyrus, orbitofrontal gyrus, anterior cingulate, motor and premotor regions (motor cortex M1, supplementary motor area, dorsal premotor cortex), striatum, thalamus, and nucleus subthalamicus. It seems that behavioural inhibition itself consists of several subprocesses: inhibition of interference, response delay, and response cancellation. All of them are linked to the activation of the right inferior frontal gyrus, supplementary motor cortex, and parietal cortex. Inhibition of interference activates to a greater degree premotor and parietal cortex; cancellation of response represents a late phase of response inhibition and is linked with higher activation of fronto-striatal circuits. Meta-analysis of fMRI studies revealed strong evidence for decreased activation of the right inferior frontal gyrus, right supplementary motor area (BA6) and anterior cingulate (BA 32), right fusiform gyrus (BA 19), left caudate head, and right thalamus during motor inhibition tasks (Go-NoGo or Stop signal tasks) in ADHD [13].

Impulsivity linked with inadequate **reward processing** that involves decision-making and reward evaluation activates medial prefrontal cortex, medial orbitofrontal cortex, anterior cingulate, hippocampus, insula, amygdala, and ventral striatum or nucleus accumbens [9, 14]. Subjects with ADHD show decreased activation within this network, with a replicated finding of hypoactivation of ventral striatum during reward anticipation [15]. Edel et al. [16] showed that there might be dissociation of the neuronal deficit during reward processing between ADHD subtypes: predominantly inattentive subtype was linked with hypoactivation of ventral striatum, combined subtype with hypoactivation of orbitofrontal cortex.

1.2.2. Attention deficit

Deficits of sustained attention belong to very common findings in ADHD. A meta-analysis of fMRI studies (that used Continuous performance, Odd-ball, or Mental rotation tasks) detected significant decrease of brain activity in the right dorsolateral prefrontal cortex (BA 8, 46), right inferior parietal cortex (BA 40), right precuneus (BA 7), right superior temporal gyrus (BA 42), left putamen, and right thalamus; on the other hand, increased activity in cerebellum was found too [13]. However, individual studies show also involvement of the left hemisphere dysfunctions – using fMRI during vigilance task in boys with ADHD found decreased activation of the left dorsolateral prefrontal cortex (middle frontal gyrus, BA 46, 9, 8), superior parietal cortex (postcentral gyrus, BA 6, 4, 2, 1, 7), and subcortical structures involved in fronto-striatal loops [17]. DLPFC activation was related to the test performance, i.e. the reduced

DLPFC activation corresponded to deficits in sustained attention. Findings of abnormal functional connectivity within fronto-striatal loop during Continuous performance task in children with ADHD [18] demonstrates that the abnormal pattern of activity affects whole networks – which might be advantageous for the TMS applications, where only selected parts of the network are accessible, and still the influence of a part of a network may affect interconnected areas as well.

Arnsten describes a comprehensible model of attention, with two systems. The "bottom-up" system represents stimuli from the environment processed in association areas (posterior parts of the brain – the occipital, parietal, and temporal lobes) and projected to the PFC according to their salience. The "top-down" system represents the actions of the PFC which chooses which stimuli will be enhanced (relevant) and which will be suppressed (distracting) according to their relevance for long-time goals processed by the PFC. The PFC uses its extensive projections back to the sensory association cortices. [19]

In addition to the disorders of attention, dysfunction of several other cognitive functions, such as working memory and executive functions can be found in ADHD [20], albeit only in a subgroup of patients [21]. They are linked to reduced DLPFC activity [22].

1.2.3. *Time processing*

There exists growing evidence on impairment of various time-processing mechanisms in ADHD that form an independent domain of ADHD manifestation: perceptual timing, temporal foresight, and motor timing reflected in abnormalities of interval duration estimation and discrimination, delay discounting, and sensorimotor synchronization [23], i.e. processing of both interval estimation and fine-grained millisecond timing of brain events is affected. Since there is a relationship between time-processing deficits and measures of impulsivity and attention deficit [23], it seems that this neurocognitive abnormality may be another source of core behavioral manifestations of ADHD.

Functional neuroanatomy of time-processing deficits in ADHD converges on the pattern of reduced activation of bilateral inferior frontal gyrus, orbitofrontal cortex (in particular, in time foresight paradigms – delayed discounting task), SMA, precentral gyrus, insula, and cerebellum [24–27].

1.2.4. *Emotion dysregulation*

Emotion dysregulation is an important component of ADHD and according to many it should be considered in diagnostic conceptualizations of ADHD [28, 29]. It was found to be linked to some ADHD variables such as greater ADHD functional impairment, lower quality of life, ADHD persistence, and higher ADHD severity in childhood [30]. Shaw et al. [31] describes emotion dysregulation as emotional expressions and experiences that are excessive in relation to social norms and context-inappropriate; rapid, poorly controlled shifts in emotion ("lability"); and the anomalous allocation of attention to emotional stimuli. In the study of Vidal et al., adults with ADHD presented higher levels of emotional lability when compared to clinical control subjects and community subjects [30].

Similarly to attention, there are different systems that regulate emotions. The "bottom-up" system is represented by emotional responses of the amygdala and ventral striatum to external stimuli. Their projections to prefrontal cortex (PFC) draw attention to emotionally loaded processes and similarly to attention, this bottom-up system stresses salience of emotions and not their current relevance. Subcortical structures, the amygdala, and the ventral striatum play a key role in generation of emotions. These areas project to ventrolateral prefrontal cortex (VLPFC), which is not a centre for emotion regulation, rather it decides if regulation is necessary. The need for regulation is signalized to the dorsolateral PFC (DLPFC), either via the anterior middle cingulate cortex or directly. The DLPFC processes the information from VLPFC and relays it to other brain structures involved in emotomotor control [32], which represents the "top-down" regulation based on relevance of the emotion for tasks and goals currently processed by the DLPFC. This ability is included in the broader concept of "executive functions", i.e. the processes that are focused on attaining long-term goals through organizing and planning.

Emotion dysregulation in ADHD may arise from deficits at multiple levels. These range from abnormal early orienting to emotional stimuli, particularly with regard to negative stimuli and reward valuation through an inability to recruit top-down regulatory effort in response to emotional stimuli. Meantime, deficits in cognitive processes, including working memory and response inhibition, may contribute to emotion dysregulation, but they do not seem to be alone to explain its presence in ADHD [31]. In children with ADHD and emotional lability, deficits in emotion regulation were associated with altered amygdala–cortical intrinsic functional connectivity (iFC). The cortical structures involved were rostral anterior cingulate cortex (positive iFC in individuals with high emotional lability). Emotional lability scores were also negatively associated with iFC between bilateral amygdala and posterior insula/superior temporal gyrus [33].

1.2.5. Motor symptoms and hyperactivity

Hyperactivity is a non-specifically increased tendency to act. The question is if it is a consequence of inadequate motor inhibition or if there are other sources for hyperactivity. Although there are no functional imaging studies of hyperactivity per se, there are reports of motor system changes in ADHD. During simple motor tasks, reduced activity of primary motor (BA4) and sensor cortex in ADHD subjects was observed [34]. Moreover, abnormal co-operation of motor system was seen as well – McLeod et al. (2014) [35] described reductions in functional connectivity at rest between the primary motor cortex and the bilateral inferior frontal gyri, right supramarginal gyrus, angular gyri, insular cortices, amygdala, putamen, and pallidum. It seems that increased lateral prefrontal cortex activity is involved in compensation of inadequate motor system performance in ADHD subjects [36].

1.3. Potential targets for rTMS treatment

From the network point of view, there seems to be an involvement of at least three distinct circuits – lateral attentional network, medial reward-related network, and fronto-cerebellar time-processing network. At present, the state-of-the-art rTMS technology enables modulation

http://dx.doi.org/10.5772/61158

of regions that lay close to the surface of the brain, i.e. lateral parts. Based on the above reviewed functional neuroanatomy, potential accessible candidate targets are represented by dorsolateral prefrontal cortex, ventrolateral prefrontal cortex, inferior frontal gyrus, dorsal parts of supplementary motor cortex, and cerebellum. Modulation of dorsolateral prefrontal cortex may lead to changes of attention, working memory, and executive functions, but through the top-down regulations it may exert effects on emotional dysregulation symptoms, and impulsivity. Inferior frontal gyrus stimulation may lead to changes in behavioral inhibition and time estimation. Cerebellar stimulation may influence time processing, cognitive functioning, and, perhaps, even the affective symptoms of ADHD. rTMS of cerebellum is technically possible; however, the tolerability due to the neck muscle stimulation might limit its clinical use. Quite recently, rTMS approaches that use a double-cone or HAUT coils demonstrated their ability to modulate activity of medial cortical regions [37, 38]. This technological advancement would enable direct targeting of medial cortical nodes related to reward processing, which may bring increased efficacy in the treatment of impulsivity in ADHD.

2. Repetitive transcranial magnetic stimulation

2.1. General description and current use in psychiatry

Transcranial magnetic stimulation (TMS) is a diagnostic and therapeutical technique based on the principle of electromagnetic induction of electric current in the brain. It uses high-density magnetic field (approximately 2T lasting 0.1 ms) to induce electric field inside cortex, which is able to depolarize neurons [39]. Repetitive transcranial magnetic stimulation (rTMS) depolarizes neurons repetitively with either high (HF) or low frequency (LF) in order to change neuronal excitability for a longer period of time. The excitability can be lowered by using a low-frequency stimulation [40], and vice versa, high-frequency stimulation is able to render the neuron more sensible to stimuli, thus more excitable [41]. Findings from the neuroimaging studies that have localized dysfunctional parts of cortex in particular diseases can be transformed into new treatment approaches. However, recent findings suggest that the effect of rTMS is more complex and the excitatory/inhibitory paradigm is not fully satisfying as some works suggest mixed excitatory and inhibitory effects of either HF or LF-rTMS [42] and the excitatory effect of HF-rTMS on motor-evoked potentials might be caused by the decrease of gamma-amminobutyric acid-mediated inhibition [43]. The method is non-invasive and few side effects have been reported so far. The complete mechanism of changes remains unclear, but it is believed that rTMS affects gene expression [44], synaptic plasticity, dopamine release [45, 46], and release of endogenous opioids [47]. The ability of rTMS to affect not only the particular area it is aimed at but also the whole functional site is crucial as it is able to modulate function in more distant parts of brain [48, 49].

Each rTMS protocol is characterized by its focus of stimulation, frequency of stimuli, intensity, frequency of sessions, total number of pulses, train and intertrain time, a total time of session, and the shape of the coil. Taking this into account, many variables which can modify the effect of stimulation are present and researchers need to consider each of them when designing a protocol. The choice of the region of the brain cortex used for stimulation is based on lesion studies or imaging data that suggest an approximate localization of the studied cortical function, e.g. dorsolateral prefrontal cortex, supplementary motor area, etc. The choice of a particular place on subject's scalp to put on the coil is based on anatomy or imaging data of the particular subject. The intensity of each stimulation is usually standardized according to a percent of RMT (resting motor threshold), determined in each individual. 1 Hz stimulation is typically used for LF-rTMS, and 5–20 Hz stimulation in HF-rTMS. Multiple imaging techniques are used for online monitoring of rTMS effect in studies (EEG, PET, fMRI).

Another form of rTMS – the Theta-Burst stimulation (TBS) – consists of 3 pulses at 50 Hz repeated at 200 ms interval (hence 5 Hz frequency). This stimulation, when applied continuously (cTBS), is considered to mimic long-term depression effect on cortical excitability, while when applied intermittently (iTBS), long-term potentiation-like (LTP-like) effect is observed [50]. However, Gamboa showed that doubling the duration of the stimulation leads to conversion of its effect [51].

Largest body of evidence supporting the efficacy of rTMS was reached in trials with patients suffering of drug-resistant major depression and this success of rTMS led to approval of this technique in this indication by Food and Drug Administration in the USA in 2008. The method is also used in neuropsychiatry for the treatment of anxiety disorders [52], child autism [53, 54], Parkinson's disease [55], and positive symptoms of schizophrenia such as auditory hallucinations [56, 57]. And for number of other diseases, this technique is in various states of research (neuropathic pain, Tourette's syndrome, stroke, amyotrophic lateral sclerosis, multiple sclerosis, epilepsy, Alzheimer's disease, tinnitus, obsessive compulsive disorder, negative symptoms of schizophrenia, substance abuse, addiction, and craving) [55].

2.1.1. Safety issues

Although rTMS is believed to be a very safe technique, several side effects were described in previous studies. Of the major concern is the possibility of seizure induction, mostly during excitatory rTMS (HF), considered the most serious TMS-related acute side effect. However, the incidence of seizures was extremely rare (0.1–0.5%) and was mostly connected to receiving rTMS exceeding previous guideline recommendations, often in patients under a medication potentially lowering the seizure threshold. A short intertrain time is considered to be one of the potential triggers of seizures during rTMS [58]. Further research and analysis should be performed to identify protocol aspects and indication criteria lowering the risk of seizures.

As rTMS produces rather intensive noise (over 120 dB) [59], considerations about its effect on patient's hearing should be taken into account. The amplitude of rTMS sound depends on the coil design and the absolute stimulation intensity. Thus, sound intensity experienced by the patient during stimulation depends directly on the subject's motor threshold which is individually variable across the population [60]. According to safety guidelines [58], hearing protection is highly recommended as some subjects with no hearing protection experienced a hearing loss or threshold shifts in past studies [61, 62].

Headache is a relatively frequent adverse effect of rTMS, but this discomfort usually vanishes within minutes with either no need for medications or it responds to common analgesics. A scalp pain or discomfort is a common adverse effect of rTMS as well and an ideal method to decrease this discomfort is still in research (e.g. local application of lidocaine) [63, 64]. However, the scalp pain and discomfort typically vanish straight after the application of pulses and eventually it seems there is a kind of accommodation as the first session is usually refered as the most painful.

Repetitive transcranial magnetic stimulation is contraindicated in patients with metallic (conductive, ferromagnetic, or other magnetic-sensitive) objects in or near the head (within 30 cm of the treatment coil), e.g. implanted electrodes, bullet fragments, aneurysm clips, stents and similar, or implanted stimulator devices in or near the head, e.g. deep brain stimulators and vagus nerve stimulators.

2.2. Repetitive transcranial magnetic stimulation in the treatment of ADHD

2.2.1. Children and adolescents

Several limitations exist for the use of any therapy in children regarding their developing brain. Every novel therapy in neuropsychiatry needs to be evaluated carefully in children, especially in the terms of long-term safety. According to the theory of "sensitive periods" (a time period within brain development when an intervention has a strong effect on the brain [65]) in childhood, neuromodulation methods might be able to affect the brain function in a more stable and effective way during these periods. Although there is no evidence of any serious side effects of rTMS in children, it has to be kept in mind that the risk of inducing maladaptive neuroplasticity during sensitive periods of development of the child brain is still present and there is great need to clearly describe the neurophysiology of the impact of rTMS on a developing brain [54].

Dorsolateral prefrontal cortex (DLPFC), and especially right DLPFC, is believed to be highly involved in the pathophysiology of ADHD – see above. Two studies reported an application of rTMS over DLPFC in children and adolescents with ADHD. Weaver and colleagues (2012) applied HF-rTMS (10 Hz, 100% of the observed motor threshold) over the right DLPFC in 9 young patients (4 of them between 15 and 17). Their sham-controlled crossover safety study revealed an overall improvement in ADHD symptoms, but no difference between the sham and the active rTMS sessions [66]. Isenberg et al. showed that LF-rTMS on the left DLPFC has similar effect in patients with depression as HF-rTMS on the right DLPFC [67]. Gomez et al. based their protocol on these findings and applied 1 Hz rTMS of 90% of the rest motor threshold over the left DLPFC in ten school-aged boys (ages 7–12) suffering from ADHD. Although this study was performed to establish tolerability and safety of this protocol in children, their preliminary results have been promising because of significant clinical improvement of ADHD symptoms (mainly inattentiveness in school and hyperactivity/impulsivity at home) as referred by teachers, parents, and partly confirmed by the attending physician [68].

Two other studies applied the rTMS in children with ADHD for different purposes. One of them successfully evaluated TMS-evoked N100 measuring by EEG as a suitable marker for online monitoring of rTMS effects in children with ADHD as they found significant reduction of the amplitude of TMS-evoked N100 in comparison to the sham stimulation [69]. Loo et al. (2006) used 10 Hz rTMS on two 16-years-old girls suffering from depression and ADHD and described improvement in depression but no change in ADHD symptoms [70]. Nevertheless, all these studies revealed no serious adverse effects in children with ADHD undergoing rTMS.

Considering the wide comorbidity of ADHD and Tourette's syndrome (60–80% according to hospital studies) [71], it is worth noticing some promising results of rTMS treatment. Two studies [72, 73] applied LF-rTMS of 100/110% of motor threshold over the supplementary motor area and showed significant improvement in tics; these improvements lasted for a minimum of 6 months [73]. However, three participants with ADHD reported no change in ADHD symptoms. Nevertheless, improving the tic symptoms can increase the compliance of ADHD patients and give the therapist possibility to better address the therapy of ADHD symptoms.

2.2.2. Adults

As the recent findings have revealed, in over 50% of children with ADHD the symptoms persist to adulthood. Adult ADHD has become a large point of interest for research. Considering the fact that attention deficit symptoms tend to persist into adulthood more often than hyperactivity symptoms, a pilot study was performed using HF-rTMS on the right DLPFC. This stimulation resulted in improvements in attention but with small clinical significance [74]. One patient in a case study reported particular dysphoria, inability to respond emotionally, hypobulia, tension, and impaired attention after the same stimulation protocol [75]. Applying inhibitory protocol on the contralateral DLPFC might be worth trying as well.

On the other hand, two studies with inhibitory protocol with LF-rTMS over the supplementary motor area (SMA) reported significant clinical improvement in hyperactivity in two women with the hyperactive/impulsive subtype of ADHD [76, 77].

Some studies focused on other functions typically impaired in ADHD (e.g. attention, impulsivity) trying to influence them by non-invasive brain stimulation in healthy population. The DLPFC was stimulated in studies measuring the effect of stimulation on sustained attention or impulsivity or inhibition. HF-rTMS over the left DLPFC led to better performance in the Conners Continuous Performance task [78]. Continuous Theta-burst stimulation over the DLPFC resulted in choosing larger delayed rewards rather than smaller immediate ones in the Delay Discounting test [79]. Similar results were reached after stimulation of the medial prefrontal cortex by HF-rTMS [80]. Interestingly, anodal transcranial direct current stimulation (tDCS) applied over either the left or the right DLPFC resulted in more careful driving on a driving simulator [81].

The performance in the Stop Signal task, which is also used for the diagnosis of impulsivity, was affected by anodal tDCS over the pre-SMA and participants performed greater number of correctly inhibited responses in comparison with the active stimulation over M1 [82].

2.3. Why are the results of studies so variable?

The differences between individual studies result from their methodology. There are great many parameters in rTMS that can be adjusted differently. The parameters are described above and studies use unequal designs. The reason for such differences is the practical absence of standard rTMS protocols for ADHD, the firm knowledge of the right technical setting is absent.

There is a possibility to use parameters that have been successful in the treatment of depressive disorder or negative symptoms of schizophrenia where the stimulation of the DLPFC is applied as well – high frequency, ideally 10Hz, above-threshold intensity (above 100% of the individual's resting motor threshold), higher number of treatment sessions (15 at least), higher number of pulses per session and totally during the treatment, and possibly the use of structural and functional brain imaging techniques for more accurate targeting of the best place of stimulation. This protocol has to be tested in trials (double-blind and placebo-controlled ideally) that could prove whether these parameters are really optimal for patients with ADHD. It is worth noting that in patients with obsessive-compulsive disorder this assumption was wrong and there is a search for a different target instead of the DLPFC. Even the protocols for much more studied disorders like depression or negative symptoms of schizophrenia differ, however, in different studies. In ADHD studies, the inter-individual variability is an important factor as extensive studies are lacking. The same protocol may lead to different outcomes in individual patients and in small sample studies the inter-individual variability can overweight the inter-group variability.

The measures of outcome can also differ in different studies. ADHD is defined by its diagnostic criteria and a lot of questionnaires are used to measure the changes in symptomatology. The functioning in individuals with ADHD varies considerably and the results in neuropsychological tests correspond to this variability. Changes induced by rTMS may be small and only detectable in testing, but patients' expectations may be higher with such a "hi-tech treatment" so patients can subjectively overestimate or underestimate the results. More studies examining patients' subjective feelings as well as objective measures of attention and hyperactivity before and after rTMS are needed.

3. Case study

An adult female patient 25-years-old with ADHD, a university student, was enrolled to the pilot study which examined the efficacy and safety of repetitive transcranial magnetic stimulation (rTMS) in adult ADHD. Although she described having had the symptoms of ADHD before starting school education at the age of 6 years, she was never diagnosed by a psychiatrist and was never treated. She was assessed by only a school psychologist who communicated to her parents that she would not be able to study at university. She, however, did not give up, and this motivated her to work harder. She had good results at basic and secondary schools even though she suffered from inattention. The results at university were considerably poorer, but with a high level of motivation she was able to finish her bachelor's degree. Nonetheless, she had to consult a psychiatrist for the first time during the studies and she was diagnosed with adjustment disorder with prevailing depressive mood and suspected ADHD. She was medicated with paroxetine 20 mg daily and also with valproate 500 mg daily for emotional instability. Her mood improved with the medication, but she still had disturbing symptoms of inattention. A year later she found our experimental rTMS study and agreed willingly to participate.

Before the procedure, she was assessed by two psychiatrists experienced in diagnosing ADHD and the diagnosis was confirmed. Consecutively, she had a neuropsychological evaluation aimed at attention. She did not meet any contraindication for rTMS (epilepsy, pathological EEG, metal object in skull, cardiostimulator, or drug pump) and thus she could start rTMS. The high-frequency stimulation of the left dorsolateral prefrontal cortex (DLPFC) was used; this alternative had been previously used in another patient with ADHD (see [74]) and seemed effective and well-tolerated.

Before the initiation of stimulation, we first localized the spot whose stimulation triggered a motor-evoked potential (MEP) in the abductor pollicis brevis muscle. Then, we determined in a standard way the resting motor threshold (RMT) as the lowest stimulation intensity that is able to trigger a MEP of at least 50 μV in the above mentioned muscle five times out of ten consecutive trials [83]. The exact stimulation localization was determined according to the "5 cms rule" – that is, a localization 5 cm more rostral from the RTM spot. The patient had ten sessions during her treatment with high-frequency (10Hz) rTMS; the intensity was 110% of the RTM; and the pulse count was 1500 in a session with the stimulation train invariably 10 seconds long with an inter-train pause of 30 seconds. The treatment was well tolerated and no adverse effects were seen during the whole course of treatment. After treatment, she did not feel any subjective improvement in attention, but the control neuropsychological evaluation showed improvements in almost all tests focused on attention. A few weeks after rTMS, she was informed she was in the second trimester of pregnancy which meant she had been pregnant in the course of the rTMS treatment. In a year, she contacted us again and reported her pregnancy without complications as well as the delivery of a healthy child. She even managed to finish successfully her university studies.

This case study supports with evidence the hypothesis that rTMS may be an effective and safe treatment option for adult ADHD. It seems safe even in pregnant female subjects; the evidence is however insufficient.

4. Summary

rTMS treatment of ADHD is in its infancy. The best treatment regimen, duration of acute treatment, neurostimulation target, and symptoms modulated by rTMS are to be determined. Although the method proved to be effective in several psychiatric indications (schizophrenia, major depression), the efficacy in ADHD needs to be studied in detail before any final conclusions. The neurobiology of ADHD is linked with dysfunctions of cortical regions that are accessible to rTMS modulation. The many regulatory functions of DLPFC enable TMS stimulation trials for many disorders. Majority of neurobiologic findings in ADHD involve

http://dx.doi.org/10.5772/61158

this cortical area, thus giving sense to the use of rTMS in ADHD. Since frequent limitation of rTMS studies is only approximate localization of stimulation targets, when trying to target specific regions linked with ADHD, fMRI-guided neuronavigation may be of crucial importance for the success of treatment regimens.

5. Abbreviations

This chapter tries to provide with current knowledge about the neurobiology of ADHD for the purpose of explaining the role of a novel treatment approach in psychiatry – repetitive transcranial magnetic stimulation. The structures of brain have usually long and complicated names. We use some abbreviations to shorten the text. All abbreviations are written in full words as they occur for the first time. Here are some of the most common for your reference.

ADHD – attention-deficit hyperactivity disorder

BA – Brodmann area

DCS – direct current stimulation

DLPFC – dorsolateral prefrontal cortex

fMRI – functional magnetic resonance imaging

HF – high frequency

LF – low frequency

PFC – prefrontal cortex

SMA – supplementary motor area

rTMS – repetitive transcranial magnetic stimulation

TMS – transcranial magnetic stimulation

VLPFC – ventrolateral prefrontal cortex

Acknowledgements

The work was supported by the Ministry of Health, Czech Republic – conceptual development of research organization (FNBr, 65269705), and by a research grant No. NT-13437, and by a research grant from the Grant Agency of the Ministry of Health, Czech Republic (AZV) No. 15-30062A.

Author details

Pavel Theiner[1*], Libor Ustohal[1], Tomáš Skřont[1], Martin Bareš[2] and Tomáš Kašpárek[1]

*Address all correspondence to: ptheiner@fnbrno.cz

1 Department of Psychiatry, University Hospital Brno and Faculty of Medicine, Masaryk University, Czech Republic

2 1st Department of Neurology, University Hospital of St. Anne and Faculty of Medicine, Masaryk University, Czech Republic

References

[1] Childress AC, Sallee FR. Attention-deficit/hyperactivity disorder with inadequate response to stimulants: approaches to management. CNS Drugs 2014;28:121–9.

[2] Schwartz S, Correll CU. New research: efficacy and safety of atomoxetine in children and adolescents With attention-deficit/hyperactivity disorder: results from a comprehensive meta-analysis and metaregression. J Am Acad Child Adolesc Psychiatr 2014;53(2):174–87.

[3] Retz W, Rösler M, Ose C, Scherag A, Alm B, Philipsen A, Fischer R, Ammer R. Multiscale assessment of treatment efficacy in adults with ADHD: a randomized placebo-controlled, multi-centre study with extended-release methylphenidate. World J Biol Psychiatr 2012;13(1):48–59.

[4] Frederiksen M, Halmoy A, Faraone SV, Haavik J. Long-term efficacy and safety of treatment with stimulants and atomoxetine in adult ADHD: a review of controlled and naturalistic studies. Eur Neuropsychopharmacol 2013;23:508–27.

[5] Watson SMR, Richels C, Michalek AP, Raymer A. Psychosocial treatments for ADHD: a systematic appraisal of the evidence. J Attention Disord 2015;19(1):3–10.

[6] Moeller FG, Barratt ES, Dougherty DM, Schmitz JM, Swann AC. Psychiatric aspects of impulsivity. Am J Psychiatr 2001;158(11):1783–93.

[7] de Zeeuw P, Weusten J, van Dijk S, van Belle J, Durston S. Deficits in cognitive control, timing and reward sensitivity appear to be dissociable in ADHD. PLoS ONE 2012;7(12):e51416.

[8] Robbins TW, Gillan CM, Smith DG, de Wit S, Ersche KD. Neurocognitive endophenotypes of impulsivity and compulsivity: towards dimensional psychiatry. Trend Cognitive Neurosci 2012;16(1):81–91.

[9] Dalley JW, Everitt BJ, Robbins TW. Impulsivity, compulsivity, and top-down cognitive control. Neuron 2011;24;69(4):680–94.

[10] Barkley RA. Attention-Deficit Hyperactivity Disorder. 3rd ed. New York: The Guilford Press 2006;p.770.

[11] Ramsay JR, Rostain AL. Adult ADHD research: current status and future directions. J Atten Disord 2008;11(6):624–7.

[12] Ramsay JR, Rostain Al. Cognitive-Behavioral Therapy for Adult ADHD: An Integrative Psychosocial and Medical Approach. Routledge, 2008.

[13] Hart H, et al. Meta-analysis of functional magnetic resonance imaging studies of inhibition and attention in attention-deficit/hyperactivity disorder. JAMA Psychiatr 2013;70(2):185–98.

[14] Sebastian A, Pohl MF, Klöppel S, Feige B, Lange T, Stahl C, Voss A, Klauer KC, Lieb K, Tüscher O. Disentangling common and specific neural subprocesses of response inhibition. Neuroimage 2013;64:601–15.

[15] Plichta MM, Scheres A. Ventral–striatal responsiveness during reward anticipation in ADHD and its relation to trait impulsivity in the healthy population: a meta-analytic review of the fMRI literature. Neurosci Biobehavior Rev 2014;38:125–34.

[16] Edel MA, Enzi B, Witthaus H, Tegenthoff M, Peters S, Juckel G, Lissek S. Differential reward processing in subtypes of adult attention deficit hyperactivity disorder. J Psychiatr Res 2013;47:350–6.

[17] Christakou A, Murphy CM, Chantiluke K, Cubillo AI, Smith AB, Giampietro V, et al. Disorder-specific functional abnormalities during sustained attention in youth with attention deficit hyperactivity disorder (ADHD) and with autism. Mol Psychiatr 2013;18(2):236–44.

[18] Li X, Sroubek A, Kelly MS, Lesser I, Sussman E, He Y, et al. Atypical pulvinar-cortical pathways during sustained attention performance in children with attention-deficit/hyperactivity disorder. J Am Acad Child Adolesc Psychiatr 2012;51(11):1197–207.e4.

[19] Arnsten AFT. Toward a new understanding of Attention-deficit hyperactivity disorder pathophysiology. An important role for the prefrontal cortex dysfunction. CNS Drugs 2009;23(1):33–41.

[20] Willcutt EG, Doyle AE, Nigg JT, Faraone SV, Pennington BF. Validity of the executive function theory of attention-deficit/hyperactivity disorder: a meta-analytic review. Biol Psychiatr 2005;57(11):1336–46.

[21] Nigg JT, Willcutt EG, Doyle AE, Sonuga-Barke EJ. Causal heterogeneity in attention-deficit/hyperactivity disorder: do we need neuropsychologically impaired subtypes? Biol Psychiatr 2005;57(11):1224–30.

[22] Dickstein SG, Bannon K, Castellanos FX, Milham MP. The neural correlates of attention deficit hyperactivity disorder: an ALE meta-analysis. J Child Psychol Psychiatr 2006;47(10):1051–62.

[23] Noreika V, Falter CM, Rubia K. Timing deficits in attention-deficit/hyperactivity disorder (ADHD): evidence from neurocognitive and neuroimaging studies. Neuropsychologia 2013;51(2):235–66.

[24] Smith AB,Taylor E, Brammer M, Halari R, Rubia K. Reduced activation in right lateral prefrontal cortex and anterior cingulate gyrus in medication-naive adolescents with attention deficit hyperactivity disorder during time discrimination. J Child Psychol Psychiatr 2008;49:977–85.

[25] Rubia K, Halari R, Christakou A, Taylor E. Impulsiveness as a timing disturbance: Neurocognitive abnormalities in attention-deficit hyperactivity disorder during temporal processes and normalization with methylphenidate. Philosoph Transac Royal Soc B 2009;364:1919–31.

[26] Valera EM, Spencer RMC, Zeffiro TA, Makris N, Spencer TJ, Faraone SV, Biederman J, Seidman LJ. Neural substrates of impaired sensorimotor timing in adult attention-deficit/hyperactivity disorder. Biol Psychiatr 2010;68:359–67.

[27] Smith A, Cubillo A, Barrett N, Giampietro V, Simmons A, Brammer M, Rubia K. Archival Report: Neurofunctional effects of methylphenidate and atomoxetine in boys with attention-deficit/hyperactivity disorder during time discrimination. Biol Psychiatr 2013;74(8):615–22.

[28] Barkley RA. Why emotional impulsiveness should be a central feature of ADHD. ADHD Rep 2010:1–5.

[29] Martel MM. Research review: a new perspective on attention-deficit/hyperactivity disorder: emotion dysregulation and trait models. J Child Psychol Psychiatr 2009;50(9):1042–51.

[30] Vidal R, Valero S, Nogueira M, Palomar G, Corrales M, Richarte V, Bosch R, Gómez-Barros N, Corominas M, Casas M, Ramos-Quiroga J.A. Emotional lability: the discriminative value in the diagnosis of attention deficit/hyperactivity disorder in adults. Comprehen Psychiatr 2014;55:1712–9.

[31] Shaw P, Stringaris A, Nigg J, Leibenluft E. Emotional dysregulation and attention-deficit/hyperactivity disorder. Am J Psychiatr 2014;171(3):276–93.

[32] Kohn N, Eickhoff SB, Scheller M, Laird AR, Fox PT, Habel U. Neural network of cognitive emotion regulation – an ALE meta-analysis and MACM analysis. NeuroImage 2014;87:345–55.

[33] Hulvershorn L, Mennes M, Roy A, et al. New research: abnormal amygdala functional connectivity associated with emotional lability in children aith attention-deficit/hyperactivity disorder. J Am Acad Child Adolesc Psychiatr 2014;53:351–61.

[34] Mostofsky SH, Rimrodt SL, Schafer JGB, Boyce A, Goldberg MC, Pekar JJ, Denckla MB. Atypical motor and sensory cortex activation in attention-deficit/hyperactivity disorder: a functional magnetic resonance imaging study of simple sequential finger tapping. Biol Psychiatr 2006;59:48–56.

[35] McLeod KR, Langevin LM, Goodyear BG, Dewey D. Functional connectivity of neural motor networks is disrupted in children with developmental coordination disorder and attention-deficit / hyperactivity disorder. NeuroImage: Clinical 2014;4:566–75.

[36] Suskauer SJ, Simmonds DJ, Caffo BS, Denckla MB, Pekar JJ, Mostofsky SH. fMRI of intrasubject variability in ADHD: anomalous premotor activity with prefrontal compensation. J Am Acad Child Adolesc Psychiatr 2008;47(10):1141–50.

[37] Krause L, Enticott PG, Zangen A, Fitzgerald PB. The role of medial prefrontal cortex in theory of mind: a deep rTMS study. Behav Brain Res 2012;228(1):87–90.

[38] Schuwerk T, Schecklmann M, Langguth B, Döhnel K, Sodian B, Sommer M. Inhibiting the posterior medial prefrontal cortex by rTMS decreases the discrepancy between self and other in theory of mind reasoning. Behav Brain Res 20141;274:312–8.

[39] Hallett M. Transcranial magnetic stimulation: a primer. Neuron 2007;55(2):187–99.

[40] Chen R, Classen J, Gerloff C, Celnik P, Wassermann EM, Hallett M, et al. Depression of motor cortex excitability by low-frequency transcranial magnetic stimulation. Neurology 1997;48(5):1398–403.

[41] Pascual-Leone A, Valls-Solé J, Wassermann EM, Hallett M. Responses to rapid-rate transcranial magnetic stimulation of the human motor cortex. Brain 1994;117(4):847–58.

[42] Houdayer E, Degardin A, Cassim F, Bocquillon P, Derambure P, Devanne H. The effects of low- and high-frequency repetitive TMS on the input/output properties of the human corticospinal pathway. Exp Brain Res 2008;187(2):207–17.

[43] Wu T, Sommer M, Tergau F, Paulus W. Lasting influence of repetitive transcranial magnetic stimulation on intracortical excitability in human subjects. Neurosci Lett 2000;287(1):37–40.

[44] Ikeda T, Kurosawa M, Morimoto C, Kitayama S, Nukina N. Multiple effects of repetitive transcranial magnetic stimulation on neuropsychiatric disorders. Biochem Biophys Res Commun 2013;436(2):121–7.

[45] Strafella AP, Paus T, Barrett J, Dagher A. Repetitive transcranial magnetic stimulation of the human prefrontal cortex induces dopamine release in the caudate nucleus. J Neurosci 2001;21(15):RC157.

[46] Strafella AP, Paus T, Fraraccio M, Dagher A. Striatal dopamine release induced by repetitive transcranial magnetic stimulation of the human motor cortex. Brain. 2003;126(Pt 12):2609–15.

[47] de Andrade DC, Mhalla A, Adam F, Texeira MJ, Bouhassira D. Neuropharmacological basis of rTMS-induced analgesia: the role of endogenous opioids. Pain 2011;152(2):320–6.

[48] Pascual-Leone A, Amedi A, Fregni F, Merabet LB. The plastic human brain cortex. Annu Rev Neurosci 2005;28:377–401.

[49] Di Lazzaro V, Dileone M, Pilato F, Capone F, Musumeci G, Ranieri F, et al. Modulation of motor cortex neuronal networks by rTMS: comparison of local and remote effects of six different protocols of stimulation. J Neurophysiol 2011;105(5):2150–6.

[50] Huang YZ, Edwards MJ, Rounis E, Bhatia KP, Rothwell JC. Theta burst stimulation of the human motor cortex. Neuron 2005;45(2):201–6.

[51] Gamboa OL, Antal A, Laczo B, Moliadze V, Nitsche MA, Paulus W. Impact of repetitive theta burst stimulation on motor cortex excitability. Brain Stimul 2011;4(3):145–51.

[52] Bystritsky A, Kerwin LE, Feusner JD. A preliminary study of fMRI-guided rTMS in the treatment of generalized anxiety disorder: 6-month follow-up. J Clin Psychiatr 2009;70(3):431–2.

[53] Sokhadze EM, Baruth JM, Sears L, Sokhadze GE, El-Baz AS, Casanova MF. Prefrontal neuromodulation using rTMS improves error monitoring and correction function in autism. Appl Psychophysiol Biofeedback 2012;37(2):91–102.

[54] Vicario CM, Nitsche MA. Non-invasive brain stimulation for the treatment of brain diseases in childhood and adolescence: state of the art, current limits and future challenges. Front Syst Neurosci 2013;7:94.

[55] Lefaucheur JP, André-Obadia N, Antal A, Ayache SS, Baeken C, Benninger DH, et al. Evidence-based guidelines on the therapeutic use of repetitive transcranial magnetic stimulation (rTMS). Clin Neurophysiol 2014;125(11):2150–206.

[56] Poulet E, Brunelin J, Bediou B, Bation R, Forgeard L, Dalery J, et al. Slow transcranial magnetic stimulation can rapidly reduce resistant auditory hallucinations in schizophrenia. Biol Psychiatr 2005;57(2):188–91.

[57] Haraldsson HM, Ferrarelli F, Kalin NH, Tononi G. Transcranial Magnetic Stimulation in the investigation and treatment of schizophrenia: a review. Schizophr Res 2004;71(1):1–16.

[58] Rossi S, Hallett M, Rossini PM, Pascual-Leone A, Group SoTC. Safety, ethical considerations, and application guidelines for the use of transcranial magnetic stimulation in clinical practice and research. Clin Neurophysiol 2009;120(12):2008–39.

[59] Gilbert DL, Garvey MA, Bansal AS, Lipps T, Zhang J, Wassermann EM. Should transcranial magnetic stimulation research in children be considered minimal risk? Clin Neurophysiol 2004;115(8):1730–9.

[60] Wassermann EM. Variation in the response to transcranial magnetic brain stimulation in the general population. Clin Neurophysiol 2002;113(7):1165–71.

[61] Loo C, Sachdev P, Elsayed H, McDarmont B, Mitchell P, Wilkinson M, et al. Effects of a 2- to 4-week course of repetitive transcranial magnetic stimulation (rTMS) on neuropsychologic functioning, electroencephalogram, and auditory threshold in depressed patients. Biol Psychiatr 2001;49(7):615–23.

[62] Zangen A, Roth Y, Voller B, Hallett M. Transcranial magnetic stimulation of deep brain regions: evidence for efficacy of the H-coil. Clin Neurophysiol. 2005;116(4):775–9.

[63] Borckardt JJ, Smith AR, Hutcheson K, Johnson K, Nahas Z, Anderson B, et al. Reducing pain and unpleasantness during repetitive transcranial magnetic stimulation. J ECT 2006;22(4):259–64.

[64] Trevino K, McClintock SM, Husain MM. The use of topical lidocaine to reduce pain during repetitive transcranial magnetic stimulation for the treatment of depression. J ECT 2011;27(1):44–7.

[65] Knudsen EI. Sensitive periods in the development of the brain and behavior. J Cogn Neurosci 2004;16(8):1412–25.

[66] Weaver L, Rostain AL, Mace W, Akhtar U, Moss E, O'Reardon JP. Transcranial magnetic stimulation (TMS) in the treatment of attention-deficit/hyperactivity disorder in adolescents and young adults: a pilot study. J ECT 2012;28(2):98–103.

[67] Isenberg K, Downs D, Pierce K, Svarakic D, Garcia K, Jarvis M, et al. Low frequency rTMS stimulation of the right frontal cortex is as effective as high frequency rTMS stimulation of the left frontal cortex for antidepressant-free, treatment-resistant depressed patients. Ann Clin Psychiatr 2005;17(3):153–9.

[68] Gómez L, Vidal B, Morales L, Báez M, Maragoto C, Galvizu R, et al. Low frequency repetitive transcranial magnetic stimulation in children with attention deficit/hyperactivity disorder. Preliminary results. Brain Stimul. 2014;7(5):760–2.

[69] Helfrich C, Pierau SS, Freitag CM, Roeper J, Ziemann U, Bender S. Monitoring cortical excitability during repetitive transcranial magnetic stimulation in children with ADHD: a single-blind, sham-controlled TMS-EEG study. PLoS One 2012;7(11):e50073.

[70] Loo C, McFarquhar T, Walter G. Transcranial magnetic stimulation in adolescent depression. Australas Psychiatr 2006;14(1):81–5.

[71] El Malhany N, Gulisano M, Rizzo R, Curatolo P. Tourette syndrome and comorbid ADHD: causes and consequences. Eur J Pediatr 2014.

[72] Kwon HJ, Lim WS, Lim MH, Lee SJ, Hyun JK, Chae JH, et al. 1-Hz low frequency repetitive transcranial magnetic stimulation in children with Tourette's syndrome. Neurosci Lett 2011;492(1):1–4.

[73] Le K, Liu L, Sun M, Hu L, Xiao N. Transcranial magnetic stimulation at 1 Hertz improves clinical symptoms in children with Tourette syndrome for at least 6 months. J Clin Neurosci 2013;20(2):257–62.

[74] Bloch Y, Harel EV, Aviram S, Govezensky J, Ratzoni G, Levkovitz Y. Positive effects of repetitive transcranial magnetic stimulation on attention in ADHD subjects: a randomized controlled pilot study. World J Biol Psychiatr 2010;11(5):755–8.

[75] Ustohal L, Prikryl R, Kucerova HP, Sisrova M, Stehnova I, Venclikova S, et al. Emotional side effects after high-frequency rTMS of the right dorsolateral prefrontal cortex in an adult patient with ADHD and comorbid depression. Psychiatr Danub 2012;24(1):102–3.

[76] Niederhofer H. Effectiveness of the repetitive transcranial magnetic stimulation (rTMS) of 1 Hz for attention-deficit hyperactivity disorder (ADHD). Psychiatr Danub 2008;20(1):91–2.

[77] Niederhofer H. Additional biological therapies for attention-deficit hyperactivity disorder: repetitive transcranial magnetic stimulation of 1 Hz helps to reduce methylphenidate. Clin Pract 2012;2(1):e8.

[78] Hwang JH, Kim SH, Park CS, Bang SA, Kim SE. Acute high-frequency rTMS of the left dorsolateral prefrontal cortex and attentional control in healthy young men. Brain Res 2010;1329:152–8.

[79] Cho SS, Pellecchia G, Ko JH, Ray N, Obeso I, Houle S, et al. Effect of continuous theta burst stimulation of the right dorsolateral prefrontal cortex on cerebral blood flow changes during decision making. Brain Stimul 2012;5(2):116–23.

[80] Cho SS, Koshimori Y, Aminian K, Obeso I, Rusjan P, Lang AE, et al. Investing in the future: stimulation of the medial prefrontal cortex reduces discounting of delayed rewards. Neuropsychopharmacology. 2015;40(3):546–53.

[81] Beeli G, Koeneke S, Gasser K, Jancke L. Brain stimulation modulates driving behavior. Behav Brain Funct 2008;4:34.

[82] Hsu TY, Tseng LY, Yu JX, Kuo WJ, Hung DL, Tzeng OJ, et al. Modulating inhibitory control with direct current stimulation of the superior medial frontal cortex. Neuroimage 2011;56(4):2249–57.

[83] Rossini PM, Barker AT, Berardelli A, Caramia MD, Caruso G, Cracco RQ, Dimitrijevic MR, Hallett M, Katayama Y, Lucking CH. Non-invasive electrical and magnetic stimulation of the brain, spinal cord and roots: basic principles and procedures for routine clinical application. Report of an IFCN committee. Electroencephalogr Clin Neurophysiol 1994;91:79–92.

Chapter 16

Updates on the Use of Natural Treatments for Attention-Deficit Hyperactivity Disorder (ADHD)

June Bryan dela Peña, Chrislean Jun Botanas,
Reinholdger Tampus, Irene Joy dela Peña,
Hee Jin Kim, Ike dela Peña and Jae Hoon Cheong

Additional information is available at the end of the chapter

http://dx.doi.org/10.5772/60840

Abstract

Attention-deficit/hyperactivity disorder (ADHD) is the most common neurodevelopmental disorder of childhood characterized by the three core symptoms of hyperactivity, impulsiveness, and sustained inattention. While the etiology of ADHD remains unknown, several studies suggest ADHD pathophysiology to involve frontal network abnormality and dysregulation of catecholaminergic and dopaminergic functions. Stimulants, which are structurally similar to endogenous catecholamines, are the most commonly prescribed drugs for treatment of ADHD, but are classified as Schedule II based on the Controlled Substances Act due to high likelihood for diversion and abuse. Non-stimulant medications, as well as antidepressants, have also been used in ADHD treatment but have been found to be inferior to stimulant interventions and to cause intolerable side effects. The search for safer yet effective ADHD treatments led to a growing interest in natural medicines and a host of other complementary and alternative treatments for ADHD. While the use of these therapies is well documented, not much is known about their safety and efficacy. In this chapter, we describe current evidence-based complementary and alternative therapies for ADHD, focusing on nutritional and botanical agents, and provide details on the performance of these agents in clinical trials. Here, we discuss the rationale for the use of natural products for ADHD, mention the potential mechanisms of action of these treatments, and highlight safety and efficacy issues associated with the use of these treatments. In conclusion, we give an exhaustive update on the use of nutritional and botanical medicines as complementary and alternative ADHD therapies for ADHD, which could potentially provide important information on the efficacy and safety of these types of interventions.

Keywords: ADHD, natural, herbal, botanical, nutritional

1. Introduction

Attention deficit hyperactivity disorder (ADHD) is a neurodevelopmental disorder of childhood, characterized by the three core symptoms of hyperactivity, impulsivity, and inattention [1]. Diagnosis of ADHD has been on the rise since it was recognized as a specific disorder in the 1970s. Currently, the worldwide prevalence rate of ADHD is approximately 5%, making it the most common psychiatric disorder among children [2]. In addition, although most frequently diagnosed during childhood, ADHD may affect an individual throughout life [3]. Given its serious academic, social, and familial consequences, along with the risk of incurring comorbid conditions and later substance abuse, it is imperative to develop efficacious treatments for ADHD [4].

2. Treatment of ADHD: An overview

Numerous treatment strategies for ADHD have been implemented over the years. Conventional treatment usually includes a pharmaceutical and a non-pharmacological intervention such as behavioral/psychosocial approaches. We describe in the following text some of the widely used pharmacological and non-pharmacological ADHD treatments as well as safety and efficacy and issues or limitations associated with the use of these interventions.

2.1. Pharmacological interventions

ADHD has been associated with dysfunctions in catecholaminergic function in the brain [5]. The fact that medications that increase brain catecholamine levels have been shown to alleviate ADHD symptoms provided solid support for the use of pharmacological treatments for ADHD [5]. Drugs used in managing ADHD are classified as stimulant and non-stimulant medications. Stimulant or psychostimulant drugs are the most common pharmacological intervention for ADHD [6, 7]. These drugs (e.g., methylphenidate and dextroamphetamine) are structurally similar to endogenous catecholamines. They work by increasing extracellular dopamine and norepinephrine levels in order to restore the dysregulated neurotransmitter balance in the brain of ADHD patients [5]. Methylphenidate (Ritalin® or Concerta®) is the most prescribed and used psychostimulant accounting for around 70% of ADHD patients who are under stimulant treatment [6, 8, 9].

Non-stimulant medications such as the norepinephrine specific reuptake inhibitor, atomoxetine, as well as antidepressants such as imipramine, phenelzine, and bupropion have also been

http://dx.doi.org/10.5772/60840

used in the treatment of ADHD [9, 10]. Similar to psychostimulants, these drugs act by increasing catecholamine levels in the brain, thus correcting the perceived neurotransmitter imbalance. However, non-stimulants have been found to be inferior to stimulant drugs on efficacy endpoints [6, 10].

Although pharmacological interventions generally improve ADHD symptoms for most children, as many as 20–30% of children either do not respond to these drugs or are unable to tolerate them due to the wide range of side/adverse effects they may produce [11, 12]. Common side effects associated with stimulant use are decreased appetite, insomnia, and headache [11]. Other side effects such as motor tics, abdominal pain, irritability, nausea, and fatigue have also been reported [9, 13]. For this reason, some parents are unwilling to medicate their children with stimulants due to concerns about the safety and risks associated with the long-term use. In addition, stimulants also have a high likelihood for diversion and abuse, and are classified as Schedule II based on the Controlled Substances Act. This is a major concern since ADHD has also been associated with increased risk of substance use disorder [14].

2.2. Non-pharmacological interventions

A variety of non-pharmacological interventions is available for treating ADHD. These treatment strategies can either be used alone or in combination with pharmacological therapy [13]. Behavioral therapy, also known as behavioral modification, is one of the most common, effective, and accepted non-pharmacological treatment for ADHD. This therapy, which typically involves reinforcing desired behaviors through rewards and praise and decreasing problem behaviors by setting limits and consequences, has shown great promise particularly in youth and adults with ADHD [15, 16]. Another form of behavioral therapy is social skills training. This is conducted in a group setting where a therapist or a teacher demonstrates appropriate social behaviors and then encourages patients to repeat and practice those behaviors [16, 17]. Other potential approaches include memory training through the use of computer software (Cogmed), electroencephalography biofeedback or neurofeedback, exercise, yoga, meditation, acupuncture, and green space [12, 18, 19]. As these therapies are not widely available, only a few patients can benefit from the effects of behavioral therapy. Despite the fact that these interventions are easy to implement, time demands, the need of a professional therapist, and participation by family members and teachers also limit the use of behavioral ADHD treatments.

Over the years, there has been much interest and controversy on the importance of food and diet and its potential role in ADHD and ADHD symptomatology [20]. Some food items have been shown to cause or worsen ADHD symptoms in children. The strategy, therefore, is to identify offensive food items and eliminate these items from the child's diet in order to prevent or minimize the occurrence of ADHD symptoms. This can be done by eliminating the particular food item (single-food elimination) or multiple food elements that are most commonly reported to cause ADHD symptoms. Common culprits include sugar, dairy products, junk foods, food additives, preservative, and others [18, 21]. Another dietary regimen that has been gaining support is the "oligoantigenic" or "few foods" diet, which entails strict removal of nearly all foods, except a limited number that have been proven to cause no problems or are deemed "hypoallergenic" [18, 19, 21]. However, due to inadequate research on the efficacy of these regimens, employing dietary modifications to treat ADHD is still controversial. Furthermore, continued compliance and nutritional imbalances are causes of concern for dietary treatments.

3. Natural health products for ADHD

3.1. Rationale for the use of natural health products

In view of the safety and efficacy issues of current pharmacological interventions, and the desire for safer yet effective ADHD treatments, there has been a growing interest in natural health products (e.g., botanical/herbal medicines, vitamins, and minerals) and other complementary and alternative medicines for ADHD [12, 18, 19]. It has been estimated that more than 50% of parents of children with ADHD treat their child using one or more of these products [22-25]. Despite their growing popularity, physicians are still reluctant to recommend these products, as they question the efficacy of these treatments. Thus, only a few families disclose the use of these products to their child's physician [18, 24, 25]. Research is still underway to demonstrate the effectiveness of natural products in the treatment of ADHD. In the following sections, we describe some of the widely used natural medicines for ADHD, discuss the potential mechanism of action of these agents, and give updates on their performance in recent clinical research.

3.2. Updates on natural treatments for ADHD: evidence from clinical studies

3.2.1. Botanical agents

Botanical agents or herbal medicines are popular alternative treatment for ADHD, as they appeal to parents looking for a more "natural" treatment for their child [12, 18]. Certain botanical agents have shown promise in the treatment of ADHD in light of the findings of clinical trials [Table 1].

Herb	Methods	Results	Proposed mechanism of action	Safety and efficacy	Reference
Pycnogenol	· Randomized, double-blind, placebo-controlled, study. · 61 children, 6-14 y/o with ADHD (n=44 pycnogenol vs. n=17 placebo).	Significant attenuation of hyperactivity and improvement of attention.	Increased production of nitric oxide that is involved in the regulation of norepinephrine and dopamine release and intake.	Mild side effects, such as a rise in slowness and gastric discomfort, were reported	Trebatická et al., 2006 [26]

Herb	Methods	Results	Proposed mechanism of action	Safety and efficacy	Reference
	· Pycnogenol (1 mg/kg/ day) or placebo treatment for 4 weeks.				
	· Randomized, double-blind, placebo-controlled study. · 61 outpatient children, 6-14 y/o with ADHD (n= not specified Pycnogenol v. placebo) · Pycnogenol (1 mg/kg/ day) or placebo treatment for 4 weeks	Improvement of attention, reduction of oxidative damage to DNA and normalization of the total antioxidant status.	Potent antioxidant properties.	No reported adverse effects.	Chovanová et al., 2006 [27]
	· Randomized, double-blind, placebo-controlled, crossover study. · 24 adults, 24-53 y/o with ADHD (n= not specified Pycnogenol vs. placebo vs. methylphenidate) · Duration of treatment is 3 weeks	Neither methylphenidate nor Pycnogenol outperformed the placebo control on any ADHD rating scale employed.			Tenenbaum et al., 2002 [30]
St. John's Wort *(Hypericum perforatum)*	· Randomized, placebo-controlled trial. · 3 adolescents, 14-16 y/o with ADHD (n=2 St. John's Wort v. n=1 placebo). · St. John's Wort (30 mg/day) or placebo treatment, for 4 weeks.	Improvement of hyperactivity, inattention and immaturity symptoms.	Inhibition of serotonin and norepinephrine reuptake.	No reported adverse effects.	Niederhofer H., 2010 [33]
	· Randomized, double-blind, placebo-controlled trial.	No significant improvement in ADHD symptoms.	Inhibit serotonin and norepinephrine reuptake	No reported adverse effects.	Weber et al., 2008 [34]

Herb	Methods	Results	Proposed mechanism of action	Safety and efficacy	Reference
	· 56 children, 6-17 y/o with ADHD (n=27 SJW v. n=27 placebo). · *H. perforatum* (300 mg) or placebo, 3 times a day for 8 weeks.				
Gingko Biloba	· Open clinical pilot study · 20 children with ADHD · Ginkgo (EGb 761®), 240 mg daily, was administered for 3 to 5 weeks.	Improvement of ADHD core symptoms.	Elevation of brain electrical activity, particularly in contingent negative variation (CNV) amplitude.	A very low rate of mild adverse effects occurred during the observation period.	Uebel-von Sanderslebe n et al., 2014 [36]
	· Randomized, double-blind controlled trial. · 50 children, 6-14 y/o with ADHD(n=25 Ginkgo biloba vs. n=25 methylphenidate) · *Gingko biloba* (80-120 mg/day) or methylphenidate (20-30 mg/day), for 16 weeks.	Gingko Biloba was less effective than methylphenidate in the treatment of ADHD.	Reverse inhibition of MAO-A and MAO-B.	Lesser side effects (headache, insomnia, and loss of appetite) than methylphenidate	Salehi et al., 2010 [35]
Gingko Biloba and Ginseng	· Open, pilot study. 36 children, 3-17 y/o with ADHD. · Combination of herbal product containing American ginseng extract, *Panax quinquefolium* (200 mg) and *Gingko Biloba* extract (50 mg), twice a day (empty stomach) for 4 weeks.	Improvement in various attributes (anxiety, social, hyperactive-impulsive) of ADHD.	Gingko Biloba can reverse the reduction of 5-HT_{IA2} and noradrenergic receptors. It also stimulates synaptic plasticity, increased blood glucose utilization, reduces lactate and pyruvate, increases dopamine and norepinephrine, and promotes nerve growth.	Five (14%) subjects reported adverse events (more emotional & more impulsive, more hyperactive and more aggressive, sweating, headache, tiredness), only 2 of which were considered related to the study medication.	Lyon M.R. et al., 2001 [37]

http://dx.doi.org/10.5772/60840

Herb	Methods	Results	Proposed mechanism of action	Safety and efficacy	Reference
Ginseng	· Observational study · 18 children, 6-14 y/o with ADHD. · Korean red ginseng (1000 mg) twice a day, for 8 weeks.	Korean red ginseng improved inattentiveness in ADHD children.	Ginseng can boost dopamine and norepinephrine levels in the brain.	Some participants complained bad taste and a degree of repulsive feeling.	Lee et al., 2011 [38]
	· Randomized, double-blind, placebo-controlled clinical trial. · 70 children, 6-15 y/o with ADHD (n=33 Korean red ginseng v. n=37 placebo). · Korean red ginseng extract (1000 mg) and placebo, twice a day for 8 weeks.	Ginseng extract significantly improved the inattention/ hyperactivity symptoms of ADHD.	Ginseng can reduce the production of the adrenal corticosteroids, cortisol, and dehydroepiandrostero ne (DHEA).	No serious adverse reactions reported apart from loose stool by one patient from the Ginseng group.	Ko et al., 2014 [39]
Valerian *(Valeriana officinalis)*	· Double-blind, placebo-controlled pilot study. · 30 children, 5-11 y/o with ADHD (n=10 Valeriana officinalis mother tincture (VOMT) or n=10 3x potency of VOMT v. n=10 placebo, for 3 weeks)	Significant improvement in ADHD symptoms was found from VOMT or 3x potency group, in comparison to placebo	Valerian's main active compound, valerenic acid, inhibits the breakdown of GABA in the central nervous system, an action similar to that of benzodiazepine drugs.	No reported side/ adverse effects.	Razlog et al., 2011 [40]
Ningdong granule	· Randomized, double-blind, methylphenidate-controlled trial. · 72 children, 6-13 y/o with ADHD (n=36 Ningdong v. n=36 methylphenidate). · Ningdong (5 mg/kg/ day) vs methylphenidate (1	Similar to methylphenidate, Ningdong granule ameliorated ADHD symptoms.	Regulation of dopaminergic activity by increasing homovanillic acid content of in sera.	Hypersomnia was reported as Ningdong granule's side effects. Methylphenidate had more side effects than Ningdong granule.	Li et al., 2011 [41]

Herb	Methods	Results	Proposed mechanism of action	Safety and efficacy	Reference
	mf/kg/day), for 8 weeks.				
Bacopa *(Bacopa monniera)*	· Open-label study · 31 children, 6-12 y/o with ADHD. · Standardized *Bacopa monniera* extract (SBME) (225 mg/day), for 6 months.	SBME significantly reduced ADHD symptom; reduced scores in restlessness, impulsiveness, learning problems, impulsivity, and psychiatric problems.	Bacopa was shown to increase dopamine levels in the cortex. In addition, it also possesses neuroprotective, antioxidant, and memory-enhancing effects.	SBME was found to be safe and tolerable in children. Only mild gastrointestinal side effects (e.g. nausea) were observed in 3 subjects.	Dave et al., 2014 [42]

Table 1. Botanical agents for ADHD

3.2.1.1. Pycnogenol® (French maritime pine bark extract)

Pycnogenol® is a standardized extract from the bark of French maritime pine (*Pinus pinaster*). This extract was reported to have a rich store of phenolic acids, catechin, taxifolin, and procyanidins, each with diverse biological effects. A number of studies have suggested that Pycnogenol® may be beneficial for ADHD and its symptoms. Of note, a double-blind, placebo-controlled study of 61 children (ages 6–14 years old) found that Pycnogenol® (1mg/kg/day) ameliorated the symptoms of ADHD including reduced hyperactivity, increased attention, and improved visual-motor coordination [26]. Only mild side effects (a rise in slowness and gastric discomfort) were reported. These benefits of Pycnogenol® on ADHD symptoms were attributed to its ability to increase nitric oxide production. Nitric oxide plays a role in the regulation of norepinephrine and dopamine release and intake [26]. Another study (randomized, double-blind, placebo-controlled) also reported that Pycnogenol® administration (1 mg/kg/day) improves attention of ADHD children, coupled with reduction of oxidative damage to DNA and normalization of total antioxidant status [27]. The potent antioxidant properties of Pycnogenol® are thought to be beneficial to ADHD given the presumed role of oxidative stress in the etiology of this disorder [28]. Pycnogenol® was also shown to normalize urinary catecholamine concentration of children with ADHD [29] and is believed to act as a vasodilator improving cerebral blood flow to brain regions involved in ADHD [19]. Contrastingly, Tenenbaum *et al.* [30] reported that Pycnogenol® failed to produce treatment effects in adults (24–53 years old) with ADHD over a period of 3 weeks. However, it should be noted that in this study neither Pycnogenol® nor the positive control, methylphenidate, outperformed placebo on any ADHD rating scale [31]. In summary, Pycnogenol® is a promising botanical alternative for the management of ADHD and its symptoms; however, more studies are needed before it can be used as a stand-alone ADHD treatment.

http://dx.doi.org/10.5772/60840

3.2.1.2. St. John's wort (Hypericum perforatum)

St. John's wort is best known for its antidepressant effects. It is an alternative option for treating mild-to-moderate depression, even in children under the age of 12, with few side effects [18]. This herb was also demonstrated to have beneficial effects on other psychiatric disorders, including major depression, bipolar depression, obsessive-compulsive disorder, social phobia, and somatization disorder [32]. It has been suggested that the effects of St. John's wort may be related to its ability to inhibit the reuptake of serotonin, norepinephrine, and dopamine [33]. For this reason, the effect of St. John's wort was tested in a preliminary study in three ADHD patients (14–16 years old) and the result showed that St. John's wort improved ADHD symptoms [33]. In contrast, a much more rigorous (randomized, double-blind, placebo-controlled) trial reported that St. John's wort (300 mg/day) did not improve ADHD symptoms in 54 children (aged 6–17 years old), after 8 weeks of intervention [34]. Thus, the effects of St. John's wort on ADHD is still unclear, necessitating further studies.

3.2.1.3. Ginkgo biloba

Ginkgo biloba is a unique species of a tree native to East Asia. The memory enhancing effects of *G. biloba* has been extensively studied, and it is being utilized as an alternative treatment for memory impairment and dementia [35]. Some studies also reported that the ginkgo has beneficial effects on ADHD. Uebel-von Sandersleben *et al.* [36] reported that *G. biloba* (240 mg, daily) improved core symptoms of ADHD in children, following 3–5 weeks of treatment. *G. biloba* (50 mg) was also found to alleviate ADHD symptoms in children (36 kids, ages 3–17), when administered with ginseng (200 mg), over the course of 4 weeks [37]. In this study, minor side effects were observed (e.g., subjects became more emotional and more impulsive, more hyperactive and more aggressive, sweating, headache, tiredness) [37]. The beneficial effects of *G. biloba* on ADHD are attributed to its various activities such as (1) improvement of cerebrovascular blood flow that may help reduce hyperactivity due to lack of focus, (2) reversal of 5-HT1A and noradrenergic receptor reductions, and (3) inhibition of both MAO-A and MAO-B in the brain [35, 37]. However, a 6-week double-blind randomized controlled trial by Salehi *et al.* [35] found that *G. biloba* (80–120 mg/day) was less effective than methylphenidate in managing ADHD symptoms in a sample of 50 children.

3.2.1.4. Ginseng

Ginseng has been shown to improve ADHD symptoms [37]. Ginseng, both American (*Panax quinquefolius*) and Asian (*Panax ginseng*), is known to produce beneficial effects on the body. Ginseng species contain a class of phytochemicals called ginsenosides, which are known as potent antioxidants and exert neuroprotective properties [38, 39]. Ginsenosides have also been reported to boost levels of dopamine and norepinephrine in the brain. In this sense, ginseng may effectively alleviate symptoms of ADHD. Indeed, an observational clinical study showed that Korean red ginseng (KRG) (*Panax ginseng*), given at 1,000 mg, twice a day, for 8 weeks, improved inattentiveness in children (18 kids, ages 6–14) with ADHD [38]. In addition, a double-blind randomized placebo-controlled trial reported that 100 mg of KRG, taken twice a day, decreased inattention and hyperactivity scores of ADHD children (ages 6–15 years old), after an 8-week treatment period [39]. Side effects associated with ginseng use included perspiration, headache, fatigue, and a degree of repulsive feeling experienced by patients due to the unique flavor of red ginseng [38]. Thus, ginseng has the potential to be used as a complementary and alternative therapy for ADHD, provided that its efficacy and safety issues are resolved.

3.2.1.5. Valerian (Valeriana officinalis)

Valerian is a perineal plant that is known to have sedative and antispasmodic effects. Valerian has been used as a treatment for insomnia, restlessness, and anxiety [12]. Its application in the management of ADHD has also been evaluated. In a double-blind, placebo-controlled, pilot study, it was shown that treatment with Valerian tincture for two weeks improved ADHD symptoms in children (30 kids) aged 5–11 years old [40]. The effects of Valerian are thought to be facilitated by the action of valerenic acid, one of its major components, on the gamma-aminobutyric acid $(GABA)_A$ receptor. Valerian is generally safe and its use on children ages 3–12 years is approved by the European Scientific Cooperative on Phytotherapy, provided that it is used under medical supervision [12, 18, 40]. Nevertheless, the use of valerian as an alternative treatment for ADHD is limited by the insufficient clinical evidence supporting its efficacy.

3.2.1.6. Ningdong

Ningdong granule (NDG) is a Chinese medicinal preparation that has been used for various medicinal purposes for many years now. As it showed therapeutic benefits in the treatment of Tourette syndrome [41], the effects of Ningdong were evaluated in ADHD patients. Accordingly, Li *et al.* [41] performed a randomized, methylphenidate-controlled, doubled-blinded trial, where 72 children with ADHD were given NDG (5 mg/kg/day) or methylphenidate (1 mg/kg/day) for 8 weeks. Results showed that NDG has equivalent effect to methylphenidate in improving ADHD symptoms, but with lesser side effects. They also reported that NDG was well tolerated by children with ADHD as revealed by blood, urine, and stool analysis, and renal and hepatic function assessments. Interestingly, levels of homovanillic acid, which is involved in the regulation of dopamine, in the sera increased in the NDG group without causing any change in dopamine concentration. Thus, the authors suggested that NDG is a promising, safe, and effective alternative therapy for ADHD. However, more research needs to be done before NDG can be used as an alternative ADHD treatment.

3.2.1.7. Bacopa (Bacopa monniera)

Bacopa also known as water hyssop or Brahmi is an Ayurvedic medicine that has been used for many centuries for its positive effects on memory, learning, and concentration. Preliminary studies have shown that Bacopa has benefits (i.e., improvement in memory and learning tasks) in children with ADHD [12]. These findings were supported by an open-label study demonstrating that Bacopa extract (225 mg/day), given for a period of 6 months, significantly alleviated the ADHD symptoms of 31 children, ages 6–12 years old [42]. The positive effects of Bacopa on ADHD are thought to be achieved via cholinesterase inhibition, dopamine regulation, neuroprotective, and/or antioxidant effects [12, 42]. Bacopa was well-tolerated by children, with only mild gastrointestinal side effects (nausea) reported [42]. Further studies (e.g., double-blind, randomized clinical trials) are necessary to verify the efficacy of this botanical agent as a therapy for ADHD.

3.2.2. *Nutritional medicines/supplements*

Studies have shown that certain vitamins and minerals may also play a role in the pathology of ADHD. Accordingly, a multitude of vitamins, minerals, and other nutritional supplements have been proposed as complementary and alternative treatment for ADHD [Table 2].

Supplement	Methods	Results	Proposed mechanism of action	Safety and efficacy	Reference
Vitamin B6 and Magnesium	· Open study · 76 children (40 ADHD children & 36 healthy children) · All children were given a magnesium-vitamin B6 (Mg-B6) regimen (6 mg/kg/d Mg, 0.6 mg/kg/d vit-B6) for 8 weeks.	Mg-B6 treatment significantly attenuated hyperactivity and aggressiveness. School attention was also improved.	Vitamin B6 facilitates the production of the serotonin. Magnesium has been shown to be a non-specific inhibitor of calcium channels, and could act as NMDA channel inhibitor. In the same way, it could also influence catecholamine signaling in the brain.	No reported side effects	Mousain-Bosc et al., (2006) [43]
Zinc	· Randomized, double-blind, parallel-group placebo-controlled · 400 children 6-14 y/o (n=202 zinc vs. n=198 placebo) · 150 mg zinc sulfate or 150 mg sucrose (placebo) daily for 12 weeks	Zinc sulfate was better than placebo in decreasing hyperactivity, impulsivity and improving socialization, but not inattention.	Deficiency in zinc is suggested to play a role in hyperactivity, concentration impairment and delay of cognitive development.	No serious side effects reported. However, metallic taste was a common complaint.	Bilici M et al., (2004) [47]
	· Randomized, double-blind, placebo-control · 44 children, 5-11 y/o (n=22 methylphenidate	Significantly greater treatment effects were observed in zinc sulfate with	Zinc regulates dopamine function, indirectly, through its action on melatonin.	Nausea and metallic taste were frequent complaints from	Akhondzadeh et al., (2004) [46]

Supplement	Methods	Results	Proposed mechanism of action	Safety and efficacy	Reference
	+zinc vs. n=22 methylphenidate +placebo) · Methylphenidate 1mg/kg/day; 55 mg/day zinc sulfate; sucrose (placebo) 55 mg, for 6 weeks	methylphenidate over placebo with methylphenidate.		the participants. Overall, it was well tolerated.	
	· Randomized, double-blind, placebo-controlled, pilot trial · 52 children 6-14 y/o (n=20 Zinc_1 or n=8 Zinc_2 v. n=24 placebo) · Zinc_1 15 mg/day (once a day) or Zinc_2 30 mg/day (twice a day) or placebo (8 weeks); amphetamine 5-15 mg/daily (based on the weight) · Duration of experiment was 13 weeks (8 weeks controlled + 5 weeks amphetamine add-on)	No appreciable difference between both dosages of zinc and placebo The addition of amphetamine to zinc supplementation did not alter the result.	Zinc is an important cofactor in the metabolism of relevant to neurotransmitters, prostaglandins, and melatonin and indirectly affects dopamine metabolism. Specific to ADHD, the dopamine transporter has a zinc building site that blocks transport.	1 patient reported gastrointestinal discomfort.	Arnold L et al., (2011) [48]
Iron	·Randomized, double-blind, placebo-controlled, pilot trial · 23 children with low serum ferritin level (<30 ng/mL) 5-8 y/o (n=18 iron vs. n=5 placebo) · 80 mg ferrous sulfate tablets or placebo once daily in the morning for 12 weeks	Iron supplementation significantly improved hyperactive/ impulsive and inattentive symptoms of ADHD.	Iron is a co-factor in the synthesis of both norepinephrine and dopamine. Iron deficiency was also strongly suggested to correlate with ADHD and restless leg syndrome.	Minor side effects were reported, such as nausea, constipation, and abdominal pain.	Konofal E et al., (2008) [49]

Supplement	Methods	Results	Proposed mechanism of action	Safety and efficacy	Reference
Essential fatty acid supplement	· Randomized, double-blind, placebo-controlled · Initially, 41 children participated but were reduced to 29 children due to side effects, 8-12 y/o (n=15 HUFA v. n=14 placebo) · *Highly unsaturated fatty acid (HUFA) supplement* (daily doses: EPA 186 mg, DHA 480 mg, γ-linolenic acid 96 mg, vitamin E 60 IU, *cis*-linoleic acid 864 mg, AA 42 mg and thyme oil 8 mg) or olive oil (placebo), for 12 weeks	HUFA supplementation significantly attenuated ADHD-related symptoms.	HUFA can profoundly influence signal transduction.	A digestive upset and difficulty of swallowing were the only documented complaints.	Ricahrdson and Puri B. (2002) [53]
	· Open-label, proof-of-efficacy pilot study · 9 children 8-16 y/o · 16.2 g EPA/DHA concentrates per day. The dosage was adjusted dependent on the ratio of arachidonic acid (AA) to EPA in the isolated plasma phospholipids at four weeks	High dose of EPA/DHA supplement improved ADHD-related symptoms	Children with ADHD were found to have low levels of LC PUFAs, including AA, EPA and DHA in the plasma phospholipids, as well as high ratio of AA to EPA.	One participant reported of loose stools while taking 30 ml of the liquid of EPA/DHA concentrate per day.	Sorgi P et al., (2007) [52]
	· Randomized, double-blind, cross-over, placebo-controlled · 132 children (104 completers) 7-12 y/o (n=36 PUFAs v. n= 41 PUFA + micronutrients v. n=27 placebo)	Significant treatment effects were found for parents rating of ADHD symptoms in both PUFA treatment groups compared to placebo.	PUFAs are key components all cellular and intracellular membranes or phospholipids, where they perform vital structural and chemical functions	No reported adverse effects.	Sinn N and Bryan J, (2007) [55]

Supplement	Methods	Results	Proposed mechanism of action	Safety and efficacy	Reference
	· Six PUFA capsules 400 mg fish oil and 100 mg evening primrose oil or six palm oil (placebo) capsules a day, for 15 weeks	Single crossover (placebo to PUFA) for another 15 weeks reiterated these results. No additional effects from micronutrients are noted.	Other nutrients and vitamins are involved in the PUFA role of synthesizing prostaglandins, chemicals with important biological roles in brain function		
	· Randomized, one-way cross-over, placebo-controlled (Phase 1 double-blind; phase 2 single blind) · 7-12 y/o Phase 1- 132 children with ADHD (n= not specified) PUFA vs. PUFA+ multivitamins/ minerals vs. placebo, for 15 weeks · Phase 2- 109 ADHD children (n=not specified) all children were given PUFA+ multivitamins/minerals for another 15 weeks · Six active or six placebo capsules per day	After 15 weeks, improvements from the PUFA group in their ability to switch and control attention compared to the placebo group. Similar observation from the placebo group after taking PUFA supplement from weeks 16-30. No significant improvements in other cognitive measures, or with additional micronutrient supplementation	PUFA have been associated with dopamine activity in the frontal lobes of the brain.	Slight nausea was reported in two patients and one report episodes of nose bleeding.	Sinn N, Bryan J, and Wilson C, (2008) [57]
	· Randomized, double-blind, single-center, placebo-controlled (15 weeks) (phase 1) followed by an open-label extension (15 weeks) (phase 2) · Phase 1- 200 children 6-13 y/o	Omega-3 supplement significantly attenuated hyperactivity/ impulsivity, as well as mood/behavior dysregulation.	Omega3 LC-PUFA has been linked to brain and central nervous system functioning, and a deficiency in Omega3 fatty acids in rats and monkeys is associated with behavioral, sensory,	No major adverse effects documented apart from gastrointestinal discomfort, atopic dermatitis, hyperactivity, tics, nausea, elevated	Manor I et al., (2012) [56]

Supplement	Methods	Results	Proposed mechanism of action	Safety and efficacy	Reference
	· 2 capsules phosphatidylserine (PS)-Omega 3 (300 mg of PS and 120 mg of EPA + DHA) or 2 capsules filled with cellulose (placebo) 2 times/day. · Phase 2 – · 150 children all participants received two capsules of PS-Omega3 daily which provided 150 mg of PS and 60 mg of EPA + DHA	Sustained efficacy were noted who continued to received PS-Omega 3 in the open-label extension	and neurological dysfunction.	serum glutamic oxaloacetic transaminase (SGOT) and tantrum episodes	
	· Randomized, double-blind, placebo-controlled · 78 children 7-13 y/o (n=39 EFA supplement v. n=39 placebo Vitamin C.) · EFA capsule (240 mg of linoleic acid (LA), 60 mg of a-linolenic acid (ALA), 95 mg of mineral oil, and 5 mg of a-tocopherol (as an antioxidant) 2 times/day or Vit. C (500 mg ascorbic acid) 2 times/day, for 7 weeks	Although both interventions ameliorated some ADHD symptoms, no significant differences were found between the groups.	Essential fatty acids (EFA) are needed for normal sensory, cognitive, and motor function	Well tolerated and no adverse effects were reported.	Raz R, Carasso RL, Yehuda S (2009) [58]
	· Randomized, double-blind, placebo-controlled · 50 children 6-13 y/o (n=25 LC-Polyunsaturated fatty	No apparent benefit was noted for the PUFA supplementation for the ADHD symptoms	PUFA supplement contains DHA. DHA is thought to reflect the proportion of FA in the brain, and a decrease of the former in the blood might mediate	Well tolerated and no adverse effects were reported.	Stevens L et al., (2003) [54]

Supplement	Methods	Results	Proposed mechanism of action	Safety and efficacy	Reference
	acids (PUFAs) v. n=25 placebo olive oil · 8 capsules of PUFA or placebo a day, for 4 months		the abnormal neuronal signaling that results in aberrant behaviors.		
	· Randomized, double-blind, placebo-controlled · 54 children 6-12 y/o (n=27 Docosahexaenoic acid (DHA) v. n=27 placebo) · 345 mg of DHA per day (n=32) or a placebo capsule (n =31) for 4 months	DHA supplementation did not significantly improve in any objective or subjective measure of ADHD symptoms.	There is a direct relationship between plasma phospholipid DHA content and metabolism of serotonin and dopamine within the central nervous system DHA and other polyunsaturated fatty acids may influence synaptic functions through effects on membrane structures.	Well tolerated and no adverse effects were reported.	Voigt et al., (2001) [60]
	· Randomized, double-blind, placebo-controlled · 40 children with ADHD 6-12 y/o (n=20 docosahexaenoic acid (DHA) v. n=20 placebo) · DHA group took fermented soybean milk (600 mg DHA/125 ml, 3/week), bread rolls (300 mg DHA/ 45 g, 2/ week) and steamed bread (600 mg DHA/60 g, 2/week) or placebo foods containing olive oil instead of DHA-rich fish oil for 2 weeks.	DHA supplementation did not improve ADHD-related symptoms.	Levels of DHA was significantly lower in the serum phospholipid fraction in hyperactive children	No serious side effects were reported in the study.	Hirayama S, Hamazaki T, and Terasawa K (2004) [59]

Supplement	Methods	Results	Proposed mechanism of action	Safety and efficacy	Reference
Acetyl-L-Carnitine	· Randomized, double-blind placebo-controlled, parallel, and multicenter · 51 children(ADHD and Fragile X syndrome) 6-13 y/o (n=24 ALC v. n=27 placebo) · Acetyl-L-Carnitine (20-50 mg/kg/day) 500 mg 2 times/day or placebo for 52 weeks	Acetyl-L-Carnitine significantly ameliorated the symptoms of ADHD over placebo on Clinical Global Impressions (CGI) parental rating, but not on CGI teacher's rating.	Acetyl-L-Carnitine was found to improve learning and attenuate the hyperactivity in a rat model of neonatal anoxia	Safe and tolerable with no side effects reported	Torrioli et al., (2008) [62]
	· Multi-site parallel-group double-blind randomized pilot trial · 112 children 5-12 y/o (n=53 Acetyl-L-Carnitine v. n=59 placebo) · ALC in weight-based doses from 500 to 1500 mg 2 times/day or placebo for 16 weeks	No significant treatment effects to overall ADHD rating outcome. Superiority of Acetyl-L-Carnitine over placebo in the inattentive subtype	Acetyl-L-Carnitine exerts mild M3 muscarinic receptor agonism in rats, simulating acetylcholine release. The compound significantly increases glutamatergic receptor binding and protects against age-related reductions in the GABA/benzodiazepine receptor binding capacity	Safe and tolerable with no side effects reported	Arnold L et al., (2007) [63]

Table 2. Nutritional medicines/supplements for ADHD

3.3. Vitamins

Vitamins have been considered as an adjunct or alternative treatment for ADHD, although no studies have systemically evaluated their effects in ADHD patients. The use of vitamins for ADHD has been based on the finding that multivitamin supplements improved concentration and attention in children without ADHD [18]. In particular, Vitamin B6 (0.6 mg/kg/day) combined with magnesium (6 mg/kg/day) improved clinical symptoms of children with ADHD following an 8-week treatment period [43]. ADHD symptoms returned a few weeks after treatment was stopped. The beneficial effect of vitamin B6 on ADHD has been attributed to its ability to facilitate the production of the catecholamine, serotonin [12, 44]. In addition, despite not directly addressing ADHD symptoms, vitamin or multivitamin supplementation can provide additional benefits for children with ADHD, who usually have poor dietary habits [18]. Caution must be exercised, however, with the use of large doses of vitamins, existing as megavitamins or megadoses, especially in young patients, considering the limited evidence to support the efficacy of vitamins in improving ADHD symptoms [18]. Double-blind, randomized, clinical studies are needed to substantiate the use of vitamins for the treatment of ADHD.

3.4. Minerals

Mineral supplementation has also been proposed to be an alternative intervention for ADHD. Mineral deficiencies have also been implicated in the etiology ADHD, and thus mineral supplementation may be useful to correct the underlying mineral deficiency and possibly control ADHD symptoms. In addition, minerals are cofactors in the synthesis, uptake, and breakdown of important neurotransmitters, also implicated to play crucial roles in ADHD symptomatology [19, 45].

Of the mineral supplements, zinc may have been the most studied and have received much support as an adjunct treatment for ADHD [19]. Low levels of zinc have been associated with deficits in several cognitive functions including information processing [19, 46]. Thus, zinc supplementation may have beneficial effects on cognition and related processes. In a 12-week, double-blind study, children supplemented with 150 mg of zinc sulfate showed reductions in hyperactivity, impulsivity, and impaired socialization [47]. Akhondzadeh *et al.* [46] also reported that zinc sulfate augmented the effect of methylphenidate in alleviating ADHD symptoms in children. Zinc is generally well-tolerated with only minor side effects reported (e.g., gastrointestinal discomforts and metallic taste). However, Arnold [48] showed negligible clinical effects of zinc supplementation in ADHD patients. These discrepant results are possibly due to differences in underlying nutritional status, genetic factors, and/or dosages of zinc used in different studies [18]. More elaborate and comprehensive clinical studies are required to solve these discrepancies.

Another mineral that has received special attention and has been evaluated in clinical trials for ADHD treatment is iron. Previous studies showed that children with iron-deficiency anemia also displayed attentional deficits [45]. Iron is a co-factor in the synthesis of both norepinephrine and dopamine [11, 19]. A randomized, double-blind, placebo-controlled study found that iron supplementation improved ADHD symptoms in children (23 kids, 5–8 years old) [49]. However, in the absence of anemia, iron supplementation in children with ADHD did not produce consistent behavioral improvements [19, 45].

Magnesium was also shown to improve ADHD symptoms. Magnesium is involved in neurotransmitter synthesis, and some studies have even associated magnesium deficiencies with ADHD [50]. Indeed, supplementation of magnesium and vitamin B6 in ADHD children improved ADHD symptoms [43].

Altogether, these findings indicate that certain minerals may be helpful in the treatment of ADHD. However, caution must be practiced when using minerals because of potential health risks associated with intake of large dosages.

http://dx.doi.org/10.5772/60840

3.5. Essential fatty acids

In recent years, there has been a lot of interest on the benefits of essential fatty acid (EFA, e.g., omega-3, omega-6) supplementation in children with ADHD. EFA supplementation exerted modest effects on alleviating the symptoms of ADHD [51, 52]. Richardson and Puri [53] reported that high-dose supplementation of EFA (fish oil; 8–16 g) improved behavior and inattention and reduced hyperactivity and defiance in children with ADHD. Another report also indicated better attention and behavioral improvement in children receiving combined omega-3 and omega-6 supplementation [54]. Similarly, Sinn and Bryan [55] reported significant improvement in ADHD symptoms (parent-rated behavior and attentional tasks) in children given EFA for 15 weeks, versus the placebo-treated group. Of note, other investigators have reported selective improvement (parent-reported benefits for restless-hyperactive symptoms in the absence of teacher-reported effects) of ADHD symptoms in subjects after EFA supplementation [56, 57]. While the exact mechanism EFAs in ADHD is not yet established, the efficacy of EFAs may be attributed to its effects on brain development (e.g., cell growth, neural signaling, and effects on gene expression) [18, 51]. It has also been postulated that increased EFA levels in cellular membranes impact dopaminergic and serotonergic activity [19, 51].

Nevertheless, other studies have also reported no significant or very minimal effects of EFA treatment in ADHD patients vs. placebo-treated group. A randomized clinical trial reported that EFAs had minimal effects on ADHD symptoms [58]. Another study also did not find any benefit of two month EFA supplementation in subjects [59]. In addition, Voigt *et al.* [60] reported that four months of DHA supplementation (345 mg/day) did not decrease symptoms of ADHD. In one study, omega-3 fatty acid supplements have even been associated with worsening of inattention [19, 57].

In summary, although some studies have reported therapeutic benefits of EFA supplementation, the current evidence for EFA as a complementary and alternative medicine for ADHD is not yet established [61].

3.6. Amino acids

Amino acid supplements have also been considered as a complementary intervention for ADHD. These include acetyl-L-carnitine (ALC), GABA, glycine, L-theanine, L-tyrosine, taurine, 5-hydroxytryptophan (5-HTP), and s-adenosyl-L-methionine (SAMe) [12, 18]. However, research regarding amino acid supplementation for ADHD treatment in children has produced inconsistent data. Various risks have been reported with their use and only short-term benefits of the supplements have been found [18]. Most research in this field has focused on supplementation with ALC, an amino acid derivative. A randomized, double-blind placebo-controlled study reported that ALC supplementation significantly ameliorated the symptoms of ADHD in 51 children, aged 6–13 years old [62]. However, a double-blind, placebo-controlled clinical trial reported that ALC supplementation has no significant effect on the overall ADHD population (112 children, 5–12 years old) [63].

4. Emerging natural interventions for ADHD and other treatment options

4.1. Novel interventions: evidence from preclinical studies

4.1.1. Oroxylin A

Oroxylin A (5,7-dihydroxy-6-methoxyflavone) shows potential as a natural intervention for ADHD. Oroxylin A is a flavonoid isolated from the root of *Scutellaria baicalensis Georgi,* a herb commonly found in East Asia. It exerted antioxidant, anti-inflammatory, and anti-allergy activities, and produced memory-enhancing and neuroprotective effects. Studies showed that Oroxylin A in an antagonist of the γ-aminobutyric acid (GABA)-A receptor [64]. Preclinical studies have shown that Oroxylin A or its derivative (5,7-dihydroxy-6-methoxy-4'-phenoxy-flavone) improved ADHD-like behaviors of the spontaneously hypertensive rat, an animal model of ADHD [65, 66]. The beneficial effects of Oroxylin A are believed to be mediated via enhancement of dopamine neurotransmission. Studies are underway to determine the efficacy of oroxylin A in ADHD patients.

4.1.2. YY162

YY162 is pharmaceutical combination of terpenoid-strengthened *G. biloba* and ginsenoside Rg3 from ginseng. A recent study has shown that YY1612 attenuated ADHD-like conditions induced by Aroclor1254 in mice [67]. It also exerted neuroprotective effects with negligible behavioral side effects. These effects of YY162 were comparable to those produced by methylphenidate. The positive effects of YY162 on ADHD-like behavior are believed to be mediated through its antioxidant properties and its ability to positively modulate the dopamine and norepinephrine transporters. Studies on the effects YY162 in patients with ADHD would be invaluable to determine its worth as an ADHD medication.

4.2. Combination treatment and integrative approaches

Because ADHD is a multifactorial disorder, a multi-modal approach may prove effective in managing ADHD symptoms. A recent and growing trend in the management of ADHD is the combination of various ADHD treatment options (e.g., medication and behavioral therapies) also referred to as combination therapy, integrative, or multi-modal approach. Multi-modal approaches are highly recommended because it is believed to provide a more "holistic" and patient-specific approach.

Due to that fact that stimulants are the most widely used treatment for ADHD, most multi-modal approaches practiced or studied employed the use of a stimulant drug coupled with a behavioral/psychosocial therapy. In a landmark randomized clinical trial known as the Multimodal Treatment Study of Children with ADHD, it was shown that the combination behavioral and medication interventions was superior compared to the individual effects of its component [68]. However, this did not go uncontested because other large-scale and long-term clinical trials have reported contradicting results [4].

http://dx.doi.org/10.5772/60840

Very few studies have evaluated the effects of medication and/or behavioral therapy combined with a nutritional/botanical component. Notably, Akhondzadeh *et al.* [46] performed a randomized, double-blind, trial evaluating the effects of zinc sulfate as an adjunct to methylphenidate. The result showed that the zinc enhanced the effects of methylphenidate in children (ages 5–11) with ADHD. This study stands as an example that natural products are very promising when used with other ADHD treatments.

5. Conclusion

There are a number of available treatment options for ADHD, however, some of them may pose risks to patients [18]. The botanical agents discussed in this study appear to be promising ADHD treatments considering their therapeutic effects and negligible negative side effects. Of the botanical agents reviewed, Pycnogenol is the most studied, widely supported, and promising ADHD treatment. Nutritional supplements are also generally considered safe, and among them, EFAs stand out as potential ADHD interventions. Although the use of natural medications for ADHD has been considered as a "safer" approach, natural products are still far from being called as standard ADHD treatments due to the lack of comprehensive and appropriately controlled clinical studies that interrogate both their efficacy and safety. Thus, more rigorous, appropriately designed clinical trials are required prior to establishing their worth as ADHD drugs.

Acknowledgements

We would like to acknowledge support from the Korea Health Technology R&D Project through the Korea Health Industry Development Institute (KHIDI), funded by the Ministry of Health & Welfare, Republic of Korea (Grant number HI12C0011)..

Author details

June Bryan dela Peña[1], Chrislean Jun Botanas[1], Reinholdger Tampus[1], Irene Joy dela Peña[1], Hee Jin Kim[1], Ike dela Peña[2*] and Jae Hoon Cheong[1*]

*Address all correspondence to: idelapena@llu.edu, cheongjh@syu.ac.kr

1 Uimyung Research Institute for Neuroscience, Sahmyook University, Seoul, Republic of Korea

2 Department of Pharmaceutical and Administrative Sciences, Loma Linda University, Loma Linda, California, USA

References

[1] Swanson JM, Sergeant JA, Taylor E, Sonuga-Barke EJ, Jensen PS, Cantwell DP. Attention-deficit hyperactivity disorder and hyperkinetic disorder. Lancet. 1998;351(9100): 429–33.

[2] Polanczyk G, de Lima MS, Horta BL, Biederman J, Rohde LA. The worldwide prevalence of ADHD: a systematic review and metaregression analysis. The American journal of psychiatry. 2007;164(6):942–8.

[3] Harpin VA. The effect of ADHD on the life of an individual, their family, and community from preschool to adult life. Archives of disease in childhood. 2005;90 Suppl 1:i2–7.

[4] Hinshaw SP, Arnold LE, For the MTACG. ADHD, Multimodal treatment, and longitudinal outcome: evidence, paradox, and challenge. Wiley interdisciplinary reviews Cognitive science. 2015;6(1):39–52.

[5] Prince J. Catecholamine dysfunction in attention-deficit/hyperactivity disorder: an update. Journal of clinical psychopharmacology. 2008;28(3 Suppl 2):S39–45.

[6] Biederman J, Spencer T, Wilens T. Evidence-based pharmacotherapy for attention-deficit hyperactivity disorder. The international journal of neuropsychopharmacology/official scientific journal of the Collegium Internationale Neuropsychopharmacologicum. 2004;7(1):77–97.

[7] Wolraich ML, Wibbelsman CJ, Brown TE, Evans SW, Gotlieb EM, Knight JR, et al. Attention-deficit/hyperactivity disorder among adolescents: a review of the diagnosis, treatment, and clinical implications. Pediatrics. 2005;115(6):1734–46.

[8] Lakhan SE, Kirchgessner A. Prescription stimulants in individuals with and without attention deficit hyperactivity disorder: misuse, cognitive impact, and adverse effects. Brain and behavior. 2012;2(5):661–77.

[9] Wong YW, Kim DG, Lee JY. Traditional oriental herbal medicine for children and adolescents with ADHD: a systematic review. Evidence-based complementary and alternative medicine: eCAM. 2012;2012:520198.

[10] Rowles BM, Findling RL. Review of pharmacotherapy options for the treatment of attention-deficit/hyperactivity disorder (ADHD) and ADHD-like symptoms in children and adolescents with developmental disorders. Developmental disabilities research reviews. 2010;16(3):273–82.

[11] Lee J, Grizenko N, Bhat V, Sengupta S, Polotskaia A, Joober R. Relation between therapeutic response and side effects induced by methylphenidate as observed by parents and teachers of children with ADHD. BMC psychiatry. 2011;11:70.

[12] Pellow J, Solomon EM, Barnard CN. Complementary and alternative medical therapies for children with attention-deficit/hyperactivity disorder (ADHD). Alternative medicine review: a journal of clinical therapeutic. 2011;16(4):323–37.

[13] Brown RT, Amler RW, Freeman WS, Perrin JM, Stein MT, Feldman HM, et al. Treatment of attention-deficit/hyperactivity disorder: overview of the evidence. Pediatrics. 2005;115(6):e749–57.

[14] Heal DJ, Cheetham SC, Smith SL. The neuropharmacology of ADHD drugs in vivo: insights on efficacy and safety. Neuropharmacology. 2009;57(7–8):608–18.

[15] Safren SA, Sprich S, Mimiaga MJ, Surman C, Knouse L, Groves M, et al. Cognitive behavioral therapy vs relaxation with educational support for medication-treated adults with ADHD and persistent symptoms: a randomized controlled trial. Jama. 2010;304(8):875–80.

[16] ADD/ADHD treatment in children: finding treatments that work for kids and teens [Internet]. [cited February 5, 2015]. Available from: http://www.helpguide.org/articles/add-adhd/attention-deficit-disorder-adhd-treatment-in-children.htm#resources.

[17] Storebo OJ, Skoog M, Damm D, Thomsen PH, Simonsen E, Gluud C. Social skills training for attention deficit hyperactivity disorder (ADHD) in children aged 5 to 18 years. The Cochrane database of systematic reviews. 2011;(12):CD008223.

[18] Bader A, Adesman A. Complementary and alternative therapies for children and adolescents with ADHD. Current opinion in pediatrics. 2012;24(6):760–9.

[19] Searight HR, Robertson K, Smith T, Perkins S, Searight BK. Complementary and alternative therapies for pediatric attention deficit hyperactivity disorder: a descriptive review. ISRN psychiatry. 2012;2012:804127.

[20] Rojas NL, Chan E. Old and new controversies in the alternative treatment of attention-deficit hyperactivity disorder. Mental retardation and developmental disabilities research reviews. 2005;11(2):116–30.

[21] Millichap JG, Yee MM. The diet factor in attention-deficit/hyperactivity disorder. Pediatrics. 2012;129(2):330–7.

[22] Chan E, Rappaport LA, Kemper KJ. Complementary and alternative therapies in childhood attention and hyperactivity problems. Journal of developmental and behavioral pediatrics: JDBP. 2003;24(1):4–8.

[23] Stubberfield T, Parry T. Utilization of alternative therapies in attention-deficit hyperactivity disorder. Journal of paediatrics and child health. 1999;35(5):450–3.

[24] Sinha D, Efron D. Complementary and alternative medicine use in children with attention deficit hyperactivity disorder. Journal of paediatrics and child health. 2005;41(1–2):23–6.

[25] Ottolini MC, Hamburger EK, Loprieato JO, Coleman RH, Sachs HC, Madden R, et al. Complementary and alternative medicine use among children in the Washington,

DC area. Ambulatory pediatrics: the official journal of the Ambulatory Pediatric Association. 2001;1(2):122–5.

[26] Trebaticka J, Kopasova S, Hradecna Z, Cinovsky K, Skodacek I, Suba J, et al. Treatment of ADHD with French maritime pine bark extract, Pycnogenol. European child & adolescent psychiatry. 2006;15(6):329–35.

[27] Chovanova Z, Muchova J, Sivonova M, Dvorakova M, Zitnanova I, Waczulikova I, et al. Effect of polyphenolic extract, Pycnogenol, on the level of 8-oxoguanine in children suffering from attention deficit/hyperactivity disorder. Free radical research. 2006;40(9):1003–10.

[28] Dvorakova M, Sivonova M, Trebaticka J, Skodacek I, Waczulikova I, Muchova J, et al. The effect of polyphenolic extract from pine bark, Pycnogenol on the level of glutathione in children suffering from attention deficit hyperactivity disorder (ADHD). Redox report: communications in free radical research. 2006;11(4):163–72.

[29] Dvorakova M, Jezova D, Blazicek P, Trebaticka J, Skodacek I, Suba J, et al. Urinary catecholamines in children with attention deficit hyperactivity disorder (ADHD): modulation by a polyphenolic extract from pine bark (pycnogenol). Nutritional neuroscience. 2007;10(3–4):151–7.

[30] Tenenbaum S, Paull JC, Sparrow EP, Dodd DK, Green L. An experimental comparison of pycnogenol and methylphenidate in adults with attention-deficit/hyperactivity disorder (ADHD). Journal of attention disorders. 2002;6(2):49–60.

[31] Sarris J, Kean J, Schweitzer I, Lake J. Complementary medicines (herbal and nutritional products) in the treatment of attention deficit hyperactivity disorder (ADHD): a systematic review of the evidence. Complementary therapies in medicine. 2011;19(4):216–27.

[32] Sarris J. St. John's wort for the treatment of psychiatric disorders. The psychiatric clinics of North America. 2013;36(1):65–72.

[33] Niederhofer H. St. John's wort may improve some symptoms of attention-deficit hyperactivity disorder. Natural product research. 2010;24(3):203–5.

[34] Weber W, Vander Stoep A, McCarty RL, Weiss NS, Biederman J, McClellan J. Hypericum perforatum (St John's wort) for attention-deficit/hyperactivity disorder in children and adolescents: a randomized controlled trial. Jama. 2008;299(22):2633–41.

[35] Salehi B, Imani R, Mohammadi MR, Fallah J, Mohammadi M, Ghanizadeh A, et al. Ginkgo biloba for attention-deficit/hyperactivity disorder in children and adolescents: a double blind, randomized controlled trial. Progress in neuro-psychopharmacology & biological psychiatry. 2010;34(1):76–80.

[36] Uebel-von Sandersleben H, Rothenberger A, Albrecht B, Rothenberger LG, Klement S, Bock N. Ginkgo biloba extract EGb 761(R) in children with ADHD. Zeitschrift fur Kinder- und Jugendpsychiatrie und Psychotherapie. 2014;42(5):337–47.

[37] Lyon MR, Cline JC, Totosy de Zepetnek J, Shan JJ, Pang P, Benishin C. Effect of the herbal extract combination Panax quinquefolium and Ginkgo biloba on attention-deficit hyperactivity disorder: a pilot study. Journal of psychiatry & neuroscience: JPN. 2001;26(3):221–8.

[38] Lee SH, Park WS, Lim MH. Clinical effects of korean red ginseng on attention deficit hyperactivity disorder in children: an observational study. Journal of ginseng research. 2011;35(2):226–34.

[39] Ko HJ, Kim I, Kim JB, Moon Y, Whang MC, Lee KM, et al. Effects of Korean red ginseng extract on behavior in children with symptoms of inattention and hyperactivity/impulsivity: a double-blind randomized placebo-controlled trial. Journal of child and adolescent psychopharmacology. 2014;24(9):501–8.

[40] Razlog R, Pellow J, White SJ. A pilot study on the efficacy of Valeriana officinalis mother tincture and Valeriana officinalis 3X in the treatment of attention deficit hyperactivity disorder: original research. Health SA Gesondheid. 2011;17(1):1–7.

[41] Li JJ, Li ZW, Wang SZ, Qi FH, Zhao L, Lv H, et al. Ningdong granule: a complementary and alternative therapy in the treatment of attention deficit/hyperactivity disorder. Psychopharmacology. 2011;216(4):501–9.

[42] Dave UP, Dingankar SR, Saxena VS, Joseph JA, Bethapudi B, Agarwal A, et al. An open-label study to elucidate the effects of standardized Bacopa monnieri extract in the management of symptoms of attention-deficit hyperactivity disorder in children. Advances in mind-body medicine. 2014;28(2):10–5.

[43] Mousain-Bosc M, Roche M, Polge A, Pradal-Prat D, Rapin J, Bali JP. Improvement of neurobehavioral disorders in children supplemented with magnesium-vitamin B6. I. Attention deficit hyperactivity disorders. Magnesium research: official organ of the International Society for the Development of Research on Magnesium. 2006;19(1):46–52.

[44] Coleman M, Steinberg G, Tippett J, Bhagavan HN, Coursin DB, Gross M, et al. A preliminary study of the effect of pyridoxine administration in a subgroup of hyperkinetic children: a double-blind crossover comparison with methylphenidate. Biological psychiatry. 1979;14(5):741–51.

[45] Rucklidge JJ, Johnstone J, Kaplan BJ. Nutrient supplementation approaches in the treatment of ADHD. Expert review of neurotherapeutics. 2009;9(4):461–76.

[46] Akhondzadeh S, Mohammadi MR, Khademi M. Zinc sulfate as an adjunct to methylphenidate for the treatment of attention deficit hyperactivity disorder in children: a double blind and randomized trial [ISRCTN64132371]. BMC psychiatry. 2004;4:9.

[47] Bilici M, Yildirim F, Kandil S, Bekaroglu M, Yildirmis S, Deger O, et al. Double-blind, placebo-controlled study of zinc sulfate in the treatment of attention deficit hyperac-

tivity disorder. Progress in neuro-psychopharmacology & biological psychiatry. 2004;28(1):181–90.

[48] Arnold LE, Disilvestro RA, Bozzolo D, Bozzolo H, Crowl L, Fernandez S, et al. Zinc for attention-deficit/hyperactivity disorder: placebo-controlled double-blind pilot trial alone and combined with amphetamine. Journal of child and adolescent psychopharmacology. 2011;21(1):1–19.

[49] Konofal E, Lecendreux M, Deron J, Marchand M, Cortese S, Zaim M, et al. Effects of iron supplementation on attention deficit hyperactivity disorder in children. Pediatric neurology. 2008;38(1):20–6.

[50] Starobrat-Hermelin B, Kozielec T. The effects of magnesium physiological supplementation on hyperactivity in children with attention deficit hyperactivity disorder (ADHD). Positive response to magnesium oral loading test. Magnesium research: official organ of the International Society for the Development of Research on Magnesium. 1997;10(2):149–56.

[51] Bloch MH, Qawasmi A. Omega-3 fatty acid supplementation for the treatment of children with attention-deficit/hyperactivity disorder symptomatology: systematic review and meta-analysis. Journal of the American Academy of Child and Adolescent Psychiatry. 2011;50(10):991–1000.

[52] Sorgi PJ, Hallowell EM, Hutchins HL, Sears B. Effects of an open-label pilot study with high-dose EPA/DHA concentrates on plasma phospholipids and behavior in children with attention deficit hyperactivity disorder. Nutrition journal. 2007;6:16.

[53] Richardson AJ, Puri BK. A randomized double-blind, placebo-controlled study of the effects of supplementation with highly unsaturated fatty acids on ADHD-related symptoms in children with specific learning difficulties. Progress in neuro-psychopharmacology & biological psychiatry. 2002;26(2):233–9.

[54] Stevens L, Zhang W, Peck L, Kuczek T, Grevstad N, Mahon A, et al. EFA supplementation in children with inattention, hyperactivity, and other disruptive behaviors. Lipids. 2003;38(10):1007–21.

[55] Sinn N, Bryan J. Effect of supplementation with polyunsaturated fatty acids and micronutrients on learning and behavior problems associated with child ADHD. Journal of developmental and behavioral pediatrics: JDBP. 2007;28(2):82–91.

[56] Manor I, Magen A, Keidar D, Rosen S, Tasker H, Cohen T, et al. The effect of phosphatidylserine containing Omega3 fatty-acids on attention-deficit hyperactivity disorder symptoms in children: a double-blind placebo-controlled trial, followed by an open-label extension. European psychiatry: the journal of the Association of European Psychiatrists. 2012;27(5):335–42.

[57] Sinn N, Bryan J, Wilson C. Cognitive effects of polyunsaturated fatty acids in children with attention deficit hyperactivity disorder symptoms: a randomised controlled trial. Prostaglandins, leukotrienes, and essential fatty acids. 2008;78(4–5):311–26.

[58] Raz R, Carasso RL, Yehuda S. The influence of short-chain essential fatty acids on children with attention-deficit/hyperactivity disorder: a double-blind placebo-controlled study. Journal of child and adolescent psychopharmacology. 2009;19(2):167–77.

[59] Hirayama S, Hamazaki T, Terasawa K. Effect of docosahexaenoic acid-containing food administration on symptoms of attention-deficit/hyperactivity disorder – a placebo-controlled double-blind study. European journal of clinical nutrition. 2004;58(3): 467–73.

[60] Voigt RG, Llorente AM, Jensen CL, Fraley JK, Berretta MC, Heird WC. A randomized, double-blind, placebo-controlled trial of docosahexaenoic acid supplementation in children with attention-deficit/hyperactivity disorder. The journal of pediatrics. 2001;139(2):189–96.

[61] Gillies D, Sinn J, Lad SS, Leach MJ, Ross MJ. Polyunsaturated fatty acids (PUFA) for attention deficit hyperactivity disorder (ADHD) in children and adolescents. The Cochrane database of systematic reviews. 2012;7:CD007986.

[62] Torrioli MG, Vernacotola S, Peruzzi L, Tabolacci E, Mila M, Militerni R, et al. A double-blind, parallel, multicenter comparison of L-acetylcarnitine with placebo on the attention deficit hyperactivity disorder in fragile X syndrome boys. American journal of medical genetics Part A. 2008;146A(7):803–12.

[63] Arnold LE, Amato A, Bozzolo H, Hollway J, Cook A, Ramadan Y, et al. Acetyl-L-carnitine (ALC) in attention-deficit/hyperactivity disorder: a multi-site, placebo-controlled pilot trial. Journal of child and adolescent psychopharmacology. 2007;17(6):791–802.

[64] Yoon SY, dela Pena IC, Shin CY, Son KH, Lee YS, Ryu JH, et al. Convulsion-related activities of Scutellaria flavones are related to the 5,7-dihydroxyl structures. European journal of pharmacology. 2011;659(2–3):155–60.

[65] dela Pena IC, Young Yoon S, Kim Y, Park H, Man Kim K, Hoon Ryu J, et al. 5,7-Dihydroxy-6-methoxy-4′-phenoxyflavone, a derivative of oroxylin A improves attention-deficit/hyperactivity disorder (ADHD)-like behaviors in spontaneously hypertensive rats. European journal of pharmacology. 2013;715(1–3):337–44.

[66] Yoon SY, dela Pena I, Kim SM, Woo TS, Shin CY, Son KH, et al. Oroxylin A improves attention deficit hyperactivity disorder-like behaviors in the spontaneously hypertensive rat and inhibits reuptake of dopamine in vitro. Archives of pharmacal research. 2013;36(1):134–40.

[67] Nam Y, Shin EJ, Shin SW, Lim YK, Jung JH, Lee JH, et al. YY162 prevents ADHD-like behavioral side effects and cytotoxicity induced by Aroclor1254 via interactive sig-

naling between antioxidant potential, BDNF/TrkB, DAT and NET. Food and chemical toxicology: an international journal published for the British Industrial Biological Research Association. 2014;65:280–92.

[68] A 14-month randomized clinical trial of treatment strategies for attention-deficit/hyperactivity disorder. The MTA Cooperative Group. Multimodal Treatment Study of Children with ADHD. Archives of general psychiatry. 1999;56(12):1073–86.